Praise for Beautiful Teams

T0220893

"Stop complaining about your coworkers. Instead to read *Beautiful Teams*. It proves the the amazin how it can happen in your company."

> —Scott Berkun, bestselling author of *The Myths of Innovation* and *Making Things Happen*

"The striking diversity of these histories, experiences, and reflections tells a broader, deeper story than any single author could manage. Somewhere in this book you'll certainly find key tips for dealing with the very team-building and team-running issues you're having today, as well as outlook-broadening views of issues that are quite outside your experience so far."

> —Alex Martelli, Google

"In *Beautiful Teams*, the many contributors step back from advancing their usual prescriptions to celebrate their own successes (and yes, challenges) within teams. In this celebration, they provide some of the best insights that we can carry forward into our own careers. Jennifer Greene draws wondrous team memories from the ashes of a dot-com failure, Keoki Andrus shares a healthy respect for innovation and creative play to inspire a team, and there are engaging stories by Karl Wiegers and many others that capture great team experiences. *Beautiful Teams* will keep you rapt like few technical books ever have."

> —Jim Brosseau, author of *Software Teamwork: Taking Ownership for Success*

"Teams build software, and if your team isn't working together effectively, you have very little hope of success at the software development game. The experiences and insights shared in this book will stick with you for years to come."

> —Scott W. Ambler, worldwide practice leader agile development, IBM Software Group, and author of *Agile Modeling*

"The good, the bad, the ugly, and of course, the beautiful. You'll read about teams who persevered no matter what, and how some famous organizations built teams. If you want to know how your team stacks up, or how to make it beautiful, read this book. The stories are captivating and all too real."

> —Johanna Rothman, consultant and author

"Anyone who's had to get a group of people to work together becomes an instinctive collector of stories: you quickly realize how complex the task is, and how limited your own experience. If you know that feeling, this book is for you. These are tales from the trenches, told with eloquence, good humor, and—for the reader as well as the writer—the occasional flash of uncomfortable recognition."

—KARL FOGEL, OPEN SOURCE DEVELOPER AND AUTHOR

Beautiful Teams

Beautiful Teams

Edited by Andrew Stellman and Jennifer Greene

O'REILLY®

Beijing • Cambridge • Farnham • Köln • Sebastopol • Tokyo

Beautiful Teams

Edited by Andrew Stellman and Jennifer Greene

Published by O'Reilly Media, Inc. 1005 Gravenstein Highway North, Sebastopol, CA 95472.

O'Reilly books may be purchased for educational, business, or sales promotional use. Online editions are also available for most titles (*safari.oreilly.com*). For more information, contact our corporate/institutional sales department: (800) 998-9938 or *corporate@oreilly.com*.

Editor: Andy Oram	**Indexer:** Ellen Troutman Zaig
Production Editor: Sumita Mukherji	**Cover Designer:** Mark Paglietti
Copyeditor: Audrey Doyle	**Interior Designer:** Marcia Friedman
Proofreader: Sumita Mukherji	**Illustrator:** Robert Romano

Printing History:

March 2009: First Edition.

ISBN: 978-0-596-51802-8

[LSI]

[2013-11-08]

This book is dedicated to Trevor Field and the rest of the people at PlayPumps International for all of their dedication and hard work bringing clean drinking water to the people of sub-Saharan Africa. A portion of every sale of Beautiful Teams will be donated to their worthy cause. We urge you to learn more about them and their work by visiting http://www.playpumps.org.

CONTENTS

Why Beautiful Teams?

WE'VE BEEN ON A LOT OF DIFFERENT TEAMS OVER THE YEARS, IN A LOT OF DIFFERENT COMPANIES AND building a lot of different kinds of projects. And over the course of writing books, articles, and blog posts about how to make projects run better, we were always nagged by a question. It always seemed like it was our job to come up with prescriptive "best" ways to run software projects: how to plan the projects, how to build the software, and how to make sure that it doesn't break. But the more we wrote and the more we talked to people, the more we questioned this idea.

We started down that path after writing our first book, which we thought of as a practical recipe book for running successful software projects. We'd done a lot of research, experimentation, and real-world project work over the years to find practices that worked for us: ways to plan software projects, techniques for developers to write better code, and ways to test the software. We took the ones that worked best for us and packaged them up into as lightweight a book as we could come up with. We've gotten a lot of great, overwhelmingly positive feedback about it over the years, and a lot of people have told us that they use it every day.

And that's where things started to go wrong for us.

Ironically, we fell into a trap that we actually wrote about in that book: we started to get a kind of tunnel vision. We saw this particular set of practices as the "successful" practices. We never intended to say that there was only one way to plan out your project, or to estimate it, or to do a code review, or to test the software. But what we found, as we started getting out into the world and talking to more and more software people, is that we were getting pigeonholed. People would say, "Oh, Stellman and Greene—you're the Wideband Delphi people? I always use that to estimate!" (Seriously, people actually said that to us!) Or, much worse, they'd tell us, "Your book talks about requirements specifications, and I never use them. But I develop software just fine. You must be wrong!"

Practices are cold. Practices are theoretical. You can sit and talk about the virtues of one or another, and have hypothetical arguments about whether they'll work in one situation or another. We've done our own share of arguing about that ourselves, talking until we're all blue in the face about when is the correct time to do requirements gathering and how to make a project more or less agile. Those kinds of things are really where people draw battle lines.

But it's not where the meat of the work happens, honestly. How you make those decisions has an impact on the project, certainly, and sometimes a big one. But it's not nearly as important as *who* you have on your team: how skilled they are, and how well they work together. That's when we realized that practices are only one aspect of building better software. And although it's the aspect we've spent the most time studying and dealing with, it took us a long time to realize that it's usually not the most important aspect.

So, we started looking for ways to get people to open up about their own projects, and to listen to each other about what they've learned. We put together a talk about best practices—because that's what we wrote about and what we knew best—and tried to explain, in as general and non-prescriptive terms as we could think of, how to use them to make your projects run better. We naïvely thought that people would be excited to hear about what we learned, both in writing our book and in running our own projects. We'd talk about the kinds of pitfalls they'd avoid, and we'd give them the tools to avoid them ("Look, here's one way you can run a productive estimation session!").

It was a disaster. One talk comes to mind as particularly bad, although not too much worse than many others that we gave. We were invited to give a presentation for a brown bag series at a major Internet company's New York office. We started in on the talk, going through the kinds of problems that software teams typically face, and outlining the practices that we found to be useful to prevent them. We could see the mounting boredom and even frustration on the faces of the developers. They were mostly young, the majority under 30, and by the time we were halfway through the talk most were checking their PDAs and laptops. Some people even got up and left. And when we got to the Q&A session at the end, we found out where their heads were. One programmer, a large guy with a long gray beard, challenged us when we mentioned agile project planning: "Agile means that you don't write anything down, you just start coding immediately." Everyone nodded their heads. We tried to redirect that—"No, that's not what agile necessarily says!"—but it didn't matter. Our message wasn't getting through, and we were clearly wasting everyone's time.

We shouldn't have been surprised that we were met with a lukewarm (at best) reception. After all, we'd sat through our own share of networking activities (project management group meetings, architect SIG meetings, software process network meetings…). And for every one that featured a really memorable talk or discussion, there were literally a dozen that boiled down to an advertisement for a consulting company, or a book, or a professional product or service of some kind, and left us completely cold.

So, we reflected on the criticism about agile we'd gotten at that talk. And to our surprise, we realized that he wasn't wrong to criticize us, even if we disagreed with him on the facts. Yes, the criticism stung at first, and we really had to take some time to figure out why the talk ended up the way it did. But in the end, his criticism ultimately showed us what was wrong with our approach. *There is no "best" practice*—at least, none that we know of that will guarantee success every time. Whether a particular tool or technique works depends on the circumstances: the project, the people, and all sorts of mushy, messy stuff that you just can't quantify or prescribe. Now, that's not to say that we don't care about process. We're not distancing ourselves from the practices that we use and that we write about. In fact, just the opposite: we still use them every day, we still write about them, and we still train other people to build better software using them because they really do work—in the right situation, for the right project, and with the right people. But sometimes the way to get something done is to do anything *but* the "right" thing. Sometimes you need to just do whatever works.

Growth for us came from realizing that there really are a lot of ways to run a project. And even though we found some practices that we're very comfortable with, there are times when they're not appropriate. We've had to get a lot more flexible over the years with our own approaches to building software, and how we work with our own teams. The reason we had to do that is because some of our projects failed. Not many, but some. And when they failed, that's when we learned the most.

That's what set us down a new path. We tried to figure out what made some projects work while others crashed and burned. It was hard to figure out one particular cause at first, and we suspected that there was no single answer. And when we started talking to people around us, people we knew, we started to hear the same thing over and over: people talked fondly about one project or another that really stuck with them, and they wanted to share their "war stories" about the terrible manager they had, or the horrible situation they faced, or another problem they overcame. In fact, simply asking people about teams they'd been on often got them to reflect on their own careers, and on their own impact on the people around them. And to our surprise, this seemed to be consistent with everyone involved in every level of software development: from the junior programmer who'd been out of school for only a year or two to the CTO who had worked his way up through the ranks from being a junior programmer years before.

The more we opened up and let other people talk about their own experiences without trying to impose our own practices and views on them, the fewer arguments we got into. And the more we talked this over, among ourselves and with other people, the more we started thinking about four distinct "buckets" (for lack of a better word) that these conversations fell into: *people* (who's on the team), *goals* (what brings them together), *practices* (how they build the software), and *obstacles* (what gets in their way). This book is organized into parts based on those ideas. We end the book with a section on groups of people that make music, because that helped us see a greater truth about what makes teams work.

Why These Contributors?

We started this project with one core assumption: the more you know about how different people run their projects, the better equipped you are to run your own. We started out by going to people who we knew personally, from our own teams and people we'd met at conferences, and from being around the software development world. We were surprised at the diversity of opinions just among the people who we knew. We were also surprised that we didn't agree with everything they said—but more importantly, we were surprised to find that we were still able to see the truth in their ideas.

That's when we came up with a cohesive goal for the book: to draw as many different opinions from as many different areas of software development as we could, regardless of whether they meshed cleanly with our own or even with each other. Yes, this would almost certainly mean that there would be contradictory ideas. But we decided that not only is that OK, but in fact it's a benefit. (It's a feature, not a bug.) It showed us that even though ideas are contradictory, they still work in different situations. All projects are unique; all teams are different. It would be very odd if there really were a single answer. There's room for all of these opinions, and there are situations in which any of them can be the right way to go.

Now, that's not to say that there are no wrong answers. In fact, just the opposite is true, which is why we included stories in this book about the teams that are *not* successful. Just as the right decision at the right time can make all the difference in a successful project, sometimes people can be truly misguided when they build software. They choose the wrong practice or path: for example, good documentation can turn bad when it's onerous and not used. But projects can fall off the other side of the spectrum, too, where people on the team don't plan at all, and everyone goes in a different direction. And that's what the cautionary stories in this book demonstrate: teams that started out with the wrong goal, included the wrong people, applied the wrong practices, or simply hit an insurmountable obstacle.

We could never have written a book that does that by ourselves. We're very limited in what we know. Everybody is. And that's why we cast as wide a net as possible, talking to people whose opinions we respect. The many people who contributed to this book represent the real spectrum of projects that people across the whole industry take on.

And while many of the opinions and ideas that you'll read about differ from our own—in some cases, they're completely opposite—we learned a lot from each and every one of these contributors. We think that you will, too.

This book includes stories and interviews with veteran team leaders from all around the software industry. We recruited contributors from as many different industries and areas of interest as possible: from defense to social organizing, from academic research to video game development, from aerospace and defense to search engines, and from project managers to "boots-on-the-ground" programmers and system admins. There are people who we met over the course of our educations and work lives. There are contributors from a wide range of companies, including people who worked (and, in some cases, still work) at NASA, Google, IBM, and Microsoft. We were especially surprised and pleased when we got contributions from people like Grady Booch, Barry Boehm, Steve McConnell, and Karl Wiegers, whose writing and teaching were central to our own understanding of how software is built. We felt honored to work with them and other people in this book who you may not know as well, but who are also doing amazing and innovative things for software development. We're especially grateful for contributions from Tim O'Reilly (whose publishing company printed this and our other books), Scott Berkun (who we've known for years and who not only contributed a great essay, but also interviewed Steve McConnell), and Tony Visconti (a legendary music producer who took the time to talk to us about his own process).

Frankly, we're still amazed that we were able to get such a wide-ranging, knowledgeable, distinguished, and talented group of contributors. But even more surprisingly, not a single contributor asked to be paid. Instead of dividing the royalties from this book among the contributors, we have the privilege of donating them to PlayPumps International, an innovative charity that digs wells to deliver clean drinking water to schools and villages in rural sub-Saharan Africa. PlayPumps is more than a charity; they've had to do their own share of engineering and innovation. You'll learn more about them and their mission (and something about teams, as well!) in our interview with Trevor Field, the founder of PlayPumps.

Every one of these contributors has something interesting, important, and, most significantly, *useful* to say about teams: how they work, how to build them, and how they break down. Each of them is a veteran team leader in his or her own right, with successes and failures under his or her belt. In some cases, we were surprised and even shocked by the stories they had to tell. And every single one is entertaining. The sum of all of these parts amounts to an experience that no single person could cobble together.

Before we delve into the four areas we chose to examine—people, goals, practices, and obstacles—we'd like to start with our interview with Tim O'Reilly because he touches on themes that you'll see over and over again throughout the book. As you're reading it, keep an eye out for each of those four things. When we talked to Tim, he was able to make a lot of these concepts concrete for us, putting words to a lot of the ideas that had been swirling around in our heads after editing the stories and interviews in the book.

We weren't really sure what to expect when we interviewed Tim O'Reilly. Between the two of us, Jenny had met him only once, at the Amazon Developer Days conference (where she'd been invited to speak), but we'd read interviews with him, and his writing on O'Reilly Radar. We were particularly interested in what he had to say about leadership and how to direct groups of people without micromanaging them.

So, if you picked up this book hoping to find the *One Correct Way*™ to run a beautiful team, we're really sorry, because that's not what this book is about. But if you're looking to gain some insight into what makes a good team tick, and what you can do to take a mediocre team and make it better—or take a great team and make it crash and burn—you're going to get a lot out of this book. We think that it's a good read, and at times a gripping one. It represents a wealth of experience, from a very wide range of people all around the industry (and a few who aren't in our industry at all). It attempts to find the general things that hang teams together, without giving you prescription, dogma, theory, or overt advice. We hope you enjoy reading *Beautiful Teams* as much as we've enjoyed bringing it together.

—*Andrew Stellman and Jennifer Greene*
March 2009

Preface

BEAUTIFUL TEAMS WAS CONCEIVED IN LATE 2007 DURING A CHANCE MEETING IN O'REILLY EDITOR Andy Oram's office in Cambridge, Massachusetts. We'd been invited to give a talk for the local PMI chapter, and we decided to take the opportunity to drop by the O'Reilly office to say "Hi" and finally put faces to some very familiar voices we'd worked with over the years. *Beautiful Code* had spent a few months at the top of the O'Reilly bestseller list, and the company was looking to follow up with another anthology. Since we've spent so much of our careers talking and writing about how projects work and how teams build software, the idea for *Beautiful Teams* basically fell out of thin air.

The original idea was just to follow up on *Beautiful Code* with a straightforward anthology about project management. Like all great projects, *Beautiful Teams* took on a life of its own. It attracted contributors of an incredibly high caliber. It became a journey for us, allowing us the opportunity to learn from some of the brightest minds in software development today. These are personal stories and experiences. Each person who contributed to this book is talking about his or her own past work life, which very few of us ever get a chance to examine. And every single contributor was happy to donate his or her time and effort without any payment whatsoever; proceeds from this book are instead being donated to PlayPumps International.

How This Book Is Organized

Here is a short summary of the chapters in this book and what you'll find inside:

Chapter 1, *Leadership*, *an Interview with Tim O'Reilly*
Tim O'Reilly gives us his thoughts on leading teams and companies, and moving the world of software forward.

Part I, *People*

Chapter 2, *Why Ugly Teams Win*, *by Scott Berkun*
Many so-called beautiful teams were never described in those words by the people on them. Scott relates his experience at Microsoft, and explains the *wabi-sabi* of ugly teams.

Chapter 3, *Building Video Games*, *an Interview with Mark Healey*
The cofounder of Media Molecule talks about what he learned building the hit video game LittleBigPlanet.

Chapter 4, *Building the Perfect Team*, *by Bill DiPierre*
Bill tells the story of how a good manager can take a disparate group of people and turn them into a great team.

Chapter 5, *What Makes Developers Tick*, *an Interview with Andy Lester*
Programming manager and Perl contributor Andy explains what motivates developers and how they can improve their relations with their teams.

Chapter 6, *Inspiring People*, *an Interview with Keoki Andrus*
Keoki tells us about how he has improved teams in companies such as Intuit, Microsoft, and Novell by understanding, inspiring, and guiding the people on them.

Chapter 7, *Bringing the Music Industry into the 21st Century*, *by Tom Tarka*
This is the story of the rise and fall of MP3.com, an icon of the dot-com boom and bust, and the people who lived through it.

Chapter 8, *Inner Source*, *an Interview with Auke Jilderda*
The inner source initiative brings open source practices and ideas to corporate teams, and Auke tells us how he implemented it, and how it affected the people on those teams.

Part II, *Goals*

Chapter 9, *Creating Team Cultures*, *an Interview with Grady Booch*
It takes work to get a team to gel, especially a distributed team. Grady talks about the challenges of getting teams moving in the right direction.

Chapter 10, *Putting the "I" in Failure*, *by Jennifer Greene*
Jennifer tells the story of her experience working on a great team with conflicting goals.

Chapter 11, *Planning, an Interview with Mike Cohn*
Through stories from his own career, Mike tells us about how understanding the context around a project means the difference between succeeding and failing.

Chapter 12, *The Copyfighters Take Mordor, by Cory Doctorow*
This is the story of how a great team that's motivated by social responsibility can succeed against a daunting foe.

Chapter 13, *Defending the Free World, an Interview with Neil Siegel*
The CTO of a major defense and aerospace company tells us about how he motivates his software developers.

Chapter 14, *Saving Lives, an Interview with Trevor Field*
The founder of PlayPumps International talks about what motivated him to leave the cushy world of advertising and dedicate his life to delivering clean drinking water to rural schools and villages in sub-Saharan Africa.

Part III, *Practices*

Chapter 15, *Building a Team with Collaboration and Learning, by James Grenning*
An early agile trailblazer and signer of the Agile Manifesto, James talks about his first experience with agile methods.

Chapter 16, *Better Practices, an Interview with Steve McConnell*
Scott Berkun and Steve McConnell discuss how better development practices can lead to high-performance teams.

Chapter 17, *Memories of TRW's Software Productivity Project, by Barry Boehm and Maria Penedo*
This is the story of one of the first successful process improvements ever done, told by a pioneer of the industry.

Chapter 18, *Building Spaceships, an Interview with Peter Glück*
Peter talks about the challenges of building software that will be shot into space at NASA's Jet Propulsion Laboratory.

Chapter 19, *Succeeding with Requirements, by Karl E. Wiegers*
Software requirements can make or break a project, and Karl uses them to ensure success.

Chapter 20, *Development at Google, an Interview with Alex Martelli*
Alex explains how better planning and agile practices improve life at a cutting-edge company.

Chapter 21, *Teams and Tools, by Karl Fogel*
Karl shows how a software tool can have an enormous impact on the way a team works.

Chapter 22, *Research Teams, an Interview with Michael Collins*
Michael tells us about his work on a security research project.

Chapter 23, *The HADS Team*, by Karl Rehmer
Building flight software for the Boeing 777 required a whole new set of tools to be written, which brought its own set of challenges.

Part IV, *Obstacles*

Chapter 24, *Bad Boss*, by Andrew Stellman
One bad manager can destroy a team.

Chapter 25, *Welcome to the Process*, by Ned Robinson
A good team can overcome even the most incredible and unforeseen challenges.

Chapter 26, *Getting Past Obstacles*, an Interview with Scott Ambler
Lots of different problems can trip up a team. Scott tells us how to get past some of the biggest ones.

Chapter 27, *Speed Versus Quality*, by Johanna Rothman
A new project manager faces stiff challenges when she joins her team.

Chapter 28, *Tight, Isn't It?*, by Mark Denovich and Eric Renkey
An improbably great team faces obstacle after obstacle.

Chapter 29, *Inside and Outside the Box*, by Patricia Ensworth
A team that's faced with poor management, terrible facilities, and interpersonal problems manages to stay together despite it all.

Chapter 30, *Compiling the Voice of a Team*, by Andy Oram
One developer can take on management when the facts are in his favor.

Part V, *Music*

Chapter 31, *Producing Music*, an Interview with Tony Visconti
Legendary record producer Tony Visconti shows us that producing records and building software have a lot in common.

How to Contact Us

Please address comments and questions concerning this book to the publisher:

O'Reilly Media, Inc.
1005 Gravenstein Highway North
Sebastopol, CA 95472
800-998-9938 (in the United States or Canada)
707-829-0515 (international or local)
707-829-0104 (fax)

We have a web page for this book, where we list errata, examples, and any additional information. You can access this page at:

http://www.oreilly.com/catalog/9780596518028

To comment or ask technical questions about this book, send email to:

bookquestions@oreilly.com

For more information about our books, conferences, Resource Centers, and the O'Reilly Network, see our website at:

http://www.oreilly.com

Safari® Books Online

 When you see a Safari® Books Online icon on the cover of your favorite technology book, that means the book is available online through the O'Reilly Network Safari Bookshelf.

Safari offers a solution that's better than e-books. It's a virtual library that lets you easily search thousands of top tech books, cut and paste code samples, download chapters, and find quick answers when you need the most accurate, current information. Try it for free at *http://my.safaribooksonline.com*.

Acknowledgments

We'd like to thank all of the contributors who generously donated their time and effort: Tim O'Reilly, Scott Berkun, Mark Healey (and the rest of the folks at Media Molecule!), Bill DiPierre, Andy Lester, Keoki Andrus, Tommy Tarka, Auke Jilderda, Grady Booch, Mike Cohn, Cory Doctorow, Neil Siegel, James Grenning, Steve McConnell, Barry Boehm, Maria Penedo, Peter Glück, Karl Wiegers, Alex Martelli, Karl Fogel, Mike Collins, Karl Rehmer, Ned Robinson, Scott Ambler, Johanna Rothman, Mark Denovich, Eric Renkey, Stan Granite, Patricia Ensworth, and Andy Oram. And we are especially grateful to Tony Visconti for taking the time to talk to us.

We want to thank Trevor Field and the rest of the great people at PlayPumps International (*http://www.playpumps.org*) for the wonderful work that they do, as well as for Trevor's contribution to this book. Please visit the organization's website to find out why we're donating royalties from this book to them.

Finally, once again, special thanks to Nisha Sondhe for her extraordinary photography.

About the Editors

Andrew Stellman started work as a programmer at a national record label after graduating from the School of Computer Science at Carnegie Mellon University. He spent the first few years focusing on technical design and architecture, but found himself increasingly responsible for leading and then managing the teams he was on. Over the last decade, Andrew has led teams of programmers and managed numerous projects. He now spends his time building his own projects and helping the people around him improve the way they manage theirs.

Jennifer Greene began her software engineering career in the early 1990s at a well-known online service. She has since built and led software engineering teams in organizations spanning finance, non-profit, natural language processing and media. She has built and managed distributed software teams and worked with developers around the world to improve their practices and build better software.

Jennifer and **Andrew** have been working together since 1998 building software and training software teams. They initially defined the software process at the company where they were working, and have since run many successful projects together. Their projects have been focused on science and public health, and they have built software for the Mailman School of Public Health at Columbia University, the Business School (also at Columbia University), and the National Academy of Sciences. They have since branched out into commercial project management and software engineering consulting, providing training, project management, outsourced project management, and professional services to both the business and academic communities.

Their first book, *Applied Software Project Management*, was published by O'Reilly in 2005, and has since been adopted as a software engineering textbook at many universities worldwide. They went on two write two books in the acclaimed Head First series. *Head First PMP* has been recognized as one of the best PMP preparation guides available, and has been used by tens of thousands of project managers to prepare for their project management certification. Their third book, *Head First C#*, spent more than a year as one of O'Reilly's bestsellers and is currently one of the top-selling programming language books on the market. In addition to writing, Andrew and Jennifer speak regularly at software development, project management, and process improvement conferences around the world. *Beautiful Teams* is their fourth book.

CHAPTER ONE

Leadership

an Interview with Tim O'Reilly

Tim O'Reilly started the company that became O'Reilly Media, Inc., which published this book (and our others, as well). We've always personally admired him and the company that he founded, not just for his impact on the publishing industry, but also for his impact on the larger world of software and software development. We've worked with people from almost every part of O'Reilly for years, and we recognize a great team when we see it. We wanted to talk to Tim to hear his ideas about how he built his team and continues to bring out the best in them.

Jenny: One thing we noticed when we started putting together this book was that everyone seems to have a slightly different definition of "team." And it turned out that some of the stories we included talk about that question explicitly: whether a team is always people who are together temporarily to build some specific project, or whether a team can be a group of people who've never met.

Andrew: We kind of pulled a fast one and just left it open to interpretation. So how do you define a team?

Tim: My own experiences are around running a company. Yes, there are team experiences in that. But most of the reflections I have are around the broader question of how you exert leadership. Let me start at the top, with a few thoughts about leadership and management, which are part of the whole team thing. I'm not quite sure where the boundaries are.

There are two quotes I want to start you off with. One is from Harold Geneen, who was the guy who started ITT, which was really the first modern conglomerate. And he said, "The skill of management is achieving your objectives through the efforts of others." So, that's kind of an interesting perspective. And the question is of the different styles of doing that, where some of them are very directive. This is the classic "manager"—the idea of somebody who figures out what needs to be done, and who needs to do it, and builds the teams with the roles, and so on.

While I completely subscribe to the concept, because the skill of management is indeed achieving your objectives through the effort of others, I have always worked with the framing of another quote, which is actually about writing. It's from Edwin Schlossberg, who wrote a magazine article I read early in my career, and it's probably one of the seminal things that took root in my brain. He said, "The skill of writing is to create a context in which other people can think."

Jenny: So, can you think of how you apply that idea—"creating a context in which other people can think"—to software teams?

Tim: I'll make an observation here, and it relates to something I call the architecture of participation. In 1998, we did a book called *Open Sources*, and we did interviews for some of the people who produced their essays on open source. And I don't think it made it into the final book, but there's something that Linus Torvalds said in an interview that stuck with me: "I couldn't have done what I did with Linux for Windows, even if I'd had the Windows source code. It just wasn't architected that way." And it really set off a chain of thinking in my mind about the architecture of open source projects, and how they're designed to allow that sort of free-form improvisation. Because there are rules that are laid down.

Andrew: It's funny to hear Linus talk about not being able to do something—it's a good reminder that SourceForge.net is littered with open source projects that never went anywhere.

Tim: I think one of the reasons why certain projects fail is because they're mixing and matching from the wrong systems. We have to have a system that has a fundamental characteristic that there are small pieces that people *can* work on independently. I think this is why, for example, people have said that they'll do books as Wikis, and it hasn't really taken off. Why not? Because a book is a fairly large, complex thing with a single narrative thread. Wikipedia is a set of pages, and the atomic unit of content is something that a single individual can make a plausible promise at, and other people can update and tweak. And the whole is the sum of many, many such small parts. I think, for example, that there are certain types of works that lend themselves to that kind of collaborative activity—being more free-form precisely because they're designed in such a way that the pieces fit together.

Unix is designed a little more like a set of LEGOs, where the design principles are that you have these "innies" and "outies" and they snap together. Thinking about pipes and filters and all of those kinds of things—that people can write completely independent utilities with the knowledge that they just fit. Most programs read standard in and wrote standard out, and there were a few simple rules.

Similarly, every atomic piece has a manpage. I've always thought, if I were given a choice between Windows with open source code under, say, the GPL, versus Windows with a manpage for every little bit of code, what you could swap out and what you could change. Yes, you'd have the license issue, but the license wouldn't be sufficient. On the other hand, the manpages *would* be sufficient, although you'd be violating a few people's copyrights.

Andrew: So, what you're saying is that a key to running a good project—open source or otherwise—is to break it down into pieces that people can understand?

Tim: What I'm saying is that there's a framework in which you organize people's creativity. And there's a whole bunch of principles there. Let me give you a concrete story. Back in 1998, when I organized what came to be called the Open Source Summit, I had this plausible story about what was happening in the industry. There were other people talking about it, notably Eric Raymond, who'd written *The Cathedral and the Bazaar*. I'd done the Perl conference the year before. We were all thinking about a bunch of things in parallel. Netscape had just open sourced their browser, so there was a lot of ferment. And I noticed something: the iconic story that was being put out by Eric Raymond and others left out the whole BSD world. It was all about Linux; it was all about GPL'd software; it was all about the ideals of free software.

Meanwhile, there was this whole other tradition that I looked at. And I looked at it and said, "Wow, that tradition has actually had more impact." So, for example, I'd go around and say to people, "Tell me the top five programs on the Internet." They'd scratch their heads. And I'd say, "Number one: BIND, the Berkeley Internet Name Daemon. Every one of you has a website that's depending on that program that's maintained by this long-haired programmer in Redwood City. Number two, either sendmail or Apache. Seventy-five percent of Net email is routed by sendmail." You went down the list, and it was all Berkeley software. People weren't seeing that story.

Jenny: I remember that at the time, there was a lot of controversy around choosing an open source license, GPL versus BSD. It sounds like you found a way to rise above that and bring everyone together. How did that happen?

Tim: I brought together all the GPL people and all the Berkeley people, and I said, "We have to find out what we have in common. We have to tell a story. We have a press conference at five o'clock. I don't know what we're going to tell them, but we're going to tell 'em something at five." I had a plausible idea that there was something really interesting going on here. But I didn't know that in the course of that day, wrestling through the issues, what that group of 20 people would do. Eric came in and said, "Well, we had this meeting a couple weeks ago, and Christine Peterson proposed this new name, 'Open Source'." Michael Tiemann of Cygnus says, "Well, we've been thinking about this, too. You know; the problem of the name 'free software'." And Linus Torvalds said, "I didn't realize that 'free' had two meanings in English." And Michael Tiemann says, "Well, we've been using the term 'sourceware'."

So we had a vote. And we said, "We're all going to agree on one name, and we're all going to start using it." We voted on "sourceware" versus "open source," and "open source" won. We had the press conference at five, and the rest is history.

Andrew: That's interesting, since Jenny and I have written about how setting artificial deadlines can have negative consequences for teams. It seems like it really helped you guys.

Tim: A lot of what happened was that we brought together a very short-term group of people. I had a sense that there was something there, but didn't quite know what form it would take or ought to take. But I knew I wanted to make something happen. So one of the team principles is that creating an artificial deadline—"We've got a press conference at five o'clock, guys"—can be a pretty powerful tool. Now, a lot of companies and a lot of people really misuse that. I've seen situations where project managers lie to their teams about deadlines, trying to create an artificial sense of urgency. That violates trust.

But when you do it right, identifying that sense of urgency can be really good. It's a little bit like what Alexander Pope said about writing poetry in rhyming couplets: that the narrow aperture makes creativity shoot out like water from a fountain.

In terms of teams, the other thing that I would just really observe is the power of having people with complementary strengths. Right now at O'Reilly, I have a very strong chief operating officer, who makes a huge difference. We're kind of two halves of a coin. I'm the big-scale storytelling, and I spend much less time on internal minutiae of the business, which frees me up to do a lot more with that. She's all over the day-to-day running of the business, and doing a better job of it than when I was trying to do both jobs. Understanding complementary strengths is really critical.

Andrew: I've got a question. A while back, Jenny and I wrote a piece for ONLamp called "What Corporate Projects Should Learn from Open Source." And subsequently, we've done a talk called "What Makes Open Source Work." And what we focused on is the practices they use, because that's been our "thing" in the past. You've been talking a lot about the team, the personalities, complementary strengths, how to work with the people. But one of the things we've found is that if you look at the most successful open source projects that we all know and love—like Apache, Linux, Emacs—you find a lot of great practices. The developers, the programmers, the people on the projects voluntarily adopt practices that, if they faced in the office, they'd find stifling, even though they're the same practices. Practices like adopting a very strict build and release process, continuous integration, test-driven development.

Jenny: Lots and lots of code reviews. We've actually been tasked with putting those same practices in place in corporate environments and gotten lots of pushback from the very same people. So why do you think that is?

Tim: Well, let me put it this way. Anyone who's ridden a horse knows that the secret of success is to have the horse think that it's doing what it wants. So, I think that when people feel like somebody else is telling them what to do, there's going to be resistance. If they think it's what they themselves want, then they sign right up.

Lao Tzu said this 2,500 years ago: when the best leader leads, the people say we did it ourselves.

When some people create something really wonderful with an aesthetic vision, it seems really obvious. Now that we have the iPod, how could you imagine not having touch-screen devices? I remember the first time I picked up the Kindle. I started stroking the screen and nothing happened, and it was like, "What's wrong?" Now the Kindle has its own pieces of truth in it, so to speak—like the EVDO connectivity, where you go, "Yes, that's how it's supposed to work."

Andrew: I think it's interesting that you're talking about how a product's supposed to work. Most of the discussions I've had about open source are about things like the GPL versus the BSD license versus Creative Commons, and I think people tend to get a little bogged down in those details. But you're talking about open source software as a unique way of realizing a vision, and I've never actually thought of it that way.

Tim: Well, you have to realize that people always get hung up on licensing as critical to open source. And while it is certainly important, I think as you guys have suggested here, the practices are much, much more important. When I think about what we've done in our business, first of all books have always been user-contributed. Most of our products are created by people who don't work for us. We have to put out a plausible idea of something we want to get done. We have to find someone who says, "Yeah, that's a good idea, I want that, too." We give them coaching, we bring in a host of other people to review their work inside the company and outside. We have to impose a management system, although it's often very loose. There are a lot of different ways to do it, which is one of the reasons I love Larry Wall's Perl slogan, "There's more than one way to do it." Because I don't think there's any one answer.

Andrew: Especially not in Perl.

Tim: Yes. And take the book *Programming Perl*. I could spend six months remaking this book to be the kind of book I'd write. Or, I could say, "Wow, it's really good just the way it is." Even though it's not the kind of book I'd have done myself. So I blessed it and sent it through.

I remember this one book we published. It's really unfortunate because the editor was really fixated on making it into a different kind of book, so she spent two years working with the authors to somehow teach them, force them, cajole them into doing something other than what they were originally imagining. She just couldn't let go. So I said, "There's a book here, but it's a different one than you're imagining." What these guys had done was written a whole bunch of disconnected pieces. I said, "All you have to do now is tell the story of the book so that this makes sense."

Jenny: I've had a lot of people on my teams tell me that Programming Perl *is one of the best programming books ever written. You had an expectation of what the book was going to be, but what you were given turned out to be different—and better.*

Tim: That's sort of another piece to all of this. How do you find what's true in what you're given? I think this is almost the root of intelligence that draws everything else. There are different kinds of intelligence. One kind is essentially algorithmic and manipulative: you're given all of this data, and you're good at manipulating it. You see people who seem like they're really bright in some sense, but they're really dumb in other ways. Like they don't see things that are obvious, they don't have any common sense. Then you see somebody else, and they're not that good at symbol manipulation, can't spell, and can't do math. But they're geniuses at looking at a situation and understanding what's really going on. And the smartest people have both of those qualities. They can look at the world fresh; they can look at something and say, "Wow, I see what this can be."

So, going back to that other book, the editor had all of this training, all of these ideas about how a book should look, and what should be happening here. And that got in the way of her being able to see the material with fresh eyes and understand that the process could be better by just helping the authors to do what they wanted anyway.

Jenny: Do you think that an editor—or any team leader, really—should try not to have a strong hand in pushing the authors (or the team) toward a specific goal?

Tim: Most of my experience is very much being a leader, not necessarily being a team member. A great deal of it comes from directing people, and I try to direct them in such a way that I have as little to do as possible. A lot of that requires seeing people's strengths, seeing a situation and saying, "Here's what we can make of it."

It's a kind of pattern recognition, which is going back to how I think about the process of editing. It's a little bit like what Michelangelo used to say about making a statue; that it's about finding the image that's hidden in the stone. I think editing a book is like that. Leading a project is like that. When I started telling the story about Web 2.0, it was looking at a bunch of data and uncovering the statue that was hidden in the stone. Same thing when I told the story about open source. I think that leading your team is like that also. How do you get a group of people to achieve their potential? By seeing who they are, and what they can accomplish.

Andrew: *Do you think it's possible to have a great team that doesn't have a great leader? That has more of a collective leadership?*

Tim: Yes, it is possible. But here's the thing. Take Apache, because I think Apache is the great example of that. Tim Berners-Lee laid down the blueprint. He said, "I've created this idea for this hypertext server, this hypertext client." And the genius of Apache was in embracing the constraints. I still remember back in the mid-'90s, this moment where Netscape had added this, Microsoft had added that, and everyone was saying, "Apache seems to be standing still. They aren't adding all these features. They aren't keeping up!" And the guys at Apache said, "Yup. What we do is a hypertext server, and we have this nice extension mechanism where people who want to do something else can add it on."

And that goes back to that architecture of participation. They didn't build this big, conglomerate, complex application. They kept to a pure vision. The vision did actually come from a visionary leader; it just wasn't part of Apache. Apache came from a group of people who were abandoned by the NCSA server team when they all went to found Netscape. And there were a bunch of customers, so they said, "We have to maintain this, and keep it going." What was wonderful about that kind of team was that they accepted the constraints that were laid down by the design of the system. They didn't try to show off their ego or their creativity.

I think a lot of the work done by the IETF (the Internet Engineering Task Force) in the early years did the same thing. There were some wonderful principles laid down, and people really honored them. If you read some of John Postel's stuff in the TCP RFC about the robustness principle, it sounds like something out of the Bible, for Christ's sake! "Be conservative in what you do; be liberal in what you accept from others." Literally, that's what it says.

The point is that if you have the system architected right, you have a better chance of success for teams. You don't want teams that are dependent on a single vision or leader, because if you lose your leader, the whole team goes "pop."

Andrew: *Speaking of things going "pop," can you think of anything from your past where things didn't go so well? Maybe a disaster or two that maybe you learned something important from?*

Tim: There are probably quite a few disasters over the years, some of them which were turned into successes after the fact.

These aren't disasters, but they are failures—they're choices, going back to an aspect of leadership. Things can go wrong. Look at what happened here with Yahoo! and Microsoft. Everybody's out there saying that they can't make up their minds whether Jerry Yang or Steve Ballmer is the bigger loser, because there was a badly mismanaged process without a clear vision of what was the right thing to do. But we might end up looking back and saying,

"Wow, Jerry was brilliant. He kept Yahoo! independent, and then he had a strategy that pulled his hat out of the fire." Can you imagine? Just like you look back at the early history of the PC, at the deal that Bill Gates had cut with IBM. What if IBM had been the sharp dealer? We'd have a very different history. So we don't really know.

Jenny: Right, what we think of as a set-in-stone success now might not even have seemed like a wise choice at the time. You make a series of choices, and the chips fall where they may. Is that how you see your own successes and failures?

Tim: I see in those kinds of moments the impact of choices. At O'Reilly, we did the first web portal. We did GNN, the Global Network Navigator, the pre-Yahoo!, the original portal of Internet sites. I was focused and I did not want to give up control of my company, so we sold GNN to AOL. I did reason correctly that unless I wanted to give up control of my company and take on investors, I wouldn't be able to keep up with the growth of the Internet. I'd read this wonderful book called *Marketing High Technology* by William Davidow (Free Press), an early venture capitalist. He said that it's simple math. Dominating a market means being more than half the market, and growing faster than the market as a whole. I looked at the Internet and said, "We can't do that, a private company that's completely self-funded. With the way that the Internet's exploding, there's no way we won't get marginalized. We have to either take in money or sell." So I sold. It was a big inexperience premium, so to speak. Jerry and David took in venture money, and went on to create a multibillion-dollar company despite the recent travails. I think, from a purely financial point of view, they did much better than we did. That being said, I was clear what my personal goals were: to keep an independent company where I could do what I wanted, and I've been doing it ever since.

I guess the point I'd make is that failure and success are relative to what you're trying to accomplish. If we'd been a venture-backed start-up, my decision would have been a disastrous failure. As a self-funded entrepreneur who was making my own choices, it was my choice to make or not. What I'm trying to get at here is that it's really important not to second-guess a "failure," because a failure may be a choice.

Andrew: But don't you need to have some sort of final accounting? In the end, a project either succeeds or it fails, right?

Tim: We have this idea that's very binary, that it's failure or success. We're trying to choose from a set of alternative futures. There's no best, there's just choice.

I think we've lost in many cases, both in business and in the design of software—the design of any work product, really—the importance of the aesthetic. Wallace Stevens wrote a book of essays called *The Necessary Angel* (Vintage). In it, one of the points he made was that we have the idea that choice matters. He had a poem called "Notes towards a Supreme Fiction." He had the idea that perhaps God was a fiction that we can all believe in. The goal in religion or even in science is to create an aesthetic vision that we can each believe in. You're trying to enroll people.

Andrew: I can hear a reader who works in a corporate environment building a database application reading that and thinking, "There's no aesthetic in what I'm doing."

Tim: And I would say, "Go look at Steve Jobs." That'd be my answer—he's a testament to the power of the aesthetic. He made a set of choices. For many, they feel that Apple screwed up because they didn't go with the dominant paradigm. They followed their own way, and their own aesthetic vision. Each time, he's been able to come back again and again because he has a compelling vision that he's been able to sell to people. People talk about the "Steve Jobs reality distortion field"—that's what it's all about. He can create a compelling vision that other people sign up for.

I remember one of my key employees laughing at me, saying, "I'd have a meeting with you, and I'd go away, and I've said 'yes' to all these things you've said. Then I go away and think, 'I don't actually believe all that stuff!'" I was able to persuade her. And that goes back to what may be an interesting observation. I remember when my company got beyond about fifty people. There was this moment when I really had to change how I worked, because I really had this experience in the early years of the company where I held people in my "reality distortion field," so to speak—everybody in the company at the same time. It was a small enough group and we were all working closely together.

I remember when I was in high school I used to sneak out at night in my father's car. So he wouldn't be able to hear, I'd have to push it out of the driveway and down the block before I started the engine. So I'd be pushing the car, and there'd be this feeling that you're pushing on this thing, and you're pushing and pushing, and gradually it starts to accelerate. I had that feeling with the people in the company—"Wow, this thing is just too heavy." So I had to let go. Then, I would talk to a few people at a time. You'd set people free to go do their thing, and then you'd check in.

There's a science fiction book I read early in my career that was very influential, a book called *Rissa Kerguelen* by F. M. Busby (Berkeley). Not that many people have read it. One of the key concepts that many people have played with over the years, particularly in the '50s and '60s (this book was written in the '70s), was the idea of time dilation. As you get close to the speed of light, one of the Einsteinian paradoxes is that the inertial frame is different and time goes much more slowly for the person traveling at high speed. Many science fiction stories would involve people going off and coming back, and everybody's very old. So this book, *Rissa Kerguelen*, had three parts, and one of them was called "The Long View." It was about how you do planning when you're about to go on an interstellar voyage, and you're going to show up 15 years later by planetary time. The idea is that you have to set something in motion, and then meet up with it. And I think there's something very powerful in that image, the fact that the things we were talking about earlier—the architecture of various systems—that's a way you set something in motion. And you can rendezvous with it, and find if it's developed in the way you expected. That was how I began to think about what I had to do in the company. I had to set things in motion and then go meet up with them.

Jenny: How did your team initially react when you started pulling away?

Tim: There are definitely cycles where people feel their own oats. They want to be the leader, and they want to take things in a different direction. And I think one thing about being a good leader is to know when somebody has the chops to do that. I'm a Celtics fan, and I remember there was a great story from the Larry Bird era. It was crunch time at the end of a basketball game—this was when K. C. Jones was coach. They'd come to the huddle, and Larry says, "Just give me the ball and everybody get out of the way." And K. C. says, "Larry, I'm the coach, so shut up! OK, everybody? Let's get Larry the ball, and everybody get out of the way."

So, sometimes people move ahead, and your job as coach or leader is to say, "Yeah, they're right, give it to them." I've had that relationship with Dale Dougherty a lot. Dale is actually responsible for a big part of O'Reilly's success. A great many things that are attributed to me, he played a major role in. He was the guy who originally got us into the World Wide Web. He was the guy who came up with the name "Web 2.0." He's currently the publisher of *MAKE Magazine*. It kind of feels like a dance in which he goes off and does his own thing, and then it comes back together. Sometimes it feels like a sibling relationship, where we're struggling over who's driving the bus. Other times we're really in harmony. You want people who will argue with you. You want people who have their own vision.

When you have a vision of something that is true—and I don't know what true means, if it's absolute truth or just aesthetic truth. When things just work, when you hear that perfect chord in music, when you see the line in a drawing or the curve of stone in a statue, and you go, "Beauty is truth, and truth beauty, that is all ye know on earth, and all ye need to know"—you know, the Keats line—that's how things come together. For me, the essence of getting people to work together is to have an aesthetic vision that you can get them to sign up for. Where you build a shared vision of the truth that you're building, where you've expressed an ideal. Because then you set people free to pursue that ideal on their own.

PART ONE

People

WHEN WE STARTED WORKING ON *BEAUTIFUL TEAMS* BACK IN LATE 2007, WE THOUGHT WE HAD A pretty good idea of where the book would go. We're techie people: we've implemented lots of practices, done lots of software projects, and seen things get better over time as we did it. We've seen our own teams improve, we've learned from our mistakes over time, and we thought we had a handle on what makes a team work.

So, we thought we'd sit down with a bunch of people who felt the way we did, write down some insightful tricks of the trade and pearls of wisdom, and everyone would be happy.

As it turns out, we were in for a surprise.

Now, we weren't exactly wrong or even misguided when we started working on this project. Results do speak for themselves, and we'd gotten good results. One of the things that made us feel quite confident about our reasonably complete understanding of what makes a good team work is that we'd read plenty other people who agreed with us.

One thing that we both agreed on when we started this project was that a good team has to have a focus on the technical skills of the people on the team. So, when we started recruiting authors and looking through their writing, we expected a lot of stories about how to make sure your team is technically capable: recruiting and hiring the right people, finding the right practices (like writing specs or doing code reviews) and training people on them, and generally helping people who already show talent and promise to develop their skills to become better programmers.

It didn't exactly work out like that. In fact, there's very little talk throughout the whole book about training people, improving their skills, or being very selective about your team members.

Now, let's be clear here. Nobody said that wasn't important. In fact, just the opposite seems to be true: all of our contributors seemed to assume that a good team starts out with at least a kernel of skilled people with the right training, background, and attitude for the job. It seemed obvious to everyone that if you have people who are incapable of doing the job, the team and the project will clearly fail. But what surprised us was that rather than being the ultimate goal, getting the right skills for the team was really more of a starting point to build on.

The truth, as it turns out, is a lot more complicated than we realized at first. It has more to do with things that are a lot harder to quantify. Sometimes the best people on the team aren't always the most technically skilled, and sometimes the most technically skilled people on the team can actually be detrimental to getting the work done. People need to be able to work together, and if they can't, it doesn't matter how good their skills are. In fact, some of the best programmers (from a technical perspective) are in danger of getting too cocky, and can actually make it more difficult to get the project done. But those are often the most important people on your team.

We were starting to get a little nervous. We were used to seeing the world in black and white: either you have a team of the best people (the smartest, most technically skilled, capable developers, testers, architects, etc.) who can do the job best, or you have a less-than-perfect team and you have to deal with it. But what we found is that *all* teams are less-than-perfect. Even the ones that are full of highly skilled, top-notch people can have serious problems that can cause the code to suffer. And *all* teams have some drama. Even if they produce something solid and amazing, they all have to overcome the same challenges that come with people working with other people.

Once we realized that, we started looking back through our own careers, and our own teams. What we found was that our most successful teams really weren't always the ones with the best programmers. They were the ones where everyone worked really well together.

In the end, teams are made up of people, and people are the most important part of the equation. Sometimes we even fell into the trap of thinking that people with similar skills were somewhat interchangeable. If you treat building software as a bean-counting exercise, it's way too easy to think of people as resources to be assigned to tasks, and their work as effort hours to be expended; you could easily come to the conclusion that good people are just cogs in a machine, and that their technical skills are just attributes that can be measured or turned on with certifications, training classes, and experience hours.

As we worked with our authors and interviewees, we were reminded just how untrue that is. And, in fact, we realized that on a few occasions, both of us have fallen into the trap of thinking of our people as interchangeable cogs, and it inevitably led to our projects running into serious problems.

The stories and interviews in this section are the ones that reminded us of those important lessons. They're about what happens when people clash on teams, and what happens when they learn to work together well. Reading these stories and talking to these people, we learned that no team is a storybook team of brilliant engineers who work together perfectly and professionally 100% of the time.

More than that, the most influential people on your team aren't always the best programmers. In fact, they're not the managers or leaders, either. They're the people who are *genuine*: they're there to get the work done, and are able to be themselves while doing it. They listen to the people around them, and understand what motivates them and makes them tick. And it's not because they read a book or took a seminar on how to be a motivational leader. It's because they're considerate to the people around them. They take the time to make sure that everyone's on the same frequency—not necessarily nice or even helpful to each other, just compatible in a way that works for them. And they recognize when they simply can't work together (for whatever reason), and try to do something about it.

Teams are messy. They're full of emotional connections, often between people who are at their wits' end trying to solve problems that may not necessarily be solvable. When you have people who, in the midst of a situation like that, are willing to be themselves, put themselves on the line, listen to the people around them, and help everyone get through the late nights and the frustration, that's what makes a team great. Not necessarily *beautiful*, but effective and good to work on. Without those kinds of connections between people on the team, the job is just a job, and the team isn't one that everyone on it will remember for the rest of their lives.

CHAPTER TWO

Why Ugly Teams Win

Scott Berkun

THE BAD NEWS BEARS. THE RAMONES. ROCKY BALBOA. THE DIRTY DOZEN. REAL HEROES ARE UGLY. They are misfits. Their clothes are wrong, their form is bad, and they don't even know all the rules. They get laughed at and are told to their faces that, dear God, for all that is holy they should quit, but they refuse to listen. In spite of their failings, they find ways to achieve, betting everything on passion, persistence, and imagination. For these reasons, when things get tough, it's the ugly teams that win. People from ugly teams expect things to go wrong and show up anyway. They conquer self-doubt, make friendships under fire, and find magic in ideas that others abandon. Ugly teams are bulletproof, die-hard work machines, and once the members of an ugly team have earned each other's trust, they will outperform the rest of any organization. Nietzsche would have been right at home on an ugly team: what does not kill the ugly team makes the ugly team stronger.

Ugly Talent

Many so-called beautiful teams were never described in those words by the people on them. Lou Gehrig and Babe Ruth, members of perhaps the greatest sports team in history, the 1927 Yankees, despised each other. America's founding fathers, Thomas Jefferson and

John Adams, feuded regularly, in public and in private. Many great music bands, such as The Supremes, The Doors, The Clash, The Beatles, and even Guns N' Roses, lasted only a few years before they tore each other apart.* We love the simple idea that only a beautiful person, or a beautiful team, can make something beautiful. As if Picasso wasn't a misogynistic sociopath, van Gogh wasn't manic-depressive, or Jackson Pollock (and dozens of other well-known creatives and legendary athletes) didn't abuse alcohol or other drugs. Beauty is overrated, as many of their works weren't considered beautiful until long after they were made, or their creators were dead (if the work didn't change, what did?). Most of us suffer from a warped, artificial, and oversimplified aesthetic, where beauty is good and ugly is bad, without ever exploring the alternatives.

Michael Lewis's 2003 bestseller, *Moneyball: The Art of Winning an Unfair Game* (W. W. Norton & Company), explored the biases of the Oakland A's baseball scouts when evaluating the ability of new players. Instead of focusing solely on results, the ability of a given individual to hit baseballs, or to throw them so that others cannot hit them, professional scouts were heavily influenced by appearance. Overweight, short, or seemingly uncoordinated players were overlooked despite statistics demonstrating their talents. Billy Beane, the Oakland A's general manager, revolutionized how the potential of a player was measured and closed the gap between what we expect talent to look like and what it actually is. He forced people to move past their preconceived expectations and to seek out less subjective measures of talent. Ugly players, or good-looking players who played "ugly" but got results, had more value than the league thought they did. His honest look at what mattered in baseball changed the way many professional sports teams evaluate and scout for players.

Similar to what baseball scouts were like before Bean's influence, we all have firm beliefs about people that we cannot justify. Over a lifetime, we passively develop an image of how a great athlete, a trustworthy doctor, or a brilliant programmer should dress, talk, or behave, and those images shape our opinions more than we realize. When it comes to teams, most of our memories of what a good team should look and feel like come from television shows and movies.† Few heroes and legends in real life were as attractive and cool as the stars who play them, and rarely did their development as individuals, or as teams, proceed in a neat little narrative easily described in 90 minutes of entertainment. Films like *The Natural, Saving Private Ryan*, or even *The Matrix* skip past all the messy, ugly struggles of how teams form and grow, presenting us only with tales of how successful, good-looking teams adopt a talented, and beautiful-looking, leading character.

Pop quiz: given the choice between two job candidates, one a prodigy with a perfect 4.0 GPA and the other a possibly brilliant but "selectively motivated" 2.7 GPA candidate (two

---

* Until a decade passes and the revenue potential outweighs their mutual hatred. See *http://www.spinner.com/2007/08/10/20-bitter-band-breakups-smashing-pumpkins/* for a longer list of famous band breakups.

† Yes, I'm aware I mentioned the films *The Bad News Bears* and *Rocky*. Even the best points have a few exceptions.

As and four Cs),* who would you hire? All other considerations being equal, we'd all pick the "beautiful," perfect candidate. No one gets fired for hiring the beautiful candidate. What could be better, or more beautiful, than perfect scores? If we go beneath the superficial, perfect grades often mean the perfect following of someone else's rules. They are not good indicators of passionate, free-thinking, risk-taking minds. More important is that a team comprising only 4.0 GPA prodigies will never get ugly. They will never take big risks, never make big mistakes, and therefore never pull one another out of a fire. Without risks, mistakes, and mutual rescue, the chemical bonds of deep personal trust cannot grow. For a team to make something beautiful there must be some ugliness along the way. The tragedy of a team of perfect people is that they will all be so desperate to maintain their sense of perfection, their 4.0 in life, that when faced with the pressure of an important project their selfish drives will tear the team apart. Beautiful people are afraid of scars: they don't have the imagination to see how beautiful scars can be.

Ugly As Beautiful

Beautiful and *ugly* are tricky words to apply to groups of people. If I say the Mona Lisa or Mount McKinley is beautiful, I'm claiming it is attractive or well crafted: I'm making an aesthetic judgment of an object we can collectively observe. I can point to it, describe it, throw tomatoes at it, or even allow you to compare your judgment of the thing as seen by your eyes with how I describe what I see in mine. I do believe beauty is in the eye of the beholder, but two people with different eyes are still talking about an object that exists outside of either person. However, to claim that a team, a club, or even a nation is beautiful makes less sense. A team is defined by a set of relationships between people, and relationships don't exist as physical things. Judging the aesthetics of non-physical things stretches the entire idea of aesthetics. It puts beauty not in the eye, but in the mind, where we cannot collectively observe the same thing. Rupert, the team captain, will have one sense of what the team is, while Cornelius, the team mascot, will have another. And certainly, people playing on a competing team will have a third. And none of them can point to "the team" as a point of reference with the same certainty they could about the Mona Lisa or Mount McKinley.

The only use of beauty applied to teams that makes sense is the Japanese concept of *wabi-sabi*. Roughly, *wabi-sabi* means there is a special beauty found in things that have been used. That pair of shoes you love because they've been broken in, and have carried your feet on long walks on the beach, has a beauty no new pair of shoes could ever have. Even if those shoes were dirty, scratched, and beat up in a way that no person looking to buy a new pair for himself would ever call beautiful, they'd maintain a *wabi-sabi* kind of beauty to you.

Sometimes the way something wears out can be beautiful to everyone. Find the oldest building in your neighborhood, the oldest tree in the nearest park. There is a majesty that

---

* Disclosure: the author's GPA may possibly resemble the one described here.

comes from how something ages that depends on the imperfections it has collected over time.* Anyone who prefers to buy used things in part because of how they look has an appreciation for *wabi-sabi*. In this sense, the ugly teams I described at the beginning of this chapter, the underdog, the misfit, represent the *wabi-sabi* teams. These are groups that share scars, have failed together and recovered together, and are still fighting as a team. And it's only through those experiences that a team can develop a character that has any approximation of beauty.

My Wabi-Sabi Team: Internet Explorer 4.0

In 1995, I joined the Internet Explorer team at Microsoft. It was a small, fledgling project manned by a handful of people. It didn't even earn a spot in Windows 95. Microsoft's first web browser was released to the world, exclusively, as an undercard feature on the $49 add-on to Windows known as the Plus Pack.† But with Netscape's rise and the industry-wide hope that the rise of Netscape would signal the end of Microsoft, the team exploded in importance. The executives at Microsoft, ever paranoid and supremely skilled at chasing taillights, famously turned the company on a dime and made the Internet a central part of every strategy and tactic across the company. By version 4.0, the project team consisted of more than 100 people, enough to dominate two entire floors of Building 27 on the north side of Microsoft's campus.

In 1997, the Internet Explorer team began its fateful voyage into version 4.0. In the history of software, few projects faced as many evils as we would in a single year.‡ A litany of reorgs, executive battles, leaked design plans, impossible goals, DOJ antitrust lawsuits, and revolving-door middle management, all while bearing the weight of responsibility to save the company from the greatest threat, at least according to the rest of the industry, it had ever seen.§ If you threw in a few plagues and natural disasters, we'd be able to check every item off the list of the major calamities no manager ever wants to face.

But the trap that would be the team's undoing had been set ourselves: despair and hubris. The first three releases had been successes. Internet Explorer 1.0 was a simple retrofit of

---

* During the recent renovation of the Parthenon in Greece, they considered restoring the building to what it would have looked like when built. But they decided instead to restore it to the ruin it is, as the aesthetic of the exposed stone and worn-out marble better fits our expectations for what the building should look like. *Wabi-sabi* trumped new and shiny.

† Even the marketing team wasn't sure if this web browser thing was going to pan out, as more sure-fire features like a desktop theme manager, hard drive compressor (hey, it was 1995), and background task scheduler earned equal or better billing.

‡ I'm not proud of this fact, but I've yet to hear a story that tops the drama of IE4 given the stage it played out on. If you have a nomination, however, I'd love to hear it. Miserable project survivors love company.

§ Don't take my word for it. Two books have been written about this period of time at Microsoft. See *How the Web Was Won* by Paul Andrews (Broadway), which is ridiculously positive about all things Microsoft. Alternatively, *Competing on Internet Time* by Michael A. Cusumano and David B. Yoffie (Free Press) presents a more balanced story told from the Netscape perspective, but focuses more on strategy than the personalities or tactics.

the purchased Spyglass browser. Version 2.0 made steady progress and was out the door in a few months. Then 3.0, the first major release, showed the world that Microsoft was not dead, had caught up, had added some new ideas, and was a contender in the game. And with a stockpile of resources in place on both sides, the fourth wave of the browser wars began. Both sides bet as big as they could, failing to recognize that the nature of the project had fundamentally changed. Like a cocky kid juggler who suddenly realizes he has more balls in the air than he can even see, much less catch, our team fell apart.

The center of our despair was called *Channels*. In 1997, the world was convinced that the future of the Web was in "push technology," the ability for websites to push content out to customers (a predecessor to the RSS feeds used by blogs today). Instead of people searching the Web, the content would be smart and find its way to people, downloading automatically and appearing in their bookmark list, on their desktops, in their email, or in desktop widgets and dashboards yet to be invented. We called this feature *Channels*, and it was led by a small team. While they scrambled to design how it would work, the business folks raced their counterparts at Netscape to court major websites like Disney and ESPN. We needed their content to make the whole thing work: having the pipes is one thing, but it's another to have something to push through them.

In the frenzy to make deals and catch up with the hype, we lost ourselves. Innovation cannot be achieved with one hand on a rulebook and the other over a fire. The deals we made forced legal contracts into the hands of the development team: the use of data from these websites had many restrictions and we had to follow them, despite the fact that few doing the design work had seen them before they were signed. Like the day the *Titanic* set sail with thousands of defective rivets, our fate was sealed well before the screaming began. Despite months of work, the Channels team failed to deliver. The demos were embarrassing. The answers to basic questions were worse. Soon, word of the Channels project's downward spiral spread across the team and the company, taking the reputation of the entire project with it. If this was the bet all of Microsoft was making, we'd already lost.

The Internet Explorer team was never a place in shortage of opinions—loud, passionate, sarcastic, and occasionally abusive opinions. Disagreements among executives grew into denial and inaction, causing the opinionated to yell louder and with more venom. No one could survive the cauldron we'd brewed for ourselves, and eventually the project manager for Channels was crushed and burnt out. Soon he was replaced, as was his manager. Then they were both replaced. In the churn, without a taskmaster to keep them at bay, the twisty tentacles of Channels spread across the project, infecting code, design, and morale. If enough big things go wrong, everyone becomes incompetent. Everyone gets ugly. People quit. Despair rose. Managers stormed out of meetings and heavy things were thrown across boardrooms. Months flew by and therapy bills rose. As other parts of the project were completed, we tried not to notice the gaping Channels-shaped black hole at our center, slowly pulling everything inside.

I don't know how it started, but somewhere in our fourth reorg, under our third general manager and with our fifth project manager for Channels, the gallows humor began. It is here that the seeds of team *wabi-sabi* are sown. Pushed so far beyond what any of us expected, our sense of humor shifted into black-death Beckett mode. It began when we were facing yet another ridiculous, idiotic, self-destructive decision where all options were comically bad. "Feel the love," someone would say. It was some kind of bad self-help jargon, but it was so far from our reality that it worked. Sometimes we'd add a smiley face after it in an email when making a request we knew was absurd. Or we'd mockingly pat each other on the back as we said it, reinforcing how phony and clichéd the sentiment was.

It worked, because we knew we were all in the same misery, and that on that particular day, more of it had landed on one person than another. On the day I saw months of people's work, including my own, being cut at random, just one slash on a list in a half-day-long marathon of slashes, without any logic or chance for defense, someone would say in an email, "Feel the love! It's IE4!" Toward the end, I once saw it scribbled on a whiteboard, waiting for us at a meeting of team leaders. Even our group manager had to laugh when he saw it, connecting with us in our sardonic lifeline of morale. That moment changed something for me and for the team: he felt the same way. If we couldn't escape our fates, at least we weren't insane for acknowledging them for what they were.

Late in the project, I became the sixth, and last, program manager for Channels. My job was to get something out quickly for the final beta release, and do what damage control I could before it went out the door in the final release. When we pulled it off and found a mostly positive response from the world, we had the craziest ship party I'd ever seen. It wasn't the champagne, or the venue, or even how many people showed up. It was how little of the many tables of food was eaten: in just a few minutes, most of it had been lovingly thrown at teammates and managers. I received the largest glob of guacamole ever absorbed by a human head, and somewhere someone has a photo to prove it.

The true *wabi-sabi* bonds grew in the aftermath. The few who remained to work on Internet Explorer 5.0 had a special bond. We had seen each other at our worst, and still felt respect. We all knew the true horrors of what could happen, and could trust each other not to let it happen again. In one of our earliest planning meetings, the entire conversation revolved around how to kill Channels and eliminate it from the face of the project. In the months that followed, my powers as a leader were enhanced by the fact that I could look certain programmers in the eye and trust them completely, having seen, firsthand, how well they'd dealt with tough situations, and they could do the same with me. We had the confidence, grown from our ugly, desperate, but collective struggles, to focus on real problems we knew customers had, no matter what hype and trends pundits were passionately guessing about. Internet Explorer 5.0 would be the best project team I'd ever work on, and one of the best software releases in Microsoft's history. That might not mean much to anyone else, but it's a beautiful thing to me.

CHAPTER THREE

Building Video Games

an Interview with Mark Healey

LittleBigPlanet has been one of the most hotly anticipated games of 2008 for the PlayStation 3, and by all accounts it's one of the best games of the year. Not only is it a ridiculously addictive platformer, but it's also a creative tool that lets gamers build and share their own levels. The combination of great game play and social networking is a winner for the game's creator, Media Molecule, which was founded a few years ago by Mark Healey. We wanted to know what it was like working on a game like this, so we sat down with Mark.

Andrew: Jenny's been utterly addicted to LittleBigPlanet, *and I love it. You guys just did a phenomenal job.*

Mark: Well, thank you very much. I've actually been quite addicted to it myself.

Jenny: It's a great game. It really, really is. That's what made us want to talk to you. We wanted to hear the story behind how this game came about. Since this book is really focused on teams and how they come about, we'd love to kind of hear the story of how you guys came together to build this.

Mark: OK, let me think. I'm going to have to use my memory, which is normally a bit of a disaster....

The company was founded by me, Alex Evans, Dave Smith, and Kareem Ettouney, with a lot of help from a guy called Chris Lee, who's the business-minded person.

Apart from Chris, all of us had worked together and been friends at our previous company, Lionhead Studios.

We were always working together on various things, and one day I decided that I was going to make a silly kung fu film over a weekend, for no other reason than to have a laugh, really. So I borrowed a video camera from Lionhead and we spent about £50 on some costumes and things. We went into the park behind my house and made an incredibly stupid kung fu film, without a script or plan; we didn't know who was going to turn up, so we just winged it on the day. I then started editing it and making it into a little film—at the same time, I was teaching myself to program C++, because I actually used to work as a programmer in the industry many, many years ago, before I became an artist. Back then I used assembler (6510), but chose to concentrate more on art because it's less of a headache.

So I was making this film and learning C++, when I put two and two together and I thought, "OK. Well, if I'm going to learn C++ I need to have a little project, so I'll make a simple little fighting game, a bit like *Street Fighter*, and use the kung fu film as cut scenes." So that was what became *Rag Doll Kung Fu*, a little indie game that eventually became the first third-party game released by Valve over their digital distribution engine, Steam. It was before Media Molecule was ever thought about.

I was working on that in my spare time, and because I knew Alex and Dave, I would often rope them into helping me with some of the more complicated stuff I needed help on. Programming is one thing, but programming a PC is a whole world of pain. It just seems incredibly complicated to me; reading Direct X documentation is ridiculous—every other word is a link to another page! Luckily for me, Alex and Dave are very brainy and technical, and can do things in 10 minutes that would take me 10 years....

I had met Kareem a couple of days before I asked him to come join in the kung fu fun in the park—we soon became the best of friends, and he ended up being involved with lots of *Rag Doll Kung Fu*: he starred as the evil boss in the filming, helped out with some of the

A screenshot from Rag Doll Kung Fu, the game that first brought the team together.

art, we made the music together on a four-track in my front room, and we even sat down and dubbed over ridiculous voices with another friend of mine, Barry, whose girlfriend, Siobhan, would later become a vital addition to the Media Molecule team as we started to grow, as executive producer.

So you see, we formed an ad hoc team through *Rag Doll Kung Fu*. And in terms of indie games, it was quite successful, really. It got a lot of attention for a game of its size, and more importantly gave us a taste for doing something bigger. We've always worked for other companies, and doing that small indie game ended up being a crash course, if you like, in the whole process from design through to production, through to localization and publishing....

Andrew: So Rag Doll Kung Fu *was the project where it all started for you?*

Mark: *Rag Doll Kung Fu* brought us together as a team. Then, through a friend of a friend, we got in touch with Chris, who has past experience running businesses (he ran Renderware) and he told us X, Y, and Z, things that we need to think about, things that we need to do. It just so happened that within a very short space of time, through a mutual friend, we got the opportunity to pitch to Phil Harrison—he was the man at Sony at the time—but the catch was we didn't have long to prepare! It was exactly in one week that this meeting would happen. We had nothing to show, so we had to put together an idea very quickly!

Mark in a live-action cut scene from Rag Doll Kung Fu.

Andrew: That had to be a rush—in every sense of the word.

Mark: It was very exciting, and I suppose it was stressful. But we always thrived off that in the past, you know, when we're given a tight deadline.

Jenny: Is that something that brought you guys together when you'd worked together at Lionhead?

Mark: Yeah. I mean, I think certainly towards the end of our time at Lionhead, people like me, Alex, Kareem, and Dave were quite often brought in to resolve some problems, but when we weren't firefighting, we had free rein to do what we wanted, really. We were put in a room and just told to make something cool. R&D is the technical term for that, I believe.

Andrew: Do you thrive in that kind of environment? Because a lot of people would find that sort of lack of direction almost intimidating, and definitely hard to work in.

Mark: I love that personally, but obviously it requires a certain amount of self-motivation. You have to come up with at least a rough plan or idea for where you want to head; otherwise, it's easy to sit down and just twiddle your thumbs or surf the Net. We were working on a project called *The Room*. I think there might be a video of it somewhere on the Internet.

Jenny: So, other than the three of you, how many are there on the team at Media Molecule?

Mark: Well, now we're about 30 people.

Jenny: And did it take that many people to build the first version of LittleBigPlanet? *How did you plan for the project?*

Mark: When we knew that we were going to do this pitch for Phil Harrison, we talked roughly about what we all wanted to be doing. The ideas were very blue sky, really, and slightly vague, so one of our main strategies for the pitch was to pitch ourselves as being incredibly creative and skillful, and that if Sony gave us some cash, then surely we'd make something awesome....

Dave had a lot of experience with physics, for example, and he made this 2D physics engine that was very cool, so we knew we wanted to use that somehow. And with the *Rag Doll Kung Fu* game, although it was a very small indie game, there were certain aspects of that that we knew people really got excited about; in particular, the fact that you could easily make your own characters and put them in the game, and that you could act. So we had this idea of user-created content and self-expression, if you like, coming into the mix.

So you could say, in a way, that I brought in the *Rag Doll Kung Fu*, and Dave brought in the physics element, and then Alex was very keen to show off his technical skills—his graphics coding (he made the rendering engine) is second to none! He was also down with the kids more than the rest of us, I think, and threw in the YouTube/MySpace element. We managed to munge all of this together somehow into a small, hands-on demo and presentation, which ended up being very cool. Try searching YouTube for "Yellow Head" and you can see what the playable part of the presentation was like. That was all put together in less than a week, thanks to some ninja physics coding from Dave.

So, this meeting was as much a pitch of talent than of a very specific idea, and thankfully, Chris had armed himself with a strange magical spell called a "business plan," which told Sony how much cash and how many people we needed to make a more fleshed-out demo.... Phil Harrison was suitably impressed with everything, and gave in to our demands, which started the ball rolling.

Following the Sony meeting, Kareem was rapidly signed up as the art director and we started to look at what and who we needed to build the team, and we quickly found some more arty people, and some more cody people, most of which were friends (all very talented). Siobhan joined to help organize us, and Mags (who had helped me deal with tax stuff related to *Rag Doll Kung Fu* earnings) joined as our bookkeeper, to make sure everyone got paid and that we paid the various things that a company needs to pay when employing people!

The design process was basically an open discussion followed up with something to play or look at on screen/paper or the other way around. My main role was always pulling together all these ideas into a single document and trying to make them make sense in relation to each other so that it could be shared with everyone. This made it clear what we were all doing/where we were heading, and became a kind of evolving design document.

Six months soon passed, and we had a very nice demo to show Sony (they had been looking at it every month to make sure we weren't just drinking the money). This is a fairly formal and pretty intimidating meeting known as a "greenlight," and is where the decision is made to continue into full production, or can it! Thankfully, Sony were very happy with it—so happy, in fact, that they decided to show it at GDC in Phil's keynote speech, in front of the world media, and well over 5,000 people!

Jenny: One of the things that's so amazing about the game to me is the level creator and the user interface for it. How did you guys come about that?

Mark: That evolved over time, really. When we first pitched the game it was very much "OK, here's a 2D physics platform game and we want to put some user-created content in there." That was effectively what we pitched to Sony. And they were actually most excited about the user-created content side, which surprised us a little bit because we thought they'd be scared about that. But once we knew they were into that, we really ran with it.

One of our big strengths is that when we went for that first pitch we actually had a playable demo, and I think that made a huge difference to getting them excited because there was something that they could actually feel and play. I think a lot of publishers get so bored looking at PowerPoint presentations.

Andrew: You're talking about getting the people you're pitching it to excited. Were you able to keep that kind of level of excitement up, first between just the core of you guys, and then once you started expanding the team? That has to be a big motivator for all of you guys. Did that have any impact on how you come up with ideas? How you build the software in general?

Mark: Yeah. This is the way we've always worked, really—we wouldn't tend to make a big design document upfront saying, "This is what we're going to make." It's very vague early on: "OK. We want it to be a 2D kind of physics platform thing with some user-created content." Just the act of doing stuff is what stirs up the ideas, and then it's like, "Oh, cool. That just gave me an idea to do this. Check this out." And we can really feed off each other. So, it's very much a sort of jamming type environment, if that makes sense, which is only possible when you're just a few people. Once you get beyond even six or seven people, you have to start being more structured. It just descends into chaos otherwise. The way we dealt with this as the team got larger was to create "molecules," which are small teams of people working on a particular area. This gives people the opportunity to still work in a jamming style.

The GDC demo was almost identical to the demo we presented at our greenlight meeting. It looked really nice, and we actually had some creative tools in there. The creative tools that we had at that time were completely irrelevant to what we've got now, but it was enough to put the seed in there. And it wasn't really until we showed the game at GDC to the public for the first time that we realized how excited by the idea of being able to create your own levels and games that people really were. It was getting that reaction that really cemented what we were making, I think.

And that made me very happy, because I'd personally always been into the idea of making something that allows people to make games easily. It's been my hobby since I was at school, and since then I was always in search of the perfect tool that makes it really easy to make games.

A thing to remember is that everyone who joined in on the adventure, particularly before GDC, took a big gamble, leaving well-paid jobs to come join a bunch of clowns! And despite various hard times (we had some hideous arguments), it's not been that hard to maintain excitement. The reaction we got at GDC gave us all a boost in confidence and then we received a lot of great support from the games dev community and the press, which was really lucky for us. Kareem also really shone as a people person, and was very good at keeping everybody's spirits up, which has been very valuable, as I can be quite introverted sometimes.

Andrew: You mentioned that once your team gets a little bit too big, you "descend into chaos." Help us understand what it means to descend into chaos, and how you get around that.

Mark: You start getting things happening on the screen and something that's playable, and then everybody throws out other ideas for where you can go with that thing. If you don't sit down and actually agree on a direction between you, then people will just kind of go off on their own tangents and start working on ideas that conflict with each other, and suddenly things don't hold together as a complete whole anymore.

I think what we've managed to do is strike a good balance there—officially, me and Dave were the lead designers of the project, but really the game was designed by everyone here. And certainly, what my role ended up becoming was kind of absorbing other people's ideas, taking them and molding them into something that's coherent, if that makes sense, and sometimes having to say, "No, we can't do it like that because that just doesn't make sense with what we're trying to achieve here now." It was just like trying to hold a vision while dealing with an ever-evolving design, I suppose, if that makes sense.

Andrew: That makes a lot of sense, and it really jibes with what a lot of people have been telling us: that you need to write something down to keep a vision. When you say "evolving design," what do you mean? Did it evolve steadily? Was there any sort of iterative thing that you had going?

Mark: Yeah, iteration is the right word, I think. Because certainly, some people might be of the illusion that you can design a game on a piece of paper, like a blueprint, and then send it to the factory and get it made. For some games that's probably possible. But in my experience, it just never works like that, certainly on the games that I've worked on. It's more that you have this high concept—it's like having an indistinct wire mesh of a statue that everyone's chucking clay at, and as you're there just trying to sort of smooth it out, it starts to present itself to you. It's not that you design it beforehand. You just work at it, and it starts to show itself, if that makes sense, and then you kind of mold it.

Jenny: Are you the one who does the molding, or is it more of a team effort? How do you keep it on vision? And how much freedom does everybody else feel to change that vision partway through?

Mark: What I've found myself doing at the end of the day was very much trying to hold that top vision: "OK. This is going to be a creative tool that allows people to make things." And to me, that's essentially what it is. Any ideas that came into the mix, I would always be looking at them in that context.

Jenny: Was there a time when someone had wanted to take the game in a different direction than you did?

Mark: There were definitely a lot of things that we would try that we would then decide, "That's just not working," so we'd go back and try something else. Because we're quite a small team, we are agile enough, if you will, to suddenly change direction. The perfect analogy is the difference between steering a speedboat and a supertanker. With the speedboat you can flick the handle and change direction. The supertanker takes ages to turn.

Early on we kind of had a bit of an internal argument, if you like, as to whether what we were making was more towards a platform game or whether it was more towards a creative tool. Some thought making a platform game was more important than the creative tools and others vice versa—I think we ended up in the middle, which was good. We made an awesome creative tool, and just so happened to make a great platformer that served as an example of what was possible with the tool!

I must confess, I would often get my way just by becoming in a very bad mood and becoming intolerable in the office, which sounds terrible, but sometimes it was like that. There were definitely some painful moments. I think at any one time all of the directors have completely hated each other and wanted to kill each other, which sounds bad, but it's good, I think. It shows that we actually care about what we're doing. There's definitely a lot of passion in there. And I think often we ended up with the best resolution.

Sackboy and Sackgirl, the characters from LittleBigPlanet.

Jenny: It's interesting you're talking about passion for the product and the end goal, because it sounds like you guys were really focused on building the right game. How do you keep track of the quality of what you're building as you're building it, especially as the vision's evolving?

Mark: Just play it all the time. I mean, I think that's one of the most important things you can do when you're making a game: just play it often. A lot of people forget that. You can sit down and you just play it and think things like, "Am I enjoying this? Am I into this? Does this feel good or is this really irritating? Is this boring? Ooh, I wish I could do this!" I think your target audience has to be yourself, initially. You have to make something that meets your own standards of something that you want to play. And then, if you're lucky, it'll be something that other people like, too. But I think if you set out to make something that's going to be impressive to other people, then you're kind of doomed to failure, really. So, I think that's probably the way to do it.

It's also always important to test it on people that know nothing about it, which can often be quite a painful eye-opener because you can become quite self-absorbed in a particular detail. You could end up getting really, really obsessed about one particular point in the game, and then you show it to somebody else that's never played the game, and what you worried about doesn't even come into their radar. Suddenly some other obvious point is really brought out into the open. I guess it's a good mixture of constantly playing it yourself, but also getting the opinions of other people. Testing, testing, testing is the bottom line!

Another important factor as well in terms of quality is having quality people. Because we're a small team and we knew from the beginning that we wanted to stay a small team, we were very careful about who we hired, and we've hired some incredibly talented people; that allows you to put trust in people. In my experience, once you get big, over 100 people, for example, it's just inevitable that you start getting deadwood, people that aren't really there to do something that they're proud of; they can be there just to get a salary. There's none of that here. Everyone here is really dedicated and proud of their work.

Andrew: How do you attract the right people? Because it's got to be more than just getting smart people or even people who have done video game programming before. They have to be right for the team, too, especially if it's a small team.

Mark: It's not easy, actually. I mean, initially in our first year, because the game wasn't announced publicly or anything like that and we were a new company, it was 10 times as hard, because you want people that have got experience, people that are good at this kind of thing. And we were expecting them to leave a well-paid job to come and join a start-up with people that they don't know, which can be quite risky.

The first six months was hard, finding good people; it was basically people that already knew us and were interested in what we were doing. But once the game was announced at GDC and it got a really good response that for us was the perfect recruitment drive.

Suddenly people are really excited by this thing, and were approaching us left, right, and center—but we had a very strict hiring process. Depending on the particular role, we'd have different practical tests that we would give to people.

Interestingly, for the level design, for example, most of the people that we took on actually had no games industry experience whatsoever. The test we designed for that role was more to test their thinking and their creativity. For the programming, it's obviously much more technical-based, so we'd give them a broken space invaders-type game and ask them to fix the bugs and improve it, make it cool.

We would also get any potential new hire to talk to other people in the team. You can quite quickly get a feel for whether you're going to get on with someone or not. And luckily, we chose pretty well. I think we've had four people that we ended up not keeping on, because we do a probation period. So, we did all right, really.

Once we found someone that we really did want, it was a case of making the proposition attractive to them. We have got a nice family atmosphere here; everybody matters. There's no small cogs. Everyone is really an important part of the team. And we've also got a very good bonus scheme! Everyone that's contributing towards this game, assuming that the game makes a lot of money, will make a lot of money, too. It's very fair like that, which is not a lot of people's experience in the games industry. Quite often, people are kind of worked to the bone and then don't really get to see a lot of the rewards, which is a depressing fact, but it's true.

Andrew: It sounds like having respect for the people on your team is really important to you.

Mark: It's essential, because I've been a member on many teams before in the past, and I've had good and bad. And when it's bad, it's terrible, really. These people are investing their life and their skills in this thing, so they need to get the just desserts from that, too.

Andrew: Hey, I had a question. It's a little bit of a jump, but I love the music. I'm a musician and I've been really impressed with the choices—they're really perfect for the game.

Mark: Oh, yeah. There's some great tunes in there!

Andrew: I've really never heard anything like it in a video game. How did that soundtrack come about? Is there a story behind that? How did it happen?

Mark: With our initial pitch to Sony, and in our monthly "show them what we're up to" meetings, we tended to use that kind of music with any videos that we presented. It helped to create a nice vibe. And it was a progression from that, I suppose. Once we started making the game, we'd set the tone with those videos. Now we had a major publisher financing the game, and suddenly they'd start telling us things like, "Well, we can license these tracks. You can use them in the game."

So, literally everyone on the team just started putting forward ideas for songs and things that they liked, and we kind of gave that to Sony and they found out whether they could get the licensing or not. That was it, really.

The original interactive music was written as a collaboration. We started working with another friend, Mat, who has a studio and access to lots of real musicians. He wrote some music for us, and then when Kenny Young joined us just after GDC, he collaborated with Mat to write all of the original interactive tracks. Kenny also managed the process of going back and forth on the licensed tracks and creating all the sound effects—quite a guy!

Jenny: And the tutorials in the game, you got Steven Fry to do the voice?

Mark: Yes!

Jenny: That's really cool. How did you swing that?

Mark: It was me who really wanted that, because with the whole creative tool and the interface, we really needed some tutorials, so I prototyped these as videos, and I kind of had in mind, "If I'm going to have someone teaching me about things, they need to sound interesting, and funny." [Douglas Adams's] *The Hitchhiker's Guide to the Galaxy* (Del Rey) immediately sprung to mind. I don't know if you've seen that film or read the books, but Steven Fry did the voice of *The Hitchhiker's Guide to the Galaxy* book in the film. And I was just like, "It would be so perfect if we could get him," not really thinking that it's a possibility. But someone in Sony heard me say that, and the next thing I know, it's like, "OK. We've got Steven Fry. He's into it."

The next thing I know, I'm in a studio, watching this huge character of a man read through the scripts to the game! I got to meet a hero! So that's definitely one of the cool things about working with a big publisher. They can make things like that happen. And we were lucky he was really excited and into the whole game. That was a dream come true, really. I do think his voice is perfect for it.

Jenny: A few times now you've said, "I wanted that and I got it." So, clearly you were leading this. As much as there were various factions within the team, groups of people who wanted to take it in different directions—creative tool versus straight-ahead platformer—you were pushing it. Do you consider yourself sort of a leader? What do you think characterizes a good leader?

Mark: I think there's a few leaders here. I'm just one of them. And at any one time one of us will shout louder than the others if we feel more passionate about it. So certainly, there were some things where I would just get incredibly moody and just make everyone's life hell until I got my way. But then with other things it would be Alex, Dave, or Kareem (or someone else) passionately wanting to take something in a certain direction. We'd go into a room and argue about it, and quite often someone would have a much better point than somebody else, so they would win....

So I would never say that I was the lead in here, but I think I'm probably the person that's capable of getting in the worst mood. It's a bit of a sad tactic, but it works. Most of the time.

In terms of what makes a good leader, it depends what you're leading, really. Someone like Kareem who leads the artists is a very good people person; he never resorts to the iron fist, and is also a damn good artist, so he is always able to lead by hands-on example. But I think the best skill a leader can have is to choose the right team in the first place, and let them lead themselves as much as possible.

Jenny: So, if there are several leaders, if it's more of a team effort, what makes for a good team? If you were trying to put together, say, a dream team for building a game, or any piece of software, what would you look for? Not just for the people on the team, but for the team itself?

Mark: You need people that are actually very skilled in particular areas. Dave, he's incredibly good at physics and maths, for example, and Alex is very good at graphics programming (and maths and graphic design, actually!). My real hardcore skill is technical art. Kareem is less technical than I am, but is much better at drawing and painting than I am; he spends every spare second he has painting naked bodies. There are lots of other essential people I haven't mentioned: a good HR person is pretty essential, and you need someone to look after the working environment (water plants, feed people working late, etc.). So you need people that are very good and specialized in their particular areas, but that are also interested in the other areas and can contribute to those as well. People are very responsible for owning certain parts of the game/company, but there's that wide enough interest so that they can contribute to everything else. And last of all, but probably the most important, is chemistry. Matching the right people with each other is essential; having two geniuses work together that get on each other's nerves is disastrous!

Andrew: A lot of people, myself included, dream of one day doing what you've done: building a great video game that a lot of people love. Do you have any advice for them?

Mark: All I can say is that it's been a painful process, but incredibly rewarding. And it's definitely taught me a lot about myself as a person, I think. I wouldn't underestimate how much hard work it is to do something like this, but also that it is completely possible, and if you don't have a go, it will never happen. If you really want to do it, you've just got to make a start, go and do it, see what happens, roll with it, and not give up when things get tough.

CHAPTER FOUR

Building the Perfect Team

Bill DiPierre

I CLEARLY REMEMBER THINKING, "MAN, I AM OUT OF THE LOOP." I SAT IN A COMPUTECH CONFERENCE room with a newly assembled team of high-powered developers. The task at hand was to port our flagship financial software from Microsoft QuickBasic to the promising new Microsoft product, Visual Basic 3. As a resident VB guru, I would bring technical expertise and hard-earned experience to a project that would determine the future of our firm.

It was hard to believe that only three weeks before, I had finished my final day of work at the large commercial bank where I cut my programming teeth. Only five weeks before, I'd met Jack, my current boss, for the first time. I'd emerged from that interview feeling a strong connection with Jack, but also insecure about how well I'd impressed him technically. And of course, perhaps hardest to believe, it was only six weeks ago that I had plunked down $11.95 at Barnes & Noble for a brand-new copy of Bill Sempf's *Visual Basic for Dummies* (Wiley).

In the conference room that day, Geoff and Mark, the two dev leads for our team, were debating some fundamental architecture questions. Mark laid out his argument, saying, "Look, I know it will be a lot of extra work up front, but I don't see any way that we can get the UI experience we want if we don't write our own user controls."

Geoff responded, "You're crazy, Mark. Do you realize how much effort that takes? I've been working with C++ a lot longer than anyone here, and I'm telling you we are biting off more than we can chew."

Mark was not deterred. "I just don't see how we have a choice. The control suite from Microsoft does not do what the design calls for."

"Then the design needs to change."

"That's not what we're about. We make the technology work to give clients what they want. We don't just regurgitate the latest technology from Microsoft and tell clients to live with it."

"Well then, why don't we give them a teleporter? Since we're not limited by technology, we might as well help them with their commute."

Sensing that the constructive portion of the debate had come to a close, Jack stepped in, saying, "All right, all right. Before we commit to building a teleporter, let's back up a step. We need more information. You guys are my experts, and I need your expertise right now. Geoff, can you put together an estimate of how long it will take to do what Mark is proposing?"

Geoff rolled his eyes and let out a big sigh. "OK, but I can tell you right now it's gonna blow our timeline out of the water."

Jack, unflappable, said, "That's all right. The dates are my problem, let me worry about them. You're our C++ man, so I need you to put on that hat and tell me what you see."

Geoff nodded. "OK."

Turning to Mark, Jack continued. "Mark, please give me a list of all the functionality we can get off-the-shelf without doing any custom work." Sensing Mark's reaction, Jack pressed on. "In addition to dates, I'm also the one to worry about the design requirements. You're going to be implementing these babies in Computech, so let me know how far you can get with the Microsoft stuff. Don't worry about what design asked for, just focus on what you can do with the off-the-shelf tools." Then, with an almost imperceptible wink, he added, "And remember: I've seen your code, so I know you can do a hell of a lot."

Mark, unable to resist a half smile at the compliment, said, "OK, Jack, I'll see what I can do."

Most of us remember the 1990s as a heyday for developers, and it was. The tech bubble was in full bloom, and venture capitalists were everywhere, looking for people to give their money to. And those people were programmers. We've all heard the stories of the rock-climbing walls and $10,000 coffee tables. The things that made it all go were the programmers. They were in demand, they could name their price—even if their price was a rock-climbing wall and an extremely expensive coffee table.

In the Computech conference room that day, the rise and fall of the tech bubble was still in the future. It was the early '90s, there were indications that software was a pretty good way to make a living, but none of us had any idea just how good. The demand for developers would quickly outstrip the supply, and turnover industrywide would reach record levels. Ten years later, I would look around the Computech conference table and see the same faces I had seen before the frenzy began. That is a testament to team solidarity. Not one of us had been lured away by rock walls or coffee tables. Actually, that's not quite true; Doug did leave, but he doesn't really count. He went on tour with the rock band he managed. I'll get to that later.

As a business, Computech was well positioned to offer a competitive product to a niche of consumers eager to get it and willing to pay for it. That's a great position to be in. As a technology, Computech was running up against serious limitations. It was written with QuickBasic and was designed to run on a single machine featuring DOS. As computer networking began to grow in the financial business sector, more and more clients were migrating their infrastructures to Windows. They wanted a Windows version of Computech. And we wanted to give it to them. Expanded network support, more robust memory management, and better development tools were just a few of the reasons Computech was determined to make this transition. Not to mention a whole new world of interface possibilities. Hey, we could use a mouse!

So there we sat. We had a reliable but limited DOS application. We had consumer demand for a Windows version. And we had a team of seven guys who needed to take the former and turn it into the latter. What a great project. It was big, it was complex, it was vital, and it was time-limited. Our need to retain a hard-won customer base meant our margin for error was small. The upside at the time seemed unlimited; this project would carry Computech into the future. It was a classic software team project.

Of course, if our two dev leads could not get along, we were in for a bumpy ride. After the meeting, my top priority, unofficially, was to try to get a handle on how this power struggle would resolve. In an attempt to get some impartial insight, I went to someone who wasn't directly involved.

"Doug, what's up?"

"Yo, Bill, how's the first month treating you?"

"So far so good, man. Meetings like that keep it interesting."

Doug seemed kind of surprised. "Yeah, I guess so."

Well, that was a non-starter. I tried a more direct approach. "So what do you think, we gonna write all this stuff from scratch in C++?"

"Huh? Oh yeah, I don't know. Jack'll figure it out. Probably do some of them and see how it goes."

Obviously, the teleporter debate did not leave much of an impression on Doug. I pressed on, saying, "Really, why do you say that?"

Doug shrugged. "I don't know, just seems like what he'll do. He's pretty mellow and he usually will try something out and see what happens."

All well and good, but I wasn't getting much sense of how the office politics factored in. Doug, for his part, seemed oblivious to them. In retrospect, perhaps Doug was not the ideal person to shed light on these dynamics. Doug was not a programmer by choice; he was a programmer by necessity. Programming paid the bills during the gestation of his real career: rock-and-roll entrepreneur.

Doug had been writing code since his teens. He started using the MIDI package on his Macintosh Plus (featuring, of course, the fully expanded 4 MB of RAM) to create records in his parents' garage. By age 27, he'd traded in the Mac for a Yamaha mixing board. His records were now circulated to non-family members. He also served as manager for an actual band. Doug spent most of his time consumed with music and was preposterously inept at downplaying this detail during job interviews. What most potential employers saw as a liability, Jack saw as an asset. Here was a kid who could bring strong technical skills without rattling the hierarchy. Doug wasn't looking to move up the company ladder or leave his mark on the software world. Doug was looking to pay his rent until his band hit it big.

That was great for our team; Doug produced a lot of code. It wasn't helping me get in the loop, though. A couple of days later, I was working with Geoff. I'd approached him for assistance understanding some old C++ code that needed to be ported. He was a big help. The code contained several optimizations that I didn't understand, but the rationale behind them was clear to Geoff. I was impressed, and told him so. "Geoff, that's pretty impressive. It would have taken me the better part of a week to figure out what we just covered in an hour."

He was almost gracious, responding, "Yeah, well, I've been writing C and C++ code for a long time. Some things start to become second nature."

"Yeah, I suppose. Anyway, I appreciate the help."

"No problem. Let me know if you need more."

That was encouraging—sincerity instead of sarcasm. I decided to press on. "Thanks, man, I will. Hey, so what's up with our UI controls? Have you spoken to Jack?"

"No, I haven't had a chance, but I will. It's a big mistake."

"Really? Seems to me like Jack is taking a reasonable approach, looking at his options."

Geoff shrugged, unimpressed. "Jack's problem is that he thinks Mark can do anything and it just isn't true."

"What do you mean?"

"I mean Mark is the main UI architect and that's fine. But he doesn't have half the C experience I do, so when it comes to a project like this he's in over his head. I don't think Jack sees that."

"Yeah, maybe. Maybe Jack just thinks it's worth the risk."

Geoff was moving from unimpressed to irritated. He fidgeted in his chair, saying, "Look, you're a VB guy and you just said you couldn't figure out this stuff without me. It's freakin' complicated. I mean, I can do it, but I've been at it a long time. It's crazy to add this onto the pile of work we already have when there's a solution out there that will do 99% of what we need."

I never said I couldn't do it without him, I only said it would have taken me longer. I let that slide. I really wanted to understand Geoff's beef with Mark, so I decided to avoid the personal slight and stick with statistics. Trying to maintain a tone of impartiality, I said, "Well, yeah, but the point is it won't do 99%. I think we're talking more like 59%."

"Whatever; it's still gonna be a big improvement over what clients have now."

I went with the loyal soldier argument. "Well, Jack said he'd take care of it, so I suppose we should let him worry about that."

Geoff found this unpersuasive. "Jack can worry about it if he wants to, but if he thinks Mark can just hop in and start cranking out C++ code, he's making a big mistake."

Somebody was getting cranky. I stuck with what I thought was the logical response. "I'm not sure, Geoff. From what I've seen, Mark seems like a pretty sharp developer."

"Sure, Mark can write code. He's good at what he's good at, but this is asking a lot of him."

Yeah, Geoff definitely was touchy about Mark. I couldn't resist asking. "Why? I mean code is code. Mark is a smart guy."

"Well, *smart* is a relative term."

At this point, Geoff leaned over to one side and reached into his back pocket, extracting his wallet. He dug around for a second, and then removed a carefully laminated card, which he handed to me. Turns out, Geoff was a card-carrying member of Mensa—literally, card-carrying.

OK, well that was quite a transformation—from sincere and helpful to complete horse's ass in about six minutes. I was fairly stunned, but I managed to mutter, "Well, that's impressive, but I still wonder if you're underestimating Mark."

Geoff shrugged, adding, without conviction, "Hmmm. Yeah, maybe. We'll see."

So the guy can write C++ code blindfolded, but he's got some serious limitations in the team player department. Clearly, Geoff thought Jack deferred to Mark, and it bothered him. I'd worked on enough projects to know the signs of someone who's about to go off the rails. This one was barreling along at full speed, and the bridge ahead was out.

The next morning I was sipping my coffee on my way past Mark's office and I popped in to see what he was working on. I'd fallen into the habit of doing this fairly regularly to help me get up to speed on our software. On this particular day, we were discussing the eventing model Mark had devised for our app. The early versions of Visual Basic did not allow public methods on forms, which made it cumbersome to manage MDI apps. Mark had come up with an ingenious and simple workaround, using the tag property of a hidden button to simulate raising events on child forms. It was fairly elegant, was easy to use, and did exactly what we needed—a typical Mark solution.

Mark and I were quickly building a nice working rapport. As a developer, he was more accomplished than I, but we tended to approach programming problems from a similar perspective. I agreed with his assertion earlier that our primary focus had to be on client needs, not technology. I wondered what he thought of Geoff's resistance.

"So Mark, how's the survey of the Microsoft stuff coming? Do you think we'll be able to avoid rolling our own?"

"Not without sacrificing some design requirements. Geoff is way too uptight about this. It would be cool to write our own controls, don't you think?"

Honestly, our personal enjoyment had never entered my mind as a viable factor in making the decision. Of course, as a developer, I could hardly disagree—it would be a great project. Still, I tried to put myself in Jack's shoes, saying, "Yeah, it'd be fun. But I'm not sure that's at the top of Jack's priority list right now."

"Well, he should keep it in mind. Keeping us happy is half the battle, right?" I couldn't tell if his grin was conspiratorial or sarcastic. Mark continued, "Anyway, Geoff acts like he's the only person on earth who can write C code. Give me a break. We'll definitely get enough benefits out of writing our own to justify it. It won't take that much longer."

Danger, bridge out ahead. "Well, if it won't take that much longer, then it's an easy decision. I guess that's why Jack is trying to quantify it."

As if on cue, Jack appeared, asking, "What am I trying to quantify?" As a manager, Jack was extremely accessible. He often took the initiative to walk around the office and drop in on people. His chats were always informal, and often had nothing (directly) to do with work. Today, however, he'd walked right into the middle of a work conversation.

I answered his question first. "Oh, I was just asking Mark about the UI controls and how much longer it would take to do our own."

Jack nodded, pointed at Mark, and said, "Oh good, I wanted to talk to you about that. I don't have time right now; let's do it tomorrow morning at our 10 o'clock."

"Sure."

Then Jack turned to me and added, "Bill, why don't you stop by, too. I'd like for you to be in on this discussion."

"OK, Jack."

"Great, see you guys tomorrow at 10." With that, he strolled out and down the hall. I looked at Mark, but couldn't read his expression. I offered, "Well, guess we'll have an answer soon enough."

"Yep. I sure hope it's the right one."

I hoped so, too, but I couldn't worry about it at the moment. I had problems of my own to deal with. Part of my role at Computech was managerial, and as such I had a single developer reporting to me. Bob had been with Computech for seven or eight years. When I first came on board I remember wondering why someone with his tenure was reporting to me and not the other way around. My confusion soon cleared up.

One of our tech guys came into my office and told me that all the color toner had been drained from our new LaserJet by Bob only one day after the cartridges were replaced. The tech was understandably upset: the toner was new, it was expensive, and it was on back order. Furthermore, he implied that Bob had wasted the toner, but would not elaborate. As Bob's manager, it fell to me to unravel the mystery of Tonergate.

I stopped by Bob's cube. After catching up on some dev issues, I got to the real point of my visit. "So Bob, have you been printing a lot of stuff? Our LaserJet has run through a whole color toner cartridge since yesterday."

Bob certainly had his faults, but dishonesty was not one of them. As such, he answered, "Yes."

Clearly, loquaciousness was not one of them, either. I prodded: "Why? Why do you need to print so much stuff?"

"I was printing menus for my girlfriend's new Thai place. Remember, I gave you one of her cards?"

I did indeed remember Bob giving me a business card when he recently described to me his new girlfriend and her new business venture. What I did not recall was any mention of Computech making material contributions to that start-up. "Uh yeah, sure, I remember that. But why are you printing the menus here?"

"It would cost us a fortune to print them at Kinko's."

Typically logical; Bob was nothing if not logical. He was a little weaker in other areas, like social convention or understanding implied things that are obvious to everyone else. "Right, Bob, but you can't crank them out here at the office just because you don't want to pay for them."

"Why not? I thought we were allowed to use the printer for personal items."

"What makes you say that?"

"Well, last week Mark printed out a picture of his daughter."

"But that's just one picture. You wiped out the printer. No one in the office can use it for a week while we wait for toner."

"I didn't know I would wipe it out."

"But you did. You can't print that much stuff."

"Well, if there's a limit for personal items, you need to tell me what it is."

By now I was aggravated. "Until further notice, your limit is zero."

Now it was Bob's turn to be aggravated. "But that's not fair. Why should I have a different limit than everybody else?"

"Because everybody's different, Bob. Everything is not automatically the same for everyone."

"Well, that's bogus. I'm gonna talk to Jack about that."

I sighed. "Fine. I'll talk to him, too."

"Fine," said Bob, as he turned back to his monitor.

That had turned into a mess. Bob was by no means a superstar developer. And obviously, he could be difficult to work with. But we needed his contribution to make our dates, and as the new guy I did not feel great about alienating him. As a manager, my job was to pull the team together, not split it apart. I walked back to my office, replaying the scene in my head, wondering if I could have handled it differently. I didn't really see another way to play it, but that didn't reduce my anxiety over what Jack might have to say about how I'd handled Bob.

Luckily, dwelling on my anxiety was not an option, because I had my Wednesday 11 a.m. to get to. Most of the team would be at this weekly status meeting. Normally it was fairly uneventful, but given the tension between Mark and Geoff, and now Bob and me, I entered with some trepidation. I planned to sit next to Doug, thinking that if fireworks started going he would most likely be out of the fray. As soon as I took my seat I regretted my decision. One look at Doug and I could tell he was wrapped up tight. He licked his lips and fidgeted around, drumming his fingers on the table. His eyes darted around the room. I braced myself. If most of the people in the room, including me, were already on edge, then this meeting could quickly turn ugly.

Doug started out, still fidgeting around in his chair. "All right, I just need to clear the air because I'm having a hard time concentrating with what's going on."

Here we go. I looked around to check reactions. Everyone looked a little surprised. No telling who would be the target of this diatribe.

Doug continued. "I'm having a hard time today because last night we had a church gig and our lead singer dropped the f-bomb."

The sound of a chuckle being stifled was clearly discernable. I put a hand over my mouth, attempting to cover a smile. Doug, apparently unaware that we did not share his distress, went on to describe in some detail the career ramifications of this inconceivably careless faux pas. I looked over at Jack who, like the rest of us, was halfheartedly trying to suppress a grin. At the time, I was unaware that Jack had taken a risk by knowingly hiring a guy with long-term plans that did not include Computech. Thinking back on it, I wonder if part of Jack's grin came from realizing how big the return on that gamble turned out to be.

A couple of hours later, I was working through some code in my office when my phone rang. I picked it up. "Hello, this is Bill."

"Hey, Bill, it's Jack, you got a minute?"

"Sure Jack, what's up?"

"Can you swing by my office? Bob is here and I want to talk about this printer thing."

"Sure, I'll be right there."

I remember thinking "crap" as soon as I hung up. I should have made a point of getting to Jack and telling him my side of the story. Instead, I'd put it off and now Bob was in there lobbying. Jack and Bob had a working relationship that spanned the better part of a decade. Jack and I, on the other hand, were still in our first month.

As I crossed the threshold of Jack's doorway, he looked up from behind his desk and said, "Hey, Bill, thanks for coming." Gesturing vaguely with his hand, he added, "Have a seat." Bob already occupied one of the two seats in front of Jack's desk, so I took the other. As I sat, I nodded, greeting him with "Hey, Bob."

Not wanting to be out-matured by me, he responded tightly: "Hi, Bill."

So much for the small talk. Jack didn't waste any time, getting right to the point. "OK, Bill, so I've been chatting with Bob about this printer thing for a few minutes. He thinks you're unfairly restricting him."

I'd been thinking off and on all morning about the best way to present my case. Ultimately, I'd decided that the facts spoke for themselves. In another environment, I may have tried to be more political. At Computech, to my well-documented dismay, I was out of the loop, so it was hard to play politics. As such, I recounted what had happened earlier, pretty much without embellishment. When I was done, I added, "I also learned that for these menus, Bob used up four reams of paper. I know we've got plenty of paper around, but it just seems like, on principle, this is excessive."

Bob was ready for this one, responding, "Well, since I've been working here I always make a point of reusing my printer paper. So after I print on one side, I reload it all and print on the other side, and I know I'm the only one here who does that. I haven't calculated it exactly, but I estimate I've saved Computech at least 10 reams of paper in the past six years."

I'm not sure, but I think that my jaw visibly dropped. There was no way Jack could go for this, could he? It was just too ridiculous. But it did have an inherent logic, and Bob had been working here for a long time. I could only assume his attitude was not a surprise to

Jack. Was it possible that Jack condoned it? I squeezed the armrests of my chair as Jack started to speak.

"Sorry, Bob, I'm with Bill on this one."

I let out the breath I'd unconsciously held in and relaxed my grip. Bob started to object, but Jack cut him off. "No one else has this problem. Everyone but you seems to understand the implied limits. You asked for a limit, and you got one, so live with it."

Bob wasn't going without a protest. "That's bogus. It's not fair."

Jack responded with a phrase I would hear him use many times over the years: "If life was fair, there wouldn't be rich people." It was kind of an odd phrase, considering most of our clients were Wall Street financiers, but it got his point across and effectively ended the protest.

That was pretty much the end of our meeting. Later that day, I popped in to thank Jack for supporting me. He responded, smiling warmly: "Hey, don't mention it. I know Bob can be a handful. You did what you had to do."

I asked, "So, you give the handful to the new guy to get him out of everybody else's hair?"

Jack grinned. "Or maybe I give him to the new guy to see how the new guy handles him."

Now it was my turn to grin. "So, how'd I do?"

"You passed."

Over the years, I've often wondered about Bob and why Jack kept him on board. Sure, he was a handy litmus test for new managers, but that hardly justified his salary. So, what was Bob's saving grace? What was the one trait that made him a crucial cog in our well-oiled machine? Was it his mediocre code? His abrasive personality, perhaps? All of the above? I think the answer is none of the above. Bob was not a crucial cog. The biggest thing Bob had going for him was that he was part of our team. Bob consumed a big chunk of Jack's time, and Jack never blinked. Jack was there to support us, to facilitate our work. That was the message he sent to Bob, and that was the message he sent to our team.

I talked earlier about the loyalty Computech engendered. It doesn't come from executive emails or dinners on the company dime. Loyalty is a two-way street. If a manager is committed to working with his most difficult employee, what message does that send to everyone else on his team? I remember years later, after Computech had been bought, and then its new corporate parent had itself been bought by a competitor, we went through a round of layoffs. The layoffs ended in December, and by the following February we were hearing from our new management about building employee pride and boosting morale. Pretty typical stuff in the world of corporate mergers and acquisitions.

I thought about Bob, who was released in the pursuit of efficiency. In a way, I was glad to be rid of him. Man, he was difficult. It was hard to argue the business case for letting him go. Or was it? Those daily morale-boosting emails we received were widely derided, considered transparent ploys to keep us docile and productive. Resumes were drafted, production diminished. Morale was low. And I thought about what would happen if Jack sent a similar email, asking us to buckle down for the good of Computech. I think we would have believed him, and done what he asked. We would have sacrificed for him, because we knew he would do it for us if we needed it. And that's what Bob brought to our team: proof that we really were committed to teamwork. He was, perhaps, Jack's most visible vehicle for showing that we were all in this thing together.

The next morning, I dropped into Mark's office a little later than usual. After discussing a few technical issues with the new build, we made our way down to see Jack. As Jack welcomed us into his office, we settled into our usual seats and began chatting about the Eagles. Jack was a huge Randall Cunningham fan; Mark and I thought his best years were behind him. That conversation (which he had several times a week) ran out of inertia and Jack switched to the topic at hand.

"All righty, well, let's talk about this UI stuff. Mark, what do you think? How much can the Microsoft stuff do for us?"

Mark responded: "Yeah, I've been looking at it for a few days and it looks like it's gonna be somewhere between one-half and two-thirds of the requirements we've been asked to do." He went into a brief description of the functionality that we would not be able to implement. Jack responded with some specific questions about which design requirements would and would not be preserved. Mark had a good handle on the scope of the work, and addressed each question. After a few minutes, it seemed quite clear to me that the Microsoft controls would handle at least two-thirds of our requirements, and probably more like 75% or 80%.

If Jack noticed this discrepancy, he didn't acknowledge it. Instead, he said to Mark, "OK, what I'd like to do is take one control and write it from scratch as a pilot. We can see how it goes, and then make a decision on the rest of them." The logic of this as a managerial decision was clear. In fact, I had the distinct impression that Jack had made that decision before we ever walked into his office that morning.

I don't know if Mark had the same impression, but I do know he was pleased with the decision. "Cool. Which one should we do?"

That was an easy one. Makes sense to do the simplest one first, eliminate complications from your pilot. My guess would be the button control. Jack, however, screwed up his face as though this detail had never occurred to him. He asked, "I don't know, which one do you want to do?"

Mark beamed. "I think the virtual listbox would be a good one to start with. It's complex, but we'll be able to use it everywhere, so we get the most bang for the buck." He paused for a second, and then added, "Plus, it'll be a fun one to write."

Jack couldn't resist a grin at Mark's enthusiasm. "OK. Virtual listbox it is. Can you give me a dev estimate by the end of day tomorrow? Also, I really need you to work with Geoff on this one." Mark's expression turned dour. Jack continued, "Don't worry, I'll talk to him. But we need to take advantage of what he can do if we're gonna be able to deliver these in a reasonable time. Otherwise, we'll be stuck with the Microsoft stuff."

The three of us chatted for a few more minutes. After we'd left Jack's office, I turned to Mark and said, "That's great, man, you get to do the V-List."

Mark was back to beaming. His face turned serious and he said, "Yeah, and I'm really gonna nail it so he lets me do the rest of them."

Of course, Mark was only half of the equation. Geoff's cooperation was critical. Jack really needed to work some more magic. Later that day, Jack caught up with Geoff for a face-to-face chat. When an ego needed soothing, Jack preferred the one-on-one format. As such, I wasn't in Jack's office for this particular session, but having talked to Jack about it later and also seeing firsthand how he operates, I can pretty fairly reconstruct it. It started with Jack playing into Geoff's ego, making him feel like his opinion mattered, saying something like, "Geoff, thanks for stopping by. I just wanted to pick your brain a little more about these UI controls. What's your feeling on the work required to get them done?"

Geoff, still on the defensive, replied, "Well, like I said, I think it's gonna be a lot of extra work. I'd estimate at least three months." He paused to maximize the effect of this shocking news. Jack, unflappable as always, nodded acceptingly, so Geoff continued: "And I don't really see the point. We don't get that much benefit for the extra dev time."

Jack tried to diffuse Geoff's stated objection. "Yeah, I hear you. Let's not worry about the dev time for now. I'm more interested in the feasibility." Then he went after Geoff's primary, if unstated, objection. "The thing is, I think this would be a good learning experience for the team, particularly for Mark. We both know he's a good programmer, but you are my top C++ guy. And I think it would make the whole team stronger if we could take your skills and spread them around to the other guys."

Geoff, somewhat disarmed, replied, "Well, sure, it's always good to have critical knowledge shared among the team, but I'm not sure this is the time to do it."

Here, Jack could call on his own experience. "Well, the thing is, there's never a good time to do it. I've never been on a project where there was extra time to devote to training. However, I've learned that squeezing the training in there almost always pays for itself before the project is over."

Geoff, feeling secure about his own skill set, was willing to cede to Jack's expertise on project management. "OK. If you think the delay is OK, then that's your call."

With Geoff more open to the change of plans, Jack went after his complete buy-in. "Yes, it's my call. You don't need to sweat that. What I do need you to sweat is helping out Mark when he needs it. Like I said, we need to spread your knowledge. What do you think?"

"I mean, I'm OK with it, Jack. I'm just not sure how effective it will be."

"Well, how about this? I'll set up an hour a week for you two to get together around this stuff, at least to get the ball rolling. Let's try that for a couple of weeks and see what happens. And try to be patient with Mark; he's used to knowing more than the other guys, so it can be hard for him talking C++ with you."

Jack had hit the right buttons. Geoff beamed and nodded OK.

"Thanks, Geoff, I appreciate it."

"Sure, no problem."

A few days later, the first of these meetings took place. Mark and Geoff started out with a weekly meeting to write a listbox in C++. At the peak of the project frenzy, they were having three or four impromptu meetings per week as they wrapped up the listbox and moved on to buttons, text boxes, and a few others, totaling half a dozen custom user controls by the time this project wrapped up. Geoff's prediction of a three-month delay turned out to be overstated by two months, mostly because the experience writing them made each successive one go faster and the knowledge that was passed from Geoff to Mark continued its dissemination to the rest of the team.

As for me, the budding VB guru, in retrospect I can see that my worries about not being plugged in were misplaced. I actually had a pretty good handle on the dynamics of our team. Yes, that's right, there was no loop. I had inklings of this early on, but it took me the better part of a year to fully accept it. Sure, it sounds nice. A team focused on their work; supporting each other in pursuit of a single goal. Yes, it really happened. Not necessarily the 10 best programmers who ever worked together. Instead, each of us brought something to the table. We each had something to contribute, guided deftly by a leader sensitive to people, aware of their strengths, and accepting of their flaws.

So, you've probably guessed by now that the Computech rewrite from QuickBasic to Visual Basic 3 was a resounding success. Indeed, it was. We had our bumps along the way. Turns out Doug did hit it big. Well, biggish. His band went on a U.S. tour. Luckily, it was toward the end of the project, so when he left we already had people lined up to fill in for him. Bob caused his share of friction, and some of his features did not make it into the first Windows release. But these were minor flaws in an otherwise overwhelming success.

Ten months after that day in the conference room, Computech's early adopters began receiving a Windows version of our software. Feedback was almost unanimously positive, reports of problems were minimal, sales skyrocketed, and executives were happy. The development team received its share of accolades. Even to this day I'll occasionally reminisce with an old Computech veteran, and they'll point out how lucky we were to get so many fantastic developers at the same time for a single project. I always respond that it wasn't luck and it wasn't fantastic developers; it was a beautiful team.

CHAPTER FIVE

What Makes Developers Tick

an Interview with Andy Lester

We wanted to know what makes developers tick, and all signs pointed to Andy Lester. He's an expert in hiring smart people and building teams that work, and he's done a lot of writing and speaking about the topic. And, as a member of the Perl development team, he knows what it takes to build great software. We talked to him to get some insight into what motivates—and demotivates!—the people who build software, and how to help them work well together.

Andrew: What makes you know about teams, how software teams work?

Andy: I've been programming for 21, 22 years professionally, on some good teams and some bad teams. First off, I program for fun. I'm able to do for a living and make good money in what I love to do anyway. If I'm not having fun doing this, it's not worthwhile. And part of that fun comes from people I'm working with. Yes, it's fun to work alone, but the social aspect—both at work and on open source projects—is undeniable. The open source world has social aspects as part of the whole thing, because otherwise, you're just writing for yourself.

Andrew: Do you think that's a big part of getting a team to work better? That need for social fulfillment is happening with everybody on the team, and not just some people?

Andy: That's hard to tell. You go back to Maslow's hierarchy of needs, and social is one of those things that's pretty low on the pyramid, meaning more basic. But what social means to some people is very different from what social means to others.

Jenny: Are you saying that in order to have a good team, you need to go out for pizza twice a week? What do you mean by "social"?

Andy: For some people, their "social" is sort of separate from the work to be done. So yes, it could be that we all hang out and have pizza, or we all go to lunch together. For some people, the social aspect is absolutely integrated into the work—"I want to work with other people." Some people want to throw on their headphones—"Don't bother me for the next four hours." Neither of those is right or wrong, they both just are.

Andrew: So, you have to be sensitive to how the people on your team work, and help give them an environment they feel is the most interesting, most fun social environment you can give them?

Andy: Yes. And people coming into an environment need to be aware of what the existing team dynamic is. If I, Andy, have someone come to me and say, "Hey, I've got a problem figuring out what's wrong with this function here," I'm glad to help out, whereas other people may see that as a gross intrusion on their programming time. I see helping other people as much a part of my job as actually writing my own code. Not everyone sees it that way.

And it's tough, because we're so set in our ways that the initial reaction when those kinds of conflicts come up is to think that the other person is wrong. "Why are you bothering me? You are wrong to be bothering me." So, I could see somebody else who's struggling on code as wrong to not avail himself of the human resources around him, and say, "Yeah, I could help you out on that." And understanding the dynamic you're getting into and already are in takes a lot of self-awareness and observing of the world around you.

Andrew: How did you learn that? Did you learn that through experiment? Did you have a bad experience?

Andy: I've certainly joined teams where I, the gregarious Andy who sees that sort of interaction as the way life should be, the way I prefer it, where that's not the case. Where interrupting the flow is seen as a cardinal sin. It didn't go well. There was constant conflict because of it, and that was very frustrating to me because I felt alone and isolated, and I'm sure the other people felt that I was a pain in the ass.

Jenny: OK, but what about other people who, once they know that they can get help from people around them, tend to lean on other people all the time? People who run into the first roadblock and, rather than Google for the answer, tap someone on the shoulder every time?

Andy: Well, the way you phrase that tips your hand as to how you see that.

Jenny: Well, I'm asking, is it possible that it's negative?

Andy: It could be negative. It all depends on what the social norms are. One thing that geeks are terrible at is social norms. And I don't just mean social norms of society—"Hey, look, bathe every day"—and I use that both humorously and with all seriousness.

What I'm talking about is social norms of any given group. And that can be really tough, because you have to have awareness of those around you. That lack of awareness can be debilitating, and actually I do have a story from yesterday, when we were having a code review. Three of us in the group were well seasoned with doing code reviews. The fourth guy, who was actually having the code reviewed, was less comfortable with them. We went in and were talking about the code, discussing it and so on, and as we kept going the guy getting the code reviewed was getting more and more uncomfortable with the things we were pointing out. And one of the other guys was becoming more and more animated, and more and more interested in explaining his point of view, and became oblivious to what the guy having his code reviewed was looking like. I was watching the reviewee, who was getting upset and frustrated at how things were going. The other two weren't paying any attention, they were pretty much just talking to each other, and that lack of awareness could have been really ugly. I saw what was going on, and said, "You know, guys, we've been at this for a while. Let's take a break." Just to let the pressure off.

Geeks—and I include myself in here—do not by nature gauge their audience well. And their audience is really anyone within earshot. In this case, there were four of us at the table, and all of a sudden it became a two-person conversation and there was no aware-ness of the other people in the room. If I hadn't stopped that, I think there would have been some real hostility popping up.

Andrew: So, I'm the sort of geek you're talking about.

Andy: God bless you.

Andrew: And it's taken me a long time to realize this and change the way I interact with people. One of the things I'm in the habit of doing—and it was a lot worse when I was younger—is that when I've got a point, I'll be overly pedantic about it and argue it to completion, whether or not the other person is interested in arguing. It took me a long time to learn that I shouldn't make overly broad generalizations, and then let the argument sort out the actual issue, because normal, non-geek people tend to find that extraordinarily irritating.

Now, I've had many geek friends over the years, many who've had similar problems and don't recognize it. In fact, they'd probably be surprised to find out that making generalizations and arguing them out is even a problem, and not the preferable way to interact with other people. What do you do when you've got somebody like that on your team? How do you help them? Or do you help them at all? Do you try to change the environment to suit them better?

Andy: A lot of it depends on what your relationship is with the offending person. For many geeks, "conforming"—that dirty word—could be seen as not only unnecessary but a sign of weakness. A lot of geeks pride themselves on being different. Difference is braggable. And that's great on its own I guess, if you want to be different. But if it hurts the team, then it's not.

Either people get it or they don't. Helping those who don't get it can be difficult, because that intrinsic need that all humans have to be understood, respected, and listened to, may be seen as a weakness by the geeks. That's a really tough battle.

Jenny: We're talking like it's just accepted that there's a certain kind of person who's in software. Is that true?

Andy: No, of course not. Not everybody is socially inept.

Jenny: Right.

Andy: But there is a not-insignificant percentage of people who are, who have grown up dealing with computers—preferring to deal with computers—because the computer does what you want, it deals with you exactly, logically. I don't have to worry about how the computer feels. I can get mad and curse at the computer, and the computer will not be upset at me for that. There are no annoying emotions to have to deal with, and dealing with other people's emotions can be annoying. Ask anybody who's been married or has had a long-term relationship. Yeah, it can be annoying. But it's what needs to happen if you're going to deal with other people.

Jenny: So how does this all come together? I'm interested in a couple of facets of what you just talked about. One is how people react to criticism in general. When you were talking about the code review example, it seemed like part of that was about people being aware of one another. But another part of it is that in a team environment, you have to put yourself out there: put your code out there, put your work out there, and allow other people to react to it, take that reaction and do something with it.

Andy: And one of the things is that you'll have somebody, for instance, who's able to separate himself—and I say "him" because it's overwhelmingly male—who will be able to logically separate himself from his code, his work. Somebody comes along and says, "Gee, you know, this code totally sucks here because you're doing blah, blah, blah." He's going to logically stand back and say, "OK, I never thought about it that way, I'll do it that way." Whereas other geeks or, more likely, normal people, will not understand, will take that as an attack, take that as an insult. "You did that wrong" is effectively what the person is saying. And that can be very harsh on the other person.

The computer guy will come around and see somebody in another department, for instance, and say, "You're doing your spreadsheet wrong, you should be doing blah, blah, blah." And he is working strictly on a logical point of view: "This work product could be better if this changed." Whereas the person whose work product it is that's not done according to the geek's standard sees it as an attack on the work that he's been doing, and that is something that's very difficult to understand. It's even more difficult to understand when it's a fellow geek who feels like that. That's the really surprising part. Because even if they learn, "OK, I don't go over to the people in accounting and criticize their spreadsheets because they do 'em wrong," they can understand that. But when it's another programmer? That's baffling! "Why does this person feel like that? That's crazy!" And not only that, because that would be almost empathetic, but, "Why are they so sensitive?"

Andrew: So, how do you help a non-geek understand this? And how do you help a geek come around? How do you help them interact? It seems like we've got potential communication problems on both sides that really require a lot of understanding.

Andy: Number one, the geek has to understand that there is benefit to respecting others.

Andrew: It sounds so simple when you say it like that.

Andy: It is! It's funny because there just was a panel at OSCON with Kirrily Robert—she runs a website called *GeekEtiquette.com*—so Kirrily and I were both on this panel. Her section was an intro to etiquette, and why etiquette isn't about salad forks and how you do your wedding invitations. It's simply greasing the wheels of human interaction.

She said, using the 80-20 rule, the three things you have to remember about etiquette are respect other people, listen to what they say, and take a shower every day. If you can do that, that's your 80%. And the reason is that if you don't do that, people will not want to work with you or interact with you.

And the thing is, it's not that tough. Her whole point is that a term like *etiquette* is a challenge, per se—yes, sometimes it takes work to actually listen to what people are saying when they're annoying you. Because, yes, it can be annoying to have to listen to what other people say for the sake of respecting them.

The key is that the geek has to understand that there is value in respecting other people, and those social interactions are necessary. Because sometimes, it's a matter of "if you're a jerk, you're getting fired." You have to understand that if you want to do the things you want to do, that requires help from other people, and the only way that's going to happen is by being a person that people want to work with, want to do things with. And then, once you're there, then you can internalize the idea that while you may not take it as an insult to have somebody pick on your spreadsheet, many other people do. Many other people are not like you. And the differences between us can be so vast, between Bob over in accounting and the geek, the differences can be so vast such that you have to stand back and say, "Wow, how can anybody think like that?" Well, you don't have to understand how or why. Just accept it and work with it. And respect that that's the way the person is.

Andrew: Wow. That's great advice. I wish I'd heard that a lot earlier in my life. But what about Bob in accounting? What's life like from his end, dealing with the geek? Can that have an impact on a team?

Andy: Bob in accounting has a tougher job, because Bob is more normal (and I mean statistically normal). You might have 100 people in the company, and only five of them are geeks, or jerks, or whatever. And he is going to feel very justified in feeling offended, because the social norm around him is, "Yes, that's the way the geeks are, and you just have to kind of put up with it." But Bob would do well to also respect that the geek's way of looking at the world is also OK. The way he looks at it is that he's just trying to improve things for the sake of improving them, because that is what he does. He wants to improve technical things around him for the betterment of the person. Bob needs to understand that as well. He may not feel that way; he may not feel like the geek is trying to improve things, but rather tear him down. But Bob should know that that's all the geek has in his heart. Really, the geek just wants things to be better technically.

Andrew: Let's take it a step back. Now, it's not just one-on-one, Bob and the geek. Let's take it to software teams. Now you need to build up your team. Let's say you're on a team, and you need to help the rest of them. You start recognizing that you've got this problem. You could be the person in charge of the team, or you could just be someone who's an intrepid team member who realizes, "Wow, this really affects me and everyone around me." What's the next step? What do you do? How do you use this knowledge to help make your software better?

Andy: Well, you're not going to make the software better, per se, but you're certainly going to build it faster. Because short of a server catching fire, there's nothing more damaging to productivity than having people hate each other, or not being able to work together, or having to go to a manager and saying, "Look, I need you to sort this out." As a manager, I dread that. It is the biggest time-suck in terms of the amount of effort I have to put into it.

I can deal with a server problem, and it's done. But if I've got people who are pissed off at each other, I may solve the problem that day, but it's not going to go away for a while. So certainly, it's in my best interest as the team leader or manager to not let that stuff happen. If there's any potential conflict between people, it needs to be dealt with right away.

Jenny: How much do you think conflict influences how your team behaves? By and large, how has conflict been an issue for you in the past in building software? Do you feel like that happens all the time, that two people on the team start to dislike each other and you end up having to have an intervention?

Andy: One big difference between Bob in accounting and the geek is how respect is seen. Society says that by default, you give a minimal amount of respect to everyone. It's ascribed. You say, "Hey, there's a person here, and I'm not going to be a jerk to this person because it's just another person." To the geek, respect must be earned. And the lack of respect—if somebody does something stupid, in many geeks' minds that is worthy of disrespect.

I was on a team once where I said, "At the very least, can we just have minimal respect for everyone here?" And I was asked quite seriously by someone else, "Well, what if not everybody on this team is worthy of respect?" And that's baffling to me as a human, but it's also not uncommon. And that minimal amount of respect is something that many just don't get.

Jenny: It makes us sound like a really angry bunch.

Andy: Many people can be.

Andrew: But it also gives a kind of "secret back door" for a geek who wants to improve a working relationship with somebody. If he needs to work with Bob in accounting, and he knows that his paycheck depends on being able to work with Bob in accounting, show Bob a little respect—even if he hasn't earned it yet. Then, he'll reciprocate and become a little easier to work with.

Andy: Yes. And the lack of respect—well, look at online culture. Why do you have flame wars? Because the person on the other end doesn't need my basic respect. I'm able to say the most disrespectful things, because the person on the other end (if you even think that far) is an actual person reading your words who is not worthy of your respect. That doesn't even have to be a conscious decision—"I'm not respecting this person." Respect doesn't even enter into it. The geek won't even think that far ahead.

Andrew: So, let's say you're a team member, and you have to get your work done. You're reading this interview and you think, "Wow, that's me. That's everyone I work with. We are having trouble with Bob in accounting." What's an easy first step?

Andy: Here's the thing. We're talking about behavior here. If I have a problem with Joe on my team and he doesn't respect me, that's not a problem. The problem is the behavior behind it. If Joe is aggressive, antagonistic, that's the problem. You need to say, "Look, Joe. You and I need to work on this project, and for that to happen I need X, Y, and Z to happen. I need to be able to have a code review without hearing insults about my code." And everything is I, I, I—this is what I need. Not "Joe, you're a jerk because you're insulting my code and you don't respect me." You cannot make Joe respect you.

And if you point the blame at somebody and say, "You are doing this, you are doing that," now you're opening yourself up for argument. If you say, "Joe, you're disrespecting me"—"No, I'm not!" And you can have an argument all day, and sometimes that's exactly what happens, about whether Joe is disrespecting you or not.

But what you can say instead is, "This is what I need. I need to have all discussion to be related to the code at hand. This is my base behavior." Because behavior you can't argue about. You can argue about attitudes or feelings or intentions. And if there's one thing about geeks that we know is that they love to argue, they love to debate. You don't want to fall into that trap of opening it up for debate about whether Joe is being a jerk, disrespecting, etc. Anytime you're talking about that, you have to keep it strictly on the behavioral level.

The other thing is that this is something for your manager to deal with, or at least be made aware of. Really, your manager's job is to remove impediments to your work. If Joe is being antagonistic and disrespectful to you or anyone else on the team, that's an impediment to the work. What you're really doing is you're saying that this is an impediment to work, just as much as if my machine crashed and I didn't get any work done today. Both of them are detrimental to the productivity of the team.

Now, if your boss doesn't understand that, if your boss is somebody who does not understand these sorts of team dynamics, that is probably a doomed team and you'd probably do best to go somewhere else.

Jenny: I want to take it up a step from geek etiquette and teams and talk more on a macro level about managing teams and working with people on teams.

Andy: Number one, you as a team leader or manager have to understand that the team has to work together. Those people problems are your number one potential impediment, and anything that gets in the way of people working together is going to crush your project. You have to understand that you may have people on your team who are a net negative as far as productivity goes. If you have somebody who cranks out 100 lines of code a day but drags everyone else's productivity down, whether that's because nobody wants to work with them, whether that's because time that was previously spent coding is now time spent wasted in meetings trying to get everyone to get along, you have to understand that from a managerial point of view.

Given that, you have to realize that the people who are disrupting the team need to modify their behavior immediately. Otherwise, the project will go down the toilet. And if that person cannot understand that the team dynamic is more important than any individual contribution, then that person is the wrong person for your team and you need to help them out. And I mean, help them out of the team, out of the company, whatever it may be.

Andrew: What about when you're putting the team together? How do you avoid that in the first place?

Andy: If you're talking about hiring people to join your team, then you need to hire specifically for that. Typically, what I've done is that when I hire someone, I have at least two rounds of interviews. The first one is merely getting past me, and basic technical chops. Can you write code? What's your level of technical understanding of programming language X? Do you understand database theory? Whatever it may be. That's not tough. And it's not very time-consuming, either, because it's just me and that person. If that person passes that initial bar of "Can they write code? Can they do the work?", the second part is "Can they do the work with the team, and will they be a fit with the team?"

I say "fit" very specifically because every team is different. Every department is different, every organization is different. And as with anything else on these interpersonal issues, it's not a matter of right and wrong. There's nothing wrong with being the kind of guy who wants to go be in his cube and not talk to anybody for eight hours a day. There's nothing wrong with that, except that you are wrong for my team. If you want to work here, that's a bad choice. It's a bad choice for that person to work with a team that I'm on, because that's not the way my teams run.

So, the second and sometimes third round of interviews is basically getting the rest of the team together and talking to the person. Technical issues will come up. But mostly, I'll sit back and watch the interactions with others, and see the kinds of things that they talk about. The rest of the team will ask things. Usually it'll be guided by senior developers. They'll come in and talk to the person and see how they expect to fit in with the team. That's when you talk about things like conflicts. "Tell me a story about a conflict you had with someone else on your group, when you thought the other person was pretty much full of crap. How did you deal with that?" Or, "Tell me about a time when you felt you were treated unfairly by someone on your team." "Tell me about a time when you've had somebody difficult on a team, and how you worked with that."

That's not the whole of the interview, but it's a big part of it. Just hearing a few of those stories—and it needs to be stories, not just "Do you get along with others on your team?" "Of course I do," everybody's going to say that—given that, you can really get a feel for what the person's going to be like in your group.

Andrew: So that second interview is not just with you, but with your team members, too?

Andy: Yes, that second interview is usually with the senior team members, and me, and maybe even my boss. There will be technical things discussed, but the real meat of what we're getting at is the interaction. What I tell people is that I'm really picky. I have one open position here, and I'm going to be really picky about who gets that position, because I love this team, I love the work I'm doing, and I'm not going to let just anyone join my group. And there are also, of course, more practical aspects to that. Number one, it's really a pain to fire someone.

Andrew: What about pitfalls for this approach? Does everybody get a veto? What if everybody likes the person, except one guy?

Andy: It's absolutely not a vote. It's certainly not a binary vote. It's "Tell me what you think." I'll ask, "Around the table, show me your thumb." But it's certainly not binary. And the fortunate thing is that I've never had that case, where it was clear that one person was out of alignment with what other people thought. I've never had a case where one person was saying, "Yeah, this guy's really great and we need to hire him," and everyone else thought he was a jerk, or vice versa. Because I find that when you talk long enough with people, it's pretty clear whether the person's a good fit or not.

And again, it's fit. "Are they going to really fit in with the rest of the team?" Now, the other pitfall that I do definitely worry about is that I don't want the team to become a monoculture. I don't want it to be where we only hire people who are just like us, because then you only get people that are just like you, and you don't get a lot of innovation. I try to look for innovation in other areas.

Jenny: When you use words like fit *and* personality, *do people ever gravitate toward hiring someone they want to be friends with or hang out with, more than really putting them through the paces to see if they're actually qualified? What does that do to the culture of the team? Do you find that it affects the culture?*

Andy: I haven't found that, not that anybody would tell me that. Nobody would say, "I want to hire this guy because I think he'd be fun to go drink with." We have enough differences in what the team is about that not everybody's alike, so I'm not too worried about that. I think that everybody on the team who comes into the interview understands the importance of hiring someone they have to deal with every day. We're hiring someone who you'll spend more waking hours with than your spouse.

Andrew: Do you think that a good team should necessarily be made up of people who like hanging out together after work?

Andy: No, definitely not! I don't think that's a requirement at all. I've been on teams where there are people that I couldn't imagine going and hanging out with because they're just not interesting to me in that way. Maybe they love to play beach volleyball, and I have no interest in that. We've got one guy here who goes and plays golf a couple of times a week as soon as work is over. Well, that's incredibly boring to me. But that's OK. By the same token, not everybody works on open source projects like I do. Not everybody plays guitar in a traditional Irish band, like Mike does; whatever it may be. Everybody has outside interests, and that's OK—they don't have to be the same. As long as we can get together for those eight to n hours a day and get stuff done.

Now that being said, sure, some people I do hang out with. And that's just natural. But it's not a failure if not everybody wants to go do it.

Andrew: So what about your open source projects? How does all of this apply to them?

Andy: The dynamics of people having to get along together on an open source project are much the same as the ones of trying to get along in a company. The difference is that on an open source project, there's nobody who can say, "Shape up and fly right or you're out on your ear."

Andrew: What do you think that does to the dynamic, that there's no one person on an open source team who can say that? Does that help or hinder?

Andy: Well, one of the things that's different on an open source project is that the leaders become leaders. Look at Perl, which I'm very involved in. Yes, Larry Wall is the leader of Perl, because it's his language, he wrote it and invented it. But aside from him, all other leadership has simply come from things that people have done. If you work on such and such, this part and that part, and you write these modules, and everybody likes your modules, and you help people out, well, then, you naturally are given respect and are seen as a leader. As opposed to "Larry has appointed so-and-so to be the boss of this group."

I think that really matches a lot of the geek tendency toward meritocracy, that the people who do the most and best work get the rewards. And if that reward is that the person is seen as a respected member of the community, then the two naturally go hand in hand.

CHAPTER SIX

Inspiring People

an Interview with Keoki Andrus

Keoki Andrus is an expert on improving the way teams work together. We first heard of him from a talk that he gave on performance and potential when he was head of operations at Intuit. He has some great ideas about how to take somewhat lofty concepts like "vision" and "potential" and turn them into practical, real-world techniques for improving the way teams run. Andrew sat down with Keoki to talk about this.

Andrew: So, how did you come to know about software teams?

Keoki: Well, I've been in the software industry for 20 years. I started at Microsoft, and I worked on the first versions of Word. I worked with one of the project managers for Office, too, when we converted it from a bundle to a suite. After that, I worked as an executive for years, running product management at Novell in project management and strategy.

This became a family joke with my wife. We would always start the engagement with a discussion of "What should we be doing with our product?" And almost always, within a few days, it became a discussion of "How do I run my company? My people aren't happy. How do we solve these problems?" And it's always because of the way the organization runs, and the cohesiveness of the organization—those things have a huge impact on the success.

Andrew: Where did you really cut your teeth on getting teams working?

Keoki: I worked at Intuit for a while. I ran a company, and I was called in there. The Orem, Utah, site was a site that they had opened up six years previously, and it was really failing. When I talked to Intuit, they had kind of made up their minds that they were going to shut it down, they just didn't have the productivity. "Morale is low, and if we don't get it turned around we're gonna have to close it. So, you're our last chance. Why don't you give it a try?" Well, I worked with that site and we turned it around from a low-morale, low-productivity kind of a scattered organization into one of the best performing group of engineers in the company. We doubled the size of the site. Some people got promoted, some people had to leave, but it ended up being pretty successful.

Andrew: That's pretty impressive. How did you do it?

Keoki: The first thing I did was that I went and just sat down with each individual in the site and tried to get a pulse from them—what they saw as some of the difficulties.

I had two objectives in doing that. The first objective was that I really did want to understand them, and what was going on from their perspective. The second thing I wanted to do was help them to understand that I truly cared. Because my doming hypothesis is that if people don't believe you care, they're not going to care about what you say.

I discovered pretty quickly that there was a lot of discontent. The team had several individuals who had very high potential and could really become high performers, but they were fractured. These people had a strong need for human connection, for good working relationships, but they had been peeled off one by one to work on projects as part of a remote team.

Now, some people can do that very well. But for people who need a day-to-day high degree of interpersonal connectivity with others that they're working with, that doesn't work so well. I noticed these people; they were leaders at the site and they were well respected, but they were grumpasaurs.

First I tried to tell them, "You've got to knock that off," but they just couldn't hear that message. Then I noticed that one of the managers at the site that I was managing was well respected by everybody. In fact, I would go beyond well respected. I would say he was loved by everybody.

And I grew to feel the same way, and I still think of him extremely highly. He's one of those fantastic human beings of high integrity, but he was getting the crud kicked out of him by upper management because of the way his people were acting. So, I pulled aside the leader among all the high-potential low performers and I said, "Here's the deal. You can be a superstar, but you're frustrated by some of the things going on." He agreed. So I said, "Did you know that your actions are hurting your manager?"

That stunned him, because he loved this guy and he didn't want to hurt him. So I sat down with him and I kind of went through his career possibilities and who he was.

By this point, he knew I really cared about him, because I hadn't pistol-whipped him even though he'd been pretty open about some things he wasn't happy with.

So, I went to his remote managers, and I worked out a transition plan for him to get back on a local team. They were happy to get rid of him, because he was so unhappy. So he saw that coming. He could see that I was going to bat for him, and once we got to that point, I sat down with him and I went point by point through each of the strengths that I saw that he had.

I said, "You know, when you add all these up, you are destined to be a superstar, but this need to be a curmudgeon, to be disruptive in this negative way, is killing you. Could we just throttle that back a bit? I know it's you, to be able to say these things that other people don't say. You're funny and you love to show that off. But could you just kind of keep that around here with the boys? Could we just not do that when we're on the phone with people at corporate?" And he turned around!

Then there was the manager. I had to help him to start to see how he could manage his people. I'd been told by the vice president about that manager, "You're probably going to have to let this guy go. He's got a lot of potential, but right now he's just dead wood, and we can't figure out a way to get him to work successfully."

So, I went and met the guy, and I went through his life with him. Then I talked to the VP and said, "You know what, this guy is a superstar. He's not marketing very well, but he's a superstar. He's just got a few adjustments to the way he interacts with others that he's got to change." So I talked to him just like I talked to the developer. Basically, I said, "Here's why you're great, here's the stuff that's holding you back. Let's work together on not advertising that one thing so much, and we'll shore up a couple of these areas and get you where you need to be."

He started working on that. Six months later, the site was really moving forward.

Andrew: It sounds like you started with a good team that had all of the right technical skills, but were being held back by that "soft" stuff that software people like us hate to think about. And it sounds like you approached the problem by knocking down communication barriers—helping them talk to other people better, advertise their strong points, tone down their weaker points in front of outside people. Is that how you operate? Starting with communication issues?

Keoki: I'm a one-on-one communicator, and I love to be with somebody face to face. I don't do as well on the phone. With that manager, it was actually kind of funny, because at first the vice president basically said, "Why haven't you fired him? This guy's a loser. You need to get a new manager in there." I had to tell him, "You know, I really think he's got some great qualities and great capabilities and we need to invest in bringing those out." That vice president actually told me, "You're the first person in six years to ever say anything positive about this guy to me. Are you sure?"

Later that year, I got my review, and my review was really good. But part of the review said, "It's so amazing how much you've managed to accomplish, seeing that you have to work with people like this guy and others who aren't very talented." I found that offensive, because I thought these guys were amazing.

So, every time they did something good, I made sure it was genuinely good. It wasn't just marketing. These people were really genuinely good, but nobody knew. So I started making sure that proper credit was given to them when they did something good. And after a while people started talking about that same manager and saying, "He's phenomenal."

And then the next year, a funny thing happened. I got my review—it cracks me up, because my review said, "Yes, your site was fantastic. But what do you expect, when you have an amazing manager like this running the place for you?" I sure wasn't going to say anything, right? Because that was what I was trying to do for him. But I thought that was hilarious.

Andrew: So, what did you learn from all of that? Is there some core principle that you took away from all of it?

Keoki: One thing that I realized was that, going back to the beginning, these people had no vision. They just saw themselves as working at a job. Nobody sees their own greatness or their own potential. So I sprang some visions.

The first vision was that this would be the greatest engineering group in the company: that people would look to us as the vanguards, the trendsetters, the ones who were always on the edge of doing the greatest, most innovative things. We would be the group that you go to when you have a hard task.

Up until now, they were the street cleaners, the garbage men. "Somebody's got to code this. We'll throw it over to them." And I thought, "We've got to change that." And one of the things that I observed was that every engineer there really was talented. They were really talented, but the problem was that each one of them had their own method for software development.

They all had their own way of doing things, writing code. They all were good at it, and they all understood each other's methods well enough to get along with each other and adjust on the fly. But if anybody new came into the group, they couldn't comprehend it. So the organization had no ability whatsoever to scale.

If you were an old-timer, great. If not, you can't swim with these guys. And from an outsider's perspective, if you're working with them you can't even talk the same language as them, even though you're a software guy. So, I brought in a group on software process, and we implemented a very hardcore process, which everybody whined at me about.

Andrew: I've been there, gone down the same process road. You must have run into some resistance from the team, because they didn't want to change the way they built the software.

Keoki: They were all saying things like, "This is terrible, it's so hard." I said, "You know what, guys? We're about scaling. We are about creating an organization that delivers super-high quality on time, and you guys are capable of doing it. I know this is miserable." I knew that these guys would want to monkey around, and that they'd rebel. I also knew that no process fits everything, and that there's always some part of a process that's stupid.

And I have a philosophy that I live by. Everybody that works with me knows this; it's on the wall: "If stupid enters the room, you have a moral duty to shoot it, no matter who's escorting it."

Andrew: Did people take that idea seriously? Even if it was your idea that they thought was stupid?

Keoki: People who work with me know that. If I'm escorting it, shoot it. I don't have any problem with that whatsoever. I will laugh if you point out how dumb I am. There's no ego with that.

What I wanted to do was get them to just give the new way of doing things a try, because everybody had this resistance of change. I was hard-nosed at the beginning: "We will do everything in the process, no matter how stupid it seems." The response was "Ugh." But at this point, they trusted me some, because the site was now getting creditability, good things were happening, they were getting treated well, they were enjoying their work, and they were sitting there going, "Well, Keoki's done these other things. Maybe this is OK, too, but it seems stupid."

So, they trusted me enough to do it. I said, "Guys, just hang on. Run with it for a while, and then when we find the stupid, and when we're sure that it's stupid and don't just think that it's going to be stupid, we'll change it." I got them to run with it for a few months. There were a couple parts of it where they said, "I don't get it" or "I know MIT came up with this, but it's dumb."

I'd say, "Well, let's talk about why it's dumb. Is it dumb because you just don't like it, or is it dumb because it doesn't fit our circumstances? If you can explain to me why it doesn't fit our system, our particular circumstances, then we'll change it." We implemented a few changes, which actually helped the organization.

We got better at the process. At the same time, they realized I live by my philosophy, that I wasn't going to make them do stupid things just because that was the way it is. We got through that phase, and then we started delivering.

Compared to everybody, the other development organization, we were on time. And our quality was insanely high; it was like a couple of quantum levels above everybody else's.

Andrew: That's a pretty impressive result. But it strikes me that you didn't do anything magical—a lot of it sounds like common sense. You mentioned that you had sprung several visions. What did you do next?

Keoki: The next part of the vision was, "Well, we have to be the greatest." Well, what do the great engineers do? They innovate. So, we launched a program of trying to really think outside the box, to figure out how do we innovate.

We started creating patents. In the first year that we started this program, where we really put emphasis on innovating to create new intellectual property, we only represented one-half of one percent of all the engineers at the company, and we innovated like seven or eight percent—we had seven or eight percent of all the patents.

In the next year, we had 16 or 17 percent of all the patents in the company.

Andrew: That's a huge jump. What did you do? Mandatory weekly brainstorming sessions?

Keoki: One way I accomplished that was I did very little screening on people-submitted ideas. I wanted the ideas, I wanted them to flow, not to criticize. Then, later, we'd let the screening people at the company screen out some ideas, and say these are the ones we're interested in.

And it was funny, because I got an email once from legal, and they said, "You know, we need to talk about what appropriate patent idea submissions are and which ones are or aren't appropriate." And then somebody got a hold of them and said, "Shut up! He's the only guy doing what we actually want him to do." And I got a nice, polite little email: "Never mind, we don't need to talk about that."

Andrew: I still want to know how you got that level of innovation, because sometimes innovation seems, well, almost mysterious to me. Where do ideas come from? I know we want to talk about teams, but it seems to me that those two things aren't unrelated. How do you get a team of people to come up with good ideas? How do you improve, how do you help people innovate in groups?

Keoki: There's a general process of leadership which is key to all of us. The first thing is to establish a vision that everybody believes in passionately, and that's a process of inclusion and ownership. Then the second thing is the how. If people own the vision, they will internally create passion that creates the innovative juices.

When we discuss these things within the team, I don't come up with all my own ideas. I socialize them into the group. We negotiate until we get to the point where everybody's passionate. I brought up this thing with the patents with them, and they got turned on about it, because it was part of our vision for being great and putting our site on the map.

Once that happened, then whenever we'd be in meetings, somebody would have an idea, someone would always ask the question, "Is that patentable?" And people would start talking about it: "Wait a minute; that could be patentable." After a while, I would go around the office—one guy had on his whiteboard a big thing just listing all the ideas that were active in the group.

It became part of the culture to figure out how we could innovate. People got excited because there was always a question: "Is that patentable?" and you've got to follow up on that. It was all part of the vision, how the team saw themselves. If you set a vision, you've got to follow up on what's important, and when people see it, if they have that personal passion, they really will create spontaneously.

The other thing is that I had to create some urgency. For example, there was this one engineer, a really brilliant database guy, and he never wanted to overstate what he can do. Like many engineers, he said, "I don't want to promise what I can't deliver." It took me over a year for these guys to realize that I would not chew them up for being bold, for learning something new that changed their schedule.

Man, be bold. That's a rule. If we learn something new, well, we're smart guys. We know that we learned something new, and that changes what we thought. Only imbeciles chew people out for not having known everything that they would yet learn.

Yet, engineers always get punished, because everybody wants a schedule from them. Well, I don't play that game. These people started to get that. This engineer, he never wanted to promise what he couldn't deliver. When I realized that, I figured, "I got his number."

He'd come into my office and he would say, "You know, we can't solve this problem. It can't be done." And I would look at him and I would say, "Jeff, you are one of the most brilliant engineers I've ever known in my life. I just have a real hard time hearing the words 'it can't be done' coming out of the mouth of one of the most brilliant engineers of all time."

"Tell you what, Jeff, you go back to your cube, and you figure it out, and at three o'clock, you come back and tell me what the answer is." He'd just look at me and say, "I just told you it's impossible."

"I know, for any normal engineer, it would be impossible, but you're not a normal engineer. You are one of the best." Now, you can't do this sort of thing if you're not sincere. If you don't have a close, intimate relationship with people, where they know you really mean it, then they can tell it's all bull.

Andrew: But you had that sort of relationship with this engineer, so he trusted you and believed you when you told him that, right?

Keoki: Right. He knew I respected him. I've done this so many times with him, and it's only him, right, because you've got to know every person individually. He'd say, "Oh, I hate it when you do this to me."

Every single time, within two hours either he'd burst into my office going, "I got it!" or I'd walk by his cubicle and he'd say, "Oh, come here, come here, come here, come here!" Because he had that brilliance, and I just had to put him in a position where he was challenged, where he felt personally motivated to tap into it.

It worked because he knew I wouldn't chew him out. Because I'd say, "If you can't figure it out by that time, then nobody can, but I think you can." And he never wanted to let me down.

Andrew: It sounds like you started with a real solid group of engineers. You had some top-level talent, a team that had the potential to do really good work that was just held back by personality, communication, and vision problems. And it sounds like one important way you got it all to work was that you figured out what makes each person tick, and you gave him exactly that.

Keoki: I had another engineer—I hope to get to work with him again. He's a god. He finishes his work ahead of schedule with great quality, then goes around the rest of the team and helps them solve their problems, and then he goes outside the team and fixes everybody else's problems.

This guy, his thing is play. He will not turn on unless he's in the state of play. He loved to play foosball and other games. Now, some people say, "Well, you're not working, you're not doing a good job." I say "bull." You have to tap into what turns on the creativity for the person so that they are operating in a state of passion.

Man, he loved to play foosball. And we had a thing in the group. There's two guys on each side on foosball. So if someone needed a game, they'd walk out and you yell, "Three," indicating that number four's already been taken. Somebody else yells, "Two," meaning we need two more, and then somebody else yells, "One," and then some gal says, "I'm in!" and we've got all four now.

You'd go play a game, and then you go back to your desk. Well, some people would say that's stupid. "You're encouraging people not to work!" But I detected that for many people, if you took 10 minutes and went and played a game, they would go back to their desk with this kind of creative, passionate energy from the competition and solve problems.

So I sat down with Jason, that brilliant engineer, one day, and I said, "Jason, tell me about how your mind works. You play games all day long, but you're the most productive engineer I've ever encountered in my career. What is the connection between play and performing at this super-high level?"

And he said, "It's just what I need to clear my mind. I get these problems, and if I play for a little bit, I go back and I can solve them." And I said, "Jason, here's the deal. I don't know if I'll say this for everybody, but if you ever feel the need to play, I want you to play, because if that's what it takes to get this kind of amazing performance, you should play as much as you need to."

And he never let me down. So, that was part of your answer to how do you get that creativity going. You have to find what turns on passion for each individual and then bring them in as a leader into that state of play.

Andrew: You keep using, it really strikes me, you keep using words like respect, passion, creativity, even love. *Plenty of people talk about respect and creativity when they talk about motivation, but I rarely hear people talk about motivation in the language of emotion. But it sounds like you use respect and love as management tools, the way engineers use engineering terms. They're almost like* jargon—*in the positive sense of the word* jargon. *When you use the word* love, *you're not using it in the wishy-washy Hallmark sort of way. It really has a technical meaning, and it turns into an important tool to help a team gel. How did you get to that point?*

Keoki: So first of all, I discovered early in my career, I'm good at observing. Engineers like to think of themselves more like Spock than anybody else. "I am logical. That is all I do."

So, I started observing how engineers would respond when somebody criticized their code. And sometimes I'd actually think, "I got a 2-year-old here. This person is incredibly emotional." The more I watched engineers, the more I realized they were as emotional—if not more emotional—than everybody else, and that emotion was a big part of their craft. They just got really good at kind of structuring the way they communicated.

I realized that they need an emotional outlet and connections, just like everybody else. So that was the first thing I figured out.

Andrew: I'm wondering if this ties back to something else you mentioned that I wanted to ask more about: when you're coming up with ideas, having an overarching vision. You seem to use vision to improve performance in a real, measurable way to improve engineering, in a way that people who would otherwise not be inclined to use that term can respect.

And it strikes me that the word "vision" is another one of those words that hardcore engineers and developers might not use. It probably sounds like business-speak, management-ese jargon. Might not—I know I haven't gotten it in the past.

Personally, it took me a long time to get any traction with the concept of a vision for a project, or for a team. I know that vision has a lot to do with figuring out who you're building the project for, with really meeting their needs, and with understanding what problem it is that you're solving. But just hearing you talk about it, I'm wondering if maybe there's a more visceral definition for vision. Can you help me understand the idea behind vision, something that might help somebody who's looking to really come up with better ideas, or to improve the way their projects are run?

Keoki: Sure, I can address that. Vision is typically botched.

And the way it's botched is like this: "Our vision is to become the number one provider of telecommunications equipment in the market." Or: "Our vision is that we're not building buggy whips anymore, we're building horse motivation tools." We come up with visions that are sterile.

If you want people to act with power, you have to tap into their emotions. Emotion is where creativity comes from. It's the source of innovation, and of long working hours, and all the other things that you want out of people. It doesn't come from holding a gun to their heads. And boring doesn't work. So, how do you get a vision that evokes that?

If the people on the team can't see it in their minds, it's not a good vision. So you have to be a little bit of a televangelist in the way you paint the picture of the vision.

Let me give you an example of a vision I had. And I think you should have vision all the time. So, my sons have been in show choirs. Do you know what show choirs are?

Andrew: No.

Keoki: Show choirs are kind of like Broadway for high school. And these choirs sing, and at the same time, they dance—they do almost drill team at the same time. It's quite amazing. My second son is a national champion, and my first son was picked as the best male performer. We were going to go on this trip to Branson, Missouri, with his group.

I live in Utah, and it's a 30-hour bus ride. We could do a plane, but people wanted to go as cheap as we could. And they went to the adults and they said, "We need some parents to volunteer to sit on the bus with these teenagers for 30 hours each direction." And parents signed up, but everybody had this attitude of like, "Well, we have to do it. I'll be swimming in a stew of fatigue, estrogen, and testosterone for 30 hours. Oh, it's gonna be awful."

And I thought about this and I said, "I'm going on this thing. What am I going to do? Am I going to just sit for 30 hours each direction and then just be miserable that I'm stuck with a bunch of teenagers? No, I need a vision." OK, well, what kind of vision could go along with this?

And I started thinking about it, and I said, "Wait a minute, these kids are going out and doing something that's one of the great opportunities in their young lives: to discover their potential. So wait a minute. I'm a guy who's totally into leadership and helping people discover their potential. Is there anything I could do?"

I thought, these kids don't know how to do any of that. What if I made it my goal to make this one of the crowning moments of at least some of their lives? It could be that thing that they looked back upon and think, "That was the time that I really felt my potential. That I really touched greatness for a moment."

That changed my job for the trip: it wasn't to babysit these kids for 30 hours each direction and while they're at the hotel. My job was to find every moment I can to show them a little way to tap into their own greatness. That was what the vision was for.

And as a result, just having that vision and looking for it every moment of that trip—well, first of all, the bus rides were a breeze for me. But second of all, I was able to take leaders aside, one by one, when I could see that they were at a moment where they didn't know what to do, and show them a little bit about greatness. And as a result, they actually accomplished amazing things, and it was a great experience in their lives. I'm still friends with those same teenagers.

I shared that with you just to kind of give you the picture of how simple a vision can be, and how mundane it can be. What I mean is, it can be associated with something so mundane, but I hope that the way I told it to you gave you that visceral feeling, where you thought, "Wow, I wish I was on that bus with those kids." And that's what a great vision does. It makes you feel like, "I want to be part of that." Even something as boring as being on a bus for 30 hours with adolescents.

Andrew: I've definitely heard about projects and thought, "Man, I wish I could have been on that team." It's probably because they had a good vision. I saw an interview once with some video game developers from one of my favorite video games, and I thought that.

You know, one of the things that I've written about, and something that I've read many times from other people, is when you start on a project, you want to get it started out right. You want to avoid problems down the road. And everyone—including Jenny and me, in our own books—says that one thing you really need to do is lay out the vision in the beginning of the project. But I never really had a good litmus test to be able to tell you that a particular vision is good. And maybe you've just given us the answer. A good litmus test of whether you have a good vision may be that just hearing it makes you want to be a part of the project.

Keoki: Exactly. And the same thing works on teams when you're recruiting. I always get the people I recruit, because when I recruit them, I don't do the boring song of "Here's what your duties will be." On my team, everybody is on their way to somewhere in their career, and it's unique for each person. I talk to them about that.

My goal as a leader is to find where that right place is for them, that they agree with, and craft a vision of where they're going. Then, my job is to help them get there in the context of them doing good work for the team. I'll teach them leadership. I'll teach them anything that they want to learn so that they can go where they want to be.

I'll give my recruits examples of how I do that with people, and then I say, "Now go talk to the members of my team. And you can ask them anything you want. Ask any member of my team." I'll let them talk to people already on my team, and they'll say, "Yeah, he's completely dedicated not to just my career, but to me as a person."

They always come back and say, "I've never encountered a job like that, and I would give anything to be in a team like that." And so, I always win.

Andrew: Wow, I've done a lot of hiring over the years, and I've never done anything like that. Let's say I want that for my team, I want that for my company. I want my teams to work that way. I can see what it will look like in the end, but how do I get there? What's my first step in getting from where I am now? You told a story of how you started with a team that had a lot of potential, and you turned them around. Let's say I've got a team, and I know they have a lot of potential. How do I turn them around? How do I get them from point A to point B?

Keoki: OK, so one thing is you can call me up, and I'll come out and help them. I do this for a living, you know.

Andrew: (Laughter.)

Keoki: But I do love doing this. The process of developing skills is a process of first recognizing that you need the skill, then learning the skill, and then processing it. Then, to actually get to a master, you need the tutorage of a master.

And you can add that as much as you can in the book, but you really do need coaching to become great at something. Now, having said that, here's the good news. People are hungry to actually be cared about. Think about that for a minute. You want to be understood, right? Everybody does. Everybody wants to feel important. It's universal.

Now, if you just try to do this by turning to your team and saying, "Oh, yes, I will do this now. I don't feel anything, but I'm going to do it," then forget it, you're just a pointy-haired boss.

But if you sincerely just reach out and start with trying to get to know your people as human beings, with the mindset of trying to understand who they are and what's important to them, trying to be a facilitator of their vision or helping them to create a vision, people will respond exponentially to being treated with care and compassion, because they've been dying for it.

They're starving to death. Imagine the old cliché of the man who's dying of thirst in the desert. How much will he pay for a drink of water? Well, people are starving to death in virtually every job, looking to actually be treated like a human being.

I've never encountered anybody, except people with borderline personality disorder, who don't want to be understood. Some people will say they don't, but just watch their behavior and you'll realize they do.

And that's what I have found as a leader that I often do with people is just sit down and go, "Oh, you know what, you missed it. Let's talk about how to succeed with it." And I know that that wasn't the greatest answer, but you can't magically jump to it, but you can have great results just by trying.

Andrew: So how does that work in practice? If I were bringing you on board, say, to help me improve the way I ran my own team? Right now our team is me and Jenny—we're working on a book called Beautiful Teams. *We're leading a team of about three dozen people who are experts at building software, and we're all working toward this one goal of writing a book that's both informative and interesting. What's the first thing you'd do for us?*

Keoki: I'd ask you to tell me more about yourself, you and Jenny. I feel like I hardly know much about you. So tell me—right now.

Andrew: Right now?

Keoki: Sure. What do you do? What's your vision? Who are you?

Andrew: OK. Well, basically, Jenny and I started writing books for O'Reilly a few years ago. We had a lot of fun writing two books in their Head First series, writing one on project management and one on learning C#.

Before that, we wrote our book on software engineering and project management. To be honest, it's really a book on quality, on making software better and software projects run better—we kind of realized at the time that our goal was to make the world a little bit better by helping people build better software. And that's really what we do: we help people build better software. It's why we write books and speak at conferences, and it's why we've done so much consulting over the years.

That's actually why we've spent so much of our careers targeting project managers. One thing we figured out early on was that project managers are an underused, under-respected resource that can really help build better software. If a project manager takes the time to understand how software is built, he can do amazing things for his team. So I guess that's our vision: we want to give people the tools they need to build better software, or maybe to help them solve the problems that are keeping them from building better software.

And other than that, I've spent a lot of my life first building software and then leading teams that build software. Jenny spent a lot of her life first testing software and then leading and managing teams that build software. I don't use the word brilliant all that often, but she's a brilliant quality engineer. Before I met her, I felt that software testing was a kind of "black art," something you're kind of born with, or maybe just feel your way through. It wasn't until I worked with Jenny, back in the '90s, that I realized that software testing is a real engineering discipline in its own right. You can understand it, you can make it transparent, and you can get a team to do it. And she does it brilliantly. I'd deliver software to her that I thought was done, and she'd find so many bugs that I couldn't believe I was willing to let it out the door. But more than that, working together we figured out how to keep a lot of those bugs from getting into the software in the first place. Doing that really made me really realize the art of quality, of building better software, as well as the science.

Keoki: There's a certain way that that type of QA person thinks and what motivates them, and if you got it, you got it. I was a QA engineer at Microsoft when I started out, and I've known some of the people I think like you're describing.

Andrew: Jenny was the first real QA engineer I met who really understood quality, really got it on a deep level. Not just on a "let's make this software not crash" level, but really understanding it's about how software works, how software meets the users' needs.

It's about software conforming to requirements—getting back to the real definition of quality. And that's what motivates her—it's what motivates me, too.

Quality's also about process—but process is more than just getting people to do things in a certain, repeatable way. It's more than that. It's about changing the way an organization breathes and grows, it's about changing the way people actually act and, hopefully, how they think about their jobs.

We were working together for a few years at a small financial software company and, through a lot of trial and error, we were lucky enough to be working at a company that was small enough and inexperienced enough to let two relatively young, inexperienced people change—completely change—the way they build software.

And we got some really good results. We also made a lot of mistakes along the way. And it was really good for both of us. I kind of feel really privileged to have been able to make such mistakes. And we dedicated a lot of our career to understanding mistakes, understanding why projects fail.

Keoki: I actually have my top 10 list of how you create passion, and one of the biggest ones is celebrating mistakes.

The one talent that virtually every person in the world feels like they have that is unique to them and they feel a moral obligation to share is the talent of criticism. "*I* am the one who can find what's wrong with this, and since I can, I must tell you what's bad. I feel obligated." And we're all conditioned: we all hate it, right, but we all are good at it.

But the thing is, have you ever been in a situation where you've been, say, in a meeting, and something bad has happened? Now, that may mean anything. Say we shipped the software, and there's a crashing bug in it, and it's terrible.

We're sitting around talking about it, and somebody says, "We need to have a postmortem on this so we can figure out what happened." And then these words come out: "So that it never happens again." Have you ever heard that?

Andrew: Yes, of course. Most of us have.

Keoki: OK, let me ask you this question then. Can any success happen in the absence of risk?

Andrew: That's a good question. Probably not, I suppose.

Keoki: You will get a zero rate of return if you have zero risk, because there's no risk, so why should you be compensated? No success ever happened without the presence of risk. But what is risk? Risk is the chance that something bad will happen. Do you buy that?

Andrew: Absolutely.

Keoki: OK, so if no success can happen without risk, and risk means that something bad can happen, then if you set out to make an environment where risk goes to zero, what else are you driving to zero? The probability of success.

Andrew: I never thought about it that way, but it does follow.

Keoki: So it isn't bad to say, "You know, we may not have assessed our risk correctly, and we may have exercised poor judgment in something we did. Let's see if we can learn what we might have screwed up on so that we can be more informed in the future."

But the next thing that happens is that once you figure out what went wrong, you go after the person who made the mistake. And everybody else sees it; the head rolls down the hallway and gets put on the city gates. Everybody learns, "Don't make a mistake." And it's in the very act of creating that stress, that stress of not making a mistake, that you create the situation where nobody will take a risk.

Instead, what you must do to create that passion environment is when a mistake is made, you say, "OK, what was the mistake? OK, well, we did that. Good job. Now we know not to do that. Now we are going to be more sensitive to that in the future." You can even give the person a reward.

Now what happens? It creates an environment where people don't feel afraid to try something that could be risky. You want to encourage people. Now, if people take risks, and a reasonable person in possession of the facts can see that a decision was made that was clearly not thoughtful, then sure, they should get it right in the teeth for that. But nobody thinks that's unreasonable.

But if they were making a reasonable decision that just turned out bad, that just means they took a risk, which means there's a probability of something bad happening. And guess what? Sometimes that's the way it comes out. And if you don't freak out, but rather embrace it, then people feel at ease to take chances. And when they take chances, they innovate, and that's where greatness happens.

And that's why often, companies that are successful start out taking a big chance. They get their success, and they spend the rest of their corporate lives trying to drive success to zero, because they're afraid of losing what they have. And the very act of trying to not lose guarantees failure.

CHAPTER SEVEN

Bringing the Music Industry into the 21st Century

One Lawsuit at a Time

Tom Tarka

WE HAD BEEN ON THE GROUND AT LAX FOR ABOUT TWO MINUTES WHEN A VOICE CAME ON THE INTERCOM and said, "Would passenger Thomas Tarka please see the attendant at the front of the plane…."

My ears perked up and my somewhat groggy mind came to attention, playing out all of the potential scenarios.

Another one of my grandparents had fallen deathly ill and I needed to call my parents immediately?

Smugglers had sequestered drugs in my bag and the International Terminal drug-sniffing dogs had already found them?

I shuffled with the rest of the coach passengers, already thrown for a loop by a simple sentence on the intercom and not able to do a thing about it other than to carry my overstuffed bag and wait for the eternity it always seems to take to get to the front of the plane after a long international flight.

And so it was that I returned to the United States after circling the globe….

Ten months prior I had been living in Boulder and working as a keyboard jockey in various forms, starting off as a software tester and eventually working my way up the food chain to webmaster at a smallish software company. I wasn't sold on Boulder, and a tip from some backpackers at a hostel in Hawaii about the relatively inexpensive nature of "Round the World" plane tickets had put the bug in my ear to save my money, dust off my passport, and check out the rest of the world.

Jobwise I was also ready for a change, in large part because I had spent the majority of my career thus far working mostly alone or as the sole tech person on projects. It was lonely, and I was jonesing for people to geek out with. Case in point: it was fun being the webmaster for the company I worked for, but the website was run by the marketing department and left me working with amazing but non-Unix/programming/techie types, and it was getting old. It probably didn't help that a few of my friends had moved to the Bay Area, and through their tales I had heard the siren song of the dot-com, with its hordes of geeks staying up all night coding, building "Cool Stuff"™ and maybe even getting rich in the process. I was ready to move on, and I was pretty sure working as a programmer at a dot-com was the next step. It didn't hurt that the economy was booming and looking for people with my skill set, and I was banking on the fact that I could get away for a few months and, in all likelihood, not have any major issues finding a job, either. And so it was that in September 1998 I had left my job as a webmaster, packed up the last of my belongings, and driven cross-country to New York City, hopping on a plane to London a scant 48 hours after leaving Colorado.

Ten months and 45 minutes later I was in the back seat of a station wagon being driven by two people I didn't know, lost somewhere in the middle of L.A., staring about in wonderment at everything: eight-lane freeways, gridlock, Christian billboards confiding to me that my taking the Lord's name in vain was the reason that I was still stuck in traffic, the funny American cars of all shapes, waxed and gleaming, squat buildings and never-ending sprawl…. L.A.—no, *America* washed over me for the first time in almost 10 months, bigger than anything I had seen in what seemed like a lifetime, or if not bigger, then just *different* in some ineffable way that mirrored an attitude which had become in so many ways foreign to me. I was home, but it wasn't my home anymore.

The driver of the car was a friend of Connie-Lynne, someone I had known online for maybe two years but had never met in person. She was also the person who had phoned the airline to leave me a message which read something along the lines of "Message for Tommy Tarka. Constance will not be able to pick you up at the airport, but has sent someone who will meet you at the gate." So, I was in a car headed for Pasadena, driven by someone I didn't know who was taking me to someone's house that I had never actually met who I was going to stay with for a couple of days until Mark arrived from Phoenix.

Mark, of course, was an old college (and traveling) buddy who had driven cross-country from Pennsylvania and was meeting up with me in L.A. after spending some time visiting family in Phoenix. He had just finished up his master's degree at Penn State and it was our intention to take a lackadaisical cross-country jaunt, exploring the United States until such a time when we found ourselves back on the Eastern seaboard, where it just so happened that my remaining possessions (including my car) were ferreted away in various attics, storage sheds, and living rooms spread across three cities.

Connie-Lynne turned out to be as amazing and nice as I fully knew her to be after two years of chatting online, Mark and I managed to rendezvous, and three days later we were in San Diego visiting friends—JV and klh—who were from different places and times in our lives but who had independently ended up there. We had just finished throwing the disc around and had retired to klh's UCSD campus apartment when I happened to mention:

"You know, I wouldn't actually mind sticking around in San Diego for a couple of months, especially since JV's wedding is only a few weeks away and the likelihood of me getting back here for it is pretty slim if I'm off gallivanting somewhere else in the country. I'd have to find some sort of job, though, so if you guys know of any frictional work for a sys admin or a Unix geek, please let me know."

It's one of those things that seem perfectly natural after backpacking for a while, floating from place to place on a schedule that is dictated more by weather patterns or where the next bus is heading as opposed to anything else more concrete. And so the words were spoken with every intention of actually doing just that: hanging around San Diego for six weeks until your good friend's wedding, but with no expectation that anything would actually come of it. Besides, after 10 months of travel, I was pretty much broke and there was no way I could stick around San Diego for six weeks unless I could find some sort of job, preferably a lucrative geek-type job to bolster the coffers. The whole thing boiled down to finances.

Which is why I was surprised when I got the response, "Oh, really? Did you tell JV that? Our friend David is working for a start-up and I think they're hiring. What do you do?"

Oh, my.

And so the connection was made. Mark and I returned to L.A., but three days later I was riding the Surfliner—the Amtrak train which follows the Pacific Coast down to San Diego—and hopping a cab to interview at MP3.com, a company I knew absolutely nothing about. Adding to the sheer absurdity of this situation—from my seeing America with fresh eyes for the first time to the "ask the universe and ye shall receive" scenario of finding out about this job—I had managed to leave the bag containing pretty much my only set of nice pants and clean/presentable shirts in the trunk of someone's car the night before. I showed up to the interview in the best clothes I had with me: shorts, a somewhat wrinkled, albeit two-button V-neck, collared shirt emblazoned with beer logos and commemorating a chapter of the Hash House Harriers club, with feet shod in, if I recall correctly, sandals. I was completely stressed out by the whole scenario, but the early hour of travel (meaning everything was closed), inability to easily reroute (as I was traveling on public transportation), and lack of time to spare between connections made it impossible to do much more than ride it out and put on my best face.

"Yeah, we were taking bets on how long you'd last," said Josh Beck, CTO, as he later recalled interviewing me that day.

MP3.com was completely hopping that day. It was the day before the IPO, and everyone was running around like mad men and women, cell phones glued to ears and fighting off a recent crash of some nature, brought on by the sudden onslaught of pre-IPO media blitz and resultant web traffic. At least half of my interviews took place on a park bench outside in the ever-perfect San Diego weather as engineers with obviously more important stuff to do took a deep breath before calmly trying to find out more about this crazy-looking guy fresh off a plane "…from where? Fiji?" and the probably-not-yet-of-legal-drinking-age CTO quizzed me on Perl modules (I knew the answers to his DBI questions but wasn't familiar with Carp at the time).

You'd think that after 10 months of globe-trotting my skills would have languished, but just the opposite was true. I spent quite a few of my days also geeking out: sitting in the Singapore library reading books on artificial intelligence, working temp programming or sys admin jobs to make some spare cash (or at least to get free coffee and Internet access in the case of the Internet Cafe that doubled as an open source software development shop, with most of the computer minders also working as developers on the side), and learning the ins and outs of DBI while working on a ride-sharing website of mine. I returned with a gap in my work history, but with reasonable programming chops in skills that, it turns out, were topical to what MP3.com did. Somehow this makes me feel better about the days that I spent in Bondi, sitting out on the porch in the beautiful sunshine and hacking away on Perl code via a strung-together 386/16 (running FVWM on 12 or 16 megs of RAM and connecting in through a 33k modem) instead of frolicking on the beach. Somehow.

Four hours later there was an offer on the table and we were discussing salary and benefits. The fact that the IPO was the next day—and that the actual contract wouldn't be ready until then, not to mention the fact that I probably needed at least a week to recover all my stuff from the East Coast—meant that I was screwed on stock options: instead of locking in at an option price of a dollar or two per share, I'd end up at whatever the stock price was after going public (my option price ended up being somewhere in the $50 to $65 range); so much for getting rich quick. I was kind of pissed, but at the same time I knew that this was my bargaining chip for an actual salary, as opposed to the peanuts some folks managed to get by on—banking, of course, on their options vesting at a price that would make the small salary moot—and did my best to use the situation to my advantage. I came away with a salary lower than I wanted, but with a promise that I would be bumped up to something more acceptable in a few months. Good enough, especially with how much I wanted the job.

And so not even two weeks after returning to the country I had managed to land the job that I had dreamed of: working at a fast-paced, up-and-coming dot-com. I was disappointed that I wasn't going to be able to travel the States a bit and felt bad about leaving Mark in the lurch with regard to our plans of lazy exploration, yet it was an opportunity of a lifetime. There would be (and was) time for exploring later; for now, I had a job!

A New Project, A New Team

Fast-forward three months and MP3.com has moved to a new location: two buildings overlooking the scenic 805 freeway. Of the two, only one is inhabited and even it is still under construction as offices are framed and erected in the empty spaces, a chain link fence is put up to keep the musicologists from eating anyone, and the building is art-i-fied—one entire hallway is tagged with graffiti while another is textured with chunky dried caulk in a peanut-butter cookie crisscross painted gold. You get the picture: these buildings are becoming *ours*. The second building is under construction and before long will house the engineering department, which is already 50 or 60 people strong and probably 40% to 50% of the total company. For the time being, however, we're in cubicle purgatory.

It's early October, and for the past three months I've been working closely with Sander van Zoest, a crazy Dutchman and one of the MP3.com founders—his title is High Geek—and David Story, programmer extraordinaire. The two are as much alike as they are different: Sander is 23 with rocking blue hair, doesn't ever seem to sleep, and is someone you would perhaps run across at one of San Diego's Goth/industrial nights wearing almost see-through silver pants. He's striking both in the way that he speaks—waiting for you to finish and making sure you have nothing more to say before carefully giving you an insightful commentary on either why the system is designed in that particular way or how the particular architecture has evolved over its development cycle, resulting in its current incarnation, complete with various hints at what might make sense for the next version—and his demeanor, which is just slightly not American (and yet is, somehow).

David, on the other hand, is 39 years young with a twinkle in his eye that belies the fact that he'd probably be happier riding around on BMX bikes with his kids all day as opposed to living in the grown-up world. Yet not only is he a tireless worker who appears to view every project with a sort of ongoing curiosity, poking and prodding until he solves the puzzle, but he exudes a calm which seems impenetrable. He is fit, dressed in nice, pressed shorts and collared shirt, and drives his barely-street-legal motocross bike to work on most days.

Their demeanors, appearances, and work habits are yin to the other's yang, but both are complete professionals: taking the time to design elegant architectures, designing to published standards when they exist (or at least aware of the fact that they're skirting the standard and why), writing and submitting RFCs when it makes sense to, and generally taking the time to "Do Things Right," if for no other reason than that they'll be portable and easier to maintain later.

This seems to be one of the common threads among the MP3.com engineers: they were, to a T, talented professionals who got things done, not afraid to roll up their sleeves and jump right in and come up with innovative solutions. I can't tell you how many people arrived at MP3.com and had absolutely no direction their first day or five as things were just going too fast for everyone around them. What happened next, however, was amazing and unique: they jumped in and made work for themselves. It was not a matter of "What am I supposed to be doing?" but rather "What can I do??!" as you wanted to be a part of the living, breathing organism around you. Besides, that's why people came to MP3.com: to *work*. They were jazzed at what the company was doing, at the team assembled around them, at the breakneck pace of just about everything: the energy was addictive. And this is exactly how I started working with David and Sander.

> "Where do you think you will be when you are listening to your music 10 years from now?"—Michael Robertson, CEO of MP3.com

> "In prison."—Christopher Giles, software engineer and fiddle player

And so it was that one early October day, the three of us—David, Sander, and I—got pulled into a meeting room with our manager, David McCollum, and three other engineers: Christopher Giles, Josh Stevens, and Mike Oliphant.

> "Now this is a top-secret project and what we are about to talk about cannot leave this room. OK? OK. You know that we have been talking to the music labels for some time, trying to work out a way to license their content. Unfortunately, we've been getting nowhere. Well, I was just in a meeting with Michael [Robertson], and he has a vision for how we can move forward, legally. He wants to build a site which allows people to leverage their existing music collection, meaning the CDs they already own, from our site...."—David McCollum, director of engineering

Say what??!

"How is that legal?" someone asked.

"Michael and the legal team are working on that and think that they have a legal solution...."

And so it began.

You see, up until this point in time, MP3.com had been a website for the independent music artist. Any musician could create an "artist" page and upload his music, and *presto!* People could listen to and (if the musicians allowed it) download the music. All for free! Not only that, but you could also upload album art and sell CDs from our site, pulling in 40% or so of the price you chose to sell it at. These D.A.M. CDs were pressed on the fly using just-in-time manufacturing, so there was no cost to you and our costs were covered within our percentage of the sale price.*

That's the overview—a site designed to allow artists to self-promote, remove the overhead of creating a music product, and eliminate the middleman (i.e., the record label) who was taking a huge cut of their sales—but it doesn't capture the buzz and excitement generated by the site. Nor does it capture what went into the daily operation of the company: a full staff of musicologists, who in addition to their other duties, tirelessly listened to track after track of uploaded music for copyright infringements (and trust me when I say that some

---

* D.A.M. (Digital Automatic Music) CD-Rs were not audio CDs, but rather contained MP3 files. This meant that the CD could not be played on some traditional players, but more than 72 minutes of music could be placed on it.

of that music was not pretty), the marketing and sales teams who somehow found ways for us to slow down our burn rate, a legal department that did its best to keep us out of trouble (a difficult proposition at best), and last but not least, the engineering that went into keeping the site up every day.

And when I say "engineering," I mean it. Keeping a website that hosts 200,000 songs and 40,000 artists running is no small feat, and so MP3.com—with $400 million in the bank—invested in quality people and an engineering team which was half the size of the company.

What did all this mean? Well, three months after the IPO, the engineering team—everyone involved—had made substantial inroads in creating a very scalable infrastructure. Don't get me wrong, the frantic pace and energy hadn't slowed down, but things seemed to be…stable. And you'll note that I'm referring to the "engineering team" here as opposed to specific individuals, as I was discussing before. It sounds cheesy, but even though the engineering team had grown to be fairly huge (50 or 60 people), it really was a pretty cohesive unit; at least to the extent that none of the individual groups could have survived without the expertise of the other groups.

Heck, the whole company was pretty cohesive, with weekly companywide meetings dubbed the "Chairman's Chat" where our CEO, Michael Robertson, would address the entire company, introduce new people, and generally let us know what had been happening from a "big picture" perspective. It was one of those things where even if you didn't know everyone in the company, even if you didn't know everything that was going on, you still had some sense of what senior management was doing, and specifically, that they were doing *something*. You might not *agree* with what they were doing, but at least you knew that they were doing something. Don't get me wrong, these "chats" were at least partly pep talks and, later on, partly propaganda to keep people focused and drinking the Kool-Aid, but they worked. And just like a family, they helped us rally around each other, especially when things started taking a turn for the worse. But that wouldn't be for a while yet….

And listening to Michael (as he was generally referred to) was always interesting because he is a visionary. You might not always agree with his vision or his implementation, but he is able to think in terms of the bigger picture and think outside the box. This can be a mixed blessing at times, as he is very passionate about his ideas and he's not afraid to tell you when you're wrong. This always made it a bit scary to interact with him, as you never knew what you were going to get: was it going to be the rush of knowing your ideas were being heard by The Boss and that you might be given carte blanche? Or was it going to be the screaming, berating Michael, someone who there was no arguing with—at least not if you valued your job—who no amount of reason could reach, no matter how you chose your words, no matter what evidence you had to the contrary: his word was the final one.

This, of course, was the rush and what made Michael great: his passion, his clear vision, his ability to envision a product seemingly in its entirety and express it, or to take a nugget of an idea and explore it, riffing off one idea after another until it had become a product.

And inherent in all of this were the confidence and certainty that took these ideas to fruition. It could be an emotional roller coaster, but there was no greater high than when you were bringing one of these ideas to life.

So, when David McCollum began to tell the six of us about Michael's idea, on some level it wasn't terribly surprising: Michael had a vision for the direction the company would go in, a vision for a path to profitability, and David was asking us to assess it and determine whether we could pull it off. The idea itself was still fairly fresh and nebulous, like a concept you're talking through, but the gist of it was to roll out "a service which has three legs. The first leg is that you should be able to leverage your existing music collection (you don't want to have to repurchase anything). The second leg is that if you buy new music, it should be immediately available for you to listen to, and the third leg is that you should be able to listen to your music wherever you are and on any device you want to listen to it from."

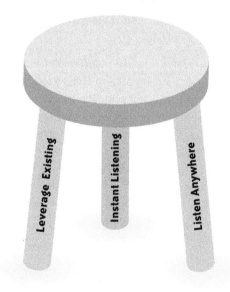

MP3.com's killer app: an online service that allows you to manage all of your music in one place, accessible from anywhere.

We were listening intently, trying to figure out where this was going, when David let us know exactly where: we were going to rip (i.e., copy a music file from a CD onto your hard drive) a whole slew of CDs, and if users could prove they owned that CD, we would allow them access to it via our site.

To explain the argument, dubious as it may or may not have been, as to why ripping tens of thousands of CDs seemed at all congruous with any sort of valid business model while all around the nation (and probably the world) the Recording Industry Association of America (RIAA) was fighting tooth and nail the notion that even creating an MP3 file, for *whatever* use, was illegal, one has to jump back to the ripe old year of 1976, when the first video recorder—the Betamax—was released by Sony. Long story short, Sony was sued for copyright infringement because the Betamax allowed you to record TV shows, movies, or whatever was on TV—something that had not been possible before and which was viewed as an infringement of the broadcaster's rights. Sony won the legal battle, and a concept called "time shifting" emerged from the court decision which states that a user can store copyrighted content to a more convenient medium for use at a later time. This is also known as the "Betamax Decision."

The corollary to "time shifting" is "space shifting," and is the concept that you can make a copy of certain media you already "own"—CDs, DVDs, records—to another form of media such as copying a CD to a tape. This concept was successfully argued in a case brought against an MP3 player manufacturer—Diamond Multimedia Systems—by the RIAA, which unsuccessfully argued that copying music from a CD to an MP3 player was a violation of copyright law.

A poster from MP3.com that exemplifies the extensive propaganda campaign that was part of the RIAA's attempt to quash music pirating.

Based on these precedents, someone (presumably our legal department) OKed the idea that we could rip a number of CDs and make them available to users who could prove that they owned the content. We were merely allowing them to "space-shift" content that they already owned. There was some additional discussion, but as Josh Stevens puts it, "We all put on our Junior Lawyer hats and set about trying to design a system that would be secure and prevent anyone who didn't own the content from getting access to that music." You see, from our perspective, we thought that as long as we could keep the system secure, we wouldn't get sued, whereas if the system wasn't secure and they (the RIAA) determined that music could unlawfully be accessed, we were in trouble.

Mind you, there was still quite a bit of grumbling about possible lawsuits, even among the six of us. In fact, I may have been one of the only people who did believe the party line and just accepted that what we were being asked to do was legal. They said the lawyers had checked it, and, well, I'm no lawyer, so I went with it. Whoops! Yet, perhaps there were other factors involved, first and foremost being the unreality field that seemed to surround many of the projects we undertook at MP3.com. I was mainly just happy to be working in this amazing environment with so many talented folks all around me.

THE PLAN

1. Rip 10,000 of the most popular CDs (based on historic sales).
2. Build web interface for managing content.
3. Create software so users can verify CDs they own ("Beam It").
4. Find retail partners to enable "instant listening."
5. Develop system to pay royalties directly to artists.

And so we started designing a system that would allow users to manage and stream music, whether the artists were on MP3.com or were from major labels (whose CD you physically owned). The system would be based upon our existing My.MP3.com website, which allowed you to do something similar with MP3.com artists. My.MP3.com would get a facelift and we would need to add significant functionality to lock down the new content, but it was a good starting point. Meanwhile, we would be taking our first foray into software, offering a tool that My.MP3.com users could download and use to verify that they owned a particular CD.

The new website would be still be dubbed "My.MP3.com," but the code name for the project was "Da Bomb": a reference both to the atom bomb, as we expected this service to change the music industry forever (much like the atom bomb had changed warfare forever), and to the Parliament lyric from P-Funk for a music reference (and 'cuz we're cool, dig?).

Independent of this, but at about the same time as Da Bomb was taking off, I started working on a side project with another engineer, Brian Degenhardt, involving user and concurrency tracking. Long story short(er), MP3.com had no way of checking if a user was currently playing a song or not. We passed around browser cookies, so we knew your MP3.com ID, but the server farm had no idea if you were logged in to multiple computers concurrently or not; it just logged that you had requested a song at a certain time. This was one of those projects where no one asked us to do it—and actually, different people told me that it wasn't something we needed—but we just decided to do it anyway. I went around and polled the people I thought might be able to use this data, and then Brian and I spent a few late nights around a whiteboard determining the project requirements and scoping out how the pieces were going to work together. It was a blast: we were both pretty young, and this was—I'm pretty sure—our first "big" project that we started designing from scratch. There was a buzz: we were modifying how all of the music on our site was served to end users. By ourselves. Because we were *allowed* to. That's just cool.

Brian was just hilarious to work with, too. He was a complete goof, straight out of college, and had this positive-world outlook that manifested itself by him just talking excitedly about the geekiest of Apache internals to anyone who would listen, able to come up with the funniest—yet dead accurate—analogies that distilled what was actually going on down to a silly caricature involving, "See, you've got this elephant, and it wants to pick up the peanut, but it can't because...." Yeah. A mile a minute and never stopping until he's figured out just why Apache isn't doing exactly the right thing that he wants it to do. I actually have no clue how we started working on the project together. Sander was probably up to his neck in other "High Geek" activities and either he directed me to talk to Brian, or somehow Brian and I just started talking to each other across the cubicle wall as we were both generally there pretty late. This was what working at MP3.com was all about: being empowered to work on crazy stuff with cool people, figuring out how to solve a problem, and then just *doing* it, learning the ins and outs along the way.

A Calculated Risk...

It's December, and Da Bomb is in full swing. The secret is out, too—at least within the company: a few weeks before, the executive VP of engineering, Delon Dotson, announced the project to the engineering staff, and Michael announced it to the rest of the company at a Chairman's Chat shortly thereafter. MP3.com was now in full "music acquisition" mode, buying all the CDs it could get its hands on, including offering employees $20 for each CD from their collection that they were willing to part with. The goal: acquire the 10,000 most popular CDs ever sold so that when My.MP3.com users buy a CD from a partnering vendor, or attempt to "Beam" (i.e., verify) a CD they have in their collection, there's a high chance that we'll have that music in our database. This is a tougher problem than expected because it turns out that for each CD there may be multiple versions. Our "Beam It" software is refined enough to detect this when you attempt to verify a CD from your collection, and if we don't have that particular version of that album, our software won't allow you to listen to it from our servers. This is good from a security standpoint—you can't listen to music you don't own—but bad from an end-user perspective: "I can't believe they don't have *Dark Side of the Moon*!" Meanwhile, there are at least eight different versions of *Dark Side of the Moon*, and even though the music on each one is identical to the listener, the master tapes were slightly different: enough that the data didn't match when comparing the files.

It turns out that 10,000 CDs is not just a nice round number: unbeknownst to us, Robin Richards, the president of MP3.com, has approved Da Bomb on the condition that only 10,000 CDs be initially loaded into the system. Why 10,000? Well, Robin has done the numbers, and with $400 million in the bank and an expected maximum fine of $10,000 to $25,000 per copyright infringement, even if we do get sued and somehow lose, we'll still have money in the bank. It is a calculated risk, but one worth taking: if My.MP3.com takes off, MP3.com has a huge lead on all of its competitors and will dominate the industry.

Meanwhile, the development teams are still going full steam ahead in intense development and QA cycles, and people are starting to get frazzled. Christopher Giles is the only engineer developing the new My.MP3.com—as he had been responsible for the pre-Bomb incarnation of the site—and the task has been daunting, including a complete redesign of the user interface, adding user handling and tracking, optimizing and reoptimizing the scripts so that they do not completely hose the database or take more than a second or two to load, etc. On top of this, it is apparent that Christopher—never one to be particularly laid back to begin with*—is chafing under David's insistent, detail-oriented (is that code for "micromanaging"? I'm not sure…) management style. For his part, David is on a mission to keep everything and everybody on schedule, and he's not shy about confronting you when he's concerned that the schedule isn't going to hold.

Things finally come to a head when Christopher calls David an "autocrat," and a minute later they disappear into a conference room. Fifteen feet away I can hear the heated discussion from behind that closed door. Ten minutes later, they emerge and it's clear that Christopher is not happy: this isn't necessarily anything new, as he's a bit of a sourpuss to begin with (although a nice enough guy once you get to know him better and/or don't have to work with him), but this time he's even unhappier than usual. David does not look too out of sorts, but he's a tough one to read (Degenhardt says: "David McCollum is an enigma wrapped inside a mystery," and I don't think he's too far off). And honestly, in two years of working with David, I think this is the only time that I saw him lose his cool with someone. This isn't to say that he couldn't hold a hard line or be insistent about what he wanted (or that you were wrong), but the man has an amazing ability to avoid direct conflict with people, usually by spinning the topic of discussion up to a high enough level of abstraction that there is no longer any disagreement. And this makes me wonder: what was it about Christopher Giles that made David lose his cool? Was it someone directly confronting him and his authority? Or was it something deeper, as I don't think I had ever seen David hound someone as hard as he did with Christopher.

One thing I have to consider is a point that a few people (including David) had mentioned to me about the MP3.com hiring process. At the time when MP3.com was hiring five or six engineers a week, the fundamental questions asked after a candidate had made the rounds were: "Can you work with this person?" and "Do you respect their intellect?" While in and of themselves these questions aren't any different from what you'd find in many workplaces, it seems like MP3.com took them to heart a bit more than most. They were explicit and at the front of your consciousness during the entire interview, resulting in more than one amazing candidate being passed on just because they were "octagonal pegs" that weren't the right fit for MP3.com.† There were a lot of criteria that could make you a good fit, interest in open source tools and/or a willingness to learn them being a

---

* Christopher had a penchant for not waiting more than 30 seconds—from the moment music had come out of your computer speakers at the lowest possible volume—to walk straight over to your cube and say in the most annoyed voice possible, "Could you turn that off? People are trying to work." Meanwhile, we're working at a music company and this sometimes requires us to have music on. I have heard that he was the sole reason we got offices, as opposed to cubes, when we moved into the engineering building.

† *Octagonal pegs* is such a great term that I can't steal it: David Dudas is responsible for it.

primary one, but it really came down to a personal assessment and the desire not to settle on anyone who was less than A level.

In many ways, Christopher did not fit into the culture at MP3.com, and he seemed like a bit of a loner and an odd man out. This makes me curious if some of the interaction between him and David wasn't dictated by a lack of fundamental respect stemming from differing world views. This lack of respect came from both parties; I suspect that accounted for at least a portion of the friction. Needless to say, I think that episode marked the beginning of the end for Christopher, as he would leave for Microsoft a few short months later.

Gentlemen, Start Your Rippers...

Ripping 10,000 CDs is a Herculean task in and of itself, but add the need to accurately enter all of the data from each album into a database—song names, year, artist names, etc.—and things start to get ridiculous. It comes out to around fifty CDs per person if everyone in our 200-person company contributed, but that assumes doing each CD only once and not having any data verification, which of course we wanted, so that put us up to over 100 CDs per person, if everyone contributes. But contribute they did. Michael announced during a Chairman's Chat one Friday that we needed everyone's help in getting this done, and lo and behold, I'm fairly certain that every employee took part: taking shifts to come down to the makeshift ripping area, using it as a break from their daily grind, and taking CDs back to their desk to work on them during downtime throughout the day. Even Michael took part in the process, although Robin Richards was out of town at the time and did not.

Over the next two weeks or so we slowly chewed through the CDs the company had purchased either from stores or from employees. It was a pretty tremendous sight to behold, and even more so it was a team-building process as you watched the office admin next to the VP of sales, the tiny on-staff masseuse, Linda, next to Paradise, one of the head musicologists as well as a founding father of hip hop. People were getting excited, and, while there was still grumbling about the legality of our situation, we were starting to get back some of the cohesiveness which we had lost as we grew from 60 or 70 people six months prior to the almost 200 that we were at now.

There's only one thing that I'm not sure anyone understood at the time: we weren't ripping 10,000 CDs.

When Robin returned, he was in for a shock: 40,000+ CDs had been ripped onto a number of file servers, just waiting to be "unlocked" by users who owned those very CDs as soon as the My.MP3.com service went live. I'm actually not sure how or when this was discovered: did Robin get back and just see people ripping away, but assumed they were working on the 10,000 he had specified, realizing only when they had finished that the full 40,000 we had acquired had been ripped? Did the engineers realize that there was a hard limit of 10,000, or did they think 10,000 was merely the goal, and since people were still ripping, they might as well go through them all? Did Michael tell people to just rip them all, fully aware that there were more than 10,000 there?

I'm sure someone knows, but by that time it didn't matter: when My.MP3.com went live, roughly 40,000 CDs had been ripped, four times as many as had been specified, with a potential fine four times as high, and enough to put us out of business. Unless we wanted to delete all of those albums—and we'd probably have to just delete them all and start from scratch, losing weeks of productivity—the stakes of the game had just gotten a whole lot higher. But we were oblivious. We were changing the world and fighting against the evil corporate music industry. Da Bomb represented the future of music and the major labels were merely unwilling to cede control. It was up to us to bring music into the 21st century, and we were going to do it in a legal way: merely allowing users to space-shift content they "owned." So what did we do? We kept ripping.

The Final Month

Meanwhile, back at the ranch, work on Da Bomb was starting to spill over into all areas of engineering. James Park was the point person on developing the user interface (UI) for the new My.MP3.com service. He was faced with the unenviable (but not altogether unusual) task of developing a UI spec for a service which didn't exist yet, and more specifically, whose performance was unknown. This last bit was key: this was the only area of our website which would be doing live database queries, and the current prototypes were slow. Having our new, premier, best-thing-since-sliced-bread-how-did-I-ever-live-without-this service (My.MP3.com) be equated with "slow" was not acceptable in the eyes of management, and it was up to James to figure out how to design a workable UI which didn't require too much data from the database, and therefore minimized the DB query times.*

But an interesting thing happened here: James pulled in two of his cohorts from the design group—Brian Callahan and Nancy Bachman—and it soon became apparent that these folks were not invited to the party. It's not that they weren't technically competent or adding value to the project—they did all of that—it's just that they weren't part of the "Cool Kids Club" (yet). Or so it was presumed from the dirty looks when James pulled them into meetings, or the lack of invitations to these meetings in the first place! It was a wholly bizarre phenomenon which seemed to manifest itself fairly frequently at MP3.com: either you were a "chosen one," in which case you could do no wrong, or you were one of the grunts who were put on whatever "this needs to get done, but it's not particularly sexy" task. No glory, just keeping the site up and running smoothly.

This had ramifications into how management worked, too. If you were the current "go to" person or manager, the high-profile projects flowed to you, and as long as you completed the project, you got more and more visibility. In the engineering department, would-be managers were constantly jockeying for position to become the next director or vice president, and this visibility was key to your ascension.

---

* IIRC, there were also some technical issues related to getting our homegrown XML-templating system to play nicely with XML data which was generated on the fly from live database queries and which didn't exist as a file on the filesystem, per se, but I may be misremembering.

Of course, being able to successfully complete these tasks was all about the team that you assembled. If you managed to get the top performers, or the team that had mad chemistry, or the guy with the amazing skills, then the work came to you. Sometimes it came because the person on your team had the skills that were the best fit for the job, and sometimes it was just because you had performed well on the previous task, but it worked.

So, managers were constantly attempting to align themselves with the top performers so that they could succeed themselves. Any management reshuffle resulted in a "kids in the schoolyard" scenario where first it was my pick, then your pick, then my pick again, without the overt trauma of waiting to see when you would be picked, but still with the knowledge that you had gotten dumped for someone "better" when things were reshuffled.

It was a mixed bag, moralewise, for the actual engineers. It was incentive to keep performing—"If I keep kicking ass, I'll keep getting the cool projects" or "If I work my ass off, maybe I'll get to work on this other project"—but could be crushing after you put in long hours, only to be shat upon. "I just worked 80-hour weeks for months and now you're going to reward me by putting me on the boring maintenance project? The hell with that…."*

While this reshuffling wasn't a constant thing, at least in engineering, it did seem to happen every 4 to 7.25 months, and one could never tell how it was going to turn out. A feeding frenzy would begin when a top manager would leave the company, or—more often—fall out of Michael's favor, and all of a sudden there would be a flurry of activity: existing top management huddling in a conference room, people being pulled aside to be asked "Would you like to work for me?" or "What do you think about managing a team of engineers?" and general upheaval, which you might miss if you weren't paying attention, but was there if you knew what to look for.

James probably rankled some egos by bringing people from "outside the fold" into the project—whether because they weren't in the right manager's group and therefore would be bringing prestige to someone else, or because of some never discussed elitism—but the three of them managed to get the job done. In fact, not only did they get it done, but the site was beautiful, and even more, sleek and slick from an end-user perspective. It just worked and was the way it should have been.

Over the course of the project, however, it became apparent that the most elegant way to solve a number of the problems at hand was to use JavaScript. I can see you sitting there wondering where I'm going with this. Well, let's take a second to remember that the year is 1999, and while JavaScript is far from new, the implementation of JavaScript varies widely across the two or three major web browsers in existence.

And?

---

* There were other incentives for high-visibility projects, with options being given as rewards for particular, *intense* projects, and they certainly helped morale, but in a slightly different way. MP3.com also paid pretty reasonable wages to begin with, which should be taken into consideration.

Well, the "and" is that we didn't use JavaScript at all on our website because, well, because there was no way we could provide a uniform user experience: different browsers supported different things, people were still browsing with JavaScript turned off, and it was generally just a nightmare because you could never be sure what would and wouldn't work. It was already hard enough to make sure pages looked the same across different browser/architecture combinations, and adding a semisupported scripting language was just not in the cards.

But desperate times call for desperate measures, and we were making the great leap forward with our very "geek-oriented" service, using JavaScript to provide the best possible service. Once again, the beauty and power of this environment were peeking through: James checked in with the director of web design on using JavaScript and then ran with it, moving the entire My.MP3.com site into a new and taboo realm.

The site was so beautiful, in fact, that said director of all things *visual* made the executive decision that we should redesign the entire website to match the branding of the impending My.MP3.com site....

Curtain rises on the engineering department of MP3.com, currently living in cubicle land. It is almost midnight on the Friday before Christmas. Both the web team and the QA department have been working for more than 12 hours on the rebranded website, reporting bugs, tweaking templates, and generally trying to get the new design finished off. One web designer in particular, Brian Callahan, has probably not slept more than three hours a night for the past four days, often leaving at six in the morning as the director of his group is coming in to the office. But it's not just that he's bleary-eyed; he's also having visions of his wife filing for divorce, especially since their Christmas party is in full swing at his apartment 10 miles away, and he's still stuck here.

Finally, Brian snaps: "Can anybody tell me why the *hell* this has to be done tonight?"

Blank stares....

Finally, Medha Parlikar, the lead QA engineer, walks up behind him, gives his shoulder a quick rub, and says, "Yeah, we're all tired. It may be time to go home."

Curtain closes on Brian driving home, finally ready to celebrate...or fall over.

I Am So Smart: S-M-R-T...S-M-A-R-T

By the time everyone returned from the Christmas break, the company was, as Robin used to say, "firing on all cylinders." Everyone was working crazy hours, especially our systems guys (who seemed to be building half a dozen new servers every day, never mind the normal tasks of installing new network appliances—the ones that didn't fall off the truck when being delivered, that is—and managing terabytes of storage) and our crack QA team, who were charged with testing each new piece as it was completed and came online. I was still fighting with both Perl extensions and Apache modules at this point, which were functional but still had some lingering bugs on the data reporting side. To me, it was an exercise in banging my head against a wall repeatedly: I just wanted it to be done. In all honesty, I was kind of jealous of Degenhardt, too: even though we had spec'd out the concurrency service together, he was the one who got to implement it. It was actually probably better that way: he did a killer job and I had my hands full, but there was a little bit of longing as I struggled with Apache and Perl day after day.

We still touched base on it periodically, bouncing ideas off one another regarding how things should be implemented (or maybe it was just me asking him questions so that I could feel like I still knew what was going on!), and one of the cooler things he did—and this was typical BMD—was to use representative MP3 files for error conditions. As in, if you tripped the security sensor, you ended up being served an "error" MP3 in your playlist instead of the song you requested. Of course, they weren't just any MP3s; they were five-second clips of Homer Simpson! Case in point: if you were trying to play more than one song at once, the servers would ding you and serve up a recording of Homer saying: "I am so smart: S-M-R-T…S-M-A-R-T!" Brilliant! (Although that audio clip will forever be embedded in my brain as a result.)

The funniest part, however, was that when it came time to test the system, QA was beat up and tired enough that they just came to him and said, "We don't understand. The server keeps playing the same song over and over again, and it's just this guy speaking…."

D'oh!

Miscommunications aside, development was moving right along. Of course, there were minor blips, like the fact that we moved our servers to a *brand-spanking new* data center a week before the release, but this was all part of the excitement, right? Right….

Well, OK, there were still other minor difficulties. About a week before the scheduled January 11 release, Michael was given his first test drive of the system and he absolutely, positively lost his collective shit. "Who is responsible for this???" In a flash, the VP of engineering, the director of web design, and just about everyone involved in the decision-making process had been herded into Michael's office. You can guess what the problem was: *JavaScript*!!! This was the darker side of MP3.com's "take initiative" mentality: it was all fine and good until you did something wrong or got on Michael's bad side. This was a shame, but it was the way it was: you went from working your ass off, following your muse, riding high and on your game, invulnerable, the chosen one, to…nothing. And you were powerless to do anything.*

Even with these issues and non-issues, however, the My.MP3.com service launched with very few issues. We went live just after midnight January 12, 2000, one day after we were supposed to release the site. The biggest issue we encountered was that only about half the

---

* Quite the Catch-22 when you think of it: either you reach for the sun, Icarus-style, or you go nowhere. Yet there's always the risk of flying too high. I was among those who didn't reach: when my manager said to me, "We were thinking about you in a management position…." I essentially responded with a "Who, me?" Probably not the best answer if you're looking to move up in the world.

servers were actually displaying the new content when we first pushed the site live, but before too long everything was going smooth as silk.

And the company? Well, the folks who were there at least, which was most of engineering, were ecstatic. There was beer and champagne, and people standing around in case they were needed, almost paralyzed in wonderment at what the future was about to bring.

Engineering Department Smokes a Collective Cigarette

It's hard to describe the attitude at MP3.com after the release of My.MP3.com as anything other than post-coital. The staff was in a daze—a good one, mind you—waiting to see what would happen next. We watched the news sites and waited for something, *anything*, to happen. We knew it couldn't be too long before the RIAA or one of the majors did *something*, but beyond some initial and relatively minor posturing, everything seemed fairly quiet; almost too quiet. And so things started to get back to "normal," or at least to "non-emergency" mode. It's not that there was a lack of work to do: quite the opposite. Things were still humming: My.MP3.com was undergoing a full redesign, we were upgrading the rest of our music-serving infrastructure to utilize some of the functionality we had designed for Da Bomb, and generally we continued with the day-to-day tasks that had fallen by the wayside during development of Da Bomb.

It was a bit weird, actually, because all of the anticipation, all of the buildup and energy that had gone into releasing My.MP3.com, just sort of dissipated. There was no project that everyone was clamoring to work on, no "this thing that is going on is something bigger than me, something bigger than the tasks I work on daily" feeling which inspired people to work what amounted to a second job just so that they could be a part of it. This doesn't mean that people weren't working 60- or 70-hour weeks, but perhaps just that we weren't working that many hours *together* as a greater organism, instead having gone back to our individual projects and small groups.

But with things returning to normal, some of the management "jockeying for position" which had lain (somewhat) dormant awoke from its slumber. More importantly, this was the first time it affected me.

The first thing to happen was that the meeting I had been trying to schedule with my manager for the past two months (and that he had repeatedly missed, which was somewhat understandable given the fact that he was managing the biggest project the company had ever undertaken) finally came about. We went into the little side office, and…

"Tom, I've got some good news for ya, buddy, you're getting a raise!"

(Conversation continues, discussing the amount and how this is going to work, with me patiently waiting to see what comes next.)

"David, I'm really happy to be getting a raise, but honestly, that's not at the level I expected given what you had told me when I was hired on. You had specifically said that I could expect to be making between X and Y within three to five months: it's now been six months and this raise doesn't even bring me up to the minimum amount."

"I'm sorry to hear that you're disappointed. Did you get that in writing when we hired you?"

(Mentally slaps forehead.)

"No. No, I didn't."

"Well, I'm sorry, Tom. There's really nothing I can do about that then…."

I was annoyed: I felt like I had taken a salary of less than I was worth with the understanding that this would be rectified within a relatively short period of time once I had shown I could perform. Was I not performing? Or was I just getting screwed because this is how *every* company works: they hire you for as low as they can get you, and then give you incremental raises, but rarely a "step" raise.

I found out the answer to whether I was performing a couple of weeks later when I got word that I was being shifted from David's group to work for Janet Delfino in the infrastructure group. While this made sense based on the projects I was currently working on, it felt like a demotion. I had been traded for one or two programmers in Janet's department, and in looking at the guys that David ended up with, I felt like I was getting shoved off to the minors. I was crushed and felt fairly worthless—or more specifically, like I was no longer one of the Blessed who got to work on the cool projects.*

Intermission: The Founding of a Panda Preserve

Two months after the rollout of the My.MP3.com service, it was finally time for the engineering department to move to its new building. For months now we had patiently waited as Randy Blumhagen, our facilities manager, worked his magic, and we were not disappointed. Walking into the building you were immediately confronted with a sweeping, curved stairway leading to the second floor (the first floor was still gutted and under construction at this point), black and blood-red carpet with sweeping flame designs awaiting as you crested into a 30 ×60-foot open space strewn with stylish furniture—gentle curves and overstated arms and backs—all designed to match a high-ceilinged, warehousey feel, bounded by a row of offices framed up on either side. To your right and left were groupings of chairs, couches, and tables—gathering places for "open room" meetings—with castle turret rounded walls and windows overlooking the 805 on one side and the identical "non-engineering" building on the other, parking lot filled with shiny cars.

All in all, the space was more a huge, high-industrial-ceilinged warehouse that happened to have a ring of offices on the outer, window-facing edge and what looked like a row of two or three shipping containers placed end to end—set about four feet from the outer

---

* This transition was not without its upsides, though, including a new manager who went to bat to get me a retroactive raise. Yowza!

ring of offices and with a half-length football field between them. There was another bank of offices, but they were dwarfed by the space, which was *huge*. And stylish: the offices were beautiful and yet modern, with designs that varied by row, some with fishbowl pop-out windows, others cave-like.

I ended up in the row of offices whose outer wall was translucent corrugated plastic, opaque enough so that you couldn't see through it but allowing some ambient light from the windows to seep in, and sharing an office with two other programmers: GK Parish-Philp and David Dudas, which, of course, is a story unto itself. You see, as the months in cubicle land went from one to the next, it seems that the occasional disquiet or minor complaints had been met with the reassurance that "once engineering moved into its own space, things would change" and the rules would be different. Everything from noise issues—whether talking or quiet music—to people not wearing shoes was met with this perfectly reasonable mantra that allowed everyone to (sometimes begrudgingly) get back to work, assured that before too long everything would be OK. I suspect that some of these even affected the way the space eventually turned out, as I'm not sure we would have ended up with offices had it not been for the squeaky wheel who was so easily disturbed, which is a testament to the appreciation that management had for the engineering staff. These good feelings continued as we were asked to pick office mates—whomever we wanted—and the like.

But by the time we were getting ready to move in, some of these promises seemed to fade away in people's minds: situations had changed, "issues" had been forgotten, and, well, any previous statements made no longer applied. One issue that came up was that of office mates. We had long been promised that we could share an office with whomever we liked, but now there were rumblings that managers wanted all of their reports sitting together. There didn't seem to be any logic behind this, other than it being a control issue and the preference of a particular manager or two, but again, the overarching management style of "keep the engineers happy" shone through, with (I believe) David McCollum going to management and saying, "This is what these guys want. Let them sit together. It's more important for the work environment to be good than for people to sit with their groups." And so it was. And needless to say, the cross-pollination ended up being a good thing as well, because it meant that the different groups—applications development, systems, web development—all had a slightly better understanding of who was working on what, and how some of the different pieces came together.

"You Realists Can Stay the Hell Out of Our Office!"

I can easily say that my fondest memories of MP3.com stem from sharing an office with David and GK. For starters, we decided that rather than have someone sit with their back facing the window, all three of us would set up our desks adjacent to each other so that two of us were sitting perpendicular to the window—just look 90 degrees and you have a view—and the third facing toward the window, forming three sides of a square with the window as the fourth and our jungle arrangement of plants in the center. Next, we brought in musical instruments—GK brought a guitar, bass, and didgeridoo, Dave brought a guitar amp, and I brought my bass amp, and, well, we were wired, instruments hanging from hooks on the wall, just calling out to you anytime you had coder's block and needed a few to get your neurons to fire around the problem instead of slamming your head against the wall.

A completely unintended consequence of this was due to the large number of amazing musicians who worked at MP3.com. I can still remember the first time Rattlesnake Ray Matthews, currently a web designer, walked into our office and, without saying a word, walked past where GK and I were sitting, picked the guitar off the wall, plugged in, and let loose with this amazing blues lick for something like two minutes before unplugging, hanging up the guitar, and leaving. Un. Fucking. Believable. I don't think any of us had even known that he could play before that. This ended up happening probably about twice a month, and it was just a welcome relief and always brought a smile to our faces. (It turns out that Ray had been a session musician for a good long while, even touring as Madonna's guitarist, I believe, and was now working a straight job to—among other things—put his kid through school.)

The dynamic in our office was one that fostered communication—or more specifically, discussion. GK was a philosophy major from Texas A&M turned software engineer, David was a vegan and a Buddhist who had grown up under interesting circumstances in Detroit, and I was, well, the consummate devil's advocate, a jack-of-all-trades, and a person with an interesting take on life. Topics ranged from the nature of addiction to the best Beastie Boys album (*Paul's Boutique* was groundbreaking, but *Check Your Head* was funkier and a better overall album with a deeper groove), dissertations on how the mind processed information to our ability to define our own destiny, and assertions from David and GK that "reality" was strictly a function of subjective perception (and therefore non-existent). There was a crazy energy about it all, and a bit of magic in the air with occurrences like a plastic bag floating up in front of our office window, cued by our discussing the symbolism of the plastic bag in the recently released movie *American Beauty*.

It wasn't all "philosophical discussions on the true nature of the proletariat in American society," either. David and I would regularly check each other's Perl code, or at least provide a second set of eyes and an ear for a sounding board. More often than not, just this process of trying to *describe* a problem you were coming up against was enough to turn on the light bulb and allow you to solve the problem yourself, but the talking it through was an integral part of the process. The whole dynamic was one that fostered a healthy work environment, where 75% of the time you sat there working in silence—headphones on, or someone choosing the next album without being asked—and the rest of the time you felt OK asking for help should you get stuck…but you waited until you *were* stuck.

I did feel bad for the folks who reported to GK, though. It seemed like once a week someone would come in and patiently wait for us to finish whatever bizarre tangent we were pursuing, sometimes sitting there for 10 minutes before we finished—or before they left because it really wasn't that important. The odd thing was that it was rare for anyone to jump in and contribute, which always just struck me as a bit weird.

Brian Callahan probably bore the brunt of our tangents, as he was frequently popping by the office for direction. When he finally left MP3.com to seek his own fortunes, he posted a long missive of fond memories and other minutiae to the internal BBS. His tribute to our office was "I dare anyone who considers themselves a realist to drop by David and GK's office" (I had since moved elsewhere), to which David promptly responded:

"You realists can stay the hell out of our office."

'Nuff said.

Not with a Bang, But with a Whimper...

Even before moving into the new offices, we had been sued for copyright infringement by the RIAA (on behalf of the major record labels), the Harry Fox Agency, which owned the publishing rights to a large portion of the songs in our "library," and a number of smaller record labels.* This had happened January 21, 10 long days after we had gone live with My.MP3.com. While this wasn't entirely unexpected, it was slightly worrisome, especially the language in some of the reports: "clear case of copyright infringement…" etc. Special "All Staff" meetings were called where we were told how this was normal and to be expected. We received updates and assurances in the weekly Chairman's Chat about how we were doing, who we were talking to, how we had enough money in the bank and were fine, but it was worrisome. Meanwhile, we hadn't stopped ripping CDs; instead, we were adding 1,500 new CDs to our database per day.

All said and done, though, I don't remember much open talk or concern about our demise. I'm not sure if this is because people had drunk the Kool-Aid and believed we would be OK—after all, it was in their best interest to believe this (who wants to be unhappy and all doom and gloom when it's your potential fortune at risk)—or if people just weren't talking about it. To be honest, there was a certain air of invincibility that we carried with us: we had a dream team of engineers assembled, had solved every challenge which faced us, had revenue streams…it didn't seem like anything could affect us. We were changing the world. It was obvious to us that this was the next step for music, that the record labels were behind the times and would have to come around sooner or later to the fact that music was going to be distributed digitally, that DRM was dead in the water and always would be, and that here we were, providing them with a tailor-made service, complete with top-notch statistical reporting so that they knew *exactly* how many times a song was played, and by whom. The data mining opportunities were endless, the opportunities in general were endless, and really, it would just allow them to reach more consumers. In fact, we wanted to pay them money in licensing. We were already seeking to pay artists directly when their songs were played, just so that they would get the royalties that they deserved. How could this not work?

---

* Songs have two types of copyrights: the publishing rights and the recording rights. Each has to be licensed separately depending on the use.

But as time went on, as more and more court dates came and passed, some of this optimism faded, too. People all over the company were leaving in dribs and drabs. They left for different reasons—some had reached dead ends because they had fallen from favor, not able to work on anything interesting, but instead just passing the time (and becoming less productive as a result), others because they were bored at the direction the company was going: we had shifted into "make money, maintain/upgrade infrastructure" mode and away from the initial "change the world" mindset which had been so exciting in the beginning. Sure, My.MP3.com was an attempt at changing the world, but it was built, and mid-flight we were merely watching to see if it cleared the earth's orbit or got sucked back down. It was our world-changing shot, and the rest of our resources were geared toward opportunities which would bring in revenue, and these were rarely world-changing.

Then, we had our first layoff in engineering. There had been culls in other departments before, but we had never really been affected up until now; we had been somehow safe. I found out recently that the folks in the other building referred to the engineering building as the Panda Preserve: the place where the rare breed got all the appropriate care and feeding and was removed from all the dangers of the real world. No more. The glass had been shattered.

Mind you, some (all?) of the people who were laid off in the first round had ceased to perform for whatever reason—morale, burnout, or just being given fewer opportunities, resulting in a general decline in productivity. It was hard to go from "top of the world" to "we're giving you the grunt work because you pissed someone off," just as it was difficult to keep up the hectic pace that a lot of people were putting in, especially when there was always someone who was willing to step up and take your place, either someone within the company or someone who was thrilled at the chance to work for MP3.com. I think my dear friend and former cubicle mate, James Park, left in that cull. He had never been the same after the My.MP3.com release: for whatever reason, be it the JavaScript, his ignorance of the hierarchy and bringing people in to meetings, or possibly something as simple as merely dropping by a My.MP3.com release party but not staying for hours to hang out with the managers and engineers who made the site work, he somehow dropped to second-class-citizen status. He had never really been given a chance to prove himself again.

Personally, I was still enjoying the work at MP3.com, but I was starting to entertain thoughts about my general career trajectory. I had entered MP3.com a person who wanted to work with other geeks, who was searching for that camaraderie and circle of peers that would provide a rapport and, in the end, raise the level of the work I performed through collaboration and the bar set by those surrounding me. The one other thing I had been looking for was the ability to change the world. Three months before interviewing at MP3.com, I had been discussing the future of music in the digital age with a fellow traveler from the Netherlands. Here I had the opportunity to effect that change.

But as the company moved on, as we stopped focusing on the My.MP3.com service—or at least, while it was in legal limbo—and as the motives of senior management started to come into question (whisperings of "cashing out" and "selling us out so they can become millionaires" being heard for the first time), I started reconsidering what I was here for.

For the first time, I started to feel like my path was actually in chemical engineering (which I held a degree in but had never pursued, as Boulder had been lacking in entry-level chemical engineering jobs). This gut feeling was strengthened by the fact that I felt slightly out of my depth "academically" with some of the people around me: I had taken computer science courses, but perhaps didn't have the same level of in-depth theory that they did. I was able to do my job, but it served as a juxtaposition: I *did* have that knowledge in chemical engineering, why wasn't I going that route and bringing all of my resources to bear? These thoughts, coupled with a feeling coming into this job that if the "being a programmer at a dot-com surrounded by amazing programmers isn't my bag, then I'm probably done in the computer industry," formed a kernel of a question in the back of my mind: nothing solid yet, but the crystal had been seeded.

Meanwhile, our legal battle was slowly sliding away. We had settled with two, then three of the major labels, but things weren't looking good for the remaining ones. Blame was placed on the judge involved, optimistic rhetoric abounded in the weekly chats, but Robin seemed a bit wearier, and some people were tuning out. Or were they? It's really hard to tell what the general mindset was, as people were still busy and there was still more than enough work to do. The big difference was that the buzz seemed to be gone. People didn't seem to be clamoring to work on projects: they did their jobs. They were still working 60- to 80-hour weeks, but it was to keep up, not to break new ground.

The final shift in mindset for me occurred over the course of a quick-turnaround, four-week race-to-market project where we built our first subscription service. It was an adrenaline rush to work on (I'm a big fan of Get-It-Done, compressed-timeline projects), but miscommunication between the QA department and the infrastructure department (that would be me) killed me. It seemed like two or three days a week I would fire off an email at 4:30 a.m. saying, "Here's what I've done. Here's what should work. Here's what doesn't work. I'm going home and going to bed. I'll be in at 10:00 a.m.," only to get a phone call three hours later from my manager saying that something didn't work. There are two problems with this: (a) I was working my ass off to try to get this thing to work, and calling me at 8:00 a.m. is not going to solve the problem, and (b), as often as not, QA had not read my email and were complaining about something which I had stated *did not work*. Ugh.

I don't blame my manager. I know that she was getting it from the VP, who was hearing it from the director of QA that our stuff didn't work.* The problem was that I was starting to have nightmares about my cell phone ringing and I felt like I was putting my heart and soul into this project and getting no respect for doing so. Not long after the project went

---

* In all honesty, Janet was a great manager in that she protected her staff and totally went to bat for us, which was awesome. She also didn't take any guff and would come straight to you to…make sure everything was going to get done right and to ensure that you had the correct "sense of urgency" that some of the engineers didn't always appear to have. Ahem. Unfortunately, while I can understand this latter management style, *I* chafed at it a bit as I'm pretty sure it's going to take me longer to accomplish a task with someone literally looking over my shoulder.

live (according to schedule), I tuned out. Sure, I got a nice set of (not-quite-worthless) stock options for my hard work, but that couldn't give me back my state of mind or make me feel like I would be respected for working hard. I was done.

I kept working at MP3.com for another year, and after a while, things got better: one of the VPs—Dan O'Neill—took me under his wing and worked with me to start performing again. It was a big deal that he took the time and energy, and it worked to a certain extent. I was getting work done and getting code written, but my heart still wasn't in it. I was working 40–50 hours a week, and that's really not up to snuff in that environment. A day after the planes hit the Twin Towers, I was gone.

Epilogue

On April 28, 2000, a summary judgment found MP3.com in violation of copyright infringement and ordered a full trial to begin in August. The "space-shifted" content in the My.MP3.com service was shut down shortly thereafter, and icons resembling a padlock started to appear next to song names on your personalized My.MP3.com page, connoting that this song was unavailable. MP3.com managed to reach deals with four of the five major record labels agreeing to pay a settlement and gaining a license to serve their content, once each copyright was verified.*

On August 28, 2000, MP3.com went to trial with the one label it could not reach a settlement with, and promptly lost the case nine days later. Before damages were awarded, however, a settlement was reached, but the damage was done.

Over the next months, MP3.com soldiered on, looking for new revenue streams, partners, and "groundbreaking" applications. They also continued to bring back the now-licensed content, and the padlock icons started to disappear from content you had verified, although sometimes only 3 or 4 of the 10 songs in an album would be unlocked (frustrating, to say the least). Six months after settling with the last label, MP3.com was purchased by the label in question: Vivendi Universal.

In retrospect, continuing to rip CDs when we clearly didn't have the money was sheer folly, but it was so very MP3.com. You see, at some point early on, MP3 had become the bad boys—maybe only in our own minds—of a certain Internet space. We went toe to toe with the major record labels and didn't back down: hell, we *countersued* after they sued us for copyright infringement!

---

* This "copyright verification" process lingered for months as the labels—who were not in the digital age—dragged their feet in responding to requests for verifications. The Harry Fox Agency was no better, and at one point we sent them two or more palettes stacked to the brim with copyright request forms (they wanted individual paper requests for each album). How many man-hours got siphoned from MP3.com I can only imagine, but I bet the look on the faces of the folks at HFA was priceless.

THE TIMELINE

1. January 12, 2000: Da Bomb drops.
2. January 21, 2000: RIAA sues MP3.com.
3. April 28, 2000: MP3.com loses summary judgment in copyright infringement suit, full trial to follow in August.
4. May 4, 2000: Major record label content in My.MP3.com service "locked" from use, but still appears in account.
5. June 9, 2000: MP3.com settles out of court with Warner Music Group and BMG Entertainment, licensing its content for My.MP3.com.
6. July 28, 2000: MP3.com settles out of court with EMI, licensing its content for My.MP3.com.
7. August 22, 2000: MP3.com settles out of court with Sony Music Entertainment, licensing its content for My.MP3.com.
8. August 28, 2000: MP3.com case goes to trial in *UMG v. MP3.com*.
9. September 6, 2000: MP3.com loses court case; Judge Rakoff orders MP3.com to pay Universal Music Group damages.
10. October 18, 2000: MP3.com reaches settlement with Harry Fox Agency, settling the publishing rights copyright infringement issue.
11. November 15, 2000: MP3.com settles out of court with Universal Music Group, licensing its content for My.MP3.com.
12. December 21, 2000: MP3.com enters into licensing deal with Warner Music.
13. May 21, 2001: Vivendi/Universal announces intent to acquire MP3.com.

In a way, this was all Michael. He defined MP3.com and made it the company it was: a company that talented people flocked to because they wanted to be a part of it. This culture, once defined, both held the company together and sent it asunder.

Eight-plus years after Da Bomb was dropped, there are still headlines about music downloads and sharing. Some of the visions of the My.MP3.com service have come to fruition—Apple opened the iTunes Music store and started selling music—while some are now obsolete or yet to be realized. A surprising number of the areas are still topical, though....

Afterword

There are thousands of things I can say about my time at MP3.com, many more than I could ever fit into one chapter. I worked there for just over two tumultuous years and it was a ride I'll never forget.

One of the most amazing things, however, is the lasting nature of the friendships I built during those two years. I keep in touch with more people from MP3.com than any other place that I've worked. And it's not just me. In talking to some of my old compatriots to verify dates and to hear their version of events, the most common comment I heard was the amazement at how much people hang out with each other and how strong the bonds are, even five or six years after many folks left. I'm not sure how much of this was accomplished upfront, by the hiring practices and making sure that only the "right" people got through the gates versus the experiences we shared, but whatever it was, it worked. Many of these same people are still working together today, although they all agree: it has never been the same as it was at MP3.com.

CHAPTER EIGHT

Inner Source

an Interview with Auke Jilderda

It has always amazed us that some of the largest, most successful open source projects like Linux, Firefox, and Apache release high-quality software under conditions that would cause most teams to crash and burn. They have large (sometimes huge) teams that are distributed all over the world and that rely on a lot of the work to be done by unpaid or undercompensated volunteers: programmers, testers, and other team members. That's why we wanted to talk to Auke Jilderda, who's had a lot of success studying how those open source teams work and applying their lessons to corporate projects.

Jenny: You've spent a lot of time looking at how open source projects work, and how companies can learn from that. How did that start?

Auke: I started work in the research department at a large European multinational. I was working at one of the laboratories in the software architecture group, where most were focused on the architectural aspects of building software.

I recognized that there are a number of spectacular successes in open source but also a huge number of complete failures. For instance, Apache beat the big players on the web server market—IBM and Microsoft—despite those trying very hard to win at the time, in an effort to gain control of the web standards. At the same time, the vast majority of projects on open source development sites are dormant, one person efforts that haven't gone anywhere. In other words, there is something to learn from open source and it is not trivial.

The company I worked for was and is good in software architectures for software intensive product families, but could learn a lot from open source communities about software processes, in particular on how to collaborate across organizational boundaries. I studied open source software development and worked on how to deploy key aspects of open source development inside a company scope. I then went on to a product division where we rolled out my inner source ideas and introduced a new development environment, CollabNet, to enable this inner source development. After two years rolling out those ideas, I was ready for a new challenge and joined CollabNet itself to do similar things for other organizations.

Andrew: Can you tell us a little about one of the projects you studied? Maybe one where you saw team-related problems that they had to overcome?

Auke: One of the projects which I studied in quite a bit of detail was the KMail project, which is a mail reader under the KDE desktop environment. That was an impressive project with some 20 people, some interesting characters that had some run-ins with each other where they didn't quite agree. For example, one wanted to be project lead, and the rest didn't quite agree with that. It was interesting to see how they handled such a conflict.

It was also interesting to see how they handled development. And at some point, they had separate work that they started linking in. They wanted to enable users to encrypt messages. They used a standard encryption implementation, and made an interface to make sure that you can actually hook into it. There I recognized how the team was working together with other teams. And they have various ways of collaborating.

I studied the projects from the outside, not actually participating in the teams. And I came up with a set of what I considered the key aspects of what makes an open source project successful. And the next step, of course, was to roll that out within a real production environment in an enterprise.

Jenny: It sounds like you looked at how the people interacted with each other, and not just at the software they built. What do you think makes open source team members work together the way they do?

Auke: What you see in open source is that people always go through certain evolutions. They typically don't start as a developer in an open source project. Nine out of 10 people start out using the software as is, and then at some point some of them start tweaking a bit with it, and then they become expert users, and then some of them go on to start contributing to the project, and then they evolve to become a developer. And what you see in successful projects is that they treat the people in a way to help and stimulate that evolution. So, you will always see that in a successful open source project, it's very easy for people to submit defect reports. They make it very easy—they help people if they run into issues, and spend time helping them figure out what the issue is. Both because they consider it in their own best interest and because it enables this evolution, to evolve from user to expert user to contributor to developer.

Jenny: That's interesting, because a lot of people have to approach software projects without understanding the domain of the problem that they're solving. You're saying one of the things that helps open source projects be successful is that they know the software as a user before they're actually involved in making changes to it.

Auke: Yes. What I've seen by far the most is that people start using it first. And then they start contributing to it, and then they start developing it. And, of course, there are orders of magnitudes of difference. Typically tens of developers, hundreds if not thousands of contributors, and then tens of thousands or hundreds of thousands of users.

Andrew: So let's say you're in a corporate environment, where you don't have that kind of ability for the developers to start off as users. Is there anything you can do to get at least some of the benefit of what you're talking about? Because that seems like a fundamental difference between a lot of open source projects and the sort of projects you'll be assigned if you're a professional developer in a company.

Auke: Well, so I saw two sides to it, and you see this in the enterprise as well. One side of open source is the software engineering, and what the key aspects of open development are. Number one, you get openness, and there's a number of things you can do to make development open. One is, of course, to make it easy to see all of the development efforts, and in an enterprise everything currently defaults to not being accessible. So, you don't get to somebody else's project, even if you're in the same company, in the same department. Information is not accessible unless you have a specific need for it and explicitly arranged to get access to it.

If I'm in a team, and you want to start using this component that I'm building, it's quite likely that you'll need to adapt it to use it. For me to make it easy for you to do that, I could make regular snapshots that I verified build and passed some level of testing, to save you and other potential contributors time in getting up to speed. In other words, I am making it more open by making it easier to access whatever I'm building. And by that I'm stimulating a lot of people to start reusing.

So one side is software engineering, and the other side is "community governance," if you will. And those two, you have to play correctly to get a successful open source project. Nine out of 10 enterprises only do the software engineering, and management covers what is done through "community governance" in open source.

Andrew: Let's say somebody's reading this right now and thinking to themselves, "Wow, the way you describe a 'closed' enterprise is exactly what I see at work every day, and I would love to get my company to have more of an open source model." But they have no idea where to start. What would you tell them? What advice would you give them? How do you get from point A to point B—what steps would you take?

Auke: That company I worked for is a good sample case. Everything around deciding who works on what, and all the project management, all the software strategy, road mapping, requirements management, commitments made to customers, that just stays in place as it has always been. But the real engineering approach, that starts to change fundamentally.

There are a couple of things that you need to do. I identified three key aspects. One is openness, or ease of access to all information relevant to development. That means source code, tracking, documentation, and developer communication. In addition, it means making it easy to get to the information. So, keep it in a central, easy to access location and not require people to jump through three hoops of burning fire before they get to the information.

Second, we introduced a clearly defined ownership and control: the team developing and maintaining a component owns and controls it while another team adapting it to their needs owns the patch. This is standard in open source but ownership and control of components is commonly not clearly defined in enterprise development projects, especially on the border of two teams collaborating.

Third, with the relevant information and assets accessible and ownership and control defined, we stimulated teams to start adapting, or patching, another team's component rather than working around and writing glue code to make it fit. Those are the three engineering aspects that you can start rolling out.

At our company, that was about 120 developers split across two locations that built a product. Basically, what they did was developed lots of components that were reused across multiple products. These 120 people were building the components. And then there were about 350 people around it working on product teams, actually building end products out of it. So, when we got there to introduce it, we gradually rolled out those key aspects, opening up access to all parts of the development, defining ownership and control clearly, and stimulating a patching approach, combined with a whole lot of "evangelizing" the different groups involved. It needs to be an evolution, gradually making more information available while educating teams on the collaboration model, before getting one or two teams to start collaborating in that model. They then become an example for others.

Andrew: And how did they respond when you first talked to them?

Auke: Well, there was a lot of politics. This product family was forced, in a sense, by the executive management that said that this was good for the division, so we have to force this through. There had to be some level of force applied to make sure that anything happens. But the price you pay is the people inside those teams—the ones that are being forced to start introducing the common components built by another team instead of using their own implementation—are not very happy that this is forced upon them. They would have wanted to have that choice entirely themselves. But, of course, they never would have taken that choice. So, there's always a bit of a chicken and egg problem: they have to apply some force, and that gets a lot of negative responses.

So, when I first started these things, there were a lot of negative responses, basically because the product teams didn't trust the product family teams.

Jenny: So, tension between teams was already thin when you started?

Auke: Yes. For instance, the product family program had made commitments to the product teams. And in the product teams, the minute I started talking to them, even though I was an outsider—I wasn't part of the product family either—their instant knee-jerk reaction was, "OK, so now that the product family wants to introduce an open method so that they no longer have to support us, they can just break commitments, and we have to fix it ourselves."

Andrew: How did you convince them otherwise? How did you get around that, knock down that resistance?

Auke: There was a whole lot of talking and explaining how this model works. The commitments were not changed in any way, shape, or form. In this case, the teams having tried to collaborate in a closed model for years had been slow to pick up the pace with this. There were other guys that were new to this product family that had just been acquired, and they didn't have the history. And there we found a good entry point, where they started to work with the product family in this open fashion. So there was one part to go through it, to get somebody else to demonstrate it, and then they would start seeing it in the other team as well.

Initially, the product teams didn't respond much and primarily just observed the initiative, how we were going through it. The initial main focus was to start opening up the whole development. First we made the source code read-only available inside this community. Then, we set up a mailing list on which everybody could ask questions, making the communication lines accessible. Up until that point, everybody had to ask questions to the "support team." This was a group that had a difficult job: they were basically in between a rock and a hard place. They received questions, and then they had to go look for somebody in the platform team—that team of 120 people—to find the person who's the expert on it, and then get the answer and get it back. So, they're the intermediaries, and there were always lots of details lost in translation. And, of course, the result is that the support didn't work so well.

A key observation that enterprise development can learn from open source development is that you typically cannot reuse somebody else's component without adapting it. Nine out of 10 cases, you need to adapt it to your needs. And that's what they ran into here as well. The common components fit maybe 80%, never 100%. They had a lot of pain. If they asked questions, they'd come to the support team who didn't have the answer themselves. They'd have to go look for it, and often just couldn't find it. So, the product teams were extremely frustrated. They were forced on board, and then had the problem of getting it to work without a decent support level.

Jenny: But it's not enough to just install mailing lists, right? A lot of companies have mailing lists that aren't all that effective.

Auke: By simply introducing mailing lists, the support team still had the responsibilities organizationally, so initially it didn't change anything. But a number of more senior developers, I got them to subscribe to the list and they started answering questions. And before you know it, the support group became obsolete. Basically. they could start doing other things—they could go to development work, rather than trying to find answers to questions. There was no longer somebody in the middle. Now everybody could start communicating correctly. The product team asked a question, they got an answer much quicker, a much better answer because there was no issue with this lost-in-translation part, where you were communicating with a third person that just never worked so well. In turn, this took away a lot of the distrust and misunderstanding between the teams. In addition, it brought our inner source initiative a lot of credibility because they noticed a tangible improvement that was clearly connected to inner source.

The problem with many generic collaboration initiatives in large companies is that it is generic, not domain-specific. This inevitably ends up with enthusiastic people publishing tons of information, but without much focus and not easy to find. The difference with this initiative is that this is very focused around the particular set of common components and the development and maintenance of those. All people in the community are using, adapting, or developing the components. That focus makes the difference. It is one thing to be able to talk, but you also need something to talk about.

Andrew: That's great! Once you got the senior guys to play ball, you were able to take this support group and make their jobs more satisfying, and give them much more important, real work to do that would be better for the whole company.

Auke: Yes. That made a huge, direct impact. It's a very tiny thing to do. It's really not rocket science to introduce a mailing list and to make source code available. But it had a huge impact and built a lot of credibility.

In the meantime, I kept doing this evangelizing thing, where I kept reiterating the same key aspects and the value it provided to the person I was talking to. The other thing that I did was that I gave it a name—the "inner source" initiative—that turned out to be a good buzzword. What always happens is that when other people hear about it, initially they don't understand it at all. They just hear the term, and they repeat the term without knowing what other people are talking about. But it serves a purpose, to have a name like that. Because then once they start talking about it, then at some point they also start getting it. Just giving it a name makes a difference there as well.

Jenny: What made you start the inner source project?

Auke: I started inner source because I knew open source delivered a number of spectacular successes and a huge number of failures. In other words, there is something to learn and it is not trivial.

There are three key aspects that in my view make the difference between successful and unsuccessful projects. The first is easy access and openness: making all development-related information easy to access, like using mailing lists for communication, making source code and tracking accessible, and providing snapshot builds to make it easy for somebody else to adapt and tinker with your component. The second is a clearly defined ownership and control of the component and the patches on a component: making it clear who's responsible for what. A component's owner controls what goes into his component. A team adapting a component controls their patch and decides whether they want to offer it to the component owner, and the component owner decides whether to accept it into his component, effectively transferring ownership of the patch. And the third is that open source projects default to patching instead of workarounds.

Andrew: That seems like a big change from how most companies do their work. How did you get there?

Auke: To deploy the approach, I did three things in parallel. First, I gradually opened up access to the development assets. So, I started by introducing the mailing lists, then making the source available, then providing snapshot builds, and so on. Second, I had ongoing, almost relentless evangelizing: with great regularity I took the time to visit key people throughout all teams to reiterate how the approach should work and what it will bring them and to actively seek their feedback. And third, I actively supported the first teams that adapted or patched another team's component.

An additional challenge that is currently common in enterprises is the need to replace their existing development infrastructure with a next generation infrastructure that enables collaboration. We had to replace the legacy infrastructure, IBM Rational, with a next generation, CollabNet, to enable the development community to collaborate across organizational boundaries and locations in an easy, secure manner. The previous generation infrastructures hampers collaboration (understandably so—they date back to a time in which this was not a requirement and they have not been designed to facilitate that).

Andrew: And you came up with the name "inner source."

Auke: That worked very well, just giving it a name. I did all of the rounds within the company's internal conferences, where every single conference—whether it was just the research department or the whole of the company—telling the story of inner source was creating a buzz within the company. And it's a huge company, so that was a lot of work, creating a buzz and getting visibility. That worked very well. And of course, every chance I got I talked about it, and talked to especially those product teams around the product family program. Doing that for about a year or so, that started paying off. They started crediting the inner source initiative with that positive influence. And then they started to take it seriously.

In the meantime, we also introduced much more openness. We started by making all the source code available, but then there are next steps to be taken as well. We also started making the communication open—not just the mailing list for support, but also for developers. So, all of the development discussions also started being on a mailing list. If you're on a product team, now you can follow the discussion the developers have. We made the tracking information much more accessible. And we introduced something that we called snapshot builds. That had been quite a battle as well with the product family team, because it's considerable work to provide a weekly snapshot build, or a biweekly one. Basically, you build a version of the whole set of common components to make it easy for the people around the product teams to work with and adapt a very recent version of the common components, in turn making it more likely for a patch to make it back into the main line. That's what we pushed through as well. And once that started being part of the standard process, once we had that automated, it also made a big impact because it made it easier for people to start adapting and, with that, using common components and increase the chance of a patch being accepted back into the main line.

Another thing we added was to write some key documentation. Really successful open source projects always had three distinct levels of documentation. They call it different things at times, or organize it differently, but they had three distinct levels. One is a README: what is the project about, and who's involved. The second level is how you start using it: how you install it, what are the runtime dependencies. It doesn't explain it in extraordinary detail. It just says, "This is how you typically start using this." And the third level is contributor information: how you build new versions of the software yourself, what kind of dependencies you need, and how you contribute something. Note that this fits the three distinct types of people involved in a community: users, contributors, and committers. The README helps people decide if they want to become users, the install information helps people to become users, and the contributor information helps a user become a contributor.

That's what we see in successful open source projects, and we copied it inside the enterprise. And again, that made a big difference. For instance, when I first arrived with the teams, I took a standard development machine from that same department, and tried but couldn't get it to build. Which meant a developer at a product team would most likely not be able to get it to build either—there was clearly information missing. I had to ask three different developers before I got it working. We worked out a short document that clearly defined the runtime and build-time dependencies and outlined how to build and run. It all goes back to making it *easy* to use and adapt to your needs.

Jenny: So, making your company more open changed the way the teams did their work. But did it have any real effect on the way they designed their software?

Auke: There is a fundamental difference between open source and the enterprise. In my opinion, open source actually found out how to properly reuse software, while enterprises are still learning it. What you see in the enterprise is that they try to design for reuse. Theoretically, that is great, but typically you don't know and cannot foresee exactly how software will be reused. The only thing you really know for certain when you start building software is that it's going to be different than you think, and it's going to be basically used differently and work differently than you had initially envisioned.

Andrew: So, designing for reuse isn't always a great thing?

Auke: It's not really a very suitable approach for software development. What you typically do in open source is that you start by building something for one use first. Then, somebody else takes it and starts modifying to their needs. And he can reuse it. And once you've done that—use and reuse—you know what the commonality is, and you can refactor out the common functionality.

That pattern you see quite a lot. Design for reuse is too static. It doesn't work that way and is a very poor fit. It may be something to strive for, but is not feasible in the foreseeable future. Use-use-reuse is a much better fit.

So, you basically build software for one case first. And you do this in the enterprise as well. At the company, they first built a certain algorithm or a certain feature in one product. Then they started evolving so they could use it in other products as well. To do this, you needed a much more open process to actually enable this evolution. And that's what we essentially did with inner source.

Andrew: So, you can't design for reuse? That seems a little drastic.

Auke: You can still design for reuse, of course. But my thesis is that whatever you're designing for, it's always a moving target, so it's never going to be a good fit. And that's also in part because while you're building and designing it, you're actually learning much more about it, and that leads to changing it as well. In essence, open source and inner source make it very easy to pick up something that fits closely but not entirely and adapt it for your own needs.

What a lot of enterprises have today is just closed source so that if you work on some software, I can't see anything of it. If I ask you for it, you'll send some installable binaries. You might send the source code, but you'll only send one version of the source code, and it's probably a stable release that's half a year old. So, I'm not going to touch that, because if I start touching it, I'm on my own. I can't feed this back to you because it's so outdated, so you won't take the time to incorporate it in your software, and I can't get to the leading edge easily.

PART TWO

Goals

LET'S SAY THAT YOU'VE GOT A JOB TO DO, AND YOU NEED SOFTWARE TO DO IT. AND LET'S SAY THAT you've got two choices. The first is a brilliantly engineered piece of software. It never crashes, has a beautiful user interface, and has great technical support. It's fast, a pleasure to use, and inexpensive, and it runs on any operating system and practically any computer. But it doesn't do what you want. The second piece of software, on the other hand, is terrible. It's buggy, it crashes all the time, and it's slow. It runs only on an obscure operating system, and needs a very expensive and very fast machine if you want it to be at all usable. It's got a terrible user interface that makes even the simplest task a chore. But it does 20% of what you need. Which one do you choose?

Unfortunately for you, you'll end up with the poorly written piece of software, because it actually does something that you need it to do. And while this seems like a somewhat ridiculous scenario, it's actually not that far from the truth for a lot of us.

The worst possible mistakes in working with teams happen when your team's goals diverge. And, unfortunately, it's a lot more common than a lot of us realize. This shouldn't really be a huge surprise. Anyone who's cracked open a college textbook on software engineering has probably seen a chart that shows that it gets exponentially more expensive to fix a bug the longer it takes to realize that it's in the software. But most experienced programmers don't need a textbook to tell them this—they've almost certainly seen it firsthand.

One of the most common ways that software projects run into trouble is that people on the team are trying to solve the wrong problem. Over the years, we've talked to dozens and dozens of developers, testers, architects, project managers, and other software people who all universally recognize that gut-wrenching feeling that happens when you deliver what you think is the final product to the customer, only to have them say something like, "Well, that looks very nice, but isn't it also supposed to do…?" We all know the feeling of our hearts sinking when we find out about that enormously important feature that nobody told us about. Is there any experienced programmer among us who hasn't had the thought, "I would have built it entirely differently if someone had told me two months ago that it was supposed to do *that*!"

If you've spent any time on an agile team, then you probably recognize the saying, "Embrace change." One reason that programmers on agile teams work well is that they keep revisiting those goals. They'll make sure those goals are out in front of everyone: the team will make sure the goals are up on a whiteboard, and they'll have meetings specifically to make sure they're on top of any changes. And they get the customers involved in the day-to-day project work, because that's the most effective way to make sure that everyone's aligned to the same goals.

But even though we know how much those changes can damage the project, it's far too easy for us, as developers, to dismiss the idea of setting goals at the beginning of the project. And it's even easier for our own customers, users, and stakeholders to send us down the wrong path before we even get a say in the matter.

Customers—the people who we're building the software for—are not very good at telling us what they need. They'll ask for solutions instead of telling you what their problems are. They'll ask for a smoother, faster, less smelly horse and buggy, when what they really want is a better vehicle that will get them from point A to point B. They don't know enough to ask for an automobile, and it's all too easy to go about building a better, more improved horse and buggy. A developer needs to know enough about the whole transportation problem to find a better solution.

On the other hand, we, as developers, have our own peculiar problems. It's very easy for us to *think* that we know exactly what software we're about to build. We habitually interrupt our customers halfway through their explanations and say, "OK, I understand what you want." Then, we go off into our cubicles and build the software that we think they need, only to find out that we completely misunderstood their problems. (We've done this ourselves on rare occasions, usually because we really wanted to work with a particularly cool new technology, and were basically looking for an excuse to play with it.)

So, understanding your project's goals is critically important, and the stories and interviews in this section show us exactly how this affects our teams. It doesn't matter how good the software is, or if it's the wrong software for the customer. One of the biggest challenges of working with a team is keeping everyone aligned to that goal so that they build the right software. And even the best teams can have conflicts around those goals, conflicts that can tear a team apart. But if you align people to those goals from the beginning, and keep everyone in the loop as they change—and they *always* change—the project is much more likely to be a success.

CHAPTER NINE

Creating Team Cultures

an Interview with Grady Booch

Few people in the software industry are as widely recognized for their work as Grady Booch. His work with Rational and IBM helped guide the industry in both object-oriented development and process improvement with the Unified Modeling Language (UML) and the Rational Unified Process (RUP). Lately, he's done a lot of work with distributed teams and platforms. We started our conversation with him there.

Andrew: Tell us a little bit about what you did in the past that taught you about how teams work.

Grady: Wow. Great question. You know, from the very beginning of my professional career, I was involved with some distributed teams. The very first project I was engaged with was when I was actually still in the Air Force. My first assignment was at Vandenberg Air Force Base, where I was first a project engineer for a telemetry system and then a project manager for a range safety system. In each of those cases, we were dealing with a really distributed system. This was back in the late '70s, early '80s. It was really ahead of its time from a commercial perspective, because we were dealing with the fusion of sensor data from radar sites around the world. So, that in itself led me to some experiences with how one deals with the architecture of distributed systems. And additionally, the people who were building these systems, most of them were collocated in the Vandenberg Air Force Base area, but we had groups that were scattered about because of the distributed nature of the system itself. Indeed, on the range safety display system, which was the one I was a project manager for, we eventually coordinated with groups at the Kennedy Center, so we were across the country in that case. So very, very early on, I was used to development across geographic time zones.

Then, when Rational began, my focus was mostly on architectural issues. I helped most of our customers deal with the transition from waterfall methods to more agile methods and also from monolithic architectures to looser architectures. It really was about 10, 15 years ago that I began to see a sea change among the customers I was working with. Many of their projects no longer fit in the same building or the same company. And you saw, for economic reasons, outsourcing or near-shoring to break up the team. Also, they were building systems assistants, which meant that their teams were not just the one team on a particular part of the system, but they were dealing with teams across the country or the world. Even more so, as I began to work with multinational corporations, you were dealing with systems that involve different companies as well. So, the natural progression of both the technology—the kinds of systems we were building—and the economics had led to natural pressures which meant organizations are distributing both in time and in space. And it's those experiences that really shaped my worldview.

Andrew: So, what's the hardest thing about working with a distributed team: different locations, different personalities, or different technologies?

Grady: It's interesting you point that out, because there are some technical issues that are still wickedly hard, which are the problems of coordinating management across time zones. But I think the really difficult ones have nothing to do with technology, but have everything to do with social issues. I'd put those in two categories: one is the issue of trust, and the other is cultural differences.

On the issue of trust, if I have a group that is geographically distributed and I may not be working with them face to face, it's difficult to calibrate their abilities and how they're going to react or how I'm going to work with them. It's very different than when I'm working in the same room with them and can see them on a day-to-day basis. This is called the "water cooler problem" because, when you have a distributed situation like that, there's no opportunity for serendipitous connections, and those kinds of very loose, opportunistic connections are very important in building trust.

On a cultural perspective, if I'm dealing with systems across countries, then the culture of developing on the West Coast is subtly different from the East Coast view, which is very different than that in India, in China, and in Japan, and so there are subtle things that go on that add friction to the development process.

So, I'd say that those two, the issues of trust and cultural dislocation, are the most difficult to overcome.

Jenny: What does it look like when trust doesn't work on a team that's distributed, as opposed to one that's working in the same location?

Grady: Well, you know, it smells much the same if the team doesn't trust one another, whether they're collocated or not. If they're collocated and they don't trust one another, then politics get very, very nasty because they're immediate. If they're distributed, you get more of this passive-aggressive behavior, where you sort of ignore the other group and just get things done and eventually certain groups become polarized and eventually disenfranchised.

And you *can* really smell that lack of trust. I mean, I've smelled it in teams that were collocated, and you just go in and you can feel the tension and hate among one another. And nothing gets done very well. There was a great article, an interview with Andy Hertzfeld recently about his experience with the Mac. He observed, and I'm paraphrasing, that conventional processes lead to conventional products. That's not necessarily a bad thing, because there are many conventional products to build, but if you're in a space that's doing some tremendous innovation, and you don't have a culture of trust, then that innovation is going to just suffer, absolutely.

So, how does one build that kind of thing? Well, I'm going to mention some exotic ideas, some exotic to simple ideas. The simple ideas are: occasionally, you do need to get people together. Having, in a distributed team, some way that I can get people together at least once really helps, or in a periodic way, moving people back and forth. On the more exotic side, there's been some interesting work in the virtual worlds in IBM, where people have built Outward Bound-type programs inside the virtual world, so that teams working together, although distributed, can work on a common task that has nothing to do with software development, but they learn about one another that way.

It's those kinds of things that can build that opportunity for trust. But it doesn't really deal with the water cooler problem, because with the water cooler problem, you need to create environments where people can serendipitously get together. This is why, on video conferences and phone calls, it's really not a bad thing to get the chatter before and after: "Hey, how's your day, how's your kid, how's your dog?" These things really help humanize the whole process—and ultimately, software development is a human experience. And insofar as you can bring that human experience to the table, then trust can find its own way.

Andrew: What about dealing with developers who just want to bury their noses and really would prefer if nobody talked to them ever and they could just be left alone to code? It sounds like you'd have to approach the whole trust issue differently with different kinds of people.

Grady: Absolutely. And you do need code warriors like that, who just totally go heads-down. But you have to be careful about them: you need to channel them, you need to interest them, and you need to keep them excited about what they're doing. In fact, the best thing you can do in those circumstances is to get out of their way. But you can't do it in a totally hands-off fashion, because they'll go off and build things that are absolutely fascinating but useless to the business. And so there is this balance one has to have between respecting the work style of individuals, but also the needs of the business itself. And any good manager is going to recognize those differences among individuals.

Andrew: What if you're on a team where you're a developer and you're not sure how to work with someone like that?

Grady: In those circumstances, you find places for common agreement. If I'm working with someone who is just a heads-down, code-warrior kind of guy, antisocial perhaps even to a degree, I have to find a common ground upon which we can work. That might be some wicked piece of code I'll try to engage him on. Also, as a developer in those spaces, I'll often try to draw them out beyond where they're heads-down about and say, "Hey, have you looked at this in the real world?" Because such people are a delight to have, but if they're going to be an enduring jewel for your organization, you have to make sure you feed them constantly, too. And that kind of feeding helps build trust.

Andrew: So, a lot of this is sort of "care and feeding of the software team" fundamentals.

Grady: There are days when I swear I need to be Dr. Phil. It is more of a sociological issue than it is a technical issue—not that there aren't technical issues, but the sociological issues as you start moving to teams of size become more and more important.

Andrew: Jenny and I have both been in the position of trying to grow teams that hit that wall of three or four or five people—trying to get past that barrier and build teams of 10, 20, 30, 50, 80. How have you handled it? Has it always worked out well for you?

Grady: Oh, not always. I couldn't give you a percentage, but some teams just simply don't fit together—it's true not only in technology but in any kind of organization. Some teams gel, some teams don't. And the key is to provide the mechanisms, and those teams will find their way. If you have too heavy of a hand in terms of process, then there's no room whatsoever for people to self-organize. But if you make it too loose, there's no organization and no degree of predictability. All of us have to realize that some people really, really do like structure. This is what attracts people to large organizations and makes them shy away from start-ups. At the same time, the mentality you need in a start-up, where you have no legacy strangling you, is a very, very different kind of mentality than if you're going to maintain that. And the people who often build things initially often get really bored quickly and really don't like maintaining the same code for years and years and years, and yet the business goes on beyond that.

This brings up another problem in the space, which is one that I call tribal memory. Every system has an architecture: most of them are accidental, only a few of them are intentional. And what I mean by this is that the architecture that we end up with is really borne from the tens of thousands of small decisions made on a daily basis. You wake up one day and you say, "This is what I have." Not to single Google out anymore, but they're in the same situation. They're saying, "We had no legacy when we started the company, and now we've got this marvelous system and we've dominated the marketplace," and they have made certain architectural decisions for their cloud that are very different than Amazon's cloud, that are very different from IBM's cloud, and yet they've made those investments so their architecture is what it is. And now as people move on, you have this interesting issue of that architecture, those details, are rarely left in the documentation, there often is no documentation, and though the code is the truth, it's not the whole truth, because it doesn't capture things like rationale and trade-off, nor does it capture things that are difficult to discern at the individual lines of code; they're the patterns that transcend the lines of code itself. That kind of stuff is kept in tribal memory. And so you'll find these tribal elders within an organization who've been around for a while, and they understand that rationale and those cross-cutting concerns. The challenge is, as the organization continues to grow, these people move on, and that IP is often walked out the door, literally.

So, the challenge is, in addition to the problems of temporal and geographic distribution, that you also have to deal with intellectual property leakage, because having it kept in tribal memory is very, very expensive—well, actually, it's very inexpensive, but it's very expensive to extract it, and it's very, very expensive when it leaves.

Andrew: Is it feasible to extract it? Is it feasible to actually take these busy people and say, "Hey, let's write down the rationale for this piece of software?"

Grady: Absolutely. I have a circumstance where I was working with a state office on the East Coast where they said, "We have these curious demographics: we've got these really young folks right out of college, we've got these older folks, and there's nobody in the middle, because they've heard the siren song of Manhattan and gone off to Wall Street." And now the older people are retiring and dying—not necessarily in that order—so my recommendation was to do oral histories. Get video cameras. Interview them and find out where the skeletons lie. Even something as light touch as that really helps.

Jenny: I want to bring it back to what you said about rationale in the code and how people are making their decisions within the team. What do you think of criticism within a team and how do you handle that in a distributed team? Also, a lot of what process is about is helping people to understand how they fit in and be transparent with one another. How do you think that works with a distributed team?

Grady: That's a great question, and I think this is a case where you really need to have the mechanisms for the team to find its own way. I really liked the phrase you used there, and

I'll rephrase it by saying something to the effect that the ideal developing environment is one that produces a frictionless environment, meaning that it allows you to collect information with minimal intervention by the developers themselves, insofar as I can instrument my change management systems to do things for me, insofar as I can instrument my tests to do daily builds and things like that; this is the kind of stuff that needs to be shown in the tools, because it allows tasks to be automated to a degree that gets out of the way of the individual developers themselves. And yet, as you point out, there will be points of tension, and there will be times when one has to make some hard decisions. In a team that has no visible leader, this can often be very, very painful because egos run high and you see a lot of tension. But ultimately, in most healthy teams, you do find some centers of gravity and knowledge. They can be self-appointed because of their experience. A good example of this is Linus Torvalds and the whole Linux project. He has risen as the intellectual leader in that space because he began it, but it's not just Linus. There are people that also drive elements of the kernel itself, and they have, through their experience, earned the right to do so and earned the respect, too. And the same thing happens in any gelled team.

As you grow larger and larger, these kinds of roles have to be institutionalized. This is why you see people getting the role of "senior designer" or "architect" or, in larger systems, you see someone who's an architect for a whole group, or for the company as a whole. In fact, there are these growing patterns of where the center of control lies as you move toward less rapid development, where there's a tremendous amount of innovation but you're also throwing away lots of code, to the point where the code begins to accumulate, becomes a capital investment, and becomes part of something of the culture itself that you can't just throw away anymore. And you have to institutionalize some of that decision-making process.

Jenny: You've been talking about the people on the team, but what about the team as a whole? What do you think are the top characteristics of a well-run team?

Grady: Well, I'll give you two that I think are the most important to me. And they're the things I can really smell when I go into a group. The top characteristic is that they're having fun. You can really tell, when you go into a group, if they're enjoying each other and enjoying what they're doing. That's a clear measure that this is a team that's working well.

And the second is that they're wonderfully reactive, but at the same time, they're producing code that meets the needs of the business. This is the difficult balance that I spoke of earlier. You can have small teams that are just running totally unconstrained and having a hell of a lot of fun just burning up other people's money and not doing anything useful, but a group that does understand its business's needs and communicates and does what it does well in building code—that's the other side. They're building good code for the business.

So, those are the two things that I think are the most important. And everything else, frankly, in my mind, is just a minor measure below that. There are lots of detailed measures, but those are the big ones.

Andrew: That's a tall order. A lot of people have probably been on teams that have been fun to work on; not that many could say that those teams were really productive.

Jenny: They tend to cancel each other out.

Andrew: Yeah—how do you keep that from happening?

Grady: The magic is hard to create, and it's something that comes and goes. Xerox PARC, in its time, was such a magical place, although they kind of failed on the equation of trying to make money about it. I think Apple is in a place, right now, where many of their developers are having fun and they're just going gangbusters in the marketplace. Google, in its earlier days, was a place with more emphasis on fun, and they made more money than God, so you didn't notice the inefficiencies—now it's going to become more challenging. IBM's a company that emphasizes the business to the extent of fun, but you still find lots of pockets of fun where people are gelling and loving what they do.

So, I don't know how you do it. You're asking me, in a sense, what are the rules that produce this kind of emergent behavior. And if I knew the answer to that, I'd own a small country.

Andrew: There won't be rules, but there are things you can do to nudge your team or your culture in the right direction.

Grady: Sure. And I'll mention two of them here.

One is to make certain that they get out a bit. In other words, you find groups that are heads-down in the code itself, and that's wonderful because you need people that are skilled in the tools themselves. But ultimately, we're building code to fill some need, and we need to make certain that the team is not insulated, not totally isolated. I think that's an important one because it gives them a context and rationale for what they're doing.

The second thing you have to do, especially as a project manager, is shield them from the rest of the world. There's a lot of really crappy politics that goes on with some companies. And for a team to obsess over the daily machinations of what goes on in the political structure—they're just going to be worried to death. And so a good project manager has to be a shield between the developers and the politics of an organization.

And in some cases, as I said earlier, the best thing a manager can do is to make certain that you get everybody out of these people's way. It's simple things like managing the stupid meetings that the organization requires as it grows—but at the same time, you don't want to make them unconstrained. It's like, Nerf Wars in the hallways are fun, too, but you want to make sure these people are focused.

Jenny: And how does a manager make sure the people on the team are focused?

Grady: Three things come to mind. One is that the best leaders I've found in this space tend to be really articulate. They can write great code, but they can also talk to people outside that space—they can rise above the code itself.

The second is they do care about interpersonal relationships. The best leaders, I find, are not just total gear heads, but people who really do understand the human experience in building software and respect that, too. People have off days—their dog dies, their kid's having problems in school, these are all things that affect the development team. A good leader understands these human issues.

Third, a good leader is able to work at many levels of abstraction simultaneously. A person who can go down to the code, then go up and talk to the CEO, these people are very rare indeed, but they're the best kind of leaders that I can find because they provide that context.

Andrew: It's funny that you say that, because a lot of times, especially early in my career, I've been on a team and thought that to myself, "I'm just not speaking the same language as the people above me." I definitely needed a "translator," and I think maybe I started out a manager simply because I had to rise to the occasion out of sheer frustration. What would you say to somebody else, somebody who finds himself thrust into that role because nobody else will fill it?

Grady: I always give this advice to such a person: please take on that role gently and without arrogance, because you're dealing oftentimes with people who are highly technically skilled, who have a certain amount of ego, and the thing that's going to irritate them the most is that sense of arrogance without any kind of respect. So, move into such roles gently. But do so boldly, and don't be afraid to fail.

Another thing that one needs to grow to in that space, and I know it's difficult for somebody starting out, because your very livelihood is at risk, but you really want to be in a position where you can speak truth to power—where you can say to management, "That is the most insane schedule possible, and no human on earth can do this. It is unrealistic." You have to be truthful; otherwise, your whole process becomes a series of lies built atop one another. Speaking truth to power is important. That's another aspect of shielding your team from the strange politics that go on.

But it's difficult to stand up, because sometimes management doesn't even understand the process of developing software. Software, to them, is just another huge cost item in the organization, and they'd prefer to outsource it all. In that case, the leader has to be one who also gently educates upper management, and that's a long process. And, if you fail, you can always find another job: life's too short to work for a crappy organization.

Andrew: It's funny—Jenny and I spend a lot of time talking to people in a lot of different companies about why projects fail. In fact, we put together a talk called "Why Projects Fail" and took it on the road. And what we keep finding over and over again is that people get really uncomfortable when they hear people talking about failure. That's a shame, because I think they need to start talking about failure if they're going to learn from it. Have you noticed that?

Grady: One of the signs that I have for the health of an organization is that they're reticent to fail. Organizations that are totally anal and refuse to fail at all tend to be the least innovative organizations, and they're hardly any fun, because these people are so fearful of failing they take the most conservative actions. On the other hand, organizations that are freer in failing, not in a way that will destroy the business, but are given some freedom to fail, are the ones that are more productive, because they're not in fear for their life with every line of code. Because, you know, every line of code you write, it's going to be wrong. You have to have the opportunity to refactor it over time.

This is a big problem for organizations transitioning from building something that doesn't have a legacy to having a legacy. I've seen this scenario happen so many times. You get a group—especially if they're using something lightweight like Ruby on Rails—and they have no legacy whatsoever. Maybe there's a database out there, but somebody says "go build X" and they go build X because they have nothing else that they have to work with. Maybe there are a few services or APIs, but they're pretty much running across virgin territory. The problem is that starts accumulating. Every line of code I write today becomes tomorrow's legacy. And you get to the point where you say, "Gee, I can blow this up and start over," but then you get to a point where you say, "I can't blow this up anymore, there's so much stuff here. I simply can't rewrite all of this." And you get to the point where you realize you have some choices. One is to abandon the code and start over, and that's rarely useful because you never get the behavior you want. Another choice is to isolate it and put some wrappers around it and say, "Let's leave it off in a corner here, it works well enough, we'll get to it eventually," although you never do get to it. There are other cases where you might want to harvest it: "Throw it away, but harvest the best things we can do, and rewrite it, although not from scratch."

Enduring organizations I encounter tend to refactor on a continuous basis, not just at the programmatic level, but at the architectural level as well. But that's a challenge because your upper organization will say, "We paid for this code already, why are we rewriting it?" And the answer is that we're doing it to make it simpler, which will give us opportunities for innovation and degrees of freedom we could not have had otherwise. But that's a tough sell, and that's part of the education process that I spoke of earlier.

Jenny: I suspect there are people who will see the word "refactoring" and immediately jump to agile development. Is that what you mean here? What does that mean for a team's productivity?

Grady: It's just a label, for me, for some best practices I've seen here for a long time. No matter what label you give it, the best process that I've seen hyper-productive organizations across domains tend to follow is this, in three parts. These are organizations that tend to incrementally and iteratively produce releases of executable architectures. So, what are the three pieces?

First, a focus on executables. Pushing out raw code as your primary product, that's the most important thing, and that's obviously an agile process. Second, doing so incrementally and iteratively means you have some regular rhythms, where you can introduce refactoring, in which you have an opportunity for failing a little bit along the way and have parallel paths that let you try things. The third element, which is less so one of the agile community and more one of the RUP community, is a focus on architecture as a means of governance. Because, from my experience, as I start dealing with systems of any kind of meaningful intellectual or physical size, there become a set of accumulated design decisions that are part of the tribal memory, and it's very expensive, if not impossible, for me to throw those decisions away and start over. And so what I tend to govern on, as I grow the system over time, is preserving those architectural decisions so I don't end up with a totally random piece of software, but I end up with one that's intentional over time.

Now, call it agile, call it whatever you want, those are the practices that I find to be consistent among the really hyper-productive teams.

CHAPTER TEN

Putting the "I" in Failure

Jennifer Greene

THE SUMMARY LINE ON MY RESUME SAYS THIS: "JENNY GREENE IS AN EXPERIENCED PROJECT AND development manager with a track record of successful projects and teams." And it's true, I've managed a bunch of teams that have been able to create the software they were paid to build on time, within budget, and with quality. I'd bet that a lot of people out there could make the same claim. But when I look back over the work I've done over the past 15 years or so, I know that a number of those successful projects didn't lead to market dominance for the companies I worked for. In some cases, they didn't even solve the problem they were meant to solve. And pretty much everything I've read tells me that I'm not alone. A lot of projects do much worse than the ones I've worked on. Some published estimates put the failure rate as high as 80% of all software projects.

A few years ago, Andrew and I started traveling around to networking events and conferences giving a talk called "Why Projects Fail." The point of the presentation is to help people make the connection between practices that they might dismiss as heavy or difficult (like code reviews and estimation) and avoiding common pitfalls. We expected it to be a bit irreverent and lively because we tried to use some of the stuff we'd learned in writing Head First books to keep the mood light. And we got what we expected—but more than that, we struck a chord with people who seemed to be dying to talk about the mistakes they'd made on their projects. I mean, a lot of people want to know, "Really. Why *did* my project fail?" More often than not, the talks turned into an opportunity for people to vent: to tell us their war stories about this insane decision from management, or that terrible programmer who was too egotistical to fix his own code, or that product that was just a bad idea from the start. In front of the audience, we'd always try to turn the conversation around to a particular practice that could help out ("If you've got problems with quality, do code reviews upfront" or "You're always missing your deadlines? Use a consensus-based estimation process like Wideband Delphi"). Those practices have helped both Andrew and me immensely in our careers. But practices won't solve interpersonal problems or make sure that the project you're working on is the right one for your company. They won't guarantee success. And away from the audience, we talked about that a lot.

I've worked with companies where the need to produce software on a regular basis was so encompassing that they'd lost track of the reasons behind that software. Places where people spent tons of money building stuff just to prove that they have a product. I've seen projects get funding without much understanding of what they'll produce, and I've been managed by insecure people who turn the screws on the team to hit crazy deadlines for projects that are really not important in the scheme of things. I've worked nights and weekends and given up vacations for products that have barely been used. I know what it feels like to work on a delivery team when your goals are constantly changing and there's no guarantee that what you're building will ever be useful to anybody. Are you successful if you build that useless product on time? Are you successful if you keep a team together under conditions like that? Frankly, it's tough to be objectively successful in that situation. The best you can do is work to challenge the need for those deadlines. Fight to give people a more reasonable set of goals, and sometimes that's a fight you can't win.

Some of the best teams I've worked with have been in impossible situations and some of the best work I've done hasn't contributed to objective success. It's the people who stick with you, and sometimes those impossible situations, that bring out some really innovative thought. When I was new to New York and still pretty early in my career, I joined the team that'll probably stick with me as one of the most hard-working and genuine groups of people I'll ever work with.

"At Gabfest Software, we think that getting a bunch of really smart people together and putting them in a room with a really tough problem can lead to magical results."

I remember the excited look on the CTO's face as he said those words. He was really enthusiastic about the work that they were doing, and it was disarming. I was interviewing for a job as a QA manager at a small start-up company that was doing amazing things. This company was going to change the way people interacted with computers: it was going to get computers to understand the way people talk. This informal chat came after a full day of meeting half the company and answering more traditional interview questions. He took me to the coffee shop next door to the office and began to sell me on his vision of the company and its future. When he said that bit about smart people and tough problems it seemed not just reasonable, but actually inspiring. Smart people can do anything, right?

At the time I thought I was pretty smart. And after spending two years testing internal software for a really conservative financial company, I was ready to try to tackle more significant problems. So, I left that company and prepared to start fighting the good fight.

My background was about as far from natural language processing as it gets. The company I'd just come from, Gridline, was a small company that built financial software that tracked stocks. They'd hired me after I moved to New York City (I'd just spent a few years at an online service testing C++ client software). The job at Gridline was great, but a little stuffy. It was the kind of place where casual Friday meant "business casual." Everybody wore suits and ties every day, the culture was sales-driven, and most of the team had been in finance for a long time.

Gridline was small. The executive team was filled with people who'd been there since the company was founded. They took pride in the company's success and felt a kind of loyalty to its founder that I haven't really experienced anywhere else I've worked. Many of the people who worked there stayed in the same job for years and years. I joined the company as a QA manager testing their internal data scrubbing applications. I was there for about two years and I really enjoyed the work. I hired and trained the test team from scratch, and documented and built the first versions of their development process. That had a big impact on the quality of the work they were doing. When the test team was built, I started taking on more and more responsibility. But I didn't see my paycheck growing along with the challenges. Eventually, it dawned on me that I could probably do better by looking for a new job. The dot-com boom was in full swing, and anybody who knew anything about computers had absolutely no trouble finding a good job.

When I took the elevator up to the Gabfest offices, I was amazed that it seemed to be the absolute opposite of the job I was leaving. There was no security desk to pass when you entered the building, no receptionist, no fancy lobby. Not one person in the office was wearing a suit or a tie. The whole office was set up as one big room full of tables. Everyone sat together with no cubicle walls and no privacy at all. I thought of the fights I'd been through when we were remodeling the offices at Gridline. The office furniture there conveyed your status; small cubes for the entry level and temporary employees, big cubes for those who'd been around for a few years, small offices with Formica desks for managers and supervisors, and big offices with real wooden desks for directors, VPs, and higher. We had endless conversations about who would sit where and what level should get what kind of office furniture. All of that stuff meant so much to everyone at Gridline. The people who worked in cubes took it very seriously that one day they might make it into an actual office, and the execs were really proud of their wooden furniture. I knew my place: Formica office with about five years of toeing the line to get to finished wood furniture. But Gabfest's office made it clear that nobody cared about any of that crap. We were all there to get the work done together. After two years of watching people fight over offices and titles and responsibilities, I was ready for a job that was all about the work.

A lot of people have written about the excesses of the dot-com boom, and now that I've read about the other start-ups in that time, I feel like I got the short end of the stick when it came to amenities. There was no foosball table, no massage therapist on staff, no organic food chef, or free lunch. It was just a big room full of people working really, really hard on some impossible problems.

They were building a product that I still don't fully understand today. A group of computational linguists had created a language processing engine that took phrases that were typed in by users and modeled out responses based on a deep understanding of the domain they were discussing. The first product they built knew everything there was to know about laptops. If you typed in "I want a fast, cheap laptop that weighs under 5 pounds" it would turn that into a SQL query and return the laptops from a database that fit your specifications. These programs would be packaged up and sold to websites that wanted to provide a more personal shopping experience for their users but didn't want to hire people to sit and talk to them.

The work began with one of the senior employees in the company. He led the team of linguists and had built the prototype the software was based on before the company was even formed. He was really dedicated to the software he'd built, and constantly interested in making it better. But he wasn't sold on the idea that it would ever be a commercially viable product. In retrospect, that probably should've been a red flag for everybody working there. But we all really liked our jobs. I mean, we all really liked the work we were doing in the meantime, so it made the direction and overall goal of the product less important.

I instantly liked the people I met. They were smart and funny, most with impressive educations and completely dedicated to their work. The software, for the most part, worked. As long as you confined your conversations to laptops, it was a pretty helpful sales tool. The group had focused on the quality of the software from the very beginning. Along with the product, they'd built an automated test tool to catch defects as early in the development process as possible. There was a sense that the people working there were so dedicated to the problem they were solving that they were really doing their best every day to expand its capabilities.

In retrospect, there were a lot of problems with the software we were building—and not necessarily technical ones. For instance, we've learned a lot about how to sell people laptops over the Internet, and it's pretty obvious that people don't shop the way Gabfest wanted them to. If you want to buy a laptop online, most companies that sell them have configuration tools that let you select the features you want from a list of what they offer. When you think about it, an interface like that is probably a lot more direct than the tool we were building. Let's face it: most people don't want to have conversations about laptops with natural language processing (NLP) engines just to narrow down the six or seven optional features they can choose from. But it was still a really interesting problem for linguists to solve, and one that it was possible to get funding for back then.

I worked really hard while I was there. Whenever there was a demo or a business development deal in the works, I would put in ridiculous hours making sure that everything worked correctly. I remember putting in overnights and weekends on an almost routine basis. Everybody did. You could rely on everyone there to do his or her part in a way that

I haven't really seen since. I was responsible for starting to gather metrics on the way the product was behaving, tracking down some nasty bugs and planning out the work of the rest of the QA team to hit some aggressive delivery deadlines. Because the testing itself was automated from the start, I needed to figure out the best way to evaluate all of the test results and track them over time. I started to find habitual problems with the development process and worked with the team to correct them. That work was interesting for me and it's where I started to piece together some of the practices that would make such a difference in the way I managed development teams going forward.

I had the freedom to make any suggestion I thought might help our products directly to the CTO, the development leads, and the developers themselves. I was able to suggest changes and see their impacts right away. We argued and discussed every change we made before we implemented it, but people were open minded and would try most ideas that had merit. I trusted the people I worked with, and they trusted me, so all in all, it really worked. After working in some pretty political places, having that kind of access to the decision makers was a welcome change.

But as rewarding as the work was, there were some major problems, too. Alongside the natural language projects were some AI projects that were being developed without buy-in from the linguistics teams. We also had a data mining team that was spinning up to track the conversations live users would have with the software when it went live. There were often heated battles about whether it made sense for us to focus on all of those goals at once.

As the company went on, the three groups of people really emerged as almost warring factions. Everyone believed really strongly in their own cause, and honestly believed that they were going to be the difference between success and failure for Gabfest when it finally hit the marketplace. There were the computational linguists. They fought to make the NLP engine as good as possible, expanding its vocabulary and its knowledge domain. There was no real end point. There are an unlimited number of ways you can express an idea, even an idea as simple as "I want a fast laptop." They knew their engine would never be as smart as a human being, but they also knew that people wouldn't trust it to work properly if it didn't understand "I want my laptop to be fast" to mean the same thing as "I don't want a slow laptop." It seems like an easy problem to describe (for anyone who hasn't really worked with it), but it turns out to be a deviously difficult linguistic problem to solve. And that's what the computational linguists were doing. They felt that the richer the engine was, the better the product would be in the end.

Then there were the artificial intelligence people. They wanted the software to be able to learn new vocabulary and even new behaviors and ideas from the people who were talking to it. Their work wasn't nearly as far along as the linguists'—they were trying to tack their functionaly onto an already working language processor. But what it lacked in vision, it made up for in cool factor. Everyone loved this idea. They wanted the software to get smarter and smarter, not because people were working on it, but just because they were talking to it.

If the company had been pulled in only two directions, by the linguists and the AI folks, it might have turned out differently. But there was a third faction who had their own goal for the company: data mining. They wanted the software to go through all of the conversations it had had with all of its users, and use that information to target advertising to specific users based on their profiles and current conversations. Everyone had an intuitive feeling that there was a lot of potential profit there. But we were all worried—even the data mining proponents—about the possible privacy issues that this raised. But it was one of the big selling points of the product. Gabfest's clients were pitched the idea that they would learn a lot more about their own customers based on their conversations with the software.

That was the three-way battle in a nutshell. The linguists basically thought, "None of this works if our stuff doesn't work." The AI people had a goal that wasn't well thought out, but everyone felt it was worth pursuing just because it was so cool. The data mining people considered themselves a profit center for the company. The problem was that we weren't big enough to do all three things well. And as smart as we were, these were very, very tough goals. We all had a sense that as a company we were trying to focus on too many problems at the same time. But that was part of the vision for what would make our product successful. But we didn't, and the leadership encouraged all three factions to go in their own separate directions.

What we ended up with was a bunch of almost "covert" projects happening simultaneously. The AI people built lots of prototype neural networks, but didn't really add anything to the main product. The computational linguists kept adding functionality to the existing product, even though its sales were still struggling to take off. And this, to me, was the real story of the dot-com boom: it wasn't about foosball tables, flexible hours, wacky job titles, open office plans, free food, or even the rise and fall of venture capitalists. It was about people being given more free reign to take bigger risks and do more interesting work than they could have imagined. It was a time when we were really encouraged to be creative. And for us, that meant doing real, cutting-edge linguistics and artificial intelligence research and trying to come up with a real business model out of it.

Everyone kept working on their own thing. But as things progressed, we had a lot of trouble coming up with a single cohesive product. I think most of us knew this, but wanted to ride it out because each and every one of us was learning something, and it was the most fun job any of us had ever had. In a way, we all got to choose our own adventure, and we were all rewarded by it—not just with paychecks, but in our careers. Every single person I worked with at Gabfest was better off for being part of it. But everyone did feel very strongly about their opinions, and the value of the work they were doing. Each person tried to exert as much influence as possible over where the company was going. There were a lot of knock-down, drag-out fights, sitting in conference rooms screaming at each other about where the company was headed.

Then one Tuesday afternoon the CTO told us we'd run out of money and the company was going to dissolve in two weeks.

I remember the night the announcement was made that we all sort of hung around talking to each other about what we'd do, for hours afterward. We opened beers, sat around and hung out, and for the first time in a long time we had a relaxing night. The fights didn't matter anymore. There was no more goal for the company. We shifted to being just people who'd gone through something traumatic together.

Then something weird happened. The last two weeks that the company was in existence, everyone who worked there showed up every day as if nothing had changed. We just kept working to try to preserve as much of the product as we could. Nobody even questioned it. We were there working 12-hour days, even though we knew we'd be out of work in two weeks. Every single person cared so much about the work they were doing that it didn't matter what would happen to the company. We had a new goal: get everything archived so that we could pick up the work again someday. And in a way, I believe that every one of us thought that would really happen.

Even afterward, we helped each other get jobs. We were all references for each other. One of my friends was eight months pregnant at the time of the company closing, and the whole company came together even after we'd disbanded to throw her a baby shower, chipping in money to get gifts for her. In the months and years after, we've all stayed in touch. Even more than a year later we were getting together. As ill-fated as the original idea was, we were all so engaged in our pieces of it that I think we all think back on the experience and the relationships fondly. We were bonded by that company. I'd happily pick up the phone and give a glowing reference for pretty much everyone I worked with there. There isn't another company I've worked with that I could say the same about.

I know I've never worked with a team before or since that was so singularly dedicated to their work. They're still an inspiration to me. But the truth is that it takes a lot more than smarts, gumption, and money to solve big problems. First it takes a unified, viable goal. We didn't commercialize natural language processing, or build products that made the web shopping experience much more personal for everybody. We didn't revolutionize the way people communicate with computers. But the work we did at Gabfest did result in something sort of magical.

Despite the industry's disturbing track record for failed projects, nearly everybody's resumes are full of sentences like the one I quoted earlier. In my case, this particular failure was worth a lot more than many of the successes I've had since. Would I consider my part in this successful? On a personal level, definitely. I grew immensely as a result. But objectively, the company and its products didn't succeed. As far as I know, our archived software never got dusted off. I know that we were smart enough and skilled enough to build any software we wanted to—the team at Gabfest was easily the smartest group of people I've ever worked with. But I've seen much less skilled people make an awful lot of money in the software industry, because they chose a product that would sell and they got it to customers who would buy it.

In general, none of us seem to think that the failures we've lived and worked through are ever our fault. And I don't necessarily think that's a bad thing. I guess I don't think that the failure I've lived and worked through is my fault, either.

CHAPTER ELEVEN

Planning

an Interview with Mike Cohn

Anyone who's followed the world of software development anytime after the late '90s has at least heard of the agile movement. One area that agile development overlaps with the work we've done over the years is in the practices used on agile projects—especially practices for planning and estimation, and how that impacts teams and the software that they build. Mike Cohn has written books and spoken frequently on exactly this topic.

Andrew: We wanted to start out by asking you about your background. How did you come to know about the things you know about how teams work?

Mike: Well, I guess I got kind of lucky in one of the first programming jobs I had. My boss didn't know what to do with us. He wasn't a manager of programmers at all, so he ended up putting me in charge, even though I didn't have a lot of experience doing that myself. I had a little bit more than the other developers that I was working with, as there were just four of us at the time. I just kind of ended up being a team lead there. From there, I ended up running various software development teams, and worked my way up to being a VP of engineering at a handful of companies. I got a lot of exposure to different types of companies from that.

Jenny: Through all of that experience, can you tell us specifically what characterized some of the better teams that you've been on, and if there's anything that they've had in common?

Mike: Normally what the better teams I've been on have really benefited from is having what's called a clear, elevating goal. They had some sort of mission that they were after and that the team really focused on. When you have something like that, it gets rid of all of the other crap and politics and stuff that get in your way.

Andrew: Have you ever felt like you understood the goal, but your team didn't quite get it? How did you get everybody in sync on the goal?

Mike: Well, a lot of times the team doesn't understand the goal right off. That's part of the project manager's job, or in agile it's part of the product owner's or ScrumMaster's job to help make sure the team understands what that goal is.

Going back to the importance of this, a lot of us have been in companies that have had the goal of "make a ton of money." That's not a very elevating goal. I'm looking for teams to have something that's a little more intrinsically valuable than that to pursue.

There's nothing wrong with making a ton of money, but that's not the type of thing that's going to pull a team together to really achieve spectacular things. Yes, they'll work hard because they think they're going to make a ton of money, but I'm looking for people to go beyond the productivity we get just from those types of motivations.

I'll give you one example. One of the companies I was at was a healthcare company. Essentially, we were the first company to put nurses on the telephone giving out medical advice. That's a very common thing these days, but back in the early '90s, it wasn't.

A lot of people in that company were there because they felt we were going to significantly improve people's lives. It would be great—you would be able to call a nurse rather than go to a doctor, and get medical advice right then.

We had some archetypal phone calls we wanted to support. One we used a lot was a young mother with a sick baby who can't get a hold of the doctor. She calls, talks to a nurse, and her mind is put at ease because she knows what to do for her baby.

What we wanted to do was make calls like this very tangible to people. We started putting out an email a day of a significant phone call that had happened the previous day. Some of those phone calls were lifesaving.

I remember one guy had called in with a question about whether he should go to his chiropractor or not. He'd hurt his back. He had pain in the left side of his back and really wasn't sure what to do about it. Should he go to a chiropractor? Should he just take some aspirin and wait? It turned out he was having a heart attack. Our nurse on the phone was able to diagnose that by using the software, plus her own nursing expertise. So she was able to figure this out and dispatch an ambulance to his house. She saved his life.

We started sending around the phone call of the day by email to team members to help them understand the impact that we were having. We did things like that to try to make a team understand why we were doing that project.

Andrew: I can definitely see how that would be huge for the morale of the team and really pull people together as a group rather than just a bunch of individuals. I'm wondering: did that also have an effect on the quality of the software? Because it seems like it might.

Mike: I guess that's a tough question. How do you ever do a double-blind study? Do you say, "Hey, you're not motivated today" and "Today you are" and compare?

I believe there's a direct correlation between a team with a clear, elevating goal and a team that writes high-quality code, lots of tests, and such.

The way I always say it is teams that go well go fast. If you write a bunch of high-quality code, you're going to go fast because there's not a lot of bugs dragging you down.

The teams that I've worked with that have had this type of clear, elevating goal as motivation certainly went fast. So, I'm assuming that we can draw the analogy they also must have been writing high-quality code to be able to do that.

Andrew: I really like the direct line you drew between getting the job done fast and getting the job done right or well.

Jenny: That's actually a really, really difficult point for a lot of people to comprehend right off the bat. It's something that takes a lot of experience for a lot of people to come to.

I know that both Andrew and I have had a tough time getting that idea across to all different kinds of people, because when you talk about investing upfront in testing and in practices that are going to help people to write quality software, it seems like a lot of extra bureaucracy and a lot of extra time sometimes.

Andrew: A lot of programmers—and just not programmers, but managers, too—often have a lot of trouble connecting the dots between spending time doing stuff other than writing code—stuff like figuring out and writing down what you're going to build and how you'll build it—and ending up not just with better code, but with better code more quickly than they would otherwise.

Mike: I think a lot of it is because we don't communicate about all of the goals of the application or the product that we're trying to build. Occasionally, it's not worth writing really high-quality code and we have to acknowledge that, and in those situations, perhaps, rush through it.

I work with some clients that do websites for advertising or marketing campaigns. Let's say we're doing a website to do a tie-in to a movie that's coming out. That site's got to last for a couple months. I don't need the same quality of code for that as I do if I'm writing something like Microsoft Office. If I expect code to live for 10 years or longer, I need to make an investment in writing good code.

Jenny: Let's go back to your initial statement that if you write good code it ends up going more quickly than if you write bad code. How does that fit with what you just said?

Mike: Well, because the payback is over time. Writing high-quality code is an investment, and if I'm only going to amortize that investment over two months of a short-lived website, I may not have the chance to earn back the investment in quality.

If the application's going to exist for years, the investment I take in going very methodically, being very careful with what I write, that's going to have much more time to pay back.

Andrew: Let me make sure I get what you're saying. Are you talking about "paying back" effort in terms of spending less on maintenance going forward? I guess I buy that. Your team is going to have a much easier time extending and maintaining the code and there'll be less of a chance for people to even run across bugs—you can live with more bugs out in the field and distributed to the users. If it's going to be there for years, users will find a lot more bugs and will put up with a lot less hassle than if they only need to use it for a couple of weeks or a couple of months. Is that part of it?

Mike: Absolutely. It sounds like there's some skepticism here. Let me prove this.

Imagine you're working on some application you've done in the past. You're very diligent; you're the most diligent programmer out there in terms of quality and code consciousness, and you want to have this really high-quality stuff. There are two parts to this application: the application itself, and a data import routine you'll run once to move data in from an old system.

It should be clear that almost everyone in that situation would write higher-quality code for the application since it's going to live for years. The import routine gets run once. It just doesn't need the same rigor that the rest of the application does.

I feel like I'm justifying writing crappy code here, so I want to be careful with that. What I'm trying to say with this is that most teams don't have this type of discussion, and they should. This should be discussed with stakeholders: "How long is this system planning to last? What are our big goals here?" We miss big opportunities with that.

I'm going to contend that if we're writing this system, and it's going to live for 10 years, I'm going to write it to a higher quality of beautiful code than I am something that's a one-time "import the data" routine. I certainly have to get the thing correct, but I run all my tests, I check it out, I run some sample data, it looks good, and I'm done.

Andrew: You know what? I'll buy that. I'll buy that at the beginning of the project you should actually choose, come up with a quality standard. In fact, from a traditional quality management perspective, isn't that what acceptance criteria are all about? Or target defect rates? That's all stuff we read about in textbooks, but it sounds like exactly what you're talking about in the real world.

Mike: I think it is something that we should talk about that isn't normally talked about.

Think of how some projects would change. I mean, I don't know that we can ever be this honest, but imagine if you had the key stakeholder who came in and said, "Here are my goals for this project. I am after my next promotion. I want this project to get done. I want it to come out well enough that I get that promotion. I expect that to be in the next 6 to 12 months. After that, I'm going to a completely different division and I don't care."

We would know where that stakeholder's incentives are. I'm not necessarily even putting that person down. That's the type of incentive some companies create. But that might be how somebody's thinking about an application, and it's why teams get pushed to write lower-quality code than they might be inclined to otherwise in most cases.

Jenny: So, how do you figure out the team's incentives? A team can really be driven to release good software, but if the quality is poor, won't that affect the team's morale? And what happens if people on the team are driving toward different goals? What if they have different ideas of what they're building and why they're building it?

Mike: I want to give a concrete example of a company I went and visited in Boston. I met with the VP, who brought me in to consult with his organization. I started by asking him about the application he brought me in to help with.

They were building a new system to replace an existing workflow system. The original system had been built around 2000–2002 and had amazing JavaScript stuff in it, what today we would call Ajax. This was built by some consultants they'd brought in who must have been absolute geniuses to have figured all this out way back then. But the application was extremely fragile because of how it was done with Ajax before Ajax existed.

I asked the VP why they were rewriting the system, and it was purely to get a stable application, one that his team didn't have to spend as much time per year maintaining. That was his only goal.

Then, I went and met with the teams. I wasn't looking for miscommunications. I wasn't looking for communication errors. But I just asked them. I said, "Why are you doing this application? What are the big goals for this project?" I got answers like "We need faster performance" and "We need faster throughput because we process more documents now."

One answer was, "Well, we're changing to a new technology because our CTO read about it in an in-flight magazine on an airplane and he decided we should switch technologies."

Not one of the five or six developers I spoke with individually had the right answer. No one gave the same answer as the VP who had initiated the project. They were making decisions that were leading them to create the same poor maintainability issues with their application.

The company had an interesting approach where they only released applications to their internal users every three months. This was interesting because it made planning real easy: "Can we meet the June 30 deadline? If not, let's go to the September 30 deadline."

So the boss had said, "Hey, I'd like it by June 30 if you can, but I can understand if it's not ready by then because I know that's a little aggressive." The team misinterpreted this as schedule pressure and was cutting quality corners to meet the June 30 date.

When I told that to the boss, he had a fit.

This was a team that didn't have that conversation at the beginning, and was going off and making completely wrong decisions.

Andrew: You know, it's funny. Hearing you talk about that, I can almost hear Jenny's voice talking about a specific team that she worked with a while back that had almost exactly the same thing happen. There were very clear goals that had nothing to do with the deadline, but she had a real disconnect with the team about that. She had a heck of a time getting them to let the deadline slip and concentrate on quality instead. Jenny, do you remember that one?

Jenny: Yeah, and the way that we were able to finally fix it was to clearly write down the scope and make sure everybody understood it. But you're right, people had a tendency to fixate on the release dates, and on making sure that everything fit into the timeline. They weren't really thinking hard enough about the actual goal that they were trying to achieve.

Andrew: I guess that gets back to the idea of a "clear, elevating goal" that you've been talking about.

Mike: Yep.

Andrew: So what about that question Jenny brought up about team morale and quality?

Mike: You mean, how is team morale affected by some of these quality issues? I think that was the question.

Jenny: The question, to me, is about the morale of a team that's building poor-quality software. I mean, if you know you're building something that's, say, slightly crappier, is that all right? How does asking a team to cut corners affect them?

Mike: Again, I want to be real careful with this, because 99% of the time when a team thinks they are being pressured to write crappy code, they aren't. Usually it's the result of the stakeholders and developers not being in alignment on the goals of the project.

Earlier I was trying to make the point that most of the time we should be writing far higher-quality code than we are, and that one of the ways to get that some of the time is to realize that not everything in an application needs to be coded to the same quality level.

One of the correlations I draw there is I remember that when I started hiring people into different organizations, I noticed something unusual about the fresh college graduates. They felt like every assignment had to be their A-quality work. They were trying to impress me with their A-quality work on everything they did.

I thought about it, and I realized that was what they were used to. You're in college; you've got five or six different professors. One professor doesn't say, "Oh, well, I'll grade you up a little bit because I know you had a hard time in biology class this semester, so I'll take it easy on you. I only need your B-quality work and I'll give you an A."

You were graded independently on each thing. I realized that as I was giving people different assignments, sometimes I had to say, "Do this the best you can." But for other times— let's make it about something other than coding, like doing a vendor assessment—I'd say, "We're going to pick a calendar widget from our application. There are eight good choices. It's not like we're going to go *that* wrong. Go spend two hours checking them out and pick one."

I'd have somebody fresh out of school feel like they had to go spend 20 hours on it and make the absolutely perfect decision. "We'll never regret this decision!" they'd think. Meanwhile, I would have preferred a good decision and 18 hours left for other work.

That's the kind of distinction I'm trying to draw there: not everything needs somebody's A-quality work. We're not even, in most cases, given the opportunity to do that.

Does that make sense? I want to make sure I'm not coming across as saying that I want crappy code. I mean, yes, I gave one example; sometimes it's OK, but normally it's not.

Andrew: That makes sense.

Mike: I still want to stick with a comment on this morale thing for a moment. It's a little bit different from anything you exactly asked, but I think it gets to the real question here. I want to tell you about a team that I worked with.

I was managing a very large project in one of the companies I worked at, and we had a secondary project going on. It wasn't as important, but any project is important. We had some people on that project who were under some very weird management restrictions.

For example, they were told they were not allowed to do any error handling. If an error happened, the boss didn't care. The application could crash. He didn't care. It was just bizarre.

I had heard about a few of these unusual things, but I was swamped with the project I had, the critical project. I didn't get involved in this other one. I just heard about some aspects of it.

A lot of nights I don't sleep well, so I'll get up and go into the office early. It was a stressful project, and I went in real early one morning, about 5:00. It's 5:00 a.m. when I get into the office, and I meet the other two developers, the two main developers on the other project, Jeff and Donna.

I said, "What are you guys doing here?" They didn't want to talk at first. But they eventually confessed: "We're here adding error handling and doing testing. The boss doesn't let us do it on the application, but our pride is tied to this thing. We can't put out an application that is like what he's asking for."

For the past three months, they had been coming in at five in the morning and working until seven. At 7:00 a.m., they would go out to the local Denny's for breakfast. They'd have breakfast from 7:00 to 8:00, show up at 8:00, and pretend they were just getting there for the day! They'd then work until 5:00 or 6:00 at night on their application.

After I ran into them that one morning at 5:00, we talked it out. I was a manager. They were programmers. They said, "Can you please help us out? Talk to our boss; figure out what's going on. We can't keep doing this." And this is where it gets at the morale question, because they were beating themselves up over their boss's insistence that they put out a low-quality product.

So I went to talk to the boss, and I said, "What is going on here? Why aren't you letting them add error handling, do testing, and write a high-quality product? I agree with them that it's wrong." I told him what had been going on. And he came clean. Here was the situation.

This was back when it was kind of in vogue to name projects after cities. Microsoft had done it and so companies were naming projects with code names after cities. I was working on a project called the Napa Project, after Napa, California. Their project was called Dodge City, like the old western Dodge City.

The boss had named their project Dodge City because of the idea of walking down a Universal Studios set—you see Dodge City on the side and it's just a façade. It's just the front of the building. There's nothing behind it. There's no depth, it's not real.

He was having them work on an application that they could demo at an upcoming trade show to entice people to renew their licenses because of the great new version that was coming. But that version would never be released. He was never going to come out with the next new version. He was going to upsell people into the related product I was working on.

These developers were on a fake application, the ultimate vaporware, which is why they didn't need any error handling, why it was meant to just be like a good, old Norton demo type of thing from the '80s.

Here was a team killing themselves to do things that legitimately weren't needed. Apart from the ethics of lying to your customer base like this, what a horrible thing for that team.

Andrew: How frustrating for them! If the boss had been transparent about everything from the beginning, had he been upfront with the team about that goal, they would have understood and probably would have done a better job making it look as good as possible in a way that absolutely didn't have to work. Because when you think about it, your hands are really tied by projects that have to work. If they don't have to work, you can do some things that look amazingly cool. All the boss needs is something he can talk about and give hints to his customers.

Mike: Right. What he needed were the paths through it that he could demonstrate at a big trade show. If there was an error, he just wouldn't demo that little path, or he'd make up some other data and go through a different path to do it. He could have a carefully scripted demo and run that only.

Andrew: I like that story—it really ties together the two ideas we've been talking about: the idea of time, quality, and morale, and the idea of how understanding the vision, understanding the main goal of the project, really does have a huge effect on quality.

I guess that brings me to one of the reasons we really wanted to talk to you more than anything else because you spent a lot of time talking about practices, about things that programmers do to make their code better, to improve the quality of the code.

Let's say I put you on the spot; you had to choose one, two, three practices that really could make a difference in quality of code and how well you plan your project. What would you—if a team that was just stuck and wasn't sure what to do—what would you tell them to do first?

Mike: The first one's easy. The absolute first thing I would want a team to do is a continuous integration approach. I just think that is the greatest thing to do.

I remember—this is going way back, it was about 1992. One of the teams I was working with had the typical C++ application of the era, where just due to some external dependencies and things like that our build times had started to go through the roof.

We didn't know quite enough about networking to set something up like a good build server. For various reasons, Novell print queues just happened to be something we'd been using with our application.

I know this just sounds bizarre, but it was fantastic at the time. We actually wrote a build server that monitored a Novell print queue. Novell print queues were wonderful. They could hold anything. We put compile jobs into the Novell print queue, and we had a build server that would just monitor it and kick off compiles whenever it noticed anything getting inserted in there.

It was a completely cheesy, crappy way to do this network communication, but just on that application it had tremendous benefits. We had a little thing you inserted into the queue and the build would kick off.

I don't know why we never took that to the next idea of having it monitor the version control system. It took another seven or eight years before I ever saw a team doing that.

That completely changed what I wanted to do. It's just such a wonderful technique.

So my first one would be continuous integration. I think that's huge for teams.

Andrew: I like continuous integration as a first step, because it's something a team can do by themselves. No manager will ever object to it, because any manager who understands it well enough will generally be in favor of it. It seems like just the sort of stuff programmers do anyway.

Mike: Yeah, great point. There's nothing you can object to about it. I think to your point it's not even one I think you have to go to your manager and say you're doing. You do it.

I'm not trying to mislead managers. I mean, I've been one for many years. But I'll meet teams that obsess about it: "How do I sell my manager on continuous integration?" You don't. I mean, how do you sell your manager on the fact that you need to compile your code? It's a fact of life. You do it.

You're right, that's not one I think you have to go and beg a lot of permission for. Maybe you've got to buy some hardware or something, but just go find an old desktop lying around and it's good enough to get started.

The second thing that I really want teams to do is to get some level of test automation in place. This can obviously tie to the first goal of continuous integration. It's one thing to have the application building continuously; at least we know that everything at least integrates at a compiled level. But I'd sure like to get some automated tests going with that. That's a big challenge for many teams.

I don't really care what level they're testing at, whether it's unit tests or what I'd call the service layer, with tools like FitNesse, or even if it's a little bit more of a scripted user interface type of testing.

I certainly have preferences on how they phase in those tests, but it's most important to just start somewhere. Often it's easiest to start with some high-level user interface tests. Automate that regression test that's sitting around that you have to run manually. Get that automated at a user interface level and then start really working on getting the other types of testing added in.

Andrew: I like that you addressed just the code and build and quality testing. But what about planning? That's something that can have a huge effect on the project, but it's also something that can be surprisingly hard to sell to the team, or to the boss, or both.

Mike: I wrote a book on planning because I got so frustrated with agile teams running around saying, "We're agile. We don't plan." This was common in the early days of agile, through perhaps 2004.

It just bothered me because my experience up until then had been as a vice president of engineering at a couple of different companies, and I'd have been furious if one of my teams had come to me with a process I didn't know about and told me how wonderful it was. "It's faster and customers like the results and it's higher quality," and all these wonderful things that we often get from agile teams. But then they threw in the kicker: "But we have to give up all predictability."

I would have been furious, because that would have been teasing me with a great process I couldn't use. I don't care how good the rest of the process is. If it doesn't allow some degree of predictability, I can't use it.

From my experience having done it with various teams, I knew that agile teams could plan. I ended up writing that book on it just because I wanted to try to dispel this myth of "We're agile. We don't plan."

I don't hear that argument a whole lot anymore, so I hope I've been somewhat successful. That and, I guess, it's mostly been a matter of time and teams proving it can be done. There are enough agile teams out there doing planning. That's what probably has the biggest impact: when you see other teams doing agile planning, it's hard to say that you can't.

I definitely want teams to plan. But your initial question was, what were the first couple things I'd want a team to go do.

Normally, the first one is not planning. Teams have to start getting their act together with a lot of other stuff before they get a chance to really worry about anybody's opinion of their planning capabilities.

Jenny: That's a good point. Initially, when we started this conversation you were saying that not understanding the goal was a big problem in keeping teams in line with what they needed to build.

I wonder—all of the tools that you mentioned were about executing the project and building the code, and not really about understanding the project's goals. Do you think that that's something that teams can work on? Are there specific practices around that that you would recommend?

Mike: Around improving the planning? Yes, absolutely. Jim Highsmith documented a number of them in his book, *Agile Project Management* (Addison-Wesley). He talks about having teams write what's called an elevator statement. This is a two-sentence statement that you can give a stranger who meets you in the elevator and asks, "What do you do?"

But beyond some of those, I've done things like have a team write the magazine review that you'd like to have come out about your product once it's done.

I did this with a company that was doing anti-spyware software. Their product had just been reviewed by a magazine as the second best product in their field. It was the runner-up to an editor's choice award. Now, one way to think about this is if I were the director of the second best movie of the year, I'd be pretty happy. I'd make a ton of money. You've got the second best movie. People go to more than one movie. But the second best anti-spyware product? People buy only one of those.

Being second best in a niche like that was not a good thing for them. So, they got serious about some of their process changes they were putting in place, and I asked their

ScrumMaster who was working with them, Erin, to have the team write a magazine review that would summarize what they wanted to have said about them six months later when the next review cycle happened.

This was about establishing their clear, elevating goal. And it worked. They wrote the magazine review, and I remember the day about six months later when the real review came out. I remember it was Halloween and I was home. I wasn't traveling or working that day. I took my kids trick-or-treating, came home, and checked my email at about maybe 10:15 at night before getting ready for bed. I had a three-word email from Erin saying, "We did it!"

A week later, when I could read the real magazine review, I noticed there were sentences in it that were very close to what the team had written in their version of the review: "Finds more spies than any other spyware product." "Removes spies that other products couldn't even find." There were sentences like these that the team had established as its goal in writing a review six months in advance.

That was a testament to the team working with its stakeholder, figuring out what it is they were trying to achieve in this release over the next six months, and then making it happen because they had that very tangible goal very clearly in mind.

Have teams do things like that to solidify that goal. The vision is then shared among all team members.

Andrew: I had one more question about planning. Specifically, I want to talk a little bit about task boards. I've seen a reasonable amount of writing about task boards attributed to you.

More importantly, what do you think of when you think about the differences between working on an agile project and working on a traditionally project-managed project? It's certainly clear that we don't have a schedule in the traditional sense, or structured estimates, or those things that you normally associate with a dry, dusty binder full of paper. But for a lot of agile projects you've got this task board, a living whiteboard that seems to do a reasonably good job of actually planning things out—in a way that programmers actually embrace.

Now, I'm a little bit torn here, because I've definitely gotten a lot of success over the years out of those dusty binders full of planning and project schedules. But I can't deny that task boards and other agile planning tools have been really successful. So, would you include something like a task board in your two or three practices that you'd tell a team to adopt immediately? Can you give us a little background, tell us how a task board works?

Mike: A task board is a practice that I would have a team start doing right off if they were doing agile. So toss it in as one of the three practices from your prior question.

I remember when I first started doing that with my Scrum teams. I wasn't aware of anyone else doing them; it was just an idea I had that I thought would help a particular team I was working with. This team wasn't getting the concept of teamwork. We had done a nice planning meeting. We had a big list of things that needed to be done. But people didn't understand that they were to be a team. They were just a group of individuals.

This was a team that had switched from a traditional process. I was introducing Scrum to them. I grabbed some big 2-foot × 3-foot sheets of paper and I said, "OK, this sheet of paper is for this user story and that sheet of paper is for that other user story." And we just taped index cards to them.

There was no logical arrangement to the cards. Each big sheet of paper represented one user story or feature being worked on. Each thing we had to do was represented by one index card.

About a week later, I could see that things had gotten a little better with this group of individuals, but it still wasn't connecting with them that they had to be a team. People would come in and we'd do our daily standup Scrum meetings, but people would only talk about their own tasks. They had no interest in anybody else's work.

We finished up that meeting, and I remember taking the sheets of paper down and organizing them onto a great big whiteboard that this company had. I stretched it out and I drew columns: "Here are the things that we haven't started yet; the to-do column." I made a column of work that's in process, and a column for work that was already done. I said, "We're just going to move the cards very tangibly across this," and it clicked with that team right off.

Since then, this has been something that I always encourage teams to do. Any sort of co-located team in the same building, I think, is going to benefit from putting an iteration plan on index cards or Post-its, and putting them up into some sort of loosely structured form—a task board—up on the wall.

The task board outlines the steps that work has to go through. Whether it's a step like the design, coding, and even testing, just something that shows this is not started, this is being done, and this is done. A task board like that is about as complicated as I ever want one to get, but I've certainly seen teams do far more with that.

Andrew: It sounds to me like it's less about what are we going to be doing in a week, two weeks, three weeks, a month, two months, a year, and more about what we're doing right now. It's about figuring out where the project stands, at a glance.

Mike: I think that's part of it. Ideally, the team walks in and they see a bunch of work up on the board and they say, "What's the most important thing for me to do right now, today? Of all that work up there, what's the most important thing for me to do?"

We're not looking out six months on a task board. Task planning is normally done at the start of a two- or four-week iteration. The task board is wiped clean at the end and starts all over again for the next iteration.

It doesn't have to be complicated. I remember when I first started doing these. I had incredible fears that as kind of the traditionally trained project manager, I would be the

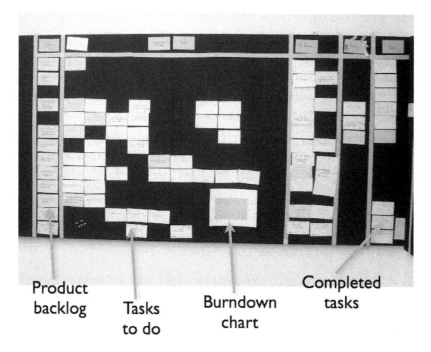

Product backlog

Tasks to do

Burndown chart

Completed tasks

A typical task board, with all of its parts labeled. (Image used with permission of Clinton Keith.)

only one to see a critical path. There'd be a critical path of work and no one would see it but me, the project manager.

I worried about that for the first, maybe, six months. After a while, I eventually realized that no matter how smart I thought I was, my team collectively was far smarter than me. If there was a critical path up there on the board, they would see it. This freed me up from having to worry about those things. I still haven't had a team that bumped up against the last day and said, "Uh-oh, there's not that many hours of work left, but there are sequential dependencies between them and now we're screwed." I've never had a team make that type of mistake.

The short time boxes and typically small team sizes that we have eliminate that whole class of issues that we would otherwise have.

Jenny: Actually, that comes back to something you said earlier about being frustrated with agile teams that say they can't deliver predictability. It's definitely clear how you can do planning for a short-term iteration. You're looking at the next three weeks, or the next four weeks, or six weeks, the next sprint or the next iteration. How does that fit with being able to give your manager enough information to plan the next six months, or the next year?

Mike: You absolutely have to be able to plan the next six months. You might even have to do a little planning the next year or two years. But the key is you have to be able to plan them with far less precision.

A task board that uses index cards held up with magnets. The lefthand side shows categories of tasks to be done ("Left Over", "Bugs", "Misc"), and the top shows the status of the tasks ("To do", "WIP", "Done"). (Image used with permission of Lisa Owens.)

I'm sitting here on October 22. There's not a project around that has to be able to say, right now, today, "OK, we've got our delivery date. It will be next September 16." I can't even imagine a scenario where that has to be the case. What would happen if it was September 15 or September 17? That level of precision is just not necessary over that longer term.

Now, I want to be careful. I'm not saying that we don't have to commit to a September 15 date 11 months in advance. But if we do, then we need to have some flexibility in the scope. The key is we don't have to lock those things down 11 or 12 months in advance. Teams need a little bit of flexibility and the business should be fine with that.

If we're looking at a project that we want out 12 months from now, we have to know a couple of different things. I have to know from the team about how long it's going to take, and I have to know from somebody in product management or marketing how much money are we going to make.

But I don't need to know how much money we're going to make down to the nearest dollar or euro, just like I don't need to know the schedule down to the nearest day. Giving me those things with less precision, as long as they're accurate, is OK. We can still make an appropriate decision, which is all that's really necessary.

Andrew: I have one more question I wanted to ask. Jenny and I have done a lot of speaking and training all over the world, and we've talked to a lot of people from all around the software industry. And one thing I've noticed is that there seems to be a small group of highly zealous agile evangelists. I think you've sort of referenced this a little bit: I'm talking about the sort of person for whom agile is a be-all and end-all answer to everything.

Now, personally, I don't believe there's one silver bullet that solves all project problems. I do believe that many agile teams use some very good practices that can help a lot of teams, agile or otherwise, to build better software. You've given some really good examples of those practices. I also believe that everyone, myself included, should always keep an open mind about the way we do our jobs, and we should always be looking for ways to improve our own software development.

But there are a small number of zealots and evangelists who, as far as I can tell, apparently claim that there's only one true way to build software, and that everyone else in the world should change the way they do things, even if their current methods work just fine.

And I've noticed that you don't do that at all. So, I want to know if you've noticed the zealotry that I'm talking about. How have you avoided falling into that? Or, on the other hand, do you think that I have it wrong? Is vocal agile evangelism—to the exclusion of all other ways of thinking about building software—a good thing that people should be falling into? I know that's kind of a loaded question, but I think you know what I mean.

Mike: Well, I don't think agile zealotry really gets us anywhere. I think the agile approaches are the right way to do things. I'm certainly a huge advocate of that. But I think two things prevent me from becoming an overzealous agile advocate.

One is that it's just totally by luck that this is how I've always done software. When I started out, in my first real job in a company (other than a very small company), I was doing software in a division of Andersen Consulting back in what was called their Litigation Information Services division. We worked on lawsuits. We worked on projects for people and companies who were being sued.

I remember working on very high-profile lawsuits. When you're working on those types of projects, you can't take a month or two to get something done. An attorney would come to you and say, "We need a program to solve this problem. We need it now." We needed to have very short cycles and turnaround periods on things like that.

I got lucky, and just kind of learned how to build software in that way back in the 1980s. I became agile just by luck and circumstance. The nature of the businesses I was in led me to do this.

I think the second thing that influences me is having lived through the object revolution. I think agile is the second wave of the object-oriented (OO) revolution. Agile is a continuation of that idea, which is why we saw that so many of the early, great OO thinkers found the agile movement. They were just continuing what started with objects.

I don't hear people saying things like, "I have to go to the OO design meeting today." They just say, "I have to go to the design meeting." Objects won; nobody talks about OO. Nobody asks, "Is this a structured design meeting or an object-oriented design meeting?" Objects won, as they should have. For the most part, teams do object-oriented development. (I know there are some applications that don't and can't.)

I want agile to be the same type of thing. I'd like the word *agile* to go away. I'd like eventually not to be talking about agile software development. I'd rather just be talking about software development. I don't know if it's another 5 or 10 years or whatever it takes, but eventually we'll stop talking about agile and it will just be how we do it.

Some projects are more or less agile than others, just like some projects make better use of objects than others. We won't need books with "agile" in the title. We won't need an Agile Software Conference. It'll just be the Software Conference.

Agile goes away as a concept and it wins. It simply becomes how we do things.

CHAPTER TWELVE

The Copyfighters Take Mordor

Cory Doctorow

THERE'S A LIMIT TO HOW MUCH OF THIS WE CAN PULL OFF. TRY TO FIND A RESTAURANT THAT 10 friends can agree on, or a wedding plan that everyone will sign off on, and you run up against some hard limits of collective action. By the time you hit the scale of a midsize company or a large family, it becomes apparent that an ever-larger slice of your "doing-stuff hours" must be devoted to "figuring out how to do stuff."

This is the transaction cost: the cost of getting stuff done, the overhead of getting everyone to agree on a restaurant, a course of action, or the truth. The cost of doing stuff that requires large groups of people and lots of labor is high enough that there's lots of stuff we don't even contemplate doing ("This weekend, my buddies and I are planning on whipping up a skyscraper!").

Transaction costs go by many names, like *overheads*, and *red tape*—but at the end of the day, the correct term for them is *bullshit*. As in, "There's no way I'm going to try to get the whole office to agree to that—do you know how much bullshit I'd have to wade through to get that done?"

As a society, we can only do stuff that produces more value than bullshit. The bigger the project, the more of the cost will be just bullshit.

But the Internet clobbers overheads.

WIPO is the United Nations' World Intellectual Property Organization. WIPO epitomizes the danger the Internet faces: a room full of diplomats meeting in Geneva in closed session, aggressively lobbied by the representatives of huge copyright and patent industries—and funded primarily by patent applications around the world, which means that these lobbyists represent the people who paid for the building they're meeting in. This is the veritable birthplace of bullshit.

Practically every rotten Internet regulation and law can be traced back to something that started at WIPO. WIPO has the same relationship to bad Internet rules that Mordor has to evil—a bottomless wellspring of dangerous foolishness backed by the power of one of the most powerful institutions ever created, the United Nations itself.

But in 2006, a multiyear, multimillion-dollar project to create a deadly new WIPO treaty collapsed under the onslaught of a tiny handful of activists who used the Internet to shatter the negotiations and replace them with a treaty that protected the public's rights to access and share human knowledge.

The Broadcast Treaty was an attempt to create a new layer of bullshit for video: a copyright-like rule governing the use of broadcast material. The idea was to create a new right over broadcast content, separate from copyright, which would belong to a broadcaster.

Say that you recorded a clip of the local city council debating school funding last night and you caught your own councilor lying about her campaign promises—you've still got her brochure stuck to the fridge with a magnet, and right there she promises that she will not approve school funding cuts, period. Feeling betrayed, you decide to make a little YouTube video using the recording, interspersed with you talking about how that promise got you to vote for her.

Copyright law says that you have the right to do this. Taking a short clip for the purposes of political commentary, parody, analysis, teaching, and other protected uses falls under the banner of "fair use" (or "fair dealing" outside the United States).

But if the Broadcast Treaty became law, copyright would be irrelevant, because in addition to the copyright on the work, there'd be a "broadcast right" that the broadcaster would control. The fair use rules for broadcast rights would be different from the copyright rules, and that means that you'd need permission from the broadcaster where you never needed it before.

So, the Broadcast Treaty would overrule the exceptions to copyright, but it went much further than that. The broadcast right would also apply to material that *can't* be copyrighted. Only creative works get a copyright; factual material does not. Many countries don't allow for copyrights on government works (if your taxes are paying to produce it, why should you need permission to use it?). All of these works would also suddenly become the property of the corporation that broadcast them.

But most importantly from the Internet's perspective was that the broadcast right would also override cases where creators had chosen to allow their works to be shared. The Internet is full of stuff that was made to be shared, copied, and remixed. A project called Creative Commons provides free licenses for sharing works, and in a remarkably short time (since 2003), more than *160 million works* have been released under these licenses, published by creators who want the public to be able to "rip, mix, and burn" the stuff they made with a minimum of bullshit. Wikipedia's millions of words are governed by a similar license, the GNU Documentation License, that also allows for free sharing of the free encyclopedia.

But under the Broadcast Treaty, a corporation that broadcast (or "webcast") a Creative Commons licensed video would be able to prohibit you, the audience, from copying, mixing, or sharing the video, *even though the artist who made the video said it was OK.*

WIPO is a huge, slow-moving juggernaut of an organization. Its meetings are attended by representatives of governments, many of them from poor countries that can't afford to send hundreds of experts on every subject to live in Geneva and participate in all the different UN agencies' treaty negotiations. Most of the delegates at WIPO are not experts on copyright, creativity, or economics; if they're from a poor nation, chances are that they're experts on agriculture or health, the kind of thing that a sub-Saharan country needs immediate action on.

So, these government delegations rely on "technical experts" from so-called "nongovernmental organizations." Most of the world thinks of NGOs as being groups like the Red Cross or Amnesty International, but at the UN, the term refers to any body that isn't a government. At WIPO, most of the NGOs are motion picture associations, broadcaster associations, pharmaceutical company associations, recording industry associations, publisher associations—the very people who stand to benefit from treaties that give more rights to companies that hold copyrights and patents.

This is the impartial, expert advice that WIPO relies on to make its treaties, so it's no wonder that every WIPO treaty has taken rights away from the public and handed them to companies.

But in 2003, all that changed. That was when UN observer credentials were granted to small coalitions of tech-savvy "public interest" NGOs, like the Consumer Project on Technology (which initiated the antitrust action against Microsoft), the Electronic Frontier Foundation (which spent a decade winning legal battles over privacy and freedom online), and Public Knowledge, a DC-based organization that did a lot of lobbying at the FCC over freeing the airwaves.

The Broadcast Treaty negotiations had been underway for years at that point. A draft treaty had been widely circulated, and the big players—the United States, the European Union, and Japan—were all agitating for a speedy conclusion. Pretty much everyone in the room thought that the treaty was a good idea—and what's more, the committee in charge of the treaty had been threatened with being shut down unless it could get a treaty out the door soon. Everyone was rooting for the Broadcast Treaty to pass and for things to move on.

The public interest groups had almost no money (sending delegations all the way to Switzerland was extraordinarily expensive for these little nonprofits) and were untrained in the diplomatic style of negotiation. The first few hours of the meeting—seen on a big screen in a side room, as the public interest groups weren't given seats in the main room—were nearly impenetrably dull. Delegate after delegate rose to his feet and said things like:

> Mr. Chairman, as I rise to take the floor for the first time in this session of the Standing Committee on Copyright and Related Rights, let me say how glad I am to have your hand on the tiller, steering us toward a speedy conclusion of this matter. My country's ministers have met recently on this matter and we wish to say that we are generally in accord with the current circulating draft, particularly in reference to proposals O, R, and W. However, we are concerned that the inclusion of webcasting at this time may stand in the way of the speedy conclusion we are all hoping for and would like to hear from our learned friends about the possibility of moving the webcasting provisions to a separate appendix or addendum that would be optional and normative, but not binding…

For hours.

The longer the activists sat there, the grimmer it looked. There wasn't even Internet access at the meetings—it seems like any meeting about reforming the Internet that doesn't provide Internet access is really about destroying the Internet. Then they had an idea. Wendy Seltzer from the Electronic Frontier Foundation created a wireless network with her laptop and fired up a piece of shareware called SubEthaEdit, a program that lets multiple people edit the same document over a network.

Minutes later, all the activists in the room were logged into Wendy's computer, writing down everything that was said. One transcriber would type, another would correct typos, a third would add editorial notes about what it all really meant. Classic high-tech de-bullshitification: rather than passing around notes and marking them up and consolidating them, everyone just worked together, all at once.

At the dinner break, a few activists snuck up to the mezzanine where the public terminals were, and unplugged one from its Ethernet cable and plugged it into a laptop and uploaded the day's notes to the Internet. The activists blogged it—billing it as the first look inside a UN copyright treaty negotiation.

By the next morning, the meeting notes had been Slashdotted—that is, posted to the enormously popular geek news site, Slashdot.com—and had gone from there to thousands of other postings. Millions of people read about the obscure machinations of a closed-door group in Geneva. The national delegations began to get phone calls from their capitals, either berating them for selling out their national interest, or congratulating them for taking a brave stand that was enormously unpopular at the meeting itself. One delegate recounted, "My capital called to say that a very important tech industry leader had called the ministry to tell them that he'd heard that our country was being very good here at the UN, having read about it on something called 'slash-dot'."

Thereafter, the activists used twice-daily blog posts to recount the goings-on at WIPO. These posts included editorial commentary and "human-readable" translations of the stilted, bureaucratic language that prevails at WIPO. They made fun of the technologically improbable predictions made by the delegates, and lionized the delegates who stood up for freedom.

The activists couldn't afford to take the national delegations out for fancy dinners or woo them at cocktail parties. Instead, they wrote daily position papers rebutting the other side's points, and then used bloggers around the world to translate them into several languages overnight so that they could be distributed the next morning before the meetings resumed. The UN administration suspended free photocopying for NGOs, a service they'd performed for the likes of the Motion Picture Association and the Pharmaceutical Research and Manufacturers of America for decades. Now that activists were using the press to hold the UN to a standard of public accountability, it was off-limits.

Before long, a mysterious person or persons began to actually *steal* the activists' printed handouts off the literature table, vanishing great piles of papers that later turned up in the toilets and behind potted plants. The Secretariat ignored requests to ask one of the many guards in the lobby to keep an eye on the table—or to review the CCTV footage to see who was systematically sabotaging the dissemination of "expert opinion" at WIPO.

The rights-holder groups and the WIPO executive went ballistic. One representative of a rights-holder group threatened to sue for copyright violation because the activists had written down his testimony and published it without his permission. The Secretariat accused the activists of "violating the UN's hospitality" and threatened a ban on the dissemination of all printed material by NGOs.

But the blog posts kept going out. The activists also used ad hoc wireless networks to vet each other's prepared statements before they were delivered, becoming superhuman with the help of a network, each comrade helping the rest to hone their talking points so that the groups were able to act as a coordinated whole.

Activist groups all over the world heard about the goings-on at WIPO through the blog posts, and more and more turned up to each meeting. One day, the rights-holder representative who'd threatened a lawsuit over copyright violations approached me with a printed sheet.

"What's this?" I asked.

"It's what I'm going to say this afternoon. I just wanted to be sure that your record got my remarks down accurately."

Not long after, the delegates of a national government approached me. "You know, we've just been transferred into this branch of the diplomatic service—a departmental reshuffle. We tried to read the official accounts but, well, you know…."

Indeed I did. The official reports from WIPO come out months after the meeting, are written in impenetrable bureaucratese, and are only published once every person "quoted" in them has had the chance to edit their remarks to remove anything they'd rather not have on record. Reading official WIPO transcripts makes memorizing the phone book seem exciting and glamorous by comparison.

"So, we tried to read the official transcripts, but we just ended up reading the reports the activists published. They're much clearer, you know—easier to follow."

From pariah to official biographer in just a few short years! The activists had fought WIPO's attempts to clobber the Net by using the Net—harnessing the low cost of collaboration and collective action to apply intelligent and unstoppable force. The other side *could* have used the Net to fight back, but they didn't; WIPO and the dinosaurs who back them have all the wrong intuitions about how the Net worked, and their efforts at grassroots Net-organizing are about as convincing as your old, white boss's attempts to rap at the company's boozy Christmas karaoke party.

Just how unstoppable was the force of Net-coordinated activists? The Broadcast Treaty was shelved by WIPO. In its place, WIPO elected to pursue a new treaty, one written by a broad group of activists, technologists, librarians, and geeks of all stripes, called the Access to Knowledge Treaty. Unlike all the other WIPO treaties, which spell out what the public *isn't* allowed to do with copyrighted works, A2K sets out the minimum set of information rights that every country has to give to its citizens, rights like the right to lend, to share, to make copies in special formats for disabled people, and to archive copies in libraries and national archives.

CHAPTER THIRTEEN

Defending the Free World

an Interview with Neil Siegel

Few jobs in the software industry are bigger than the chief engineer of Northrop Grumman's 35,000-person Information Systems sector, one of the largest defense and technology organizations in the world. Not many people (ourselves included) outside of the defense industry know much about the world of defense and military projects. Neil Siegel gives us a rare look at the defense industry, and what motivates the people who work in it.

Andrew: Start off by telling me a little bit about Northrop: how you came to be there, and how you came to learn about how teams work.

Neil: Northrop Grumman is one of the key participants in the U.S. defense and aerospace industry, with many important contributions over the years. The company took its current form over the last 10 years through a series of mergers, bringing together a set of synergistic companies with long and proud legacies of accomplishment. We think of ourselves as a "company of immigrants," respecting those legacies and achievements, while at the same time trying to combine our skills into something synergistic that is better than ever. My current job is sector vice president for Technology and Advanced Systems; I've been doing that for about seven years. Before that, I ran one of the businesses within the company, called Tactical Systems. Tactical Systems created vital, life-saving capabilities for the U.S. military—what the military calls "battle command" and "command-and-control" systems, primarily for the Army, but also for the other military services. Tactical Systems was a very successful business organization, which grew on average 25% a year during each of the seven years that I ran it.

Andrew: And what kind of projects did you work on?

Neil: We built equipment that allowed our soldiers to communicate and coordinate on the battlefield, to know where everyone (friend and enemy) was, to make and share plans, and to monitor the execution of those plans. It was a very team-oriented business; 50% of our revenue was derived from vendors and subcontracts, which meant that we had not only to build effective teams inside the company and with our customers, but also with a large number of other companies. Interestingly, the typical contract inside the company at the time had 70% or 80% of the content done by our own company, so this was an organization that depended very heavily on its ability to form teams not just with other parts of our own company but with other companies. And that was a lot of fun, and yet at the same time, very hard.

Andrew: What made it hard? What's harder about working with teams from a bunch of different companies?

Neil: It's about achieving alignment of objectives. Everybody has their own set of motivations and goals, and it's very rare, even inside the company, for two different people or two different organizations to have exactly the same motivations and goals. But this potential for misalignment of motivations and goals is even more exaggerated when you are working with people from other companies. For example, you might team with companies that would actually prefer that they were in charge of the job; for various reasons, you are able to talk them into being your subcontractor to team together for a job, but maybe there's the thought in their minds through the whole job that they could have just gone off and won this by themselves…and then they would be the prime contractor! In any case, there are always factors like, "We want to have a little more credit", or "We want to have a little more visibility", or "We want to have a little more work", or "Why is she giving the work to this other party? We could do that better."

So, all those things that are perfectly normal even inside one company are all magnified a little bit when you are partnering with other companies, because every work assignment has to be done as a subcontract, or as a teaming agreement—every aspect of the relationship is controlled by a very formal business arrangement. Every issue is resolved through formal negotiation, and the resolution documented through modifications to the subcontract. Actually, in some sense, there's an advantage inherent to using outside partners, because it forces you into that formality, which gives you the possibility of eliminating ambiguity in what you've agreed to, and ambiguity can be a real enemy to effective team operation. Ambiguity is a major source of conflict, due to mismatch of expectations.

Andrew: That sounds like a delicate balancing act. I get the sense that you had to learn that the hard way. Not a lot of people get the opportunity in their careers to learn a lesson like that. How did you learn that?

Neil: Let me go back a little bit in time to when I was running the Tactical Systems division. We bid and won a large Army program, and we produced a very important warfighting system (one that is still in use); I think at the time we submitted the proposal we had about 10 companies on our team. Some of these companies were providing what you might call components: they were very specialized, they had very clear scope, and as a result there was little conflict, little ambiguity about how we would work together on this job. But others of those companies viewed themselves as generalists who could bring a full range of capabilities to the partnership, and yet to be a part of a team that large, they had to narrow their scope to do just one or two specific things. As a result, some of those companies came to the party with the feeling that they'd subverted their ambitions so as to increase their likelihood of a win, and while that made sense intellectually, emotionally many of them felt like there were additional pieces of work on the job that they could do and would like to do. So, there was really a possibility for misalignment, and even conflict.

It was a very exciting activity—first of all, to talk all these companies into being your subcontractor rather than submitting prime contractor bids competing against you, or teaming with some other bidder. You basically have to convince them that their total expected financial and strategic return is higher because the probability of win is higher. Maybe their work share—the dollar value of work they'll do—is smaller, but the probability of win is so much higher that the total financial package is better for them. That's a hard sell, at times.

And then, when you have so many companies on one team—and in this instance, for various reasons, that was really necessary—then obviously none of these companies could be doing a very large portion of the total job; they start asking, "OK, I'm good at that, but I'm also good at these other things, so why aren't I doing that? Why have you given that work to this other company?" So, it's a real negotiation challenge; you have to get everybody aligned and working toward the main goal (and continuously keep them aligned!), and then you have to get everybody motivated, because this team might have 10 companies on it, but it has to look to the customer as one team.

Andrew: I've never had to deal with a project team as complex as one with people from 10 different companies, but I definitely recognize the need to get people aligned and motivated. How do you do that?

Neil: In our business, we have some advantages and we have some disadvantages. The first thing that we do in the defense business to get people aligned and motivated is sell our mission: we are defending the free world. I was the general manager of this business throughout the dot-com boom. The dot-com boom created a huge demand for technical talent. Recruiting talented software people for our company became a big issue because the dot-com boom was sucking up a lot of talent and paying very high salaries. And so I used that opportunity to recruit shamelessly, based on the value of our customers' mission. I would say things like, "You're a talented software person. You could go to work for a telecom company, and your life's work could be routing telephone calls successfully. Or you can come to work for us and maybe we won't pay you quite as much—although none of our employees starve—but you'll be saving the free world."

Andrew: I can see how that would be a motivator—not for everyone, but definitely for the kind of person you'd want working there. Did it take a lot of work to find those people?

Neil: It's kind of a self-selection process. The people who resonated with that motivation came to work for me. The people who were absolutely out to get the best salary offer didn't come to work for me. I had a strategy of trying to pay just a few percent less than the prevailing wage in our area so that I would be picking off those people who resonated with our customers' mission, playing to one of the natural strengths our industry has: we do something that's important and easy to explain. We also do something that's interesting. I view it as every bit as interesting as the telecom companies or Microsoft—that's a personal judgment—but it's most definitely interesting. It's high-tech, very leading-edge. So, I could really play on the combination of *important, interesting,* and *reasonably compensated.*

So, the people who joined my team had self-selected against those criteria. This is important: the first vector of alignment wasn't around our company, and wasn't around me, but was around "here's a way to contribute to national defense." This particular program had very high visibility in the Army—we routinely met with the chief of staff of the Army, and so forth; this made working on this program a very visible opportunity to do something that was clearly important. Furthermore, the Army was trying to do this reasonably fast. When you're trying to do something big in the defense industry, sometimes it takes seven years, or 10 years, or longer; it takes seven years to build an aircraft carrier. But the government wanted to do this particular innovation much faster than normal. So, not only could you do something interesting and important, but you could also get to the job satisfaction of seeing the thing done in about three years.

That gave me an opportunity to create alignment around these bigger-than-us factors like national defense, and the United States Army, and the first-ever digitization of the battlefield, and saving soldiers' lives, and saving marines' lives. That provided a strong message around which to start a process of reaching alignment within our team. I suspect that this might not translate so directly to other fields, but with a little bit of creativity, almost every business has something about their business that is essential and important in some way.

Andrew: I'm actually a little surprised by the fact that what you just said is very similar to what I've heard from open source people: a feeling of working toward a higher cause. Your higher cause is life-and-death, but for a lot of us, I suspect we can still find that kind of motivation in our own projects. What do you think?

Neil: National defense is a very tangible thing, but I suspect that many fields have some aspect that can be important. For example, working for the electric company can be important, because delivering uninterrupted, reliable electric service is important. One can create an ethos within your team that what they are doing is vital to the community. There's probably something in every industry that you can attack from that angle.

Andrew: So, let's get back to those 10 companies you had to balance. How did you do it? I can see how you'd motivate your individual team members, but how do you keep all of these companies working toward the same goal?

Neil: There are some obvious things that they want: they want revenue, they want profit margin, and they want predictability. But those are really, in my experience, weak things to build alignment around. The better thing is, "What are the strategic goals of that company?" If you're dealing with people at a sufficiently high level in your partner companies, you can have discussions about what the strategic goals are and what you can do—things that may or may not have to do with near-term revenue—that can maybe help reinforce a capability that five years from now will be strategically important to them.

So, one spends a lot of time trying to understand the strategic goals of your partner companies. It's a little difficult, in that they're not going to tell you everything, because you're still potential competitors on other jobs. But just ask what makes them tick, what their strategic goals are, and what you can do that will not only satisfy their near-term need of revenue and jobs, but will also create strategic value out of the relationship. Even just the act of asking such a question and listening to their answer, engaging in dialog, is creating an air of respect: a sense that this project isn't just about me and my glory, or maximizing the glory and revenue of my company, but includes them, too. And that's obviously a long, slow process—one conversation is never a basis for building a relationship of trust—but it's a very tangible thing. You can find mutually agreeable things in a teaming relationship that create strategic value for the partners.

And that works for partners, and also with other organizations within our own company. The nature of the discussions with organizations inside our own company is maybe a little different—there's actually a perverse clarity that comes with having these discussions with other companies—but if you look like you're trying to reach beyond the obvious work scope and revenue, and trying to make this work for them in a longer-term strategic sense, that can create a lot of satisfaction in the teaming arrangement, even if the immediate revenue is less than that for which they hoped.

Andrew: I'm really interested in the day-to-day of what it's like working on one of your projects. I assume that you guys have to go through a pretty big information-gathering phase at the beginning of a project, talking to the guys who are actually using what you'll be working on. Can you tell me a little bit about how that works?

Neil: First of all, this information gathering is a huge opportunity for realizing the alignment that I talked about first, the alignment around the mission. Because really, this is a chance to get people seduced and resonating emotionally with the mission of the users. The officers in the U.S. military are, in general, extremely capable and motivated people who are great representatives of their mission. It's wonderful for me to be able to connect our people with them.

Andrew: Are they good to work with? What's it like working with them?

Neil: They're a good customer! They believe in their mission, and know how to talk about that. Of course, the U.S. military is an even bigger bureaucracy than Northrop Grumman; we're a hundred thousand people, they're a million people, and there are some potential disadvantages with that. On the other hand, they understand that the quality of what *we* do can affect *their* life: in a literal life-and-death sense, not just in a sense of whether their milk is fresh or stale, or whether their newspapers arrive on time; their very lives can depend on the quality of our work. So, they're very motivated to make sure that they convey information to us as effectively as possible: what they do, how they do it, what they want to be able to do. It provides great clarity. So, we love for our people to get deeply immersed in our customers' problem. We call that "acquiring domain knowledge."

We like our people, especially our more senior technical people, to become real experts in one of our customers' specific problem domains. When they acquire that expertise, we now have the engineering knowledge, the technology knowledge, and the domain knowledge all resident in one brain…and in my experience, that's when the magic happens. Then we can create these great ideas that in turn get the customers very excited that we can really do something that will improve things for them.

Andrew: "Where the magic happens"—can we delve into that a little bit?

Neil: I have an opinion that, in the typical business—and I've done some commercial IT and other things in my career—they all kind of look the same. There are people who work for our customers who are designated to talk to the contractors, to describe what they need and how they work. Sometimes customers are their own worst enemies. They probably understand quite well what they do today, but sometimes their vision of tomorrow is three seconds from now, not three years. They can have a very narrow view of what they need.

So, we do things like sending our senior employees to spend a year with the National Security Agency or the National Reconnaissance Office, or we bring Army officers to live in our facilities for a year, or we send engineers out to observe maneuvers at the National Training Center, or even send engineers to Iraq and Afghanistan to ride along with units on patrol. Because typically the customers' designated experts, who may understand their current practices, and may or may not have a sufficiently long-sighted vision of the future, probably don't have a grasp of the technology...and therefore don't understand the art of the possible. On the other hand, the private industry people have technical experts who understand a lot about technology, but if they don't understand the problem domain, you need an interpreter in the middle: "He said this, but what he really means is this," and so forth. We used to really concentrate on developing these interpreter–translators. But we realized it takes a long time to turn domain experts into engineers or scientists; we hire a modest number of retired military people because they can come in and tell us about how the organization works. But at the same time, what I've found is that what works better is to immerse our engineers into a customer's problem domain to acquire domain knowledge. Then I don't need a translator; there's no barrier between domain knowledge and technical skills. One person can merge both, develop new ideas, and help visualize the future.

So, that's what we aspire to: getting our technical staff to acquire a pretty good level of domain knowledge about a customer. Now there's no filter or barrier between the domain knowledge and technical knowledge, and that's where the "1 + 1 = 3" ideas for seeing what the future could be occur. That's how you get out of the "future is three minutes from now" bottleneck—you start thinking about how you can use technology to create revolutionary improvements in this mission. That's how we work with customers.

Andrew: Are there any specific practices or tools that come to mind that help you deal with this?

Neil: We have lots of specific mechanisms. For example, we have something called "user juries" where we take ideas out, and walk actual military users through how a system would work: a day in your life after we built this new system. Then, we discuss whether that will help them, and how we would measure such improvement; we try to measure projects not in terms of technical improvement, but in terms of operational utility. There are lots of other mechanisms; it's all about trying to eliminate or minimize the effects of the barrier between domain knowledge and science and engineering.

Andrew: I would love to hear a story from an actual project where you could tell us a little bit about what you were building, and how you actually applied these mechanisms.

Neil: Sure. I'll give you an example. On one of these military command-and-control systems we were building, we had an interesting conceptual breakthrough.

Andrew: I'm not familiar with military systems—what's a command-and-control system?

Neil: An information system for military commanders. It allows them to communicate with each other, and allows them to maintain situational awareness: where everybody is, what their status is. It's how a commander can understand what's going on. Battlefields used to be small areas—a commander could stand on a hill with a pair of binoculars and could see what was going on. But by about 1900, the battlefield started getting so big that you couldn't stand on the hill like Napoleon did. You had to start using technology to "see" the entire battlefield. And the systems that do that are called "command-and-control systems."

A soldier in the field using a command-and-control system built by Neil's team.

So, we were building a system like that. And we had in our head a model that was kind of like email: I've got a piece of information and want to send it to somebody, so I get the information into the system, and then I tell the computer the name of the person to whom I want to send it. One of the big "aha!" realizations we had is that that was actually a very low-value way to build one of these military information systems; the users eventually realized that actually they don't want to have to know whom (by name) is the right person to receive a piece of information: they wanted the system to figure out from the intrinsic nature of the information who are the people who would be interested in receiving that information, and then to send it to them automatically. If you're on the battlefield and you see something, and determine it's a potential target—for example, the Army and the Marines use a process called "call for fire," saying, "I want to tell somebody to shoot that tank for me"—maybe I'm just an observer and don't have a weapon or don't have the right kind of weapon or I need to stay concealed, so I can't shoot it, but I want to tell somebody to do so. But I don't know who that should be. So, let the computer figure that out, and automatically get the information to the right person.

So, we finally realized that they want to address a call for fire to the *system* (and *not* to a specific named person), and have the system figure out who they should ask to shoot it. Because there are a lot of different options: you could have the Air Force drop a bomb from an airplane, or you could have a helicopter fire a little missile, or you could have another tank shoot it, or you could have artillery stand 10 miles away and shoot shells at it. And you don't want this person on the battlefield to have to decide which mechanism to use. He might not make the right decision: he doesn't know who's in the area, who's ready to shoot, which kind of ammunition to use. His job is to recognize that there's a bad guy out there, and that we should shoot him. It's somebody else's job to decide what kind of ammunition to shoot, and what kind of delivery mechanism to use.

It took an amazingly long time for us to communicate with each other, and to realize that the "right" approach was for the system to figure out who would be interested, rather than having the originator of the information have to address the information to specific people by name. That's an example of the tension and the suboptimization that can happen when the user is speaking in one language and the scientists and engineers are speaking in another, and how the processes of getting engineers to become domain experts and having user juries and so forth can get you to have the "aha!" moment of "Oh! This is how I can do what you really need!" The users hadn't thought about it that clearly, either, and so we were all struggling with this useless idea of how to build the system.

Andrew: I love that story. One thing that's interesting to me is that a lot of people think of military contracting and associate it with bureaucracy and paperwork, but the way you describe it makes it sound really tough but really interesting.

Neil: I wouldn't trade my job for any other job on the planet. I'm the chief engineer of a 35,000-person organization that does really important and really interesting things. This is a wonderful business for an engineer or a software person. Yes, there's a bit of bureaucracy inside the company because we're 100,000 people, but on the other hand, you can have 99,999 really smart colleagues. If you can harness that size to your advantage, it can be great.

I've worked in small companies. It's a lot of fun, and it's really easy—there's 20 of you. But if you needed an expert in some other field, chances are there isn't one. Here, there's an expert in almost any field that's relevant to what we do. Since I'm the chief technology officer for a big chunk of the company, either I know who these people are, or I know who to call among my counterparts in the other portion of the company to find them. There are thousands of world-class experts inside this company and, if we can get organized, that size works to our advantage. So, when we are at our best, this is a very exciting and wonderful business. It has its bad days, like all businesses, but this is a great and exciting business for software people. And we have a completely insatiable demand for software people and system engineers, with the one caveat that they almost always have to be U.S. citizens.

CHAPTER FOURTEEN

Saving Lives

an Interview with Trevor Field

There are a lot of charities out there, and no shortage of places for you to donate money. But few organizations are as effective or innovative as PlayPumps International. It's hard to imagine a better use of money than bringing clean drinking water to people in villages in sub-Saharan Africa who desperately need it. And Play-Pumps does it in a unique way: by driving the pumps with merry-go-rounds or roundabouts, which the children in the village play on. Not only does this give clean water—which both nourishes the people and prevents water-borne disease—but it also frees up women, who in many villages have to literally spend their entire day fetching water, often from polluted sources. Trevor Field, the founder of PlayPumps, inspires us not just because he does great work, but because he does it through great innovation, engineering, and teamwork, which is why part of the proceeds from every copy of Beautiful Teams sold will be donated to PlayPumps International. We had the privilege of speaking to Trevor about his organization.

Andrew: So first of all, thank you so much for talking to me. Jenny and I are really impressed with everything you guys have done. Since this whole book is about engineering teams and how to make them work better, it occurred to us that you had put together more than just an organization that does really good things in the world; really, it amounts to a major civil engineering effort. We wanted to talk to you about how you put it all together, the history of it, and the challenges you faced.

If you could start by giving us a little bit of a background: tell us how you started PlayPumps, and a little bit about what the organization's about.

Trevor: Water is the source of life on this planet, and it's always been very interesting to me. Some years ago my father-in-law came up to visit me with his wife. While my wife and my mother-in-law went out shopping, I took my father-in-law to an agricultural show in Pretoria, which is about 50 kilometers north of Johannesburg.

At the show, there was a guy called Ronnie Stuiver. He was a driller, showing a drilling rig and compressors, that kind of stuff. And he had a model of a PlayPump system. It was a different one to the ones that we've got now, but I saw the concept—I saw how this could possibly work. The problem he had with it was that it had a lot more steel attached to it, and when compared to a hand pump like an Afridev or a Mono Pump, the price was just ridiculous. I'd been involved in outdoor advertising and advertising in magazines for a long time, and I just loved the idea of this thing. I approached him and got him to give me the exclusive rights to sell the idea. And it was born from there.

I thought that the easiest way we can make this work is to get the private sector involved. And the way to do that was to be able to pump the water into an overhead storage tank, and then put advertising messages around those tanks. Rural people are not exposed to television or the Internet or magazines or newspapers. You go into the very rural areas, and there's no advertising whatsoever.

A water pump is like the focal point of the community. If we could put messages up there that advertise the kind of stuff that local, rural people bought—sugar, tea, coffee, and these days, cell phone rechargers, and all that kind of stuff—it should work. That's what we did; that's how we started.

And it's grown hugely from there. We bought the patents from that chap, Ronnie Stuiver, and we redesigned and reengineered the whole thing. We've got our own factory in a place called Modderfontein, just up the road. And we employ 36 people in my factory. The factory's capable of producing a hundred units a month with ease. That's how the concept basically started.

Andrew: When you reengineered the pump, what needed to be done? Was there an interesting or difficult design challenge?

Trevor: It was that the chap had made a model. From a model we had to actually design the actual working unit, which is what we did. He actually made some units for us in the early days. But Ronnie, you know, he was a farmer, with a workshop on his farm. He used to build things by hand, and hammer them out—it wasn't polished.

We were concerned with the equipment. It was OK here in South Africa because we could maintain the equipment ourselves. But when you're looking to export into other countries, you need an export-quality product. So, we bought the patent from him, and we reengineered the whole thing—not from scratch, but basically we had every piece tested for stress and tolerances. And we made a new model that we were confident that we could go and put into the bush and leave it, and it would work.

So that was the challenge there.

Andrew: A lot of people who read this book who build software will definitely recognize that—the idea of starting with a prototype, something that they've built themselves, and having to harden it in order to get it to the state where it can be shipped out to people who will use it in the field every day.

Trevor: That's exactly what we had to do. I mean, you have to leave this thing in the middle of nowhere and just hope that it's going to continue to work. Plus, you've got a responsibility to the kids. I've seen 70-odd children on one of these roundabouts, all piled on top of each other. The average weight of a child that's playing on a roundabout is about 30 kilograms. You've got 20-odd, 30 children of 30 kilograms each and you're talking tons of momentum. You've got to make sure that the thing doesn't break. So we had to make sure that all of the bearings and all of the moving parts were extremely strong and all had tolerances way in excess of anything that the kids could throw at it. I think the main bearings have a breaking strength of about four and a half tons; huge compared to what it's actually going to receive.

Andrew: And I'm sure the kids are going to play with things in ways that you never even thought of, right?

Trevor: Absolutely. That's why we use a positive displacement cylinder. Without getting technical, the thing goes up and down. As the kids turn round and round, the mechanism transfers that motion into reciprocal vertical motion, so the pump goes up and down. You do get pumps that go round and round, such as an Archimedes screw principle. The problem with that is that they only go in one direction and you can't reverse it, because if you reverse it, it just undoes all the piping.

And if you put a brake on it—well, that's exactly what the kids are going to do. They're going to try and brake it, because they want to go the other way, you know.

Andrew: That has to be enormously motivating for everybody who was working on the engineering, and for the guys in the factory actually building the pumps. I mean, you don't get a lot of products where you're actually doing real, honest-to-God good for the world.

Trevor: It's a shame that you can't come here and see a real one, because we could take you to the factory. We've got guys at our factory who are just pop-riveting steel onto frames, and it doesn't look like anything to them. So to motivate them, we had posters of the PlayPump blown up. You know, we did have an outdoor advertising company, a professional one that used to do huge billboards on the side of the road. (We sold it and disposed of all our assets to concentrate solely on PlayPumps.) We printed these massive posters of what these PlayPumps looked like, and we hung them up in the factory so the guys who are actually making them get motivated.

And you know, my partner's a bit of a creative guy, so the pumps get painted red, yellow, green—bright, bright colors, the kind of stuff that kids like. So, we painted the whole factory like that. All the handrails are red, yellow, green. I mean, it looks like Charlie and the Chocolate Factory!

The PlayPumps factory.

Andrew: It's one challenge just to get the pumps to the point where you can manufacture them and they can stand up to the punishment of being left to do the job. But getting them out into the field, that's got to be a challenge, too.

Trevor: That's a huge challenge. I mean the fuel price alone—I don't know what a gallon of gas costs in California these days, but in New York it's going to cost more or less the same. Problem with Africa is it's difficult to transport this stuff around, and it's heavy. Very heavy.

The price of fuel in South Africa is about $1 a liter or thereabouts. But the price of fuel in Uganda, for instance, is more like $7 per liter. You can't plan anything with those kinds of variables. It really does mess up the logistics in a big way.

And in places like Zimbabwe, they've got no fuel at all. That's one of the reasons why we're not there, apart from, well, obviously Mr. Mugabe's going to have to disappear before we go there at all. And that's a pity, because we want to help the people in Zimbabwe. They're suffering, and it's not their fault. They were just born in the wrong time zone. And it's our neighbor. I could drive to Harare from here; it's like driving to the coast for Christmas holiday. The roads are good, but the border guards want a 35% import duty on a gift. Well, not in my lifetime, we're not going to do that.

Andrew: It sounds like working with other countries and their governments and borders brings its own set of challenges.

Trevor: We get import waivers from all of the countries that we're working on because we raise funds from America, Britain, all over the world, and we make these pumps and we actually give them to the recipient communities within that country.

We insist that the government gives us a customs duty exemption. So, that's one challenge, getting that import duty exemption. Another is getting through the borders, because all the borders have some very cavalier ideas on what's supposed to happen with imports and exports.

And then you've got other problems, as well. The road system is not really great in other countries. For instance, I think you'd call it an 18-wheeler, a big double semitruck; it carries two containers, a 40-foot and a 20-foot. We would call that an interlink. You can't put an interlink on the road, because they won't allow them in Mozambique. And they won't allow them in Zimbabwe because they damage the roads so much. We could get 25 units in an interlink, but we can only get 11 on a semi, which is a fixed-body truck. So consequently, you know, you've got to send two, which doubles your costs.

We've just done a deal with Malawi, so I've got a Malawi MOU, Memorandum of Understanding, with the government. They're very happy to accept the pumps, and they've given us the customs duty exemption. But to get to Malawi from here, we've got to go through either Mozambique or Zimbabwe. And that's a challenge: the fuel's a problem, and the costs vary from one transporter to the other hugely, with massively different prices.

Andrew: I was just thinking about the kinds of administrative and bureaucracy issues software people face in their jobs. The next time I find myself groaning about having to come up with a report for Bob from accounting for my project, I'll remind myself that at least I don't need to negotiate a Memorandum of Understanding with a government. You must get caught up in a lot of red tape—and language barriers, to boot.

Trevor: Yeah. Well, with respect to the people I deal with, the majority of them speak pretty good English, because they are at a ministerial level. But there are still idiosyncrasies that they don't understand.

And you have to spell it all out, physically go there to sit and take time, explain the whole process and how it is going to work, where we're going to put these PlayPumps, and when they arrive in a country who's going to store them. We want to know if it's secure, because we don't want people running off with bits and pieces. Because every part of the machine is put together at our factory, and every nut and bolt is counted and double-counted and checked into a nylon sack that's got all of the little bits and pieces in it. You don't want an installer to be 300 or 400 kilometers from Dar es Salaam in the bush trying to install this thing, and then he finds in his sack that he's missing two bolts.

That makes it a tad of an operational problem, you know. We have to send up spare units and spare parts for the installers. The model we use is basically the same in every country as it is in South Africa.

Installing a PlayPump.

Andrew: Do you do most of your work in South Africa? How does installation work? Maintenance? It's got to be a challenge.

Trevor: How it works is that in South Africa you've got nine provinces. We work in five main provinces: the Eastern Cape, KwaZulu-Natal, and Mpumalanga, Limpopo, and Northwest. Those are provinces that are historically the most deprived from a facilities point of view.

We've got an installation crew in each province. What happens is that we'll send a truck with, say, 25 units on it to KwaZulu-Natal. It usually goes to the municipal buildings in that area, where we'll store the equipment. Our installer in KwaZulu-Natal will go in every day, load up a couple of pumps, go out to the sites, and start the installations.

Andrew: Maintenance has to have its own challenges. Have you had to get creative to handle those challenges? How does that all work?

Trevor: When the installer finishes the installations, he becomes the maintenance guy for those pumps. On the tank stand itself we used to put a free phone number, our 0800 number. So, if a pump broke down, a person could write that number down on a piece of paper and go to a telephone, go to a local store or a spaza shop, get hold of a telephone, make a free call to our offices in Joburg, and report the pump out of order.

But that was an absolute disaster, because what happened was in reality a pump would break down, the guy who got to the pump would write down the telephone number for the pump repair, go to the phone, and phone us up. We'd ask, "Which pump is it?" And he'd say, "I don't know, it's the one by the school," you know. And we'd say, "Which school?" And he'll say, "Ambabulla School." And we'd look on our database and we haven't got an Ambabulla School because they've got seven different names for the same place.

That was a real problem, one we really wrestled to try and overcome. Eventually we cracked the idea of using text messages on cell phones. Because it didn't matter which rural province you're in, or how poor the people are, somebody's always got a cell phone. It's amazing.

So, what we do now is we've got a number on the tank. Well, we've always had numbers on the tank to identify them—in KwaZulu-Natal it would be KZN001, for instance. That would be the unique number for that particular pump, which is GPS'ed on our database so we know where it is within 5 meters, and we see it on Google Earth, too, so that's another, you know, advantage.

What we came up with was that we'd say, "SMS or text this number, KZN001, to this phone number." That way, we'd see which pump number it is on the message, which means we could identify it straightaway. And then we can phone the guy back, because our phone identifies his phone, his phone number, so we can communicate with the person who is reporting the pump out of order.

That worked a lot better. And it's a simple thing, but it took a bit of working out, I can tell you.

Andrew: Sometimes simple, elegant solutions to complex problems are the hardest ones to come up with. And it worked well?

Trevor: Yes, it worked really well. The only saving grace was that you know when a pump does break down, because it is a person's supply of water. You get way more than one or two calls, you get lots of them.

Andrew: In addition to the organization that gets the pumps out into the fields to deliver the water, you're also running a charitable organization. I'm sure that had a different set of challenges, establishing PlayPumps and getting it all set up. Was this something you'd done before?

Trevor: No, I'd never done it before.

Andrew: So you had to learn a lot to do this.

Trevor: What happened was that in 1999, about eight, eight and a half years ago, we were running a fully commercial operation called Roundabout Outdoor, which we still run today. We were selling the advertising on all four sides of those water towers for commercial gain. We had a launch in the south of Johannesburg at a place called Reitfontein. Former President Nelson Mandela was there—there was huge excitement, thousands of people turn up whenever he's around. He came and looked at the pump. That was the first and only time that I actually shook his hand. A whole lot of different people were there, from the World Bank, from UNICEF and CARE and Planet International, all sorts of different people.

I was talking to a guy from the World Bank, a guy called Dr. Ross Paul, who's retired now in Australia. I asked him, "How can we get, you know, funds for this system?" And he said to me, "There's a competition called the Development Marketplace Competition. Why don't you enter that?"

So we did, in a very, very rushed fashion—the deadline was approaching for submissions. I went to his office and spoke to him about what we did, and he typed it in on his computer, and we put the online application in to the competition. We got short-listed, and I went and presented it in Washington, DC. We won the competition. They gave us—I think it was $165,000 in those days. We used that money to put more pumps in the ground. That's how it started.

But what happened after that was that people had seen the system. Instead of us amortizing the advertising against the cost of the equipment, people started giving us money out of the blue. One guy from Ireland gave us like 10,000 pounds, and somebody else just sent us money in the post, another did transfers into our bank account. We were a for-profit organization accepting donations. It was getting a bit awkward.

So I spoke to the Ministry of Water at the time, a guy by the name of Ronnie Kasrils, and I asked him what he thought we should do. He referred this to the Finance Department, and they wrote letters between each other. Then I was called into the SARS in South Africa—you'd know that as the IRS. I almost had a heart attack when they gave me the call, because I thought it was my personal tax they were looking at. But they wanted to talk to me about the structure of the company.

I went there and basically they said, "What you want? What do you want us to do?" And I said, "I want you to work out some sort of incentive that would enable or encourage a company to give us more money, because when we make a pump we're going to put it in the ground. It's not mine, and it's not the company's, it's not Anglo American's [a South African mining company that contributes to PlayPumps]. It belongs to the people. So where's the inducement to get Anglo to give us more money?"

I was anchoring for them to give us a tax incentive. And they did! They worked out a structure: they said, "OK, you need to open another company and make that an NGO." Then they said that Ministers want to do this so much that they'll make it a PBO, a Public Benefit Organization, because the work we do is ostensibly what public works should be doing.

We opened up the NGO and we called it Roundabout PlayPumps. We kept Roundabout Outdoor, our original company, because we have telephone numbers and faxes and computers on all the business cards and letterheads. The NGO accepts the donations from various quarters, and Roundabout Outdoors was designated the implementation organization for that NGO. So, that's how the structure works. But yes, we've had challenges like you can't believe.

Andrew: Wow. It sounds like you've really come a long way. That's really inspiring. Do you have any advice for someone who wants to do good things, but might be a little intimidated by the size of the problem? How did you keep motivated, even when you weren't sure how it was going to turn out?

Trevor: Well, look, from a motivational point of view, I'd come up with this idea in 1989, and my wife actually put the first two pumps in the ground in KwaZulu-Natal in 1993. I couldn't give up my day job at the time—it's the same old story, you know.

How anybody gets anywhere is that you just have to adopt the Nike slogan: just do it. You just go do it, and that's what I did. One day I walked out of the job that I was in, and decided I wanted to do this full-time.

We had two pumps then, and lots of people laughed at me. "Ha, ha, ha, a children's merry-go-round that pumps water, yeah, yeah, sure, OK, you know. You will be all right, just keep taking the pills, whatever."

Well, they're not laughing now. We had First Lady Laura Bush, Bill Clinton, and Steve and Jean Case from the Case Foundation standing on the stage at the Clinton Global Incentive, in the States, awarding a $16 million investment into PlayPumps globally for a 10-country expansion.

So, from two pumps that we started with in 1994 to 4,000 pumps across Africa affecting 10 million people. Yeah, you've just got to stick to your knitting and just make it happen. And that's exactly what we've done.

Kids playing on a brand-new PlayPump.

Billboards carry education, health, and consumer messages.

The storage tank carries essential social messages.

PART THREE

Practices

ALL TEAMS—EVEN TEAMS WITH GREAT PEOPLE WHO WORK REALLY WELL TOGETHER—HAVE HABITUAL problems. And when they do, the problems are bigger than the individual people on the team. It's both frustrating and difficult when you just know your team is technically capable of solving their problems, but somehow they keep succumbing to them.

That's where changing the way you work can have a big impact on how your team works. And that's what practices are all about: finding a better way to do things so that your team doesn't get stuck on the same old problems.

The world is full of books about building software: some great, some good, some not so good. The not-so-good books claim to tell you "the right way" to build software. The good and even great ones will tell you that they have a good way—not necessarily *the* way—to build software. What they all have in common is practices.

It's pretty easy to get overwhelmed with practices, because it seems like there are dozens of ways to do any one thing on a project. Just deciding how you'll describe how your users will use the software can be a challenge. Will you use user stories? Use cases? Textual use cases or visual, UML-style use cases? Or maybe more traditional stimulus-response sequences (which predate both use cases and user stories)? Do you write them down in a document, or pin them to a wall? Do you use index cards? Post-its? An Excel spreadsheet? There are literally dozens of ways to write down what amounts to the same information. It all depends on how your team works best and there is definitely no single right answer.

And that's just the problem of writing down how your users will interact with the software. Almost every programmer has a different idea of a perfect code review. Or how to document the architecture the team's come up with. Or how to write down a project schedule—some people hate, hate, *hate* Gantt charts, others can't live without them.

It's hard to overstate just how dangerous change can be to a team's culture. In fact, not just its culture; a change can threaten its very existence. There are two big risks that teams face when they try to adopt a new practice. One is that the practice itself is stupid, but the person pushing it doesn't know that. One of the most popular and unfortunate practices that teams suffer through is the useless status meeting. That's not to say all status meetings are useless. (Ask anyone on a well-run Scrum team, and they'll tell you about their way of having effective meetings!) But there are definitely status meetings that are universally useless, usually done solely for the benefit of a project manager or senior executive. Everyone on the team sits around a table, and each person waits his turn (usually checking his email when he's not speaking). When it's a team member's turn, that person summarizes everything he did in the past week. It's not clear whether that information is ever recorded anywhere, but it's generally not used for anything other than some senior manager's ego gratification. Nobody hears anything anyone else has said, and the whole thing basically just sucks several hours a week of the team's time, with no useful product whatsoever.

A practice such as the useless status meeting is bad for the team, because invariably, nobody ever asks anyone on the team if he gets anything out of it, or if it improves the software. If someone did ask this question, the meeting would be halted immediately.

But what about when the practice is smart, and the people on the team just don't get it? That's the second big pitfall. A lot of teams have run into exactly this problem when trying to put code reviews in place. A lot of programmers agree that code reviews are a good idea. Look at most successful, high-profile open source projects—for example, Apache, Linux, and Firefox—and you'll see a culture that's built up around code reviews. But it's very common for a team to fail to actually put them in place, because the programmers themselves moan and groan every time there's a code review scheduled. When a code review does happen, very little comes of it, because the people participating didn't really believe in its value, and didn't work very hard to review the code. And that creates a self-fulfilling prophecy: everyone decides that the code reviews don't work, and stops doing them. The same thing happens anytime the team doesn't really believe in the value of the new practice.

If you want to put a new practice in place on your team, you need to do two things. First, you need to convince everyone on the team that it's worth doing. And second, you need to get the people who are paying the bills to understand the value of taking the extra time and effort—or, in their view, money—to do the practices. Because a good practice pays for itself in the long run, but that's definitely not intuitive for a lot of people (especially ones who don't actually write the code). Try telling your boss that you want to adopt a new practice that will cause it to take twice as long to build the project, but the testing and deployment will go so much more quickly that it'll be worth the extra time spent upfront, and you'll see what we mean.

It takes a visionary to see the value in a new practice. It takes a salesperson to convince management to pay for it, and to convince the team to do it. And in a lot of cases, it takes an above-average team to be open-minded enough to change the way they work.

The way your team chooses to work has a big impact on how successful your projects will be. And although there's not one correct way, if the team doesn't come to some sort of understanding about how they'll build the software, they risk working against each other.

The stories and interviews in this section are about practices. But more than that, they're about teams finding their way to better practices that suit them, because there's nothing more dangerous to a team's culture than imposing a change that doesn't work for them. We chose these stories because they're about important, pioneering teams who did this well, dramatically changed the way they worked, and had great results. These team leaders saw serious, habitual problems that were preventing the teams from building better software, and they found a way to get their people to embrace a better way of building it.

CHAPTER FIFTEEN

Building a Team with Collaboration and Learning

James Grenning

AROUND THE TURN OF THE MILLENNIUM, I HAD A GREAT EXPERIENCE. I WAS BROUGHT IN TO HELP ONE of our clients get a new project started. They were new to object-oriented (OO) design, and I was supposed to help them get an OO architecture defined and an initial plan in place. As it turned out, I spent almost half a year with them every other week. This was a time of great learning for them and for me. Not only did we have some fine accomplishments, but we also spent some time in turmoil.

The company, call it By the Book Systems (BBS), was very structured and prided itself on its quality and conformance to its processes. Like many big companies, BBS sometimes did things that hurt itself. In this tale, we'll see some of the brave and great things that were done at BBS and some outright blunders that can kill team morale and stifle progress.

Starting a new project is fun. I've had the pleasure of starting quite a few projects in my career, and it was good to be part of a team at BBS. As a consultant, I am too often an outsider, being on the team for only short periods of time. In this case, I was with BBS almost every other week. So, I really became part of the team.

The team started small: initially Johnny (the systems engineer), Alan (the lead engineer), and me.

The first order of business was for Johnny to brief me on the requirements of the project. He had a 30-page requirements document written by the book with the shoulds and shalls just as prescribed.

The requirements document had plenty of good information in it, but in that form it was almost totally unactionable. Even with the requirements prioritized, it was not clear what the software had to do. Software does things; we needed an inventory describing what the software had to do. Thankfully, there is a popular solution to this problem. Use cases are used to catalog and define system behaviors. Use cases would really help us get a handle on what the software should, shall, and must do.

We had a small problem, though. Johnny had not used use cases before. If use cases were not part of the standard process, we might have to do some formal justification. We pulled out the process manual and discovered, much to our pleasure, that use cases were one of the acceptable forms for requirements articulation. That was good news.

Johnny and I locked ourselves in his office. As we read the requirements document, we discussed what the requirements meant and what the implied system behavior was. We named use case after use case, capturing them in a spreadsheet. After about a week's effort, we had extracted 105 use cases from Johnny's requirements document and we identified nine actors outside our system's boundaries. We understood the system boundaries and the system behaviors, at least at a talking and planning level. This activity is called *use case identification*. The idea is to name all the behaviors.

Around that time, Kent Beck published his book, *Extreme Programming Explained* [1]. It was all the buzz. Wars raged on the newly formed Yahoo! Groups and the established comp. object newsgroup. A great opportunity presented itself. Object Mentor, my employer at the time, had cornered the market on Extreme Programming (XP). Well, that's not really accurate, but it sounds cool. What really happened is that Bob Martin, Jim Newkirk, and Lowell Lindstrom (the Object Mentor management team) had formed an alliance with Kent Beck, Ron Jeffries, and Martin Fowler to train people in XP. Lowell invited me to attend the first XP Immersion. I took the week off from BBS to get immersed in XP. What an impact that unexpected week at the Deerfield, Illinois, Marriott had on me. It amazes me how small events can have such a profound effect.

I must admit, most of the world knew very little about XP and I was in the same boat. What I had heard concerned me. How could something called *Extreme* really be a good idea unless it had to do with skiing? Were helmets required, or elbow pads? Would I need a new life insurance policy? I think Kent was being provocative and I am glad he was. If it had been called something like *Sensible Programming*, everyone would have yawned, and the waterfall process would have been kept as the ideal. As it happens, that simple, small book has made many people challenge the status quo.

After my week at Immersion, I returned to BBS with the enthusiasm of the newly converted. OK, I am exaggerating. I was never religious about XP, but thought many of the ideas could really break some logjams at BBS.

I started telling my colleagues about the interesting and revolutionary techniques in XP. They were interested, but reserved. "The quality people will never let us do something called Extreme," said Alan. Johnny was worried that more upfront design work and documentation were needed than XP prescribed. The big process culture made it difficult to imagine that a lightweight process like XP could be a good idea.

Selling Management

After a few more discussions about XP, Alan and Johnny were warming up to the idea. We briefed our manager, Fred, on XP and he was all for trying it, but we needed to go to the boss, Bud, our director. We knew there would be some contentious issues, specifically around keeping the process police at bay and providing the level of documentation that was needed. The documentation requirements at BBS were heavy. But it was my job as the team's mentor to challenge their current practices and help them grow.

I prepared a presentation on the practices of XP. We anticipated some of the issues that would come up and built a case for our recommendations. The presentation ended with a few open-ended questions to get a dialog going.

Bud: "This all sounds very good, but how will we handle the technical reviews required by our process?"

"We need to take the reviews off the critical path," I told Bud. I told him something he already knew: that the reviews temporarily block progress. Preparing for reviews was time-consuming and we also had the logistical problem of scheduling the senior engineers for our review meeting. We discussed how the current approach reviewed untried design ideas.

I explained, "Your most experienced people spend all their time in reviews rather than building the product. You need an experienced designer on each team." We talked about how design is a daily activity, not an event that ends when the sign-off happens.

Bud: "I think I understand. Are you saying we don't need reviews?"

"I'm not comfortable giving up reviews, but we will change what is reviewed and when," I responded. We knew that periodic reviews could not be avoided completely, but that we could find a more effective way to do them. The reviews stop the team's forward progress until the review meeting is held and the design is signed off. We told Bud that by moving the reviews off the critical path we could keep the team moving ahead doing continuous design, implementation, and testing.

"Currently, you use the most experienced people for reviewing the designs rather than creating the designs," I told him. We discussed how by having just one experienced designer on the team we could, with daily design discussions and pair programming, keep the design quality high.

Bud asked: "OK, but what will be reviewed?"

PRACTICES OF EXTREME PROGRAMMING

Extreme programming is a set of principles and practices for incrementally creating high-quality software. It's one of the original members of the agile development methodology family.

Customer team member

Teams have someone (or a group of people) representing the interests of the customer. The *customer* decides what is in the product and what is not. The *customer* is responsible for acceptance-testing the product. This means the customer team will likely have skilled QA team members.

User story

A user story represents a feature of the system. Stories are small; small enough to be completed within a single iteration by a single person. If the story is too big to complete in an iteration, split it into smaller stories. A story is like the name of a use case.

Planning game

In the planning game, the customer and the programmers determine the scope of the next release. Programmers estimate the effort required to complete each story. Customers select stories and package them into iterations that do not exceed the team's capacity. Stories are ordered by the customer according to their value and cost.

Small releases

The system is built in small releases. Each iteration lasts two weeks. A release is a group of iterations that provide valuable features to the users of the system.

Acceptance testing

Acceptance tests demonstrate that the story is complete. They provide the details behind the story and are defined before the story is started. Customers own the acceptance tests. The bulk of the tests must be automated so that they can be run at any time, usually multiple times per day.

Open workspace

To facilitate communications the team works in an open workspace with easy access to other team members, equipment, and project status information.

Test-driven design

Programmers write software in very small, verifiable steps. First, a small test is written, followed by just enough code to satisfy the test. Then another test is written, and so on.

Metaphor

The system metaphor provides an idea or a model for the system. It is part of the high-level design, facilitating communications. It provides a context for naming modules, classes, and functions in the software.

Refactoring

Refactoring is the process of keeping the design clean, incrementally. When systems evolve, the design will get messy. The idea of refactoring is to detect, identify, and fix design problems as they come up, while they are small and easy to fix.

Simple design

The design is kept as simple as possible for the current set of implemented stories. Frameworks and infrastructure evolve with the code through refactoring.

Pair programming

Two programmers collaborate to solve one problem. Programming is not a spectator sport. Both programmers are engaged in the solution of the problem at hand.

Coding standards

The code must have a common style to facilitate communication among programmers. The team owns the code; the team owns the coding style.

Continuous integration

Programmers integrate and test the software many times a day. Big code branches and merges are avoided.

Collective ownership

The team owns the code. Programmer pairs modify any piece of code they need to. Extensive unit tests help protect the team from coding mistakes.

Sustainable pace

The team needs to stay fresh to effectively produce software. Too much overtime will result in reduced quality, burnout, and unpredictable outcomes. Everyone works hard but at a sustainable pace.

Source: "Extreme Programming and Embedded Software Development," by James Grenning [2].

"We will review what was built and tested rather than what we anticipated building," I told Bud. We discussed that during each iteration, we would capture the important architectural decisions and constructs. If design problems were discovered during the reviews, we could make changes with confidence. Our automated tests would lock in the behavior. Any changes required by the reviews could be fixed in the next iteration.

"Let's be clear on the purpose of the design document. Its purpose is to provide a high-level road map of the system," I added, "The details will be where they belong in the code and its tests."

Bud: "Wait a second, there is no detailed design documentation?"

"Not at all," I responded. "Using test-first programming we are going to have many automated unit tests. The test cases are the detailed documentation." We discussed how each test case is a focused code example with a specific precondition and desired outcome.

I added: "The tests are an executable specification." Once people learn to read the tests, the tests become a very effective form of detailed documentation. It's not like prose documents that you have to read and interpret. This spec can be executed and we can see if there are any deviations, now and in the future. "It's the gift that keeps on giving," I added.

Being a little uncertain, I added, "Bud, as you know, we are new to this, but we think it makes sense. And anyway, with the one-month cycles, we can try this approach and revisit our decision each month."

Bud: "OK, we'll make continuous improvements." But then he added: "How do we know the tests are right?"

"We've been thinking about that one." I paused, and then continued: "We plan on pair programming helping us, but we think we should review the test cases. We want to make sure the module is doing the right thing and has a usable and well-engineered interface."

Bud: "OK, we review the tests to check that the interface is right, and also make sure the tests are testing the right stuff."

"Yes, that's the idea." We went on to further discuss and convince ourselves we were making a good decision. The key points we settled on are that the specific implementation details may not be as critical as having a good interface and the right behavior. Those things impact the larger architecture. I added: "Don't forget that if some implementation needs improvement, we have the tests backing us up to make sure that during refactoring the external behavior is preserved."

Bud: "OK, but our process requires code reviews, and they have helped us quite a bit. When do those happen? Does pair programming take their place?"

"We think so. That's one of these *Extreme* things that we are a little concerned about," I added. "Code reviews happen continuously with pair programming." I took a little time to describe how pair programming works. We take turns working with each other, maybe a few hours at a time. It's like a live code review, but could actually be better in some ways, and maybe worse in other ways. Two people are involved in making design decisions and naming the classes, functions, and variables in the code. The downside is if the pair gets shortsighted together.

Bud knew they were investing a lot in code reviews. There was plenty of preparation and meeting time. We discussed that pair programming can eliminate much of that overhead. He liked what he was hearing. We all thought that combining pair programming with reviewing test cases would result in better quality than today's document-driven process.

Bud: "We get the code review in real time to make sure our format standards are met. The test cases show what the code is supposed to do and confirm that it does it."

Bud was great. He knew the current process was slowing the teams down and believed that the common-sense XP practices could help accelerate our progress. He knew change was needed. He was excited about the potential for improved schedule predictability, improved quality, and improved fun at work. He said if he got just one of those and the other two did not decline, he would consider this XP project a success. Bud gave us the green light to "go Extreme." We also got a "get out of jail free" card with the process police. "I'll sign any process waivers you need," Bud said.

In hindsight, Bud made me see one thing that enables a great team to form: a manager with vision, bravery, and a willingness to support his team. Bud supported us, believed in us, and made it safe for us to go outside the established norms.

Getting Started

Early on, we had the option to grow the team, but we decided to wait a month until we had an iteration under our belt. This way, we started the learning process, building our experience. In an iteration or two, we could coach the new people with a lot less guesswork.

Johnny, now our *customer*, Alan, and I wrote all our use cases on note cards. We wanted them to be easy to manipulate, just like Kent and Ron taught me at Immersion. At Immersion, I learned about *user stories*. To me, it seemed that a user story and the name of a use case were virtually equivalent. We considered changing our practice from use cases to user stories, but Johnny warned me, "If we decide to use user stories, we are going to have to write a justification to deviate from our standard process." Johnny also was concerned about the informality of user stories, and added, "Besides, I think that a user story is too light on detail. We would never get that approved."

We decided to continue using use cases; after all, it was an accepted BBS practice. We figured that we were going to push the envelope in many other areas, and uses cases seemed to be the right vehicle for us. We decided to pick our battles carefully and save our "get out of jail free" card for when we really needed it.

Just before we were to begin our first iteration, Johnny and I worked out the detailed steps for the core use cases. The core use cases had the highest value and the most architectural impact. We were ready to start iterating.

Looking into the future just a little: after the first iteration, we started considering the XP practice of automated *acceptance tests*. Like Kent and Ron suggested at Immersion, we built an application-specific testing language. We tried to make it readable and not too programmer-ish; the goal being that a domain expert could read and write the tests without being a programmer. After a few iterations, it became clear to us that the information in the use cases and the information in the acceptance tests was a form of duplication. Duplication is one of the wastes and liabilities that XP tries to prevent.

Eventually, I built a case for not detailing out the use cases at all. Instead, we would write the acceptance tests before the iteration, providing the details that were in the use cases. Acceptance tests would be an executable specification! And we would replace the use-case elaboration effort Johnny had to shoulder with writing acceptance tests.

As it turned out, this was too extreme for BBS. We kept doing both use cases and acceptance tests because that seemed easier than bucking the system yet another time. I guess that's what Jerry Weinberg would call becoming a pickle. Put cucumbers in with the pickles, and what happens? "Cucumbers get more pickled than brine gets cucumbered." [3] XP got a little pickled, as did I.

Let's get back to getting our first iteration started. After estimating a few stories, I mean use cases, Johnny chose the first iteration. The initial use cases described core functionality, functionality that encompassed the most common operations the system would be expected to do thousands, if not millions, of times per day. Alan and I got to work. Ellen, a part-timer on the team, joined in and worked with us from time to time. She was a senior engineer winding down from her last project. She was ready to go Extreme with us. We agreed that all production code would be created using pair programming. It's good we had a third team member because with all the meetings that Alan got pulled into, it was good that I had Ellen to pair with when we could not keep Alan out of the meetings, and vice versa.

Our first iteration was a success. We delivered most of what we planned. Looking back, I see that this was quite an accomplishment. At Object Mentor, we came to know that first iteration as "iteration zero." Not just because we computer geeks like to start counting from zero, but because so many first iterations accomplish nothing. It was our first XP project. We did not know we were supposed to fail, so we delivered working core functionality instead.

This team did not fight each XP practice. As I later experienced as a coach, the teams desire to learn and try new things made the project a success. Sure, Ken Beck wrote the book, but it was our process.

We learned some of the ins and outs of test-first design and incremental development. Our manager, Fred, was thrilled with the output. "I used to get only a draft requirements spec after a month, but we've got working code!"

We had the base learning and initial code in place. It was time to ramp up the team.

Growing the Team

Now that Alan, Ellen, and I had a grasp on our technical practices, we added a couple of bright, new engineers, Paul and Alex. They were glad to be on the team learning OO design and XP, and contributing to a new product.

It was a good team; we worked well together. There was collaboration, cooperation, and excitement about our progress and learning. We pair-programmed, wrote CppUnit tests, refactored our design as we went, and created our own application-specific language to drive acceptance tests. We accomplished a lot.

Pressing the Envelope and the Process Police

The process police, lead by Marilee, were on our tails because of our lightweight documentation approach and deviation from the waterfall-style milestones process. Just having Bud's "get out of jail free" card gave us some distance. But we did have to deal with breaking from the norms quite regularly.

At our first review meeting, we had completed a small handful of use cases. The design was simple, so writing the documentation was easy. It took only part of a day. Consequently, there wasn't much documentation. We had two reviewers, Jim and Art. Consider them the informants of the process police. They were not used to such thin documentation packages. Hey, come on! It covers only one month's work.

The fact that we had Bud's approval to push the status quo made all the difference. Our design decisions must have been good enough, because we spent most of the time discussing process and how we could get away with such thin documentation.

We gave a little more the next review, but they still wanted more. But no one could really say why. So, we settled on continuing to evolve our thin architecture document, well-refactored code, and comprehensive unit and acceptance tests.

Learning

Paul and Alex were fairly new employees at BBS, with one or two years of experience, if I remember correctly. I got to spend the most time with them. The senior people kept getting pulled into meetings, so the three of us had plenty of time to work. Being the seasoned journeyman, it was like having two apprentices. We worked day to day, incrementally developing. Like I mentioned earlier, I was at BBS only every other week, on average. So on Fridays, we would plan the next week's work.

Paul and Alex were great. They always got everything done that we planned on doing. The code was well tested and it delivered the desired functionality. As their mentor, I reviewed their work when I returned the following Monday. They always got the code to work, but they usually put some code in the wrong place. What I was detecting was something that Martin Fowler calls "feature envy" [4].

Code problems now have names! Fowler and Beck did a fine job naming and describing a small catalog of "code smells." Feature envy was where one class was doing the job of another class. There were others: long method, large class, long parameter list, lazy class, and shotgun surgery, to name a few. Just having the name for some undesirable code quality helped us detect problems early and keep the code clean.

So, Alex and Paul would leave these small code problems around, but it was no big deal; Monday became refactoring day. We had the tests, so it was easy and low-risk to move the envious code to its proper home. It was a learning experience. I would never have known to call it *feature envy* before XP. Paul and Alex could have been defensive about their work, but the learning spirit avoided hurt feelings. They also taught me plenty during our pairing sessions.

After a few cycles of this, it became a game. Paul and Alex would get the work done, and start hunting for code smells. On Monday mornings, I would come in, get a coffee, and find them. Paul would say, "James, we got all the tests passing, but there are a few things you are not going to like." They were building skill in the first step to being successful refactorers! They had to find and identify code smells. They did not always know how to solve the smells, but they learned how to recognize the problems. Awareness is the first step toward change.

Pair programming really helped break down communication barriers. When you sit next to someone for a few hours you reveal your own strengths and weaknesses. It's a two-way street. With the right people and the right attitude, learning happens and trust grows. Our team atmosphere was such that it was safe to make mistakes and to learn.

Requirements Versus On-Site Customer

Johnny was an expert in the system. He was the designer and programmer on the original system years earlier. During my work on the project, his role was systems engineer. From his vast knowledge of the system, he wrote the requirements spec. We worked together to extract the names of the use cases implied by the requirements. Johnny would elaborate the requirements just in time for us to design and implement them. Johnny was always under pressure to deliver the next batch of use cases. Sometimes it took him longer to figure out the use cases than it took for us to implement them. That always upset him. It was working quite well. I really came to appreciate having an on-site customer.

One day, Johnny, Paul, and I had finished reviewing the use cases and went to start the development work. We worked out the impact of the new use case on the existing design. We used a high-tech tool known as a whiteboard. The system design was in our heads, so we extracted enough of the design, putting it on the whiteboard, and talked through the changes. Once we were happy with our direction, Paul and I went to Paul's cube to get started.

Within minutes of starting, we had a problem. We read the detailed use case again. There was an area of interpretation. We had just discussed it with Johnny a half hour before, but Paul said, "Johnny said we should retry the transaction under these conditions." I said, "No, in this case, we are supposed to log a message and continue. You're thinking about use case extension 4B; that's next week's work."

Of course, we discussed it (argued civilly about it) for 20 minutes. Then it dawned on me. We don't have to guess. We have an on-site customer. "Let's ask Johnny." I popped my head up over the cube walls. There was Johnny in his office with the door open 5 yards away. I'm surprised he did not hear us. Johnny settled the discussion in less than a minute. No emails were needed. No voice mails were left unanswered. No requirements review cycles were spun. We asked Johnny, he settled it, and we got back to work.

Some might say we needed a better spec; others would add that the use cases needed more detail. The documents would have been great to have, but I don't think that effort would have helped or have been cost-effective. The document would never be detailed enough and usable enough where we would not need clarifications from our customer. The only form of requirement that has all the details is code.

There were other occasions where we needed clarification on the requirements. Many times Johnny asked for time to go off and study the existing code base. The legacy application that we were redesigning a part of was our de facto requirements document. It was the only document detailed enough to answer some of our nitty-gritty requirements questions. If all those nitty-gritty requirements had made it into a document, that document would have been as detailed as the code and probably not too helpful.

Trouble in River City

Things were going great until one ominous Monday morning. Wally, our newest engineer, showed up unannounced and with an attitude. He had some history with Ellen, and right away he started with a rude form of humor, cutting deep into her. After I told him to cut it out, he insisted he was kidding, but you could see it hurt her. The knifelike kidding did not stop.

Big companies have this bad habit of treating people like parts in a machine. The first sign is referring to people as *resources*. Someone in management thought that Wally was a plug-replaceable programming unit. Through some magic of "resource availability" and project priority, we got Wally this fateful morning.

Wally was bright, but he had no idea what our team culture was. Our team was collaborative, and we were excited about taking on the process and technical challenge the project offered. All the team members identified with the team, and wanted to be part of it and to live by the standards and work ethic we had adopted. Wally did not get or want to get why we were writing tests. He did not get why we were not doing a big design first. He did not get the short iterations and, surprise: he was no suitable pair partner. His *humor* disrupted standup meetings and pair programming sessions.

I recognized right away that Wally was not going to work out. Fred wanted us to try to integrate him into the team. We tried, but sand does not go well with contact lens cleaner—it's too abrasive. In the end, Fred saw it our way and got him off our team. In the short time he was with us, our morale and output dropped.

Teams Are Made of People, Not Resources

There is an important lesson here. People are not plug-replaceable. One bad attitude on a team can bring the whole team down. A bad apple can be especially poisonous in a collaborative team. I suppose someone like Wally could hide in a cube and be given individual work. He might even be able to be quite successful. But that was not our team or how we chose to work. In my career, the times I most enjoy are collaborative times like these. The least enjoyable times were made painful by a bad attitude.

When Wally finally did ship out, we recovered. Work was fun, and lots got done.

Companies Make Their Own Troubles

One of the XP practices is to adopt an open workspace. The practice involves giving the team its own space to work. In the center is a big table. Project information is plastered on the walls. Computers are set up on the table so that it's easy to collaborate.

We did not have an open workspace and we discovered that working in cubes was not great. The monitors were in the corners and that made working together tough. We started talking about taking down some cube walls so that we could have a good space for communication and collaboration.

I asked Johnny about moving some walls. He said, "We can't do that; we have union people who configure all the furniture. We have to go through them." I had envisioned how Peter Gibbons, the frustrated programmer from the movie *Office Space*, unfastened his wall and it toppled, freeing him from his cube. That was not going to happen. It was time to visit Bud.

I said, "Bud, the cube walls are hurting our ability to communicate. We should take down a few cubes and make a space for the team."

"Save your energy for something else; that one is a non-starter. We have a policy for furniture reconfiguration," Bud sighed. "Once a wall or office is changed in an office area," he said as he gestured to a lattice of 50 or more cubes, "the whole area must be brought up to the current office specs."

I replied: "Yeah, so what does that mean? Can we have an open workspace area?"

Bud: "I am not sure of that detail, but if we change one wall," he answered, pointing to the private offices along the outside wall, "all those senior engineers and managers will lose their private offices and doors. You can't make this one happen." Bud consoled us that if it was our process, he could do something about it. "But moving a wall gets the union involved, and there is no flexibility there."

This battle was over before it started. We could have pouted and whined. Instead, we got back to work and lived within what was possible. Pickled again.

Future Projects

After the success of our first project, Fred wanted to get a few more teams to go *extreme*. This turned out to be more difficult than expected. First of all, Fred wanted to run each of the other teams the same way as our original team. "This is the way we do pilot projects," Fred told me. Of course, BBS has a process for trying new things, and we could not break that mold!

I warned him not to force each team into the exact same practices. I did not think it would work. Each team is unique and each team member has unique skills. There will be differences, and they won't own the process the way we did.

Well, we tried it anyway. The projects were successful, delivering two to three times more high-quality software per plug-replaceable-programmer days than the standard BBS development project. But as much as we tried, we could not get each team to follow the exact same practices. Of course, much of the core was the same, but there were many variations. Each team found its own way.

Some of the biggest obstacles I encountered were cultural. Their culture included pride in the processes they developed and followed. Those processes helped them do many great things. But they needed to get faster. Something had to change, but the culture resisted change. A year later, I spoke to a lead engineer in a nearby group and asked him whether his team was doing XP. He told me it was too much trouble. A team that wanted to go Extreme, as Bud called it, had to put together a 30-page process justification approved by the process police. Not many project teams volunteered to be the next XP project.

Collaboration Success Factors

We demonstrated that it is possible to improve on the status quo. We challenged the current practice and gained new understanding on how to get things done. It showed me again how important a good team is. A good team, working together, can get a lot more done than a group of individuals. How do we get a gelled and collaborative team?

In a blog by Alistair Cockburn [5], I found some interesting insight into team dynamics and collaboration. Alistair said, "People collaborate when they want to," and continued, "But what gets them to want to?" Through an informal study, he discovered that certain actions lead to an atmosphere of improved collaboration. Here is an abridged form of the top action categories:

- Lift others: recognize others.
- Increase safety: support others, challenge but adopt ideas.
- Make progress: success breeds success.
- Add energy: challenge, contribute.

In recalling this story, I can clearly see Alistair's action categories at work.

Bud's confidence in our team and willingness to give us the go-ahead really provided a huge lift to our team. Our learning and teaching styles lifted individuals. A counterexample was the assignment of Wally to the team. He did not lift people; he brought people down.

Bud's "get out of jail free" cards and approval of our proposed process changes gave us the safety to try new things. His realistic expectations added to this safety.

We had good people on the team. They were skilled but did not claim to know everything. The team's can-do attitude and continuous learning made work a joy. The early success gave confidence and provided a big boost in our journey. We found things that worked; we made our progress visible. Each day had new accomplishments that relied on the team's collaboration. We challenged each other and the organization. It was a memorable team experience. Even though I could not convert the pickles to cucumbers, we changed the flavor of the brine!

References

1. Beck, Kent. 1999. *Extreme Programming Explained*. Reading, MA: Addison-Wesley.

2. Grenning, James. 2002. "Extreme Programming and Embedded Software Development." Embedded Systems Conference (San Jose, CA).

3. Weinberg, Jerry. 1985. *The Secrets of Consulting*. New York, NY: Dorset House Publishing.

4. Fowler, Martin. 1999. *Refactoring*. Reading, MA: Addison-Wesley.

5. Cockburn, Alistair. 2008. "Collaboration: the dance of contribution"; *http://alistair. cockburn.us/Collaboration%3a+the+dance+of+contribution*.

CHAPTER SIXTEEN

Better Practices

an Interview with Steve McConnell

Steve McConnell has influenced both of us for as long as we've been working in software. He was one of the first people either of us read who was able to write about complex software engineering and quality topics in an easy-to-read, conversational tone. More than anyone else, Steve has been a huge influence on our own writing, both in our topics and in the way we choose to express ourselves. In some ways, it's Steve who showed us that it's possible to write a serious book that sounds like you're just talking to someone casually.

Scott Berkun was our other great influence, since if it weren't for him we wouldn't be writing for O'Reilly today. Scott invited Andrew to be a technical reviewer for his first (and excellent) book, *Making Things Happen*, which is where our relationship with O'Reilly started. (He was an enormously valuable reviewer for our own *Applied Software Project Management*.) So, when Scott offered to interview Steve for *Beautiful Teams*, we jumped at the chance to have these two people whose work we admire sit down and talk about teams.

Scott: So, the first thing I want to ask you is does the phrase "a beautiful team" mean anything to you? Is that a phrase you ever used or heard used before, and in relation to software products you've worked on or teams you've been on or managed?

Steve: I tend to be pretty literal, and so the idea of a beautiful team doesn't resonate all that well with me. When I hear "beautiful team" I assume people are talking about something different, and maybe they're talking about a high-performance team or a high-quality team or something like that.

Scott: Or a team of supermodels.

Steve: *(Laughter.)* Which is going to be hard to come by in software. So yeah, the term itself doesn't automatically make me think of anything in particular. I guess it makes me think of a team that's highly functional, has highly cooperative, collaborative, working relationships where everybody on the team feels like they are part of something elite, where the team works on something that ends up being successful.

I don't think it's good enough for the team to just feel like it's doing something special. I think whatever business context they're in it actually has to result in something that the business or the market agrees is special before I really say that that was a beautiful team.

Scott: Whenever I think of high-performance teams, beautiful teams, whatever adjectives you want to use, the core question, the first thing I think about, is whether we're talking about the means or the ends. Is it something that you can observe only while the team is working, or is it something you can evaluate only after they're done?

Steve: Well, for some reason, my mind's kind of going back to the notion of quality, and in particular, Deming's definition of quality, which is conformance to requirements. And if I'm trying to put some shape to the idea of a beautiful team, I naturally am thinking, "Well, OK, a beautiful team maybe is a team that conforms to requirements."

And the requirements can vary an awful lot from one context to another for a team. Some contexts you might really need a high degree of innovation. Another context, you might need a really high degree of operational efficiency. Other contexts, you might just need an extraordinary level of focus.

In many contexts, I think one of the implied requirements that get short-changed is sustainability, where a team does something great one time but they're too burnt out to do something great the next time. And I think whether that's good or bad just depends on what the organizational requirements are.

There certainly are cases where the organization needs to get a great product out in a short amount of time, and if the team is burnt out, that's just the cost of succeeding at that time, but there are other organizations that are in more of a sustaining mode, and in those organizations, I think, if they're burning out teams, then they're really jeopardizing their long-term viability.

Scott: What's the best software team that you ever worked on, and why?

Steve: One of the best teams I ever worked on wasn't even really a team. It was just more of a workgroup, and I say it wasn't a team because we weren't really all working toward any common objective. We all worked for the same company, but we were working on different projects for different clients.

But it was a very fun working environment. What made that a fun team—I don't know if it was a beautiful team—was that we were all young, we were all in the same life circumstance. We all had similar senses of humor. None of us had any real significant outside attachments.

So, we were able to spend time together outside of work as well as in work. And we all had a common enemy, namely our boss, and I think that we felt like we were getting an awful lot done. I mean, we were getting a lot done, we felt, in spite of our boss, maybe not because of him. And was that a team? I don't know. It was a cohesive workgroup, but we were really aiming at the same thing.

Scott: So, you weren't actually working on the same project at the same time?

Steve: We were all doing different projects for different clients, but we happened to all be in the same room. Our work overlapped a lot. We would switch off who was working for which client and who was working for which project, and so there was a pretty high degree of collaboration across the small projects that we were working on. So I don't know; it's hard to have a conversation like this without getting all nostalgic about the good old days.

Scott: Nostalgia's fine. I mean, that's part of the story here. There are very few people who will read this book who are aware at the moment that they are currently on the best team that they'll ever work on. We always think of the best as something in the past, and even if the team we're on right now is the best, we won't fully realize it until after we've moved on.

Steve: I agree, and that actually matches the experience I was just describing quite well. Much of the time I was in that circumstance I was longing for the group of people that I had hung out with in high school. It wasn't until I had been in that circumstance for maybe a year, where one day I woke up and realized, hey, you know, this is actually pretty cool, too.

And I'm not sure what it is about the way my mind or emotions work that would cause me to not pay as much attention to what I'm working on now as to what I was working on before, but that seemed to be the way it was in that case.

I worked on a graduate school project that was also interesting.

Scott: What was the goal of the project?

Steve: Well, one thing that made it a good team was that we were quite explicit about what the graduate school's goal was versus what our goal was. The graduate school's stated goal was to deliver some software to a customer. Our real goal was to graduate on time.

And we were always very clear within our team about the distinction between what the school thought the goal was versus what we, as team members, were very clear our goal was.

Scott: Interesting; the beautiful and subversive team.

Steve: We actively managed our project to try to achieve our real goal, which was to graduate on time, and the thing that was nice about that team was that we started out with most of us not knowing most of the other people on the team at the beginning of the year.

And we went through an unusually long period of just kind of feeling each other out to see who was good at what, who wanted to do what, who was sensitive about what, and so on.

At the time, I was impatient about it, but once the project was underway, I recognized it had been very healthy. There was enough flexibility from each person on the team that we were all willing to give where we needed.

And so everybody worked on stuff they thought was interesting, and didn't get over-committed. And as a result, I think the team was quite resilient. I mean, we had one guy whose wife was pregnant, and they actually lost the baby. We had another team member who went through a divorce. We had a couple team members who were traveling often, and even with some pretty significant trauma going on, the team held together fine. Everybody pitched in where needed.

All the more remarkable, I think, was that this wasn't our main job.

We had real jobs that were demanding our attention, too. So that definitely stands out in my mind as a team that functioned at a very high level as a team. The whole was greater than the sum of the parts in many ways.

Scott: This is an unfair question, because I'm going to ask you to give a number to something that's abstract, but I'm asking anyway. What percentage of teams do you think are high-performing teams?

Steve: Oh, I think true high-performing teams are fairly rare.

Scott: Is that 10%? 5? 1?

Steve: Based on the hundreds of companies we've worked with over the years, I would say it has to be less than 10%. I mean, some of it is by definition. When you say high-performance team, you are implicitly saying this is a team that stands out from an average-performing team. It becomes a question of how many teams do we see that really stand out as being markedly different from just the rank and file teams that we work with. And every once in a while we see a team that stands out in some way or other, but I'd say 10% or less.

Scott: OK, 10%. Do you think that there are unique attributes about those teams that are difficult to replicate, or is there some way to copy them? Let's say I run a company of 100 and have 10 teams within that 100. And I recognize what high-performing teams are and believe I have one. The question is: how can I help the other nine teams to be more like the high-performing team? Or is it impossible, since what makes a great team is tightly wrapped up in the unique relationships between the people involved?

Steve: Well, this may be controversial, but I don't think that there's anything mysterious about creating a high-performance team. And I realize that can be interpreted as maybe an overly confident statement, but I think I have a basis for saying that.

My company has received awards the last two years for being the best small company in Washington to work for. And we do that because of having really high staff morale, which has been created through the kinds of practices that I'm here to talk about.

If you have people who are selfish and they only want to do what they want to do, it will be very tough to establish a high-performance team. You may have an assemblage of individuals, but that's all you're going to have. So, there has to be goodwill and flexibility. Maybe not even a super high amount, but some.

If you have some goodwill and flexibility, then I think there's a kind of template that you can follow. First, the team leader needs to establish an elevating vision or goal, and I think that this is truly a leadership function, not just management. It goes beyond the management function. An awful lot of thought should go in on the part of the team leaders into what is the team's goal and what is it about it that is not just trying to trick the team into thinking they have a goal that's elevating or inspiring, but to come up with one that truly is.

A classic example is if you're out digging ditches, that's not very elevating or inspiring. But if you're digging ditches to protect your town that's about to be attacked by an enemy, well, that's more inspiring, even though it's the same activity. And so the leader's job, really, is to try to determine or frame the activity in such a way that people can understand what the value is.

So, some amount of goodwill, an inspiring, elevating vision or goal. The next step is lots and lots of communication in all directions—between the team members and the leader and between the leader and the team members. And I think facilitating communication within the team in all possible directions is good, too.

Next, I think it's useful to establish a sense of team identity, something I've seen Microsoft, in particular, do really, really well over the years with team members getting team T-shirts and going on team trips and getting team awards and so on, just to foster that sense of team identity. Whether it's mugs, posters, t-shirts, jackets, beach towels—it doesn't matter. If you do this, you get two benefits. One is team members feel appreciated, which is just good for morale, in general. Two, if you do it right, they can actually develop a sense of team identity, which is very positive, too.

And then there are group activities. I mentioned fostering informal interaction, but I would also focus on group bonding activities. I have seen teams where they joke about doing bonding activities, but they still enjoy them. And I think everybody knows what you're trying to do, but the fact is a lot of companies refuse to spend the minimal amount of money it takes to actually do these activities.

So, maybe to put it a different way: putting some work into trying to create the team is, in itself, helpful. So, those are a handful of things that come to mind.

In the book *Peopleware* (Dorset House), Tom DeMarco and Tim Lister explicitly say they don't know how to create a team, but they know how to kill one. They talk about teamicide. And I've seen all the same things they describe—ways to keep teams from forming, or if they do form, how to disband them quickly, and companies do that all the time. They'll take a team that works really well together, and then they'll disband it and lose all the benefits.

Scott: Why do you think that happens so often? I think you'd agree that teams are critical. That the reason why that exceptional work happens is because of the team structure around people that enables really good work to happen. One complaint I always had during my years at Microsoft was that the rewards structure is entirely individually based. And so the performance structure, the way you're actually given bonuses and raises and promotions, is based on your individual performance.

Yet there is this genuine interest in building team identity, which is true. There are team events, team clothing, which can create bonding effects. But I never worked on a team or saw a team that said if we make our dates, everyone gets a 2% bonus, as a team. My gripe, my persistent complaint there, was that the reward model never matched the rhetoric model.

There was always the rhetoric of teams, but then when it's performance review time, oh, you were the best programmer, so you get the stock grant or whatever. Why do you think there's always a disconnect between the two?

Steve: Well, there's not always a big disconnect. We've worked with a handful of companies that actually do rewards at the team level, and they don't break it down further than that. Whether that actually works, I think, is an open question.

But I've seen the same thing that you described. And you know what you're talking about is what Gerald Weinberg would describe as a lack of congruence.

Scott: Yes.

Steve: The words say one thing, the actions say something else. And I think in general I agree with the idea that the more congruent you can be in your behavior, the better things will go.

Scott: Here's another idea. If these high-performing teams are rare, do you believe there are other things you can do to create them? They're not impossible, but they are uncommon. So once you have a high-performing team, what most software companies do, once that project has been completed, is disband the team. Those resources now need to be distributed to other projects. But the alternative model says the high-performing team is really the most valuable asset you have, suggesting you want to preserve that team, find a way to keep them together on whatever the new project is. And you sacrifice domain knowledge or optimal resourcing to protect the team. Have you ever seen anyone who put the team first in their management philosophy, as opposed to last, which is generally what I've seen? And aside from whether you've seen it or not, do you think it's a ridiculous idea?

Steve: It's funny, because what I would say, contradictory to what I said a minute ago, is most companies value the domain expertise a lot. And one of the side effects of valuing the domain expertise so highly is they're reluctant to move people out of an area once a person has acquired experience in that area.

And so while they may reconfigure how people are working together, over time, once people start working in one area, we see the opposite problem more often. That is to say we see the problem of staff getting bored in an area and wanting new opportunities, and their company is reluctant to move them when they've made an investment in that particular area.

We see that more often than we see the problem of the company just scattering staff to the four corners, or to the four winds once a project is done, and losing all of that staff expertise. I guess part of what I'm thinking is that we don't necessarily see really high-performing teams working together all that often. I'd have to get a larger sample of high-performing teams before I could make any statements about what companies usually do with them.

Scott: All right. It's an unfair question. However, I think many people would agree, who've worked on good teams, that there's not enough protection for those teams. There's not enough reward for those teams to stay together and they're disbanded too often. I'm just thinking, what if they went to the other extreme: bet that an intact team that does well is the most important asset and makes things work around them.

Steve: I think DeMarco and Lister have talked about this. Someone proposed the idea of allowing intact teams to bid on work within the company. And so basically, the notion was the team will say, "If you leave us together, we'll commit to get this project done in four months." And some other team might say, "Well, we're committed to get it done in five months." The idea is you take a nominal estimate for a non-intact team, and if you can get a better deal from a team by keeping it intact, and the team says, hey, it's so important to us to stay together that we're willing to work extra to come up to speed in the area or whatnot, then that could be an attractive model for a company.

To my mind, the Achilles' heel in that argument is that the team can say whatever it wants, but that doesn't mean they're necessarily going to deliver.

Scott: And you're also creating an environment where those teams are competing with each other for projects.

Steve: It has the potential. So I mean, I'm purely going on analysis here, because I can't point to any examples where I've seen this actually done, but it seems like it would have the potential to lead to a sweatshop model over time, and ultimately, you can kind of imagine a scenario in which a team works together once, has a great experience, commits to a meat grinder project on their second project, and then voluntarily disbands after that because they would prefer not to sign up for another meat grinder project.

Scott: Do you think it's possible for a high-performing team or a great team to make horrible software, or for a horrible team to make great software?

Steve: Well, so much of that just comes back to how you define a great team and a poor team. I think that you can have teams where everybody on the team is highly motivated and they're having a great time, but they're completely out of touch with business reality, and the people on the team might feel that that was a great team but the business does not feel that way.

Scott: This is sort of like your graduate student project in a way, right? That you can have a team that for their own goals feels like they've done a great job, but for the goals of their boss or their company, they've failed.

Steve: In one of the first consulting engagements we had, we were brought in by the president of the company, who was a non-technical guy, and he said, "I acquired this company, and I've taken over active management of the company, and I've got a release date. My technical guys keep telling me, 'Yeah, yeah, we're gonna make the release date,' but I've lost all confidence in their ability. And frankly, I think these guys are just entranced by how cool the technology is and don't care whether we ever ship at all."

And my reaction at the time was here's another classic business guy who has no sensitivity to his staff. I'm sure his staff is working really hard and he's just not being sensitive to how hard they're working. So, we went in and conducted extensive interviews with the staff, and to a person, he was right. The stuff they were working on was special effects software for the movie industry. It was incredibly cool, and truly the staff didn't care whether they ever shipped anything or not. They had no sense of business urgency or of getting revenue-generating software out the door, and they were having an awesome time doing it. I think that is a great example of a case where they might have thought they were a great team, but the president clearly didn't think they were a great team, and that supposedly great team would eventually have run that company out of business.

Scott: So how about the opposite: can an underperforming team or horrible team—a team where everyone is unhappy and doesn't like each other—is it possible for them to make a great piece of software?

Steve: I think so. But it's because even a blind squirrel finds a nut every once in a while. Morale and motivation usually go the same direction, but not always. One of the distinctions that was made clearly to me a long time ago was the distinction between motivation and morale. A lot of times people can conflate those two ideas, but you can have high motivation with low morale. And you can have high morale with low or misguided motivation.

You can look at sports analogies for the ins and outs of what teams work and what teams don't. One of the things that you can find lots of examples of in sports teams is that you can have high-performing teams where the team members love each other, and every once in a while you see a high-performing team where the team members hate each other. It isn't common, but it does happen.

You can have high-performance teams where you've got really strong, standout individuals. You can have disastrous teams where you have some strong standout individuals. You can also have great teams where you've got no real standout individuals, but as a team, they work really, really well together.

And then you can have teams that are just plain mediocre. The individuals don't stand out and the team is mediocre. I think all those configurations can be found in software teams also.

Scott: So, you studied computer science, right?

Steve: Yes.

Scott: How much of the curriculum—the projects you did, the assignments you had— had anything to do with learning about teams, or experiencing teams?

Steve: Well, so my undergraduate degree is in philosophy, and I had my—

Scott: There's not much teamwork in philosophy.

Steve: *(Laughs.)*

Scott: Unfortunately.

Steve: There is probably more than there was in computer science.

Scott: Oh, boy.

Steve: I got a minor in computer science and I don't know that I had any multiperson assignments. When I went to graduate school, one of my explicit goals was to get more experience and to get better at working in teams. And one of the things that was attractive about Seattle U's Master in Software Engineering program was that many of the assignments were team assignments. It wasn't just the final-year project, but many of the assignments, especially the bigger assignments, throughout most of the classes were done in teams.

Scott: And was that useful in helping you to understand how teams work?

Steve: It was, and now that you mention it, I think it would have been helpful if the program had actually spent some time talking about how to succeed on team assignments versus as individuals, but we stumbled on some good insights anyway. But I think it would have been possible for other groups of students to not stumble on those insights.

Scott: Your experience fits the experience I had at Carnegie Mellon University. There were projects when you reached junior level, junior year, that were team-based, but by and large, everyone I knew in the class formed teams with people they were already friends with. And there was no guidance provided on even things as simple as the five most likely kinds of conflicts you're going to have. It would take a half hour, a short class discussion on the five most common kinds of conflict and how to resolve them. But there was nothing. And the reason why I asked the question is there is definitely a gap here between how people are taught. We are taught you are an individual programmer and your goal is to be a master at the craft of programming yourself, yet once in the workforce they are put into environments that are exclusively team-based.

Steve: I think there's always a gap between the craft and the things you care about in your craft versus what you get taught academically in school. I agree that the example you gave would have been very helpful in my context. Five things that you can do to have a smooth team project—that would have been really helpful. Five ways you can mess it up, five things you can do to help it go smoothly. That would have been helpful. And I don't think that's unique to software. I was involved in a legal dispute a few years ago, and I went in and the attorney for the other side made some decisions that I thought were just incredible blunders. And even though they benefited me, I thought it was not doing their clients much of a service. And so I talked to a friend of mine who had gone to Harvard Law School, and said, what do you think about this? Is this uncommon that my attorney would pay attention and the other party's attorney wouldn't? And my friend's response was surprising.

He said, "Well, one of the things I would do before I went before any judge or commissioner, if I hadn't been in front of that judge before, I would call people and find out what that judge was like, and I would learn everything I could about that judge. I would learn what their hot buttons are. I would learn how they tended to rule in the past. I would look up their opinions that they've written on similar issues. So that when I go into the courtroom, I know how to expect that judge to behave." And I said, "Did you learn any of that when you were at Harvard Law School?" And he just laughed and said, "No, we didn't talk about anything this practical."

And yet, that ends up, as far as I could tell, being somewhat decisive in whether you're going to win or lose. I think any academic program has to strike a balance between theory and practice, and there is some level where we're probably just getting a little bit too practical. It's more like a trade school than an education if you get overly practical.

At the same time, you'd like to think that there are labs or studios or something where you could actually get some practical experience and maybe what we're saying is there's more of a need for some kind of guided studios in software than we often find.

Scott: I'm convinced there's an obligation colleges have. If you are putting students in an environment where they're experiencing something for the first time, and we know this replicates an experience they will have the rest of their careers, there's an obligation to at least say, "If you're having problems on your team, go to this website, go read this book or come to this workshop." In my experience—and again, my experience was almost 15 years ago—there was nothing. There was not even a conversation about it. You could go to your TA (teaching assistant), but your TA was not there to listen to what they would see as your social problems. There was a machismo marine suck-it-up attitude about anything not related to code. It reinforced the idea that to be a good programmer was based exclusively on what you could convince a compiler to do, rather than what you could convince a person or team to do.

I admit it's a separate skill set. Being good at programming and good at teamwork are unrelated: you can be great at one and suck at the other. But when I think of beautiful teams, that's where I go. I ask people questions like, what was the first team you were on, how did you learn, how did you have any idea what a good team is like. They have to at least have an idea of how it is supposed to be, and some notions of what behavior are more likely to make the team work well. The fact that most CS graduates are highly ignorant of these things is a travesty. It's irresponsible, given the nature of how most professional programming is done.

OK. I feel better now. This does all lead to a more practical question. Do you think that certain software development methods promote greater teamwork than others?

Steve: Well, definitely. There are certain practices I think contribute to high-performing or effective teams.

In Scrum, for example, I think that communication you get with the daily standup meeting is helpful. There are an awful lot of teams where people do not see each other face to face every day. In addition, the sprint planning, which is typically done at the whole team level, is a chance for the team to get together in an in-depth way, in a task-focused way, approximately once a month. These activities can be used on essentially any kind of project, but they get done on Scrum more often because they're built into that particular approach.

I think there's a point of diminishing returns with in-person communication in programming. In Extreme Programming, there was a heavy emphasis on pair programming. We see very few companies that have retained any emphasis on pair programming. We see organizations that make selective use of pairing, but if anything, it's just more communication and more interaction than most programmers want.

One of the common developments we've seen is an almost universal presence of multisite teams. I think that there are various things you can do to make the best of teams that are distributed across different time zones, but that's exactly what it is. It's making the best of it. We almost never see a case where the multiple sites end up providing any kind of a net advantage. If it's done really, really well, then it's not that much of a net loss.

Scott: So, were any of the high-performing teams that you've seen virtual teams? And by virtual I mean that the majority of the team does not see each other face to face.

Steve: I can't think of any. And then the other question is what if the team is split across two or three different sites or two or three different time zones? And I think that you can do reasonably well with two sites. But once you get above two sites, it gets much more difficult to do well. You risk having extremely low efficiency and lots and lots of communication mistakes and tons of rework that arise from communication problems.

Scott: I asked you before about the best team experience that you had. What was the worst team experience you've ever had? I'm hoping for a horror story to balance out the good ones.

Steve: I think I've been lucky in my career. I can't think of any teams where I thought the team was a bad team. I can think of lots where I felt the team was not an exceptional team, but I can't think of any where I thought the whole team was just bad. I've had a few experiences where there were one or two individuals on a team that really detracted from my personal enjoyment from working on the team, but does that make it a bad team?

Well, maybe the interesting question is, can one really bad team member ruin a team? And in my experience, I would say yes. It depends how bad the person is, but if the person is obnoxious enough, then I think it can be pretty bad. I worked in a group earlier in my career, in which there was one team member who was extremely territorial about the team documentation.

And so if you went and got the design notebook that had the design for a particular section of code you were working on, even if you were scheduled to be working on that code for two weeks, she would come at lunchtime and grab the notebook off your desk and put it back in her area. *(Laughter.)* And so then you'd have to go ask her for it again.

She wasn't using it. She just wanted to be really sure that it didn't stay in your area longer than it needed to. And when you're working on something for a couple of weeks, and you have to go get the notebook 20 times when really you should have had to go get it only once, that sort of thing can get irritating. And of course, that's just the tip of the iceberg.

Scott: Well, here's a more specific situation. If you're on a team that's functioning OK, but there's one person that you believe is causing the most problems, they are creating the most turmoil, are the most difficult to work with, the most sensitive to criticism, but the challenge is they happen to be the most talented engineer you have on the team—what do you do?

Steve: Well, Gerald Weinberg, in his *Psychology of Computer Programming* (Dorset House) book, made the blanket statement that if you have a programmer that's indispensable, you should fire him.

And I read that first in 1989, and when I first read that, I thought that was too extreme. But as years have gone by, I have come to see the wisdom in that advice. In some organizations, firing may be too harsh. But in some way get them off the team, or at least get them off the critical path. And my reason for that is the longer you let them work in that mode, the bigger the risk becomes of them leaving.

It is just bad risk management to have a single point of failure on a project, and the lowest point that your risk is ever going to be with somebody like that is *today*. It doesn't get lower by waiting. It just gets higher. And so the sooner you can take some kind of action to bring that risk down, the better off you'll be.

I've also usually found that that person who seems indispensable usually isn't. Usually there's somebody who's quietly doing their job who's actually a much stronger contributor than the difficult, visible, uncooperative person. And I'm sure that there are exceptions, but I think the first-order approximation is that that person is probably not as good as you think they are. So number one, they represent a super-high risk to your project. Number two, they're probably not even that good.

Number three, they're a drain on everybody else on the team, and so the manager in me says, try to find some way to coach them to be better, and if that doesn't work, try to find a way to coach them out of the organization. The business owner in me says get rid of them as soon as you can, because they're just costing you.

There was an interesting insight in Larson and Lafasto's study on high-performance teams where they described a survey of team members and of managers, where managers said that they felt that one of their strengths was dealing with problem team members, whereas team members said they felt that one of their managers' greatest weaknesses tended to be dealing with problem team members too slowly.

I think what this says is it says that there's a pretty big gap in perception between how effective managers think they are in dealing with these issues and how effective they really are, and I think in general, when the manager finally takes action on a problem team member, the team's reaction is typically not, "Oh, that's so unfair." The team's reaction is typically "What took you so long?"

Scott: How can managers avoid falling into this gap between perception and reality?

Steve: Working at Construx for the last 12 and a half years, we have really explicit company values, and two of our values are openness and accountability, and we have pushed those principles a lot further than I have seen at any other company. And after living those values for the last 12 and a half years here, I simply do not understand how you can run a company or how you can run a team without having very strong support for both openness and accountability.

And the reason I mention those as a pair is I don't think you can have one without the other. You can't have real accountability if you don't have openness about who's doing what and how they're performing, and whether they're hitting their dates, and whether their quality level is good. If that's all sort of kept secret, then it's just too easy to not hold people accountable.

You have to throw it out in the open. Otherwise, it's too subject to gaming and you don't get input on whether you've really got the right information, all that kind of stuff. Likewise, if you have just the openness but you don't have the accountability, then people think you're incredibly inept, or that you're just asleep at the switch, because you're seeing that some people are doing well and some people keep missing their dates, and you're not doing anything about it. So, if you don't have accountability there, then the openness actually becomes a problem rather than an asset.

And just in terms of being able to manage workflow and address personnel issues in a timely way, and address all the zillions of little teamwork issues that come up, if you're constantly saying, well, should we expose this item or should we tell so-and-so about this, it just becomes this incredible drag on your efficiency, as you're spending half your time talking about who should know what and how are we going to protect so-and-so's feelings and that kind of thing.

Whereas if you just throw everything out on the table, it makes it really easy, and I know that's not the only possible way to run an effective organization, but for my personality, I just cannot imagine going through all the overhead of doing it any other way. I don't know how you can have an effective organization without really strong accountability. And I think most organizations give lip service to the accountability word, and don't have anything that would look to me like real accountability.

Scott: What you're saying is terrifying to most people, especially to people in power. Whoever's in charge has the greatest to fear in being open and accountable, because they have the largest number of people who can challenge their authority.

Very few people, in my experience, who seek out power, are simultaneously interested in being as open and as accountable to the people that they want power over. It's rare. It's not impossible. There have been managers and executives I've worked for that I feel embody the same thing you're talking about, but it's rare. I think it's probably rarer than high-performing teams.

Steve: Yeah, I just don't know how else you could do it. The interesting thing about a software organization is you're basically talking about directing how people are thinking. That is what we pay people to do. We pay them to think, and you cannot stand over somebody with a whip and tell them what to think.

You have to make them want to think the things that they're paid to think. And there's a very real sense in which you give over your soul as a programmer in ways that you don't give over your soul if you were operating a piece of heavy machinery or standing behind a counter, talking to people. Because when you're doing those operations, you can think whatever you want to.

Your mind is your own, but as a programmer, you are actually renting out space in your brain, and hopefully, a significant amount of space in your brain, to somebody else for commercial purposes. And so the idea that when you're paying people to think that you can somehow keep things a secret and deceive them into thinking what you want them to think, I just don't think that makes any sense. I think maybe you can get away with it in the short run, but I don't think you'll ever get away with it in the long run.

Scott: I agree with you, but I can't explain the practices, the actual behavior that I see at a lot of the companies that I visit and speak to. I agree with you in principle, yet I'm convinced the majority of work environments don't live up to anywhere near the standard that you're describing. And part of me wants to say that it has something to do with the size of an organization. That the more layers there are, the harder it is to maintain in the whole openness and accountability. You have pockets.

Steve: Yeah.

Scott: And a manager might say, "my unit, my team, my group" is open. There are often pockets within the group where there is openness and accountability. But across the company, across a division, there isn't. There's a tribalness to it. Beyond the size of a small tribe, it's extremely hard to maintain.

Steve: The bigger you get, the harder it is.

Scott: Right.

Steve: And we do have an asset of being small, and having said that, I have worked for several companies as small as or smaller than we are now that have been highly political. So, it's not a foregone conclusion that when you're small, you are automatically open.

Scott: OK, here's your last question. So let's say I am an individual contributor. I'm a programmer on a team that is not functioning well. It's a bad team. Your list of criteria for high-performing teams, we embody the opposite for all of them—not all of them; we are semifunctioning. We're a dysfunctional team, but it's not a good team, and before I decide to leave, what's my list of things I should be thinking about doing to try to help the team environment for the team that I'm on? Is there anything I can do?

Steve: Yeah, I think so. You can lead from the front as well as leading from the rear, and I think most of the things that I've described as being critical to team formation can be done by an individual contributor.

You can define an elevating vision. You can figure out why what you're doing matters and communicate that to the rest of your team. You can organize team activities, both at work or outside of work. The first team that I mentioned was, I think, very much a case of that, where the team formed in spite of the boss, rather than because of him, and, in fact, a big part of the team identity was that we all thought the boss was a greedy jerk.

And so I do think that it does require that somebody exercises some leadership, and by leadership, I mean they figure out where they want to go and then they try to lead other people to wherever that is. And where you want to go is part of it and how you want to get there is another part of it.

One of the things that you see in technical organizations is the distinction between the official management hierarchy and the unofficial expertise hierarchy. And a lot of times the unofficial expertise hierarchy affects day-to-day operations a lot more than the official management hierarchy. It's interesting, because there's some guy who doesn't show up on the org chart who is the guy who everybody goes to to get their question answered, or who everybody defers to when it comes down to key technical strategy questions. And most orgs eventually identify those guys and they show up somehow or other on some corner of the org chart, but that's a form of leadership where there's no budget attached.

There's no title necessarily attached to it, but that person is demonstrating some leadership, and I think that person is in a position to make the team experience better or worse for everybody else.

Scott: We've talked for over an hour now. What key idea do you think most people haven't heard about regarding teams?

Steve: We see far too seldom any effort or thought put into even trying to create teams. The kinds of practices that I described earlier might not be guaranteed to create a beautiful team, but not doing them is almost guaranteed to prevent a beautiful team. And I don't think companies have to spend a lot of money. I don't think they have to have a great deal of expertise in trying to make their teams work better together. I think even a little bit really can go a long way.

I would say that less than a third of the companies we work with have any sort of explicit morale budget or team event budget, and that's just shocking. The companies we work with that do have those budgets, the budgets aren't large. They're a few hundred or a couple thousand dollars a year, maybe, where you're looking at payroll cost for a team is probably a million dollars. I mean, for a small team, the payroll cost is a million dollars, and we're talking about a couple thousand dollars for team building? It's a tiny percentage, but very, very high leverage.

CHAPTER SEVENTEEN

Memories of TRW's Software Productivity Project

A Beautiful Team, Challenged to Change the Culture*

Barry Boehm and Maria H. Penedo

Background on the Software Productivity Project

IN THE EARLY 1980S, I (MARIA) WAS LOOKING FOR A JOB AFTER FINISHING MY DOCTORATE IN computer science at UCLA. I was full of enthusiasm for the field I was in and a little concerned about the kinds of jobs I would find. I wanted a place where I could follow my passion and make contributions. I had met Barry at one of the conferences where I presented some of my research results, and thus went to interview with him at TRW. During the interview, Barry described the environment around the company and told me about this new project he was starting whose objective was to revolutionize the way the company developed software.

Barry told me that he had conducted a software productivity study [1] in the company, which performed an economic analysis to determine whether a significant level of investment into software productivity aids would be justified. The factors that led to the analysis

---

* Editors' note: if you've worked on a software team in the past 20 years, you have been influenced by Barry Boehm. He was one of the first people to take a systematic approach to estimating and planning software projects. And many people (including us) believe that his pioneering Spiral Model is the direct predecessor to the modern idea of iterative development.

were driven by an overall corporate focus on industry and international competitiveness, but also included increased demand for software, limited supply of software engineers, rising software engineer support expectations, and reduced hardware costs—do they all sound familiar even today? This study led to the project that he wanted me to work on, the Software Productivity Project (SPP) [2,3]. He told me it would not be easy, since we would be trying to *change the culture*. Well, it seemed the perfect challenge for my first job in industry, so I accepted the offer and went to work on the project, together with a fantastic team of TRW veterans and newbies. We were going to attempt to change the current ways of developing software by providing a software development support environment for the aerospace part of the company.

Before it was acquired by Northrop Grumman, TRW was a conglomerate which included a large auto parts company (Thompson Products in Cleveland) and a large aerospace company (Ramo-Wooldridge in Los Angeles). It included a number of software-intensive product lines, including TRW Credit Data, and divisions producing point-of-sale systems, telecom switches, and industrial process control systems. In the mid-1980s, TRW was ranked number two in world software sales in the annual Datamation 100 lists, well behind IBM.

In the 1960s, TRW's aerospace sector pioneered in going from the code-and-fix approach to software development to the requirements-driven waterfall model, as described in Winston Royce's classic 1970 paper [4]. In the 1970s, TRW developed a set of waterfall-oriented software development policies, standards, review procedures, training courses, and requirements-driven software tools. These were a good match to TRW's engineering, science, and real-time control systems of the time, and the culture became strongly waterfall-oriented. By the late 1970s, though, TRW's applications became much more people-interactive, and the waterfall model didn't work well with requirements that were emerging as the project progressed.

At that time, the environment for projects included managers coordinating the people and activities, secretaries who typed the project's documents, meetings to plan and produce the project's activities and tasks, and system engineers and developers producing the designs and the systems. Only developers used software development tools and they had to work in batch processing mode or go to special bays with limited numbers of terminals for interactive development, using mainframe computers. Well, in the SPP we developed a new work environment where all members of the project (managers, system engineers, software developers, secretaries, and controllers) had individual offices with workstations, and communicated electronically via a local area network (LAN). Its architecture was based on the Unix operating system and it included commercial off-the-shelf (COTS) and locally developed tools in support of the full life cycle (e.g., requirements definition, traceability, design and development, forms management, and office automation tools). For this new project, we had to cope with significant technical and stakeholder-conflict risks, and with emergent requirements that could not be specified in advance; thus, we had a great opportunity to apply an early version of the risk-driven, concurrently engineered spiral model developed by Barry [5]. Those changes created culture-clash challenges, especially for the waterfall-oriented veterans and interactive-oriented newbies on the SPP itself. We can still recall heated meetings where TRW veterans would say things like, "But the policies don't allow you to prototype this early! Prototyping is coding before you have passed your critical design review!"

The project was very successful (with significant productivity gains—a factor of two or more, depending on reuse), but it was not easy to institutionalize the changes and convince the personnel. We also learned that productivity gains require an integrated program of initiatives in several areas and an ongoing and sustained effort. Even though this project happened long ago, the stories we tell in this chapter describe points that are still valid today, in spite of all the advancement in tools and technologies, both in planning and in executing productivity activities. *Changing cultures is difficult, and it is even harder to keep up with the fast pace of technology in large organizations.*

Making the Project a Reality

Getting Started: Being Ready with Options When Management Calls

Scene: Bob Williams' office, late 1979. Bob is the vice president/general manager of the 2,000-person Software and Information Systems Division, one of six divisions in the TRW Defense and Space Systems Group (DSSG). Barry is his chief engineer and advanced technology business area manager.

Bob: I've just come back from a DSSG General Managers off-site about improving productivity. Corporate in Cleveland is making a big push to get the auto parts division to be more competitive with the Japanese, and wants everybody in TRW to focus on improving their productivity. It looks like the company will put up money for productivity initiatives if there's a good business case for them. I think it's worth a try. Do you think you can put something together for us?

Barry: Definitely. This fits with a lot of improvements we've talked about but haven't found funding for. Our Constructive Cost Estimation Model (COCOMO) provides us with a good framework for a business case. It shows how much our productivity goes up or down as we change some of the cost drivers like tool support, turnaround time, reusing components, and people factors. This last driver would fit with your ideas about multiple career paths for our people. We could probably use some of our local area network technology to get everybody interactively working and communicating. And we could probably get added support from some of the Defense Department's Ada initiatives. Are they looking for a full-up proposal?

Bob: Well, if we were proposing to the government, that's what we would do. But since this is an internal company initiative, the sponsors want a clearer idea of their options, before they commit to spend a lot of money. So, we have a couple of months to put a white paper together. Why don't you do a part-time study with Ray Wolverton and a couple of the Ada guys and put a draft together? And, let's get everybody involved by doing a survey of what people think would best help them improve their productivity.

Barry: Great. We'll get right on it and give you a progress report in a couple of weeks.

Evaluating and Selecting Options: Applying the Spiral Model

The project's incremental versus total upfront commitment was the first opportunity to fully apply the spiral model of software development [4] to incrementally explore options, refine scope, and obtain higher levels of management and user buy-in at the end of each spiral cycle. After the first white-paper cycle ended with approval to proceed, the second cycle of the spiral involved visits to advanced technology centers such as Xerox PARC and IBM Santa Teresa, LAN and workstation architecture and market analysis, more detailed manager and developer needs surveys, demos, and prototypes. Three operational concept options were prepared at expenditure levels of $2K, $10K, and $50K per person, resulting in selection of the $10K/person alternative, although the Xerox PARC workstations were tempting.

Scene: Bob Williams's office, mid-1980.

Bob: Good news! We've been selected to develop our proposed Software Productivity System. You guys did a great job in the Round 1 white paper, which got us support to develop the operational concept options. With the help of the productivity data from IBM and AT&T's initiatives, they bought into our $10K-per-person option with the local area network, the lower-cost version of the IBM private offices, the Unix-based support system for not just programmers but everybody on the project, and the complementary management and career path initiatives. So, we're funded at $1 million per year to do this, but we'll need to pass a review based on a set of prototypes, specifications, and plans, and find an early-adopter project to work with you on building what they need. I think I can find a good pilot project. Do you have anything further you need to get started?

Barry: That's great! I'll need some help in working with the facilities people on reconfiguring and wiring the private office complex, and on letting the TRW LAN people know that we'll have to do a competitive analysis of their product's maturity and performance. Also, we'll need to hire some top technical people with extensive Unix experience. There are a couple of people at UCLA and UC Santa Barbara that I think will be very interested.

Bob: Fine. You can put together a presentation on this for the next staff meeting, and I'll identify people to work with you on those.

Getting Started: A Balanced Team, a Committed Pilot Project, and the Niceties of Unix

The productivity project was fortunate that its early-adopter partner project was a portion of a very large real-time application with an open-minded manager and many performers who, after some resistance, appreciated the ability to have dedicated interactive workstations and electronic communication. And the Software Productivity Project team had a good balance of experienced TRW software developers and new-hire Unix environment experts. The Unix key experts from UCSB (Art Pyster) and UCLA (Maria Penedo) were very good in coming up with creative and new ideas, engaging the team members, and showing how Unix capabilities could improve automation, support rapid prototyping/ development for both tools and target software, and shortcut some of the frequent difficulties projects would encounter. The pipe and filter and other features of Unix made it possible to respond regularly to those kinds of customer requests; we could put together simple solutions to problems and respond quickly to customer requests because of the flexibility of the Unix environment.

Scene: An early Unix demo to the partner project people, mid-1981.

Skeptical old-timer: All of that is very interesting, but can it do anything useful for the project, like create a specialized telephone directory?

Art: Sure. We'll just do a "grep" on the names in the project roster and the names in the company phonebook, "pipe" it to a new file…and there it is.

Project Stories

The Team

Yes, we formed a team, a beautiful team, with 20–25 performers. Some were experienced TRW veterans, but most members of the team were in their 20s (the GEN-Ys of today), a few fresh out of college including undergraduates, some with master's and PhD degrees, a good mix of male and female personnel, a few non-natives (from South America, Asia, and the Middle East), and a lot of enthusiasm. It did not take a long time for the team to gel, with many having lunch together most days (do people still do that these days?), others even becoming good social friends. And of course, we also had your typical "nerds" who produced tons and did not like socializing much (we will tell you more about that later). Keep in mind that most of the members were totally comfortable with the new technology since they were coming from universities that were pioneers in the Internet (like UCLA). The target community, however, represented much of the standard company personnel, used to the "old" ways.

The Challenge

Our challenge was to convince the typical project personnel to adopt a new style of development and collaboration as a team and use the new technologies we were bringing. The SPP was aiming at changing the culture, establishing LANs, and bringing all members of the project to communicate via email and to use automation for the development and non-development activities. (Remember: that was in the '80s…. On the other hand, things haven't changed; we can observe the same issues with established personnel in large corporations that hesitate at the introduction of the latest technologies like social networking, Wikis, and virtual worlds.) We were matched up with another project that was to use the new tools/processes that our team generated and we have many interesting stories about this matchup.

Educating the Boss

We had a wonderful boss, very friendly and open-minded—after all, he took the challenge to manage this "revolutionary" project. However, he had been in the company for more than 20 years and was very accustomed to the culture. We, the young, set out to change his habits. He was enthusiastic about most of the proposed tools to automate the life-cycle process, but we noticed that he never used email (none of the managers did at that time). So, one of us played a trick on him; she scheduled a meeting with him and, upon arriving in his office, she promptly said she was going to teach him how to use email. You should have seen his face; the look of astonishment. He was used to telling his staff what to do, not the other way around. To make the story short, he could not refuse, and after learning, he really became a part of the team by participating in the online discussions and conversations, understanding the issues, and sharing the news. By avoiding the change, he was missing on much of the project chemistry. Sometime later he confessed that he "couldn't type" and therefore was embarrassed of showing his shortcoming. But this staff member and her boss became very good coworkers and friends, as the project progressed due to his openness to change. Those were key ingredients toward the success of the project.

Can We Have a Private Office?

The status quo of projects was to have offices for managers and cubicles for project personnel; developers used a development bay where a pool of shared computer terminals were located. Among the "new" ideas being implemented was to give each project person a private office independent of his or her status, and access to computers via individually assigned terminals connected to a LAN. Good ideas. The LAN idea caught on like fire; they had access to the computers from their offices at any time. Unfortunately, economics didn't allow the "individual office for all" idea, not then or now. And we tried; at that time, we knew that when the crunch for spaces hit, that wouldn't hold. Thus, the proposal was made to make the individual offices just big enough according to company policies so as not to allow more than one person. That worked for the project, and folks really enjoyed their privacy while it lasted. Unfortunately, that was one of the change proposals that did not get migrated into the rest of the organization; we were not able to prove the value proposition or to fight the economic pressures.

As a side comment, there was a lot of jealousy from those outside the project because we had private offices, terminals on our desks, and so on. We had to find ways to not aggravate that jealousy by pointing out that we were the "guinea pigs" for something that might not work, and that if we were successful, they would eventually get what we had.

Choice in Technologies: The Importance of Trade Studies

The selection of technologies didn't run that smoothly all the time. And the choice of a commercial versus in-house bus interface unit for our LAN was an issue. There was an in-house product that was immature but being pushed by upper management, which is quite understandable since it was our own product. A careful trade and testing experiment was carried out, but there was a need for plenty of political outreach to convince management that there would be less risk if we went the commercial route. Does that sound familiar?

Converting the "Guinea Pig" Project

As we mentioned before, a project was assigned to use the new environment/tools being developed. The LAN idea was very welcomed, but the operating system (we were introducing Unix into a DEC VMS-oriented culture) and some of the new tools were not welcomed by all. To make it harder, the partner pilot project was using the VMS operating system, which already came with a few good automated tools. Also, several personnel in the assigned project complained that Unix on the VAX ran much slower than did the VMS operating system. That was true, but they missed the fact that that was a development environment and that overall productivity was improved because the people were the more valuable resource at that point (they still had the mindset that machine time was more important than people time). Over the course of the project, some became converts, some never did.

What was interesting, however, was to observe how sometimes something very small can have a huge effect on user acceptance. We have two examples to tell, both involving showing the value added in the new automation. The first one was about a secretary who typed most of the documents for the project and dealt with quite a few of the project personnel; many of the documents she typed had many equations for which she had to leave space to type, even if she used an automated word processor. That was both cumbersome and slow for her and her customers. Once she found out that Unix had the "eqn" tool that automated equations, she became a convert and was able to convert many more in her circle of work, including managers and system engineers, who were by then also being converted to use word processors. The other example was a savvy administrative assistant/ data manager, who figured out she could automate some of their forms needs using Unix "scripts" as well as providing configuration management with the new tools; her boss was so impressed with the results that he mandated all his staff to use the system/tools. She used her creativity to solve a problem and had an open-minded boss who also dared to mandate (sometimes that is the only way to get some people to change).

Standardization

Technology adoption has many facets, but we found that, even if the technology is good, sometimes adoption happens only by standardization or mandate. It happened for this project after the tools proved themselves, and it still happens today within the organization. Examples include standardizing on PCs, using Microsoft products, and other examples including SharePoint, eRoom, Livelink, and so on. Management made those decisions and the users just went along with it. On the other hand, where possible, standardizing on interfaces is better, particularly for custom software houses like TRW that have to deliver software and support tools that are compatible with different customers' environments.

Users Should Be Part of the Team

Technology acceptance is easier if users are invested in its success. If they are involved from the very beginning and participate in the requirements definition, analysis, and design processes, or if they participate in the review process during its development, they will feel ownership and are more likely to defend and less likely to criticize and/or reject the technology. This was a lesson we learned the hard way. Some team members expected to spend their time developing state-of-the-art research tools, and were somewhat disappointed when users said they wanted simple (for Unix) things like putting change bars in the margin to indicate where the next version of a document had been changed. But they felt a lot better when they saw the positive impact that their amenities had on the project users.

Making All Inclusive

Every project has its lone wolf, who, for reasons unknown to most of the team, appears to not want to be part of the team, lacking bedside manners. We had one of those, an extremely smart and talented person who had no patience for the "normal" people. He was extremely fast and constantly surprised us with his innovation. We remember that he got the Forms Management package to speed up performance by a factor of 4 or 5 because he just dug around into Unix until he found a few obscure interface calls. All that was said to him was that the package was running too slowly for many. He grumbled about how they should appreciate what they had, walked away, and came back two days later, all smiles and with a new version that ran four or five times faster…and we didn't even know that he was working on it.

But his aloofness turned out to be very difficult for many. It bothered the team; we wanted to bring him in, we felt it would really improve team collaboration since he was one of the most knowledgeable in the group. We don't know exactly what caused the change, but one of the members of the team, a smart lady with degrees in both music and computer science and with great wit, became his friend and broke through his glass shell. We think after that, he started trusting and actually enjoying some members of the team. Life in the project became so much better after that. The lesson here is that if people care and take their time, ways can be found to include everyone.

Training Managers, Not Your Usual Student

The project started a training program about the operating systems and its many tools. We then noticed that the managers were not coming to the class. Was it lack of time or hesitancy to show their lack of knowledge of the capabilities? We found out that the latter was true for many. As risk mitigation, we started separate classes for managers (which were not that different in content, maybe just a little more high-level) that made them feel more comfortable being within their peer group; once they were more familiar with the technology, they were more prone to use, recommend, or mandate it.

Tasting Our Own Cooking

A great lesson learned was to make the SPP use the tools that it was developing. That wasn't done at first, which led to the inability to understand some of the users' needs and which hurt the acceptance process. Once the project started to use the tools, such as the requirement traceability capability, a better understanding of the user community occurred and that led to many improvements to the tools themselves, which then led to better acceptance.

Is Email a Boost or a Hindrance?

What would we do without email these days? (Actually, the email of yesterday may equate to the Instant Messenger or social networks of today.) We institutionalized email across the projects with the new environment. But of course, that brought about issues, which still apply to date. Email has many benefits: it enables people to communicate or broadcast messages instantaneously to multiple recipients across a great distance, it allows one to leave messages when the recipient is not at his or her desk, and so on. However, it can also incur negative productivity in that, instead of picking up a phone to talk to another person to solve a problem or to discuss some ideas, one defaults automatically to writing an email message. That can waste time on both sides, taking longer for resolution of issues when a short phone call would satisfy. There were many frustrating moments of people not addressing issues posed in an email because they either didn't read their email carefully or they misunderstood the email.

Also, the problem of sending cryptic email can create hurt feelings and misunderstandings. Due to the non-interactive and non-personal nature of email, the "quality" of communication often suffers. Misunderstandings develop and sometimes are not clarified or remedied until significant cost in time and labor is incurred. A side effect of the SPP environment occurred when some people stopped stepping out of their private offices to talk to each other. They sent cryptic email messages rather than popping their head into their neighbor's office to ask a question or discuss an issue. That led to some team issues that had to be solved by an all-hands where management encouraged the team to "talk" to each other rather than defaulting to email as a means of communication.

Also, email is not efficient for assigning action items or important items. One should never assume that the email was read correctly on the other side, if read at all. And sometimes over-reliance on email multiplies the inefficiencies—for example, if "Reply All" is used indiscriminately or accidentally.

Becoming Word Processors

The same negative productivity applied to tools like word processors (e.g., LaTeX and others). Whereas being able to type their own documents made this task much faster and great for maintenance purposes, users complained that they ended up spending too much time on the aesthetics (getting the formatting just right), rather than the content of the documents. Because the document generation switched to being prepared by the engineers themselves (except for managers who had secretaries), the cost per hour was ultimately higher and the content suffered because more time was spent on debugging the document format. Of course, the advent of WYSIWYG word processors solved that problem; well, almost.

The Difficulties of Innovation, Timing, and Commercialization

Led by the projects' needs, a forms management system was created that included many of the fourth/fifth-generation DBMS capabilities of today; those did not exist at that time. It was an excellent system which could have been commercialized, had our company been in the commercial market. That did not happen since we were (and are) a large aerospace company who works mostly on contracts. Keep in mind, as mentioned before, that the team had many young, entrepreneurial, and very creative folks who thrived in the environment being brought about by this innovative project. As a result of the lack of interest in commercialization, a few of those folks left the company, some to try new endeavors, others to work on their own to build tools that could be commercialized.

The Iron Law of Software Maintenance

The Iron Law of Software Maintenance says that for every dollar you put into development, you will have to spend $2 to keep the product viable over its life cycle. The Software Productivity System began as a free service to projects, and it became too hard to switch to having projects pay for its maintenance. Thus, as time went by, the project had fewer and fewer resources to add new features. For example, the forms management system was the world's best system of its kind in 1982; by 1986, it was still the world's best 1982 system of its kind, but had become eclipsed by commercial forms management systems with broader financial and user bases.

Champions

Throughout this and many other projects, we identified the need for "champions," that is, people who will adopt and are passionate about the technology, both on the development and the user sides. We all know that sometimes passion can move mountains. And many times, without such champions, the momentum tends to die. However, the life of a "champion" is not always easy; it depends on the need for the technology, the economics, and the goals of the management in charge. Champions are at the heart of change; they need to be nurtured and rewarded.

The Challenges of the Rapid Change of Technology

The reason the project started in the first place was to bring new automated tools into the organization for the purpose of enhancing software engineering productivity. However, we found out that the pace of technology changed very rapidly and had to create means to keep looking toward the future in order to fulfill the goals of the project, to continuously bring in and deploy new technologies (that was before IT took such central places in enterprises). It wasn't (and still isn't) trivial. In parallel with the program, a future-looking activity evolved, and from workstations we moved into bitmap displays, computers at the desktop, and so forth. As this project moved on into other improvement activities, we found out that in-house technology or tools development within the organization was generally short-lived and invariably overtaken by commercial products. Each one of the efforts started with high hopes, made some progress, and caused changes and improvements, but organizations need to be constantly reinventing themselves. Many of those efforts served an excellent purpose in introducing the concepts into the consciousness of the user community and in illustrating the need and the benefits of the technologies, but many of them ultimately lost momentum due to the Iron Law of Software Maintenance and the relatively small user base across which to amortize changes to the custom in-house tools. That is the reason why, in today's world and age, most tools in use come from the commercial world, and those by themselves carry their own challenges of robustness, cost, adaptation to user needs, and evolution.

Learning and Assimilating Changes in User Behavior

Both the productivity project manager and the pilot user project manager commented on the ability of electronic communication to flatten traditional management hierarchies. An example comment was, "On my previous project, I was never sure what was happening two levels down, and I always felt that I was too late in responding to project problems. Now that I see a lot of the email traffic, I have more advance warning of problems coming up and a clearer picture of how each part of the project is doing." Also, the fact that all of the artifacts were electronically analyzable meant that we could better identify and fix bottlenecks in such processes as change management and defect closure. A key advantage of the private offices coupled with passionate people was the ability to achieve the state of productive flow emphasized in Tom DeMarco and Tim Lister's *Peopleware* [6]. As the project went along, a sort of door code emerged. A closed door meant, "I need to concentrate," and an open door meant "Come in and talk." This led to examples such as the following:

Scene: The productivity project office suite, 4:00 p.m.

Steve emerges, saying, "I'm hungry. Anyone ready for lunch?"

Sue responds, "Steve, it's four in the afternoon. You've been in there programming all day."

Steve: "Well, I guess it's true that time passes quickly when you're having fun."

Conclusion

The productivity project was fortunate to have a number of the features that distinguish successful from unsuccessful software projects: top management support, capable and enthusiastic team members, realistic budgets and schedules, concurrent requirements and solution development, and iterative development. However, many projects have had all of those factors, but have fallen short of having a *beautiful team* experience. In comparing the productivity project with some of these other projects, we would say that some of the key *beautiful team* enablers were:

- Identifying and involving all of the success-critical stakeholders
- A lot of work upfront on listening, exploring, and team building
- Developing a shared vision for the product and its results

- Identifying a manager with an open mind and good listening and team building skills

- Encouraging creative ideas from outside and within

- Paying attention and addressing the team's needs

- Respectfully redeploying incompatible performers

- Negotiating win-win resolutions of stakeholder conflicts

- Carefully monitoring progress and proactively addressing win-lose threats

References

1. Boehm, B., M. H. Penedo, et al. "A Software Development Environment for Improving Productivity." *Computer Magazine*, May 1984, pp. 30–44. Also in R. Selby (Ed.), *Software Engineering: Barry W. Boehm's Contributions to Software Development, Management, and Research*, IEEE Computer Society Press/Wiley Interscience, 2007, pp. 245–268.

2. Bitar, I., M. H. Penedo, et al. "Lessons Learned in Building the TRW Software Productivity System." *Proceedings of Spring CompCon*, San Francisco, February 1985.

3. Penedo, M. H. and E. D. Stuckle. "TRW's SEE Saga." *Proceedings of the International Workshop on Environments*, Chinon, France, in *Lecture Notes in Computer Science*, No. 467, Springer-Verlag, September 1989.

4. Royce, W. W. "Managing the Development of Large Software Systems: Concepts and Techniques." *Proceedings, WESCON*, August 1970.

5. Boehm, B. "A Spiral Model of Software Development and Enhancement." *Computer Magazine*, May 1988, pp. 61–72. Also in R. Selby (Ed.), *Software Engineering: Barry W. Boehm's Contributions to Software Development, Management, and Research*, IEEE Computer Society Press/Wiley Interscience, 2007, pp. 345–365.

6. DeMarco, T. and T. Lister. *Peopleware: Productive Projects and Teams*, Dorset House, 1987 (2nd Edition, 1999).

Acknowledgments

Our thanks to the contributors and reviewers of this chapter, including Christine Shu, Frank Belz, Art Pyster, and others who participated and made this a beautiful team. We would also like to dedicate the chapter to the memory of Don Stuckle, the productivity project manager and a truly beautiful person.

CHAPTER EIGHTEEN

Building Spaceships

an Interview with Peter Glück

Is there any geeky kid in the United States who didn't grow up wanting to be a part of NASA? We sure did. That's why we were excited when we got in touch with Peter Glück, who's been working on and running software teams for NASA's Jet Propulsion Laboratory (JPL) for more than 20 years. We wanted to know what it was like to work on a NASA team, and even more, what it was like to send his software into space, where it has to work and you can't just walk over and patch it.

Andrew: Tell us a little bit about your background, how you came to be at NASA, and the kinds of projects you've worked on.

Peter: I have a master's degree in aerospace engineering and a bachelor's in mathematics. I actually went on a field trip in fourth grade to the Jet Propulsion Laboratory here in Pasadena, and came home that day and said, "Mom, when I grow up, I want to work at JPL."

Andrew: So, you've wanted to work with NASA since you were a little kid.

Peter: Yeah, so I was kind of focused as a youngster. Actually, at one point, I wanted to join the Air Force and fly jets, but my vision precluded that.

I went to Cal State Northridge, and while I was there I had a class with a girl whose father worked here. She got me an interview, and I've been here for 22 years. That's how I got started at NASA.

Andrew: Tell us a little bit about the projects you've done, especially in terms of the kind of software. We want to talk about teams in general, and the kinds of teams that build software in particular, and teams that work well together.

Peter: Teams can be a challenge. Getting people together that have the right mix of skills and the right mix of personalities can sometimes be a challenge.

I worked on many flight missions here at JPL for my entire career, from Magellan back in the 1980s—which was a Venus radar mapper—to Mars Observer, which made it to within three days of Mars and then disappeared. I worked on the TOPEX/Poseidon mission which was an Earth-orbiting oceanographic satellite, and then on the ground systems for the Cassini mission.

Deep Space 1 was my first leadership role where I led the flight systems control software team doing the Deep Space 1 mission for three years.

I was on Phoenix for the last four and a half years. I was the project software systems engineer responsible for the overall development of both the flight and ground software for the entire mission. I have since moved on to the advanced optical systems program at JPL.

Andrew: It sounds like you've had your hands full with a lot of really big projects over the years.

Peter: Yeah, a lot of different stuff, including a couple I didn't mention.

Andrew: So, you said that getting teams together can be tough. What's tough about it? Specifically, what challenges have you seen in the past?

Peter: Well, there're two things. One is finding the right skill mix. You need people of different capabilities and different tastes, frankly. You can't have a team that's just a bunch of code hackers, because you need people who can also do the documentation and the systems engineering and can run the test program. You need people that can interface with the customer.

In any successful team, you're going to find that there's a variety of people; so one aspect is the technical skills of the team members.

The second aspect is the personalities. Some people are more withdrawn, some people are more outgoing, and to some extent you can't have it all skewed one way or the other. You need to find the right balance in personalities so that people can get along. You have too many people with strong personalities and they're going to lock horns.

On the other hand, if you have too many people who are meek, then you might not get the best ideas coming forward. You need to have a balance. And you need to have an environment where people feel safe in communicating their concerns and their ideas.

Jenny: Can you think of a time that stands out where in a team you worked on everything just meshed well, where you had an ideal mix of talent and personalities?

Peter: I guess I've been pretty fortunate that most of the teams that I've been a part of have been pretty good here; some better than others.

But in general, I guess I'd say the Deep Space 1 team was a pretty tight-knit team. Our software team, especially, was a very good team. I think we had a lot of good relationships. There were some members of the integration and test team that used to lock horns a bit, but overall I think that was a really good team.

The Phoenix team was also really a great team to be a part of. The software developers were all very sharp, mostly very willing to accommodate whatever the project needed.

Andrew: Do you think that locking horns is something that always tends to be good for a project, or is it something that can go either way?

Peter: I don't think it's always a terribly good thing, actually. I think that there needs to be a forum for discourse, but at the end of the day, you've got to have people that are willing to accept whatever the direction of the project is.

We have some very, very bright people here at JPL, much brighter than I am in many respects. I have seen those people just deadlock the entire team to the point where you can't get a solid direction one way or the other, because you've got these two or more individuals who simply won't budge from their righteousness, and that's counterproductive.

To some extent, you need some healthy skepticism, some healthy exchange of differing viewpoints. But at the end of the day, there needs to be one decision to go down a certain path and everybody needs to be able to accept that and contribute for the good of the project.

Andrew: It sounds like if there has to be one decision, that's a role for a team leader, somebody who has not just the authority, but maybe the respect of the team to get everybody to move past the disagreement and accept the decision.

Jenny: Do think that has an effect on the ability for the team to gel? When you're leading a team, is there anything in particular that you do?

Peter: That is an interesting question.

The job of a team leader is an awful lot of diplomacy, at least on Phoenix. The last four years I've had to deal with three different large institutions: the University of Arizona, the Lockheed Martin Space Systems Company in Denver, and the Jet Propulsion Laboratory.

I had developers each independently developing their own software at all three institutions. And not to mention all of the contractual agreements and the management chains of command and all that. Diplomacy is a skill that you have to have in that kind of environment.

In terms of getting the teams to gel together, one of the things that I like to do is provide some team-building activities. Now, when you're scattered across time zones like this, it's a little difficult. And it may sound silly, but one of the things that I used with some success is fantasy football.

I invited everybody to join a fantasy football league, and I got about a dozen people to join it, not so much in the software team, but across the different teams that we worked with. There were members of the operations team, members of the integration and test team, members of the software team, and members of the systems engineering team all involved in this activity, and it's just a little something that you can talk about, and kind of humanizes everybody.

Otherwise, you end up where you're always dealing on a professional level. I think it's easy to lose sight of the fact that there is a person back there who has feelings and does the same things that everybody does.

That's definitely one technique that I try to use.

The other thing that I do is I try to make myself available to anybody who has any questions or concerns. I have an open-door policy. Anyone can come and talk to me about anything that's concerning them at any time. If there's a serious problem, we'll try and get it resolved. Sometimes they just want to get something off their chests, and it doesn't go any further.

I think those are probably the two most important things in my toolbox.

Jenny: And what about in the way that you build software in general? I know that NASA is known for being pretty process-heavy. Do you want to talk about how the process itself impacts your team and how you feel, as somebody who's working on software that's scrutinized a lot?

Peter: Well, process-heavy, I don't know—it may very well be that the manned program is far more process-heavy than we are. Actually, to be honest, in the last 10 years, we've become fairly process-oriented at JPL. And frankly, our industry partners have been well ahead of us in that area, although I think we're beginning to gain parity with them.

But we do have certain rules we have to follow, and we have a coding standard like any good software house would. We have a design life cycle that we follow. We have some institutional standards and practices.

One of the things that you have to do as the leader of the team is to make sure, a) that everybody is aware of the standards and processes; b) that they're trained on how to interpret them and use them; and c) that they actually get used so there's an aspect of verification that goes with that.

But I haven't generally had problems with that in the past. People are generally pretty receptive, at least the ones that I've worked with, to accepting the limitations of being in this environment.

Jenny: Can you take a few minutes and describe the process that you guys use to build software?

Peter: Well, I have to be a little careful here because I do have to be conscious of ITAR restrictions.

Andrew: What is ITAR?

Peter: International Traffic in Arms Regulations. It's a federal law that prevents us from disclosing details about defense-related technologies; spacecraft are classified as a defense-related technology.

So, I can't give you any specifics, but we use a standard waterfall-type life cycle here. Sometimes it's iterative, so you'll have a series of builds that you'll establish and you'll build up functionality, moving towards your end goal of a fully functional system.

You have your requirements, your design, your integration phases. People are pretty familiar with that here. There have been new people that come in and become familiar with it very quickly.

Andrew: I'm kind of having a bit of an almost disappointing, "I put my pants on one leg at a time" moment. I always imagined that NASA had some incredible, intricate way of building things. But it sounds like you guys just do the same things that everybody else does, except you need to be a lot more careful and maybe rigorous about it. And I guess it's because your software has to work millions of miles away, where there's no you way you can get to it.

Peter: That's true.

Andrew: How do you cope with that?

Peter: A lot of testing. We do a lot of testing, and we have a lot of systems engineering that goes into it. We have an integrated team. Frequently, you have people who are members of both the systems engineering team for the spacecraft or the mission and also members of the software team.

Where it tends to come together is in the area of fault protection. You'll have a team of two or three or four fault protection engineers who are systems engineers that are looking at the entire system, what can go wrong with the system and what, if anything, you can do to correct it. They're also part of the software team and helping to write the specifications for the software that has to do that.

That's really where it all comes together. Fault protection and fault management is a big part of what makes our missions able to survive for extended periods of time without any direct interaction from the operators.

Andrew: I know that there are some people who are going to be reading this who aren't quite sure exactly how fault protection works, how testing works in general. Without breaching any federal laws, can you tell us a little bit about how you guys go about testing this kind of software?

Peter: Yes, I can give you the general overview. It's important to have—let's see, one, it's important to have visibility into what the software's doing, so you don't want to have any hidden commands, data, features.

Everything needs to be accessible so that you can actually see what's going on inside the software to the largest extent possible. Obviously, you're not going to publish every counter or every loop variable or every intermediate state. But to the extent that there's a hardware measurement available, you want that to be visible from the user's perspective.

The second thing is you need to have platforms that you can test on. In the last 10 years, what we do largely is a software-based simulator.

You have a software simulator that can run on a workstation and it basically models the environment that the spacecraft software operates in. You have models of the avionics systems. You have models of the vehicle dynamics; by that, I mean the rotational and translational motions of the vehicle. You have models of the planets and whatever external factors are of importance to your system.

Then, you can operate software in an environment that simulates what it's going to expect to see in operations. You run tests in that way and you confirm that the behavior is what you expect it to be, both nominal and off-nominal cases, so that you can identify places where fault protection is working correctly and maybe places where you need to beef it up in some way.

We also take advantage of hardware test beds. That's your highest-fidelity test bed. You actually build duplicate electronics and you put them in a hardware test bed, and then you command the software in a flight-like way. You observe how it behaves, and hopefully it behaves as you expected it to.

That's the best way to do it, but you're limited by the fact that hardware generally operates in real time. There are two problems there. One is the time it takes, and the other is that it costs a lot of money to get the extra set of hardware. So, you're really limited to only a couple of hardware test beds and can't do a whole lot on them. You rely on software test beds because they can generally run faster than real time, and you duplicate those on as many workstations as you can buy.

Andrew: First of all, thank you for the explanation; it's really interesting. It occurs to me that if you went to, say, your typical programming team building typical business applications at a company, and you expected them to put in that kind of testing, that level of quality engineering, you'd have a minor revolt on your hands.

Peter: Which is the reason why our missions to Mars cost $400 million, and your typical business application only costs $1 million to develop. You're looking at a difference in scale and in cost of failure.

The cost of failure if a business application doesn't work quite right is a few irate customers. It can be bad for the business if they really get it wrong, but chances are in the nominal cases it's going to work fine, and in the off-nominal cases they'll get some complaints and they can issue a patch.

If we get it wrong in the off-nominal cases, we may not get a second chance.

Andrew: I'm guessing that unlike a business team, the actual team members, even just the most junior programmers on the team, will have a more focused attitude towards quality, an appreciation of quality among the people who are actually building the software. And maybe even an appreciation of the project itself.

Peter: Yes, I think that people who work here generally feel privileged to be here. I know I certainly do. It's a unique place to work. There are certainly some disadvantages to being here, but there are an awful lot of advantages with respect to just the opportunity to work on the things that we work on.

I think that most people here are very conscientious and really trying to do the best they can. They understand that the things we're doing are difficult, and therefore require attention to detail.

And to the extent that we might miss something because we're all human, we have a robust test program that tries to shake out all of the major defects. We certainly aren't going to get every defect, but if we can get all the major ones, then we're doing well.

The goal is to make the spacecraft survivable so that nothing that we did during development is going to cause it to be lost. That's the main thing: to make the spacecraft robust so that it can protect itself until we can figure out what went wrong and correct it.

Andrew: I'm guessing that all of that attention to detail, that attention to quality, the awareness of the need to get it right, and just the general feeling of being privileged to work there, that's got to have a positive effect on teams and their ability to gel quickly and actually get moving in the same direction.

Jenny: I have another question. One of the things that some of the people we've been talking to have brought up as a problem in making teams gel is that a lot of times people will have divergent goals. They'll understand the project a little bit differently from their teammates.

Do you think that that's something that you've encountered in JPL, or is that something that pretty much everybody gets? We're sending a spacecraft to Mars, and that's the goal of the project.

Peter: Yeah, I think on the flight projects that I've worked on, people are pretty well oriented towards the goal and what the project's supposed to do.

On a day-to-day basis, you occasionally have someone who heads off in the wrong direction and does something that's not exactly what you expected, but generally the high-level goal is understood and everybody understands the seriousness of what can happen if we don't get it right the first time.

Andrew: Does that have an impact on how well people work together?

Peter: I think the things that probably affect the day-to-day operations of the team are, one, the natures of the personalities, as I mentioned earlier. And two, it's not all rainbows and roses here. While we are certainly honored and privileged to be here, along with that comes a lot of responsibility.

I tend to be more laid back, but I know people who really do stress out over the fact that what they're doing is so critical.

There are often long hours for many months. We have to hit planetary launch windows that are about three weeks long and only come around once every two years or so. You really don't have an option to slip a launch.

If you slip a launch, it costs tens, if not hundreds of millions of dollars, because you've got to then keep being staffed up for the time that you are waiting for the next window to come around. You've got equipment to store. You've got additional facilities to keep running. There are all kinds of costs involved. We really do try very, very hard to meet the launch window.

There's a lot of stress involved, too, and there have been many documented cases of personal problems occurring as a result of the work schedule that we sometimes have to adhere to.

Jenny: So, given that kind of stress, and given the fact that the team is under such strict, strict deadlines, do you find that that makes it more difficult for them to get along? Or do you think that that's something that brings them together?

Peter: I think that it depends on the person, and where you are in the mission timeline.

Now, frankly, the people that really can't handle the stress eventually drop off the team. They either leave for another job or they just get reassigned. There's really no room in this business for someone who can't do the work. To that extent, I think that there's a lot of cooperation and general agreement on how to do things.

As far as the teams go, the teams tend to work pretty well together. On the ones that I've been on, there hasn't been too much discord. Sometimes there are differences of opinion on how to proceed, but generally, once a direction is given, you proceed pretty well.

Where we have gotten into trouble, and this is my personal opinion, is reuse. There have been several attempts to produce reusable software architectures that can then be used to reduce costs and bring our overall project costs down and make our projects more affordable.

And frankly, I think that the lack of a solid deadline to hit on those has contributed to the fact that people tend to disagree more on which direction to go in, and they tend to not make as much progress on those particular projects.

Jenny: That's really interesting. A couple of the other people that we've interviewed for this book have also brought up the idea that reuse as a goal in and of itself can sometimes actually be an obstacle.

Peter: Yes, I think that's an accurate statement.

Jenny: The interesting thing to me is that reuse is something that people have really touted as a big goal of a lot of projects. I've worked with or heard of a lot of teams who designed entire software packages to make them reusable, especially over the last five or six years. That seemed to be happening industrywide.

In your experience, even with the kind of rigor you guys put in, do you run into trouble delivering software that's meant to have lots of layers of abstraction, where the goal is to be reusable?

Peter: I think we do. It's something we've been trying to do for 20 years. I'm not sure that we've still gotten it right, to be honest.

What tends to happen is that you get an initiative going to build some kind of reusable platform, and it's not just software. It also applies to the hardware and the avionics and various components that we use.

Then you get a bunch of smart people together, and those smart people tend to not really agree on what the best way to do things is, and so they debate and they talk about it and they make some progress. But eventually what happens is some project comes along that wants to use the system or needs to use the system, and suddenly the system becomes dedicated to that project.

That's when you start to get some progress in terms of getting to a real functional system, but it loses its reusability aspects because now the project owns the system, and doesn't want to spend project money to help the next project out. They need to spend their project money to get their project going and to make their project the best that it can be.

It's really a tough nut to crack. I haven't seen anybody at JPL successfully complete a reusable platform yet, to be honest.

Andrew: Do you think that maybe what happens is that once the common, well-understood goal of putting a spacecraft in orbit around a planet is gone, the goal becomes more amorphous? Do you think that the lack of that clear goal might be making the team less cohesive?

Peter: Yes. And you get into philosophical arguments, and once you descend into abstraction—you could think of it as ascending—but once you get into that abstract level of thinking, then it becomes much harder to justify a particular direction as the right one.

Whereas when you've got a concrete goal—"We've got to put this functionality together, and it has to be here by this date, or we're going to miss our launch window"—eventually people fall in line. They say, "OK, well, this isn't the way that I would really like to see it done, but it's going to work, and it's good enough."

What you lose is that "good enough" aspect when you're going for something reusable. It's natural to do that because you're trying to find the best solution and not just the good enough one. But that tends, as you said, to be an obstacle to actually accomplishing something.

Andrew: It sounds like you fall right into that locking-horns trap that you talked about before, except in this case, there's no longer the trump card of, "We have to get the mission out. Our launch window is at this date for these three weeks, and if we spend the next six months locking horns, we're going to miss our launch window." That trump card's gone and the situation just devolves into locked horns, into deadlock.

Peter: That's exactly right. One of the things that we also suffer from here at JPL, and it's sort of unique to the business we're in, is that every one of our missions is unique. I've yet to see two missions that are identical or even very similar.

I mean, even if you look at the Mars Pathfinder and the MER and the Mars Science Laboratory, which is currently in development, all three are Mars rovers. Yet each mission is very unique in the hardware that's onboard, in the methods used to arrive on Mars, and in the instrument packages that are onboard.

What you have is a situation where technology outpaces the life cycle that we're in. It takes three to five years to get a mission from concept to launch. Technology moves at roughly that same rate—even faster, actually, if you look at how quickly computers become obsolete.

We end up with a situation where even if we can agree to develop a certain platform using a certain language on a certain piece of hardware, by the time we get it ready for the first mission, technology has moved ahead. That makes the job even that much harder to actually come up with a standard, reusable platform.

We're still trying, and there are still some smart people thinking about it and trying to figure out what to do. And perhaps someday, with pluggable architectures, we'll finally come up with something that is more universal.

Jenny: A question hit me as you were talking about the testing team earlier. One of the big tenets of agile development that both Andrew and I really like a lot is the responsibility for quality that's put on developers, the fact that they're expected to unit-test their own code and that through continuous integration, it gets easier and easier to monitor changes that are made in code. So I wondered, do you guys use any of those techniques?

Peter: I am not aware of anybody using agile development here.

Jenny: Not agile development, per se, but more quality-related activities that are done by developers themselves.

Peter: Yes, we do expect our developers to unit-test their code before they deliver it for integration.

We tend not to do continuous integration. It's more along the lines of everybody gets together, we figure out the requirements and the design for the current cycle, we then produce those modules, unit-test them, and they come together at once.

Andrew: I have a question about integration testing. What you just said reminded me about when I first read about integration in general, back when I was first learning about software engineering.

If you guys didn't invent the term integration with respect to software, you certainly were some of the first to popularize it back in the '80s and early '90s. For those of us purely working on software, where every system in the project is a software system, integration just means integrating modules together. But I'm assuming that when you say integration, you're using the larger, original meaning of the word, where you're integrating the development of the software and the development hardware, too. And if you go back to that meaning, the term unit—as in "unit testing"—had a specific meaning, too. So, is that what you mean by "integration"? Integration of your software with a hardware component within the larger system that you're working on?

Peter: Yes. So, there are two levels of integration. We develop independent software modules, or units, which are pieces that are small enough that a single person or a couple of people can actually get their arms around them and adequately implement them and test them.

Then those come together in our software integration. We put those together, and those get linked together, and then we run some software integration tests on, say, one of our SoftSim test platforms that I mentioned earlier, or perhaps even on a hardware test bed if we have one available.

Then, once the software is integrated and ready to go, it's declared ready by the software manager, and it gets sent to the hardware test beds for certification. It then goes to the vehicle.

One of the phases of the mission is called ATLO—Assembly Test and Launch Operations. That's also known as Phase D, which is just a letter designation for that particular time in the project life cycle. That starts from the delivery of hardware to integration on what you could call the factory floor, although we attempt to do it in a clean room.

You start to get hardware together, and the hardware gets assembled. Once you have a sufficient critical mass of hardware assembled together, you can upload the software onto the avionics system, and then you can start to test it out and make sure that a) the software correctly commands the hardware, and b) the hardware works properly when you command it.

We test as much as we can on the ground. Typically, that runs about 9 to 12 months prior to delivery to the launch site. That's our ATLO phase. When a new software build is ready, it goes to the hardware test bed, and then it goes to ATLO for integration with the vehicle and the testing that occurs there, so we do have several levels of integration that occur.

Andrew: So, I guess for somebody who when they first heard you say, "We don't do continuous integration" wasn't sure why not, that should explain it. I think it's safe to say that if your integration process involves a clean room, it probably precludes automated integration.

Peter: True. We don't have automated integration. Now, I have seen systems at some of our industry partners where they will do, for example, a nightly build of everything that has been checked into the CM system for that day. The reason they do that is to make sure that the whole build system hasn't been upset or broken by some changes that were made.

Then there is a process where at some designated point or when everybody says thumbs up, we designate that that particular build is ready for integration and it all gets pushed forward in the process.

As I understand continuous integration, I think the way you're using it, anybody can basically say, "OK, my module's ready," and just stick it in and start to work with it. We really can't do that. It's really a much more coordinated effort.

Andrew: One of the things that people really like about continuous integration or an automated integration process is that it's very efficient, and it enforces a certain quality level. People don't have to spend a lot of time coordinating with each other to build the software, and they can trust that the software does have a certain level of quality because they can depend on the system to make sure that it builds cleanly, passes its unit tests, etc. Now, you can't do that level of automation, for the reasons you just outlined. But are there other ways that you make your process more efficient? And are there ways that you make sure that the quality of the code is always high?

Peter: What we will do is we sometimes run those cycles in parallel, so you'll have build two in integration, and build three will be in the design phase. You'll have people working on different aspects of the system in different phases of the life cycle at the same time.

Yes, we do expect people to deliver quality, unit-tested code. And not only that, it has to adhere to the coding standards. It has to be well commented. They have to deliver documentation associated with it that describes what it's supposed to do, what problem reports are addressed by the current revision, what problem reports are still outstanding. We keep track of all the defects that are found in integration and tests, and we have to address all of those before launch.

We also have a NASA facility called the Independent Verification and Validation Facility in Fairmont, West Virginia, that does independent audits of our processes and our code and helps us to locate any residual issues, defects, requirements, problems.

Jenny: Like an external SQA group?

Peter: Yes, exactly like an external SQA group. We have independent SQA here at JPL that is not reporting through the project management, but reports to our SQA organization. Then, on top of that, we have an outside, external SQA, which is provided by NASA.

Jenny: It sounds like it's very transparent. People write code. They write documentation around that code. They go through many levels of review by themselves and then with the team, right?

Peter: Yes.

Jenny: Which sounds really great in terms of finding defects as early in the process as possible. But one question that I have about that is I've noticed in my career that a lot of developers get really, really defensive when other people look at their code, or even when people have negative comments about code, or find defects, even. Do you feel like the culture where you are is different than that?

Peter: I guess I do. The developers that I've worked with have all been fairly responsive to having people review their code and point out places where there might be problems. In fact, we go through review, a code walkthrough, of every module that we put onto our spacecraft.

There's a certain amount of professional pride, of course. People don't like to see their code picked apart, but on the other hand, if there really is a problem, I've never known anybody that wasn't willing to accept the fact that there was a problem and then fix it. In fact, a lot of times they're really happy when you say, "You've got a concurrency defect here and you could have a potential deadlock," and they say, "Oh, yeah, I guess that's true. We'll have to fix that." Haven't had any real problems with that.

Jenny: And what about the relationship between the testers and the developers? Is there a good relationship there?

Peter: Generally, yes, I think there is. In some cases, it's the same person, really. We don't always have independent tests. We have independent review of test results. So, a developer will do their unit tests. We have a unit-test review, and then when we get to integration, it is frequently the same developer that is writing the tests for integration and sometimes even executing it.

But we always have a second set of eyes, someone from the systems engineering organization or someone from the subsystem organization that's responsible for that piece of equipment that the software's supposed to operate.

We always have someone from systems engineering look at the test and verify that the software looks like it's doing the right thing.

Andrew: I really can appreciate how careful you guys have to be with your quality, and the results speak for themselves in the missions you fly.

But I can just see some of our readers reading this, maybe somebody who's used to being a down-and-dirty developer who has to fire things off really rapidly, and often in not the most rigorous environment. I could see them getting an interoffice mail package from an IV&V group or an SQA group, opening it up, and groaning because it's yet another report from someone who I don't even know who's looked through all my code and come up with all these problems, these bugs I've introduced.

Peter: Well, it's no picnic. It really is something of a burden to have to deal with these things.

On Phoenix, there were over 800 technical issue memoranda that were generated by the NASA IV&V group. I had to review every one of those technical issue memoranda to ensure that there wasn't anything in there that was critical to the health of the spacecraft.

I think there were roughly half a dozen of those that were significant enough that we needed to fix them. There were many of them that we caught in our own internal reviews or testing. Then, there were some that were what you might categorize as nits where you say, "Yeah, you know, I understand what you're saying, but that's not really going to be a problem because we're either using it in a different way, our use precludes the problem from occurring, or it's just a minor point that, geez, stylistically it would look nice, but we're not worried about it."

Andrew: Do you think that if you asked everybody on the team to give their honest opinion, would the general consensus be that it was worth all of the effort or not worth all of the effort? Are these half a dozen defects things that would have actually crashed a spaceship into a moon?

Peter: None of them were things that we would call mission-critical. That is, we wouldn't have lost the mission if we had failed to fix those. But they would have been annoying. We might have lost a couple of days on the surface, maybe even a week, trying to figure out what happened and get it corrected.

It's good that we found them. Was it worth the effort? I guess I would say, yes, I think it was. It's like eating your vegetables. Sometimes you don't want to do it, but you have to because it's good for you in the long run.

Andrew: I think that's very interesting. If you were going to plot out software and quality practices on a scale of least onerous to most onerous, or from least overhead to most overhead, you guys would be at the very end of that scale. And you, the guy who actually has to review the memoranda, still feel it's worth it. It was worth the time and effort you and your team put in, simply based on how much better it made the final product.

Peter: I think so. If you look at Phoenix, we had very, very few problems in flight. I can't think of any major or even significant software issues that we had prior to landing.

And post-landing, we had one issue, a problem that was related to reuse of a telemetry system that was designed for an orbiter, where it wasn't expected that you would be rebooting it frequently.

On the surface, we shut down and wake up several times a day, and there was a counter that wasn't managed quite right. When that counter rolled over, we had a problem that caused the spacecraft to go into what we call safe mode, a protective mode where it basically shuts all of the science down and tries to maintain a good power environment, and communicate back to Earth and wait for instructions.

Fortunately, we were able to identify the cause of that problem rather quickly; within about 24 hours, we understood what happened and got it corrected within a few days.

But, really, as spacecraft go, missions that I've been involved in, this mission had the least amount of software problems that I can remember.

Jenny: Just one more kind of general question, Peter. Is there anything in particular that characterized the best team that you've worked on? Something that you want to drop out as a pearl of wisdom for readers?

Peter: I think that the best teams that I've worked on and worked with have really had a common goal. You're working to the same goal and you appreciate each other. You have a respect for everyone's skills, and even though somebody's the project leader and somebody else might be the chief architect, everybody really understands that contributions are being made all around.

It's funny; the most satisfying projects are not necessarily the ones that do the grandest things, but the ones where the team is cohesive and everybody is respected for their contributions.

CHAPTER NINETEEN

Succeeding with Requirements

A Drama in Three Acts

Karl E. Wiegers

The Setting

AUTUMN 1994. THE RESEARCH LABORATORIES OF A LARGE COMPANY, CONTOSO PHARMACEUTICALS (a real company, but not its real name).

The Cast

Paul
  Manager of the Health and Safety Department at Contoso Pharmaceuticals

Dana
  Manager of Contoso's chemical stockroom

Sarah
  One of the chemists who works in the Contoso Research Laboratories

Jonathan
  A member of the Purchasing Department

Janet
  A project manager and analyst from the research labs' IT department

Devon
> A programmer/analyst from the research labs' IT department

Karl
> An internal consultant for the Contoso Research Laboratories

Prologue: Paul Is in a Pickle

Paul is feeling some heat and he isn't happy. New government regulations require Contoso Pharmaceuticals to supply specific quarterly reports describing how it acquires, stores, uses, and disposes of chemicals. Hundreds of Contoso scientists have vast arrays of chemicals in their labs and thousands of additional containers are stored in the chemical stockroom. The only way Paul can comply with these reporting regulations is to have a robust Chemical Tracking System (CTS) that can monitor the location and status of every chemical container in the company.

Paul has been aware of this need for some time, but now it has become critical. Two previous teams from a corporate IT department had taken a stab at the Chemical Tracking System. Each team sat down with Paul to discuss his requirements, but neither team ever produced a written requirements specification and eventually both efforts were abandoned without delivering anything. Now Paul is under increasing pressure to deliver these reports for regulatory compliance and he has nothing to show for the previous efforts. Knowing how critically this application is needed, the research labs' IT department charters a new team to beat the project into submission.

Act I: Girding Our Loins

Wherein we develop a strategy and assemble the cast.

The initial goal of the project team is to develop a requirements specification that is sufficiently accurate and complete to allow the software development to begin. The decision to build the system in-house or to outsource part or all of the development is deferred to a later date. Our requirements analysis team consists of three people:

- Janet is an experienced developer and analyst who is taking on her first significant project management role. She will plan the project activities, track our progress, and serve as one of the requirements analysts. Although fairly young, Janet is mature, doesn't get rattled easily, and has a calm demeanor.

- Devon is a more junior developer. Bright and energetic, he's looking forward to building some analyst skills. If the CTS software is implemented in-house, Devon will be one of the developers.

- I'm Karl. I've worked at Contoso for 15 years as a research scientist, software developer, software manager, and quality engineer. Having pursued ways to improve requirements engineering for some time, I frequently serve as an internal consultant. I will work half-time in an analyst role on the CTS project.

Janet meets with Paul and explains that our team of analysts is going to do our best to meet his needs. But first, of course, we need to understand his requirements for the CTS. Paul's frustration is evident. "I gave your predecessors on the two previous teams my requirements," he says. "I don't have time to talk about requirements anymore. Build me a system!" This becomes our mantra for the project: "Build me a system!"

Facing a hostile, disillusioned, and somewhat intimidating lead customer, our challenge is clear. We need to overcome the distasteful legacy left by the preceding groups and somehow engage Paul and other customers in an effective and collaborative requirements development process. It looks like an uphill struggle.

It's not unusual for the requirements development process to be strained and maybe even adversarial. The participants sometimes forget that they are (or at least ought to be) on the same side, working toward the common goal of successfully delivering a useful product. Our first step is to begin forging a collaborative partnership with Paul. He needs to have confidence that this time will be different, that we really will move him toward his goal of meeting the regulatory requirements. And we IT people must concoct a plan for delivering on that expectation.

Expectation Management

Too often, teams begin working on a project without having discussed just how they will collaborate. The team members make assumptions about the activities involved and how the participants will interact with each other. People have different communication styles, various understandings of the problem, diverse perceptions about just what "requirements" are, and so on. Many groups don't explicitly agree upon how they will make the myriad decisions that arise in the course of every project. Neglecting these issues can lead to mismatched expectations, ineffective collaboration, and hard feelings. It's well worth taking some time at the outset to discuss how the team will operate.

Janet begins by promising Paul that this analyst team will use more effective approaches to understanding his requirements for this application. Furthermore, we'll document what we learn in a way that serves as a suitable foundation for the development work that will follow. Janet also sets expectations for what we need from Paul if this collaborative effort is to succeed. Notwithstanding his previous frustrating experiences, the fact is that we have to start over with the process of exploring requirements. So, we're going to need time from Paul and perhaps his colleagues so that we can understand just what kind of a system would meet his needs. Paul reluctantly agrees to play along.

Classy Users

Paul is not the only stakeholder for the system, and the members of the Health and Safety Department won't be its sole users. We apply the concept of *user classes* to identify other groups of users who will have largely different sets of needs. Members of different user classes might need different functions or features, have various educational or skill levels, work in different locations, or have other distinguishing characteristics.

Based on input from Paul and the analyst team's understanding of Contoso's research environment, we identify the following four major user classes:

Health and Safety Department staff
> Led by Paul, these people are responsible for generating the necessary government reports that describe how Contoso Pharmaceuticals handles its chemicals.

Chemists
> Contoso employs hundreds of chemists in the research labs, product development areas, and manufacturing. These chemists acquire new chemicals, store them in their labs, use them in experiments, and dispose of leftover chemicals that are no longer fit for use.

Chemical stockroom staff
> Although few in number, the people who work in this stockroom are central to the chemical tracking process. They place requests for chemicals to be purchased from vendors, stock and dispense thousands of chemical containers, manage supplies of new chemicals invented by the research scientists themselves, and dispose of outdated chemicals.

Purchasing Department staff
> Like the Health and Safety Department staff, these people will never touch a chemical. They serve as the interface between Contoso employees who need to buy chemicals and the vendors who supply the chemicals.

These user classes have certain needs in common. For example, both chemists and the chemical stockroom staff will place requests for new chemicals periodically and dispose of chemicals. However, each user class also has a distinct set of requirements for services they expect from the CTS.

Our next analysis challenge is to find the right individuals with whom to explore these needs. We must then consolidate those needs into a cohesive software requirements specification. This requirements exploration will include resolving requirement conflicts and setting priorities to reach the best balance of timely and cost-effective delivery of a useful— and usable—system.

Who Ya Gonna Call?

In 1986, my small development group at Contoso realized we had to learn how to interact more closely with our users so that we could properly meet their software needs. We conceived the project role of *product champion*, a key user representative who works closely with the requirements analyst. The product champion serves as the literal voice of the customer for a particular user class. Product champions typically are experienced users and subject matter experts in their domain.

Our next step on the CTS project, therefore, is to identify champions for the four user classes. My previous group had created a list of possible product champion activities that the CTS analysts can present to each candidate champion so that they understand what they're getting into. Negotiating the exact responsibilities that each champion is willing to accept is an important part of crafting that vital collaborative customer-development partnership.

As the key manager on the spot and a hands-on user of the future system, Paul is the obvious product champion for the Health and Safety Department. Our project manager and lead analyst, Janet, will work with Paul to define his requirements. A member of the Purchasing Department named Jonathan is willing to present requirements for the CTS from his community's perspective. Our second analyst, Devon, agrees to work with Jonathan on Purchasing's requirements. Dana manages the chemical stockroom. She's the natural product champion for that user class, although she'll obtain additional input from the members of her staff who perform the day-to-day operations. Janet will do double-duty to lead requirements elicitation with Dana.

Finding a product champion for the chemist group is more challenging. Dana tries to help. "Before I became the chemical stockroom manager, I was a laboratory chemist," she tells us. "Therefore, you don't need to talk to any other chemists about their requirements. I can tell you everything you need to know."

Although Dana is sincere and means well, she is wrong. And it's really hard to convince her that she's wrong. The first problem is that she's no longer a member of the chemist user class. She is literally the best person in the world to describe the needs of the chemical stockroom staff. She isn't, however, a practicing chemist anymore. I learned long ago that it is best to have actual members of the user class participate in requirements development, rather than using surrogates or former members of that user class. In some cases, particularly on commercial product development projects, you don't have direct access to appropriate user representatives, so you must use surrogates, such as product managers or marketing staff. That isn't a problem for this internal corporate project, where we can arrange to work with actual users.

The second concern we have with Dana's offer is that she has a narrow and parochial view of the chemists' requirements. She is also very adamant about her opinions on such matters, and she is prone to crying when discussions get a bit tense or her opinions are not immediately accepted. (Dana isn't all that much fun to work with.) Relying on Dana's strong opinions alone would not provide the rich understanding of chemist needs that we need to get. So, we politely decline Dana's offer and go searching for a suitable chemist representative.

We find one! A highly experienced and respected chemist named Sarah offers to serve as the product champion. Although she isn't terribly sophisticated when it comes to computers, Sarah recognizes the value that the Chemical Tracking System will provide to her and her colleagues. It's common that the people best suited as representatives for their user class are already overextended in their own work and are reluctant to commit much time to requirements-related activities. We really luck out with Sarah, though. She promises to create time in her busy schedule for requirements elicitation discussions and review sessions. Since my own educational background is in chemistry, I will be the analyst working with Sarah to understand the requirements that chemists have for CTS.

We realize it's just not realistic to expect even an experienced chemist like Sarah to know the full spectrum of requirements for all the chemists at Contoso. She needs some help. We establish a backup team of five additional chemists drawn from various departments across the company. They will have many requirements in common, but these representatives know about specific needs that pertain to the kinds of chemical work going on in their own areas.

We don't expect Sarah alone to produce the chemists' requirements, or even Sarah plus the backup team. Each of our product champions is responsible for interacting with other members of his or her user class to collect ideas and get feedback on proposals. The product champion also will resolve requirements conflicts that arise between individual members of the user class, which makes the analysts' lives much easier. So, in this representative engagement model, the primary pipelines through which requirements flow are from each product champion to the corresponding analyst, with extensive interactions behind the scenes between the champion and other users. The analyst will need to work with the various product champions to resolve requirements conflicts that arise between the user classes.

Now we're ready to roll. Table 19-1 shows the complete cast of key participants in the requirements elicitation activities we are about to launch. But exactly how should we proceed?

TABLE 19-1. Requirements elicitation participants for the Chemical Tracking System project

User class	Requirements analyst	Product champion	Backup team?
Health and Safety Department	Janet	Paul	No
Chemical stockroom staff	Janet	Dana	No
Chemists	Karl	Sarah	Yes (5)
Purchasing Department	Devon	Jonathan	No

Act II: Use Cases, Schmuse Cases

Wherein we try some requirements development techniques and see what happens.

Traditionally, requirements analysts have often opened an interview or workshop by asking users, "What do you want?" This is the least useful question you can ask when exploring requirements. A related nearly useless question is "What are your requirements?" People aren't sure just how to answer these vague questions, and often they yield random bits of important, but unorganized, information. We don't want to fall into that same trap on this project, so we need a better way to hunt the elusive and secretive requirement.

The Case for Use Cases

Several members of our IT groups routinely attend technical conferences on software development. The conference attendees then present summaries of the talks they heard at our weekly group meeting and we all contemplate how we might apply new techniques to our own projects. I recall that one of my colleagues recently attended a conference presentation on a requirements elicitation technique called *use cases*. This sounds like a potentially useful method so I borrow his copy of the presentation slides.

As I pore over his notes on the use case method, I get the feeling this just might work for the Chemical Tracking System. We don't have much information about use cases available, and none of us has any experience with them, but the concept surely makes sense. The main theme of the use case technique is to focus requirements discussions on what the *user* needs to accomplish with the system, rather than on system features and functions. That is, we will take a usage-centric approach instead of a product-centric approach. So, instead of asking our users "What do you want?" or even "What do you want the system to do?" we plan to ask them "What do you need to do with the system?" It's a small change in the question, but a profound shift in perspective. Each of these "things the user needs to do with the system" is a potential use case—literally, a case of usage.

Since we've never tried use cases before, we aren't sure how this is going to work and we face some learning curves. Use cases will also be unfamiliar to our product champions. We'll need to educate them about their role in this new approach and explain why we're trying this route rather than holding a more traditional requirements conversation.

Working in the Shop

Instead of conducting many individual interviews with user representatives, we decide to hold a series of facilitated requirements elicitation workshops. Each analyst will meet periodically with his or her user representatives to learn about the goals those users hope to accomplish with the help of the CTS. The analyst will serve as the facilitator and recorder for each workshop (although we soon learn that sometimes it's helpful to split these two roles). Having teams of users put their heads together saves the time often needed to resolve the conflicts that arise when individuals are interviewed sequentially. The synergy of a group discussion also generates new ideas and helps the participants reach a shared vision of the ultimate product.

We elect to hold workshops for the different user classes separately. We've subdivided our users into multiple user classes with largely different requirements, so it doesn't make sense to have them all participate in the same workshop sessions.

I lead the workshops with our chemist user representatives—the product champion, Sarah, and the five members of her backup team. In keeping with the spirit of having teams agree on how they're going to collaborate, we establish some ground rules for each workshop group. One of our ground rules is that the sessions will begin and end on time; we don't wait for people who straggle in late. Another rule is that the participants who show up to a workshop constitute a decision-making quorum. If someone is unable to attend, he's invited to submit his input beforehand or to send a delegate. He'll also be able to review the results of each workshop. But those who attend will make the necessary decisions so that we can move along expeditiously. Agreeing on these and other ground rules is an important part of defining an effective and efficient collaborative team experience.

Before we hold our first workshop, I invite the chemists to think of "things chemists would need to do with the CTS." Each of these "things to do" becomes a candidate use case that we will explore in the workshops. Some are big things (Request a Chemical); some are small (View a Stored Request). I schedule our first workshop, planning to start with what seem to be the most important use cases.

Not certain exactly how to proceed, I refer to the conference presentation notes I mentioned earlier. The speaker described a technique for using flip charts and sticky notes to capture the essential components of a use case. These components include:

- Use case name

- Name of the actor who will execute the use case (to a first approximation, an *actor* is a type of user)

- A brief description of the use case and its priority

- Preconditions that must be satisfied before the system can initiate the use case

- Postconditions that reflect the state of the universe at the successful completion of use case execution

- The normal flow, which describes the most typical set of interactions between an actor and the system that lead to a successful outcome

- Alternative flows, which describe other ways the actor might perform the use case (branching options and other variations)

- Exceptions, which are possible ways the use case might fail to complete execution successfully

I am pleased when this flip-chart approach appears to work well in our workshop. I'm further pleased when my chemists are receptive to the use case approach. Use cases are comfortable for many users because they relate directly to their business and how they anticipate using the system in that business. As we gain experience, I learn how to facilitate the workshops more effectively, to limit them to about two and a half hours in duration, and to time-box the discussion on each use case so that we don't get bogged down. I also learn that it's important to keep the use case discussion at the right level of abstraction. We avoid drilling down into excessive detail, such as user interface specifics, prematurely.

I am Lewis (or maybe Clark) in this use case exploration. We don't know anyone who has applied use cases before, so I do my best to blaze the trail. Once the chemists get into a rhythm and start making progress, the other analysts sit in on one of my workshops to observe our approach and determine how they want to adapt the method to their own user groups. Janet and Devon hold their own workshops in a similar style and also make good progress with their users. The three analysts work independently, but we share our experiences and insights so we can all learn to do a better job. All software team members can work more effectively if they learn by looking over the shoulders of their colleagues.

Use Cases Aren't Enough

As I examine the products from a use case workshop, I realize that we've done a good job of describing how users would interact with the CTS to achieve various goals. That is, the use cases are a good way to describe *user requirements*. However, they don't seem to provide all of the information a developer would need to implement those capabilities in the system. Also, the way information is packaged into small chunks in the use case isn't ideal for handing off to a developer. We conclude that use cases alone will not be a sufficient deliverable from our requirements elicitation activities.

To take it to the next level, we need to derive the associated *functional requirements* from each use case. As a former developer myself, I understand that developers don't implement use cases. Developers implement specific bits of system behavior—functional requirements—that, in the aggregate, allow a user to perform a use case. So, after each use case workshop, I analyze the information we collected and begin growing a software requirements specification (SRS). For each use case, I write a set of functional requirements that, if implemented, will enable a user to accomplish the goal described in the use case.

Some of this functionality is straightforward, particularly regarding the dialog of interactions between the user and the system. However, I can derive additional functionality that is not so evident from the use case description. For example, the use case preconditions give no clue as to what the system should do if a precondition is *not* satisfied. Some of the actions the system must perform aren't visible to the user, so the use case doesn't describe them. These functional specifications provide a richer description of expected system behavior than developers would get if we simply handed them a stack of use cases and said, "Call me when you're done."

Beyond Functionality

People seem to learn best from painful experience. I reflect back on a previous project for which we did an excellent job of specifying functionality but did not explicitly explore the users' quality expectations. As a consequence, the newly released system met serious resistance because of less-than-ideal trade-offs between system efficiency, usability, and other characteristics. Not wanting to repeat that unhappy experience, we elect to also discuss *quality attribute* requirements as part of specifying the CTS requirements.

Quality attributes describe not *what* the system does—that's the functionality—but rather *how well* it does the things that it does. Quality attributes include usability, portability, maintainability, installability, availability, performance, efficiency, robustness, and security. Users have implicit expectations for certain of these quality characteristics. Unfortunately, they often do not spontaneously share those expectations. Users have difficulty articulating their quality expectations in a way that provides helpful guidance for architects and developers.

Simply asking a user, "What are your robustness requirements?" isn't likely to yield useful information. So, we take a different approach. We think about what "robustness" might mean to our users, and then we write some questions to help the user think through some aspects of robustness. An example is, "What do you think the system should do if the network connection fails partway through submitting a new chemical order?" We do the same for other quality attributes that are likely to be important to the success of the system. We analysts ask our user teams to answer these questions and to rate the relative importance of each attribute from their perspective. Patterns emerge that help us determine which characteristics of the system are critical and which are less important. Those quality attribute requirements go into our SRS; they are every bit as important as the functionality descriptions when it comes to satisfying customers.

The Rules of the Game

During one elicitation workshop, the chemists discuss a use case called View a Stored Request. A member of the backup team says, "I don't want to see Sarah's chemical requests, and Sarah shouldn't be able to see my requests." The chemists agree that this is a good policy. We record it as being a *business rule*. Business rules can come from various sources:

- Corporate, organizational, or project policies, such as security policies for accessing information systems

- Laws and regulations, like those for generating reports on chemical handling and disposal

- Industry standards, such as file formats for importing and exporting chemical structures

- Computational algorithms, perhaps to determine price discounts on large orders purchased from a single vendor

Business rules are not in themselves software requirements. However, a rule can serve as the source of functionality that must be implemented so that the system complies with or enforces the policy. The rule that constrains who may view which orders implies the need for functionality to authenticate each user's identity before he can view a request. During the elicitation workshops, each user class identifies (or invents) numerous business rules. These rules help to establish a framework to make sure the software developers color inside the lines.

Test Before Coding? Are You Mad?

Requirements are all about describing what we're going to have when we're done. But as I'm working with the flip charts from one workshop, I have a revelation. The use case thought process appears to flow naturally into identifying tests we can use to tell whether we have in fact built what we intended to build. I had never heard about this connection between use cases and tests before, but it certainly makes sense to me.

So, I begin writing tests from the use case description, thinking about not how I might implement the use case, but rather how I might tell whether I had implemented it correctly. These are conceptual tests, free from implementation and user interface specifics.

In the process of writing these tests, I discover some errors in my use case. It's another "aha!" moment. Perhaps I can use these conceptual tests, developed early in the requirements process, to find errors long before any design or construction takes place!

I build on this theme. As I mentioned earlier, I had been deriving functional requirements from the use case description. In principle, if a developer implements that functionality, the user can perform the use case. Now I'm deriving tests from that same use case, using a different thought process. I compare those tests to my functional requirements, looking for two things:

- Is each of my functional requirements covered by a test?
- Could each of my tests be "executed" by firing off a particular series of functional requirements?

As I go through this analysis, I find missing, incorrect, and unnecessary requirements. Some of these indicate problems with the use case and some with my decomposition of the use case into functionality fragments. I also find missing, incorrect, and unnecessary tests. After I fix all of these problems, I have a lot more confidence that my requirements are correct.

I also realize it would be even better if different people, using entirely separate brains, were to derive the functional requirements and the tests from each use case. Disconnects between their results could indicate ambiguities and omissions in the use case that lead to different interpretations. I now know that I can begin testing a software application immediately after I've written its first requirement. This surely beats testing at the end and then spending a lot of time and money to fix the errors that originated in requirements.

I invite my product champion, Sarah, to review the tests I wrote for the chemists' use cases. She offers additional corrections and improvements. In a final workshop, all six chemist representatives walk through the tests to make sure we all share a common mental image of how the CTS would work. We all have different ideas of what the screens might look like, and we'll work through that when we get further into design. For now, though, we feel confident that we share the same expectations and understanding of what the CTS will do for the chemists.

Act III: Look Over My Shoulder

Wherein we do lots of peer reviews to find as many requirement errors as we can.

Simply documenting the requirements an analyst hears during interviews or workshops isn't sufficient to give confidence that the requirements are correct. There are so many opportunities for miscommunications and misunderstandings that validation is an essential step in the requirements development process. *Peer reviews* constitute one of the most powerful mechanisms for finding errors in requirements. During a peer review, someone other than the author of a work product examines that work product for possible defects and improvement opportunities.

Peer reviews are a type of static testing, a way to filter out requirement problems before writing the first line of code. Reviews provide a way for users to confirm that their input has been interpreted and recorded properly. They also provide a way to detect ambiguous requirements, which helps all stakeholders reach a common understanding of what the requirements are trying to say. If I could perform only one quality practice on a software project, that practice would be formal peer review (also called *inspection*) of all requirements information. Given this appreciation of the power of peer reviews, we build them into our requirements activities in two ways, informally and formally.

The Casual Style

Following each use case elicitation workshop, the analyst supplies the documents he or she creates to the workshop participants. Such documents include use cases, portions of a growing SRS, graphical analysis models, data definitions, and other knowledge acquired during the workshop. The workshop participants then examine these materials informally on their own, looking for omissions, errors, misinterpretations, and any other issues.

And, boy, do we find a lot of problems this way! Sometimes, the analyst misunderstood something or put his own twist of interpretation on the requirements, which the users catch and correct. In other cases, a user realizes we overlooked an alternative flow for a use case. Or perhaps he concludes that an error condition should be handled in some different way than we originally envisioned. Sometimes the act of reviewing the requirements triggers an idea for some additional functionality that users would find helpful. These individual, incremental, informal, and inexpensive reviews greatly improve the quality of our growing body of requirements information. The types of problems we find also give us insights into how to improve our future requirements elicitation and specification activities. In addition, the reviews provide clear evidence to Paul and the other project stakeholders that we are making real progress on understanding and recording their requirements for the CTS.

The analysts on the team try different review approaches. I am holding workshops once per week with my chemists. Within two days following each workshop I deliver my write-up of the workshop outputs to the product champion and members of the backup team. Reviewing these materials helps anyone who missed a workshop get caught up. My users do a great job of finding errors, which they share with me at the beginning of the next workshop.

Our least experienced analyst, Devon, takes a different tack. He's holding daily workshops with his users, so he must quickly write up the workshop information and get it to the representatives to examine before they meet again the next day. This puts a lot of time pressure on the participants. More significantly, Devon reports that his users aren't finding many problems. Unfortunately, the problems are there; the reviewers just aren't catching many of them.

The insight here is that when you review a document shortly after thinking intensely about it (either while creating it as an author, or while contributing to it as a workshop participant), you don't really review the document—you mentally recite it. You're less likely to find problems than if you get some mental "settling time" before revisiting it. In contrast, when you come back to a document after a day or two, during which your short-term memory has faded, you look at it with a fresh perspective. You're more likely to spot disconnects, omissions, and other problems. Perhaps you've been mulling over the matter in the back of your brain for the past couple of days and you have some ideas for how to improve on the original work. Ever since I had this realization, I've always tried to set my own writing aside for at least 24 hours before I review it myself. This helps me look at it with a sharper eye than if I review it immediately after writing.

The Formal Style

The type of individual, informal peer review I described in the preceding section is called a *passaround*. Our passarounds yield many improvements, but they aren't a substitute for the more rigorous type of team peer review, called an *inspection*. In an inspection, several participants examine the work product on their own and then pool their observations and questions in a meeting. The interactions that take place during the inspection meeting often result in discovering problems that no inspectors found during their individual preparation.

For requirements specifications, inspections provide another advantage: the ability to catch ambiguities. An ambiguous requirement is one that can be interpreted in multiple ways by different readers (or sometimes even by the same reader). Suppose each inspector reads an ambiguous requirement on his own during a passaround review. The requirement makes sense to each of them, but it means something different to each of them. Each reviewer will say, "This is fine," and the ambiguity goes undetected. During an inspection, though, one member of the team called the *reader* describes in his own words what he thinks each requirement means. The other inspectors can compare the reader's explanation against their own understanding. Sometimes this reveals a difference of interpretation—an ambiguity—that could cause big problems if not caught until much later.

Given these powerful benefits, we decide to inspect our compiled SRS. Janet takes responsibility for editing together the partial requirements specifications and associated materials that the three analysts have developed. We end up with a 50-page SRS, with about another fifty pages of back matter, including analysis models, definitions, and other supporting information.

We invite our four product champions, our three analysts, and one additional project stakeholder to participate in the inspection. Eight is a fairly large inspection team. I have performed inspections for several years, so I serve as the moderator, which helps keep us on track. Devon serves as the recorder, logging the issues as they come up in the discussion. We realize that we can't possibly cover this volume of material in a single session, at least not if we're serious about scrutinizing it closely for problems. So we schedule three inspection meetings on a Monday, Wednesday, and Friday in the same week, with a maximum duration of two and a half hours per meeting (this is still a fairly rapid inspection rate). Marathon review meetings are useless because after a couple of hours, tired eyes contribute little additional insight.

Our inspection is a success, at least if one measures success by the number of errors detected. Every error we fix now is one we won't have to fix later on at considerably greater cost and aggravation. Devon keeps running out of the room for more blank copies of the inspection issues log. It's a bit discouraging to find so many defects because we've all worked hard on the requirements. But we also realize that each problem found at this stage is a "good catch."

The Outcome

Our inspection identifies no fewer than 223 defects and issues. Most are minor, but some would have had a major impact on the project had we not found them at this early stage. Finding so many errors makes us glad we took the time to look. It's clear that the cost of performing the inspection, although not trivial, greatly outweighs the potential loss had those defects lingered into the final requirements we will present to developers and testers.

Following the inspection meetings we correct the many errors the inspectors found. Paul and the other product champions agree that the revised requirements documents accurately state their requirements for the Chemical Tracking System, so far as those requirements are known today. Next we define a *baseline* for our SRS. A baseline doesn't mean that the specification is frozen or that changes can't be made in the future. The reality is that requirements *will* change, for many reasons. Customers think of things they forgot, analysts get bright ideas for useful new functionality, we might spot more requirement errors during design and coding, and the business itself can change during the development period. But our baseline serves as an agreed-upon foundation for the subsequent project work. Even though we acknowledge that the requirements are not perfect, achieving this baseline milestone gives all the participants a good feeling that we have accomplished what we set out to do on this important project. The requirements are "good enough" for development of the Chemical Tracking System to continue.

Epilogue: Let's Eat!

As time goes on during requirements elicitation, we detect a thawing of the ice we encountered in our early conversations with Paul. He sees that we're making real progress in understanding both his needs and the needs of other CTS stakeholders. Paul observes that the new techniques we're using do a better job of eliciting the right requirements than did the approach the earlier teams had taken. The result is that Paul believes the final set of requirements really will, if properly implemented, let him comply with the government reporting mandates, as well as providing many other valuable services for a wide variety of users.

We also experience a clear sign of a culture change as a result of our team approach to requirements on the CTS. Shortly after baselining the SRS, Paul throws a lunch bash for the analyst team, the product champions, and other key project participants. It's quite a spread. A good time is had by all and nobody goes home hungry. Paul's mood is much improved compared to that of four months earlier.

Coda: Then What Happened?

Since I became an independent consultant in 1998, I have primarily worked with clients on an intervention basis. I provide training, coaching, or assistance with particular problems a client is experiencing. I often do not get to see how the project turns out as a result of my involvement. That was true with the CTS project—at first.

Following our successful requirements development effort, I moved on to other activities and shortly thereafter moved to an entirely separate division within Contoso Pharmaceuticals. Two years later, I left Contoso and started my own software training and consulting company. I use several examples from the Chemical Tracking System in my training courses to illustrate techniques and insights for requirements development.

In 1999, I was presenting a requirements course at a client site. When I shared some of our experiences on CTS, one student in the class said, "Hey, I recognize that project!" This student happened to work in marketing. His previous employer was the company that Contoso approached for outsourcing the implementation of part of the CTS. Intrigued by this coincidence, I asked him how the implementation went and what the developers at his former company thought of the CTS requirements. I was relieved when he said that the project went well and that the requirements were a major factor in that success.

Despite its rocky beginning, the Chemical Tracking System turned out to be an illuminating case study. We learned how to selectively and thoughtfully apply several new requirements development methods. We found ways to effectively engage diverse customer representatives in the process. We enjoyed some cultural benefits through our collaborative approach, as Paul and the other lead customers realized that it was indeed possible—nay, essential—to work closely with IT representatives to make sure that the right product comes out the other end of the process. Best of all, this application is still in use at Contoso Pharmaceuticals, 13 years after the requirements development experience described here.

Useful References

1. Ambler, Scott. 1995. "Reduce Development Costs with Use-Case Scenario Testing." *Software Development* 3(7):53–61.

2. Collard, Ross. 1999. "Test Design." *Software Testing and Quality Engineering* 1(4):30–37.

3. Gottesdiener, Ellen. 2002. *Requirements by Collaboration: Workshops for Defining Needs*. Boston: Addison-Wesley.

4. Kulak, Daryl, and Eamonn Guiney. 2004. *Use Cases: Requirements in Context, Second Edition*. Boston: Addison-Wesley.

5. Wiegers, Karl E. 1996. *Creating a Software Engineering Culture*. New York: Dorset House Publishing.

6. Wiegers, Karl E. 2002. *Peer Reviews in Software: A Practical Guide*. Boston: Addison-Wesley.

7. Wiegers, Karl E. 2003. *Software Requirements, Second Edition*. Redmond, WA: Microsoft Press.

8. Wiegers, Karl E. 2006. *More About Software Requirements: Thorny Issues and Practical Advice*. Redmond, WA: Microsoft Press.

Acknowledgments

I appreciate the many valuable review comments provided by Jim Brosseau, Barb Cardenuto, Chris Fahlbusch, Kathy Getz, Andre Gous, Shannon Jackson, Lori Schirmer, and Moe Stankay.

CHAPTER TWENTY

Development at Google

an Interview with Alex Martelli

It seems like everyone we know wants to work at Google. We hear about all sorts of great perks—from developers being able to spend some of their time working on their own projects, to massage therapists on staff to make sure everyone's nice and limber. But Google takes its software development very seriously, and Alex Martelli, originally hired by Google as an "über tech lead," has been working on the serious side of software development there. We wanted to hear what he had to say about building teams at Google.

Andrew: How did you come to know what you know about how software works?

Alex: I started out as an electrical engineer designing computer chips for Texas Instruments and then IBM Research. I found myself drifting from doing the hardware, the chips, to doing the system, to doing the microprogramming, because the research operation was just building a few prototypes at a time—to get the chance for the prototypes to actually be used by our target audience of scientists and such, we basically had to make it easy for them to get to there with, say, FORTRAN or APL. They definitely weren't going to be happy doing microcode. So eventually, after a few years of drifting, I had to realize I wasn't designing hardware anymore. I lost track of exactly what was happening in hardware design and for chips and technologies, and resigned myself to being a software person instead.

Shortly after that, I joined a start-up where everybody basically had to do everything. Given that I was probably the most experienced developer in the group, I was by default tagged as a managerial type who was supposed to organize the team and make it work. It didn't really work that well the first time. Fortunately, I did manage to avoid killing the company and actually found somebody who had a little bit more of a clue about management, and I went back to doing mostly software development. Then, learning from what I'd done wrong the first time, I tried my hand at management again, and gradually got more comfortable and more skillful at balancing the purely technical contribution with organization and management and leadership points.

In 2004, I went to Google and interviewed for them and just at the end of the year they sent me an offer to join them with a job description too cool to refuse: "Über Tech Lead." It basically means what I'd been doing for the last few years in my career, with a lot of technical aspects and a lot of management and leadership points as well. The "Über" part has to do with the fact that I've never been responsible for a single software development team at Google, but rather each team has its own tech lead. But I was responsible to oversee and integrate many teams in a certain area of the business.

Andrew: Let's talk a little bit about that first attempt at management you were just talking about. What happened?

Alex: I think the main thing that interfered with my performance at the time was very related to a deeply seated trait of my character, which is an abiding faith in human nature. I use the word *faith* advisedly because it's something you just have to believe. From observing the world, you cannot really come to the conclusion that human beings are fundamentally good—experimental evidence doesn't appear to support that very well. I guess I just have it in me.

So, for example, we had this guy who had been brought on board because he worked with another of the founders on a previous venture. But the other founder wasn't actually a software developer, so they didn't realize that he was bringing in somebody who really wasn't up to the extreme pressure that you experience in a start-up. He probably did well in a large company, where he could take limited responsibilities and execute them decently without making waves. But to make a start-up survive, you just need a completely different level of intensity, of involvement, and skill. One thing he definitely had learned from his previous stints at large companies was to make very credible excuses.

Andrew: That's hilarious, but surely a bit of an exaggeration?

Alex: I don't remember him ever coming forward with "The cat ate my software," but we kept falling for it. So eventually, I was facing the near—not rebellion exactly, but the rest of the team were not stupid. I wasn't stupid, either, just too optimistic and too trusting. And they were realizing that this guy was basically dragging them all down. His productivity was negative. He was actually able to work intensely. He wasn't a shirker, but he'd work intensely for three days and make seven days of work for somebody else who had to fix all the bugs he had introduced. I kept giving him a second chance, third chance, fourth chance. And in that, in retrospect, I make myself sound silly. I assure you that with the amount of things to be done all the time in that kind of setting, it's only in retrospect that I recognize the patterns.

Eventually, I had to face the guy and do what is really the hardest thing to do for a manager—and one of the most crucial things to make a team work well. I had to say, "Even though you have been with us from day one, it just isn't working." That was the very first time in my life I had to terminate somebody, or heartily invite him to look for other opportunities, and I didn't expect how heart-rending it would be. But in the end that was absolutely indispensable to let the team survive. It's like one bad apple in a bushel can spoil everything. If management is too kind-hearted and, particularly, if the way the team is formed is based on those acquaintances and friendships, it's even harder to say these very unkind, but true and necessary words to somebody you count as a personal friend.

The fact that he just can't hack software well enough doesn't mean he's a bad person. And I'm sure part of why his excuses were so credible to me, beyond my incredible optimism, was that he probably deluded himself that they were the real reason he wasn't delivering. In the end, having to communicate that message worked. I'm sure people who are particularly skilled can do it without even breaking the friendship, but unfortunately, I'm not as good at that. It's like terminating a personal relationship that isn't working, but you've given it chances and chances and chances. It's heartbreaking, because when the relationship has become a part of yourself, you don't want to hurt this person. But it just isn't working, so what are you going to do? So, that was probably the harshest lesson I ever had to learn.

Jenny: Do you feel like before you did that, there were problems in team dynamics because of this one particular person and his excuses?

Alex: Yes, exactly. Everybody was very much invested in the success of the whole enterprise because it's a start-up. You're getting pocket-money-level salaries, and your big payday is supposed to be when the firm triumphs and takes the market by storm. So, you don't have just a professional involvement in the firm's overall success, your whole life has been poured into that. So, keeping somebody in your team who is actually doing damage to your chance of success is really pointless. And it's difficult to communicate because, hey, isn't that the manager's job to realize that? And the answer is yes. I was not doing my job—not all of my job. I had more work to do, between managing and technical contributions, than I could deal with, but this part I obviously didn't do well and it was a very important one.

The rest of the team was fine among themselves. When I stepped back to individual contributor and found another pretty good guy to hand the management reins to, things really soared. First, because I was now able to use 100% of my time and energy to actually develop software, and second because this guy was obviously a better, more experienced manager than I was at the time.

Andrew: What would you tell someone on a software team who sees that his manager is having that particular problem? Is there something that one of your team members could have told you to help you realize how bad the situation was getting, so you would deal with it sooner?

Alex: There are many possibilities, and believe me, I've done a lot of introspection about it. I'm pretty sure I wasn't deliberately deceiving myself. There is a strong human temptation to just make believe it's not happening, and maybe it will solve itself on its own. It's just like someone who doesn't want to go to the dentist because he strongly suspects that he has something wrong with his teeth, but he's really afraid of how painful it will be to fix, so he keeps not going. It's wrong, but it's very human. We don't really like to face harsh realities that may require painful action and consequences.

So, take the guy you mentioned hypothetically—the one who recognizes, "OK, we've got this six-person team that would be absolutely great if it was five people because that person is just doing damage instead of giving positive contributions and the manager is totally, totally blind to that." It's particularly important if it's a small firm or start-up so that the success of the whole team is paramount to everybody. And that includes the manager.

How does he tell the manager? It's going to be almost as hard as it is for the manager to tell the underperforming person, particularly if it's not a one-on-one thing. If he's realized that there's this one person who just isn't pulling their weight, probably some other teammate is just as aware of that. If it's two or three people going to the manager and basically showing their bad perception here, it's going to be more effective. The manager obviously needs to be hit with a two-by-four, and if you can get two or three teammates together to supply the bad news, do so.

Incidentally, this is something where you really want to be face to face. I just can't imagine myself doing it in email or on the phone or instant messaging, because when you give bad news, you want to leave open the communication channel for emotions that body language and face-to-face communication provide. At the same time, it's absolutely crucial that you will be able to offer emotional reassurance. "You're doing a bad job doesn't mean you're a bad person. It means you've gone awry, and should do something different." That is something that is really much better communicated face to face, like most bad news.

Jenny: So how much do you think the success or failure of that team relied on your role as a manager, and how much of that do you think came from the team dynamic itself?

Alex: Well, it relied on the success of the team's manager because, basically, that's the same thing as success of the team. But it didn't have to be me. Indeed, I stepped back to be a senior individual contributor and somebody else took the management reins, and things went much better. That was about 20 years ago, but I don't think human nature has changed very much. Technology, incredibly. Human nature, not so much.

There are technological and methodological aspects that would have made things much clearer—like, for example, if 20 years ago we'd had a properly structured agile team organization with daily standup meetings. One thing about agile, which is a very big plus for actually working, but a potentially big risk and why so many people are afraid of adopting it, is that it makes truth emerge much sooner than the traditional channels of communication.

If everybody is standing around for five minutes in the morning and basically telling each other what have I accomplished yesterday, what I'll accomplish today, what stands in my way that maybe somebody could help with, you can't keep hiding bad performance day after day after day for very long. It becomes pretty evident. That is just one example of how agile structured methods provide so much better communication, and therefore, for better or for worse, make it extremely difficult to hide things from yourself or anybody else. The classic example is how agile estimating—burn-down charts and so on—gives a very clear picture of progress. It makes it painfully obvious to everybody: "Hey folks, this is our velocity. This is the amount of work we're actually able to get done. If we insist on having all the features that we originally accepted, this thing is going to be two months late." That happens to a lot of software projects, and is normally the kind of thing that people don't want to admit to themselves. They may start doing overtime and then maybe even burn themselves out, but in the end they just delay the inevitable. And if it appears far too late to do anything about it, it can be a disaster.

With the high visibility of agile methods, the painful reality will have to be faced much sooner. The earlier you face the reality, the less painful—although still painful—it is to fix it. You might have to drop some features and slide a couple weeks on the delivery time if you realize things early enough. But if you realize them way past deadline, then it's too late to do anything as relatively painless as that.

Andrew: Do you think there's a shortcoming to the agile approach?

Alex: The shortcoming is that you can't hide, and that is very scary for many developers and managers. Eventually the project will probably be a disaster, but in most particularly big corporate situations it may be that two weeks before you are scheduled to deliver and will not make it, there is a big reorg and the project disappears, and you don't get a bad mark on your record. That's like winning the lottery in a sense, but people keep hoping for that to avoid damage to their careers. I don't really think it's a minus from the point of view of the team or of the corporation or whoever wants the software delivered and wants to use it, but it's definitely scary for the manager and for the developers on the team because there's nowhere they can hide. It makes things so clear, so obvious to everybody involved.

Another thing, which I already mentioned about giving bad news, is that in my modest experience I don't know how to make agile work in a distributed team. I know people who claim otherwise and I really admire them, but in my experience, if the team is not collocated, all the extra amounts of communications going on are just missing. Not that I have any better solution—if you have to work with a totally dispersed team, I don't have any magic bullets to make that work. But I suspect that the usual Scrum experience just doesn't stretch that well to it.

Andrew: I think it's interesting that you brought up two really important sorts of things that go on in a team: transparency, or not being able to hide, and being able to have that constant flow of communication.

Jenny: I think pretty much all development methodologies, agile or otherwise, focus on transparency, on trying to make sure that people understand who is accountable for what and how they progress on that. You're saying that things like burn-down rates and projects will actually make that information much clearer for other people. I'd like for you to drill down into that a little bit more and tell me why you think those specific practices might make it clearer than, say, I don't know, earned value management, or other tools that have been used in all sorts of projects—software and otherwise—for decades.

Andrew: You know, you're right. I never thought of it that way, but burn-down—a staple of agile projects—isn't really all that different from earned value. Is it all that much more effective than stodgy 50-year-old project management stuff that they used to build, say, a nuclear reactor or the space shuttle?

Alex: So, the reason I think burn-down charts work particularly well is that they form an easily understood, shared language among any member of the project. And let's never forget the external stakeholders, the people who are rooting for the right software to be delivered on time and on budget. They may be internal customers if you are doing internal enterprise development, or they may be product managers, or marketing people if it's supposed to be sold in the marketplace; whoever plays the role of the customer for the specification discovery process.

There's the problem of quantifying exactly what it is that we need to do and what would just be nice, what we don't have to do, and how much will it cost to actually get those tasks done and deliverable to the user; all of these issues are absolutely crucial to the team. (I'm including the customer in the team, as is the best agile tradition.) And these issues are very effectively communicated by the burn-down charts. You don't call something "finished except it still needs QA." If it still needs QA, or anything else, then it is not finished. Finished means finished. Finished means something you can ship tomorrow.

Any code that has been checked into the trunk, approved, accepted, whatever your detailed procedure for calling a feature finished, should be ready to ship today. That's crucial. So the meaning of the word *finished* doesn't stretch in agile as much as it does in other methodologies. And the costs that come with estimating and planning "what do we do first, and what do we do next" are just as transparent. There is no magic wand that tells you those things for free. There isn't in any software development project. It's always a substantial part of the project's workload to determine exactly what is being done, and to change it in mid-flight and keep responding to the exact needs of the customer or of the stakeholder.

Andrew: A lot of what you're saying would probably come as a big surprise to someone who thinks that "agile" is synonymous with "we don't plan our projects."

Alex: With agile development and burn-down charts, all of those factors that could otherwise end up stretching the projected delivery dates well beyond what the more rigid, more traditional methodology shows are fully accounted for as part of the software development process—which is exactly how they should be, because really, they are at the beginning or at a crucial cyclical time in the process of developing software. This doesn't really have all that much to do with the team aspect, but it has a lot to do with the development that the team is supposed to be doing. So, I guess these are basically two faces of the same coin.

If you count the stakeholders or product managers or customers as part of the team, then I guess you can say it has to be the team, but I haven't seen that done except in agile development shops.

Andrew: I find it very interesting that you drew a straight line from burn-down charts to talking with the customer. Burn-down charts are all about answering questions about the effort we've put in and the work we've done. I like that you used the phrase "right software," and talked about figuring out how you know when the project is finished, if there's still work to be done, specifically calling QA and testing in particular as something that people keep doing after they consider the project "done." I like that a lot, because if you crack open any traditional quality textbook—and I'm not even talking about software quality, I'm just talking about engineering quality in general, going back 50 years, going back to Deming and Juran—you'll see those are practically the textbook definitions of quality. Yet you brought them up in the context of agile development.

Jenny: Building the right software, conforming to requirements, fitness to use—we might not use those traditional quality terms today in an agile shop, but I think it's really interesting that they're still behind the ideas you've been talking about. It's almost drawing a straight connection to the team adopting this practice, having this meeting every day where they look at these charts, having a task board up there, where you actually see traditional quality practices showing through. I think a lot of software people wouldn't make that connection.

Andrew: And it all has a big impact on the team—how they work together, their morale. There are other traditional quality ideas that are clearly part of agile, too, right? Embracing change is an important part of an agile process. But responding to changes, and making sure your stakeholders have a channel for making changes, that's also an important part of traditional project management. And doesn't that have an impact on the team's morale?

Alex: I believe that in this particular case, the periodic enrichment nature of most agile processes actually helps. If you do, say, a monthly iteration for some very large project, or bi-weekly for something possibly smaller and moving faster, you do fully expect things to change at the end of the iteration, because you devote some time at the end of the iteration to do a retrospective: "OK, what did we do in this last iteration? What went wrong? What went right? Is there some new thing we learned that we should apply in the future either to avoid mistakes or to take advantage of the best practice?" That means that change is systematically going to happen, not at random and unpredictable times, but on a schedule. There is a huge advantage in being time-driven. By time-driven I mean meeting every Thursday or Wednesday or something like that, as opposed to, "OK, whenever we're done, we're done."

Andrew: Does that help you keep your project's schedule under control?

Alex: It helps you pull into a stride, a rhythm, where you know that this is the deadline and everything that is not tested, committed, accepted by the deadline is not in this iteration. Even if a work is still in flight, you know that nevertheless, this is when you do retrospective introspection. Why did we end up with three tasks in flight where we've already done a lot of work on them and we have nothing to show for that? Well, they were harder than we expected, maybe, or my darn computer kept breaking down. So, there are solutions that are completely different. One is to redo the estimate of the remaining tasks: maybe through much more layering we'll have many more, smaller tasks, and so we are not going to be blindsided by one of them proving to be much bigger than we had originally thought.

So then at the beginning of the next iteration, it is absolutely crucial that upper managers or other stakeholders are there, because this is their occasion to change things. This is when they get the priorities right for this iteration, which may require dropping or postponing some features and tasks, moving others ahead, injecting completely new ones, saying that something that sounded like a great idea at the time is unfortunately not going to help, so it shouldn't be part of the shipment—and so on, and so forth.

Again, this is not random change that happens out of the blue, and strikes you as a team member by surprise. It's planned. It's forecast. You don't know exactly what will change, but you do know that something will change more likely than not, because the underlying business reality has changed.

Andrew: It sounds to me just from what you're saying that a big part of making sure that your team actually is successful and builds good software is not just setting the expectations of, say, the managers and the customers, but actually managing the expectations of the team themselves.

Alex: That's a very good observation. It's a two-way street. The engineers and developers in general and the team leader must be talking regularly to the people who are hopefully burningly expecting the software to be delivered.

Jenny: A couple of things kind of ran through my mind when you were talking about expectations, and meeting the expectations of the customer. I've worked personally on a few agile projects that have gone kind of crazily awry because of just those two factors. I've had customers before who, while they were involved in the entire process as agile dictates, decided to change their mind drastically during various iterations—to the point where we had to rewrite the entire premise of the thing that we were doing, to the extent that maybe we shouldn't have built the software in the first place until they had worked some of those out.

That's one thing that I would bring up. Another thing that's happened to me working in an agile environment is I've had developers who kind of refused to rein in their creativity, and have felt the need to add a lot of gold plating, features that the stakeholder never asked for and didn't need, but which the programmers thought were a great idea. Sometimes that resulted in better software, so people didn't say anything negative about it, but it almost always led to serious quality problems.

Alex: Yes. Engineers, particularly those who are young and brilliant but with not yet enough scars on their back to have fought many battles, do tend to overengineer. I totally agree with that. So, what I've found works well for that is a practice that I already found well established at Google when I got in, and I absolutely love. I tried to make it happen in the past, but it's so hard to actually make happen in the real world unless it's already in the culture: mandatory code reviews. I would give credit for this to employee number one, Craig Silverstein. No piece of software gets into the code base unless it's been examined and approved by somebody else on the team. That's not the kind of structured code review that people had in mind in the '70s, with hours and hours of preparation and projection and a whiteboard, that sort of thing.

It's really a lightweight process, and it's perfectly suitable to happen in email or with lightweight web-based tools. The point is that if you can keep an eye on all the change sets and all the code reviews firing back and forth, whether you're directly involved or not, you'll never get blindsided by some change when it hits the code base. Now, I'm talking about changes done internally by the team itself—such as the gold-plating aspects that you were mentioning—as opposed to changes requested by the customers, which is a very different kind of issue.

Andrew: I could definitely see how that sort of code review could help the second problem Jenny talked about, the engineering, gold-plating problem. What about the first thing she mentioned, which I've definitely seen, too. I definitely remember what she was talking about, when her team just got destroyed by people on the business side who were asking for things they never should have been asking for in the first place. Jenny's team faced a terrible problem on that project. The customer completely and unexpectedly changed direction, and they really did have to practically rebuild the entire code base from scratch. I'm sure that she's not the only person who has run into that problem. Is there a good agile approach to that particular problem?

Alex: It boils down to going to the two big objectives of a development team, which are do the right software and do the software right. Much of what we've been talking about is do the software right. Given that the software has to do this and that, make it happen. Nice, solid, well-performing, bug-free, and so on.

But maybe even more important is to do the right software: the software that has the feature set that will really make the company succeed. I realize that if you have never been on the business side of things, it may seem that those changes, those totally absurdly drastic changes you're being asked for, are capricious and arbitrary. But they do make sense, unless you're working for a seriously dysfunctional company—in which case I would suggest printing your resume on the good laser printer.

If it's not a dysfunctional company, put yourself in the business guy's shoes. The world is changing under them, and it's all they can do to stay afloat.

There is one aspect in most schools of agile programming, that I don't entirely subscribe to: that generalities are shunned. Some generality costs you, but some generality is actually a savings of time. So making—though it may be a silly example—a routine that computes the remainder of a division by three, a very specific task, is probably going to be more costly than doing a routine that computes a remainder by anything and passing it three as an argument.

So, if you have a good nose, a designer's nose and, to a lesser extent, an implementer's nose, for where generality comes free or even makes your work cheaper, then you as part of embracing change and being prepared for change build classes and modules and packages and routines to be configurable for situations that are a little bit different.

The point is that if the total amount of your work is more than starting from scratch, then this is a sad reality that just has to be faced. If there is reusable code in there, then it can actually be worth reusing. If the business-side people are being totally arbitrary and capricious and wasting the firm's money and your time and their own time and so on, then it's laser printer time. But more likely than not, they are doing the best they can in an extremely challenging, difficult, and changing world.

Andrew: All this discussion about agile reminds me of something that happened a few years ago. Jenny and I were brought in to do a talk at a prominent company about improving software development. At the end of the talk, we got into a discussion with the audience about agile development, which I think it was a little bit newer at the time. Then a developer stands up. He clearly had been there for a while. He was a big guy with a big, gray beard—he really looked like a very stereotypical developer—and other people in the room clearly deferred to him. So he gets up and…Jenny, do you remember exactly what he said?

Jenny: He said, "Agile means that you don't write anything down, you just start coding immediately."

Alex: Right; I have a pretty famous colleague who would basically be applauding this guy's theories. He's a pretty well-known blogger, Steve Yegge. He works over in the Seattle area. Let's just say that we have our own dissents on the technical plane.

Search for him and "agile" in the blogosphere, and you'll find a million posts of his essentially condemning the whole idea, and explaining how the only right way to do software is basically what that developer was advocating. Just start hacking, and things will start to happen on their own. Don't just accept my summary of his theories; go read his own posts. They are well written indeed! And to be perfectly honest, to play devil's advocate, there are examples in which this has worked. My favorite one is—do you know the software company called Autodesk?

Andrew: Sure.

Alex: Have you ever wondered, what does their business have to do with desks?

So, the story is they wanted to do an office automation application. Before Microsoft Office or other integrated suites, they wanted to do the automatic desk. And a couple people, very senior engineers in the start-up who actually didn't really like the idea very much, on their own spare time hacked on a computer-aided design application instead.

Andrew: And they built AutoCAD just like that?

Alex: Yes. They thought it would be more fun than doing invoice filing and all that stuff that the businesspeople said there were huge markets for. So the "AutoDesk" application never actually happened, but AutoCAD took the world by storm. The company didn't change their name, but despite their name, Autodesk, they are still flourishing in the computer-aided design business after 20 years or more. There's a great book, by the way, by one of the founders, explaining all these things and the history of Autodesk. So, that would be the counterexample, where the guys on the team actually doing things on the proper channels were, as it turned out in the end, not really producing anything marketable for the company. And the rebels, who basically were off on a ledge doing something completely different and "wasting" company resources to make something happen that has nothing to do with the company's business model…actually saved the company and made it a huge success.

But that's basically a story of people winning $137 million with a lottery ticket. It happens, but I wouldn't bank on it.

Andrew: Is that different from a classic skunkworks project?

Alex: In my mind, a skunkworks project is something that upper management is actually supporting. The team is hidden from the rest of the company, particularly middle management. Middle management's main role at a large company is to stop any change from ever happening (or at least it seems that way if you ever work with them). Good engineers in the trenches and, funny enough, some of the top management, may actually have vision, and so they may make something happen by hiding in a corner. This project, as far as I can understand from the history that Autodesk has published, was actually the group of engineers deciding entirely on their own.

Another example would be Microsoft Internet Explorer 1, the first edition. Some engineers had this idea that this new Internet thing was all the rage, and that Microsoft should have a browser…and the long chain of middle management totally killed that stupid idea. Nobody will ever make a penny with browsers. So the guys hid in a corner and starting writing a browser anyway. Then suddenly the CEO at the time, Bill Gates, issued a memo explaining that the Internet was everything, including the company's future, and that everything must change on a dime. And those guys had more or less working software ready the next day.

Again, that may be something you'd call a skunkworks project, but again, it's not something I would bank on. If you are working in a company that is dysfunctional, then maybe that's the only way to survive. But you know that there are other companies. If everybody in the company is pulling in the same direction, and we're all interested in getting the customers good software and making money that way, there should be no need to hide and go do your own thing instead of pulling the cart together with everybody else.

Jenny: In an environment like that, do you think that a more structured, more traditional agile approach would work a lot better?

Alex: I think it probably would, because the idea of change is baked in, in a way it isn't in otherwise good processes—like the Rational Unified Process, for example. The continual iterations and the concept of timing them, fixing dates, and so on, are optional in RUP— it's something you can do, but it's not the core of the process. The core of the process is drawing a huge stack of diagrams that are illegible to anybody outside of the "priesthood" of your experts. I think that many teams love to produce very tall stacks of paper, because they basically can use them as walls to hide themselves from the rest of the organization, which might otherwise demand accountability and transparency. OK, I'm being a bit snide here, but you know what I mean.

The idea of building an enormous amount of specification before you start coding—eek! That is the kind of dysfunctional behavior to which the programmer you were quoting was basically overreacting in the other way. "Everybody is doing far too much rigid specs, so let's not do any at all." Well, there's a feasible middle way, you know?

CHAPTER TWENTY-ONE

Teams and Tools
Karl Fogel

This chapter is about the transformative effect that good tools can have on a team's ability to collaborate.

Consider that for years the World Wide Web consisted mainly of static pages that required technical expertise to write, and that readers could not influence except by sending email to the appropriate *webmaster@* address. Then, a few visionary souls started making software that would allow anyone with basic computer skills to cause text to appear on the Web, and other software to allow readers to comment on or even edit those pages themselves. Nothing about blogs or wikis was *technically* revolutionary; like the fax machine, they could have been invented years earlier, if only someone had thought of them. Yet once they appeared, they greatly increased people's ability to organize themselves into productive networks.

This chapter tells three stories about how good tools (or the lack of them) made a difference to a team. The tools discussed here are much narrower in scope than blogs and wikis, but their specificity makes them well suited to teasing out some principles of collaboration tools. As my experience has mostly been with open source software projects, that's what I'll draw on, but the same principles are probably applicable to any collaborative endeavor.

How Open Source Projects Work

If you've already taken part in an open source project, you can skip this section. If not, let me introduce the basics of how such projects work so that the tools discussed in this chapter will make sense.

*Open source software** is software released under a free copyright, allowing anyone to copy, modify, use, and redistribute the code (in either modified or unmodified form). Much of the software that runs the Internet and the World Wide Web is open source, and an increasing number of desktop applications are as well.

Open source programs are usually maintained by loosely organized coalitions of software developers. Some volunteer their time, others are paid by corporations in whose interests it is that the software be maintained. Because the participants are often spread across many time zones, and may never have met each other, the projects rely to an unusual degree on highly sophisticated collaboration tools: bug trackers, email lists and archives, network-based chat rooms, version control repositories, wikis, and more. You don't have to be familiar with all these tools; I'll explain the ones that figure in the discussions that follow as they come up.

Each open source project must decide how to organize and govern itself. Usually this is resolved by informal means: projects tend to be started by a small group of people anyway (sometimes one person), and over time, as interested volunteers show up and get involved, the original core group realizes it would be to the project's advantage to invite some of those newcomers to become core maintainers, too.[†] But once a project has many contributors, it can be difficult to keep track of them all and to identify which ones to cultivate as potential core maintainers. The first tool we'll look at grew out of one project's need to solve this problem.

---

* The older term *free software* is synonymous. There is not space here to explain why there are two terms for the same thing; see *http://producingoss.com/en/introduction.html#free-vs-open-source* if you'd like to know more about this.

† You may be wondering what it means to have a "core group" of maintainers when open source means that anyone has the right to change the code. Doesn't that mean that anyyone who wants to be is a maintainer? Not quite. In open source, anyone is free to make a copy of the code and do what she wants with that copy. But when a group of people get together and agree to maintain one particular copy *collectively*, they obviously have control over who is and isn't in that group. Similarly, anyone who wants to translate the Bible is free to do so, since it's in the public domain, but no one can force one group of translators to work with another, and if two groups don't work together, the result will be two independent translations. In open source software, this situation is known as a *fork*, as in "fork in the road": two independent copies with increasingly diverging sets of modifications, growing increasingly apart over time. In practice, however, forks are rare: more often, programmers coalesce around one particular copy in order to pool their efforts.

The Contribulyzer

Like most open source projects, Subversion[*] is continually trying to identify potential new core maintainers. Indeed, one of the primary jobs of the current core group is to watch incoming code contributions from new people and figure who should be invited to take on the responsibilities of core maintainership. In order to honestly discuss the strengths and weaknesses of candidates, we (the core maintainers) set up a private mailing list, one of the few non-public lists in the project. When someone thinks a contributor is ready, she proposes the candidate on this mailing list, and sees what others' reactions are. We give each other enough time to do some background checking, since we want a comfortable consensus before we extend the offer; revoking maintainership would be awkward, and we try to avoid ever being in the position of having to do it.

This behind-the-scenes background checking is harder than it sounds. Often, patches[†] from the same contributor have been handled by different maintainers on different occasions, meaning that no one maintainer has a good overview of that contributor's activities. Even when the same maintainer tends to handle patches from the same contributor (which can happen either deliberately or by accident), the contributor's patches may have come in irregularly over a period of months or years, making it hard for the maintainer to monitor the overall quality of the contributor's code, bug reports, design suggestions, and so forth.

I first began to think we had a problem when I noticed that names floated on the private mailing list were getting either an extremely delayed reaction or, sometimes, *no* reaction at all. That didn't seem right: after all, the candidates being proposed had been actively involved in the project, usually quite recently, and generally had had several of their patches accepted, often after several iterations of review and discussion on the public lists. However, it soon became clear what was going on: the maintainers were hesitant to solely rely on their memories of what that candidate had done (no one wants to champion someone who later turns out to be a dud), but at the same time were daunted by the sheer effort of digging back through the list archives and the code change history to jog their memories. I sensed that many of us were falling into a classic wishful postponement pattern when it came to evaluations: "Oh, so-and-so is being proposed as a new maintainer. Well, I'll save my response for this weekend, when I'll have a couple of hours to go through the archives and see what they've done." Of course, for whatever reason the "couple of hours" don't materialize that weekend, so the task is put off again, and again…. Meanwhile, the candidate has no idea any of this is going on, and just continues posting patches instead of

---

[*] Subversion is an open source version control system; see *http://subversion.tigris.org/*.

[†] A *patch* is code contribution, such as a bugfix, sent in a special format known as "patch format." The details of that format don't matter here; just think of a patch as being a proposed modification to the software, submitted in extremely detailed form—right down to which precise lines of code to change and how.

committing* directly. This means continued extra work for the maintainers, who have to process those patches, whereas if the candidate could be made a maintainer himself, it would be a double win: he wouldn't require assistance to get his patches into the code, and he'd be available to help process other people's patches.

My own self-observation was consistent with this hypothesis: a familiar sense of mild dread would come over me whenever a new name came up for consideration—not because I didn't want a new maintainer, but because I didn't know where I'd find the time to do the research needed to reply responsibly to the proposal.

Finally, one night I set aside my regular work to look for a solution. What I came up with was far from ideal, and does not completely automate the task of gathering the information we need to evaluate a contributor. But even a partial automation greatly reduced the time it takes to evaluate someone, and that was enough to get the wheels out of the mud, so to speak. Since the system has been up, proposals of candidates are almost always met with timely responses that draw on the information in the new system, because people don't feel bogged down by time-consuming digging around in archives. The new system took identical chores that until then had been redundantly performed by each evaluator individually, and instead performed them *once*, storing the results for everyone to use forever after.

The system is called the Contribulyzer (*http://www.red-bean.com/svnproject/contribulyzer/*): it keeps track of what contributors are doing, and records each contributor's activity on one web page. When the maintainers want to know whether a given contributor is ready for the keys to the car, they just look at the relevant Contribulyzer page for that contributor, first scanning an overview of his activities, and then focusing in on details as necessary.

But how does a computer program "keep track of" what a contributor is doing? That sounds suspiciously like magic, you might be thinking to yourself. It isn't magic: it requires some human assistance, and we'll look more closely at exactly how in a moment. First, though, let's see the results. The first figure on page 273 shows the front page of our Contribulyzer site.

If you click on a contributor's name, it takes you to a page showing the details of what that contributor has done. The second figure on page 273 shows the top of the detail page for Madan U S.

The four categories across the top indicate the kinds of contributions Madan has had a role in. Each individual contribution is represented by a *revision number*—a number (prefixed with *r*) that uniquely identifies that particular change. Given a revision number, one can ask the central repository to show the details (the exact lines changed and how they changed) for that contribution. For r22756 and r18324, Madan found the bugs that were

---

* To *commit* means to send a code change directly into the project's repository, which is where the central copy of the project's code lives (see *http://en.wikipedia.org/wiki/Revision_Control* for more). In general, only core maintainers are able to commit directly; all others find a core maintainer to shepherd their changes into the repository. See *http://producingoss.com/en/committers.html#ftn. id304827* for more on the concept of "commit access."

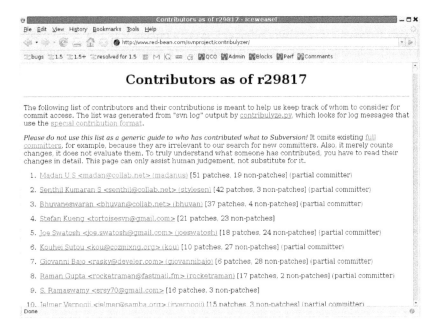

The Contribulyzer (main page).

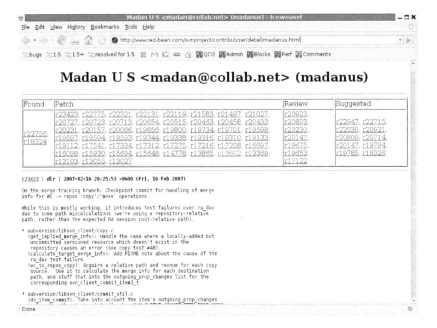

The Contribulyzer (contributor page).

fixed in those revisions. For the largest block of revision numbers—the "Patches"—he wrote the change that some maintainer eventually committed. For the remaining revisions, he either reviewed a patch that someone else committed, or suggested the fix but (for whatever reason) was not the one who implemented it.

Those four sections at the top of the page already give a high-level overview of Madan's activity. Furthermore, each revision number links to a brief description of the corresponding change. This description is known as a *log message*: a short bit of prose submitted along with a code change, explaining what the change does. The repository records this message along with the change; it is a crucial resource for anyone who comes along later wanting to understand the change.

If you click on "r20727", the top of the next screen will show the log message for that revision, as shown in the next figure.

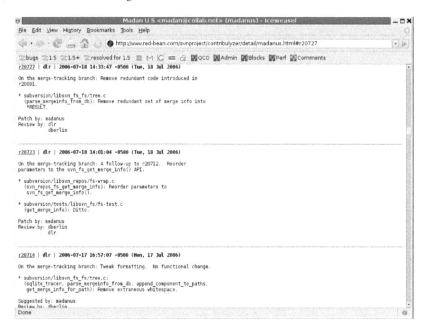

The Contribulyzer (revision entry).

The revision number here is a link, too, but this time to a page showing in detail what changed in that revision, using the repository browser ViewVC (*http://www.viewvc.org/*); see the first figure on page 275.

From here, you can see the exact files that changed, and if you click on "modified", you can see the code diff itself, as shown in the second figure on page 275.

As you can see, the layout of information in the Contribulyzer matches what we'd need to jog our memories of a contributor's work. There's a broad overview of what kinds of contributions that person has made, then a high-level summary of each contribution, and finally, detailed descriptions for those who want to go all the way to the code level.

But how did all this information get into the Contribulyzer?

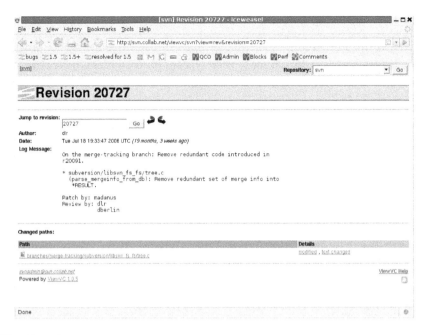

ViewVC revision page.

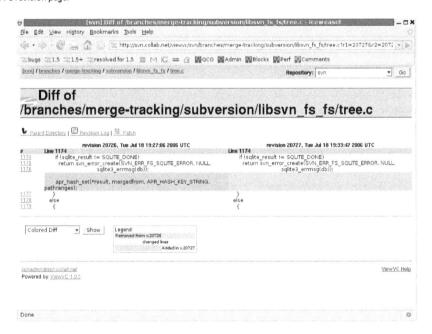

ViewVC file diff page.

The Catch

Unfortunately, the Contribulyzer is not some miraculous artificial intelligence program. The only reason it knows who has made what types of contributions is because *we tell it*. And the trick to getting everyone to tell it faithfully is twofold:

- Make the overhead as low as possible.

- Give people concrete evidence that the overhead will be worth it.

Meeting the first conditon was easy. The Contribulyzer takes its data from Subversion's per-revision log messages. We've always had certain conventions for writing these, such as naming every code symbol affected by a change. Supporting the Contribulyzer merely meant adding one new convention: a standard way of attributing changes that came from a source other than the maintainer who shepherded the change into the repository.

The standard is simple. We use one of four verbs (for the expected types of contributions), followed by the word *by:* and then the names of the contributors who made that type of contribution to that change. Most changes have only one contributor, but if there are multiple contributors, they can be listed on continuation lines:

```
Patch by: name_1_maybe_with_email_address
          name_2_maybe_with_email_address
Found by: name_3_maybe_with_email_address
Review by: etc...
Suggested by: etc...
```

(These conventions are described in detail at *http://subversion.tigris.org/hacking. html#crediting*.)

One reason it was easy to persuade people to abide by the new standard is that, in a way, it actually made writing log messages easier. We'd been crediting people before, but in various ad hoc manners, which meant that each time we committed a contributor's code, we had to think about how to express the contribution. One time it might be like this:

```
Remove redundant code introduced in r20091.  This came from a patch by
name_1_maybe_with_email_address.
```

And another time like this:

```
Fix bug in baton handoff.  (Thanks to so-and-so for sending in the patch.)
```

While the new convention was one more thing for people to learn, *once learned* it actually saved effort: now no one had to spend time thinking of how to phrase things, because we'd all agreed on One Standard Way to do it.

Still, introducing a new standard into a project isn't always easy. The path will be greatly smoothed if you can meet the second condition as well, that is, show the benefits *before* asking people to make the sacrifices. Fortunately, we were able to do so. Subversion's log messages are editable (unlike some version control systems in which they are effectively immutable). This meant that, after writing the Contribulyzer code to process log messages formatted according to the new standard, we could go back and fix up all of the project's existing logs to conform to that standard, and then generate a post-facto Contribulyzer page covering the entire history of the project. This we did in two steps: first, we found all the "@" signs in the log messages, to detect places where we mentioned someone's email address (since we often used people's email addresses when crediting them), and then, we searched again for just the names—without the email addresses—harvested from the first search. The resultant list of log messages numbered about one thousand, and with the help of a few volunteers (plus some rather labyrinthine editing macros), we were able to get them all into the new format in about one night.

Thus, the proposal of the new standard coincided with a demonstration of what it could do for us: we had the full Contribulyzer pages up and running from the moment the Contribulyzer was announced to the team. This made its benefits immediately apparent, and made the new log message formatting requirements seem like a small price to pay by comparison.

The Limits of the Contribulyzer

There is a famous saying, much used in open source projects, but surely long predating them:

> The perfect must not be the enemy of the good.

The Contribulyzer could do much more than it currently does. It's really the beginnings of a complete activity-tracking system. In an ideal world, it would gather information from the mailing list archives and bug tracker as well as from the revision control system. We would be able to jump from a log message that mentions a contributor to the mailing list thread where that contributor discusses the change with other developers—and vice versa; that is, jump from the mailing list thread to the commit. Similarly, we would be able to gather statistics on what percentage of a given person's tickets in the bug tracker resulted in commits or in non-trivial discussion threads (thus telling us that this person's bug reports should get comparatively more weight in the future, since she seems to be an effective reporter).

The point would not be to make a ratings system; that would be useless, and maybe even destructive, since it would suffer from inflationary pressures and tempt people into reductively quantitative comparisons of participants. Rather, the point would be to make it easy to find out more about a person *once you already know you're interested in her*.

Everyone who participates in an open source project leaves a trail. Even asking a question on a mailing list leaves a trail of at least one message, and possibly more if a thread develops. But right now these trails are implicit: one must trawl through archives and databases and revision control histories by hand in order to put together a reasonably complete picture of a given person's activity.

The Contribulyzer is a small step in the direction of automating the discovery of these trails. I included it in this chapter as an example of how even a minor bit of automation can make a noticeable difference in a team's ability to collaborate. Although the Contribulyzer covers only revision control logs, it still saves us a lot of time and mental energy, especially because the log messages often contain links to the relevant bug-tracker tickets and mailing list threads—so, if we can just get to the right log messages quickly, the battle is already half-won.

I don't want to claim too much for the Contribulyzer; certainly, there are many aspects of running an open source project that it doesn't touch. But it significantly reduces our workload when evaluating potential new maintainers, and therefore makes us more likely to do such evaluations in the first place. For one day's investment in coding, that's not a bad payoff.

Writing metacode rarely feels as productive as writing code, but it's usually worth it. If you've correctly identified a problem and have seen a clear technical solution, then a one-time effort now can bring steady returns over the life of the project.

Commit Emails and Gumption Sinks

This next example shows what can happen when a team doesn't pay enough attention to tool usage. It's about how a seemingly trivial interface decision can have large effects on how people behave. First, some background.

Most open source projects have a *commit email list*. The list receives an email every time a change enters the master repository, and the mail is generated automatically by the repository. Typically, each one shows the author of the change, the time the change was made, the associated log message, and the line-by-line change itself (expressed in the "patch" format mentioned earlier, except that for historical reasons, in this context the patch is called a "diff"). The email may also include URLs to provide a permanent reference for the change or for some of its subparts.

Here's a commit email from the Subversion project:

```
From: dionisos@tigris.org
Subject: svn commit: r30009 - trunk/subversion/libsvn_wc
To: svn@subversion.tigris.org
Date: Sat, 22 Mar 2008 13:54:38 -0700

Author: dionisos
Date: Sat Mar 22 13:54:37 2008
New Revision: 30009

Log:
Fix issue #3135 (property update on locally deleted file breaks WC).

* subversion/libsvn_wc/update_editor.c (merge_file): Only fill WC file
    related entry cache-fields if the cache will serve any use (ie
    when the entry is schedule-normal).

Modified:
    trunk/subversion/libsvn_wc/update_editor.c

Modified: trunk/subversion/libsvn_wc/update_editor.c
```

```
URL: http://svn.collab.net/viewvc/svn/trunk/subversion/libsvn_wc/update_editor.
c?pathrev=30009&r1=30008&r2=30009
==============================================================================
--- trunk/subversion/libsvn_wc/update_editor.c Sat Mar 22 07:33:07 2008 (r30008)
+++ trunk/subversion/libsvn_wc/update_editor.c Sat Mar 22 13:54:37 2008 (r30009)
@@ -2621,8 +2621,10 @@ merge_file(svn_wc_notify_state_t *conten
   SVN_ERR(svn_wc__loggy_entry_modify(&log_accum, adm_access,
                                      fb->path, &tmp_entry, flags, pool));

-  /* Log commands to handle text-timestamp and working-size */
-  if (!is_locally_modified)
+  /* Log commands to handle text-timestamp and working-size,
+     if the file is - or will be - unmodified and schedule-normal */
+  if (!is_locally_modified &&
+      (fb->added || entry->schedule == svn_wc_schedule_normal))
   {
     /* Adjust working copy file unless this file is an allowed
        obstruction. */
```

When done right, commit emails are a powerful collaboration tool for software projects. They're a perfect marriage of automated information flow and human participation. Each change arrives in the developer's mailbox packaged as a well-understood, discrete unit: an email. The developer can view the change using a comfortable and familiar interface (her mailreader), and if she sees something that looks questionable, she can reply, quoting just the parts of the change that interest her, and her reply will automatically be put into a thread that connects the change to everyone's comments on it. Thus, by taking advantage of the data management conventions already in place for email, people (and other programs) can conveniently track the fallout from any given change.[*]

However, another project I'm a member of, GNU Emacs,[†] does things a little differently. Partly for historical reasons, and partly because of the way its version control system[‡] works, each commit to GNU Emacs generates *two* commit emails: one showing the log message, and the other containing the diff itself.

The log message email looks like this:

```
From: Juanma Barranquero <lekktu@gmail.com>
Subject: [Emacs-commit] emacs/lisp info.el
To: emacs-commit@gnu.org
Date: Sat, 08 Mar 2008 00:09:29 +0000

CVSROOT:      /cvsroot/emacs
Module name:  emacs
Changes by:   Juanma Barranquero <lektu>    08/03/08 00:09:29
```

---

[*] For more on this practice, see *http://producingoss.com/en/vc.html#commit-emails* and *http://producingoss. com/en/setting-tone.html#code-review*.

[†] GNU Emacs is a text editing tool favored by many programmers, and is one of the oldest continuously maintained free software programs around. See *http://www.gnu.org/software/emacs/* for more.

[‡] CVS (*http://www.nongnu.org/cvs/*).

```
Modified files:
    lisp            : info.el

Log message:
    (bookmark-make-name-function, bookmark-get-bookmark-record):
    Pacify byte-compiler.

CVSWeb URLs:
http://cvs.savannah.gnu.org/viewcvs/emacs/lisp/info.el?cvsroot=emacs&r1=1.519&r2=1.520
```

And the diff email looks like this:

```
From: Juanma Barranquero <lekktu@gmail.com>
Subject: [Emacs-diffs] Changes to emacs/lisp/info.el,v
To: emacs-diffs@gnu.org
Date: Sat, 08 Mar 2008 00:09:29 +0000

CVSROOT:        /cvsroot/emacs
Module name:    emacs
Changes by:     Juanma Barranquero <lektu>    08/03/08 00:09:29

Index: info.el
===================================================================
RCS file: /cvsroot/emacs/emacs/lisp/info.el,v
retrieving revision 1.519
retrieving revision 1.520
diff -u -b -r1.519 -r1.520
--- info.el     7 Mar 2008 19:31:59 -0000      1.519
+++ info.el     8 Mar 2008 00:09:29 -0000      1.520
@@ -3375,6 +3375,8 @@

 (defvar tool-bar-map)
 (defvar bookmark-make-record-function)
+(defvar bookmark-make-name-function)
+(declare-function bookmark-get-bookmark-record "bookmark" (bookmark))

 ;; Autoload cookie needed by desktop.el
 ;;;###autoload
```

Together, those two emails contain the same information as a single one like the one I showed earlier from the Subversion project. But the key word is *together*. They are not together; they are separate. Although the programmer committed a single change,* there is no single email containing everything a reviewer would need to understand and review that change. To review a change, you need the log message so that you can understand the general intent of the change, and the diff so that you can see whether the actual code edits match that intent.

It turns out that if people don't have both of these things in one place, they're much less likely to review changes.

---

* Some people use the word *changeset* for what I'm talking about here: the situation where perhaps multiple files were modified, but the modifications are all part of a single logical group. We can call that overall group a "change" or a "changeset"; the two words mean the same thing in this context.

Or so it seems from my highly rigorous* survey comparing the two projects. In February 2008, there were 207 unique threads (from 908 messages) on the Subversion development list. Of these, 50 were follow-up threads to commit emails. So by one reasonable measurement, 24% of development list attention goes to commit review (or if you want to count messages instead of threads, then a little over 5%). Note that follow-ups to Subversion commit emails are automatically directed to the main development list via a Reply-to header, so the development list is the right data set to use.

Meanwhile, in February 2008, the Emacs development list had 491 unique threads (from 3,158 messages), of which, apparently, zero were review mails.

Stunned at this result, I loosened my filters for detecting review mails and scanned again. This time I came up with, at most, 49 emails. But spot-checking those 49 showed that most seemed to be reviews of patches posted to the list from elsewhere, rather than reviews based on commit emails; only two were definite review mails. However, even if we count all 49 (which is almost certainly overly permissive), that's at most 10% of the development list traffic being commit reviews (or 1.5%, if we count messages instead of threads). Because Emacs does not automatically redirect commit email follow-ups to the main development list, I also searched in the commits list and the diffs list archives. I found no review follow-ups there in February, and exactly two in March, both of which were from me.

Now, the two projects have different commit rates and different traffic levels on their development lists. But we can partially control for this by approaching the question from the other side: what percentage of commits gets reviewed? In February 2008, Subversion had 274 unique commits, and Emacs had 807.† Thus, the ratio of review threads to commits for Subversion is about 18%, and for Emacs is somewhere between 0% and 6% (but probably tending low, around 0.2%, if there really were only two true review mails).

Something is happening here, something that makes one project much more likely than the other to do peer review. What is it?

I cannot prove it, of course, but I think it's simply the fact that each Emacs commit arrives separated into two emails: one for the log message and another for the diff. There is no way, using a normal mail-reading interface without extensive customizations, to view the log message and the diff at the same time. Thus, *there is no convenient way to review a change*. It's not that review is impossible, or even hard. It's neither: if I wanted to, I could review all the Emacs commits, and so could the other developers. But each review would require shuffling back and forth between two emails, or clicking on the URL in the shorter email and waiting for a page to load. In practice, it's too much trouble, and I can never be bothered. Apparently, neither can anyone else.

---

* Read: "extremely anecdotal."

† If you're checking these numbers against primary sources, note that when counting Emacs commits, you shouldn't count commits that affect only ChangeLog files, because (due to certain oddities of the way the Emacs project uses its version control system) those are duplicates of other commits.

There's a sobering lesson here: adding a few seconds of overhead to a common task is enough to make that task uncommon. Your team isn't lazy, just human. Put light switches at roughly shoulder level and people will happily turn off lights when they leave a room; put the switches at knee level, and your electricity bill will skyrocket.

What is the cost to a project of not getting code review? Pretty high, I think. Looking over the Subversion commits for that month, 55 indicate that they follow up to a previous specific commit, and 35 bear a special marker (see *http://subversion.tigris.org/hacking. html#crediting*) indicating that they fix problems found by someone else. In my experience with the project, such suggestions are usually the result of commit review. Thus, probably somewhere between 12% and 20% of the commits made in Subversion result from review of previous commits. I cannot easily come up with the comparable number for Emacs, because Emacs does not have standardized attribution conventions the way Subversion does. But I've been watching Emacs development for a long time, and while it's clear that some percentage of commits there results from reviews of previous commits (or from just stumbling across problematic code in the course of other work), I do not believe it reaches 12% to 20%.

Besides, the benefits of timely commit review cannot be measured solely in further code changes. Commit review sustains morale, sharpens people's skills (because they're all learning from each other), reinforces a team's ability to work together (because everyone gets accustomed to receiving constructive criticism from everyone else), and spurs participation (because review happens in public, thus encouraging others to do the same). To deprive a team of these benefits because of a trivial user interface choice is a costly mistake.

They're Staying Away in Droves: A Tale of Two Translation Interfaces

In 2005, I wrote a book on managing open source projects,* much of which is about exactly what this chapter is about: setting up tools to make teams more effective.

A while after the book was published, and its full contents placed online, volunteers started showing up to translate it into other languages. Naturally, I was extremely pleased by this, and wanted to help them as much as possible, so I set up some technical infrastructure to enable the translators to collaborate. Each target language generally had more than one volunteer working on it, and having the translators for a given language work together was simply common sense. In addition, certain aspects of the translation processes were common across all the languages, so it made sense even for translators of different languages to be able to see each other's work.

It all sounds good on paper, doesn't it? But what actually happened was a deep lesson in the consequences of failing to understand a team's tool needs.

---

* *Producing Open Source Software* (O'Reilly; *http://producingoss.com/*).

What I Gave Them

The infrastructure I set up for the translators was basically an extension of what I had used myself to write the book: a collection of XML master files stored in a Subversion repository, written to the DocBook DTD, and converted to output formats using a collection of command-line programs driven by some Makefiles.

Let me try saying that in English:

I wrote the book in a format (XML) that, while a bit awkward to work in, is very easy to produce web pages and printable books from. For example, here's what the beginning of Chapter 3 looks like in the original XML:

```
<chapter id="technical-infrastructure">

<title>Technical Infrastructure</title>

<simplesect>

<para>Free software projects rely on technologies that support the
selective capture and integration of information.  The more skilled
you are at using these technologies, and at persuading others to use
them, the more successful your project will be.  This only becomes
more true as the project grows.  Good information management is what
prevents open source projects from collapsing under the weight of
Brooks' Law<footnote>, <para>From his book <citetitle>The Mythical Man
Month</citetitle>, 1975.  See <ulink
url="http://en.wikipedia.org/wiki/The_Mythical_Man-Month"/> and <ulink
url="http://en.wikipedia.org/wiki/Brooks_Law"/>.</para></footnote>
which states that adding manpower to a late software project makes it
later.  Fred Brooks observed that the complexity of a project
increases as the <emphasis>square</emphasis> of the number of ...
```

Here is what that becomes after being run through the converter to produce web output:

Chapter 3: Technical Infrastructure

Free software projects rely on technologies that support the selective capture and integration of information. The more skilled you are at using these technologies, and at persuading others to use them, the more successful your project will be. This only becomes more true as the project grows. Good information management is what prevents open source projects from collapsing under the weight of Brooks' Law[8], which states that adding manpower to a late software project makes it later. Fred Brooks observed that the complexity of a project increases as the *square* of the number of....

One can certainly see the similarity between the two texts, but there's no doubt that the XML master files are harder to read. For me, that was OK: the inconvenience of working in XML was outweighed by the ability to produce different types of output conveniently.

I managed the collection of XML files using a version control system called Subversion, which is very familiar to programmers, but less widely known outside the programming community. Similarly, the converters—one for web output and another for printed output—were powerful and flexible tools, but somewhat hard to use, especially for non-programmers. Just to set them up you must first have various other supporting programs installed on your computer. The overall process is difficult under any circumstances, but it's a bit less difficult if your computer runs on a Unix-like operating system (again, common among programmers, but not other demographics), and a bit more difficult on Microsoft Windows.

All of this was fine when I was the only author. I'm a programmer anyway, I was somewhat familiar with all those tools already, and since I was putting in a lot of effort to write the book in the first place, adding a little extra overhead to learn some tools was well worth it. I knew it would pay off in the long run, and it did—for me.

But the situation for the volunteer translators was completely different. They were *not* all programmers, most had no prior experience with these tools, and they therefore faced a steep learning curve right at the start (always the worst place to face a steep learning curve!). Furthermore, since any given translation was being done by several translators, for each individual the ratio of tool-learning to real work was worse than it had been for me: each translator paid the same tool-learning cost I paid, but each translator was not writing an entire book, and therefore had less benefit across which to amortize that cost. The translators showed up with one particular kind of expertise—the ability and desire to take English text and rewrite it in another language—and found themselves asked instead to take on a task completely unrelated to that expertise: that of learning a whole new set of tools, tools that they might or might not use elsewhere in their lives.

The wonder is not that some of them rebelled, but rather that we got any useful translations at all. We did get some: as of this writing, the German translation is draft-complete, the Japanese is about 80% done, the Spanish about 60%, and so forth. (The French are a more interesting case; we'll get to them in a moment.) But seeing what the translators had to go through to get this far makes me wonder how much *more* could have been done if I hadn't imposed such a high tool overhead on the process. Take a look at the translator guidelines I wrote up at *http://producingoss.com/translations.html#guidelines* to get a sense of how much engineering was required of the participants. (I'd just show those guidelines here, but they'd take up too much room, which already tells you something.)

What I Should Have Given Them

Unfortunately, for a long time I didn't realize how punishing the aforementioned system was. I knew it was less than ideal, but it's very hard to tell why any particular translator isn't doing as much work as he said he would—and it's impossible to notice when a translator doesn't volunteer in the first place because he's daunted by the requirements.

Eventually, though, we got a wake-up call from France:

```
From: Bertrand Florat <...>
Subject: French translation
To: ProducingOSS Translators Mailing List
Date: Sun, 17 Feb 2008 16:54:32 +0100
```

```
Hi Karl,

Just to keep you in touch, Etienne and myself moved to the Framalang
wiki to finish the book translation. We plan to port all its content to
docbook format once done (it's about 90% done now).

I think it could be a good idea to link the French translation from
http://www.producingoss.com/fr/ to
http://www.framalang.org/wiki/Producing_Open_Source_Software so people
can benefit from the almost-done translation right now, and it could
bring new translators.

What do you think?

Cheers,

Bertrand
```

In other words, the French translators decided to *route around* the technical infrastructure
that I had set up to help them translate the book. Instead, they copied all the English data
over to a wiki, where they could do their editing in a convenient, familiar environment.
When they're done,* they plan to port the translation back to XML.

That's a pretty searing indictment of my infrastructure, I'd say. And looking at the Framalang wiki site (*http://www.framalang.org/wiki/Producing_Open_Source_Software*), I can't really
blame them. It is much more suited to the task of coordinating translators than the ad hoc
system I'd set up. At Framalang, the original text and translation are displayed next to
each other, in different colors. There are special functions for tracking who is responsible
for what portions, for giving feedback, for providing a centralized list of agreed-on translations for common terms, for labeling what work remains to be done, and so on. All of these
things can be accomplished in my ad hoc system, too, of course, but the difference is that
they aren't handed to the translators for free: the team is forced to reinvent the wheel over
and over, whereas Framalang just gives out the keys to the car (see the figure on page 286).

Bertrand's announcement prompted another translator to voice some dissatisfaction with
the homegrown infrastructure:

```
From: "Manuel Barkhau" <mbarkhau@googlemail.com>
Subject: Re: French translation
To: bertrand@florat.net
Cc: producingoss-translators@red-bean.com
Date: Sun, 17 Feb 2008 17:21:35 +0100
Reply-To: mbarkhau@gmail.com

Bonjour mon amis,

on a different note, maybe you would like to share you're experience
with the wiki format vs. subversion. How much participation have you
received apart from the main translators. How many translators joined
```

---

* In fact, they finished their first draft of the translation while I was writing this chapter.

your effort, quality of their work etc.
Something I especially miss with the current format, are reader
statistics and feedback.

ciao,
Manuel

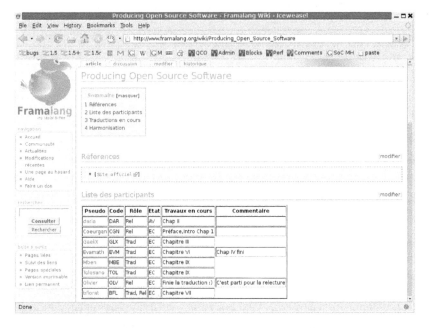

Framalang translation wiki.

Seeing this on-list correspondence made me think back to private conversations I'd had with some of the other translators. Many of them had had problems working in XML. Even though the translators themselves generally understood the format well enough to work with it, their editing tools often did not. Their word processors (particularly on Microsoft Windows) would sometimes mess up the XML. This was something I'd never experienced myself, but that's only to be expected: I'd chosen the format in the first place, so naturally it worked well with *my* tools.

Looking back, I can correlate the conversations I had with frustrated individual translators with dropoffs in their contributions; a few of them actually stopped doing translation altogether. Of course, some turnover is to be expected in any volunteer group, but the important thing is to notice when dropoffs happen for a specific reason. In this case, they were, but because I was personally comfortable with the tools, it didn't occur to me for a long time that they were a significant gumption sink for others. The result is that I effectively turned down an unknown amount of volunteer energy: many of the translations that were started have still not been finished, and some of the responsibility for that has to lie with the awkward tool requirements I imposed.

Conclusion

From the preceding examples, we can distill a few principles of collaboration tools:

- Good tools get the fundamental units of information right.

  For example, with commit emails, the fundamental unit is the change (or "changeset"). When the tool failed to treat each change as a single logical entity, and instead divided it across multiple interface access points (in this case, emails), people became less inclined to inspect the change.

  Getting the fundamental units right does not merely make individual tool usage better. It improves collaboration, because it gives the team members a common vocabulary for talking about the things they're working with.

- When you see necessary tasks being repeatedly postponed ("I'll try to get to it this weekend…"), it's often a sign that the tools are forcing people into a higher per-task commitment level than they're comfortable with. Fix the tools and the postponements may go away.

  The Contribulyzer didn't help with any of the interesting parts of evaluating a contributor's work: one still had to review the actual code changes, after all. But it did remove the *uninteresting* part, which was the manual search through the revision control logs for that contributor's changes. That dismaying prospect, although less work than the actual evaluation in most cases, was significant enough to be a gumption sink, in part because it's simply boring.

  Removing it, and replacing it with a pleasant, lightweight interface, meant that team members no longer had to make an emotional commitment to a major effort when deciding to evaluate a contributor. Instead, it became like a decision to sharpen a pencil in an electric sharpener: there's no effort involved in starting up the task, you can stop in the middle and resume later if you want, and you can do as many pencils as you want without multiplying the start-up overhead.

- When your team starts routing around the tools you've offered them, pay attention: it may be a sign that you're offering the wrong tools.

  Not always, of course: there can be cases where people don't initially appreciate the benefits a tool will bring, and need to be taught. But even then, the tool is probably at least partly to blame, in that it didn't make the benefits clear enough from the outset. At the very least, grassroots workarounds should make you sit up and investigate what's motivating them. When the French translators of my book defected to a wiki-based interface, at considerable start-up cost to themselves, that was a clear sign that something was wrong with the interface I'd been providing.

- A change in a team's demographics may require a change in tools.

  With those XML book chapters, as long as the "team" consisted of programmers who had prior experience working with version-controlled XML files—which was the case for as long as the team consisted only of me—the tools I'd set up were fine. But when new people came on board, simply extending the existing framework was not the right answer. Instead, the tool environment needed to be rethought from scratch.

- Partial automation is often enough to make a difference.

   Designers of collaboration tools love 100% solutions: if something *can* be fully automated, they feel, then it should be. But in practice, it may not always be worth the effort; a hybrid model is often the better choice. If you can get 90% of the benefit with 10% of the effort, then do just that much, and remember that the team is willing to make up the difference as long as they'll get clear benefits from it. The Contribulyzer, for example, completely depends on humans following certain crediting conventions when they write log messages. It takes time and effort to teach people these conventions. But the alternative—a fully automated intelligent project watcher that infers connections between mailing list messages and commits—would require a huge amount of effort with no guarantee of perfect reliability anyway.

   Actually, that's one of the often overlooked benefits of hybrid tools: because they cause humans to stay engaged with the data at more points, such tools can prove *more* reliable than allegedly fully automated ones. The point of good tools is not to make humans unnecessary, but to make them happy. (Some might say "to make them more efficient," but an inefficient team is rarely happy anyway, and you surely wouldn't want a team that is efficient but unhappy.)

Despite the benefits to be had from good tools, my experience is that most teams' actual tool usage lags behind their potential tool usage. That is, most teams are failing to take advantage of potentially large multiplier effects. I think this is because of two built-in biases shared by most humans.

One bias is that trying new things costs too much. Since most new things are likely to bring little benefit, groups tend to be selective about adopting new tools, for the overhead of changing habits can be a drag on both productivity and enjoyment. (I do not mean to imply that this bias is unreasonable. Indeed, it is usually well founded, and I share it myself.)

The other bias is subtler. Because successful tools quickly become second nature—blending into the mental landscape until they are considered just part of "the way things are done"— people can easily forget the effect a tool had *at the time it was introduced*. Examples of this phenomenon are not hard to find, starting with the text editor in which I'm writing these words. Fifty years ago, the idea of editing and reshaping a text while simultaneously writing its first draft would have been a writer's wishful dream;* now it is so commonplace that it's probably hard for schoolchildren in the developed world to imagine writing any other way. And even computer text-editing starts to look like a mere incremental improvement when compared to a truly transformative tool like universal literacy.

---

* Whether it results in *better* text is, of course, open to question.

Imagine trying to get a team to cooperate without depending on its members being able to read and write!

And yet, consider how your team would react if someone came along and advocated the following:

> I know a way to make you many times more productive. Do what I tell you, and your group's ability to collaborate will increase beyond your most optimistic projections. Here's the plan: first, everyone's going to learn this set of symbols, called an *alphabet*. Each symbol is called a *letter*, and the letters map, more or less, to sounds in a language that is native to some of you and non-native to others. Once you've learned the basic sounds of the letters, I'll show you how to arrange them in groups to form written words. Once you've memorized between 5,000 and 10,000 of those words, you'll be able to transmit arbitrary sentences, and then your productivity will increase by *a whole lot*!

Literacy is a classic example of a high-investment, high-payoff tool. Everyone spends a lot of time in training, but after they make it through that part, it pays off for years to come.

Usually, the tools that get people most excited are low-investment, high-payoff. But it would be a mistake to consider only such tools: literacy did pay off in the end, after all. A dedicated team can make non-trivial tool investments when necessary, especially if everyone bears the burden together and thus is able to strengthen his sense of community by learning the new tool as a group. A tool that makes obstacles go away and makes new things possible will justify a lot of investment. For people working together on a technical project, few things have as direct an effect on daily experience as the tools they work with. The more you understand their experience, the better tool choices you can make.

CHAPTER TWENTY-TWO

Research Teams

an Interview with Michael Collins

The area that Michael Collins works in interests us for two reasons. First, Michael spent much of his career working on research with teams in an academic setting. But second, that research has been oriented at solving concrete, real-word security problems for serious customers inside and outside government, and the work that he's done spans both academic and commercial areas. We wanted to hear what he had to say about that.

Andrew: You were working on a research project to try to detect intrusions into networks.

Michael: Mostly what we were trying to do was model normalcy. Most of what I do falls into the field of anomaly detection, which falls under the field of intrusion detection. Most anomaly detection is trying to build a model of normal behavior, so when you see that all of a sudden you're falling outside the domain of normal behavior, you get curious as to why that's happening.

A credit card example of this is that you've got normal spending habits. And if all of a sudden you start spending in Katmandu, that's when the credit card company calls up and asks, "Are you in Katmandu?" And the answer is no. That's anomaly detection, as done with credit cards. You do the same thing with network traffic.

Andrew: So, your goal was to look at the data from routers, and just by looking at the gigabytes of daily data from router logs you can detect successful and unsuccessful attempts at intrusion?

Michael: That's the Holy Grail. But the first step was just to model what was going on. But to do that, you don't know the types of questions you're going to ask. And this is the cornerstone of research: you don't really know what you will need yet. Oftentimes, you build and rebuild your tools all the way through the process.

Now, the client at this point could conduct one query every five hours or so. It was something in the nature that they were literally conducting the query of the day. They'd put up the graph and say, "This is what we found today." We got that time down from five or six hours to about 10 minutes on a dual-processor Pentium box (in 2001). We put out our initial report, which led to the question, "How are you able to do that many queries?" We came up with our explanation as to how we'd shrunk down the data and formalized the query process. And the response from the client was, "We want that."

Andrew: And suddenly you have a software project.

Michael: Exactly.

Andrew: And you need a team to build it.

Michael: Yes. Our original group was four people. Two of us were doing code, and neither of us were considered "programmers." Specifically, the one time I referred to myself as a programmer, my boss, Suresh, yelled at me for about five minutes and said, "You might do woodworking, but you're not a carpenter. You're a researcher. You write code to answer questions, you're not a developer."

Let me make a couple of points here. We'd actually already prepared the environment for tough work, for lack of a better term. So, our file type headers, for example, already had a versioning system built into them. We'd been prepping for forward and backward compatibility.

We'd had enough experience with engineering environments to know that prototypes are something of a luxury, in the sense that the difference between your prototype and your production may sometimes be that you simply changed the label on it. So, we were not expecting the reaction we got, but we also treated the development of the system as a serious problem from square one.

Andrew: One thing I've seen when doing research projects and talking to people who've done research projects is that, like your boss Suresh said, researchers are not programmers. If you were talking to someone who's just starting their Ph.D. research or starting a research project in a university environment, how would they apply the lessons you learned to their own project? What did you do differently that a more naïve research team might not think to do?

Michael: I think one of the big things—and this is very true, especially of grad students—is that there's a tendency to build a lot of stuff out of spit and bailing wire without necessarily thinking about the solution ahead of time.

One of the big things that we did was that we tried to chop the work into discrete, tiny, well-defined "project-ettes." And one of the major reasons for doing this was to make sure that the code in project-ettes was robust. When you get to the architecture of SiLK* (the name of the system we were building), there's kind of a core library that manages reading files, I/O, a lot of this stuff. And then there are about 40 applications that have been written at this point.

Research has a very high failure rate. So, the ideal is that as long as we kept the development effort involved in these tiny projects, which we could then test, see if they were useful, see if they answered a question, and if they didn't, they went away. We expected to expend time, but at least this way we weren't expending huge amounts of time. The stuff that really mattered got folded into the central SiLK library. One of the key things was that because we spent a lot of time worrying about versioning, and making sure that the central library was robust, I think we saved ourselves from the headaches you usually see with research projects where you end up with this blob of software that keeps expanding all the time. I think that's because when you do research, you slap in things an awful lot. You're going to have an idea, you're going to try out that idea, and hope that idea becomes useful. We were actually fairly ruthless about cutting off things that didn't work and acknowledging when we had failures. We also spent a lot of time rebuilding and keeping the central core of the system small and robust.

Andrew: So, it sounds like there's an architecture perspective, where basically you keep it to the scope, acknowledge that something didn't work. And when it doesn't work, you get rid of it, you get it out of your solution so you don't end up with a lot of cruft over time that makes it harder and harder to maintain your code.

Michael: Right. The difference between research and feature creep can be really, really fine.

---

* SiLK, the System for Internet-Level Knowledge, is the collection of traffic analysis tools that Michael and the team were working on. It's been released as an open source project, and it can be downloaded from *http://tools.netsa.cert.org/silk/*.

One of the things we also did as time passed: let's say that tool X did something, but later tool Y did something that X did, but better. Then we would try to deprecate and remove tool X. Now, it turned out that since the system was being used live, that some people at the client would stay with tool X. But it no longer became a high-priority development task for us. One of the key things attached to this, because people were using the live system, was that there was a lot of documentation associated with it: there's training, there's manuals, there's meetings. And there kind of became a training course and training manual that defined how someone used the system. As we deprecated a tool, we would remove it from the main part of the training course and put it into the back section.

Andrew: So, there's the tools and the architecture, and that's one area where you tried to optimize what you did towards building software. You changed the way you did your work in order to keep it more maintainable. What about the way you worked together? The people aspect of it? Did you feel like you had to do something differently from the way a lot of research projects were? Is it something you guys gave a lot of thought to? An environment that would evolve over time?

Michael: Well, that was an interesting problem, because we ran into some interesting skills stovepiping issues. You had a couple of people who were researchers, primarily from statistical or higher-level software engineering backgrounds, who really don't know code. And then you had people who were hired primarily as developers. But our ideal was to find people who sat in the middle: if you could do statistical analysis, and you could write C code to do numerical analysis, then that was what we were looking for on the whole. And part of the reason was because it's easier to justify a researcher than a coder in our line of work. So, our goal eventually was to have everyone as a kind of semiautonomous coder/researcher, with a couple of people who basically were "guardians" of the architecture. It didn't really work out that way in the long run. I think the stovepiping ends up being inevitable, simply because people have specialties and interests and skill sets.

One of the problems we ran into early on was with a senior researcher who was explicitly *not* a coder. So, if he ran into a problem and there was nobody around to write code for him, he had to basically sit around and twiddle his thumbs, and that was a running problem we had to figure out how to address. Eventually, we ended up getting utility developers who would work with people like him and give them the code they need.

Andrew: So, you've got this problem to solve, where you've got some of your team members—pure researchers, scientists, mathematicians, statistical analysts—who aren't coders. In a software company, what you'll see a lot of times is that you'll have a team working with business clients. But in this case, those non-programmers were really part and parcel of the team.

Michael: Yes. We ran into a different requirements extraction problem. The researchers served as the engine for new ideas. That's part of the reason we were looking for hybrid researcher-developers. These were people who'd have a problem, they'd go build a tool to solve the problem, and the tool would have to be viable in multiple situations. And we then had a couple of people who tried to figure how to take what had been built and plug it into the entire system. So, you'd have these prototypes the researcher-developers would build, and you'd have a couple of people in the back thinking about how this would go into the architecture. One person would think about how to plug things into libraries, and I'd think about where we were generally moving: here's our gaps in what we've done so far, here's a place where we can probably plug those gaps. We've got these tools, so how about we expand the functionality of these tools to do this additional stuff, and now we've got a coherent view of the problem.

The advantage was that as we did more and more of those things, the pure researchers would not be writing C code, but they might be doing scripting or something like that to plug the tools together. Then, we'd have a solution—a slow one—and we could use something better here. So, then we could devote some development effort into developing an optimized version of it.

Andrew: So since, at the core of this, this was a project to build software as much as it was a research project, the team members who normally might not have been coders were contributing something codewise in a way that hopefully connected some dots to help move on to the next interesting research question.

Michael: Right. The idea there was to reach a middle ground. First off, you'd never expect a pure researcher to contribute to the code base. But if we have a collection of tools, and a researcher could write a shell script to use the tools, that's not onerous to him and it's not destructive to us. It's something where he can go forward and come up with an initial answer to the question, and we can use that information to say, "Now it's time to build system X."

Again, we're getting to that idea that we don't know if what we're producing is going to be valued.

Andrew: How often did you find yourself going down false paths that required you to remove code from the software? Because when you pull features out or change code, you often end up introducing as many problems as you solve.

Michael: The way we avoided that was that SiLK had two layers. There's the architecture—the filesystem, the file storage, things of that nature—and then there were the tools around it. Research, from SiLK's perspective, consisted of either implementing or gluing together a set of tools to answer a question. As a rule, the research orbited the tools. If we came up with an idea, and we implemented it as a tool, no harm, no foul to the central architecture.

Andrew: From an architecture perspective, you made things highly modular, to the point where you had different programs glued together with shell scripts, which is about as modular as possible. And from a team perspective, you tried to make sure that people were, from a technical perspective, as flexible as possible technically.

Michael: Yes. That said, we did end up with somebody who became the guardian of the architecture, and that's a technical job.

Andrew: Did you ever run into any conflicts between people on the team?

Michael: The research group was composed of strong-willed, largely autonomous people who were drawing in their own funding. Argument was the default state of affairs.

Basically, arguments fell into two categories. The first category of arguments are research arguments: I should try idea X, I should try idea Y, I should try idea Z. As a rule of thumb, you'd try out the idea, and if it turned out to be fine, you went with it. If it didn't work out, you didn't. However, we were also producing things that did go to the client. We did all of the prototyping with our tools, and if our tools turned out to be useful, we'd produce a module and a training course, and we'd teach people to use the tools. And one thing I'd do is elicit requirements from people who used the tools, because they usually had a better idea of what they were looking for than we did. We were using the tools for research; they were using them to actually find people!

So, we had that class of arguments. And the other arguments we had were about things like the integrity of the code base, things of that nature. There was a spectacular, legendary argument that Suresh and I had, and this was more a vanity thing on his part. He'd been in jury duty for two weeks. He was coming out, and we were going to ship something, Goddamn it. Basically, I refused to let that happen until I had tested things. The reason for this was that at this point in time, we hadn't yet coalesced into having the guy who was the guardian of the code base. And one of the things I specifically was brought on to do was to be the system reliability guru. I was the guy who worked out all of the fault trees for how everything failed, and I wrote documents describing to the sys admins how to use these things so if the system fails in fashion X, here's how to handle that kind of recovery. So, I wasn't letting anything out. It was a four-hour argument, and basically boiled down to me sticking to my guns. That was a major thing for me, because by that point I'd always been junior to him. This was the point where I had taken ownership of the project sufficiently that I wasn't going to let my name be damaged, because quite frankly, he'd been in jury duty and was feeling salty.

The key part of that, really, is just that when you're an academic, reputation tends to be a big item. When you write a paper, you bet your name on the paper. And that was one of the key things about this: we had a culture that was generally dedicated to the idea that when we put something out, that was our reputation on the line. That was taught to everyone within the group. You're representing us, your work represents us, and when something goes wrong you have to own up to it, fix it, and be cautious about releasing things.

This was eventually streamlined to the point where we had a sort of jury system for moderating releases. We had screw-ups, which I handled internally as appealing to personal pride. One time there was a glitch in the system that resulted in two fields being swapped, and I ended up privately talking to the developer and saying, "Look, you made me look like a fool in front of the client. I took that bullet, but don't do that kind of thing again." And after that, he was extremely conscientious and diligent about making sure that never happened again.

I came from a background that was theoretical, very driven by the idea of what engineering design is. We were all trained with the idea that we don't have a monopoly on the truth. So, we expect arguments to take place. We also placed a cultural emphasis on the idea that the arguments weren't personal. I tend to say that I expect the most productive environments are composed of people who respect each other but are personally neutral to each other, the reason being that they will provide unbiased judgments and they won't treat each other as fools. They're not interested in being nice to spare your feelings, and they're not interested in being nasty to hurt your feelings. As a group, you have the courage to argue with each other, and the objectivity to actually reach a consensus at the end.

One of our rules about arguing was that you have to reach some kind of consensus finally. Then we could go at each other full out. Most of the time the arguments we had were technical or experimental or something of that nature, so at the end of the argument we'd have to conduct a test to find out who's right. The thing is that most of the people we were dealing with were PhD-educated. This is part and parcel of the process: if you don't know if something's true or not, you have to test.

CHAPTER TWENTY-THREE

The HADS Team

Karl Rehmer

IN ANCIENT TIMES, THE BUILDER WHO WAS IN CHARGE OF BUILDING AN ARCH WOULD BE REQUIRED TO stand under the arch when the supports were first removed. If the arch failed, it would come tumbling down on the builder. I felt a bit like the arch builder the first time I got on a Boeing 777 airliner. I had written some critical parts of the flight code and been part of a team that built the software tools that were used to build a large portion of the flight software for the plane. It's an amazing feeling to realize that your life depends on the quality of the software you have written. As with building the arch, the final product was not the result of one person's efforts. The builder would know the history of the project, and sometimes knowing what was done could make him quite nervous. Though I knew a lot of the background of the development of the flight systems and some of the problems encountered during development, I didn't have to be nervous like the arch builder. The airplane had undergone extensive flight testing before it was ever put into service. I wasn't the first to stand under the arch. It is exciting to board a plane, knowing that your team played a big role in helping to produce the flight software. The story I'm telling here is the story of the HADS team, the team that built the compiler, runtime, linker, debugger, and other support tools used by the developers of the flight software for the Boeing 777. This small team developed, adapted, or maintained by the HADS team was roughly the same amount of code as for the entire 777 flight systems that had hundreds of developers. Every one of the project deadlines was met. Working on this team was one of the highlights of my software engineering career.

I suppose some teams start off beautiful and stay that way. I know that some teams start off ugly and stay that way. The HADS team didn't start out as beautiful, and at the end, it just kind of faded away. But in the middle there, it was beautiful, and while it was beautiful, it was really beautiful.

The Background

You might wonder how Honeywell Air Transport Systems ever got involved with making the HADS tool set, since its purpose is to produce avionics for commercial aircraft.

The origin goes back to the 1980s. Sperry Flight Systems was making the transition from building analog flight controls to using digital computers and software for the controls. At one point in the process, Sperry designed its own computer chip and had a software team make a hybrid version of Pascal for this processor. They recognized that the type checking provided by Pascal provided some safety advantages and added some features that were important to writing software for flight systems. When the Ada language became a standard, they became interested in the language for developing software for safety-critical flight systems.

In 1985, Sperry Flight Systems began looking at Ada for a fly-by-wire system for the proposed Boeing 7J7. The target processor was to be a member of the Intel 80×86 family with an Ada development system from a compiler vendor named DDC-I. DDC-I was respected as a compiler vendor, especially for the quality of its tools and runtimes for the Intel 80×86 family of processors. It also helped that DDC-I had a sales and engineering office in Phoenix, Arizona, where Sperry Flight Systems was located.

As part of the software development process for flight-critical software, all routines included in the system must be well documented and have tests written to ensure code coverage. An effort was undertaken to document and test the DDC-I Ada runtime system to the level required for DO-178B, the FAA guideline for software. In the middle of this process, Sperry Flight Systems was sold to Honeywell. The part that dealt with large aircraft such as commercial jetliners was named Honeywell Air Transport Systems Division.

Meanwhile, my wife and I were working as assistant professors at Indiana-Purdue University in Fort Wayne, Indiana. In the summers we did software consulting at a Magnavox facility in Fort Wayne. Magnavox was an early adopter of Ada, working on the first really large Ada project, called AFATDS (Advanced Field Artillery Tactical Data System). In 1988, we decided that my wife would continue her education by working on a Ph.D. in computer science and I would support the family by finding a job in industry.

My Ada experience matched Honeywell's needs, and I was hired to be a member of a small team that was to reverse-engineer, document, and write coverage tests for the DDC-I Ada runtime system that was to be used for the 7J7 project. For speed, the runtime was written in assembly language, so the first part of documenting the runtime was to reverse-engineer the code and write a higher-level pseudocode description of each of the algorithms. The purpose of each subprogram and when it would be called was also documented. This team got to the point of having the runtime documented when the 7J7 project was cancelled by Boeing.

Honeywell Air Transport Systems had a continued interest in Ada, and knew that it would have future Ada projects, so I began working on developing design and coding standards for Honeywell's use of Ada. I also developed an in-house training class for Ada. Both of these were important because few software developers at Honeywell had any Ada experience or experience using many of the software engineering principles that Ada was designed to support. In short, I was the in-house Ada guru.

It wasn't very long until Boeing began to develop its next airliner, the Boeing 777. Honeywell Air Transport Systems was awarded large portions of the software.

Among the software to be developed was a system called AIMS (Aircraft Information Management System). This system was to be written completely in Ada. Previous flight software would have one CPU per line replaceable unit (LRU). AIMS integrated the functionality that had been distributed into multiple LRUs into a single system. A single processor would run several applications. For software that was flight-critical, underlying software needed to guarantee that one application could not steal time from or corrupt the data of another process. Because multiple time-critical applications that shared information were to run on a single processor, AIMS required a powerful processor.

Weight on an aircraft is always important. Every pound that is flown requires fuel. As part of the weight savings, AIMS was to be passively cooled—no fan was to be used to provide for cooling.

The hardware engineers at Honeywell did an extensive study of the available processors and rejected the most popular Motorola and Intel chips as either consuming too much power (therefore being too hot to passively cool), or not having enough processing power to handle the job. The analysis and the fact that the hardware engineers were able to build some early prototypes led the engineers to require the AMD 29050 processor for AIMS for the 777. The host system for development was DEC VAX computers running VMS, and later, DEC VAX workstations.

This presented an interesting problem, because Honeywell had promised Boeing that it would do the AIMS software in Ada, but there were no Ada compilers available for the AMD 29050. In my role as Ada guru, I recommended that the choice of the 29050 should be revisited. Since the quality of the compiler and support tools would have a great impact on the development, I felt that the choice of a mature compilation system was vital. The hardware engineers insisted that only the AMD 29050 would meet their needs, so Honeywell needed to find a development system. They approached a number of Ada compiler vendors about producing a compiler and related tools, but for various reasons, none of these worked out. So, Honeywell decided to make its own compiler and development tools. After all, it had made compilers before. It did realize that an Ada compiler and tools was a more complicated task than creating a Pascal compiler, so it formed a partnership with DDC-I. It would use the DDC-I frontend technology as the starting point. In addition, two DDC-I employees would work as consultants on the project. Several engineers from Honeywell's Software Tools section were also to work on the project. I was not one of the original members of the team. I was to continue my guru role. The product to be delivered was called HADS, the Honeywell Ada Development System.

DDC-I had just completed a project of making an Ada development system for the Intel I960 processor. Since it and the AMD 29050 both are RISC-like processors, the source code for that project was selected as the starting point for the project. An Ada compilation system involves much more than just a compiler that generates source code. It also requires a runtime system to manage tasking, exception handling, and storage management. Ada's tasking is a way, within the language, to allow for communication and synchronization of independent threads of control. Exception handling, while now common in languages like C++ and Java, was not a well-known concept at the time. Ada's storage management allows for the management of a general heap as well as other specialized heaps.

The compiler and linker are host tools, and DDC-I had used its DEC VAX native Ada compilation system as the tools for developing its Ada I960 compiler, so this was a natural choice for writing the HADS compiler and linker.

The runtime portion of the compilation system is code that runs on the target. Since the HADS compiler was not yet available for generating the needed code, the runtime was written in C and AM29050 assembler. The portions of the runtime that would be included in the safety-critical portions of final AIMS applications would need to be documented and tested to DO-178B standards.

Since I wasn't originally on the team, my recollections of the initial team are based on things I could overhear while I was sitting in my nearby cubicle, as well as things told to me later. Some developers' names I will be using are not the correct names. Some of this is because I truly don't recall the name of a person, and some to avoid any possible embarrassment.

The Initial Team

While sitting in my cubicle in the same area as the members of the HADS team, I was able to observe the initial work of the team. The start-up was anything but promising.

Tom and Dave were the DDC-I consultants working on the project; Tom had been the project leader for the DDC-I I960 project. Among other things, Dave had played a vital role in one of the most difficult parts of the code generation process: the task of making efficient use of the registers on the hardware. None of the Honeywell engineers had any experience with building compilers other than perhaps in a class in school. Tom was not initially the project leader for the HADS project, but was always closely consulted.

Aside from setting up initial schedules, the first major task was to analyze the differences between the Intel I960 and the AMD 29050 to try to understand what pieces of the previous project could be retained, what could be modified slightly, and what would need to be completely rewritten. Engineers from Honeywell were to do this work with consulting help from Tom and Dave. Chris was to analyze the architecture differences that affected linking. John was to look at the architectural impact on exception management. Cynthia looked at linking issues. Waleen looked at storage management issues. Ajit looked at issues related to Ada tasking. Ajit also looked into issues related to what is called the User Configurable Code, since it interfaces closely with the scheduling portion of Ada tasking. The engineers doing these analyses would be designers of these portions of the tool set. Implementation would use some additional Honeywell engineers, including Dan, Fred, Willis, and Henry.

It's interesting to observe how differently people work. From my nearby cubicle, I could get a lot of impressions of how things were going. John didn't ask for much help, and mostly studied documents by himself. Waleen usually didn't go to Tom and Dave for help. Since we had worked on the 7J7 documentation project together, she would often come to me to ask a question or two. Chris spent a lot of time with Tom, but mostly he would moan about how impossible his task was. Tom was not entirely sympathetic and would not take over Chris's task, but he would try to point out to him some areas that needed to be looked at and to point him to the documents where the information could be found. Fred was one of those guys who has a lot of great ideas, but then doesn't seem to follow through with them. I can remember several times thinking how glad I was to not be on that team.

After a few weeks, John decided that he was not up to the task and asked to be moved to a different project. Because of my past experience documenting an Ada runtime, I was asked to take his place. In spite of my misgivings, and because it would not have been politically wise to refuse, I joined the team with my first responsibility being the exception management. The first meeting to go over the differences was not too far away at that time, but John had actually left behind some pretty good documentation. By the time of this first high-level design meeting, I was able to speak to the major architectural issues that would impact exception management. Still, the fact that I was given a late start on the project put this part at risk.

At this same meeting, Chris made his presentation on the architectural differences that would impact code generation. It was obvious to everyone at the meeting that he had done virtually nothing. He had clearly started with one of the DDC-I documents for the I960 and made some editing changes. Frequently, entire sections were about the I960 with nothing said about the AMD 29050. In some places, it looked like he had just used the editor to substitute "AMD 29050" for "I960" and he made some statements that were clearly false. This was really bad, since generating code is obviously one of the most important parts of a compilation system. I guess I was too amazed by the presentation to remember much about the reaction at the meeting. I don't recall any direct criticism of

Chris, but certainly errors and omissions in his presentation were pointed out. The meeting didn't do anything to increase my confidence in the success of the project.

Dave later told me that as they were walking back to their cubicles, he and Tom were discussing how poorly Chris had performed. They couldn't believe the lack of progress. They decided to go to the section head for the Honeywell Software Tools group and have Chris removed from the project. Interestingly, Chris had gone straight from the meeting to ask to be removed from the project. Some other areas of analysis, while not quite this bad, also seemed to be in trouble. The first major deadline, being able to compile, link, and run a "Hello World" program, was in jeopardy. Many on the team were not pulling their weight.

Getting It Right

Something had to be done to get the project on track. The team was reorganized, and, in spite of looming deadlines, made smaller. Chris was not replaced. Fred moved off to a different project. Willis and Henry moved off to a different 777 support role, working with the C compiler that was used for a small portion of the 777 code. Peter, an additional consultant from DDC-I, was added. Tom officially took over as project lead. The team divided the work not previously done, identifying the unique features of the processor that affect code generation and the runtime implementation. The frontend of the compiler could be used without change. Only a very small amount of the code generation and a minimal amount of the runtime are necessary to compile and run "Hello World". Though it was close, the first deadline was met.

Following this, some team members began the detailed design and implementation of the storage management, task management, and exception management of the runtimes. Others continued with more code generation.

Waleen did the design and implementation of storage management. At a high level, many of the algorithms could be similar to those used for the I960. The biggest challenge was that this was being written in assembly language, so a complete rewrite needed to be done. Waleen also had to learn the assembly language.

A low-level body of code called the User Configurable Code (UCC) allows for the writing of a very small portion of code to allow interfacing of the runtime with the actual hardware. Some examples of code in the UCC are low-level code for I/O, code to manipulate timers, and code to handle traps and interrupts. This was designed and implemented at this stage. Ajit worked on the UCC.

For the most part, the task-management algorithms could be used as they were from the I960. The challenges had to do not with the Ada tasking constructs, but with general handling of independent threads of control, such as how to do a context switch and handle interrupts. Since handling interrupts and doing context switches are very close to the hardware handling that is done by the UCC, Ajit also worked on this portion.

I worked on the design and implementation of the exception management. The general form and purpose of the algorithms did not have to be changed, but the low-level implementation involved a lot of architectural differences. This portion of the code was written in C. A C compiler for the AMD 29050 was available from Metaware, but there was no source-level debugger. An instruction set simulator provided the ability to run programs and to do machine-level debugging. It was possible to have the compiler generate mixed source and assembly listings, so this was used to relate the source code to the generated machine code for debugging. The lack of source-level debugging can be cumbersome, but with practice, the listings and machine-level debugging provided an adequate development environment. As a side benefit, I was forced to learn quite a bit about the machine language. This was helpful later when I did some work on portions of the code generator.

Cynthia continued working on linker issues and the other members of the team areas of code generation for additional constructs.

As part of the standard for Ada (Ada 83), a suite of tests called the Ada Compiler Validation Capability (ACVC) was defined. In order to be validated, a compiler and associated runtime must pass all the applicable tests of the ACVC for its environment. After the first deadline of being able to run "Hello World", subsequent deadlines of passing increasing percentages of ACVC tests were defined.

One defined deadline was to pass 80% of the non-tasking ACVC tests. When this deadline was met, the first release of the system was made to the users for the 777 team. Some groups were far from ready to begin coding at this stage, but others were ready to do some prototyping. One particular group led by Joel was especially anxious since he had heard rumors of Ada inefficiencies. Though many of the so-called inefficiencies can be met by turning off the default, language-defined runtime checks after initial development, the group was concerned. Immediately upon getting the first release of the compiler, they did an analysis of the output of the produced machine language. They concluded that the performance of the compiler was not good enough. In spite of the fact that we told them that the emphasis on this release was not on performance, and that subsequent releases would have much more optimization, they began to look for alternatives. They didn't really have much choice since Honeywell had committed to using Ada and there were not other compilers. They decided that for much of their code they would use Ada's machine code insertion mechanism. When this is done, the user essentially writes assembly language and the compiler merely assembles it. This would technically meet the mandate to write the code in Ada, but give the desired performance. After about the fourth release of the compiler, the HADS team revisited the original code from this team and found that the compiler generated much more efficient and smaller code than the "assembly" version. This is not surprising, and was shown to be true in a number of published studies. A high-level language compiler—and in particular an Ada compiler—can keep track of and take advantage of more global knowledge than a programmer can keep in his head. The compiler developers are also generally more knowledgeable of architecture features that can be used. The HADS team had to continually "sell" the product.

The project had one great piece of good luck related to the AMD 29050 processor, which was the existence of a very good and complete simulator. This meant that the team could develop and test while the actual hardware was in the early prototype phase. It turned out that any code that would run on the actual hardware would run on the simulator as well. There were only a couple of timing-related areas where code that was not legal on the actual hardware would run on the simulator. The simulator was a big factor in letting the team stay on schedule.

Though some deadlines were close, the HADS team met all deadlines on the way to producing a compiler that passed 100% of the ACVC tests. After meeting this goal, the work was far from done. For example, Ada defines and allows for a number of implementation-dependent features. These include things like the ability to precisely describe the layout of data structures such as records and arrays. Features appropriate for the AMD 29050 and for the 777 project needed to be implemented. Also, the promised optimizations needed to be added. Since the UCC portions of the project were finished, and the Ada tasking was working, Ajit left the project to work for one of the 777 project teams.

Dealing with User Issues

One of the major tasks that we had to undertake was education and support for the users of the tool set. Most were unfamiliar with the Ada programming language, few knew any details of the processor architecture, and the tool set was new to all of the users.

Aside from dealing with some of the myths about Ada, the HADS team had to struggle with a general lack of Ada knowledge among the 777 developers. Ada is a powerful language with a lot of features that make it ideal for safety-critical embedded systems. These days it would not be considered to be a complex language, but at the time, it was considered to be a very complicated language to learn. Many of the software engineering concepts that Ada was designed to assist were foreign to the majority of developers. The HADS team had to take on a role as informal instructors in the use of Ada. For example, Ada's strong type checking can lead to difficulties getting programs to compile. This is an intentional attempt, in the design of the language, to catch inconsistencies as early as possible (during compilation) rather than at runtime. But struggling users tend to blame their tools. We were often called to help out some user with a compilation problem. Since most of us on the HADS team were very familiar with Ada, this was not difficult, but time-consuming. It also could lead to some tense encounters.

I remember being asked to go help Frank who was having some difficulties getting his code to compile. I went over to his desk and we sat down to go over his code. He definitely was having some type-mismatch problems with the subscripts of an array and the elements of the array. So we struggled through getting the types straightened out. Frank was quite frustrated with the strong type checking. I think he came from the school that feels that anything should compile and then you debug the result. Finally we got his code to a state where it would compile, but it seemed overly complex. I said to him, "You know, there is a better way to do this," and told him about some Ada features that would make the code clearer and probably generate more efficient code. Frank got all upset, feeling insulted that I was criticizing his code. I was taken aback, since in the HADS project we did this all the time, and the team members considered it helpful. Of course, the members of the HADS team knew that they were good and didn't feel threatened. Frank had just gone through a lot of frustration just to get something to compile, and was then told there was a better way.

Passing all of a test suite does not guarantee that a compiler is bug-free. The ACVC tests are a rigorous set of tests for the basic features of Ada, but combinations of features may not be tested and implementation dependencies are not included in the suite. Naturally, the HADS team had to deal with bugs in the releases. One thing that we did well was, when possible, to duplicate a bug with a small test which was then added to our own regression test suite that was run in addition to the ACVC tests. Producing such a test case can be difficult.

One time Paul came to the team with a bug report, and after looking at it, we agreed that this did seem to be a code generation problem. Unfortunately, Paul said that he could produce the bug only in a large, complex system, and that whenever he would try to simplify it, the bug would go away. Clearly he had found some obscure corner case. Luckily, as part of Honeywell, we had no difficulties getting permission to get all of Paul's code. By turning on some output of the internal workings of the compiler, we were able to see what the compiler was doing, and we were able to reduce the original case consisting of several thousand lines of code down to a test program of about twenty lines. Sometimes it was not as easy as this, and we might spend several days creating a small test case. Still, the effort was worthwhile since finding a correction for a bug in a small program is much easier than trying to find the correction in a large program. The small program also provided the basis for the regression test.

I've often said that software tools are at the bottom of the food chain. By that I mean that when all else fails, users blame their tools. We had to deal with this issue a great deal, since not only was there a tool to blame, but it was a "homegrown" tool, and therefore was more mistrusted. One day, I got a support call from Frances who was complaining about a compiler bug. When she was writing to an array, erroneous code generation was causing another nearby variable to be overwritten. This kind of behavior is possible, perhaps even likely, when using a language like C that doesn't check that an array subscript is in the proper range. With Ada's compile and runtime checks, this behavior should be caught. If it is statically known at compile time that a subscript will be out of bounds, a warning will be emitted at compile time. At runtime, checks will raise an exception if an attempt to access an array with an out-of-bounds subscript is done. Such runtime checks do generate extra code and can create inefficiencies, so Ada compilers allow an option to turn off some or all runtime checks. Frances had done her build using an inherited build script that turned off runtime checks. A small amount of investigation and debugging showed that the source code was written so that values were written beyond the end of the array. The compiler was generating code to do exactly what it was instructed to do. We had to continually educate users on the tools' command-line options and their effects.

We had to deal with many bug reports that turned out to be user error. Unofficially we called these UIB (User Is Bozo) errors.

Once the ACVC tests were passing and several releases with some implementation-dependent features were made, the team began working on creating a source-level debugging environment for the HADS system. About this time, Cynthia was taken from the team to work on the 777 project. The remaining members of the team did the initial work on the debugger. Tom, Dave, Peter, Dan, and Waleen then returned to compiler issues, while I finished the first release of the debugger. Tom concentrated on peephole optimizations, Dave concentrated on efficient use of registers, and Dan and Waleen concentrated on general choice of optimal machine code generation for a construct.

One of the things that Dave needed to do in providing for efficient use of registers was "live/dead" analysis to determine when a register is holding a variable and when that variable is no longer used. As a side effect of doing this analysis, it was easy to determine whether a register was being read before it was written to. This would mean that an uninitialized variable was being used. Dave generated code that would emit a warning about an uninitialized variable being used. Once this was released to users and they began to get the warning, they began to call, asking for help to find their uninitialized variables. Dave found a clever way to analyze the inputs to the register allocation whereby he could output the name of the uninitialized variable. He implemented this and wrote several small test cases that showed that it worked properly. We included this feature in the next release. Almost immediately, we started to get complaints that the compiler had slowed down, and as we looked into it, we found that it was this uninitialized variable analysis. For one system that had compiled in under five minutes with the previous release, we aborted its compile after a day and a half. Naturally, the compiler was not any slower when there were no uninitialized variables, but it was clear that the ability to name any uninitialized variable detected was not worth the expense.

Adding information about the uninitialized variables was just one example of a request for a feature that came from our users. Since we were in-house and since many of the users had gotten to know us, we were often individually approached to add a feature to one of the tools. This began to get out of hand and we soon adopted a policy of "just say no" to any such request. We referred all of the requestors to our project lead, Tom, who would decide, along with the rest of the team, whether the request should be added to our work and what priority it should have.

We also instituted a "top 10" list for each person. Each person had a list of his top 10 priorities. That way, he knew what he should be working on now and what was coming up next. Tom might revise these lists daily, but if we disagreed with the priorities, he was open to discussion. We also had weekly meetings, on Friday afternoons, where we discussed the progress of the previous week and helped set priorities for the coming week. A small amount of technical discussion might also occur at these meetings.

When we were making the source-level debugger, much could be taken from previous DDC-I work, but many areas of debugging are architecture-specific. The handling of debug information is architecture-specific, and each target has specific ways of doing things such as setting breakpoints. Because the simulator was so useful to the team, a debugger that supported both the simulator and actual targets was made. As with the compiler, the release of the debugger was not a "big bang"—rather, a series of releases, supporting more and more features, was planned.

With the release of the debugger, more user support was required. One issue that was particularly perplexing was variables in registers. The code ported from the DDC-I baseline did a good job of indicating the initial location of a variable in a register, and where the register was stored if a subprogram was called while in the scope of the variable. But when we started to add optimizations to reuse registers, we found that we did not have information about how a variable might be moved from the register into memory and the register given to another variable. Users would ask for the value of a variable at a point where it was dead and its register reused. They would get an incorrect, confusing value when really the correct answer was that the variable was no longer available at that point in the code. It was a significant task to design a system to track this and to implement it in the debugger and in the register assignment portion of the compiler.

Many users are unfamiliar with using source-level debuggers, having mostly used print statements to get information about their programs. Educating users about how to use the debugger was an ongoing task. It seemed that no one reads manuals. As users would get familiar with the debugger, they would often ask for the addition of a feature that would make debugging easier for them. Usually it was easy to "fill" these requests since the feature was already in the debugger and the user hadn't read the manual.

Even with source-level debugging, sometimes it is useful for users to be able to debug at a machine code level to examine the low-level behavior of the code. Of course, when debugging at this machine code level, it is useful to know something about the architecture of the machine and its assembly language. Unfortunately, many users didn't bother to read that documentation either. One day, Sam called me up and said, "Either this debugger is broken, or there is something wrong with the simulator." So, I went over to his cubicle to see whether I could find the problem so that we could fix it. He was debugging at the machine code level where he could step individual machine instructions. He said, "Look, here I am ready to execute a call statement, but when I step into the machine code, I end up at the statement after the call rather than in the called routine." It was hard not to laugh. The architecture utilizes a "delay slot" to keep the instruction pipeline full when doing a branch or call. So, the behavior that Sam was seeing was the correct behavior.

A similar experience came when Helen called up to tell us that the compiler had optimized an important statement of her code. She was stepping through the code at the machine code level and got to a call statement. The source window was reflecting the source code positions that corresponded to the machine instructions executed. She said, "See, the assignment that is done just before the call was not done." Our optimization had moved the assignment into the delay slot. If she had executed one more machine code step, she might have been surprised that she didn't immediately get to the called routine, but she would have seen her assignment being done.

Epilogue

Developing a large tool set like HADS can be an expensive proposition. In addition to acquiring rights to the frontend compiler technology, external consultants and Honeywell engineers were used on the project. While this was not a large number of people, it still had a cost. Some of the managers on the project seemed to resent the expenditures. At one point in the project, an Ada compiler for the AMD 29050 from an external source became available. Since there was not much of a potential market for a compiler for this target, it is likely that the target customer for this compiler was the 777 project. It may be that some at Honeywell were encouraging the compiler vendor to develop the tool set to replace HADS or as a fallback position if the HADS team should fail. One day in a hallway, Bruce, one of the managers, came up to me and said, "Since there is an off-the-shelf compiler available, they are going to kill the HADS project." Naturally this was concerning, not for the sake of my job, as there was plenty of work to be done, but because we took pride in the quality of what we had done and didn't want to see it go to waste. But Bruce was known as a guy who liked to spread a lot of rumors and who liked to make others uncomfortable, so we didn't do anything special. We just continued on with our plans. By the time the other compiler came out, the HADS team had demonstrated numerous successes. Some evaluation of the other compiler was done, but the HADS compilation system was clearly superior.

The small HADS team was very successful, producing a large, quality system without missing any of its deadlines. Of course, we had some advantages that the 777 team did not have. For example, there is a standard for what it means to be an Ada compiler, meaning that the basic requirements for the product were known from day one of the project. Another big advantage we had was that we did not need to produce the volumes of customer documentation that the 777 project's waterfall life cycle required. Except for documenting those parts of the runtime that required DO-178B certification, we produced only the internal documentation it deemed necessary for reference and only external user documentation. This made things quite a bit easier for the HADS team than for the 777 team.

But there were also some things about the team that led to its success. What were the things that turned an initially ugly team into a beautiful, successful team?

The most obvious change was that a number of people who were merely going through the motions were replaced. The result was a smaller but much more dependable group. Having people that you can't depend on is not good. With a larger team, someone who is not "pulling his weight" can be overlooked for quite a while. With a small team, it is obvious what each person is doing. We found it much better to have a small group of dependable people. The small group that did the majority of the work was also highly competent. Many of us had not worked on compilers and related tools, but we all had worked on difficult projects and had developed a great deal of competence in programming in general. Experience in developing compilers did not seem to be highly important, but experience that involved proper use of software engineering principles did seem to be important.

It was much more than dependability and competence. A collegial attitude also developed. We all shared several characteristics that led to success. Most importantly, we all knew we were good. Because we knew we were good, we didn't worry about taking credit or getting blame for individual accomplishments. Because we knew we were good, we would ask others for help when faced with a particularly nasty problem. Because we knew we were good, we did not take offense if someone else offered a possibly better solution to a problem. Because we knew we were good, we were willing to take time to help out others. Because we knew we were good, we recognized the competence of our colleagues. Because we knew we were good, we didn't feel that it was necessary to get our own way, but could be insistent when it was important. Some have said that HADS was a very egoless team, but I think that the team members all had pretty big egos; however, the big egos did not need to be fed. We all had a confidence in our abilities and the abilities of our colleagues.

We all worked very hard, and each of us worked to the maximum of his or her abilities. We worked very little overtime, but each of us came in on time and put in a hard, full day every day. Because we would ask others for help when we had problems, and because we could see our colleagues working hard each day, we always had confidence that the work was progressing.

During most of the development, each developer had the primary responsibility for developing a particular area. Some example areas were the storage manager, the exception manager, providing the linking capability to the AIMS requirements for separation of applications, register assignment, and optimizations. Since we knew the person primarily responsible for an area, it was easy to talk with the right person about an issue.

In addition to the competence and personalities of the team members, there were several practices that the team used that led to success.

Since the HADS project was being developed in-house, and the engineers on the 777 project got to know the HADS developers well, it was easy for the project engineers to approach one of us about a particular feature or optimization that he desired. This could have led to a lot of "feature creep" or conflicting requirements. We avoided this problem by insisting that all requests go through Tom, the team leader. He decided what requests should be worked on, as well as the priority of these requests. He did a good job of shielding the rest of the team from a lot of outside pressures. I'm sure that it was a difficult balancing act to protect the team and also be responsive to the 777 project.

A really helpful practice we used was to have a short (half-hour) meeting at the end of the day on Fridays. In this meeting, we assessed the progress of the past week and set the general priorities for the next week. This was pretty much a democratic process, though Tom, as team lead, had the final say. Very little general problem solving was done in these meetings, but we were allowed to give opinions about things to look into as a possible solution to a problem. Many agile teams currently use a similar concept, though they have shorter, daily meetings.

We had deadlines that were rigid on data and fairly rigid on content. The weekly meetings determined the primary focus for the next week. The "top 10" list allowed us to continually readjust focus onto the short-term problems that must be solved in order to achieve the long-term goal. The combination of longer-term deadlines, goals for the next week, and the ability to change daily through the "top 10" list provided for an agile development environment.

The development of a regression test suite, based on issues found either internally by the team or by users, provided continual feedback on the quality of the product. It also made it easy to find regressions introduced during development. When a regression was found, its seriousness could be evaluated to determine its priority and when (and where) it should be added to someone's "top 10" list.

The HADS project was quite enjoyable to work on. Much of this had to do with the beauty of the team and the success of the project. It is difficult to know whether the success—and the practices that led to success—caused the team to be beautiful, or whether the beauty of the team led to the successes. I suspect that they grew together.

Any project winds down as it either fails or produces what is needed. For the HADS team, the wind-down was gradual. Several members of the team were moved to areas of production for the 777 project where their expertise in Ada and their intimate knowledge of the tool set were beneficial. Gradually, the consultants were removed until the team was down to two people. In a final round of layoffs, I was laid off and transferred to the Honeywell Technology Center. After a few months, the one remaining team member grew tired of working by himself and he left Honeywell. Maintenance of the project was taken over by a completely different set of engineers. An irony of the project is that after all of the primary HADS developers had left the team, the HADS project was given Honeywell's Highest Technical Award.

The perspectives given in this narrative are my own. Others on the team may perceive things quite differently. Perhaps, though I doubt it, some of the primary developers would not feel that the team was beautiful. But for me, my experiences on the HADS team were one of the highlights of my career as a software engineer.

PART FOUR

Obstacles

SOME OF THE HARDEST PROBLEMS YOU DEAL WITH WHEN BUILDING SOFTWARE ARE THINGS YOU CAN'T control. Sometimes accidents take down your project. Sometimes unforeseen issues do. And unfortunately, sometimes things are done to the team on purpose to undermine a project. Building software is hard enough without dealing with obstacles that are put in the team's way. But we work in the real world, and real-world projects run into problems that are bigger than the team and the software.

One of the biggest obstacles is a bad manager.

Have you ever had a manager who refused to accept a reasonable estimate? Or who consistently undersold your efforts ("The team says it'll take six weeks? I'll promise it in four; that'll light a fire under their asses!") and makes you work weekends to meet the crazy expectations? Bad managers come in all sorts of flavors, and every one of them presents a serious, sometimes even insurmountable, obstacle to the team. Some managers seem bound and determined to make your project fail. They micromanage the team, constantly change the goals of the project, and always seem to be made of Teflon when things go wrong, blaming the team for the problems and never questioning, even for a minute, their own direction or management.

A bad manager can be impossible to work for. But a team that's got a bad manager does have options. Sometimes it starts with recognizing that the manager is working against the team, and working around him. Sometimes you can actually change a bad manager: if you can gain a manager's trust, and get him to have confidence in the team, those things can work themselves out. Either way, the first step is recognizing the obstacle and figuring out how to handle it.

Not all obstacles are managers, or even people. Sometimes an obstacle is as simple as a technical constraint: having to work with terribly old hardware, having to make the software backward-compatible, unexpected and serious performance problems, or impenetrable spaghetti code that's difficult to maintain.

Some problems are an unavoidable result of the environment the team is working in. It could be a problem with the facility or the building. Some teams have to cope with time zone issues, when they're divided into groups across the world from each other. There are weather problems, traffic problems, transportation issues, noise problems…all sorts of obstacles that the team simply can't avoid.

Any of these problems can sink a project. But if you have a team that trusts each other and works well together, they can overcome even the craziest, most seemingly insurmountable obstacles in their way. In fact, getting past a serious problem can bring a team together. After all, you're all in it together. If you've got a serious problem that affects everyone on the team, then you'll all have to work together to get past it. And once you do, you've all got a shared experience that bonds the group tighter—much more than any cheesy corporate team-building retreat exercise ever could. In a lot of ways, it's adversity that makes a team gel.

Obstacles are hard for people to talk about. They're painful to go through, and not much fun to think about. And more often than not, serious obstacles really do cause projects to fail. If you open any software engineering textbook, you can read about all sorts of statistics and studies about project failure. (Some textbooks put this number at a staggering 80%!) But how many people have you talked to who really spend any time talking about their own failed projects?

It's human nature to avoid talking about our own failures. Most people's resumes highlight the successes, and try to find a silver lining in a project that failed. Few (if any) people ever see their own work life or careers in terms of failed projects, and certainly nobody will ever cast his own career as a series of failures, one after another. But if 80% (or even half that number) of projects really do fail, then our resumes and our lives should be littered with them.

And, in fact, when we've gone around to actual teams and talked to them about their own projects, that's exactly what we've found. There really are a huge number of failed projects: projects that went woefully over budget or came in very late, projects that built unusable software that the users rejected, projects that were so behind schedule that the problem they were built to solve substantially changed, and projects that simply failed to deliver anything at all. In fact, we've given many talks over the years about project failure, and at each of those talks, we ask the audience, "Is there anyone here who hasn't been on at least one failed project?" We've never seen a single hand go up.

The stories in this section are about teams overcoming all kinds of problems. There are stories that deal with good people facing difficult companies, awful managers, serious technical problems, and true evil. Some of them are preventable, frustrating, and insidious. Some of them are simply heartbreaking and utterly unavoidable. In every case, the obstacles had a profound effect on the team: on how they worked together, and on how (or whether) they got past it. But in every case, there's an important lesson to be learned, and people who were made stronger for the experience, even when they outlasted the team itself.

CHAPTER TWENTY-FOUR

Bad Boss

Andrew Stellman

IT WAS THE MID-1990S. FLANNEL WAS IN STYLE, THE THEME FROM FRIENDS WAS A BILLBOARD HIT, and I was working as a programmer at a small suit-and-tie financial company on Wall Street. I joined as a junior programmer, and by this time I'd worked my way up to senior developer. I'd gained a reputation for being able to get big jobs done quickly. I also had a reputation for speaking my mind, even when it wasn't always the most tactful time to be running my mouth. My boss, Peter, once referred to me as a "loose cannon that he learned to point in the right direction." I had no problem with that.

The dot-com boom hadn't quite hit New York yet, and the company where I worked was somewhat traditional and a little stuffy. It was the sort of company where the title "manager" carried a lot of baggage. Only capital-M Managers got offices, and when someone was promoted to Manager it was a big deal. There was a lot of competition for one of those prized Manager slots. The company had a culture where people went out of their way to be more than a little obsequious to the boss, and there was a bit of a cult of personality around the CEO. I'd heard of someone who had been fired after his first day for referring to the CEO as "the old man" to a coworker, who promptly reported the gaffe to her boss.

I didn't mind. Despite the suits and ties and stuffiness, I felt that I'd really carved out a nice niche for myself. I got to work with a lot of new technology, and I was getting a lot of work done. Peter trusted me to do my job, and gave me bigger and more critical assignments over time. I definitely felt like I made a difference to the company—the software I built had a big impact on the bottom line. And I was working with a team that I really liked. Everyone got along really well, and I don't remember any major arguments or fights among any of us—at least, not up to this point.

The company was a value-added data reseller: we provided financial data to investment banks. Most of the software I worked on had to do with reading data we got from several of our dozens of data vendors, performing arcane and complex financial calculations, scrubbing the data (usually by comparing it against multiple sources), and sending it off to our clients, who used a custom frontend program to access it. Our little team was only a small part of the company; most of the employees either entered financial data into programs that we built, or worked on the sales team talking to clients.

Aside from me, there were five other people on the team. There were three other programmers: Paul, who had an advanced degree in mathematics and spent his time writing financial algorithms and low-level code; Diane, a really talented GUI designer and a good all-around coder; and Lenny, who'd been with the company for years in the data entry group, and had worked his way onto our team after spending a few years writing scripts for the other data entry people. And there were two testers, too. Ellen was an amazing QA engineer: there were many times that I turned my "finished" code over to her thinking it was done, only to get a heaping pile of bugs back from her that needed to be fixed. Anne was the newest team member, a junior tester that Ellen had taken under her wing.

We all reported to Peter. He'd been at the company since it started. He was a jack-of-all-trades who had wired up the company's first network, negotiated with data providers, configured network servers, Unix boxes, firewalls, and routers, and, because one of our data providers needed it to feed us stock quotes, he even spent an afternoon in the rain strapping a microwave radio receiver to a post on the roof of the office building we were in on the corner of Wall Street and Broadway. I had a lot of respect for him. He worked longer hours than anyone else in the company, and he was always willing to get his hands dirty. And even better, he never made me call him "Sir."

We'd been working on a big project for the past three months. It was an important project for the company: it had to do with reading our clients' stock portfolios, calculating their returns, and comparing them with a bunch of stock indexes. The sales team was anxious to have it complete, because it was going to be a major service that they'd sell to our customers. And the data team wanted it done, too, because it would automate a bunch of the most tedious work that they did. I was the project lead, and had spent weeks talking to the salespeople, data entry group, and senior managers before coming up with the spec, architecture, and database design. Diane had designed the user interface, and now Paul and I were busy building the code. Ellen and Anne were busy building a test plan and test cases, and putting together a pretty extensive set of test databases for us all to use while we were building and testing the code.

Our big project was going pretty well, but things weren't perfect. We'd broken the project into three major phases where we delivered fully functional pieces of the final product, and we were about to deliver the first phase. (Later on in my career, I'd learn about iteration. But this was the mid-1990s, and the best we had at the time was phased releases.) We were just about done with the first phase. There was a piece of the program that the data people would use immediately while we finished the last two phases. And there was one small portion of it that the salespeople were planning to show to clients to prime the pump for future sales.

It was time to demo our work, so I gathered my five teammates into a conference room, and asked Peter to call in Agnes, the VP of the data entry group; the head of sales (who brought his top two salespeople, because they happened to be in the office that day); and the CEO. I proudly demonstrated the software we built, showing them the ins and the outs of it. We were all excited to see the looks on their faces when they saw the software we built. Excited, that is, until we actually *saw* the looks on their faces.

After I was done, there was a long silence. Finally, Agnes said, "Well, that looks great. We'll definitely be able to use it." She didn't sound convinced.

"But…?" I asked.

"But, well, wasn't it supposed to read the client portfolios from the network?" she asked.

Ugh. I had no idea it was supposed to read client portfolios from the network. Somehow, in all my discussions with them, I'd missed that point. This was a disaster, and it was entirely my fault. Nobody on the team was making eye contact with me.

The meeting ended at a quarter to four. I took the team out to coffee, my treat, for the rest of the afternoon. We needed a plan. We argued. We went through denial, anger, bargaining, and acceptance. We came up with a plan. We'd bring everyone together for a meeting to really hash out exactly what needed to be built. We'd work with them together. We'd work with them individually. We'd write everything down, and we'd walk through it all with everyone. We'd fix the software. We'd get the rest of it right.

And that's pretty much what happened. We were lucky—the data and salespeople had a pretty good idea of what they wanted. They really wanted the software done right, and they were willing to sit down with me for days to work through their problems. I took a step back and really tried to figure out what they wanted. I asked a lot of questions.

And I learned from my mistake. I didn't go it alone. No, I got the team involved—any time there was a question about how the users would work with the software, Diane was there to help us figure out the GUI. Lenny knew the data vendors and their formats really well, and sometimes I needed a translator (since I spoke programmer, and the data people spoke data). And Paul really had a knack for the calculations we needed to do. Ellen and Anne insisted on sitting in with us through most of the meeting. I wasn't really sure what they were doing, but they took a lot of notes and grabbed samples of pretty much every data file we had to work with. (Eventually they came back to us with a complete test database that made our development job much easier, along with a really thorough set of test cases.)

Two weeks later, it seemed like we were past the problem. The people from data and sales were great—they sat through at least three different walkthroughs, which must have been enormously tedious for them. But I really got the feeling that we were on the right track.

And, more importantly, we were rolling along again with the project. And all six of us on the team were getting along really well again. I must have pulled all five of my teammates aside at one time or another to make sure they weren't mad at me. "Absolutely not," said Anne, when I talked to her. In fact, I got the sense, after talking to each of them, that we were actually somehow closer-knit. It was trial by fire, and we'd survived it.

The only problem was that Peter was becoming a bottleneck for us, and he knew it. We had to pull him into a lot of meetings. There were a lot of decisions that he had to be a part of, especially when it involved pulling people off other work to help plan the project. At one point, he pulled me aside.

"Look," he said. "I just added four new tech-support guys, and they need a lot of my time."

We spent some time talking about what the team needed. He felt that a lot of his job had amounted to being a "negotiator" between us and the other managers. It turned out that he spent a lot of his time "running interference"—protecting us from an almost constant barrage of requests for changes, alterations, and new projects that probably weren't needed. But just as the programming part of his job was getting more and more demanding, so was the IT side. The company was growing, and he'd gotten approval to build a new data center to house our increasingly large network infrastructure.

So it came down to this: Peter said that we needed a full-time manager. We needed to split IT and development into two teams. He'd work with the IT folks directly, and he needed to put someone in charge of the development team.

He asked me whether I wanted the job.

I'd never really thought about management, except that I knew I wasn't really all that interested. "Look, I'm flattered you asked me. But I just don't think I've got the experience to do it."

I could see that he was disappointed. But he didn't push me.

"I'll start looking for a new manager," he said.

Over the next month and a half, Peter interviewed at least a dozen people. He rejected most of them. Apparently, it's hard to find a good manager. Then one day he called me into his office.

Peter said, "Meet Eric."

There's a big guy sitting in front of me. He's easily six foot four, mostly bald, wearing a three-piece pinstripe suit and what looked like a very expensive watch. His tie clip and cufflinks matched. He definitely looked like he'd fit in with the company's culture, probably better than I did. He was coming to us from one of the large investment banks—he was a vice president at our biggest client, as it turned out. He'd worked with large development teams before, and said that he'd have no trouble with our small team. It looked like Peter had found his manager!

We were all pretty excited. The first person I ran into after meeting Eric was Diane, and she was really happy about it. It turns out that Peter had had Eric talk to her. Eric had told her that he thought she'd done great work, and was thinking about giving her a bigger role on the team (which she wanted). I talked to Paul, who told me that Eric had dropped a few hints that he'd give Paul a big raise at his next review. All in all, we were all pretty excited to get someone on board who might help us keep from repeating the problem that cost us weeks on our big project.

Two weeks later, Eric came on board. They gave him Peter's office—Peter moved to a bigger one that was closer to the IT people. Eric brought in golf trophies and a few awards from his old job at the investment bank. He had a photo of a big boat—presumably his—on his desk in a wooden picture frame with a fancy nautical clock inlaid into it. It looked like a capital-M Manager's office.

Eric brought all six of us into a conference room for a big team meeting.

"I really respect good developers," Eric said. "And you're a really good group of developers. I respect that."

So far, so good. He told us that he wanted to "get out of the way and let you do your job." OK. He talked a little bit about sailing, and how a good captain steers the ship and everyone on the crew did their jobs. He talked about habits of highly effective people. He talked about trust, and wanting to earn our trust.

Then he talked about an executive training retreat at his old investment bank, where they had the VPs go out into the woods with a former Navy SEAL. OK. I didn't quite see where he was going with this. I was never a fan of the sort of "trust falls and group hugs" mandatory corporate retreat, and Eric seemed to really like them. But I was still willing to give him the benefit of the doubt. I looked around the room to see how the rest of the team was taking it all. Diane and Paul looked like they were buying it. Ellen and Anne, less so.

Eric closed out the meeting by telling us that things would be changing. "I'm not like Peter," he said. "I'll show you respect, and fight for you." That was a little weird. I never really got the impression that Peter had anything but respect for us, and I wasn't really aware that he hadn't fought for us in the past (or that he'd needed to). Lenny looked a little uncomfortable. Paul, who usually had a good poker face, was frowning.

I pulled Ellen aside after the meeting. Ellen and I had a really good working relationship. We'd spent a lot of time talking about software development over the last couple of years, trying to figure out how to make things better. A lot of the meetings that I had with the data and sales people to fix the big project were actually her idea, and they worked really well. What's more, Ellen was generally an excellent judge of character, so I wanted to know what she thought.

"Honestly, I could be happier right now," she said. "Did you notice that he never actually spoke to me or Anne? He only talked about programming. I think he might have a problem with us."

I completely dismissed her. (I've since learned that it's generally a mistake to dismiss things that Ellen says.) I told her, "Look, I'm confident that he's a good manager. We just need to give him a chance." For some reason, I'm often optimistic like that about people, especially about people I report to. This wouldn't be the last time that kind of optimism would come back to bite me in the ass.

Later that week, Eric asked me to come to his office. He sat me down and grinned. He had an unnerving grin.

"I've been talking to the people at the top of the company. They need two things, and they're both top priority. The first priority is an intranet."

"Um, Eric, I'm not quite 100% clear on what you mean by that." We already had an internal network, behind the firewall that connected us to the rest of the Internet. (It was the mid-1990s, so we just had a 56k line.) We had a few web servers running some internal applications on an early version of IIS, and we had some shared file servers. What more did we need?

"I talked to the top managers, and they want more than that. They want a full-scale intranet application, a single launch point for all of our internal applications. It should have a deep menu system. It should be fully configurable. It should let you access every internal resource we have: every program, every file, every piece of data. It should have a database browser, a file viewer, and a message board. And they want you to build it."

OK.

"So, what's the other thing they want?" I asked.

"Their second priority is that we expand the team. I had to fight for this one, but I convinced them to add a slot for another developer."

I wasn't sure why he wanted another developer on board. We didn't really have a huge backlog of work. Everyone had enough work to do, but nobody was clamoring for extra software to be built. In fact, I was under the impression that we had the opposite problem: we had enough trouble getting the people from the business side—the salespeople and data people—to take time out of their schedules to meet with us. We already spent too much of our time waiting for them. In fact, I thought that was part of the reason that Peter wanted a new manager for the team.

Clearly, that's not how Eric saw it. "I went to bat for you guys, for the team. I made a big stink with the higher-ups, and after a fight I got them to add another slot for a programmer. That's how I take care of my team."

Over the next few days, I spent about five hours talking to Eric about the intranet. At first, he seemed to have a good idea of what the senior managers wanted. He spent about an hour talking about a "grand plan." I didn't quite follow, but I did take a lot of notes. He talked about menus, and options, and databases, and a data browser, and a bunch of other features that would probably take me a good three months to finish.

I got started with the project. But when I went back to my notes, I definitely got the sense that while like Eric may have had a "grand plan," his actual plan for the software came up short. So, I went back to him and asked for more details. Like the menus—what did he mean by "configurable"? Did he want to configure it using files or a database? Did he want a GUI for that, or was it enough to edit the database or files directly?

Eric's response was less than satisfactory. "You're authorized to make those decisions yourself," he said. Then he said he had to take a call. I wasn't sure what he meant by "authorized." I didn't need authority, I needed answers. Eric didn't have any. He didn't answer my emails for the next two days. So, I started building the intranet, doing the best I could from my notes. I kept going for a few weeks. Luckily, I'm pretty imaginative, and came up with my own idea of what an intranet would look like for our company. That whole time, I didn't get much direction from Eric—every time I talked to him, he didn't really seem to know what I was working on. But when I showed him the progress I'd made, he said he was really happy. Apparently, I was doing a great job and building exactly what he asked me to do.

Well, he was the boss. He was happy. So I was doing my job…right?

A little over three weeks had gone by since Eric had come on board. I was working on building some obscure part of the intranet when Diane knocked on my cube wall.

"Have you met with Eric yet?" she asked.

It turned out that while I got my share of face time with Eric, he hadn't even had a single one-on-one talk with her. After she finished with the GUI for our big project (which she finished long before Eric arrived), she moved on to a new project for Agnes, the VP in charge of the data entry group. She and Anne had been working with Agnes since then, and about two weeks after Eric came on board they'd delivered the final product.

Over the past week, there were a couple of bugs that Agnes's team had run into, and Diane fixed them. But other than that, she'd been sitting around without much work to do. She'd sent a few emails to Eric letting him know that she was ready for the next project, but he never responded to any of them. She'd left him a voicemail, which he apparently ignored.

I thought that was weird. There was definitely work for her to do. I was preoccupied with the intranet, so I wasn't working on the big project. That left Paul and Lenny on it, and they could definitely use her help. Which was great, since she wanted to work on it. It was an important project, and she'd put a lot of work into the GUI design already. But the last time she talked to Eric was when she ran into him in the hallway, and he told her that she should "absolutely not get involved with it under any circumstances." That was two weeks earlier, and she hadn't heard a peep from him since then.

I told her, "Don't worry, I'm sure there's just something weird going on. He'll definitely be on board when we explain the situation to him."

I was naïve. I sent Eric a long email explaining everything. I told him about all the work that Diane had been doing, talked about her valuable contribution to the big project already, and that she was ramped up and ready to go. I made it clear that I had a lot of respect for her, and that it made sense for her to get started on it.

No response. Nothing.

I dropped by his office and knocked on his door. He wasn't there. Apparently he was out to a long lunch with one of his old buddies from the investment bank. I asked around later, and found out that he told one of the salespeople that he might be able to get our company on an "inside track" with that bank. That wasn't really his job, but I figured it was good for the company, so it must be OK…right?

He was back in his office by a quarter to four. I started to tell him about Diane.

"Yeah, I saw your note. Don't worry about it, I'll take care of it."

Great! But, well, what exactly was he going to do?

"I said, don't worry about it." He seemed agitated, and eager to change the subject. Then Eric handed me a thick stack of paper. It contained nearly fifty resumes. "We need to fill that open developer slot," Eric said. "Here's a stack of candidates. Go through them, call them up, and find the best ones." I hadn't really spent much time going through resumes before. I thought that was *his* job. There was a reason I didn't take the manager position when Peter offered it to me.

"What about the intranet project?" I asked.

"This takes priority," he replied.

I decided to drop the Diane issue. I felt bad about it, but it was pretty clear that I wouldn't be able to do anything about it. I went back to her and told her what happened. She took it well, but still didn't know what to do. I told her that she should just start working on the big project. There was a piece that wasn't being worked on, and I had a pretty good idea that she'd be able to handle it. She'd already designed the GUI for that piece, and had a good idea of how the internals needed to work. Yes, Eric told me he'd take care of it. But he didn't say what he'd do, and I had a feeling that he was just going to leave Diane twisting in the wind. And I was starting to get the sneaking suspicion that Eric might not really care all that much either way. So, I told Diane that she should go ahead and join the big project.

"But what about Eric?" she asked.

I told her to let me worry about it. "If he raises a stink, I'll take the blame. I'll say that I misunderstood him." I invoked one of my favorite rules (which, incidentally, I'd learned from Peter): sometimes it's better to apologize tomorrow than ask permission today. I met with Paul and Lenny, and we all carved out a piece of the big project for Diane to work on. They were happy for the help. Eric may not have cared about the project, but the team did. They were glad to have her on board.

After that meeting, Lenny pulled me aside. "Look, I need you to talk to Agnes."

Apparently, Agnes had been coming to Lenny at least once every day or two asking for him to maintain some old scripts he'd worked on. That was a problem. When Lenny officially left her department to move over to Peter's group two years back, Agnes had promised that he wouldn't have to maintain those old scripts. They had another person who was perfectly capable of doing the job, and we needed Lenny to keep moving on the big project. But Agnes wanted that other person to do "more important" work, so she kept bothering Lenny about those scripts.

That was one of those "running interference" jobs that Eric was supposedly hired to do. And when Lenny talked to him two days earlier, he told Lenny that he was absolutely confident that Agnes would stop. He told Lenny that he'd "ripped her a new one" and promised that would be the end of it. But just yesterday, Agnes came over yet again with another request for a script modification.

Something was definitely weird there. I'd just had a meeting with Agnes a few hours earlier, and she seemed her normal self: smug, overconfident, and generally obnoxious—the same old Agnes we'd come to know and love over the years. If Eric had really "ripped her a new one" then she would have been irritable and cranky instead. (As far as I could tell, Agnes had only those two moods, so she was easy to read.) Instead, she actually went out of her way to point out how well Eric had been doing recently. Things were not adding up.

So, I promised Lenny I'd talk to Agnes and see whether I could get her to stop. It wouldn't be too hard—she wanted the big project done, and I figured that she just didn't realize that Lenny was an important part of it. I figured that if I put it in that light, she'd agree to back off. And when I went to talk to her, that's exactly how the conversation went. Lenny was definitely happy to be off script maintenance duty, and we got our programmer back.

By this time, I was spending more than half of my time dealing with hiring a programmer for the slot that Eric fought for. My work on the intranet project had fallen off substantially, because I'd been spending a lot of my time on the phone with recruiters or conducting phone screens for Eric. Not only that, but I was giving assignments to the team, running interference with the managers, and generally doing all of Eric's job. That left me wondering exactly what he was doing.

After poring through dozens of resumes and talking to more than 10 candidates, I finally found a programmer who would be perfect for the job. I brought her resume to Eric. She was a really good fit: she'd spent 15 years as a programmer at a consulting company, and before that she'd been an analyst at an investment bank for another 10 years. She already knew the language we were using, and had been building financial software for years.

He looked over her resume for a minute. "*She* graduated from college in 1961. That would make her, what, in her early 50s?" He put a lot of emphasis on the word *she*, in a way that made me very uncomfortable.

"I guess so," I replied. "I didn't ask her age."

"Humph," said Eric. He looked at the resume some more. I watched the minute hand of the nautical clock built into the picture frame on his desk jump. "I'll give her a call and tell you how it goes."

I went back to my desk. Fifteen minutes later, Eric calls me back into his office.

"She's not right for the company."

I asked him to explain himself. He declined. "It's my decision. I'm just not comfortable with some of her, um, *attributes*." I asked him to be more specific. He told me that he couldn't really say any more than that. "You know, it's because of her, well, her age and her gender. It's just not a good match."

I was floored. I know I should have told him that it was blatantly illegal—not to mention personally offensive to me—to reject our best candidate because she's a woman and she's over 50. But I just didn't know what to do. So, I walked out of his office, called up the candidate's recruiter to say that we had to pass on her, and went home early for the day.

The next day, Eric told me to clear my schedule after lunch. He'd done a phone screen with one of my second-choice candidates, and now he was coming in for a face-to-face interview. I thought that was odd, since I didn't give Eric any second-choice candidates. He handed me the resume. I didn't remember seeing it before. The guy didn't have all that much experience, but I didn't see any red flags.

The interview was scheduled for 1:00 p.m. At a quarter after, I got a call from the receptionist. She sounded a little giddy, and said something about Elvis arriving for his interview. She was always giggling and cracking jokes. I walked to the front of the office, and sure enough, Elvis was standing there. He wasn't quite the young Elvis—he was definitely a little pudgy—but he wasn't quite the old, fat Elvis, either. He had hair slicked into a mini pompadour, long sideburns (remember, it was the mid-'90s, and thanks to Luke Perry on *Beverly Hills 90210*, sideburns were back in style), and sunglasses.

I brought Elvis back to an empty conference room and did the interview. He'd exaggerated a bit on his resume, but for the most part he seemed to have a reasonable idea of what he was doing. He'd done some programming before, mostly with databases. He'd probably be able to maintain some of the scripts that Lenny had written a while back, so there would definitely be work for him. When he was done, I dropped an email to Eric recommending him for a junior position.

The next day, there was an email from Eric to the rest of the team announcing that we'd just hired a new senior programmer. He was pleased to let us know that this senior programmer would take over a major part of the big project that Paul, Lenny, Diane, Ellen, and Anne were working steadily on. That new senior programmer…*Elvis?!*

No, no, that had to be a mistake. He wasn't senior, not by a long shot. And there was absolutely no way that Elvis could handle that job. He could maintain some simple scripts, maybe do a little minor database work. But he had neither the skills nor the knowledge required to take on any part of the big project. I tried to find Eric, but he was out at a long lunch again. By the time he got back to the office, the day was almost over. I told him that I thought Elvis would crash and burn. Eric told me to have some faith. My faith was definitely starting to run thin.

Two weeks later, Elvis showed up in the cube across from me. He arrived late, the last one on the team to show up. He was still wearing those sunglasses. He made small talk with the receptionist. (She told me later that he'd hit on her when he showed up for the interview.) We had a team meeting that afternoon about the big project. Paul and Lenny had come up with a plan to try to bring Elvis up to speed. Elvis never showed up.

The next day he told Paul that he'd had a personal emergency and had to leave early. Paul was irritated—he'd spent all morning putting together material for that meeting instead of coding. They were starting to fall behind on the big project and needed all the time they could get.

Two days later, Elvis didn't show up for work at all. He didn't show up the day after. Eric didn't say anything. He seemed to be acting like nothing happened. Later that day, I ran into the receptionist in the elevator, who told me what happened.

"Elvis failed his drug test, so we had to let him go," she said.

The company had a policy that required all new employees to take a drug test. Every candidate is told about it in the first phone interview. Elvis knew about the test, and had over two weeks to get clean.

"Wait a minute," I said. "I know that one of the IT guys tested positive for pot, and they let him slide."

"Yeah, but Elvis tested positive for coke. According to the test, he did it in the past two days," she said. "Elvis has left the building."

I can't say that I was sad to see him go. I didn't tell anyone about what happened, but later that day I heard it from at least three other team members. Apparently everyone knew about Elvis and his drug problem.

Eric took it all in stride. He handed me another stack of resumes, and asked me to call at least 10 of the people in the pile. This was getting ridiculous. I hadn't had time to work on the intranet project in over a week, and again, Eric didn't really seem to care. So, I decided to talk to Peter. I don't normally like going over my boss's head, but I'd been working with Peter for a long time. I felt comfortable talking to him, and I wanted to get the straight scoop.

"What intranet project?" he asked.

That's when I discovered that nobody else in the company even knew I was working on the intranet project. I couldn't believe it—Eric told me that it was a critical project that the senior managers specifically asked for. Peter was in all of the strategy meetings where the senior managers discussed the new projects, and it had never been brought up. In fact, Eric was never even *in* any of those meetings, so there's no way that he'd have any idea what the senior managers were asking for. Apparently, Eric had decided all by himself that it was a priority, and I'd spent months of my life working on a project that nobody else at the company needed or wanted.

I went back to Eric, who seemed genuinely irritated that I wasn't on the phone with candidates to replace Elvis. He didn't really want to hear about the intranet project. He wasn't interested in the progress, and to be honest, it seemed like he'd forgotten about it entirely. I told him that I could really help Lenny, Diane, and Paul on the big project.

"Look, don't worry. You're doing a great job," he said. "Leave the big project to the rest of the team. You've got more important things to work on."

I wanted to ask him whether "more important things" meant not working on the intranet project or actively discriminating against people on the basis of their age and gender. To this day, I wish I'd had the *cojones* to do it.

I was back at my desk stewing about my missed opportunity to run my mouth, when I heard Eric shouting at the top of his lungs. I peeked into his office—his door was open—and was pretty shocked to see that he was yelling at Ellen and Anne. From what I could hear, apparently there was some sort of emergency with a client's data.

After the onslaught ended, Ellen and Anne left. Anne was sobbing quietly at her desk. Ellen looked like she wanted to kick someone's head in. It turned out that there was a problem with a piece of data that one of the bigger clients used. That client threatened to cancel the account. The thing is, both Ellen and Anne knew perfectly well that the problem had nothing to do with them. And not because they're testers—it wasn't even that they'd missed any sort of bug. The problem had originated at one of the data vendors that provided the data that we sent on to clients. There was absolutely nothing that we could have done about this. If anyone was at fault, it was Agnes and her data entry group for missing the data problem. But Agnes was particularly good at avoiding blame, so she came down on Eric. And Eric, in search of a scapegoat, apparently decided to let Ellen and Anne have it.

Ellen and I took Anne out for coffee. She was beside herself. The entire office heard Eric yell at her, thanks to the fact that he'd left his door open (apparently on purpose, specifically to embarrass them). We got her calmed down, but she didn't get any work done for the rest of the day. She ended up taking the following Friday and Monday off to visit her mother. She still looked upset when she came back on Tuesday, but at least she was able to get back to work. I asked her whether she was OK.

"Yes, Andrew," she said. "I'm OK, mostly. I want to see the big project through. I've put a lot of work into it. But when we're done, will you be a reference for me when I'm interviewing for a new job?"

I told her I'd be a reference. I was just glad that she'd be there for the rest of the project.

And she was making progress on it. The whole team was. As surprising as it was, everyone on the team seemed truly committed to delivering the big project. I only wished that I could be a part of it, rather than being stuck with doing Eric's job for him. By now, I was the only person who wasn't actively working on it. The rest of the team had gotten through the second of the three phases, and this time, both the data entry people and the salespeople loved what they saw. Agnes even sent them a congratulatory email, which was uncharacteristically kind of her. They were extremely happy—so happy that they were only slightly miffed at Eric's obnoxious reply (cc:'d to everyone in the company) taking credit for the success.

The company was expanding. When I first arrived, we took up only about half of the seventh floor of the building. Now we took up the entire seventh floor, and had recently signed a lease for half of the eighth floor. This was lucky for the team. They started using a conference room up there, which caused Eric—who routinely complained about having to go up a flight of stairs whenever there was a meeting up there—to stop dropping by their team meetings unannounced and giving long speeches about his time as a vice president at his old investment bank.

Later, Paul pulled me aside. He told me that his cousin worked at the same investment bank where Eric had worked. He said that his cousin was also a vice president, and told him that they handed out vice president titles like they were party favors. The idea, apparently, is that when a small Midwestern customer calls up demanding to talk to someone, they can always be connected with "Vice President So-and-So," who personally handles their account. This is an effective sales tool, because it makes a small customer feel like he's being treated like a big shot.

That explained a lot. Eric no longer seemed particularly impressive. According to Paul's cousin, the fact that he was a vice president from that investment bank simply meant that he wasn't a janitor.

(To be honest, I was starting to suspect that the janitor who cleaned our office would do a better job than Eric. I'd talk to him occasionally when I stayed late working on a project. Despite his prison tattoos, he was a nice guy. His name was Mike. Unfortunately, the building eventually switched to a non-union janitorial company, and he left. The service workers' union went on strike against the building, and I felt weird about crossing their picket line outside and started using the rear entrance.)

It was about this time that Ellen had her annual review. She wasn't really sure what to expect, since the only interaction she'd really had with Eric by this point was being yelled at. Still, she's always very professional about these things, and she'd been promised a raise at her last meeting with Peter. Unfortunately, as soon as she sat down for her review, she saw something she wasn't supposed to see. Eric had written up my performance review already, and had left it face-up on his desk—and at the bottom, in big bold numbers, was my salary.

It was approximately twice as much as hers.

Ellen had been at the company about as long as I had. She had more experience than I did, with more years in the software industry. Yes, testers tended to make a little less than programmers. But she had really made a difference to the company, and it was outrageous that I was earning twice the money she was earning. This was clearly unacceptable. Ellen wasn't sure what to do, so she picked up the review, turned it over, and handed it to Eric.

Later, she pulled Eric aside.

"Look," she said. "I didn't go looking to find out what Andrew made. But now I know. We both know it's not right that he makes twice as much as I do, and I hope you can do the right thing here." She let him know that she didn't need to be making exactly the same as I was, but that she should at least be in the same order of magnitude.

Later that day, Eric came back to her with bad news. He wasn't going to bring it up with anyone in senior management. And Eric pointed out that we've all seen the statistic about how women don't make as much as men, so she should be used to it.

A week later, Ellen gave notice and left the company.

Eric couldn't have been happier. Now he had two openings in his group: the one that he told me that he'd fought for, and now another one to replace Ellen. He handed me yet another stack of resumes to go through.

I went through them. I noticed that there were no testers or QA engineers anywhere in the stack, just programmers. I asked Eric about it.

"Aren't we going to replace Ellen? Otherwise, Anne's really going to have her hands full with the big project."

Eric wouldn't hear any of it. He told me that he had no use for testers, and that one programmer is worth five testers. He said that he felt that the industry didn't really need testers at all, and that we should all just hire interns and even smart teenagers to do testing.

I told him that I thought that he might be a little hasty in dismissing the entire field of quality assurance. He told me to get back to my job. Then for some reason he went off on a long tangent about how he was personally related to a branch of the Kennedy family, that his relatives have a huge amount of money and own the building on the corner of Broadway and Astor Place, and that he doesn't even need to work. (I stopped myself from asking him why he kept showing up at work, then.)

So I sucked it up, went back to my desk, and started through yet another stack of resumes to see whether I could find anyone to fill the two slots. I spent the next day and a half doing phone interviews and talking to recruiters. Eventually, I found three candidates who seemed to know what they were talking about. I thought they all had a lot of potential. And, just as importantly, I felt that their personalities would be a really good match for the rest of the team.

I was dismayed to find that of those three people, absolutely none of them ended up in our office. Instead, Eric hired Noam and Dustin within days of each other, and without letting me or anyone else on the team interview them.

Noam seemed to be a competent programmer. Eric was very excited about him, because they spent over two hours in the interview and Noam seemed, in Eric's words, "to have a lot of respect for authority." The problem was that while Noam was a good programmer, he was the most argumentative person I'd ever met. He picked fights with everyone: salespeople, data people, his teammates, me, Agnes, Peter; he even got into an argument with the CEO of the company in the elevator. (I'm not sure whether he knew exactly who he was talking to, though I'm pretty sure he wouldn't have cared either way.) Most of his arguments seemed to end up the same way: with him relating a story about how he was an Israeli tank commander on the front lines in Lebanon, and that he got shot at on a daily basis. This always seemed to end whatever argument he'd started.

The stories about Noam seemed to get weirder and weirder. A data person told me that one of her coworkers said he caught him sniffing the seat of her chair before work one morning. One of the salespeople pulled me aside and told me that they were so creeped out by him that they started calling him "Babies-in-Jars Noam" behind his back. The rumors were flying, and none of them were good.

In the meantime, Noam seemed to spend far more time arguing with people than programming, and wasn't actually getting any work done. Luckily, Paul and Lenny figured out early on that they didn't want him threatening the success of the big project. They were able to convince Agnes to let him start maintaining some of Lenny's old scripts. The rest of our team quickly learned to avoid Noam.

Unfortunately for Noam, things didn't end well. One of the receptionists complained to the human resources person that he'd been making inappropriate comments to her about her religion. Apparently, she was a Jehovah's Witness, and Noam got into a big argument with her about the New Testament.

Eric pulled me aside and told me that the "Nazis" above him were making him fire Noam. He told me that he didn't want to do it, and he understood how nervous that would make me and the other people on the team. He seemed to be under the impression that we'd assume that any of us could be fired at any time. He didn't understand that we were unanimously happy to see Noam go.

"Stick with me," Eric said. "If you make sure you keep your allegiance with me, I'll make sure I've got your back."

I wasn't sure exactly what he meant by that.

Meanwhile, Lenny, Diane, Paul, and Anne were finishing up the last phase of the big project, and it was coming out really well. And now that Eric had stopped asking me to review resumes, I could get back to work on it. Ellen was gone, and I knew I couldn't replace her as a tester. But I needed to fill in where I could, and there was testing that had to be done. So, I spent some of my time testing—luckily, she'd left behind a complete set of test cases—and the rest of my time programming. It was great to be back with the team. When we were working together, it was a little like all of the irritating problems that had been plaguing us were left behind in another world. Especially when we met in that eighth floor conference room, where Eric couldn't find us.

Eric's other new hire, Dustin, put an end to some of that temporary peace. Everyone else at the office wore a shirt and tie to work. That was the rule—a rule that apparently didn't apply to Dustin, who showed up in jeans, a hooded sweatshirt, and a wrinkled t-shirt. If that were the extent of the problem with Dustin's deportment, it might have been OK. But the real problem was that there were other rules that also apparently didn't apply to Dustin. Rules like showering at least once or twice a week.

Dustin smelled terrible. And, unfortunately, I seemed to be the person that everyone complained to about him. Every single team member—Lenny, Paul, Diane, and Anne—independently came to me to complain about his body odor. So did Agnes and at least two of the salespeople. Unfortunately, when I went to Eric to complain, he didn't seem particularly interested, and definitely didn't intend to talk to Dustin about it.

Eric demanded that we assign part of the big project to Dustin. We were in the final stretch of the project, and it was difficult to divide the work. Basically, the only thing we hadn't started was the online help, so we assigned it to Dustin. He spent the next four weeks working on it. But he wasn't actually doing anything useful. It turned out that he was trying to do some weird Win32 API trick to add a help option to the Windows menu (the little menu that appears when you click in the upper-righthand corner of a window). There was absolutely no reason to do this—it would have taken about three minutes to add a "Help" option to the program's main menu. But Dustin really wanted to add it to the Windows menu instead, where our users would never be in danger of actually finding and using it. I asked Eric about it. He said that not only was it fine, but the CEO of the company had, in fact, personally asked Eric for that feature.

Dustin never finished his project. He finally quit to join one of those newfangled, up-and-coming dot-coms. After he left, I looked through his work. There was absolutely nothing of value there. We threw out every line of code that he wrote.

I was more than a little skeptical that the CEO really asked for the weird help system, so I decided to ask Peter about it. Did the CEO really request that feature personally? Peter had no idea what I was talking about. That was when we were both sure that something was seriously wrong. Eric had been less than honest with us for a long time.

But we didn't really have time to talk that over, because Paul, Diane, Lenny, Anne, and I finally finished the big project. Once again, I called a meeting with Peter, Agnes, data entry group members, and salespeople. And this time, it went really well. There were no awkward "but isn't it also supposed to do *this*?" moments. Everyone—Agnes, the data entry people, the sales people, Peter and the rest of the team—seemed genuinely happy with the way the project turned out.

Everyone except Eric. After the meeting, he pulled me aside and asked what I thought about Diane and Anne. Did they really contribute to the project, or did Paul and I do all the work? I told him I thought they were indispensable.

"I talked to Peter," he said. "He thinks the entire team should be outsourced. Don't get me wrong—I think you're great. But Peter is trying to convince his boss and the CEO that there are serious problems with the team. I hate to be the one to say this to you, but he thinks you should all be fired."

I was floored. I'd never heard anything like that from Peter. I couldn't believe I was going to be fired. Eric told me not to worry. He said that he knew he had my "allegiance," and that he had my back. He still knew people at his old investment bank who would hire our whole department at any time.

That was the last straw. I always had a good working relationship with Peter, so I went to him. I told him I couldn't believe that he wanted to fire us and outsource the whole team. I started to make my case.

"Andrew, I have no idea what you're talking about."

It turned out that Peter had just talked to Eric, who told Peter that he had thought Diane and Anne were doing a good job. But then he told Peter that after seeing their work on the project, it was *me* who decided that they needed to be fired. And who was Eric to second-guess his top team member?

It turned out that Eric was lying to everyone. He lied to me, he lied to Peter, and he probably lied to pretty much everyone else he talked to. And as if the lying wasn't bad enough, he'd racked up a steady stream of failures from day one: the intranet project, Elvis and his drug test, Ellen and her salary, the disasters that were Noam and Dustin. Even worse, that position that he said he'd fought for, back when he was first hired? There was no fighting. It turned out that when Peter brought Eric on board, he'd worked with the senior managers to add an extra programmer to the team. Eric knew that all along, and lied about it to my face for months.

The next day, Eric was fired.

Later that week, I was feeling really guilty about how the team was treated. Ellen was gone, and I was worried that Anne, Paul, Diane, and Lenny were in really bad shape, moralewise. I was worried that they resented me for not doing more about Eric, and I wouldn't have blamed them all for putting in notice. I'd been avoiding them all week, because I figured they all thought I let them down. I got a call from Peter, who asked me to come to his office.

"I talked to the rest of the team," he said. "We need a new manager to replace Eric, and every single person said that you should take over. The manager job is yours if you want it."

This time I said yes.

CHAPTER TWENTY-FIVE

Welcome to the Process

Step Inside, Step Inside, and See the Show

Ned Robinson

IT WAS APRIL 2001, AND THE GRAY SKIES OF WINTER IN NEW YORK WERE GIVING WAY TO THE CRISP blue skies of spring. A 20-year programming veteran, I had spent the previous 5 years running the software division of RePlay Technologies, a music software company. The company had done relatively well for a small start-up, but after five years of almost breaking even, RePlay was sold and I was out of a job. So here I was, back in the financial district of NYC looking for a job.

My first few interviews proved that the American corporations had not changed their software development practices during the previous five years. They were still paying little attention to formal processes and good project management. Every company I interviewed with sang the same refrain: work 60 to 70 hours a week, projects will succeed because of your superhuman efforts (red cape and beeper will be handed out on first day of job), and yes, expect the sponsor to be changing requirements constantly. When can you start?

The problem was that I no longer wanted to be a superman developer. I had done that for too long already and was burned out. I hadn't minded when I was still in my 20s and trying to make a name for myself in the industry. Whatever the project, whatever the obstacles, I had spent many sleepless nights writing line after line of code to accommodate incomplete and half-articulated and thought-out requirements that lasted only until the boss came in the next morning with some new ideas that wiped out 80% of the work I had just done. The adrenaline rush of handing my boss a working program with the changes he had requested the night before as he left the office had long ago lost its luster. I no longer wanted to live in the world of constant scope creep. I no longer wanted to be part of a team of half-asleep, over-jolted programmers.

All of these thoughts were in my mind as I entered the lobby of the World Trade Center, Building 2, for an interview with Benchmark, a small software company that specialized in desktop stock evaluation software for asset and portfolio managers. I rode the elevator up to the sky lobby on the 78th floor and entered the office.

The offices were beautiful. Spreading out on a portion of the 78th floor and the entire 77th floor, everywhere I looked I saw unobstructed views of the most incredible New York City vistas. As I walked up to the reception desk, I could see the Statue of Liberty from the window on the right. This was a pretty cool environment, I thought, from a physical standpoint. I was hoping that the job lived up to the surroundings. After checking in with the receptionist, I awaited the arrival of the software development manager.

When Curt arrived at the reception desk, I was quite surprised (and equally excited) by his dress and demeanor. He was dressed in black jeans, a button-down collared black shirt, and black army boots. He had his straight black hair pulled back in a ponytail and there was a 2-inch streak of purple hair on the right side. An earring completed the picture. All of a sudden, I had hope that this job might offer something different from what I had been imagining.

Curt and I went down to his office on the 77th floor. His office was littered with all kinds of hardware, hard drives, motherboards, memory chips, and so on. Our conversation started off easily as I related my work history. It turned out that Curt was also a musician, having played cello in school and now playing bass in a punk band. We talked about music and about how I developed a suite of music processing algorithms for RePlay Technologies. We shared war stories about writing code in beta versions of Microsoft compilers, about writing 16-bit code in a limited memory model, and how to handle users who always seemed to wait until you were just about finished to ask you to add just a few more fields (to all the screens and reports). We even spent a few minutes discussing the pros and cons of FORTH and reverse polish notation.

He then told me about the development team that he was managing and the process reengineering that he had already started. This is getting interesting, I thought. He told me about getting his undergraduate degree at Carnegie Mellon, the home of CMMI (the Capability Maturity Model Initiative) and his efforts to date to bring the company to Level 2 compliance on the CMMI scale. After he concluded his very brief introduction of CMMI, he said the following sentence that won me over even before the job was offered: "If you ever have to work more than 40 hours a week, then I have failed at my job as manager. You have not failed at yours. My job is to hire good people and stand back and let them do the job that they were hired to do. For software developers, this means department or companywide adoption of time-proven processes and methodologies that clearly define all project work and scope and have a strong change management component."

Wow! Was the ground going to break open and swallow him up for blasphemy? Did he just say there is a way to manage scope creep? Could any more noble words come from a boss's mouth? Did he really have senior management buy-in for this? While I still had a lot of questions, so far this looked like the job for me. Over the next couple of days, I met the members of the development team, and took a technical test, a personality assessment, and a drug test. Within a week, I had a new job.

I was the fourth developer on the software development team. The team worked well together, and each member had a particular area of strength that the other team members relied on. Mary was great at developing user interfaces. Dmitri was the bit guru and wasn't scared of getting down and dirty with the code. Peter liked decomposing the business requirements and creating the software development plan. I was intimately familiar with Windows internals, object-oriented design, and multitiered architecture. We all had our strengths and would prove to be the nucleus of a growing team that worked well together and loved writing code.

The team also worked well with the other departments in the SDLC: business requirements, quality assurance, project management, operations, and frontline business users. They worked so well together that one of the developers married one of the QA testers. In the spirit of continued family harmony, we did our best not to put them on the same project!

There was a spirit underlying the entire company that created a really positive work environment. Many of the approximately 200 employees had been with the company for 5 to 10 years. was All of them were committed to seeing the company grow and to feel like they were a part of it. This was promoted from the top level of the company down. Customer milestones were tracked, and whenever a new milestone was hit (every 100 new desktops or 10 new customers), each employee received a wooden plaque and a crisp $100 bill. For those who had been with the company for a long time, their cubes were proudly tiled with plaques from floor to ceiling.

Things were good at Benchmark. While the company had been bought by a large financial information firm, Benchmark was still operating pretty much independently, although rumors abounded about being folded into the larger corporate family. But, at the moment, Benchmark would be able to follow its own processes and methodologies.

My first project was to write a program that continuously monitored critical backend data collection processes. The program was to check that data was flowing into the company's servers from a number of data providers and that the data was being automatically converted, saved, and made available for redistribution to our customers. It also had to make sure that the delayed security price request system was working and providing accurate quotes. This Watchdog program updated a frontend monitoring program that Dmitri had written and that ran on an IT workstation 24/7.

As I started to write my use cases, I began to understand why Benchmark had such a bad record of delivering quality software on time and to spec. In order to write this Watchdog program, I had to know what each system being monitored was supposed to do. As I looked for information on each system, I discovered that many of the systems had no documentation or that the documentation had been a preliminary specification that in no way matched the final deliverable. For example, the data files from one vendor had to be converted to a specific layout with a checksum added to each row and to the end of the file. Unfortunately, the final data layout of the imported file had been changed by the vendor and fields were added to both the middle and end of the data structure. Since I had to check specific fields and compute a checksum, I had to make sure that I was reading the right fields. To make matters worse, the developer who had originally written the import program was no longer with the company. I tried talking with Nancy, the head of the department that managed the data feeds. Unfortunately, she had no patience for requirements gathering and told me that she didn't have time to discuss it and to just figure it out myself. In the end, I had to do just that: open the import source code and decipher what was going on.

I continued to hit these types of walls as I worked to complete my use case analysis. The only smooth part of the requirements gathering was when I had to figure out how to interface to Dmitri's monitoring frontend. When I asked Dmitri how to do it, he sent me a link to the complete and up-to-date API spec! With a complete requirements document in hand, I was able to finish the Watchdog program a few days before my required delivery date.

As this project was coming to a close, Curt assigned me to work on another internal project for Benchmark. One feature of the software was to track the comings and goings of all the top Wall Street executives: what companies they worked for, their previous and current titles, promotions, salaries, bonuses, and so forth. Curt gave me a rough draft of a requirements document that Nancy's team had given him: a one-page brief description and a couple of hand-drawn screens. A kickoff meeting was scheduled for the following week.

As the meeting began, all of the participants were introduced. Nancy had brought six members of her staff to the meeting while all the other departments had one or two representatives. One of Nancy's assistants introduced the purpose and scope of the project. After they finished, Curt asked Nancy when her team was going to deliver the completed requirements document. Nancy said that she felt what she had delivered was enough to understand all of the requirements of the project and that they were too busy to do any more writing or analysis. Since there were no business analysts available to work on this project, the software developer would just have to figure it out himself. Curt and I looked at each other with shock and dismay. We couldn't believe that she was serious. Curt made some comments about what Nancy had promised to deliver and Nancy made some counter comments about how the software developers had to be nimble and be able to go with the flow.

Curt stood his ground and told Nancy that the project would be on hold until more requirements were available. Curt wasn't going to cave in like other managers I have had in the past. At that point, the project manager ended the meeting and said that it would have to be continued after the issues with the requirements had been discussed offline. As we left the conference room, I smiled as I realized the street credit that Curt had just gotten.

As summer 2001 was coming to a close, I felt at home at Benchmark, like I had always been a part of the team even though I had worked there for less than six months. As I arrived at work one morning in late August, I walked off the elevator and was greeted with an incredible view of the Statue of Liberty framed against a crisp Carolina Blue sky. I had my headphones on and was listening to Gershwin's "Rhapsody in Blue." That was one of those moments that I will never forget: the music, the view in front of me, the blue skies above. I sighed and walked just a little lighter to my desk.

Less than two weeks later, that view would be gone forever; even the possibility of stumbling across the nexus of that view and that music, at the same time in the early morning light—that possibility would be gone, and the only artifact remaining through eternity of that experience would be the recording of it that is burned in my memory.

It was 8:30 on the morning of September 11, 2001. Some of the team was already in the office and working on the day's tasks. I was going over a list of questions I had on the Nancy project. It was a quiet morning on what I thought was going to be a quiet day. I took a short break and checked in on Barry Bonds and his quest to break Babe Ruth's home run record. I was just about to get my second cup of coffee for the day when all of a sudden we all heard a loud explosion. Peter and I walked over to the window, and as we looked out, a large plume of fire shot past us, followed by smoke and ash. Due to our viewing angle (we were looking out east, over the Hudson River) we couldn't see what had caused the explosion or the fire shooting past us. We waited a couple of minutes, waiting for an announcement from the building staff, but nothing came. Alice (a business analyst), Peter, Megan, and I all sat near each other, and after a few minutes of discussion, we decided to start walking down the stairs in the fire escape, figuring that we would get some direction soon. As we entered the fire escape, it seemed that a lot of other people had had the same idea. The speed of our descent on the stairs slowed, but did not stop as everyone walked down in an orderly fashion. Some people had handfuls of tapes, some had tapes and the tape backup units as well. Many others were carrying piles of CDs and other personal belongings. I was carrying my laptop in my shoulder bag.

As more and more people entered the fire escape, the going got slower and slower. The apprehension around us was made all the more eerie by the fact that we still did not know what had happened. Was it a terrorist bomb? Was it some kind of Con Ed situation like a manhole cover exploding? Whatever it turned out to be, not one of the thousands of people on that staircase would have thought that it was caused by an airplane flying into Tower 1, the next tower over. Nor did we suspect that a second plane was heading for Tower 2 and was about to crash into us.

The four of us stayed together, helping to keep all of our spirits high. After about 45 minutes, we had gotten to the 50th floor. We faintly heard an announcement being made in the hallway, so everyone emptied the fire exit to hear. The fact that there was no PA system in the fire exit must have been a design flaw, no?

The crackling male voice told us to remain calm, but no information was given about the cause of the explosion. The voice just reassured us to remain calm, that the situation was in Tower 1 and was under control, and, here's the kicker, that we should all head back to our offices and wait for further instructions.

Here was a real dilemma. We were all trying to stay organized and follow the instruction we were given. Unfortunately, at a gut level, this instruction didn't make sense to anybody. So, what to do? Do what our gut was telling us to do and get the hell out of there, or do what we were being told and go back to our offices? Megan and Peter stepped off by themselves to discuss it, which left Alice and me to come up with our own decision.

After going back and forth on what the right course of action should be, we finally agreed that we should go downstairs, get a cup of coffee, and see what was going on. Alice and I headed back into the fire exit, which was now empty as everyone else was still deciding what to do. We were actually able to run down the stairs. We ran and ran, and then suddenly felt a huge explosion. The stairs started to sway back and forth, a good three feet in either direction. I grabbed on to the railing, half expecting it to pull out of the wall as the stairs were turned into a pendulum. For some reason, I had a vision of Shelley Winters in *The Poseidon Adventure*, holding on to a steel ladder that just pulled out of the wall when she grabbed it before being dumped into the water. But, to my great relief, the stairs in Tower 2 held and the swaying eventually stopped. I noticed that we were on the 43rd floor. To my amazement, there was absolutely no damage to the stairs. The lights were on, the staircase and railings were solid, and there was not a chip of paint or plaster anywhere to be seen. Alice spoke first and said that we needed to keep going. I agreed and we continued to run down the stairs until, once again, other people had entered the fire exit and the descent again slowed to a crawl.

It took us about 45 more minutes to get out of the building. As we entered the World Trade Center shopping pavilion, fire department and other emergency service personnel were lined up every 5 to 10 feet, creating a corridor for us to walk through up and out by Building 5 (or was it 7?). They were proud to be doing their job, helping us get out. Every day I have prayed that they, too, were able to get out before the building collapsed.

All in all, the company of 200 employees lost four people that day. We had all felt like one big family. The beautiful office space that the family had struggled to attain, which was a symbol of our success and unity, was gone. We were homeless, made that way by a tragedy that will never be forgotten. And we had lost four comrades. But, like any good team, we pulled together and worked tirelessly to get the company back on its feet, to support each other emotionally and spiritually and in any way that we could.

There are many stories of escape from Tower 2, and I would like to share a few team members' efforts to survive. I also want to mention that when the plane hit Tower 2, it had crashed right into our conference room on the 78th floor. This conference room was the showpiece of the office. The side facing outward was all glass and there was an incredible view of the southern tip of Manhattan. It was such a special place that our parent company would frequently use the conference room when making important presentations. That morning, two people from the parent company were there early to set up for a presentation later that day. Unfortunately, they did not survive the attack.

Aparna was a member of the QA team. She was eight months pregnant on 9/11. She had decided to stay near her desk when we heard the first explosion. When the plane hit Tower 2, the ceiling panels on the 77th floor fell, filling the entire space with dust and debris. Aparna could not hide under her desk to escape because of her pregnancy. All she could do was stand there and get showered with debris. When the dust had started to settle, she began to call out for help. Rick, the manager of the QA department, and Tony, the manager of data operations, both came running. They helped Aparna to the fire exit and the three of them walked down the 78 flights of stairs together.

When they got outside, EMS immediately took Aparna to a local hospital to ensure that she and her baby were OK. They were, and one month later, Aparna had a healthy baby boy. Rick was covered in dust and EMS gave him oxygen. He was sitting on a curb on Church St. with the air mask on. All of a sudden, the police started yelling for everybody to run as fast as they could. The building had started to collapse. Ripping the oxygen mask off, Rick started running for his life. He ran down John St. but there was no place to enter as most businesses had closed by then. Suddenly, he saw an open bar and grabbed the door handle and pulled himself inside. As he closed the door, the rolling cloud of the remnants of Tower 2 blew past, leaving Rick safe inside the door.

Bernie was the director of IT. He had come in that morning and gone directly to the conference room on the 78th floor to help the visitors prepare for their presentation, making sure the advanced A/V system was working. With everything in working order, he accidentally left his briefcase on the 78th floor and returned to his office on the 77th floor where he was when the first plane hit Tower 1. He spent some time coordinating with people on his side of the building and was getting ready to leave when he realized that he didn't have his briefcase with him. He picked up the phone and called Violet, who sat next to the conference room.

"Violet, this is Bernie. I'm looking for my briefcase. Can you tell me if it is in the conference room? And, by the way, what are you still doing there?"

"Bernie, yes, your briefcase is in there. I can see it from my desk. I am just going to put the phone system on night standby, and then I am going to get out of here," Violet replied.

"OK, thanks," Bernie replied. "I have to call my mother to let her know I am OK, and then I will get the briefcase and head on out myself. Thanks."

Bernie quickly spoke with his mother, and as he said goodbye to her and hung up the phone, Violet, who was still at her desk, saw a dark shadow cover the conference room window and then "POW," the second hijacked plane crashed through the window and Violet, now frozen in her chair, watched in shock and horror as the plane's wing flew right past her, just a few feet from her face. Luckily for Violet, she was able to get herself moving and headed right for the exit stairs.

Bernie also headed to an emergency exit. The first one he went to was jammed shut. He tried to push it open, but something was blocking the door on the other side. He ran down the hall and found another exit. He pushed, and this time the door opened easily. However, the stairwell entrance was flooded and some kind of liquid was leaking down from the ceiling above Bernie's head. He thought it smelled like kerosene and assumed that a pipe in the heating system had cracked. He didn't know that he was being dowsed in jet fuel.

Another worker, Anthony, came running into the stairwell, holding a flashlight in front of him. Together, he and Bernie ran down the stairs. As Bernie grabbed the railing, he noticed it was wet and sticky. He assumed that the kerosene was leaking on the railing as well as on him. They ran down about thirty floors when, all of a sudden, the lights went out. Total darkness. Anthony switched on his flashlight and the pair had to slow their pace for another 10 floors until they came to a place where the stair lights were working again. In the new light, Bernie took a moment to look down at his hands. They were covered in blood. The liquid that was on the railing on the upper floors had not been the same kerosene that had soaked through Bernie's shirt. It had been human blood.

Bernie and Anthony had made it to the lobby of the WTC and were now running out to the street. An EMS worker came right up to Bernie who was soaked in blood and jet fuel. Immediately, the EMS worker made Bernie take off his shirt. As he was lifting the shirt above his head, they heard the police yelling "Run!" Bernie started running, but he didn't have as big of a head start as Rick did. Instead of being able to find shelter, Bernie just kept running, even as the debris cloud caught up with him and coated him the same way it coated Lower Manhattan.

As that September day went on, I was able to speak with all the members of the software development team and confirm that everyone was safe, alive, and accounted for. I was also asking for volunteers to go to our small Philadelphia satellite office to rebuild all the backend data servers that had been in New York and to establish the numerous operational procedures that were involved in the nightly push of data to our clients.

Unfortunately, at 12:30 that night, just as I was getting ready for bed, my phone rang.

"Hello, Ned?" the caller said. "I am a friend of Barbara's husband. You work with Barbara at Benchmark, right?"

"Yes, I do," I replied.

"Well, no one has seen or heard from her since the attacks this morning. Her husband wants to know if you might have seen her since then."

"No," I whispered helplessly. "I saw her at the coffee machine very early in the morning. But our desks were on the opposite sides of the building, so I didn't see her after that."

"OK, thanks," the friend said. "Her husband just wanted to call everyone possible."

I hung up the phone. Barbara was never found and was eventually counted as one of the four Benchmark employees who were killed that day.

By the next day, 15 people from Benchmark had arrived at the Philly office. This office was home to a small group of software developers who were responsible for writing and maintaining the frontend application. There was one conference room which was going to be repurposed as a data center, and many developers were already sharing small cubicles. The office quickly began to look like a small college campus during finals week.

The goal was that by the time the stock market reopened the following Monday, our software would be fully operational and we would be able to push data down to all of our clients. That meant that there was less than a week to get data feeds and servers installed and configured and to establish the three-man nightly operations center that was required to support the software.

Curt and Dmitri represented the software group. They worked tirelessly over the next week making sure that all of the custom software was loaded on the servers and correctly configured. The rest of the software team that had stayed in New York were communicating with them constantly to help stress-test the data feeds as they became operational and to ensure that the customers would be able to use the software. Sleeping was rare, and so were hotel rooms. It felt like we were working at NASA during a lunar mission! Pizza boxes were stacked floor to ceiling in any corner that wasn't occupied by a data server or a developer with a laptop.

By the time the stock market opened the following Monday, our software was ready to go, albeit with a few Band-Aids in place. However, our clients were happy that at least one of the data providers was working.

Dmitri stayed in Philly for a few extra days to do an inventory of our backup source code servers. We had to make sure that all production software could be compiled and run according to specification. Dmitri called me at home with utter despair in his voice. He told me that while the SourceSafe server that contained all of the company's documentation had been backed up nightly, the server that contained all the source code had never been added to the nightly backups. Oops! No one had bothered to test the integrity of the server backups. All of the software that Dmitri had written at Benchmark for the previous seven years was gone.

We spent a lot of time over the next few weeks trying to figure out what source code we did and didn't have. We checked our home computers and any laptops that we had with us. Fortunately for Dmitri, his last big project had been saved by one of our process improvement initiatives. We had instituted peer reviews between the New York and Philly offices and had recently sent the Philly group a large project that Dmitri had worked on. The source code was safe on the Philly development manager's computer.

In the end, senior management decided that since so much source code was lost, only production software that was in immediate need of an upgrade would be reproduced. This allowed most of the software team to begin working on new development work. The only question now was where we would be working from.

A few weeks after 9/11, the entire company got together at the Union Club in New York City for a company meeting. This was the first time we had all gotten together after the attacks. In a way, the Union Club's requirement of formal dress helped to create an atmosphere of importance. Dressed in our Sunday Best, we came together and together mourned our lost coworkers. One of the people who had been killed was George, a salesman with the company for many years. I was speaking with one of his fellow salesmen who said he had been at the dentist that morning and, as he was sitting in the dentist chair, was in utter despair as the TV reports started coming in. All he wished for was to be back at the World Trade Center with his team. He had spent the previous few weeks feeling guilty about not being there. His thinking was that if he had been there, perhaps he could have saved his friend. I have heard the same sentiment from many people: people who were just getting off the subway, people who were still in their cars driving to work but could see the planes as they attacked us, people who lived just down the street in Battery Park. It seems irrational, but people want to feel connected in whatever way they can.

At the Union Club, Nancy spoke with Curt and me about permanently sending the developers to work in the Philly office until a new location could be found in New York. She didn't believe that developers could be productive working at home and that they needed to be closely supervised. Curt told her that the conditions in Philly were extremely overcrowded and that he wasn't going to have the developers share hotel rooms for an indefinite period of time. He wouldn't give in, and Nancy walked away frustrated and angry.

It turned out to be six months before we were all relocated together in our new office space. During this time, everyone worked from home but remained highly productive, and we constantly communicated with the rest of the company. We IM'd each other, teleconferenced, had impromptu meetings in New York City restaurants like America and Zen Pallate in Union Square, and did whatever we could to stay productive. I even had a three-hour meeting in Starbucks with one of Nancy's assistants to try to hash out the requirements for the stalled project. It just so happened that the assistant had some downtime. Nancy had told her to work on the requirements if it wouldn't interfere with other activities. By the time we moved into the new space, the requirements were complete, inspected, and approved, and the coding was 50% complete.

At the end of February 2002, we settled into our new office space. We had the entire fifth floor of what used to be a dot-com start-up company in the West Village. There was a foosball room, a yoga room, and lots of curved walls and oddly angled corners. It turned out that there had been a bar in Philly that had a foosball table and some of the people who had worked there got quite good at it. The yoga room was turned into a meeting room but the foosball table stayed!

Another change was in store for us. Curt had made the decision to return to Carnegie Mellon to get more involved with CMMI and process engineering. He resigned and I was given his job. We also expanded the team to include two new developers and one consultant. The team was changing right before our eyes. But our shared experiences of the previous six months had created an invisible bond between us that could never be changed. The way we thought about each other, the way we worked together, the way we could look at a problem and know the solution the other person was thinking of without saying it—no, nobody ever talked about it, but we all felt it and honored it.

One department benefit that I instituted right away was for each developer to be able to work from home one day a week. We had proved that we could be just as productive from home as in the office. The only constraint was that we had to do it on the q.t. because one of the other managing directors did not agree with this policy (guess who?).

The team continued to work hard. Now that we had some unplanned time, we took the opportunity to create a strong code foundation. Each developer was responsible for writing reusable code and, for every project he worked on, he had to create at least one reusable component. This could be a backend processing DLL or a user interface widget. At our weekly department meetings, one developer would have to present his contribution to the rest of the group. He had to include code samples on how to use his contribution as well as showing the group the code he wrote to create his object. As a senior developer on the team, it was soon Dmitri's turn to make his presentation.

Dmitri resisted. He came to see me and told me that he wasn't comfortable speaking in front of the group. He had a thick Russian accent and felt that he couldn't communicate that well and that he would ruin the meeting for everyone. I said, "Dmitri, you are always meeting with one or two people, showing them how to write code or helping them debug a problem. Everyone understands you just fine. Don't worry, these are your friends!" We spoke some more and I told him that if he really didn't want to do the presentation, he could skip this round. He thought about it and eventually agreed to give it a try.

The day of the presentation came. Dmitri got so tied up with making his handouts that he was late to the meeting. We sent out a search party and found him at the copy machine, battling the automatic collator. The search party helped him clear the paper jam and finish making the copies. They all came back together and Dmitri began his presentation. He had written a DLL that standardized the format of error logs, and the output could be directed to either a text file, the Windows Event Logger, or both. This was something that the developers really needed and they were anxious to start using Dmitri's DLL. As he began writing his sample code to his interface with the DLL on the whiteboard, you could tell he was nervous. He spoke with his back to the group and his handwriting was hard to read. He stumbled through his presentation and, thinking he was finished, sat down, visibly perspiring, and asked whether there were any questions. I am not sure who started it, but there was a look of utter despair on Dmitri's face and we all just started to laugh.

Even Dmitri started to laugh. And that was enough to get rid of all the tension in the room. And the meeting changed from a formal presentation to just another session where Dmitri was showing the rest of us how to do something that he knew backward and forward. The meeting continued, and before we knew it, we had run out of time and the next group was knocking on the conference room door to get us out.

Megan had the same aversion to speaking up in large groups that Dmitri had. She was one of the QA testers. She had the dogged determination needed to uncover even the most obscure bugs. When she walked over to the development area, the programmers took cover. Unfortunately, she was not much of a contributor to inspection meetings. One day I happened to be sitting next to her at a requirements inspection meeting. We all had our copies of the document. When I glanced down at Megan's copy, I was impressed that she had red marks on just about every paragraph! She had really taken the time to read this, I thought. However, she didn't say anything during the meeting. I figured that she had her reasons and didn't say anything at the time.

Later that day, I walked over to her desk.

"Megan, you have a sec?" I asked.

"Sure. What's up?"

"I was just curious as to why you didn't bring up any of your comments at the meeting this morning."

I could tell she was getting very uncomfortable with the conversation and didn't want to answer me. Since I wasn't her manager, I decided to not push the issue with her. But I did speak with her manager later on and the two of us began to gently encourage her to be more assertive.

A few months later, I was at another requirements meeting with Megan. We were quickly moving through the document when all of a sudden Megan raised her hand and said, "Excuse me, I think I found some mistakes on the previous page. Does anyone want me to point them out? I don't know how important it is. I'm sorry for stopping everyone." We all turned back to the previous page and Megan showed us the two mistakes she had found. They were two small, non-critical errors, but everyone was glad to have them pointed out. "Great catch, Megan," I said. She started to apologize for finding them and wasting everyone's time, but I quickly stopped her: "No, you were 100% correct to point them out. Remember, we are so much better off finding all the defects now rather than waiting until development or testing. Good job." Over time, Megan became respected as the most thorough document inspector in the QA department.

As the group manager, it was important for me to recognize that everyone had different strengths and desires when it came to writing code. Mary was excellent at creating user interfaces. Peter was our process person. Together, Peter and I went through all the nooks and crannies of the Rational Unified Process and created what we called the Benchmark Unified Process. This project lasted a few months and the end result was a complete road map that any developer could follow to ensure that his project followed the software development life cycle process and had all the needed documents and deliverables. This became an invaluable part of the department's assets and the core for writing quality software. Our adoption and adherence to this process and the focusing on each other's strengths, not weaknesses, was the main reason why, over the next three years, the software development team had a perfect track record of delivering software on time and on budget and with the features promised. We were the department that everyone wanted to work in and be a part of. I had to keep a list of people who wanted to transfer into my department.

One day, my boss, Bernie, came to see me. "Ned," he said, "I have a favor to ask you."

"Sure," I replied. "Go ahead."

"There is a guy over in the IT department that has been writing little utilities for us in VB script. He's pretty good at it, too. I just did his annual review and he is bored working in IT. I think that if I don't involve him in more development work, he might leave the company."

"Bernie," I said, "do you realize that I already have official requests from five other people to transfer into the development group? Are you going to open up six positions for me?"

"Well, of course not," said Bernie. "But I don't want to lose Doug. Give him a regular interview, and if you think he is a good match with the group, I'll work out the transfer myself."

"How about if I do take Doug, I get to also take one other person from the top of the list. You know these are all junior programmers and it takes time to train them. We can have them sit with a more senior developer for a few months and they'll get some good experience. Plus, if it seems that they are not going to be good developers, we will find it out soon enough before any real harm is done."

Bernie said: "I can't make any promises now. See how it goes with Doug. If it works out, I'll see what I can do to open another job req. OK?"

"Fair enough," I said. "I'll meet with him and get back to you."

By the end of the month, the development group had two new junior programmers, Doug and Henry.

Although we were successfully adopting and adhering to our process and proving beyond a shadow of a doubt that software process does work and that the more time spent planning up front guarantees excellent results, there were still one or two senior managers who continued to fight the process whenever they had a chance. Mary had been working on a group of reports for Nancy that "somehow" continued to fly under the process radar. One of the outputs on the report was a custom calculation. We had no specs on how the calculation was supposed to work as Nancy and her staff told Mary to just stop by whenever there was a question. But it was a very complex calculation, and the business users themselves didn't really understand it. Mary had just delivered her third redo of the report and the end users were still finding problems with the calculation. Mary came to my office not knowing what to do to get consensus on this one calculation.

I called a meeting with all the stakeholders, including Nancy, her staff, Mary, and me. There were about 12 people in the meeting. I stated that we had been coding the calculation as we had been told, but it seemed that the developers were never told about all of the different scenarios that could affect the calculation. As a result, the calculation was being asked to do different things under many different circumstances. We then asked the business stakeholder to draw out on the whiteboard his understanding of the calculation.

After 20 minutes, we had a whiteboard filled with flows. Everyone participated, and there was finally consensus among the group. Yes, they were all ready to sign off on this change. That is, until another stakeholder asked about a condition that was not represented on the whiteboard. Everyone gasped as they realized they had forgotten one specific condition that would affect the calculation about 15% of the time. We then worked that into the whiteboard flow. Again, everyone agreed with the change and was ready to sign off on it. Then, the main business stakeholder, Nancy, who was the most senior person in that meeting and the one who had always resisted process and process improvement, came up with a user workflow that would again totally change how the calculation worked in 50% of the cases! Everyone else had missed it. We added that to the flow on the whiteboard and thought that we finally had the calculation defined.

Mary's head was spinning, but she did her best to do one final walkthrough with the group. When she was finished, Nancy looked at her, stood up, and said to the group, "I guess this is why process is so important. We should have done this work when the project was starting and I apologize to the group for skimping on the requirements for this. Let me take this back to the business unit for a few days, get a business analyst assigned, and we will then write up a document of exactly what we want. There is no need to spend any more time coding until we do our work."

I nearly fell off my chair! This was a huge victory. Curt and Nancy used to argue all the time about the need for process, and I knew that this statement from Nancy was a moral victory for Curt, who had left the company by this point. Having Nancy onboard with process was also a moral victory for the entire software development team.

As we walked out of the conference room, Nancy waited for me outside the door. While we were walking to our offices, she said to me, "Ned, it has come to my attention that you allow your group to work from home one day a week. Even on Fridays." Oh no, I thought. There goes that! I started to mumble something, but didn't know what to say.

"Don't worry," Nancy continued, "I just ask that you keep it among yourselves and don't let the other departments know what you are doing. I see that it works well in your group, but it would never work in mine."

"Sure," I said, "no problem. See you later."

I went into my office and sat down at my desk with a wide grin on my face.

CHAPTER TWENTY-SIX

Getting Past Obstacles

an Interview with Scott Ambler

Scott Ambler helped lead the software world through two revolutions: first in the move to object-oriented analysis and design in the 1990s, and then in the adoption of agile practices in the decade that followed. He's spent a lot of his career focused on making enterprisewide changes, and doing that successfully means having to overcome obstacle after obstacle. We wanted to hear how he managed to make change work on that scale, especially when people around him weren't sure that it would work.

Jenny: We're interested in talking to you about your experience, and how you came to know about how teams work together.

Scott: Right now I'm the practice leader for agile development for IBM Software Group. For the most part, I help customers become more agile and more effective at what they're doing. I also work with IBM itself. A lot of that is helping people to work together more effectively, often in teams. I've written a few books, and done a lot of work in the agile community. I'm the guy behind Agile Modeling, the Agile Data Method, and the Enterprise Unified Process.

As far as my background in teaming, it's a lot of hard-earned experience, I guess. Software is developed in teams, for the most part. As a result, you either learn the easy or the hard way—and I guess for me it was the hard way—about how to work in teams.

Jenny: Getting companies to adopt the kinds of practices and techniques you talk about means convincing a lot of people to change the way they do their jobs—and the way they think about those jobs. How do you go about making those kinds of large changes?

Scott: I think a lot of it is just trying to get stuff done. Software's hard, software's complex, and you need to work with people. I think the first obstacle you have to overcome is yourself, in recognizing that you can't do it all. You're going to need help, and you're going to need to learn from others.

As far as obstacles go, a big one is being able to observe when the team is not working well, because it's not always obvious. If people are shouting at each other, then something bad *might* be happening. But I worked on one team where an observer from the outside, if they were to look at us, would think we were about to kill each other. But for whatever reason, the way we worked together best was to argue. We could argue something out, and we'd be shouting sometimes—you'd think we were about to kill each other. What was happening was that we were working together really effectively. Some of it was just because we'd grown to respect each other. And even though we'd never really talked about it, we knew that our process was to talk about it and argue things through. Invariably, nobody had it right going into the discussion, but through the argument we came to a much better conclusion to whatever we were working on.

My point is that you can't always tell when a team is dysfunctional. Because in that case, an outsider would have thought we were dysfunctional, but we were actually phenomenally effective. If there's negative shouting and screaming, that's a problem. But sometimes, you can be on a team where everyone's trying, but nobody's communicating, and nobody's reaching their goals. It might not be explicit, but there's a slippery slope that occurs where everybody can work really hard for a long time, but in total, you're not accomplishing much. The easy analogy is that during the day you've got people digging a hole, and at night other people are filling it up. Everybody's working really hard digging and filling holes, but in the end nothing of value is actually occurring.

That can happen on dysfunctional teams, and it's not always obvious that it's happening, particularly if the team is large and distributed. When you haven't bonded and you're not close, it's difficult to observe that.

Andrew: So, the way that the team communicates can be an obstacle, not just to getting the work done if the communication is problematic, but even to recognizing whether or not a team is effective. And it sounds like personality conflicts can be a real problem. If the team has the right stuff technically, but the people don't mesh for whatever reason, it can keep work from getting done. I'm guessing that someone who was very introverted and avoided conflicts whenever possible would have had trouble joining your team, right? Even if they were perfect, technically, to fill a slot that's open on your team, I have a feeling that they'd be lost. But sometimes, you end up in a situation where there's a personality mismatch. What would you do about it?

Scott: So, say there was an introvert that ended up getting caught in the crossfire, or however you want to describe it. Someone would have to notice. The introvert would have to step up and say, "You know what? I really don't like this." But that would be really hard for them. So, say that's not happening. Then somebody else would have to notice, which is easier said than done. In that environment, our manager would have noticed.

Andrew: Do you think it's the manager's job to notice?

Scott: I would hope so. A good manager or team lead should be responsible for looking out for everybody on the team, which is easy to say but hard to do in some situations. Whoever's in the team lead role or the manager role should be looking out and asking themselves, "How is this person doing? How are they fitting in? How can I help them? What problems are they running into?"

And they need to have techniques to help them notice these things, and status reports might not do it. The introvert probably wouldn't write in a status report, "I hate working with these guys. I'm not getting things done, and I'm not fitting in." The team lead needs to observe that.

Say that someone observes that this person is running into trouble and not fitting in well. I would hope that person would bring it up amongst the team, or point it out to the extroverts who are shouting at each other: "Hey, this is working for you, but Sally over here is really having a rough go of it. Can you try to bring her into the conversation, and maybe calm things down and try to find ways to work with her?" Everyone else on the team would have to find different ways to work with Sally, and Sally would have to maybe step up a bit. We'd all have to take the opportunity to learn; which, to me, is the mark of a professional. You should always be trying to improve how you're doing and how you work. In particular, you've got to get good at collaboration, working together with others and working on a team.

For technical people, this can be a challenge. This industry rewards people for their technical skills, and many of us are really geared for being technical, but we often shortchange the softer "people skills," or whatever you want to call them. As a result, we don't focus on them as much. And those are important things, at least in software development. People are a primary factor of success on a software team. The way you act with each other matters a lot more than whatever cool new technology you're working with today. This is something we don't appreciate as much.

Andrew: I think a lot of people would be a little bit surprised sometimes to hear that, since you've spent so much of your career talking about architecture, development, and practices: object-oriented development, UML and software modeling, agile development, planning, and process in general. But, when asked about the biggest problems that face teams, the ones you bring up are people-based, how people work together. Were you surprised to figure that out? Or is that something you knew from the beginning?

Scott: Yes, I was surprised, but I figured that out fairly early, I guess through observation and experience. I figured out pretty early that there's more to it than just technology. I didn't actually fall into this people stuff right away. I guess my first step was to realize that we need to look past technology to process and practices. When I went back to school for my master's degree, I started focusing on Computer Supported Collaborative Work (CSCW), which is a fancy academic term for groupware. I guess that's what gave me an appreciation for software people issues, because that's what CSCW is all about. In this case, how do we use technology to get people to work together more effectively? That's how I became more aware of these software issues.

Jenny: You've also spent a lot of your career talking and writing about practices. Have you ever found that the practices themselves that people are using can help you get past those obstacles to team building that you were talking about? Or, on the flip side, can those practices themselves be an obstacle?

Scott: In non-solo development, techniques like pair programming—or from Agile Modeling, modeling with others—you can start to get that recognition that you have to work together on a regular basis. A lot of people in the agile community practice what they call "promiscuous pairing," where not only do you work in pairs, you swap pairs on a regular basis. When you do that, not only does the quality of your work improve, you learn a lot from others from working with them. By swapping pairs on a regular basis, that really forces the issue, and the team has to learn these softer communication skills to survive in this environment.

But like you pointed out, that in and of itself can be a challenge, and not everybody can work this way. This is one of the challenges that the agile community faces. In a way, the software skills that we're talking about and trying to improve upon are a barrier to entry to some people. Some people really do just want to focus on the technology, and really do want to work by themselves. And that's OK. That, I think, is something that an organization or team needs to recognize: that not everybody's the same, and some people just don't want to work on teams. There are some jobs where it is solo work. I think that's an important observation.

Andrew: Throughout doing the research for this book, we've talked to many people who have told us about agile practices and agile in general. And everyone seems to have a slightly different definition of what agile actually means. Can you tell us a little bit about how you got started with agile? What kind of project did it solve? And also, what kinds of problems did it cause? Because nothing's a silver bullet. We'd love to hear your thoughts on that, and on what agile really means to you.

Scott: Definitely. On the Agile Modeling site (*http://www.agilemodeling.com/*) I've got my definition. I've actually got it on the screen here—let me read it to you: "Disciplined agile software development is an iterative and incremental (evolutionary) approach to software development which is performed in a highly collaborative manner by self-organizing teams within an effective governance framework with 'just enough' ceremony that produces high-quality software in a cost-effective and timely manner which meets the changing needs of its stakeholders."

Now, there's some "motherhood and apple pie" stuff in there. But I think those are all important features, and a lot of it is teamwork-based. So, for example, all of the talk about working in a highly collaborative manner and on self-organizing teams, that's more obvious from a team perspective. But one of the things that a lot of agilists don't talk about, which I think is unfortunate, is the governance framework aspect to it.

No team works in a vacuum. There's an overall organization and environment that the team is working in. And the work of that team needs to be governed, and governance in some ways can be a good thing. Unfortunately, it's not always done right, which is why some software professionals cringe when you use the term *governance*. But you do want to make it lean, and you do want to make it as effective as possible.

Working closely with your stakeholders is absolutely critical, and that's a teaming issue. In the agile world, we talk about the "whole team" concept. That may or may not be a practice, depending on your point of view. People should have enough skills on the team to get the job done, and you're going to work together to do whatever that job is. And that's a very good thing. But what's often missed is that someone needs to keep an eye on that whole team, and make sure that whole team is actually staying on course and whatever it is they're trying to achieve actually makes sense in the overall organization. That's something I think isn't discussed enough in the agile community.

Andrew: Those two things—governance and self-organizing teams—sound like opposites to me.

Scott: They're really not. Everybody is governed, and this is something that often gets missed. "Self-organizing" doesn't mean that you're out of control and doing your own thing. It means that the team members themselves decide how to meet their goals. But the goals themselves, the resources they use, the time frame they have to do it, those are governed by the organization. Somebody's paying the bills. Just the financial issue alone is an issue, because if the organization doesn't like what your team is doing, they can pull the plug. Now, that's a harsh governance mechanism, but it's fairly realistic. How did the team start up? If it's a software development project, there must be some kind of goals you're trying to achieve. There has to be an initial vision. And setting that vision, the mission—that's a form of governance as well. The rights and responsibilities of the team, the reporting chain: that's governance. For example, the junior programmer might not have the same decision rights as the senior technical lead. That's a form of governance as well.

So, governance is given short shrift, I think, in many situations. It's always happening, but we don't recognize it. And it's a shame if we ignore it, because one of the things I see in the agile community is that we're so paranoid about bureaucracy and wasted time that things like governance will instantly be beaten up. "We don't need any governance; it's a waste of time!" Well, no. Bad governance can be an obstacle to leadership. Let's try to be effective at governance, because the value of governance is to help us make good decisions and go in the right direction. Let's keep the baby and throw out the bathwater.

Andrew: So, a team can be governed by the vision, by the goal of the project, as well as by the expertise and limitations of the team and the company. Now, I've personally seen plenty of software projects go off the rails because the project governed the vision, and not the other way around. I guess that's one way you can describe scope creep.

Scott: Yes. The vision should evolve over time—and rightly so, because the situation evolves, too. But what happens, for whatever reason, is that long before the project actually starts, somebody has this idea that you need to do X and achieve whatever goals, for whatever business reason. There's always this long list of opportunities that an organization has. But there's only so much funding, so they have to choose what they want to do, and hopefully do it effectively. The reason for that project really does direct the effort, because you really want to make sure that you're achieving those goals. And if the goals are changing, you want to make sure they're changing the right way, and you want to manage that evolution. You should be doing a reality check every so often, which doesn't happen as often as it should.

I ran a survey through Dr. Dobb's a year or two ago about how people define success, because we don't have many numbers on this. It's my philosophy that if a project is in trouble, someone should actually say, "Hey, this project is in trouble!" Somebody has to make a decision about how to get this team out of trouble. If nobody knows how to get the team out of trouble, we need to cut bait now, and stop throwing good money after bad. Now, that's my philosophy, but I didn't know how many other people thought this way. So we asked. And what we found was that something like only 41% or 42% of respondents said that in their organization, if a project is in trouble, it's considered a success to cancel that project—which is a real shame, because if I recognize a project is in trouble, I want to get it out of trouble as soon as I possibly can. I would consider stopping a project as early as possible. That's obviously not a good idea, but I'd rather waste half a million dollars and learn the hard way than waste three or four million dollars and learn the hard way.

The only way that you can actually make that work is to monitor what's going on, and ask these sorts of questions. Is this team still succeeding? Does this project still make sense? Because teams can become blind to that. A team can be phenomenally successful in whatever the scope of the project is. But the environment could have changed, and they may not have recognized that. Whatever reasons there were to start that project may have changed, and we need to stop it.

So, for example, in the fall of 2008, we had the financial crash. For a lot of financial institutions, their business environment changed dramatically from September to October. I'm sure that some of them put some projects on the shelf, because the business environment changed so radically that some projects no longer made sense. It's no fault of the development team at all. Still, why throw good money after bad?

Andrew: The idea of aligning the project to the company, of having somebody looking out to make sure the project we're building is the right project to build, reminds me of a problem that I suspect a lot of agile teams face. But I've never heard anyone talk about it, and maybe you can help shed some light on it. One of the bread-and-butter practices that a lot of agile teams follow—and, I think, a good one!—is to bring a business representative into the team. Sometimes this is part-time, sometimes it's even full-time. I can see that embedding a stakeholder or business person in the team itself can do really good things for communication and information sharing, and for making sure the scope doesn't creep in the wrong direction. Now, to be honest, I've never really seen this done all that well, because I've rarely come across stakeholders who feel that they have that kind of time, for better or worse.

But, for a team that does manage to embed a stakeholder into the team, I worry that they may run into a problem where they also start to be affected by that very same blindness that you just mentioned. If you bring the stakeholders from the business side into the team, and everybody suffers from the same blindness, then who's looking out for the project's goals to make sure they're still aligned with what the company needs?

Scott: There are a couple of things there. Sometimes the outsiders go native. It doesn't matter who you're bringing into the team. If you work closely with an existing team enough, you'll start relating to that team, start relating a little bit less to where you came from, which in this case is the business side of things. And this can be a problem.

One of the risks of the "whole team" concept is groupthink. The basic concept of groupthink is that if a group of people work together long enough—and this can be several months—they start to think the same way, and start to become blind to the same issues. Psychologists sometimes talk about this in relation to risky decision making. For example, you might not be willing to bet $100 on a horse race. But if you're out with your friends, and one of them bets $100 on a horse, and then another bets $100 on a horse, then betting $100 starts to seem less risky to you. So, the entire group together would together make what they perceive as a very risky decision, but because you're in a group, suddenly that risk has gone down. And that sort of thing happens as well.

So, there are these interesting team dynamics that you have to watch out for. Nothing's perfect, right? And this is something that governance efforts have to watch out for. The challenge with governance—and this is the reason I think that people are bitter about IT governance—is that a lot of organizations facing a problem like this will go into "command and control" mode. The people doing governance will think that they're managing.

They'll try to direct the project, and they'll get too actively involved, or they'll place too much of a burden on a team. They'll start asking the team to produce regular status reports or attend the monthly control board meeting, or they'll have these milestone meetings every couple of months to ask the team to justify what they're doing. That throws a lot of extra unnecessary burden on the team. Good governance should be about enablement and about motivation. It shouldn't be about command and control, and it shouldn't be a burden. Obviously, there will be a little overhead, but it shouldn't be too much. If it's too much, the governance effort becomes detrimental, and that's a very serious challenge.

Jenny: So, how do you approach that challenge? What's the first thing you do to make sure that you're not forcing a team to have to put up with detrimental governance?

Scott: You want to automate as much as possible. Per Kroll and I wrote a white paper on this about a year and a half ago called "Lean Development Governance"; the philosophies there were to automate as much as possible, to make it as easy as possible to report accurate metrics, and for the person doing governance to understand that different teams are in different situations. The people doing governance need to be flexible, and understand that a team of 5 people will work differently from a team of 50. A team building a data warehouse works differently from a team building a website. Your team building a website will work differently from my team building a website. We're different people, and we're different teams, even if we're building similar things with the same technology. And as a result, those teams need to be managed in different ways.

A very common mistake that governance people make is that they try to inflict the same process and the same governance structure on different teams, and it just doesn't work because different teams need to be governed in different ways. The goals might be the same, but the way that you reach those goals will be different. The way I like to say it is that you should be aiming for repeatable results, not repeatable processes. But that can be a challenge for the more rigid and bureaucratic among us.

Jenny: That's interesting to me, because when you talk about engineering a lot of automated solutions to deal with this stuff, that can actually get to be as heavyweight as writing a lot of documents. Creating a lot of test frameworks and putting automation scripts in place, and putting all the practices in place that you need to automate your quality activities upfront, and the engineering effort needed for that, seems like it can be very heavy.

Scott: That's a very good observation. If you're toolsmithing all of your own tools, it is quite heavy. This, I think, is another challenge to the agile community. Many agile teams rely on open source software, and for very good reason. But there are limits to that, and one of the limits is one of integration, and particularly one of governance and accurate metrics reporting. You need to go beyond some of the agile rhetoric.

For example, there's an example called Jazz, and if you go to *http://jazz.net* you can download demo copies of it. But in Rational Team Concert, which sits on top of Jazz, we automate all of this. All of the stuff that agile teams are hand-jamming—their defect trend reports and their burn-down charts, whatever it is that they may or may not be reporting on—that they're either doing manually, all of that gets generated automatically in real time. So, there's no real curtain there. But that's because it's already implemented.

If you had to implement it all yourself, it'd be a phenomenal amount of work. So, there's limits to some of the things we see the mainstream agile community doing right now. There are some challenges there.

No development team in a bank or an insurance company would think of developing their own compiler. That's something you buy or download free of charge. So, now you're starting to see better-integrated tools that are providing the information you need to govern effectively. But you definitely don't want to be hand-jamming all this and implementing it yourself, because that's a huge burden.

Andrew: We've been talking a lot about obstacles to building software, but we'd really love to end on an upbeat note. Can you tell us about a great team that you've worked on?

Scott: One of the best teams I was ever on wasn't a software team. It was at my karate dojo. I trained in karate for about 10 years until an injury sidelined me, which is unfortunate, but that's the way it goes. There are some very interesting philosophies that a lot of teams can benefit from. One of the philosophies or rules in North American karate is the concept of belts: you go through a white belt, then a yellow belt, and so on, all the way up to black belt. And one of the rules was that somebody who's a lower belt, somebody who's not as experienced, can always go up to someone with a higher-ranking belt and ask them for help. That person is responsible for helping them to the best of their ability. Now, part of that help might be to say, "I don't know how to describe this to you, but this person over here can help us, so let's work on this and get better at it."

The willingness to ask for help is critical. But the willingness to give help is critical, too, and one of the principles of martial arts is that you learn more through helping and teaching than you do by just trying to work things through by yourself. This is something that many people can relate to.

If it's just orange belts in the room at the time you can still work together on things, and help each other achieve what you need to achieve. That willingness to work with each other that I learned in karate, I try to apply on software teams. It's interesting to me that the agile community does coding katas and runs coding dojos. I think a fair number of people are bringing martial arts ideas into software development. The martial arts have been around for a long time, and they've figured out how to teach people. Because it's pretty much all voluntary: as an adult, you go to a martial arts class because you want to learn, or get more fit, whatever your goal is. But you're there because you want to get better.

Andrew: It's really interesting to me that you say that. I've been studying another Japanese martial art, aikido, for about 10 years. And one thing I really like about aikido training is that everybody always trains together. And teaching more junior people is considered an important part of your training, especially as you get more senior. One of the things that I've found over and over again—I didn't expect to find this, but I did—is that I actually learn more from teaching other people than I do from being taught by other people.

That's another thing that I think translates well to the programming and software world. For example, when Jenny and I wrote Head First C#, *our book on teaching people to program, I learned a lot by figuring out how to explain some of the concepts to somebody new. I mean, I definitely understood, say, core principles of object-oriented development going into the project. But I really feel that figuring out how to explain to a new C# programmer why they care about encapsulation, or the difference between interfaces and abstract classes, in a way that they'll actually understand and connect with, brought me to a whole new level of understanding.*

And I found that this all translates directly to my job. I found that as a manager, especially, when part of my job is to train people on my team and help them not just do their jobs but develop professionally, I'd learn from them, often unintentionally but sometimes intentionally. Sometimes someone who's only been programming for a few years has some really good ideas that I've never heard before. So, I definitely relate to what you're talking about.

Scott: It's interesting, especially if you look at some of the pair programming research into different combinations. If a novice pairs with an expert, for example, what they found is that both people benefit. Obviously, the novice will pick up a lot from working with the expert. But the expert learns from answering those questions. And the question might be something straightforward: "Why are you doing that?" Well, it's because...wait, why *am* I doing that? It forces you to think through some of your practices, which is an opportunity to improve. "This really doesn't make a lot of sense, and maybe I can do it better."

Andrew: Wow. What you just said is almost exactly the same as something Jenny and I wrote about in our first book. Actually, I've got it right here—it's from the section that's about pair programming teams that have a junior member and a senior member: "Often, a junior team member will ask a seemingly 'naïve' question about the code that turns out to identify a serious problem. This is especially common with problems that the senior member has been living with for so long that she no longer notices them. Sometimes the extent of a code problem only becomes clear when it is explained to somebody else." That sounds exactly like what you were just talking about.

And that begs the question for me: why is it so damn hard to get programmers to do it? Of all the practices, agile or otherwise, that I've had my own teams work with and talked to other people about, pair programming is the one practice that I've had an almost impossible time getting teams to adopt. It's even harder to get them to do that than to start doing automated unit tests and test-driven development.

Jenny: I think there's sort of this intuitive notion that having two people on the same thing is just inherently wasteful, and people just don't want to do it.

Scott: There's a lot of that. Also, people just aren't comfortable with it. There's something to be said for being at your desk by yourself, doing your own thing. It's interesting; pair programming's tiring. You do it for five or six hours, and you're exhausted, because you're actually working.

One of the things I do, and it's a bit harsh, is to really force the issue. My technique is that I'll bring the idea up with the team: here's what it's all about, here's how you do it. But it's hard. We'll talk it through, and talk about why it's hard. And what I'll get the team to agree to is to try it out for a month. We'll swap pairs on a regular basis—every day, you should work with someone new, not whoever you worked with yesterday. We're going to talk it out. We're not going to tolerate solo programming for that entire month. And at the end of the month, then we'll make the decision about whether or not we want to keep doing it. And what I've found is that by forcing the issue, and by really keeping people's noses to the grindstone, is that by the end of the month very few people want to go back to solo programming. But it takes a while. It's a "no pain, no gain" kind of deal—I'm sure there's other rhetoric, but sometimes you've just got to suck it up and do it. And pair programming is one of those things where you just have to force the issue for a while. Because it *is* uncomfortable at first. It feels strange, and for many people it's outside their comfort zone. So you've just got to do it. What I've found is that on the teams that choose to do it, very few—maybe 5%—of the people go back to solo programming. But it takes a month.

Andrew: Do you think that's because it's hard for someone to put himself in the mindset of someone who's actually doing it if he's never done it before?

Scott: I think so. Pair programming is initially a hard thing, but there are a lot of benefits to it. There's an intrinsic benefit that's very hard to observe directly, and that's the problem. It's one of those things where it's easy to say, "Well, there are two people working at the same desk, so they're half as productive." So, it's easy to knock if you've never done it. But once you've experienced it, it's pretty good.

Andrew: Do you think that's something that might be a general rule for getting teams to accept changes? That once they've tried it, they won't want to go back, no matter how much whining there was at the beginning?

Scott: The general conclusion I'd draw is that if there's something where there's so much discussion out there and so much evidence that it works, then it's worth trying. I'm not sure if you're at the point of your life where eating a lot of bran is a good thing—eventually, you'll get there, believe me! It's not something you want to do to begin with. But after a while, you think, "Eh, that's pretty good for me." So eventually, you'll need to just tough it out and do it.

CHAPTER TWENTY-SEVEN

Speed Versus Quality
Why Do We Need to Choose?

Johanna Rothman

DURING A PROJECT WHEN I WAS THE PROJECT MANAGER, I HAD THIS CONVERSATION WITH A SENIOR manager at a company:

> *Big Cheese:* "Stop those code reviews. They're slowing down the project."
> *Johanna:* "But then we won't know where the bugs are. We need the code reviews."
> *Big Cheese:* "Stop them or I'll fire you."
> *Johanna:* "You'll fire me for doing the right thing?"
> *Big Cheese:* "In this case, the right thing is to finish the project as fast as possible. Stop those code reviews."

Pretty strange conversation, eh?

I wish I could say this was an isolated incident. But even though this particular conversation occurred almost 20 years ago, it still happens every day someplace. This is the story of a team that refused to buckle under management pressure to do it fast. The team knew that they if they did a great job, they *could* do it fast, by doing it right.

How Did We Get Here?

If we turn on the Way-Back machine to the beginning of the project, Big Cheese brought the project team together and said, "I have great news. I sold a new version of ProcessControlApp. But it has to do these three things faster, and have these five new features. And, we need it in six months."

The project team of six developers got together and discussed the problem. They'd worked as a team for several years. The newest team member had 18 months of experience working on the product with the team, and the most senior developer had initiated the product four years before. They knew each other and how to work together.

ProcessControlApp had no GUI because it was integrated into a manufacturing line. All of the access into and out of the application was through the command line or through an API. ProcessControlApp did a visual inspection of the material on the line, made some decisions about the material, and commanded the line based on its decision. So, although there was no GUI, ProcessControlApp was a highly complex application, where performance (how fast could the software make the decision?), reliability (how much uptime did the software have?), and accuracy (how many false positives or negative decisions did the software make?) all counted.

For the previous two releases of ProcessControlApp, they'd all worked together, along with two testers and a writer. They knew how to work together as a team. They told the VP of software engineering they needed that same writer and two testers.

I was the SQA manager, so it was my job to assign testers to different projects. When I met with the engineering VP, Nancy, I explained I had no testers available. "But you have to give them two testers. They can't get the project done without them."

"I have no testers. Look, here's where everyone is allocated." We discussed the other projects and their relative priorities [1]. Nancy agreed that I had no testers to provide. I asked about hiring more people, and Nancy told me I had no budget to hire more people.

I thought for a minute and suggested, "Hmm, I can't do the testing, and I can't give them testers. But here's what I can do for the team. I can be their project manager, help them see options, and remove obstacles so that they can get work done. Since this is a process control application with no GUI, this is possible. Difficult, but possible. Is that OK with you?"

"Talk to the team and see if it's OK with them."

About the Team

This team was a true team, not a group [2]. The team chose its own practices, which is part of what made it so successful. But a big part of what made this team successful was the trust the team members had for each other.

Although I was the project manager, the team trusted me differently than they did each other. They were happy for me to make suggestions about what they could do, but they never blindly took my suggestions. They always discussed each idea thoroughly. If they didn't reject the idea, they adapted the idea so that it would work for them.

Becoming Part of the Team

I set up a meeting with the team for the next day, and explained, "I can't give you testers; I have no one to give you. I can't do the testing myself—I still have my management work to do. But I can offer you my services as a project manager, especially if you need someone to run interference and remove the other obstacles that will arise."

This was my first meeting with the team. I'd known these guys for a while—some for more than 10 years socially. Here's how I remember that meeting.

Dan, one of the longtime team members and one of the original developers, said, "Well, Johanna's OK as a tester and better as a project manager, but we really need more testers, not another manager. Sorry, Johanna." Dan gave me that lazy smile and leaned back in his chair.

Fred agreed: "JR, it's nice of you to offer, but we really need testers." Fred was also one of the original team members. He drummed his fingers on the table and his knee-thumping kicked up a notch. Fred was a great developer, and had a few nervous habits.

"Well, I can't give you testers. I have no one available, and no money to hire more people. I offered to be the project manager not because I think you need management, but to help you with ideas about how to work differently than you're accustomed to. It's clear to me that the team had a great process that worked before. But that process depended on the testers. I can't give them to you."

Clyde asked, "Why? What's the problem?"

I pulled out the testing assignment sheet from my conversation with the VP and explained how the other projects needed the testers and that this project, while important, was lower priority than the others.

Dan frowned: "That's just stupid."

I leaned forward. "I already checked with the VP and Big Cheese. This project is number six on the list, and I have testers for only five projects. I am not trying to make your lives miserable. I know it sounds like 'I'm from the IRS and I'm here to help.' Except that I'm from management.

"But you guys know me. You know that I know a lot about projects and that I don't want to tell you how to do development. I can help you think of alternative ways to do this project. But only if you want me."

Dan leaned back in his chair and exhaled loudly. "OK. Why don't you go away for a while and we'll discuss it?"

"OK, I'll be back in my office. Call me there."

I received a call about fifteen minutes later and returned to the conference room.

Fred said, "JR, the team discussed it, and we'll take you. But you better have some good ideas. Not everyone is convinced we need you."

"That's fine. If you don't need me, fire me. Well, not really fire me, just tell me you don't want me, and I'll stop helping. OK?" I asked.

Everyone nodded or said OK.

We talked about how they wanted to work and how I could help. I had a few tasks, including setting up a standard meeting time, helping them get conference rooms for reviews, and seeing whether I could get a few cycles from the testers who'd worked on previous projects to see if they could fix the regression test scripts.

"How did the regression test scripts break?" I wanted to know what had happened, so I could understand how much time the testers needed to provide, to see whether this was even a possibility. One of the more junior members, Sam, blushed, and explained that he had improved a global class, and now several things didn't work. He had looked at the regression tests, but he didn't understand how a couple of them worked.

"So, maybe I should see if the testers could spend an hour explaining how the regressions are set up for the whole team. And then spend some time with you, unraveling this problem."

"Yeah, that would probably work."

Starting Off Right

This team had more going for it than many other teams. They knew how to work together as developers. They were talented people who all wanted to do a good job. And they were open to working in whatever way the project required them to work to do a good job and meet Big Cheese's commitments.

The team had a "gentlemanly" culture. They didn't swear when things went badly. They did let off steam with pranks. It was acceptable to call each other "brain-dead" when someone made a dumb mistake. But it wasn't acceptable to use profanity or be late for meetings.

Technically, they had other assets. Their automated regression test suite had worked for the most recent release. They had an automated build system. And they were familiar with code review, unit tests, and continuous integration.

Before the team started on the performance work or the new features, they decided to fix the regression test suite, so they would know that the current builds worked without having to do manual testing.

The developers and the previous testers convened a regression test meeting.

Jack, a tester, started explaining how the regression tests worked. "OK, everyone look at page 3, that's where the central loop for the tests is."

Sam interrupted, "No, that's not the central loop. Look at page 6—that's the central loop."

Jill, the other tester, piped up, "No, you just don't understand how it works. Look at the main part on page 2. See the sequencing?"

Sam glared at Jill, "Do you think I'm brain-dead? Any fool can see that the loop is on page 6."

Jill looked at page 6, and said, "Oh, now I know why you think that. Look at this call over here and look at that loop over here." She pointed to the different pages, explaining where she was each time.

"Oh, that makes a little more sense. But why didn't you write anything about that in the comments?" asked Sam.

"Because I ran out of time, and thought I would be working with you on the next project. It never occurred to me that the company wouldn't put testers on this project," replied Jill.

Everyone turned to look at me. "Hey, I'm sorry, but I can't put people on this project who don't exist. Jack and Jill, you know your project has more revenue at stake." They nodded. "Well, this team will figure out what to do to make this work, even though it's not the best situation."

The testers walked through how the regression tests worked, covering the tricky part that had stumped Sam. The team discussed how they wanted the regression tests to work, and divided them into several chunks, assigning different team members to the chunks. Sam took the tricky part "to get more experience with this test framework" and the testers agreed that he could ask them questions if any arose.

Within a few days, the developers had the full regression test working. In addition, they had chunked it into pieces so that they could use pieces of it to take performance measurements and verify that the new features wouldn't break anything else. Now it was time to start on the new work.

Everything seemed to go swimmingly until it was time for the first feature to be integrated. Every piece of the regression test suite blew up.

Solving Problems As a Team

It would have been easy to blame the developer, Fred, who had integrated his feature. But that wasn't the team's culture. There was a rousing chorus of "brain-dead code" at our meeting. I suggested we do a quick root-cause analysis at our team meeting, to see what had gone wrong. I was sure we had several issues at work, and it would be worth our while to see what was happening. The team agreed.

The team discovered several things had occurred (see the following figure):

- No one had looked at the code before it was checked in.

- The team was no longer using their multiple levels of check-in.

- "Too many" people had checked in on the same day.

- No one had added anything to the regression test suite to check for new features.

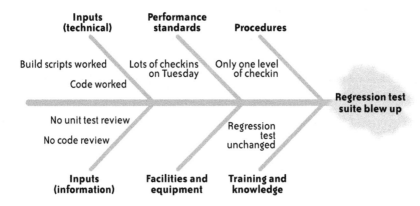

Root-cause analysis diagram.

Dan took the lead. "OK, what do you guys want to do?"

Fred replied, "Look, we all know how I can be." Everyone except me nodded, grinning. "I really want someone to review my code each and every time. I'll write unit tests, especially since we don't have testers, do we, JR?"

I replied, "Nope, we don't. Unit tests are a great idea. They aren't the same as system tests, but they should prevent this problem."

Dan said, "But we're not done yet. Just code review and unit tests aren't going to be enough. We're going to have to go to multiple levels of check-in, like we did on the last project."

I replied, "You don't have to do that. You could all just check in all the time, and let the build and unit tests catch the problems."

"No, are you brain-dead?" asked Sam. "That will never work. We need multiple levels of check-ins."

"Well, let me explain how it works," I started.

"Look, you might have used that on a team with testers, but without testers it ain't gonna work," replied Sam.

"Well, if you feel that strongly about it," I replied.

"You bet I do."

"How about everyone else?" Everyone else nodded. "OK. Let's see how the multiple levels of check-in work before we consider an alternative, OK? I'm going to want to build a rolling wave schedule [3] with you so I know what's going on and can track it."

Sam was concerned. "This rolling wave schedule—what is it and how will it help me? Am I going to need to do anything more than my work?"

"Well, you'll all need to spend about 30 minutes getting the schedule ready the first time. Then, we'll update it with your status reports and my one-on-ones with you. If we run into trouble, we'll have to spend another 30 minutes all together, but that's it. Will that work for you?"

"Uh, OK."

"Sam, you know, JR isn't brain-dead, at least not yet." Fred started, and everyone chuckled. "You haven't worked with her before, have you?"

"Nope."

"She pretty much leaves us alone, but she runs interference. If Big Cheese comes to you with a request, you suggest—politely—that he go to JR, and she'll take care of it. Besides, if we don't like what she's doing, we can fire her. Right, JR?"

"You bet!"

Now the team had some safeguards (the multiple levels of check-in) for managing the issues of people working independently and wanting to check in at the same time. They decided to add code review back into their practices. In addition to code review, all developers were now required to write unit-level tests for all their code.

The team decided not to add anything to the system-level test regression suite. They could not imagine they would have enough time to manage the development and that level of testing. But they were quite happy to write unit tests for all their code.

What Code Review Looked Like

The team chose to use a modified Fagan-style code review. Each code review had a moderator and several reader-reviewers, and the author was the scribe. In a true Fagan code review, the reader-reviewers would each read the code individually in advance, and read the code out loud at the review. But this team chose not to read the code out loud during the review. The moderator would ask, "Does anyone have any issues on page 1?" Everyone would respond with "No," or "Yes," and explain his issue. Similar to a Fagan code review, the reviewers would hand their small issues to the author at the beginning of the review.

One of the reasons for not reading the code aloud was to save time. If the developers had chosen to read every line of code aloud, the team would have had to schedule many more code reviews, because each one would have taken much longer. With these code reviews, the team could review 50 pages of code in one sitting.

The team realized they had to trust each other to explain at the beginning of the review if someone hadn't finished reading the code. In those cases, the review stopped where everyone had finished reading and another review was scheduled for the next day.

If the author had concerns about how he was supposed to fix a problem in the code, the author and the moderator managed those concerns together.

Unit Tests

The developers knew they had to keep up with testing. But as one developer said to me, "I'm just not nasty enough to be a tester. I know how to do unit tests, but I'm not very good at system tests."

Nancy and I and the team agreed that we would incur the technical debt of not having enough system-level tests. But the team agreed that there was no way they could meet the deadline without having unit tests for all of the code they wrote.

The developers wrote their code and then wrote their unit tests. One of the developers started using McCabe's tools (there was a freeware Unix version) to check that he had written enough unit tests for each of his classes and modules. As the developer explained, "I'm really good at writing tests for everything that works. I always seem to miss the piece that doesn't work. With McCabe's, I'm less likely to miss that one thing."

Check-ins

I tried to convince the team to use continuous integration, but they didn't buy it—at least, not from me. But the team developed another approach to continuous integration, by staging the integration in a way that made sense to them. They chose three levels of integration:

Raw
    The code that had been compiled and unit-tested

Cooked
    The code that had been through code review and any issues fixed

Golden
    Code that had passed a build and all the existing regression tests

Each developer was responsible for compiling and unit-testing his own code. If a developer fell behind, he was supposed to tell me, and I would work out the scheduling issues with the team.

Builds

The team chose to kick off an automated build every night at midnight. Every night, all the code labeled "golden" was built, and all the unit tests and regression tests were run against it. The results were emailed to each team member.

As soon as someone checked in code, he labeled it "raw." Every developer built a raw build locally, to make sure he hadn't broken anything. Once the code had been through code review, it was labeled "cooked." Once a developer had "cooked" all his code, he promoted it to "golden."

Schedules

We had a meeting the following day, just to start develop the rolling wave schedule. I posted the months on stickies across the top of the wall, along with the known major milestones, such as internal demo, initial customer demo, and customer release, under their correct months. I listed the features down the side on a piece of flip-chart paper, in the order the developers told me they were going to implement them.

I asked, "What will it take us to get to these first two features?"

Dan replied, "No, JR, we're working in parallel. That's the wrong question. The real question is who will do what when?"

"OK, as long as we don't plan the whole darn project at once. The idea of doing this on stickies is to make sure we can figure out a Plan B if this plan doesn't work. Remember, when you write your tasks on stickies, make the tasks as small as possible."

Everyone wrote his tasks on stickies. Most of the tasks were one or two weeks long.

"OK, guys, I'm in trouble now."

"Why?"

"Because I am not going to know for too long if anyone is in trouble. Neither will you. You have to make smaller tasks. I bet each of you does something every day, right?"

Heads nodded.

"OK, then write all those things down, just for this first week. If you know enough about the second week, add that, too."

After they'd revised their first two weeks of stickies, I explained, "OK, I'm not going to ask you every day what you're doing. You're going to tell me if you don't make the progress you think you're going to make. If you know why, tell me that, too. Some tasks you'll finish on time, some might be early, and some might be late. My job is to figure out if you're late on a task how that matters to the rest of the team and the project. If it's a systemic problem, we'll address it in a group meeting. If not, the two of us will discuss it.

"I won't bug you for status. You'll email me status on Friday mornings, and we'll have one-on-ones on Tuesdays. That way I know if I need to do something a couple of times every week. OK?"

Sam frowned, looking concerned. "Johanna, this seems like a lot of work for us. At least for me. Do I really have to break down all my tasks into small pieces for the rest of the project?"

"I don't know how to effectively manage this project given the tight schedule and technical risks. Do you have a better idea?"

"No."

"Well, try it for two weeks and we'll see how intrusive it is. If it takes too much time or you think it's a waste of time, we'll address it at a weekly team meeting. But this has worked for me before. You need to plan only the next two to three weeks in detail. Not any more than that."

Status Reports

As the project progressed, the team members did email me their status on Friday mornings. I collated and sent out status by Friday afternoon, so everyone knew what everyone was doing. We used our team meetings to solve problems, such as the performance issues.

I prepared a monthly status report for Nancy and Big Cheese. The first three months were fine. But for the fourth month, we had encountered several problems with the performance enhancements, and were behind on them. I sent an explanation with my status report, and we continued.

Go Faster Now!

Nancy mentioned that the team was behind in our one-on-one. She said, "What are you going to do about it?"

"Huh?"

"Well, they're behind by a week or two. What are you going to do to make up the time?"

"Nothing."

"What do you mean, nothing?"

"Nancy, the team is working as fast as they can. They are working only on this project. They are doing what they can. Some of them are working overtime already, which is not good because we still have six weeks left on this project."

"Well, why don't you cut out the unit tests and reviews? That would free some time, wouldn't it?"

I was stunned. "Nancy, you are joking, right? Without the unit tests, we would have no testing at all. Without the unit tests, we have no way to know if what we're doing is good or not. You want to release this product in six weeks, right?"

Nancy nodded.

"Then let my team work the way they need to."

"But what about the code reviews? Maybe they can forget them. That might save some time."

"Nancy, it's been a long time since you wrote code, right?"

Nancy nodded.

"Well, it's harder now than it was for you. Did you ever write code that worked the first time?"

"Yeah, a couple of times."

"So, you wrote code that worked the first time, maybe five times in your 10 years as a developer? Were you dealing with pointers? I thought you were writing in assembler."

"Yes, it was assembler. The pointers were not like the pointers in C."

"So, why do you think that eliminating the code reviews is going to help us finish faster? That's just going to make it slower at the end, when we won't know what's wrong."

"Why are you asking me about this anyway? What's going on? Are you under pressure?"

"Yes. Big Cheese is telling me my job is on the line if we don't deliver in six weeks, not eight."

"Well, doesn't he tell you that about every project?"

Nancy grinned, "Yes, he does."

"So, why are you believing him now?"

"I really want to make sure you are doing everything you can."

"Look, if Jack and Jill can stop their other project, and come back here and do system testing, this might speed up the project. But the developers can't work any faster than they are.

"I'll tell you what. In our next team meeting, I'll ask the developers if they can think of something that will help them work faster. Whatever it is, I'll let you know, OK?"

"OK, but see if you can do something."

Looking for More Speed

At the next team meeting, I asked the developers whether they had any ideas about going faster. Dan answered first. "Well, if you got us those testers...."

"Sorry, not going to happen. I checked with Nancy, and I can't take them off their current project. Does anyone else have another idea?"

Fred cleared his throat. "We could start working overtime every day and a day on the weekend."

"Do you really want to?" I asked.

"No."

"Then let's not bring that up as an option. Overtime this far in advance is not a good idea. Sure, if it was the last week, maybe we could put that extra effort in. But now, we'll just make ourselves miserable. Any other ideas?"

Tim said, "I'm almost done with my last feature. Fred, do you want me to help you with the performance? Maybe we can work together on it."

Fred agreed.

"Is anyone else just about done with his work? Maybe more doubling up will help?" No one else was almost done. "OK, keep at those little tasks. Let me know if you run into trouble. I'll look for your status on Friday."

Losing a Week at a Time

By Friday, it was clear that Fred was struggling with the performance enhancement. He hadn't made any progress yet. Tim had just finished his feature work, and was ready to work with Fred. I sent my status report to the team and the higher-level status report to Nancy and Big Cheese. I was reviewing everyone's tasks to see whether we could rearrange anything to help Fred. I was pretty sure he needed Dan's help, too, to see other options.

Big Cheese arrived at my office, and said, "I need to talk to you now, Johanna." Big Cheese strode in and stood over my shoulder.

I glanced up at him, and said, "OK, let me just save what I'm doing."

"No. Stop doing that and listen to me."

I turned around, and asked, "What's the problem?" I motioned to my visitor chair. He shook his head.

"I have no problem. You, however, have a big problem. Stop those code reviews. They're slowing down the project." Big Cheese shook his finger in my face.

"But then we won't know where the bugs are. We need the code reviews."

Big Cheese stood yet closer to me. He shouted, "Stop them or I'll fire you." By now his face was red.

I stood up. "You'll fire me for doing the right thing?" Big Cheese wasn't a tall man, but I'm not tall either. I came up to his shoulder. But that was better than sitting down, at gut-height. Big Cheese took one step back.

"In this case, the right thing is to finish the project as fast as possible. Stop those code reviews. I expect to see more progress next week."

Big Cheese left my office. I took a deep breath and walked over to Nancy's office, but Big Cheese was already there, screaming at her. I decided to wait to talk to her.

What to Do Next

I was in a bit of a quandary about what to do next. I wasn't going to tell the team to stop unit-testing and doing code reviews—I felt as if those two activities were going to save us. But I did want to be able to keep my job. And I didn't want to lose more time on the project. I decided to talk to Dan now. Dan was the laid-back type. He thought before he spoke, and not much ever seemed to faze him. Aside from being an original developer on the product, he would help me think through the problem. He wouldn't freak out.

I emailed Dan asking for about 30 minutes of his time for help with this problem. He should let me know and I would go over to his office. Dan has that lazy look that masks a brilliant brain. He's the kind of person who ambles rather than strides, who looks as if he's half-asleep and then says something that stuns you with its brilliance. If anyone had ideas about what to do, it would be Dan.

About 10 minutes later, Dan sauntered over. "Hey, thanks for coming over. Want to go to your office?"

"Nope, I bet you have all the task information here."

"You're right. Let's take a look. I don't want to lose another week. I also don't want to stop the code reviews—or the unit tests—but Big Cheese is having a bird. I need to show some progress next week."

"Did he threaten to fire you?"

"Yup."

Dan paused for a minute and frowned. "Uh-oh. He usually only threatens to fire Nancy. The last time he threatened to fire a manager, he did."

"When was that?"

"Two weeks ago."

Oops. I was in trouble.

"Dan, I am not going to change what the group is doing. The code reviews and unit tests are working. But I would like to keep my job—at least for a few more weeks. Do you have any ideas about what to do?"

"Well, we could have a whole-team review of Fred's code to see where the problem is. Has Fred instrumented the code, so he knows where it's slow?"

"He told me he had, but I didn't review the instrumentation. Maybe he's missing something?"

"Yeah, maybe it's time to review the instrumentation. Maybe we need more data, too, about where and why Fred thinks it's too slow."

"Dan, let's talk about where you are. I think Fred needs more help, and you have as much experience with this code base as he does. If you help him, what do we need to do about your work?"

Dan and I discussed options for his work, and decided not to change his work yet. Dan would ask Fred about performance tests, and suggest a test review and a code review. Dan might suggest an instrumentation review. But that's all Dan would do until I met with Fred on Tuesday—unless Fred asked for help.

I was still concerned. It's not every day a senior manager threatens to fire you. But it was clear to me that the team had accepted me because I was helping them get their work done. I wasn't going to prevent them from finishing the work. But I did need a plan.

Retaining Integrity

I was caught in a bind I hear many managers and project managers discuss. If they do the Right Thing, they're in danger of losing their jobs. But if they cave in to what a senior manager wants—no matter how misguided—they lose the respect of the team. In this case, we would have also endangered the schedule.

I chose to keep my integrity and the integrity of the team. To be honest, it was an easy decision. If I'm working with a team that's working well, why would I do something to disrupt their flow?

The Rubber Meets the Road

We decided to use our next team meeting to review the instrumentation and performance issues in the code. I played the role of scribe, since I didn't know enough about the code to usefully comment. In preparation for the meeting, I suggested the team consider reading the code out loud and that we plan to spend two hours on the review. I added a note at the bottom of the email: "Remember, don't tell anyone we're doing this long of a code review—Big Cheese will have my head." At the time I thought I was joking.

We slowed that code review down to a crawl. After two hours, we'd gone through 15 of the 30 pages. Fred had a number of ideas about how to re-instrument the code, but no ideas about how to work faster. We'd been at this for two hours and had no more mental energy.

"Let's stop this for today," I suggested.

"No, we can finish," Sam said.

Tim, a.k.a. "Silent Man," piped up. "Sam, no."

"No?"

"No way. We're tired. We've been focusing on this code and the instrumentation, and it's gotten us somewhere. But just spending more time right now isn't going to help. We need a little distance and a break. I need a bike ride."

"Look, Tim, I know you get all these great ideas on the bike, but—"

"No, I'm learning. So are you. JR, can you book us a room for 10 to 12 tomorrow? I think we can finish then. And if not, we'll figure out what to do next. Sam, listen to me. Go play with your dog or work out or take a shower or something. But do not look at this code anymore. Got it?"

"Uh, sure." Sam looked shell-shocked.

As Tim left, Dan chuckled. "Sam, you didn't realize that Tim is really the power behind this group? Time you learned."

I booked a conference room and emailed the ideas we had so far to the group, as well as the conference room location for the next morning. The only problem was, it was on Exec Row, near the senior management offices.

At home that night, I explained to my husband what I was doing. "Honey, remember that conversation about code review I told you about a couple of weeks ago?"

"Yup."

"Well, we're doing a two-hour review tomorrow right near Big Cheese's office. I might be home early, looking for a job."

"Well, it won't be the first time you've been fired, will it?"

"I prefer the term *layoff*. That's what it was."

"Oh, fine. Just start on your resume tonight. Oh, and call me at lunch to tell if you're still employed."

The next day, we all arrived at the conference room and started on page 16. We made some progress. At 10:40, Big Cheese barged in.

"Johanna, what are you doing? This looks like a code review."

"Does it? We're trying to figure out how to make up time on the project. We don't have a plan yet, but we're getting there."

"Glad to see you've come to your senses. You knew I was right."

After he left, everyone cracked up. Tim was the first to speak. "JR, you can't play poker, but you can lie without blushing?"

"I told the truth—at least, partially. We are working on a plan. It's just that we're using a tool he doesn't like." Everyone laughed again. "OK, let's get back to this."

By noon, we had two more suggestions for instrumentation, and one suggestion for changing the code. Fred and Tim were developing their inch-pebbles, coordinating who would do what, and promised to let me know by the end of the day what their plan was.

I spent some time reviewing the schedule and floated the idea of a phased release to the team. We could release the new feature set on time, and release the performance enhancements two weeks later. I asked the team to consider that as an option we could discuss at our next team meeting.

Success at Last

The team agreed to the phased release. They kept up with the code reviews, unit tests, and multiple check-ins. I maintained the projectwide inch-pebbles. As other team members finished their features, they worked with Fred and Tim on the performance issues. We got lucky. At the desired date, we actually had everything done: the features and the performance changes.

The next day, we had a little celebration with ice cream sundaes and we discussed what we'd learned.

Sam started. "Johanna, I had no idea that breaking tasks into small chunks would really help that much. But I'm even more impressed with the code reviews and the unit tests. I could never have done all this without them."

Fred added, "I wish I'd asked for review earlier. We wouldn't have needed that overtime."

Tim said, "Maybe now you'll believe me. Now all I have to do is to get you to start eating organic food." Everyone laughed.

I added, "I'm really impressed with what each of you accomplished, separately and together. Thanks for the opportunity to work with you."

Epilogue

I stayed with that organization for another few months and then was fired. (It was the best career move of my life.) That team stayed together for another two years. Big Cheese separated them when it became clear they worked well as a unit and were influencing other teams.

I've maintained ties with some of them. Several still work together. A couple have moved on to management positions, where they're working on re-creating that great team experience. I'm thrilled I had a chance to work with a beautiful team.

And the product? It won a Japanese award for quality. Big Cheese accepted the award, and said, "The team was inspiring in their dedication to quality."

References

1. Rothman, Johanna. 2009. *Manage Your Project Portfolio: Increase Your Capacity and Finish More Projects*. Raleigh, NC: Pragmatic Bookshelf.

2. Rothman, Johanna, and Esther Derby. 2005. *Behind Closed Doors: Secrets of Great Management*. Raleigh, NC: Pragmatic Bookshelf.

3. Rothman, Johanna. 2007. *Manage It! Your Guide to Modern, Pragmatic Project Management*. Raleigh, NC: Pragmatic Bookshelf.

CHAPTER TWENTY-EIGHT

Tight, Isn't It?

Mark Denovich and Eric Renkey*

Only Pawn...in Game of Life, or "What's a Dazzling Urbanite Like You Doing in a Rustic Setting Like This?"

IN AUGUST 1998, I RECEIVED AN EMAIL IN RESPONSE TO A RESUME I HAD POSTED ON AN ONLINE employment website. I didn't think much of the contact at the time, but then I've failed to recognize all the major turning points in my life. A quick reply with my phone number led to a return call from the founder/president/CEO of the company. I could not predict that I was just days away from joining an extended train wreck of a company and becoming part of the most improbably great team I have ever known. The sum of my formal education was going to be dwarfed in comparison to what I would learn over the next six years.

Now, my words can have an uncanny habit of coming back to haunt me, and this story is definitely no exception. It would be convenient to claim that everything that follows is a work of fiction, but I'm not that good at making things up. I might also like to rely on my admittedly poor memory as a possible defense. But I had a great deal of help with the story from my once former and now again current coworker Stan Granite. His humor, his

---

* Editors' note: while this story was written by Mark Denovich and Eric Renkey (with help from Stan Granite, who wished to remain anonymous), it's told from Mark's point of view.

unique perspective, and his superior recall (often supplied with supporting text from his email archives) helped make the story far too accurate. He was also responsible for coining many of the nicknames that became part of the company lore. In most cases, I've used those names to cover my ass, along with a few additional substitutions of my own when I deemed it necessary. Unfortunately, the guilty will still recognize who they are. I know words can hurt, so I can only hope that when they read this and think back, they will laugh as much as I have and have mercy on me.

Upward of 160 different people worked for the company during the six years I was there. Headcount ranged from a low of six or seven when I was hired to a watermark of 42. Turnover was remarkably high, when you excluded the development team, who our CEO grudgingly acknowledged as a necessary and indispensable evil. But when any cash was available, it was soon lavished on a host of VPs and directors, often of dubious pedigree and even more dubious strategic purpose. When times were tight, they were the first to be shown the door, generally with little ceremony. But, through thick and thin, the core development team remained surprisingly stable. Starting from nothing, a core of eight developers produced a product with a Windows client comprising nearly 800 screens, totaling 700,000 lines of code, and a database tier consisting of 750 tables and 800 stored procedures containing 400,000 lines of T-SQL. All of this was developed while simulta-neously delivering a score of custom projects, which were needed to help keep the lights on. I was too naïve at the time to appreciate how impressive a feat this was. We were all too naïve, and this was probably the key to our success. Anyone with some sense would have quickly understood that even our best efforts were no match for a string of comically poor decisions by management and the criminally bad behavior of our customers that resulted. In my defense, I had assumed anyone with the courage to risk his own money and that of his investors would be someone who was sure he had a winning strategy. My assumption was right, but I failed to consider that the same person could also be perfectly delusional. But then, I had never met anyone like Hedley Lamarr.

I met Hedley in an office building in downtown Pittsburgh. I remember our first meeting clearly, only because it was exactly what I expected. He was smartly dressed in suit and tie, was well spoken, and had a respectable office with a nice view. Hedley described Rock Ridge as a bespoke software shop, specializing in the energy industry. He seemed to clearly enjoy being a businessman that day. An hour or so later, I left smiling, convinced that I had delivered another commanding interview performance. A phone call confirmed it, and after some quick salary negotiation (20% over the first offer), I was hired. "Finally, a real job." Previously, I had worked in a few Mickey Mouse operations during school, spent a few months at a crooked dot-com hopeful that was run by the insane, and most recently was a poorly paid independent consultant. I wasn't looking forward to the dress code (shirt and tie), the start time (8:30 a.m.), or the commute, but I was happy to put all that silliness behind me and begin my career in earnest.

My new job enthusiasm quickly wore off. My few coworkers were odd, but uninspiring; I made a mental note to continue ignoring them. A busy hallway door opened without warning almost directly into my cube. Possibly worse was the diabolically bad coffee. I also didn't see much of Hedley again. What little direction I received was in intense but brief conversations from a harried (and hairy) software development manager, later to be dubbed C$. My task, I gathered, was to design the UI and application framework for a new project, a VB and Microsoft SQL Server-based utility billing system. I didn't have the experience to question the project's lack of any real requirements, specifications, or processes. So, when I wasn't exploring the limits of how much I could goof off, I made up the design as I went along. Two weeks later, I was introduced to another new hire in the next cube, Stan Granite. I was only beginning to take in what I was seeing as I reached out to shake his hand. This guy was completely out of proportion with everything in the office. He was a giant. He did not look comfortable in a shirt and tie, and looked especially uncomfortable in his tiny cube, which might now be doubling as a veal pen. When his junk heap of a computer immediately gave him trouble, I guessed it wouldn't be long 'til I heard "Hulk SMASH!" or words to that effect.... I began to consider my escape route. But what I really wondered was, "What in the hell was this guy doing here?" Stan apparently was wondering something similar. I asked him about his first impressions:

> Even though our team eventually became close, it took a while to reach that point. There's an old saw about marriage that states that the traits that you thought were charming before you got married are the ones that drive you crazy later on. For me, it was exactly the opposite in regard to our team: the traits that eventually provided us with hours of entertainment were those that initially made me wonder if I'd last three months.
>
> When I first started working at Oxford Center, there were six or eight of us packed in a cube arrangement that looked like an ice cube tray and which wasn't much bigger than one. I received about three minutes of instruction and was given a PC that was out of service more than in service—facts that were dismissed when I was berated by C$ at the end of my first week, which concluded with the line, "I'm not even sure why I'm paying you."
>
> I barely interacted with Hedley until we started working on the VPC version of Candygram, so my first memory of him is a 10x scale customer invoice, drawn with more detail than a Hieronymus Bosch painting. Nearly a thousand square inches focused entirely on layout, without any context given to the data. I mean, who mocks up a bill with a marker on an easel pad and feels the need to draw an accurately scaled, fully scannable PostNet bar code and account numbers rendered in MICR font? I think that if he'd written "bar code goes here," we'd have gotten the idea. If I were more perceptive, all of that exquisite layout detail with no substance to speak of would have given me some early insight into his personality.
>
> And then there were my teammates: Friar Tuck is exactly the opposite of C$ as far as first impressions and lasting outcomes. Initially my impression was positive. He at least acknowledged my presence, which is more than I can say for The Mad Shitter (TMS), who appeared to be a modern-day Harpo Marx, or Rain Man (the guy that ritually arranged all of his pens, markers, and pencils on his desk, by type and size, making sure they were in perfect alignment before leaving each night). But after spending half an hour trying to help Friar Tuck remember the name of this amazing new restaurant he found (we finally determined it was Chick-fil-A), I got suspicious. It didn't take me long

to figure out that he had all of the prodigious computer programming prowess and well-honed powers of logical thought I'd expect from a [decidedly non-technical subject] major.

Mark was prone to making seriously controversial statements. Like…murdering babies wasn't nearly as serious as murdering adults. He'd explain, "It only takes two years to replace a two-year-old. I represent 25 years of investment, and I'm at the beginning of my economic prime." And when he wasn't on my ass, C$ had a habit of ceaselessly reminding everyone that they had no talent compared to him [by any measure]. I had not yet learned to appreciate the entertainment value of their antics.

I think the turning point with C$ happened one night when we were working late. He was regaling me with tales of how powerful his brain was. C$ explained that he had four brain quadrants, each capable of working independently to solve the world's problems. One quadrant must've realized he was hungry, and he proceeded to leave to get something to eat. But not before he pointed in the general direction of his head, saying, "This thing needs a lot of fuel to keep it going." I replied, "C$, I couldn't tell: were you pointing at your brain or your mouth?" It was the first time we'd ever seen C$ speechless. Granted, it lasted only a few seconds, but it seemed to me that after I made that comment, he started treating me less like a minion and more like a peer.

Somehow we all survived the following month and a half to see the opening of the Software Development Center in the heart of Pittsburgh's South Side. Probably 50 bars and restaurants were now within a 10-minute walk of the office. Hedley was happy that the technical staff (the help)—below Hedley's standards, even with the help of the dress code—were no longer disrupting the professional image he was trying to project in the downtown office. But he still had his concerns. Stan writes:

Most of the developers were in their 20s and male, so Hedley thought that we needed supervision, and he appointed a woman a decade or two older to keep us in line. Her sole contribution during her brief tenure at Rock Ridge was to institute a "whereabouts board," and she instructed us that each person was supposed to indicate his or her whereabouts and estimated time of return if they were not in the office. If someone was going to run downstairs to get a bagel from the bagel shop, it was supposed to be noted on the board. The whereabouts board was a contributor to team unity in that it was nearly universally reviled by the core team members. The fact that Mark completely disregarded the board, as did I, was probably my first sign that he was OK. Well, that and the fact that his lunch would occasionally consist of only a 10-fluid-ounce gimlet.

Mark's note: to potential prospective employers, voters, or members of the jury…I'd like to clarify that when I complemented his recall, I was not suggesting that Stan's memory was 100% accurate.

Stan's note: Mark is correct…on occasion, the gimlets might have been as small as 8 oz.

With two offices, the company now got together only for special occasions (like Christmas, happy hours, and the periodic mass layoff). When the first happy hour found us all at Dingbats in town, the company was up to about 15 or 20 people.

Editors' note: the authors put us in touch with Stan Granite. Andrew interviewed Mark and Stan, who filled in some of the more interesting details of the story.

Andrew: So, I have two questions. One, how did you end up developing so much working code with such a small team? And two, why did you guys stick around to do it? It seemed like a kind of difficult environment to work in, even after the move to the South Side. It sounds like you had some real challenges. But you put out an enormous amount of code, and from what I understand, it actually worked.

Stan: Let me answer those two questions as succinctly as I can; maybe we can flush them out. One, we built everything that we did because we worked like beavers on meth. And two, the team stayed together because every day was like going to work with an improvisational comedy troupe. I mean, you had to be on your game, and that was fun. If you said the wrong thing, man, you were getting crushed.

Andrew: But working like demons isn't enough. I've been on teams where we worked like demons, and basically produced nothing of value. In fact, what I've seen in the past is that for some teams, the harder they worked the less they produced, because they spent most of their time ripping things out that they'd built last-minute in a panic and that didn't actually work. You guys, on the other hand, got something out the door that's used now every day by a major energy company to manage their core business, and it works well enough that it's become critical to their operation. So, it's got to be more than working like demons. I want to try to figure out what that "more than that" was.

Mark: I think part of it is that we didn't have a lot of overlapping or competing skills, so our ego problems didn't descend down to the code level. Or, maybe, there was one person, C$, whose ego was so enormous that it couldn't be subverted, so we had some consistency there.

But I don't think there were too many conflicts when it came to figuring out what to do. I think we had the right ratio of people that were there to get the work done, and enough people looking a little bit ahead who would say, "This sucks, and we need to do this better. If we don't, this will hurt." So, I guess we had some sensitivity to pain.

Stan: But the thing about ego that you said—it really didn't extend to the code. Even C$, while proclaiming that he was the world's greatest SQL programmer on the East Coast, could face it. He took a lot of flak for the hidden text box thing after the fact.

Andrew: What was the hidden text box thing?

Stan: So, when we started developing Candygram, there was a previously existing version, version 2.5. (We'll talk about that later with the Turducken story.) Candygram 2.5 was a Visual Basic 4.0 application. Mark and I started looking at the code, and we saw these hidden text boxes used to store state all over the place. We were immediately all over C$, making fun of him—"Are you unaware of the form-level variable?"—which, of course, irritated the crap out of him. We obviously had to do a bit of code cleanup there. He always claimed that was how you had to do it in Access 2.0, where there was some bug that if you used a variable it'd lose its state under certain conditions, and that got carried forward.

Mark: I think he was just being lazy by using a hidden text box with the built-in data binding, because otherwise he'd have to write a line or two of code.

Stan: Everybody was open to listening to new stuff. We occasionally would have design sessions where somebody would get pissed, but everybody would just shake it off. Even if people didn't admit it, they learned a lot from working collaboratively.

It was getting rid of Friar Tuck that actually allowed that to happen. He was the one that was holding us back.

Mark: I think that's probably pretty important. There were no bad apples when we were at our peak. Friar Tuck, on the other hand, was a jackass. He was the kind of person who sucked the life out of the projects he was on, because he did things poorly. You ended up having to do more work when that guy was around, because not only did he mess up your work, you also had to fix *his* work. He made you think he was working on things that were worthwhile, until it was time to get it out the door and you realized that you had to backfill everything he did. And then you'd be punished later because you had to maintain his terrible designs.

Once we got rid of him, and one or two other people who were marginal at the time, you were working with people who you genuinely respected. Each person had their own area where they were competent and even talented. Nobody was such a jackass that you were demotivated by it. Once we got rid of the bad apples, you kind of felt guilty if you weren't getting a lot of work done, because you could look around and see that everyone else was busting ass and doing what they had to do, so you'd do it, too.

Stan: There's a famous story that C$ still references every now and then. Early in the Candygram project, C$ had a meeting to talk about code and the standards everyone had to follow. People made their arguments for doing this or that, then C$ made a decision and that was the standard going forward. There were a handful of items—seven, eight items—on the agenda. Mark and I were arguing for the right way to do it, and Friar Tuck was on the other side of virtually all of the decisions. So, we have this meeting, and C$ basically ruled on all eight items in our favor, because it was basically Code Complete kind of stuff that nobody in their right mind would argue with, except for Friar Tuck. Tuck basically evaluated every technique in terms of how little typing it would require; that was his primary motivator. He's a big fan of whatever syntactic hacks required the fewest keystrokes.

So, we had this meeting, talking about how we wanted to approach these things and what our standards would be. C$ was always big on code standards. If he has a strongest point, that would be it—he always hated people doing things in eight different ways because that made it hard to maintain. It was probably close to a two-hour meeting that we addressed this. So we get to the end, and C$ asks if anyone wants to talk about anything else. And Tuck gets up and says, "I don't like the scent that we have in the bathroom. I don't like the spray that's in there. It's a berry scent, and I don't like that." And C$ turned bright red.

He said, "Look, we bought that with our own money. It was all the store had. Is there anything *real* that anyone has to bring up?" That was Friar Tuck in a nutshell.

Andrew: And getting rid of him?

Mark: That was when things started to get interesting.

CMM Level Subzero, or "Processes, We Don't Need No Stinking Processes!"

> Mission Statement: To give our clients a competitive advantage by applying advances in technology that enhances their customer relationships.

To describe our early software development practices as primitive would be an extreme understatement. After several months of slow progress, we reached a level of technology in software development equal to that of the clan of monkeys in the opening sequence of Kubrick's *2001: A Space Odyssey*, with similar levels of wild shrieking and skull crushing. In the plus column, I had previously seen the light—and had been delivered from evil—by the power and the glory of source control. From the start, we employed source control for our Visual Basic code. However, the vast majority of our business logic, a hundred thousand lines of T-SQL, remained unsaved in the limbo that was our development database. The extent of our SQL change management process started and ended with C$. All changes went through him. We had to assume he had some method to his madness. He was, after all, the self-professed greatest SQL Server developer in Pittsburgh (or was it the entire East Coast?). In his defense, he was not entirely conceited. He often brought up a developer and tech columnist who might have been better "but he died when his snowmobile crashed into a tree!…" And after his trademark paroxysm of laughter, he'd somberly say, "I feel really bad for his family, he was a father of three."

We rarely even knew what we were supposed to be doing. [Imagine Colts head coach Jim Mora's voice when you read the next quote.] "Detailed specifications!? Detailed specifications!!?" We were lucky to have detailed conversations. C$ was always on the move, and always in a hurry. Human communication was too limited to keep up with his quadrants. When he had time, you might get an email describing what we should have been doing. Failing that, if you were lucky, you might get a phone call. I wasn't the only one who recognized and complained about many of our process shortcomings, but no one was in a position to take unilateral action. Most team members were supposed to be working on Edsel, a system for managing petroleum exploration partnerships, but much of the application's design referenced functionality that existed in an AS/400 application—an application that none of us had seen and none of us could access.

Secretly, I was still holding out for signs of a plan. Maybe we were to beaver away day and night, like the World War II allied code breakers in Bletchley Park, cracking the German Enigma cipher, each focusing on some tiny chunk of the whole, never seeing enough to know what we were building. And one day, the last piece of the puzzle would be put in place, and Hedley's and C$'s grand vision would be revealed: our state-of-the-art, multi-utility billing system we'll call the Candygram [because "the bitch was inventing the Candygram"]. We'd leverage the technical architecture we'd built for Edsel, and Rock Ridge would be positioned to take on the brave new world of the deregulated energy market. More likely, we were like a lot of the other companies that were struggling to get a foothold in a promising market; we often just sucked at what we tried to do.

But there was soon some reason for optimism in the atmosphere (and thanks to our new office, more than just optimism was in the air). Stan was revealed to be a surprisingly gifted employee. Most importantly for us, he had a personality bigger than even his physical presence, and he could program, too. The team recognized this, and for the rest of his time at Rock Ridge, he was its center of gravity. This meant his cube or office also served as a social center, which would remain a career-long drain on his productivity. Now the team had a chance to solidify, and with the help of a few more hires, it became an effective counterweight to C$. The improved group dynamics blunted some of C$'s rougher edges and helped to fill in the void left behind when his time was demanded elsewhere. With some success, trust started to take root and this found C$ delegating more and more. He was even becoming occasionally receptive to opinions other than his own. We had a long way to go, but soon we at least began to develop processes, standards, and what was the start of a truly impressive billing system. We had passed another critical point. Crucially, the nucleus of the team was forged while our roles were still malleable, and before anyone significant had a chance to defect.

Candygram's first customer would be a small division of a large utility company. We were lucky to have VPC (Very Patient Company) as its first user. And not just because the second biggest deal the sales team ever inked was our bar tab when our sales manager accidentally left it open during a much extended happy hour. VPC was like a homely and not-too-bright first girlfriend. They put up with our poor-quality releases and our sloppiness, and they gave us the chance to refine our technique on a real, live customer for a change. I just don't think they expected any better.

We were still a year or more from having any sort of repeatable release process. The best we had were some batch files that automated the application of the release's scripts to the database. Determining exactly what belonged in a particular release, and how to make those changes without corrupting the data, was an entirely manual process. Two developers working independently from the same code base were not guaranteed to create the same end result, so the final product varied depending on who built it and on what computer it was built. As a result, components and/or database objects were often missing or improperly configured, causing all sorts of downstream errors.

I got to see just how tolerant VPC could be, firsthand, when I got fingered to deliver the latest database release, as I was already going to update the client app. C$ had tapped a relatively new guy to assemble the database package: The Sigh Guy (TSG), a bright, hard-working, and chronologically young man. You could almost see the weight of the world prematurely aging him right before your eyes. I was shocked some months later when I found a picture of him from his college days. He was a portrait of vitality, but now it looked as if he had been made of wax and left in the hot sun. C$ ensured that he got no respite at work. I tagged him with the nickname (we all had many), because if he was around, you were soon to hear an exasperated sigh. The external pressures rendered him only about 90% great, which doesn't sound too bad, unless you consider it in terms of things like airplane safety, or more relevantly, database code. TSG was a pathologically bad typist. His typos were often so improbable that they seemed to have been made on purpose. Working from one of his designs, I created a half dozen dialogs implementing "Colon Batch" functionality. I knew it couldn't be right, but he couldn't have so consistently typed "Colon" instead of "Clone," right? That was worth a good laugh, but it wasn't so funny when I began to update VPC's Candygram database. I liked TSG from the start, so there was little hesitation that afternoon when I initiated the upgrade. It had been "tested." Seconds later I was treated with an exception, and a database table was now empty of all its data. While the client's DBA restored the database, I remained on the phone with TSG. Finding an errant keystroke, we started again. We would repeat this cycle of events—Execute, Error, Debug, Apologize, Restore—for the next six hours.

One thing even C$ had difficulty exaggerating, where he was a master of his domain, was in his encyclopedic knowledge of the Candygram System. Our lack of change control, specs, and processes meant we relied on it almost completely. It was self-perpetuating, too. He was the only one who knew the whole story, which meant he had to be consulted on everything. Delegating the release process in those early days could be especially disastrous. Because the company needed the cash, we had prematurely released the system fully aware that significant functionality was far from complete. We now had the joy of developing and maintaining a live system critical to the client's business. Worse still, a host of quality issues turning up daily in production kept one of our SQL experts fighting fires on-site for weeks at a stretch. Since time was of the essence, we were often developing directly on the live system. The pattern of bad decisions leading to and from money problems would cripple all our efforts every single day.

I understood the definition of quality before I started working there, and it was something we all desired. I knew the non-linear nature of the cost of an issue versus product timeline. But it still took a while to learn just how absolutely fundamental it was to the success or failure of a company. It was more important than any decision we could make in technology, hiring, or strategy. It wasn't just the raw number of issues, either. Perception mattered, and first impressions especially so. Once we lost the faith of one of our customers, no amount of effort, negotiation, or groveling seemed to win it back. Quality issues would poison our relationships, led to poor references, killed future sales, weakened our bargaining position, and led to unreasonable promises, piling more stress on an already overstretched development team. Hedley never seemed to grasp this. While we survived long enough to become much better developers, we were never good enough to break the cycle.

Date: 04/22/1999 04:59 PM
From: Cash Money *cdollar@rockridge.com*
To: Rock Ridge Personnel
Subject: Candygram System 3.0

As everyone knows, Rock Ridge has been consumed with the Candygram System 3.0 (CS3) development for VPC Retail Services. Our entire organization has been working very hard to reach our goal and I would like to the time to acknowledge the effort. Thank you.

The Beta date for CS3 is now May 5, 1999. This Beta version will include customer inquiry; order, adjustment, and receipt batch processing; service cycle processing; bill processing and posting; as well as master and support table functionality. We will also implement security roles and permissions and robust error messaging. We have been Beta testing the Candygram System Import (CSI) Utility at VPCR over the past two weeks. The CSI was written for the VPCR custom data feed between RSSC (a VPCR system) and Candygram. The CSI will also handle lockbox data loads. This testing has been very valuable not only to work the kinks out of the CSI, but also to avoid the same issue in CS3. VPCR plans to begin using the CSI to load 130,000 Customers for the Beta testing period. CSI coding will be complete April 26, 1999.

We need to continue to focus and work towards our dates. Overall the system looks very good and I am pleased with the cohesiveness of the team. Soon the project will transition to an implementation and support phase, where other members of the organization will carry the torch handed off by the designers and coders.

It's not easy being the best. We just need to make it look easy.

Quality issues were like landmines: able to lay dormant for extended periods. At what seemed to be the most inopportune time, they'd cripple us. Issues with Edsel, the project that functioned as an organ donor to Candygram, hit us well over a year after delivery. Just in time to hobble us in the lead up to our biggest Candygram development push. We'd have to work heroically to make up that time that was already overpromised to our biggest client, a multibillion-dollar company that had spent years waging multiple wars of attrition with companies much larger than ours, and which had only red ink, derelict billing system implementations, and ongoing lawsuits to show for it. Was this the recipe for success?

Date: 09/29/1999 08:31 AM
From: Hedley Lamarr
To: Cash Money *<cdollar@rockridge.com>*, Stan Granite *sgranite@rockridge.com*
Subject: Edsel Training/Implementation

Finally, there is quite a bit of history concerning JJ, Whiney, and the Edsel development. They are very bitter and angry that the system has taken so long to develop. Actually, it was shelved for a year by Sisyphus after which they said that Sisyphus would not use it. Less than two weeks ago Sisyphus decided to implement it and gave us only a week to do it. Sisyphus management knows that not all aspects of the system are completed. We will be limiting the scope to possibly the generation of commission amounts and a request for check form. Also, we will be transferring data to and from the AS/400 in Akron. In summary, I anticipate a lot of work on Edsel for several months to come.

P.S. JJ can be combative and abrasive. He is rough but he knows his stuff. I think that generally we should give him what he wants. Whiney on the other hand does not have a firm grasp of the concept of databases. I would strongly suggest that we implement none of Whiney's changes unless they are approved by JJ.

The Brown Hole, or "I'd Say You've Had Enough"

The Software Development Center (SDC), while being in a prime location, was far from an ideal office environment. But then, lasting friendships are probably more often forged in a foxhole than in a corner office. On first inspection, we would now be working in a clean, well-lit, open-plan form office, complete with a dinette. There was plenty of natural light from the windows facing the main and side streets. We were on the second floor, conveniently located above a Bruegger's bagel shop. Parking was on-street, but free and not too hard to find in the surrounding blocks, a definite improvement over downtown. Next door was Fat Head's, our favorite bar and official hot wing vendor of the Rock Ridge development team. What could be better?

A number of months after the move, another seismic event forever changed the office. It started like any other day. C$ was up to his usual antics, as he held court at the meeting table. This meant everyone within 50 feet was in his meeting whether they wanted to be or not. I can't remember the trigger, but J-Pax must have had his fill of being harassed by C$. It seemed like the office suddenly got quiet when I heard J-Pax say, "Fuck you, C$… I'm tired of this shit…and here's your fucking pen back." I may not have remembered the quote exactly, but I clearly remember the first office-launched F-bomb. I don't know what was holding us back to that point. J-Pax had seemingly opened some sort of Pandora's Box of swearing. Overnight, the standard office chat went completely blue.

The insanity of having one phone, located centrally but not conveniently, for everyone proved to be an interesting social experiment. It would ring, and heads would begin popping above cube walls like prairie dogs to see who would be forced to answer it. Eyes would swivel back and forth, head fakes and false starts followed, before someone would finally cave. It was as though some evil genius had studied the book *Peopleware* and applied the opposite of all that was learned to create the ultimate productivity killer. When it wasn't disrupting "the flow" (a state of greatly heightened productivity that comes after approximately 45 minutes of uninterrupted effort) of almost everyone in the office, it served as a convenient petri dish for whatever cold or flu variant was in circulation.

Spending a few more minutes surveying the 50×50-foot office, you'd quickly realize that the 20 or so half-height cubicles were densely packed and were unlikely to provide much peace and quiet when fully populated. Who was going to get the two tall cubes, one on either side of the office? And that solitary cordless phone sitting in the middle of the office might seem a little worrisome. This is when you would finally take notice of the two doors on the far wall. One was a utility closet, and the other was *the* toilet. One toilet, with no vestibule or hallway. One closet-size toilet in full view of the office. Twenty people, living on a diet consisting chiefly of hot wings and coffee, relying on one toilet. This was going to get ugly.

Andrew: OK, I'm not quite sure I get this. Why's a toilet worth mentioning?

Mark: It was the essence of working at Rock Ridge.

Andrew: Seriously? Was it like that when you first came on board?

Mark: No. In fact, at the first office, shirt and tie was the standard, and it was a normal, boring downtown business office. That was the way Hedley wanted it run. And the first guy I was going to pick fights with or tease a lot wasn't going to be Stan—he was an imposing fellow, as he filled an entire cube.

We rarely saw C$ back then and the other characters who worked there at the downtown office were so boring that it wasn't even worth engaging them. It wasn't until we hit the South Side that C$ started spending more and more time there and we were free from the office drones that it kind of just happened.

It was a way of diffusing tensions. C$ has a really strong ego, and so do I, and so does Stan. And when you're talking about something in a meeting, you have to let off that steam. Making fun of people was a way of establishing that we're all on the same page. C$ liked to throw his weight around, and had a fairly important title compared to the rest of us. But we could always keep him on our level by harassing him on a personal level.

Stan: C$ didn't start treating us like human beings until we started ripping on him.

Andrew: But it's got to be more than poking fun. It sounds like you guys did this to an incredible extent. A lot of people would be driven to tears having to come in every day to the environment that you guys at Ridge Rock thrived in. Can we get to the bottom of that? And how did the toilet come into play?

Mark: The toilet was fertile ground for developing jokes. It was an ever-present actor, and that's why it came up a lot.

We wrote code and did our jobs in order to get back to making jokes about each other. That's the approach we took at meetings. "All right, let's stop for a minute and get some code done, so we can get back to so-and-so being a *[expletive deleted]*." And that's kind of how it went. As someone was speaking, you were either coming up with a new idea about the code, or a new idea to rip on somebody about. It just kept the meetings going. Our meetings were incredibly productive, I think, despite all of the constant interruptions. No one was ever in the meeting talking because they just wanted to talk. And if they were, they weren't talking about the product because they wanted to talk. They were talking about somebody's *[expletive deleted]*. I think that also kept our work focused. Real work only came up when the idea was so good that it warranted stopping the hilarity to talk about it.

Stan: People actually liked going to meetings, which is probably in contrast to every other company in existence. We actually liked to get together to meet and talk, because you knew that was going to happen. So, nobody dreaded going to meetings or tried to avoid them, because of the entertainment.

Mark: Nobody ever looked at a laptop when they were in a meeting.

Stan: Exactly.

The other thing about the poop stuff was that it was sort of the Rosetta stone, the lingua franca of humor. If you have 10 people in the room, the one thing you know you can make a joke about that everyone's going to find funny is poo.

Andrew: And that's where the toilet came in.

Mark: So, the toilet actually came into the story before the incessant humor really emerged as the dominant culture on the team. We'd just come over to the South Side office, and we were dealing with the fact that 20 of us were all using the same toilet right in the middle of the office, in an open environment with no real walls or anything to limit the impact. It was the giant elephant in the room. It was something you couldn't *not* notice. And I think it was the initial pressure valve for us with talking about funny stuff. The first thing we could all agree about was that the toilet situation was pretty awful.

Everyplace else you work you hide the toilet. It's a safe place, and nobody talks about how you have to go there. At our office, it was in your face all the time. We could see the toilet door, we could see when somebody walked in, we could see when somebody walked out, and everyone knew exactly how long they were in there. There was no way to get away from it, and you were aware of it all the time—in every sense of the word. So, the subject would just come up. You can imagine that it had a huge impact on how we worked together as a team.

So, it started with the toilet, and pretty soon the jokes were flowing about progressively more off-color things. But the toilet was as far as it went with some people, because poop is a pretty safe subject.

Stan: There were two pretty key factors there, if you step back from it. One, we couldn't have had that culture and camaraderie develop if we didn't have the South Side for it to incubate. There was no way that culture would have taken hold in the older, ice cube tray office, where the hallway door opened into Mark's cube, where we had all that terrible coffee, and where it was isolated: there was nothing around, no restaurants, no bars, nothing at all. But we moved to the South Side of Pittsburgh, where the developers were in our own office in a part of town that was a much more casual, 24-hour neighborhood where you could be there off-hours and still have things to do when you got off work. And it had the toilet. Without all that, the culture never would have loosened up and developed the way it did.

Mark: Nobody was there just to log time. It wasn't presenteeism. You were there because you wanted to be. It was either going to be funny, or you'd get work done so it could be funny when you were done. Or you were there because you were going to go out to a really good lunch or possibly dinner afterwards. Going to work was easy. And sometimes you'd actually say to yourself, "Man, I'm tired of making jokes, so let's do some work so we can reload." I think that's important to capture how critical the South Side—and the toilet—were. You were only ever really working for a short sprint at a time. You'd do a sprint, then go out to lunch, and do another sprint in the afternoon or evening. You weren't just sitting there watching the clock, because you could leave whenever you felt like it.

Stan: It was actually challenging. Whether it was ripping on each other or doing work, there were challenges there. It was a tough crowd, and you had to be on your game in order to not get destroyed when people were ripping on each other.

But we also had those ludicrous goals for our projects, and that was part of it. If we'd actually done the kind of stuff that "responsible" teams do regularly, where you plan the work first and take on projects that are realistic, it wouldn't have worked. There was a gallows humor around the kind of absolutely ridiculous demands that were put on us. I think it helped us bond against that external enemy—a ridiculous schedule for not very much money—that helped us all come together.

Mark: Somehow we were consistently being surprised by Hedley. Even though it was the same pattern over and over again, somehow we still managed to be shocked.

Stan: It's like the frog that gets boiled slowly. "OK, I see you guys can make this deadline, so let's tighten it by a week."

Mark: Or cut a third of the team, and keep the same deadlines.

Stan: Let's let the negotiations for the contract drag on for three months, but keep the due date the same. Oh, that didn't faze you…we're going to give you three weeks to turn it into Spanish. You made that work? OK, now make it work in Pakistan for 25 times more customers than your largest previous installation. And we'd just deal with it with relentless humor, and somehow that made it work.

Andrew: It almost seems like you took one obstacle after another—your terrible working environment, insane business deadlines, layoffs—and turned them into something that encouraged work, albeit not in a way that you'd read about in business school.

Mark: Right. You're not going to read in *Peopleware* that you should put a composting toilet heap in the middle of the office to help the team gel.

The daily unpleasant reminders of our limited sanitation facilities, combined with the office demographics, led to many scatological discussions. There were even meta-scatological discussions. The most infamous, after a particularly late programming session, led to some groundbreaking work in theoretical scatology. I believe the eureka moment was inspired by JDog, our technical writing manager, and the sole female employee willing to endure direct exposure to some of our more eccentric topics of debate. Exasperated, she noted that when there were enough guys in a conversation, sooner or later it invariably turned to the topic of poo. I had dreams of becoming a theoretical physicist, before my adviser at Carnegie Mellon University noted that my lack of academic rigor made me more suited to a career in computer science. Using Stan as a sounding board, I noticed striking similarities in the observed phenomenon to the implications of the Chandrasekhar and Tolman-Oppenheimer-Volkoff limits in stellar astrophysics. The TOV limit is upper bound in the mass of neutron stars, beyond which the force of gravity will exceed the neutron degeneracy pressure with a subsequent collapse into a black hole. Similarly, I proposed that any conversation involving enough men will soon collapse under its own weight, forming a super-dense discussion from which no non-scatological discussion could escape, dubbed a brown hole. The theory has agreed well with considerable observational data. Possible refinements include factors to account for the apparent increased speed of the collapse in the presence of alcohol. Also, collapse may be prevented by having enough women in the conversation, but we have been unable to collect the necessary observational data to support the hypothesis.

Some of These Envelopes Contain Stock Options, or "I'm Through Being Mr. Goodbar, the Time Has Come to Act and Act Quickly"

After we had staked out our respective cubes and started to settle in, Hedley arrived to take stock of his minions in their new habitat. Hedley being Hedley, he immediately noticed that a few of us had moved our monitors from the middle of the desk to a position a little off to one corner or the other. This unauthorized cubicle customization was quickly proscribed. That should have been a clear signal to recirculate my resume. Someone unable to properly consider the costs of this affront to his aesthetic sense in comparison to the comfort of the developers, and more importantly, the message his decree would send to the team, should not be trusted with the helm. I mostly saw it as a slap in the face. Hedley could not have more clearly communicated his evaluation of the team. We were clearly not highly educated, highly skilled professionals who were an asset to the company. C$ picked up on the sudden onset of tension in the office, or maybe he saw my posture change to something a bit more hostile. He quickly shooed Hedley out of the office and immediately tried to downplay the situation. It worked. I was now focused on the immediate problem, which for me had an easy solution: "Fuck him." I was going to put my monitor where I wanted the damn thing. But I should have remained focused on the fact that Hedley clearly had issues. I missed a clear signal to jump ship. It became a moot point when we came to realize that Hedley was unlikely to ever step foot in the office again.

The promise of alternative work schedules took a long time to be realized, too. When we did get movement, we were immediately disappointed.

Notes from our first meeting at the SDC:

> Alternative Work Schedule—We're still working out the details of the Alternative Work
> Schedule. To clarify, the envisioned Alternative Work Schedule is not a flex schedule.
> Employees will be offered a variety of start/end times from which he/she may choose.

He was implicitly trusting us with the fate of his company, but he was unwilling to explicitly trust us to come to work without punching a clock. Another sad message: I need a
clock to evaluate your performance because I can't/won't be concerned with what you
actually do. Hedley was also showing us his knack for highlighting the cloud instead of the
silver lining. We'd see this several years later, when a company bonus scheme was rolled
out. The company was seriously tight on money; benefits and any non-critical employees
were cut again. It was correctly feared that people were soon going to bail, and we
couldn't afford to lose a single person with so little staff remaining. A bonus was
announced for those willing to ride it out. The details were typically fuzzy, but if the company made money, and we stuck it out, we'd get a cut. I wasn't counting on seeing a dime
of it, but we appreciated the gesture. Sadly, I don't remember the bonus ever being promoted as an incentive again. When we did manage to hold the lines, and the company
actually survived to make some profit, Hedley did not seem to be happy. There was
enough delay and so little mention of when we'd actually get the checks that most
assumed we had been screwed (it's what we were expecting anyway). We were all pretty
shocked, at a company meeting, when the checks were actually handed out. Through his
words and body language, he managed to make an unexpected payday disappointing.
That layoff cycle was just one among many. However, there was one round of layoffs that
forever changed the SDC and probably was an event that unleashed the full potential of
the core development team.

"Some of these envelopes contain stock options; the others contain letters of reference. I
ask that you wait to open them until after I leave." Hedley may have said more, probably
about our always favorable sales pipeline, but that was all anyone heard. The entire company (about 35 of us) had been called to the SDC for this meeting with no explanation.
We had been organized into a large circle in the center of the office before the envelopes
had been handed out. He was walking out the door, while the employees were left clutch-
ing identical manila envelopes and staring at each other in stunned silence. Eyes darted
back and forth looking for answers, or for a signal to start opening the envelopes. Some
seemed to be trying to determine their envelope's contents without opening it, like a child
at Christmas shaking his gift-wrapped package. My envelope was of little interest to me;
instead, I had remote, but potentially more pressing, concerns. Namely, who was the most
likely to snap and shoot us all, or, more worryingly, who might shoot me? I had recently
been promoted to software development manager; all it really meant was that I had the
excuse to get more pay and to lay claim to one of the two tall cubes. And, after that day, to
call dibs on the only parking spot attached to the office. The org chart described an alter-
nate reality. The entire dev team were listed as my direct reports, while I reported to C$,
the VP of engineering. There was never any doubt in my mind or in the team's mind that
anything would change in practice. C$ was still the alpha and omega of the Candygram

System, and by having everyone reporting to him, it would stay that way. So, although I had no real managerial responsibilities or control, I did get a sneak preview of who made the cut. The meeting was downtown the day before. The fact that I had been wearing a tie signaled I was there. I wonder if anyone thought I had some input in the layoffs.

Envelopes were opened, and soon the silence was broken with sounds of crying. With surprisingly little encouragement or organization necessary, we filed across the street to another favorite watering hole. We spent the entire afternoon commiserating, with some being a bit smoother than others. Empathy has never been my strong suit, so I stuck with the developers who had come out unscathed. The Cold Lamper, a.k.a. the Blind Guardian, was a more recent addition to the SQL team. He was a big, strappin', lantern-jawed lad from coal country. From his warm and thoughtful personality, he probably had some Boy Scout or altar boy in him in the past. Seeing her alone and clearly upset, he bravely went to console our office/QA manager. She wasn't very talkative. So he proceeded to tell her how sad it was that she lost her whole team, wondered aloud what they would do next, about how they would have a hard time finding work, and how it was a shame what the changes meant to her role. She cried just a little bit more with each thing he said. Finally, she stopped him, telling him she had been fired, too.

After what became known as Black Tuesday, the office environment changed dramatically. The remaining employees were almost exclusively male, with an average age of around 29. The oldest employee at the SDC was a ripe, old 34. With no "adults" present, the office quickly devolved. Within a week, it was one part *Animal House* and one part *Lord of the Flies*, an office situation in which virtually anything was allowable. Every statement uttered was a potential starting point for a filthy riposte. To this day, I avoid certain words/phrases that were sure to be pounced on. (Recently, even in the presence of civilized company, I was at a loss as to how I could convey that the ground animal product packed in casing was too rich in sodium chloride for my palate.) The depravity was not confined to water cooler talk. During design reviews, comments were made that would make even Redd Foxx blush. Surprisingly, though, if one could ignore the filth, it was the most civil and egalitarian office environment I've ever had the pleasure to work in. Office politics, at least within our group, ceased to exist (other than some griping over good snacks being hoarded during the brief period that a selection of snacks was provided by the company). I suppose anyone who did not share the mutual respect of the group would have long since quit. But in spite of the enormous workload, it still was a remarkably easy office to drag myself into every day.

During this time period, the Hand Circle Game (*http://www.urbandictionary.com/define. php?term=The+Circle+Game*), which we played for pride and shame, not punches, became a daily ritual. Within days, simple attempts to catch someone with the circle were rendered useless. Cold War mentality set in with attacks and counterattacks becoming more intense and creative as the weeks passed. Two months later, virtually every surface capable of concealing a photo had been booby-trapped with a picture of a team member making a legal hand circle. This list included the refrigerator, kitchen cabinets, bathroom vanity, toilet paper roll, file cabinets, and even CD-ROM drive trays. One intrepid team member (the

Cold Lamper) managed to get on the Jumbotron between innings at PNC Park, shaming more than 20,000 people with quick thinking and a cunning display of the circle. (I know what you're thinking: "There's no way 20,000 people were attending a Pirates game." But this was the year the park opened, and a lot of people were there just to see the facility. Plus, at that point, the Pirates' streak of consecutive losing campaigns stood at a mere eight seasons, so most fans hadn't yet given up hope completely.)

Now, you might understand why working there was almost fun, but you also might be wondering when we got anything done. We had almost zero turnover in the team. Between the filth, communication was clear, rapid, and effective. Management in the traditional sense was completely unnecessary. We did what we had to do, making considerable progress on the Candygram System. We ignored the company's fiscal uncertainty. And we somehow also made time to produce a number of custom systems to keep the trickle of cash flowing. The camaraderie and rituals that developed during this "Lord of the Flies" period kept us going, even following the shuttering of our communal second floor space in a vibrant, walkable neighborhood and the subsequent move to a sterile, isolated, sprawling space with private offices on the 52nd floor of a high-rise on the edge of Pittsburgh's downtown ("dahn-tahn" in Pittsburghese).

The circle game survived the move to the 52nd floor, although occasionally the intersection of the game and employees unfamiliar with its ways led to some awkward moments. One evening, a group of "regular" employees were leaving the office while several developers were trying to finish a design meeting before the Cold Lamper had to go for the day. The Lamper walked toward the elevator while continuing the design conversation. He recognized that the other employees and the just-arrived elevator presented a previously unused, and therefore unexpected, chance to drop the circle. As the other employees had boarded the elevator, he reached around the Colonel (as our accountant was known), flashing the circle. Unfortunately, the Colonel, being unfamiliar with the game, was also unprepared to have a large man, now standing closely behind him, reaching around with his hand making the circle in the approximate location of his groin. The Colonel's face, as he was clearly unsure of what this particular elevator ride was about to have in store, showed a mixture of shock, apprehension, and disgust; his expression is forever etched in the mind of more than one Rock Ridge developer.

A subsequent and final move to a suburban office park (chosen for its proximity to Hedley's house and its lower taxes) did not kill the game, or the shared insanity powering it. Lesser combatants eventually admitted defeat and left the battlefield, leaving two developers locked in battle until an epic one-on-one best-of-seven series broke the deadlock employing a clever gambit involving barbecue potato chips.

Although the game survived the moves, the close communication that knit the group together did not. With increasing financial woes, engineers were sent to work at customer sites in an attempt to salvage projects that had gone off-track and to log important billable hours. The physical separation disrupted the careful balance. Punch lines and joke setups that had been passed around Harlem Globetrotter style now were falling flat. Without the fun, it was just a job—and not even a good one.

The Blitz, or "Break's Over, Boys, Don't Just Lie There Gettin' a Suntan…"

Earlier in 2000, we signed our biggest deal with Succubus Corp., a major gas utility. Phase I would be implementing existing functionality. VPC had helped as a reference, but I'm guessing it was the wildly optimistic promises, timelines, and budget-friendly price of Phase II that sealed the deal. The thinking was that we might not make any money, but they'd cover the development costs. Then we'd starting making the big bucks, or at least that was the thinking. Weeks earlier, we had an event to celebrate the "merging and e-merging" of our company. We would be joining forces with a virtual company that controlled our IP and was bankrolled by a real estate company. Hedley would leverage the parent company's credit to swing a sublet of Alcoa's former headquarters on the 52nd floor of the second-tallest building downtown. The mayor, who was on hand to say a few words, seemed to be a bit suspicious of our projected revenues of $250 million in just a few years, and paused a moment for a sideways glance as he spoke the numbers. A number of recently bestselling books will attest to the many pitfalls of scaling up even the most successful small companies. But reality was never a significant input to planning decisions, so why should we let it start interfering now?

The Candygram System's current incarnation was able to handle basic customer functions and retail product and services billing. In Phase II, we had agreed to develop a much more sophisticated billing and customer care functionality. We needed to be able to support a wide range of features needed by regulated gas utilities, deregulated retail and commercial energy companies, and gas transportation and pipeline businesses. We were still implementing Phase I, concurrently with the new development. But that wasn't all; we had a few demos for other larger clients that needed some new features, too. This was in addition to our regular load of existing customer support and custom system development.

Recognizing that we were unlikely to start working smarter, doubling or trebling our productivity overnight, a bold plan was hatched: we would work harder, much harder.

> Date: 10/31/2000 9:17 AM
> From: Cash Money *cdollar@rockridge.com*
> To: Development, QA, Tech Support, Training &Tech Writing, Implementation
> Subject: November Work Blitz
>
> Rock Ridge NOVEMBER BLITZ
>
> Rock Ridge Corporation has four major initiatives during the month of November: "Squeal Like a Pig" Demonstration; Much-Too-Large-For-Us Gas & Light Presentation; Succubus Phase I (Products & Services) Enhancements; Succubus Phase III (Transportation & Work Order) delivery. These initiatives overlap with continuing Succubus Phase II (Gas Utility) testing and coding, training, implementation, and developing technical documentation, online help, and courseware as well as supporting VPCR. Achieving these goals will prove to clients, investors, and ourselves that we are a small company with large abilities.

To achieve these goals I realize that we will need to work extended hours. In an effort to make November more productive (and not go insane or require a divorce) Rock Ridge will sponsor the following activities:

* Compensatory Time

* Weekday Dinners

* Weekend Lunches

* Mid-Month Dinner Outing

* End-of-Month Event

The effort rested squarely on the development team as we represented the long poles in this project plan. Training, documentation, and implementation would be, at best, playing catch-up. We had no real specs from which they could coordinate their efforts. We were making it up as we went along. Soon they were struggling just to stay abreast of new functionality spewing forth from development.

Even with the pressure of developing our real product, much effort was spent pulling off one of our most impressive tricks: creating a software equivalent of the Turducken. The Candygram System (technically CS3) developed during the spring was completely unrelated to previous generations of the product. However, one of those previous generations had an implementation of a gas-specific billing module that the new version did not yet have. Apparently noticing they had the same name, ownership suggested that we port the gas-specific module to the new system, and in fact had promised that we would demo exactly that concept at an upcoming trade show. At first, the development team laughed at the idea, but the owner was serious, so we had to find some way for it to work. I'm ashamed to admit that I found a package of Windows API calls that enabled screens from a compiled Windows application to appear as child windows in our new system. With the "hard part" out of the way, all that was left was the not-so-minor issue that the systems were using completely different databases. A few hundred hours of development and data mapping made for a convincing-looking system, albeit one that resulted in no revenue, but the owners were not discouraged.

Their sales claims, and by extension, the company website, became a ripe source of joke material for the development team. A prime example is the following excerpt from an energy industry research firm's 2002 CIS report:

> Candygram…Rock Ridge's flagship product, is an Internet-based, advanced software solution…Rock Ridge says that it has the functionality to manage all forms of energy including gas, electricity, oil, propane and other products and services such as water, telecom, security, and cable.

In 2002, the Candygram System was a Windows-based client/server system. The J2EE web-based version of Candygram was christened with the unintentionally dark but hilarious name "Candygram: The Final Solution" by Hedley at our first product planning summit. It remained a joke six years later, as each attempt to ramp up our Java™ efforts was soon scuttled by another development emergency.

The claim that the Candygram System could "manage all forms of energy" still makes me laugh out loud. I can just picture one of the owners at a sales presentation listing all of the forms of energy, à la Bubba in *Forrest Gump*: "Gas energy, electrical energy, thermal energy, kinetic energy, chemical energy, nuclear energy, rotational energy, potential energy, gravitational energy, nervous energy, sexual energy…" That claim soon had me crafting a host of regular expressions to transmute our core gas module's VB and SQL code into whatever energy market was targeted that week.

But we still had hope, and all the "fun" things about the office and our group were now amplified by 80+ hour work weeks. Running jokes no longer had an evening or weekend to fade. They were handed off from shift to shift, becoming more twisted with each iteration and compounded by weeks of accumulated sleep deprivation.

> Date: 12/04/2000 10:47 AM
> From: Cash Money *cdollar@rockridge.com*
> To: Development
> Cc: Hedley Lamarr <*hlamarr@rockridge.com*>, HR *t1000@rockridge.com*
> Subject: November Blitz
>
> November Blitz is over….
>
> I first want to specially thank each of you for your exceptional effort. Not only did we "meet" the deadline, but we were able to produce two new modules with minimal issues. I would also like to recognize Stan Granite and The Sigh Guy for their effort in architecting and designing the new modules. This was a new experience and I believe the modules are better because of their involvement.
>
> Second, I know that most of you have 80+ hours of comp-time. Please see to it that you use that time to do nothing, Recharge! First quarter of 2000 plans to be active and we need everyone thinking clearly. Mark Denovich has a spreadsheet that will be used to coordinate time off.
>
> Third, for those of you who are at the office when others are recharging, we are not done improving the Gas, Work Order, and Transportation modules. We have a lot of reporting, interfaces, and polishing to complete. Succubus is very pleased with the Candygram System, we cannot afford to let up now. Our implementation team will be ensuring that Candygram System meets their needs and will work with the development staff through December and January to fix any glitches that may exist. I would like to have another installation of the Candygram System for Friday of this week.
>
> Fourth, planning the end of November Blitz event. Originally we were planning a Penguins game or the like. Some of you mentioned that you would rather have meats and cheeses delivered to the office. The seven of you can vote on what the event should be (of course I have final approval). Please let me know the consensus as soon as possible.
>
> Once again thank you, and Great Job!

No animals were harmed in making this message and only two exclamation points were used.

We not only worked hard, we played hard. We parlayed the end-of-Blitz event into a company-funded party at my house to coincide with the AFC/NFC championship games. We had gourmet food from all across the Internet, enough top-shelf booze to kill W. C. Fields, with the guest of honor being a 15 lb. USDA prime rib roast, flown in from Chicago.

The celebration turned out to be a bit premature. Against the odds, we met our customer's deadline, or so we thought. What we didn't realize is that while we were toiling away, the customer was also busy moving the goalposts.

Our Invite to the Number Six Dance, or "What Is It That's Not Exactly Water and It Ain't Exactly Earth?"

Christopher Hawkins, founder and principal developer of a custom software development firm, posted a piece titled "11 Clients You Need To Fire Right Now."* In the piece, Hawkins describes 11 client/customer behaviors that he considers abusive, any one of which he feels is sufficient reason for terminating a business relationship. By my count, Succubus engaged in at least seven of these behaviors on a regular basis during the more than three years of its relationship with Rock Ridge:

> THE SOMETHING-FOR-NOTHING consistently increases the scope of the project but refuses to pay for the additional work.

> THE BLACKMAILER consistently refuses to pay an invoice until you perform additional work at no charge…a special subset of the something for nothing…Blackmail is always win-lose, and anyone who believes in win-lose in a business relationship needs to be cut off.

> THE SLOW PAY consistently pays invoices late.

> THE FLAKE consistently is late meeting responsibilities, but still holds you to the original schedule.

> THE LIAR consistently lies to you.

> THE CLINGER consistently makes unreasonable demands regarding your availability.

> THE MONEY PIT consistently is unprofitable…they take up far more time and effort than the fees you are able to charge them are worth…this can be a client who demands cut-rate prices, extra unpaid support, or who repeatedly does things that require you to work harder.

---

* Christopher Hawkins. "11 Clients You Need To Fire Right Now," *http://www.christopherhawkins.com/06-13-2005.htm.*

Succubus had at least two previous failed CIS replacement projects before the Candygram project started, which should attest to some of the difficulties its business partners and suppliers faced. Also, as a long-established and regulated utility, it had a culture that had been warped by the long exposure to the perverse incentives resulting from the intersection of business, government, and labor. Standard operating procedures included adversarial negotiation, maximizing gains within existing legal agreements, and cost containment. The legal department had a great deal of influence within the company, and they were never hesitant to take a matter to court.

Their approach left a business like ours that operated informally and with small cash reserves at their mercy. Unfortunately, the lure of a big payoff at the end meant that ownership was willing to submit.

The abusive cycle started with THE SLOW PAY, which turned into THE BLACKMAILER scenario when payment became overdue. Multiple change orders containing substantial free work would be agreed to in exchange for prompt payment of outstanding invoices. This would be followed by THE SOMETHING-FOR-NOTHING angle, in which scope would be added as the acceptance criteria would be "clarified."

THE FLAKE maneuver was also a favorite tactic. Project specification negotiations would drag on, in one instance six weeks past the desired project start date. The only non-negotiable point was the delivery date, which did not change. It was also a common occurrence for key Succubus people to be consistently unavailable when they were required. Their delay was solely our problem.

I'm reluctant to imply that there was a regular pattern of duplicitous behavior. But, there was one notable example of THE LIAR behavior involving a high-ranking member of the project team. One might speculate that other similarly underhanded incidents occurred without detection. This particular incident involved the primary analyst/developer of the existing mainframe system; let's call him R. By most accounts, R was the most knowledgeable person in Succubus about the existing CIS system. Not just on merit, but also because R jealously hoarded this information for his personal gain. Even his employer was at his mercy. If they wanted features or logic added to their system, you had to make it worth R's time. R understood the threat of any new system, and took a key role on the project to neutralize this threat. His role made him the judge and jury over new Candygram functionality. Just how far he was willing to go was seen firsthand by our project manager, PButt, who was helping with testing on-site. That day, they were testing a fairly complicated financial calculation that could be controlled by several configurable parameters. R caused a great deal of commotion, pointing out that calculations were wrong when a particular configuration parameter was enabled. What he didn't know was that PButt, knowing that this calculation was a high-priority item, had tested the functionality himself before releasing it to Succubus. He demanded evidence of the problem from an on-the-spot test run. R ran the calculation and provided the damning evidence. After confirming it worked on his test system, PButt created a new test scenario in the production system. R again ran the test, and again produced data showing we remained in error, and pronounced the software a failure. On a hunch, PButt checked the system's auditing tables, which recorded configuration changes. These tables were created to aid our testing and support efforts, and were not part of the advertised system functionality. User and time-stamp data showed that preceding each test run R had turned the config parameter OFF, reenabling it once his evidence had been produced. Confronted with the audit tables, R impishly admitted, "Oh yeah, I guess I was doing that." A fistfight was narrowly averted, but untold damage had already been done. PButt was later able to recount this tale during R's lawsuit claiming wrongful termination.

THE CLINGER behavior became more and more obvious as the "go live" date asymptotically approached. Near the end, roughly 40% of our company personnel were working on-site full-time. We didn't protest too much, as they were technically billable hours, but the payment games being played meant this much-needed revenue was never seen.

There can be little doubt that Succubus was a classic MONEY PIT customer. Without the reserves to absorb the abuses, we were forced to the brink of bankruptcy twice during the project, each time being forced to lay off nearly half of the work force.

> Date: 11/20/2001 2:31PM
> From: Hedley Lamarr *hlamarr@rockridge.com*
> To: Personnel
> Subject: Candygram System Enhancement Project for Succubus
>
> As a company, we have an incentive to deliver prior to January 25th in the form of a cash bonus....
>
> I believe that if we meet the December 7th deadline with a product that is defect-free, we stand a very good chance of actually receiving some of that incentive bonus."

It was even obvious to Hedley that the payment was not something to count on, especially considering the impossibly high hurdle of "defect-free" software. Still, we limped on.

In late July 2004, having failed to land a deal for the largest natural gas company in Pakistan (a fanciful reach by even the most optimistic standards), we were facing our most dire cash crunch. The triumvirate (Hedley, PButt, and a reluctant C$) agreed to a two-pronged approach to the problem: 1) immediately initiate yet another layoff, and 2) a proposal to sell the source code to Succubus *and* to waive the employment contracts of any remaining Rock Ridge employees identified as necessary to continue the project internally at Succubus. Those employees selected for the layoff revealed Hedley's thinking.

They included the only employee devoting significant time to quality assurance testing, and Stan, the client-side developer with arguably the best understanding of the system, and who in six years had unarguably logged the most overtime. Adding insult to injury, his reprieve came from Succubus, which expressed interest in signing him. Those who were kept included two employees hired in the previous six months. They lacked knowledge of the system or of our existing customers, but they had the superficial qualities of the kind of employee Hedley wanted to hire. S, an implementation analyst, looked and talked like a businessperson. He dressed in dress slacks and long-sleeved name-brand shirts. More importantly, he sounded right to Hedley. He used the sort of buzzwords that were en vogue at the time. He did have a considerable CV, but lacking the ability to generate short-term revenue, his potential was irrelevant. The other employee was of even more demonstrably poor value. Although Pong claimed a right to the title "senior developer," what little code he did produce needed to be reworked or scrapped. Worse, in the course of his efforts, he was a productivity leech, relying on a revolving selection of team members for easily sourced information. What he did have was an ability to unflinchingly spout the world-class bullshit Hedley was desperate to hear. Hedley had had his fill of reality.

Some of Pong's finest work can be seen in Rock Ridge's Quality Assurance procedures contained in a system RFP. The reality was that the minimal QA procedures we did have were now the sole domain of a part-time employee who had no formal training. But in Pong's contribution to the proposal, the truth is stretched to imply that we were clearly at the forefront of our industry, with enough weasel words to stop short of outright lying. This was something Hedley could relate to.

RFP excerpt:

> The foundation of Rock Ridge's quality assurance begins with nearly all of our technical staff having an excellent foundation in Computer Science and/or Software Engineering. There is also a significant influence from Carnegie Mellon University and the Software Engineering Institute, as a number of our staff are Carnegie Mellon graduates. The significance is the nearly universal awareness through out the technical portion of the organization of the Software Capability Maturity Model and metric based repeatable software development processes derived from it.

Translated:

> Three members of the technical team had ties to Carnegie Mellon. One left after posting a cumulative GPA < 1 in a non-CS major, but before being formally asked to leave. The second was formally asked to leave, but later returned, barely graduating, again in a non-CS major, while the third was married to someone who worked for the SEI, but had left the company a few years later. Additionally, several of our staff understands the CMM well enough to know how laughably bad our practices really are, by almost any metric, with one being so inspired by the disparity as to write a book on software project management.

By the end of summer 2004, the deal for the code and employees was nearly finalized. Hedley requested a meeting with each developer. The meeting's goal depended on your fate. If Hedley hoped you would remain a Rock Ridge employee, the meeting was to sell you on his vision for the newly reinvigorated company. If you were on Succubus's list, the meeting was somewhat more complicated. The deal was conditional on at least two of the named chattel to accept an offer of employment from Succubus. He desperately needed to convince those on the list to agree. But the years of dealing with Succubus left a bitter taste in his mouth. He made the pitch, but not without suggesting in a roundabout and hopefully legally defensible way that you might also abandon Succubus as soon as you were able. Never seeing a back he didn't feel like stabbing, he had already provided, without any consent, all relevant HR records (including salary), effectively destroying any bargaining power those employees might have had.

Having the luck of being one of the first people hired meant I started with a choice assignment: building the Candygram client framework. By completion, everyone was fully committed with project work, which meant I would be the only one available for the next choice assignment. Rarely having significant involvement in the business logic, I was off Succubus's radar. It also meant I had a hand, sometimes more, in nearly everything, including the mail and network infrastructure. So it wasn't much of a surprise, when I was the last to be scheduled, and when Hedley gave me his best sales pitch to stay. I was offered the position of CTO. In a second, maybe two, my emotions ran from joy, to pride, to doubt, to loathing, before settling on a mélange of despair and resentment. I was being offered the captain's hat on a visibly sinking ship. That's also when I realized that the SME mentioned in a footnote of the business plan was me.

> Rock Ridge will depute an SME to Gurgaon, India to carry out the knowledge transition. The duration for this is expected to be 3-4 weeks.

We were going to offshore development. One of our longest-running jokes involved our eventual Indian replacements. I wasn't offended by the prospect of my teammates being replaced by cheaper labor. I just couldn't comprehend how, after the lessons of the previous six years, he expected our salvation would be an unknown offshore team, billable on an hourly basis, who was not directly accountable to our company and who had no knowledge of, or loyalty to, our product. My email after the meeting:

> Date: Tue, 14 Sep 2004 10:48AM
> From: Mark Denovich *mark@numbersix.com*
> To: Stan Granite <stangranite@cablecompany.net>, Tubman <tubman@tubman.com>,
> BeatUntilCreamy *buc@barestearns.com*
> Subject: re: I'm meeting with Hedley in AM
>
> Fuck me.
>
> —Mark

At least I merited 30 minutes of his time for an individual meeting. Realizing that Hedley seemed to be having a hard time making room for their individual meetings (his three-week vacation in Europe having something to do with it) Stan, TMS, and Tubman proposed a group meeting. He agreed, and it meant that they would have the unique opportunity to hear both pitches. Hedley first gave the stay pitch. "TMS, you've worked for me for nearly a decade. We've stood together with you for that long, and we're not going to stop now. I want you to know that you'll always have a place at Rock Ridge as long as I'm running the company." He then turned to Tubman. "Tubman, I really appreciate what you've done for the company. The Cash Drawer project has really been a big help to our bottom line, and I want you to know that if the Succubus deal falls through, you'll be a part of any Plan B that might come about." Finally, Hedley appeared ready to give the same pitch to Stan Granite. With the Succubus deal still unconsummated, Hedley got right to the point: "Stan, you'll be off the payroll August 31st." Without a moment's hesitation, he then broke into his standard, "The future looks bright, the sales pipeline has never been stronger, and if we pull together as a team" speech that he'd given a thousand times before.

And thus ended an era.

Epilogue, or "Nowhere Special...I Always Wanted to Go There"

Honestly, the end had come a few months earlier at a fateful lunch at Fat Head's. The team had already suffered a few high-profile losses by this point. Someone had the bright idea that we should all get together for lunch.

It was just like old times, like back at the SDC. The conversation was fast and furious. The witty comebacks, put-downs, and general filth still had the same crisp timing and delivery. Our lunch hour stretched into two because no one wanted to leave. But soon the table was cleaned, and the last drinks were emptied, and we reluctantly headed for the door. Outside the weather was perfect, the sun shining and the air crisp as we exchanged a few goodbyes. I stopped almost mid-stride on the way back to my car. It hit me, like I was shot—shot with a diamond bullet, a diamond bullet right through my forehead. *"My god, I'm going back to work."* BeatUntilCreamy, a friend I had only recently brought into the company in a desperate attempt to help us address process and quality issues, spotted the change the very moment it happened. It took the sharp contrast of the lunch and the prospect of another day at what was left of Rock Ridge to drive it home. What was keeping us going was a memory. The office wasn't fun anymore, and it probably stopped being fun a few years earlier. We just didn't notice it. Once we got back, we lingered long enough to confirm we all had similar realizations. We took off early. The next few months we'd just be going through the motions.

Some of us still work for our big client—lodged deep inside their former tormentor, making sure the Candygram System continues to kick ass. A few of us have regrouped to work at a very differently run company (most importantly, a profitable one). And surprising to me, at least, some part of Rock Ridge soldiers on. I expect its pipeline is still packed. Hedley, however, was forced by financial circumstance to sell the company. He is reportedly doing well.

Andrew: Stan, I understand that you left Rock Ridge and stayed away from Candygram for a year and a half, but now you're back working with C$ for Succubus. Are you a glutton for punishment? Is it like an abusive relationship, where you know you should get out, but he just keeps sweet-talking you back? How did you end up back in the fourth ring of hell, so to speak? Start out by telling me about what you guys ended up with at the end of the project.

Stan: It's easiest if I start talking about where we are now. Believe it or not, while we are working at Succubus, C$ and I don't actually have anything to do with Candygram anymore.

At the end, Rock Ridge's code ended up being sold to Succubus, and obviously they originally brought us in—me and C$—to be the caretakers of Candygram. I guess it was just the way we worked at Rock Ridge, but C$ and I didn't try to horde our knowledge of the system.

Andrew: Even though that would obviously be a good way to ensure your own job security.

Stan: Right. We tried to give people an opportunity to know what we knew. And it turned out that they had no idea how to develop software there at all. So we tried to institute better source control, better processes generally. We wanted to help them improve their careers by learning the stuff that we'd developed at Rock Ridge through trial and error over all of our projects.

Eventually, I think we were successful enough at that, that I left to join Mark at the company that he'd left Rock Ridge for. One other Rock Ridge person, Tubman, was there, too. I was there for a little bit over a year and a half.

C$ got moved out of the Candygram group. Since both of us had done a number of projects that were successful, they wanted to move C$, and then later, me, when they hired me back, into the central IT organization so that we could do projects for the rest of Succubus. And that's the position we're in now.

Andrew: So you and C$ are basically taking some of the better practices you developed— mostly under fire, to cope with the insane obstacles you faced at Rock Ridge—and teaching them to the people at the same company that was the source of some of those very obstacles.

Stan: Exactly. I mean, we still do occasional projects with the Candygram team. But Succubus has the least amount of IT resources and expertise in other areas that are at the core of their business. So that's where we are now. Now, ironically, now that we're not there at Candygram, they brought in a major outside consulting company for an engagement where they're evaluating all of the processes around Candygram: whether they're spending enough money on maintenance.

They're trying to cut costs, and the management was under the impression that Candygram was expensive. Well, it turns out that the consulting firm told them that they're actually spending less on the system than their competitors do on theirs. And there's other people that know it now.

Andrew: It sounds like Candygram has had a real impact on the way Succubus runs their business.

Stan: Before, when they were on the mainframe system, they had no visibility into that part of the business. Now, with Candygram, they have a data warehouse, they have tons of reports and data extract, and they actually have a whole team of business analysts that can get the data they need about their operations to do something about it, which is something they didn't have before.

Andrew: And that's all based on the stuff you guys developed over the few years at Rock Ridge?

Stan: Yep.

CHAPTER TWENTY-NINE

Inside and Outside the Box

Patricia Ensworth

OUR STORY TAKES PLACE IN NEW YORK CITY. AS WITH MOST NEW YORK DRAMAS, THE PLOT REVOLVES around real estate.

The main character is an office building in Lower Manhattan, a bland 12-story box constructed soon after World War II whose afternoon sunlight was eclipsed a quarter century later by the towers of the World Trade Center. The building has the honor of being the only authentic, intact, and unadulterated element of this pseudomemoir. Lawyers and colleagues please take note: all else (the company, the people, the events, the narrator) is a collage of facts which individually are true but collectively are fictional.

I first laid eyes on the building during my job interview at Pharaoh Investment Guides, Inc. I was applying for a position as a software tester, and as soon as I walked in the door, I liked the feel of the place. Although Pharaoh was a world-class publishing company specializing in financial news and analysis, an international dynamo with offices around the globe, its headquarters seemed serene and friendly. The outside of the building might have been plain, but the inside was tastefully decorated, the lobby resplendent with gilt and marble architectural detail. People smiled and greeted each other in the hallways like residents of a small town.

The hiring manager, Jacob, was a thin, scholarly, nervous man who supervised the development on Pharaoh's book-formatting system.

"We don't have any full-time testers now," he admitted. "We hired a guy last year, but after a few months he decided he wanted to be a developer instead. Mostly our end users and clients have been doing the testing. I can't give you the details unless you come on board, but they've missed a few things that came very close to putting us out of business. We need somebody to come in and help us implement a more structured approach."

He squinted at my resume. "So…you have a master's degree in anthropology. Did you get involved with computers on an archeological dig or something?"

I explained that I had studied the structure and function of cultural systems with a focus on business activities. During graduate school I had earned money by writing software documentation, and then by testing software. I discovered that I had a knack for writing test cases based upon an analysis of how human beings used the software as a tool to communicate within their own cultural systems. I was currently employed by a global financial services firm to run usability tests on software that had been developed in the United States and would be deployed in its international offices. However, there had been a reorganization, and I didn't like my new boss.

To my surprise and delight, Pharaoh offered me the job. I had gotten along well with Jacob and was looking forward to working for him, but the Friday before the Monday I was supposed to start, he called me with some disturbing news.

"Sorry about this, but I'm leaving. I got a great offer from an Internet start-up in Silicon Valley. Today is my last day. Don't worry—you'll do fine here."

On Monday morning, the person who came to pick me up at the reception desk was an elegant, statuesque African-American woman about my own age. She introduced herself as Barbara, the project manager for the editorial systems. I followed her into an elevator and up to her area on the 6th floor, where I met the PMs for the other applications. Louise, a plump, grandmotherly, former human resources manager, looked after the HR systems amid a forest of lovingly tended plants. The PM for all internal and external web-based applications was Caitlin, whose tight skirt and low-cut blouse, stiletto heels, long manicured fingernails, and glamorous haircut made me wonder by what path she had arrived in the realm of software engineering. The fourth PM was Nick, and he worked on the production systems that fed the publications to the printers and websites. Nick told me that he had served in the Air Force during the first Gulf War—a fact corroborated by his erect posture, his clean-cut appearance, and his respectful demeanor.

From this informal PMO Gang of Four, I learned that in addition to the systems they worked with, there were a few others whose development teams got along without any project manager: the financial systems, the sales systems, and the internal reporting systems. Pharaoh did not follow a defined methodology for project management or software engineering. The project managers' role was limited to coordinating resources, monitoring budgets, and filling out status reports. The real power resided with the executive director-level development managers to whom the project managers and developers all reported.

"So, who am I reporting to?" I finally asked.

There was an awkward silence.

"Jacob hired me," I went on. "He said he was lead developer on the software that formats the content for the books. Is that editorial or production?"

"Production," Nick replied. "But there has been a reorganization. The ED who was development manager for internal reporting was promoted to managing director of systems development. All the EDs now report to him. Did you meet Dave?"

"Probably," I said, trying to recall all the people who had interviewed me during my three visits to Pharaoh.

"Dave thinks there is a greater need for testing on the sales systems," Barbara said. "But the ED who is dev manager for those systems doesn't agree. And there is no PM in that area."

"So who *am* I reporting to?" I asked again.

"The dev manager for sales systems," Caitlin smirked. "His name is Scott."

Sensing the onset of an anxiety attack, I forced myself to take several slow, deep breaths.

"Let me get this straight," I said. "My new boss is a development manager I've never met who doesn't think he needs a software tester."

Louise patted my hand. "It's only temporary. Things will get sorted out, you'll see."

Nestled under Barbara's protective wing, I was taken around and introduced or reintroduced to various members of the systems development group, and then delivered to my new manager's doorstep. Scott's lair was located midway along a corridor of identical offices, but it stood out from the others because it was dim. Its occupant had unscrewed the fluorescent bulbs in the ceiling, substituting a stylish, high-tech halogen lamp on his desk and a Tiffany-shaded living room lamp on the credenza. An Indian mask hung on one wall—Tlingit or Haida, I guessed—across from some framed underwater photos. The room smelled of stale cigarette smoke.

Scott himself stood out from the other denizens of software development in that he seemed dazzlingly overdressed: suit pants with a sharp crease, business shirt, tie, cufflinks, shoes polished to a glossy shine. At the time, I jumped to the conclusion that he must have been in costume for a presentation to senior management, but I soon found out that it was his everyday attire. He seemed to be in his mid-30s, average build, fit, with thick, longish brown hair, brown eyes, and a space between his front teeth. He was handsome, but not my type.

I sat down in the chair opposite his desk with my left hand on my knee to display my wedding ring. He opened the credenza and took out a notepad. Before he closed the door I spotted a pack of cigarettes and a half-full bottle of vodka.

We regarded each other in silence for a moment. Eventually he bared his teeth in a sort of smile, though his eyes remained unfriendly.

"So…you're our new scapegoat," he said.

It was an inauspicious beginning, but things did indeed gradually get sorted out. After Scott ignored me for a couple of weeks, hoping I'd go away, Dave (the managing director) intervened. Though I would continue to be responsible for testing the sales systems, he reassigned me to report to Nick the project manager, and he told Scott bluntly to change his attitude.

Scott managed the development of three sales applications: a content management database for the sales force, a database of marketing analytics, and an order fulfillment system. As an entry-level developer several years earlier, he had designed and built all three based upon requirements given to him by a friend in the marketing department. The applications had been very successful, and the business sponsor had been promoted to vice president of sales and marketing. Scott had been promoted, too. Each application now employed its own lead developer and a couple of junior developers.

However, Scott was in way over his head. He had been an excellent developer, but during his ascent to the ED position, he never had the time or inclination to learn about software engineering or project management. The high rate of failures and defects in his systems was the result not of shoddy code, but of chaotic development processes. His stellar reputation was based upon the fact that he would do anything to please his user community, including developing a unique version of the application for a single individual and personally installing it on that user's computer.

It didn't take long for me to realize that Scott knew he had crawled out on a dangerously weak limb and was worried that it would break underneath him. If he fell from his lofty ED perch, his wealthy, prominent family who had been disgusted by his decision to play around with computers rather than go to law school would be able to gloat. Also, everyone he worked with was aware that he drank enough beer at lunch and vodka at his desk to qualify as a borderline alcoholic.

Fundamentally, I liked Scott. I thought he was smart, hardworking, creative, and honest. Nick encouraged me to address the process issues plaguing the sales system. But I couldn't get through the fortress of Scott's defenses with my test strategy or defect metrics, and my patience finally wore out. One day when he came back woozy after lunch, I confronted him.

"Scott, I wish I could convince you that we're both on the same side," I told him. "I'm not here to spy on you for Dave, or criticize you, or undermine you. I'm supposed to be making you and your team look good. Like a coach, or an editor. I really do want to help."

Perhaps Scott sensed that I was on the verge of quitting and worried about Dave's reaction, or perhaps he felt he had nothing to lose by changing course. Whatever the reason, after that day we were no longer adversaries and instead became colleagues.

Ironically, I was now in over my head, too. I knew how to create, execute, and report on tests—but the software engineering and project management process improvements demanded knowledge I did not already possess. I bought books, and my fourth-grade daughter and I studied together in the evening. Nick supported my training requests and Dave approved the budget. My husband put in extra hours for housework and child care while I took classes and attended conferences.

Over the next few months we made slow but noticeable progress. Working closely with the eight sales systems developers, Scott and I tackled configuration management, version control, change management, and defect tracking methods. It was a struggle, but there were many moments of humor in between the fights, and we grew to respect each other's judgment. I felt like a physical therapist whose patient finally starts doing the necessary exercises on his own, and the improvements showed in the declining defect rates. Our most contentious episodes involved the concepts of code freeze and feature freeze. Nick was very helpful in my crusade against scope creep: he was firm and unflappable, and had the kind of mature perspective on day-to-day crises that probably comes from surviving in an actual combat zone.

Other ED development managers began to take an interest. I was asked to help hire and train testers for their systems. Within a three-month period, Irene took on the financial systems (accounts payable, accounts receivable, billing, cash management), Randall joined the operations team (editorial, production, internal reporting, legal, HR), and Felipe signed on to the web development juggernaut. Louise the project manager was reassigned from HR to financials, and Irene reported to her. Randall reported to Barbara, Felipe reported to Caitlin, and I continued to report to Nick. Though on the organization chart the PMs and testers were all dispersed among development groups supporting different lines of business, in practice, Barbara was team captain of the PMs and I became team captain of the testers.

It was an interesting and enjoyable time. All the new testers brought in fresh ideas and approaches, and since both Irene and Felipe came from well-known software vendors their expectations helped raise the bar for standards across the entire group. Dave permitted every development team to establish its own practices, so there were no serious turf battles.

Our office building fostered a sense of community. There was a cafeteria—its food wasn't great, but it provided a neutral and comfortable place to get together for purposes ranging from impromptu discussions with developers to inter-team Scrabble tournaments. The fitness center in the basement enabled us to sweat out stress and exchange a few words with end users. The library was a welcome sanctuary from the hubbub around the cubicles for anyone who needed peace and quiet to read, write, or think. Another popular hideout was a vast, empty two-story storage space on the ground floor that had once housed a bank branch. Though it lay behind a heavy locked door, everyone knew the security code for the buttons—as well as the unwritten code about not interrupting or disclosing anything illicit that went on in there.

Yes, things were going well, productivity and morale were high…until Scott's girlfriend broke up with him.

Suddenly, Scott was morose and irritable, and began taking longer liquid lunches. He and I had never talked about our personal lives much, so I heard the news from Randall, who had become Scott's workout buddy at the fitness center. The lead developers on the sales applications complained to me that Scott had begun radically revising their software, as if by immersing himself in coding again he could distract himself from his troubles.

One Thursday evening, the entire systems development group was invited to a party at Windows on the World celebrating a major release of Pharaoh's public website. It was fun, and the sunset view of the harbor was spectacular, but I had to leave while the party was in full swing because I needed to get home and relieve my babysitter.

The following day Scott was absent, our cubicle area was eerily quiet, and everyone in our group seemed tired, cranky, and hunkered down. Assuming that the average blood-alcohol level was still in the hangover zone, I went about my business and cleaned out my email folders.

But on Monday Scott's office was empty—as in vacant, cleaned out, devoid of all personal possessions. Even the fluorescent bulbs overhead were back on.

I found Anupam, the lead developer for the marketing analytics application, and asked him what happened. He shook his head, drew his finger across his throat, shrugged, and resumed typing.

My search for Nick brought me to the cafeteria, where he and Caitlin were finishing their breakfast. Without waiting to be invited I pulled up a chair.

"Hi there! Do either of you have any idea—"

"Would this be about Scott's untimely departure?" Nick inquired.

"Yes, it would."

Caitlin laughed. "You missed quite a scene at the party."

"Scott got totally shitfaced," Nick said. "He grabbed Dave in a headlock and started insulting him."

"Well, I suppose physically attacking your boss could be grounds for termination," I said. "Did Scott complain about Dave's management?"

Caitlin laughed louder. "Not quite. He called Dave a pansy and said his only qualification for his current job was the fact that he's having an affair with Bob Wheeler."

"Wheeler? The head of the Latin American region? But he's married, and so is Dave."

Caitlin stopped laughing. She and Nick exchanged a world-weary glance, and then both of them looked at me pityingly.

I blushed, feeling like a kid who has been invited to sit at the grownups' table and then knocks over a burning candle.

"But this…this is incredible," I stammered.

"It gets better!" Nick said brightly. "Scott wouldn't let go, and Dave started to pass out, so Paul stepped up and punched him hard enough that he sailed backward into a table. Scott crawled away under his own power, but I hear he broke a few ribs. Dave's neck is sprained."

"Wow. And I thought I was having an exciting evening helping my daughter glue pictures onto poster board for her science project."

It was pretty hard to focus that day. Nick advised me to just keep on doing what I had been doing until the smoke cleared. I met with Anupam and the two other lead developers on the sales systems for a routine status update. Late in the afternoon, I received a call from Dave's chief of staff summoning me to his office at once.

The corner office Dave occupied was three times as large as any ED's office. I had never entered it before, and it seemed like a long way from the door past the couch and conference table to the chairs in front of his desk. A quick scan of the room turned up no family pictures or personal decorations except for a framed photo of a beagle. At Dave's gesture I sat down and squinted through the afternoon sunlight that shone directly into my eyes.

Dave was a small man in a large leather executive chair, and he was wearing an orthopedic collar around his neck. He had slender hands, delicate features, and fine blond hair gelled into a fixed flat plate. I had spoken with him a few times, but we had never engaged in a conversation of any length or substance. Now when he spoke to me his voice was so low and mild that I needed to lean forward to hear his words.

"You know, software testing is considered an overhead cost," he began with a pleasant smile. "Sometimes, it's hard to demonstrate the value of it to the business. Quality assurance initiatives are always the first to go during budget cuts."

"I understand," I said. In fact, I was thoroughly confused because his words and his facial expression seemed contradictory.

Based upon these preliminary remarks, I assumed I was about to be laid off. However, the opposite happened: a promotion. Dave informed me that he wanted me to lead an official QA group. I would report directly to him. The testers would report 50% to their ED development managers and 50% to me.

In other organizational changes, Anupam the marketing analytics developer would replace Scott as development manager for the sales systems. A new project manager and a replacement tester for the sales systems would be hired. Following the same model as the QA group, Barbara was being promoted to lead a new Project Management Office.

The PMs would report 50% to their ED development managers and 50% to her. Dave expected Barbara and me to collaborate in implementing process improvements for project management and software engineering across the group.

As Dave described my new role, I felt excited and honored but also a bit apprehensive. Reporting to him, I sensed, would be very different from reporting to Nick. Dave had no background in software engineering whatsoever. He was an MBA whose involvement as a "power user" of the internal financial reporting systems had persuaded the chief information officer that he would do a good job supervising the software development. At the ED development manager level he had surpassed his peers in delivering functionality on time and in controlling costs—but also in staff turnover.

It was a big shake-up. The development managers were reluctant to share the supervision of their testers and PMs with another manager. Our former peers felt awkward about reporting to Barbara and me. We were concerned about the matrix reporting relationship, and wondered how we would negotiate with the development managers about setting the PMs' and testers' priorities.

Among the new obligations Barbara and I acquired was attending Dave's biweekly status meetings for his direct reports. Before our first appearance, Dave asked each of us to prepare a presentation about our objectives and strategies. My anxiety over this debut performance reached the point where I needed to carry around a paper bag to breathe into when I started feeling dizzy. I knew exactly what I wanted to say, and I rehearsed it thoroughly with my family's patient coaching, but the idea of trying to persuade an entire group of development managers at once gave me terrible stage fright.

At the status meeting, I sat down at the conference table for the first time with EDs I knew only by reputation. In addition to Dave, his chief of staff, Barbara, and Anupam, there were four new colleagues I would soon be dealing with on a daily basis.

The ED for the financial systems, Mark, was a loose-limbed, easygoing, cheerful VB developer and RUP aficionado. At 35, he looked 10 years younger. He had married his high school sweetheart immediately after college, and they had already produced three kids. Outside of work, his favorite pastime was leading his son's Boy Scout troop. He could always be counted upon to make generous contributions to whatever charity anyone was collecting for.

Glowering beside him was Paul, the ED for web development and the hulk who had broken Scott's ribs. A burly, overweight, but muscular powder keg of simmering resentment, he lived alone inside a den of electronic musical instruments and disassembled computers. In a brief hiatus from writing C++ code he had accidentally fathered an illegitimate child whose mother frequently sent him subpoenas. His spare time was devoted to riding his Harley in Adirondack Park. He was also the group's senior drug dealer.

Across the table sat Zvi, ED for the operations systems. Zvi was in his early 50s and had been around since Pharaoh's mainframe days. He was an Orthodox Jew who always dressed in a shapeless black suit and threadbare white open-collared shirt. He wore thick wire-rimmed glasses that made his eyes seem unnaturally large. As far as anyone knew, Zvi did not have any extracurricular hobbies because he lived with his wife and six children in Rockland County and had a two-hour commute each way. Zvi could sit absolutely still for an extraordinarily long time, and he was a very attentive listener. People from all the development teams who had difficult technical and political problems dropped by Zvi's office to ask his advice.

The fourth person I was formally introduced to that morning was Carol Chu. Unlike other managers who were referred to simply by their first names, everyone always said "Carol Chu" when talking about the ED for database development. Carol stood 4 feet 8 inches tall in her running shoes, and she was nearly always smiling. Born and raised in Shanghai, she had earned a Ph.D. in mathematics at Cal Tech. Her husband was a professor of physics and their 10-year-old son was a chess champion. It was said of her that within the terabytes of data stored on Pharaoh's servers, she knew the location of every pointer in every index at all times. Although she frequently sent email messages between 2:00 and 5:00 a.m., she treated her staff kindly, like a large extended family, and she never missed an opportunity to celebrate their birthdays.

Following some chitchat about the Mets' dismal performance and the new falafel restaurant that had opened down the block, Dave called the meeting to order. He welcomed Anupam, Barbara, and me to the team, then his chief of staff distributed the agenda. It was Dave's first day without the orthopedic collar, and he made a lame joke about not sticking his neck out too far.

The first item on the agenda was a team realignment. Dave said he wanted Li, the lead developer on the contact management database, to switch roles with Rachel, the lead developer on the HR system.

"But we're just a few weeks away from a major rollout," Anupam protested. "Li has been working on this release for almost six months."

"Rachel also," Zvi said. "It's her first release since I promoted her. She's very excited and proud of her work. She'll be unhappy if she has to move now."

"But that's exactly my point," Dave said. "We don't want any of our developers to get too personally attached to their code or to a particular user community. This development group is a team, and I want every player to be prepared to rotate positions as I see fit."

In the silence that followed this speech, I glanced around the table, and from the body language I got the feeling that Dave the MD was not well liked by the EDs who reported to him.

My presentation went fine, though in truth it seemed nobody was paying very close attention. Afterward, there were a few polite questions, and Dave smiled at me, so I counted it a success and breathed easier.

But the job turned out to be much harder than I anticipated. If my process engineering efforts with Scott and the sales systems team had made me feel like a physical therapist, now I felt more like a community organizer. Apart from paying my salary, Dave provided very little support to me—and no incentives or penalties for the EDs to cooperate with me in achieving the QA goals. He evidently expected me to negotiate with each team and come up with standards and procedures that everyone could agree upon.

It was slow going, particularly when the EDs used the discussions to enact their turf battles. The testers who reported to me had their own agendas and aspirations. Yet we inched forward. We decided it was not feasible for all applications to use the same documents or follow the same methodology. In the end, we settled upon templates and checklists with mandatory and optional components for requirements definition, test planning, test execution, test results reporting, defect tracking, change control, version control, and configuration management.

Barbara was in a similar situation with her Project Management Office. In some respects, she had more clout because Dave's boss, the CIO, and the influential business sponsors of our software wanted more insight into our group's development activities. In essence, they hoped to better understand how and where and why their money was being spent. Her first step was the introduction of a mandatory Scope Document for all new projects, along with a review process that determined funding, resourcing, and scheduling. When that innovation proved successful, it was followed by templates and checklists for the Work Breakdown Structure, Gantt Chart, Responsibility Matrix, Risk Matrix, Integrated Project Plan, and Closing Report.

After almost a year, Anupam, Barbara, and I were all promoted. Anupam became an ED, and Barbara and I rose to the rank of director. I got stock options and an interior office with a door.

Barbara and I celebrated with a shopping spree. It was the beginning of the holiday season, and I had discovered that our office building had a basement-level passage into the subway that continued to the underground concourse of the World Trade Center. We liked the WTC mall because its low ceilings gave it a cozy atmosphere. It offered a wide range of stores, from the mundane (shoe repair, photo processing, pharmacy) to the glamorous (clothing, electronics, jewelry). Best of all, it was a place to stroll around in bad weather. I bought a cocktail dress, Barbara bought some fancy boots, and we both bought necklaces for our daughters.

The economy was booming. Pharaoh's business was expanding rapidly. In mid-February, after the bonus checks had been handed out, Dave announced that to keep up with the demand for new functionality in our software, we would begin outsourcing maintenance. The plan envisioned that within a year, a third of our group's total headcount would comprise developers and testers who were employed by a vendor. Initially, these outsourced resources would be located here in our Pharaoh headquarters building, but eventually, they might be located at the vendor's facility elsewhere in the United States or offshore. No Pharaoh employees would lose their jobs.

There followed an intense round of vendor presentations, strategic sourcing meetings, and briefings by consultants. It seemed as though many of the important decisions were being made by procurement specialists and lawyers who knew very little about software engineering. Anupam lobbied heavily for an Indian firm, but in the end our CIO selected Quogue Consulting based upon reviews in Gartner and Forrester reports and conversations with people in his own professional network.

A new face appeared at Dave's biweekly direct reports meeting. Frank, the service delivery manager for Quogue, was a weather-beaten man in his 40s with a jet black brush crew cut and a tic in his jaw. His forearms, biceps, and chest had the overinflated look of a serious weightlifter. During the meeting, he sat hunched over, taut like a coiled spring. We learned that Frank had been with Quogue for five years. Prior to that, he had served in the Navy, had worked as an operations manager on a rubber plantation in Malaysia, and had supervised the staff aboard a cruise ship. When the meeting adjourned, and we stood to go, I saw that around his neck he wore a medallion in the shape of a gargoyle.

On our way out he intercepted Barbara and me.

"Ladies." He was smiling, but his tone seemed more appropriate for a sailor in a brothel than a gentleman at a reception.

"Welcome," I said. "We look forward to working with you."

"I wanted to tell you that on my last engagement my team achieved CMM Level 3. I'd be glad to share our lessons learned with you if you're interested."

The arrogance and condescension in his voice irked me, but Barbara had the opposite reaction.

"That's great! Thank you. I'm sure we can learn a lot from your experience," she beamed.

The Quogue invasion commenced right away. My staff testers were redeployed to the applications with the largest product backlog of new functionality, while outsourced resources were brought in for changes to the more stable legacy systems. My tester for the sales systems had quit to go back to school, and Frank replaced her with Rafiq. Alex became the tester for the accounts payable and accounts receivable systems. Natalya joined the production systems team.

My involvement in the hiring process for these testers was: zero. The EDs and lead developers were likewise excluded from the recruitment of Quogue programmers. Following the "staff augmentation" model, Frank wanted us to provide job specifications and let him deliver warm bodies. He also insisted on managing the outsourced resources' workflow, so in the beginning, he attended all development team meetings and got copies of all emails regarding tasks to which his people were assigned. Partly this was because Quogue had its own internal tracking procedures, but it also seemed that he was looking for opportunities to point out our group's weaknesses to Dave so that he could make a sales pitch on how he could do things better and thereby expand Quogue's engagement. In particular, the lead developers considered Frank a nuisance, and they resented his obstructive behavior as gatekeeper when they were trying to integrate the outsourced resources into their projects and teams.

Meanwhile, Pharaoh's business continued growing. Soon it became evident that the data architecture implemented when the company was one-third its present size no longer adequately supported its operations and would seriously undermine future expansion. As much as everyone hated the idea of IT root canal surgery, we were compelled to redesign the central data warehouse and modify all the upstream and downstream systems. Just thinking about it made all the EDs break into a sweat. Our first requirements gathering and test planning meetings featured mood swings from hysteria to despair, followed by a mass updating of resumes.

On the bright side, it was an opportunity for me to lead a very large, mission-critical, cross-functional testing project, and I was excited about the challenge. To ensure that the project management approach and the testing strategy aligned with the Quogue internal processes, Barbara and I began meeting regularly with Natalya and coordinating our teams' efforts.

Our most memorable meeting took place at lunchtime on a beautiful day in July—one of those rare summer days in New York when the humidity is low, the temperature is mild, the air is clean, and an ocean breeze reminds everyone that the city is a seaport. Unable to bear the thought of staying indoors, we got some food to go from the cafeteria and ate it by the sculpture in the World Trade Center plaza.

Natalya was slightly older than Barbara and I, perhaps in her early 40s. She had two children, a daughter who was a freshman in high school and a son in seventh grade. She was short and stocky, with a broad face, prominent eyes, and curly auburn hair. Originally from the Ukraine, she spoke heavily accented but fluent English. She lived with her family in Brooklyn and was in the process of buying a house on Staten Island. Her automated regression tests were the most compact and effective I'd ever seen.

Under the influence of the fine weather, we disposed of our business matters quickly and moved on to personal topics. We chatted about our daughters, our work/life balance or lack thereof, our difficulties with the public schools. Eventually I asked Natalya why she had left the Ukraine.

"I am from Chernobyl," she replied.

It took a moment for the implications of this fact to sink in.

"Were you evacuated?" Barbara asked.

"After a while. For many days we stayed. The government pretended nothing had happened. We found out the truth from the BBC radio. We left with one suitcase each and did not return."

"That must have been dreadful," I said. "And your health…?"

"So far so good. Many of our old neighbors have grown cancers. I do not care so much for myself, but I worry always about my children."

Soberly we pondered the helplessness of mothers in the face of the world's evils.

All of a sudden Natalya grinned and pointed at a stage on the west side of the plaza. "Oh, look! There is going to be a band now!"

At lunchtime in the summer, the World Trade Center often presented a band: one day for jazz, one for rock, one for oldies, one for country. As a tall woman in a cowboy hat shouldered her electric guitar and strolled up to the microphone, I surmised today was country. Sure enough, soon she was belting out a rousing, twangy anthem accompanied by a bass player, keyboardist, and drummer. In front of the stage a man in a turban, an Asian woman, two Latino teenagers, and an elderly white couple began to dance. Others followed—some tentatively, some zestfully—but all happily.

"I like the music," Natalya said. "I have never heard this kind before."

"Usually I'm more of a jazz person," I said, "but it's really catchy."

"It makes me nervous," Barbara said.

"Why?" Natalya asked.

"Well, my people are from North Carolina, and when we heard this kind of music we used to cross to the other side of the road as a precaution."

"Why?" Natalya asked again.

"Because..." The music got louder. "Oh, I'll explain later."

The next song was about a woman who gets fed up with her life, packs her bags, stuffs them in the trunk of her car, and drives off down the open road fearlessly. It was irresistible, and together the three of us joined in the dancing.

After Labor Day, when the back-to-school mood had begun to settle in, and the Quogue outsourced resources were productively contributing to their teams' projects, and the database reengineering initiative was ticking off milestones on their project plan, the Pharaoh chief operations officer announced a large-scale simultaneous musical-chairs internal move that affected every department except IT. As the company expanded, employees had been doubling up inside offices and carving workspaces out of every spare nook and cranny. The Facilities manager hoped to address this problem by reshuffling everyone into smaller but more ergonomic quarters. The Quogue people, who had been scattered at random throughout the building, were to be housed inside the old bank branch storage space. The IT group was being spared because the architect had taken one look at our electricity and cabling requirements and pronounced us Not Worth The Trouble, but nonetheless, we realized that the chaos among our end users would have a destabilizing effect on our project plans.

At Dave's status meeting immediately following the move, all the EDs reported delays and problems on their projects. However, two weeks later the situation remained unsatisfactory. The metrics I had gathered and developers I had questioned indicated that the Quogue outsourced resources were responsible for most of the issues.

"There has been some disruption," Frank agreed cheerfully. "But the new space is much quieter. It has larger desks and better chairs. From where I sit I can see everyone and keep track of what they are doing. We're going through a period of adjustment, and I expect we'll be back on course soon."

This confident prediction unfortunately proved overly optimistic. Deadlines were missed. Defect rates soared. The Quogue people, formerly admired for their exemplary attendance records, called in sick much more often. Frank stared at his shoes when he walked around the hallways.

Since the initiation of the project, the database reengineering status meeting had been held every Wednesday afternoon in our group's largest conference room. Representatives from all the upstream and downstream application teams summarized their progress and described any issues they had encountered. The database developers discussed changes they were incorporating in the next version they planned to install on the QA server. Testers and project managers also attended the meeting to stay informed. As a time commitment, it was long, boring, and necessary.

Six weeks after the big move, during this Wednesday meeting, Natalya distributed some documents that were covered with dark smudges. As it happened, at the end of the meeting everyone else bolted, and she and I were left alone at the conference table while we packed up.

Casually, I pointed out the smudges on her papers.

"Does the printer in your new space need maintenance?" I asked.

"No, it is the soot."

"What soot?"

She clapped her hand over her mouth and looked horrified. Shaking her head, acting disoriented, she started to rise from her chair.

"Nothing. It is nothing," she said vehemently.

"No, wait. What soot? What's the matter? Why are you upset?"

To my astonishment she sank back into her seat, covered her face with her hands, and began weeping.

And so the story came out. The ancient HVAC system in the bank branch area had not been cleaned before the new office furniture was installed. When it was finally turned on, after everyone had moved in, decades of accumulated gunk started raining down. Every morning, the Quogue people needed to spend at least half an hour cleaning a thick layer of soot off their desks, monitors, and chairs. By the end of the day, the soot had built up again. Papers had to be kept inside drawers.

"Everyone is coughing," Natalya sobbed. "Vikram's asthma is very bad, and Olga has bronchitis."

"How could Facilities get away with this?" I said. "It must be an OSHA violation."

"What is OSHA?"

I gave her a brief overview of the Occupational Safety and Health Administration, American labor law, and worker protection rights. She seemed skeptical.

"These principles are very nice, but they apply only to citizens," she informed me.

"That's not true. Where did you get that idea? Look, we can fix this. I'll talk to Dave and we'll set up a meeting with Facilities."

"No, no, please don't!" she wailed. "I'll lose my job. I'll have to pay back $50,000. We just bought our house...."

"Natalya, what are you talking about?" Listening to her fearful visions, I wondered whether the nuclear power plant accident had made her paranoid.

But no: it turned out she had good reason to be afraid. She explained that the Quogue employment contract was based on a two-year "probation." If an employee were terminated during that period, he or she would be obliged to repay the entire amount of wages received to date. Immigrants also risked the loss of their Green Card sponsor and possibly deportation. Frank had forbidden the Quogue people to complain about their new workspace, and had made it clear that anyone who did would be fired.

When Natalya finished speaking she leaned back in her chair, exhausted. Her eyes were dry and she gazed at me with resignation. Never before had I experienced the emotional weight of an adult putting her fate in my hands.

"OK," I said. "I get it. This conversation never happened. But we are going to fix the problem."

I went back to my office, shut the door, and looked for some music to help me think. In my pile of CDs I found one I'd bought recently by the country music band we had heard on the World Trade Center plaza. To the accompaniment of their rousing songs, I called Barbara.

"Have you ever visited the bank space since Quogue moved in?" I asked her.

"No, their people come to us for meetings. It's always been that way, even before the move. Why?"

"Well, it occurred to me maybe the reason they've got adjustment problems in the new space is that they never had a housewarming party."

She laughed. "I didn't know you were so superstitious."

"I thought it might be a nice team-building gesture to surprise them with some breakfast goodies tomorrow morning. You want to join the party?"

"Sure, what can I bring?"

At 8:00 a.m. we arrived outside the locked door bearing doughnuts, bagels, croissants, juice, and a camera. I punched in the security code, but it no longer worked.

"That's odd," Barbara said. "Did you get an email about changing the code?"

At that moment, Rafiq came up behind us and let us in. He looked pleased to see us at first, then apprehensive.

We strolled along a short hallway into an open area surrounding a copy machine and set our boxes and cartons down on top of a filing cabinet.

"Good morning Quoggies!" I called out. "Breakfast is served!"

Heads popped up above cubicle walls.

"Holy Mother of God," Barbara gasped. "It's filthy in here!"

The soot was thick enough to write a person's name across the desks and cabinets. Rolls of paper towels stood sentry at each cluster of cubicles. Many of the Quogue people wore black sweaters and shawls to protect their clothes, and hats or scarves on their heads. A fine black snow wafted down from the HVAC vents overhead.

"Looks like some problem with the ventilation," I observed.

Barbara brushed soot off her yellow silk shirt. "Where's that camera?"

Frank came bounding out of his glass-walled office and tried to stand in front of the camera.

"Ladies! Nice of you to visit. Thanks for the food."

Barbara stepped around him and began taking pictures. I noticed that the vent inside his office was covered with a makeshift cheesecloth filter.

"What does Facilities have to say about this air-quality situation?" I asked him.

"They're working on it. They're looking for a special kind of contractor to come in and clean the ducts."

"Have you spoken to Dave about it?"

"Yeah, he told me to keep following up with Facilities." He shrugged. "I've seen worse."

"I can imagine."

The pictures did not do justice to the scene, so Barbara and I took it upon ourselves to spread the word. We spoke to every development manager and lead developer who had outsourced resources on their team, and most of them made the time to visit the Quogue workspace. I put an item on the agenda for Dave's next status meeting. I was confident he would recognize the urgency of the problem, and I was well prepared for the discussion with several alternative suggestions.

The initial results were disappointing, to say the least.

"Dave, I believe there is a relationship between the air-quality issues in the Quogue workspace and the decline in key performance indicators for the engagement," I said when it was my turn to speak. "I'd like to recommend that we escalate the—"

"What do you think?" Dave asked Frank.

"I don't really see a connection," Frank said, "although it would be nice to get those ducts cleaned."

"This is a matter for Facilities," Dave told me. "Frank is handling it."

"I understand, and I know he has been diligent, but it seems—"

Dave raised his finger to cut me off.

"In the future," he said sternly, "I would like you to remember that your quality assurance role is limited to software."

I looked around the table for support and encountered a wall of blank faces. In my imagination I heard a sickening thump as my career hit the rocks.

After the meeting, I was on my way to the ladies' room to sulk when Mark grabbed my arm.

"Hang in there," he said. "This was only Round One."

Behind him, Zvi nodded in agreement.

Round Two consisted of a four-pronged under-the-radar publicity campaign. Following Barbara's script, the project managers for all applications that employed Quogue outsourced resources arranged meetings with their business sponsors and described the negative effect the environmental problem was having on the development process. Nick, whose PM portfolio included the legal systems, was dispatched on a mission to review the Quogue contract and to inquire about whether OSHA rules covered vendor employees working on Pharaoh property. Carol invited the CIO to a birthday party in her group, then lured him away for a glimpse of the Quogue workspace. On the pretext of acquiring a Ping-Pong table for the fitness center, Mark visited the Facilities manager and questioned him about the plan to clean the ducts.

Dave was not pleased to see the air-quality item on the agenda again for his next status meeting. This time it was Mark who had added it, so I was out of the line of fire.

"I'm not sure why we're still talking about this," Frank said. "Many of the adjustment issues are being resolved, and the engagement metrics have improved."

He had a point. Relieved that someone was finally paying attention to their plight, the Quogue people had recovered some of their earlier commitment to Pharaoh projects. Unfortunately, this did not help their cause.

"We're still talking about it because it is a disgrace," Mark retorted.

Dave told Frank that he was excused from the meeting. After Frank had gone, he faced Mark angrily.

"The moral context you're projecting on this situation is out of scope," he said. "Facilities has indicated that if we want the ducts cleaned we have to pay for it, and it is not in our budget."

"We should not force anyone to work in such an unhealthy environment," Mark said.

"Who's forcing them?" Paul said. "It's a good steady job. If they don't like it they can leave."

"They can't leave," I said. "They have no choice. They're like indentured servants."

"Everyone has a choice," Paul growled. "We make our choices and we live with the consequences."

"How long is the Quogue contract?" Anupam asked. "If we outsource to India instead, we won't have to worry about American laws and standards."

Zvi reached out his hands, palms up. "It was a mistake. The architect, the Facilities manager…they forgot, we forgot…who knows; it's done. It needs to be fixed. Let's get all the parties together and figure out a solution, and then we'll see who pays."

"Zvi is correct." Carol Chu was not smiling. "But the systems development budget should not pay. Our CIO should push back."

"Believe me, our CIO is not going to push back." Dave sighed. "Look, we're dealing with contingent labor here. We brought them in to reduce costs. It's not like this is a meatpacking plant."

Being a novice in an ongoing tournament of management politics, I assumed we eco-crusaders were checkmated. Carol Chu assured me that the game was not over yet. The sooty ducts in the Quogue workspace had become hot gossip throughout Pharaoh headquarters. A groundswell of popular sympathy for our outsourced resources was causing ripples in high places.

The participants in Round Three were senior executives attending an off-site strategic planning meeting: the chief operating officer, the chief information officer, and the general counsel. Whether they were motivated by a sense of justice or by a fear of contract disputes and embarrassing leaks to the media, they decided that the problem was serious enough to warrant immediate attention. As soon as they returned from their retreat, the COO replaced the Facilities manager and hired a contracting firm that specialized in HVAC systems. The general counsel opened negotiations with the architect in charge of the renovation over liability for the duct cleaning costs. The CIO directed a writer from corporate communications to draft an article for the weekly company intranet bulletin honoring Dave for his humanistic principles and his ability to combine fiscal responsibility with a concern for all his workers' health and welfare.

Quogue Consulting's management expressed its displeasure with Frank's behavior during this episode by summoning him to their headquarters for several days of interrogation, penance, and remedial training.

During Frank's absence, I got an email from Rafiq requesting that I come to the Quogue workspace to look at some test results on his computer.

The former bank branch space was now immaculate. On two consecutive weekends, the contractors had scrubbed out the decades' accumulation of filth. No soot was falling from the vents. Morning sunshine gleamed off surfaces that were as clean as the night before. The Quogue people had shed their protective layers of dark clothing.

It turned out that the test results were a ruse, and what awaited me was a kind of surprise party. With their boss away, the developers and testers had assembled around the copy machine. Rafiq led me over to the group. Shyly, Natalya handed me an envelope containing a card. On the front it said, "Thank You." On the inside everyone had signed their name. Later, when I showed the card to my unimpressed adolescent daughter, I tried to explain to her that the most meaningful achievements of one's career can't always be articulated on a resume.

And so the sick part of our building was healed. Life went back to normal for both Pharaoh employees and Quogue outsourced resources. We completed the database reengineering project—not on time, nor within budget, but the business was satisfied with the result, and we felt we had laid a solid technological foundation for the future.

Yet the future for our building and our people was to be anything but solid and normal. On September 11, 2001, the terrorist attacks on the World Trade Center dropped fragments of airplanes and human bodies on our roof and enveloped our neighborhood in a toxic cloud.

For the next week, all was chaos and confusion, and nobody did much work. The following week, we were back in business at an IT disaster recovery site across the Hudson River in Jersey City.

From our conference room window, we could see the burning rubble and a corner of our building. Our group was set up in a huge open area, like a trading floor but with fewer screens per workstation. None of our employees had been killed in the attack, but everyone knew someone who had lost someone. Our new Facilities manager, a healthy 43-year-old, had died suddenly of a heart attack September 15 while inspecting the damage to our building.

During that time, all of us were not quite sane.

At Dave's first status meeting, we watched the hellish smoke rise from the pit while we discussed absence codes for the PMO's project tracking database.

"Should we code last week as sick days?" Frank asked.

"I think personal days makes more sense," Carol Chu replied.

"But then they'll be deducted from each employee's reserve," Barbara pointed out.

"The HR system and the timesheet system will be affected," I said.

"Isn't there a category for absences outside your control, like snow days?" Zvi proposed.

"What about overtime?" Paul asked.

"Speaking of overtime," Mark said, "I want to make sure that Natalya gets some recognition for what she's doing."

"We're *all* doing more than is humanly possible," Dave snapped.

"That's true," Zvi said, "but Natalya is running a hotel. She has eight developers sleeping on her floor—ours and Quogue's."

"Why?" Frank asked.

"The developers live downwind in Brooklyn," Mark explained. "Her house is on Staten Island. It's upwind of the smoke."

"We've never tracked overtime," Dave said, "and we're not going to start now."

A roar and a series of loud crashes interrupted our debate. Due to our twitchy reflexes, the entire management team around the conference table leaped up to investigate. We discovered that in the lounge area a man was assaulting a vending machine.

It was Dominic, a Java developer on the accounts payable system. Bald, round-faced, middle-aged, and built like a wrestler, in a frenzy of rage he was smashing the machine with a metal folding chair and throwing in a few vicious kicks for good measure.

"Give me my fucking money back! I want a candy bar!" he howled.

Mark shook his head sadly.

"Poor Dominic. His uncle is a firefighter. He told me that since last week he's gone to seven funerals."

The other people who had been in or near the lounge had withdrawn, forming a semicircle at a safe distance.

Dominic wheeled around and glared at them.

"It ate my last dollar bill!"

The bystanders took a step backward, afraid that he would hurl the chair in their direction.

"I'll call Security," Barbara said.

"No, don't," said Paul. "He's got enough problems already."

"Let me see what I can do," Mark said.

But before Mark could move, Natalya emerged from the cluster of people and calmly walked right up to Dominic.

"*I'M SO ANGRY*!" he shouted at her in a tone that made me flinch.

But not her. She reached out and touched his cheek.

"Yes," she said. "Of course you're angry. It's not fair."

It was like popping a blister. Immediately Dominic's fury began to evaporate. He put down the chair. After a moment he glanced around and seemed startled by the mayhem he had created.

"Come," she said.

She led him to the couch in the lounge and sat down next to him, putting her arm around his shoulder. He rested his elbows on his knees and buried his face in his hands, a picture of devastation.

That evening I ran into Natalya at the elevator when we were both leaving. As we waited, we compared notes about how our kids were coping. We agreed that teenagers were unlikely to disclose their feelings to their parents and needed careful observation.

"You know, I've been meaning to ask you something," I said. "How does this disaster compare with the Chernobyl accident?"

"Oh, they are completely different." She smiled ruefully and shook her head. "In Chernobyl, the government pretended everything was fine, and the news told us nothing. We had no idea what was going on. Here the news tells you everything. I am very glad to be living in a country where the government does not lie to the people."

We moved back into our office building at the end of October. Pharaoh was one of the first major businesses to resume operations within the military security zone. The same contracting firm that had cleaned the HVAC ducts in the Quogue work area was hired to do a much bigger job of scrubbing, decontaminating, and filtering. Despite the acrid odor of burning flesh and other unknown elements that gagged us every time we stepped outside, the air in our neighborhood was declared safe by the EPA.

Inevitably, we moved on. A year later, I left Pharaoh to become a consultant and teacher. Anupam finally succeeded in convincing senior IT management that outsourcing offshore was a good idea. When Quogue Consulting's contract expired, an Indian firm took over their projects and moved the jobs to Bangalore. The engagement grew rapidly, and this time there were many layoffs among Pharaoh employees.

Most of my former colleagues continued their careers in publishing and financial services IT. Scott moved to Australia and started a business organizing scuba diving trips to the Great Barrier Reef. After his divorce, Dave took a very senior job at a major consulting company advising its clients on how to cut costs by moving work offshore.

Barbara became the PMO director at a company that designs and manufactures several high-end brands of clothing.

Our office building no longer exists. Having survived terrorism, it fell victim to the Manhattan real estate market. It has been demolished, and in its place are now luxury condos.

The one person I'm sorry to have lost touch with is Natalya. I think of her often, especially when the curriculum in the business school classes I teach focuses on teamwork. I hope one day some social networking website will help us reconnect. I want to know how she and her family are doing. I'd also like to ask her that elevator question again and find out whether she still has the same faith.

CHAPTER THIRTY

Compiling the Voice of a Team

Andy Oram

COMPANIES COME AND GO. THE LASTING ASSET IS THE PEOPLE WHO WORKED FOR THEM. PEOPLE BRING TO their new jobs the sum of their experiences—not just technical skills, but interpersonal patterns that they build up through years of dealing with colleagues and managers.

In this light, we can balance the importance of a project's formal, stated deliverables against the seemingly peripheral impressions its staff get along the way. I'd bet that you could cite very few projects from your own career whose deliverables are still in use. Taking this observation into account, I've always felt that a project's impact on the growth of its staff is just as important as the defined project goal. In fact, I see that as the premise behind this book.

This principle carries the most force in extreme cases where projects are headed inexorably for failure. I had the misfortune of working on just such a project 20 years ago. The only positive result I can remember was a moment of illumination during which I pulled together the collective wisdom of the contributors and gave it a voice.

Personal survival becomes a triumph on this kind of project, because the project challenges your professional judgment on a daily basis: the need to square jerry-rigged solutions with the team's long-term responsibilities; to maintain your integrity and your friends under unbearable scheduling pressures; to hear and nod at requests that both the bearer and the recipient know to be unfeasible, then take them back to your cubicle and adjust them to engineering realities.

Projects that threaten survival also expose the tender boundary where the ego—which is responsible for civilized behavior—threatens to dissolve back into the frenzies of the id. I hit this boundary once during the project described in this chapter. But an intrepid suggestion by my manager directed my anguish into a surprising recovery—giving a voice to the individual contributors on the project in a way I believe helped us all survive.

Looking back on our audacious stroke, I also see in it the seed of a new relationship between individual contributors and management. My manager and I were groping toward a view of corporate behavior that is currently hawked by leading management consultants in business journals and books facing out on bookstore shelves. We were yearning for a flattened, less vertical command structure based on direct communication up and down the hierarchy, and were exploring the power of digital technology to implement that structure.

In short, through an impulsive gesture, I anticipated a vision that would be articulated by organizational experts two decades later.

A Gem from the Computing Past

Close your eyes and travel back—using your memory if you have been in the computer industry long enough, and your imagination if you have not—to a simpler and more innocent time when a small computer company could create and market a complete system from the ground up. In the 1970s and 1980s, with computer chips and other components as building blocks and a total staff of just a few hundred people, a company I will call Edom Engineering manufactured Unix systems with unusually powerful data processing capabilities. It could be considered a supplier of low-cost systems meeting high-end needs, and was very popular with small scientific and engineering labs whose research aspirations outpaced their budgets.

The eccentric personalities at Edom Engineering, many of whom you'll encounter during this story, made work constantly stimulating and sometimes pleasurable. I treasure my memories of these people, with whom I shared so many critical moments. Many of them are likely to read this story and recognize the incident I'll describe. I hope they forgive me if their recollection of the events differs from mine; I have done my best to reproduce the feelings and facts of a time that is more than two decades removed from now.

Edom Engineering occupied a low-slung warehouse-like facility on Boston's Other Technology Highway (Route 495, as opposed to the more famous Route 128). The bottom floor held a manufacturing facility and the top floor contained the engineering teams. The company was a class society, but a harmonious and very efficient one. A range of hardware from motherboards to data acquisition devices were created from scratch and tightly bound to specialized operating system software, compilers, and other tools.

Not many teams nowadays hold the kinds of conversations I sat in on, where compiler writers discuss bugs in register allocation heuristics and how to squeeze an extra bit of precision from a square root function. The engineers at Edom Engineering, including a high percentage of doctorates, were a smart bunch with a wonderful esprit de corps.

Our compiler group was tasked with reproducing all the features of the classic, industry-dominant FORTRAN compiler that Digital Equipment Corporation produced for its VAX line. One engineer got so carried away with this mission that she discovered the algorithm used by Digital's random number generator (actually, of course, a pseudorandom number generator) and made sure our RAND function produced the same sequence of numbers as the Digital library's RAND function.

I remember asking her, "Did the project requirements really make it necessary for you to produce the same exact random numbers?"

She shrugged and answered, "I just figured it out, and decided I might as well make our library conform as much as possible."

It was just such a combination of flamboyant showmanship, competitive zeal, and the sheer fun of creation that led Edom Engineering staff to retool the Unix operating system and all other software components to maximize the effectiveness of the company's well-regarded hardware. Our marketing staff boasted that we had the industry's broadest support for a wide range of features in both System V and BSD Unix, the two fundamental sources for Unix systems of that time.

Projects were organized around a cross-disciplinary model that became popular in the 1970s, largely influenced by Digital's adoption of matrix management. Engineers on each team interacted intimately with the marketing person, tech support staff, and technical writers who worked on the project. These contributors attended all project meetings and checked in with each other on almost an hourly basis.

The company's concern for good manuals and respect for documentation staff led me to join the firm as a technical writer. I was associated most closely with the compiler team, but enjoyed the chance to work on a variety of projects.

And indeed, Edom Engineering's manuals were known throughout the industry for the same high quality as the rest of the company's offerings. Programmers could actually understand our manual on device drivers, and could produce a working driver after reading it. My first year was devoted to documenting the entire FORTRAN language, which looks like an exercise in redundancy, but was actually necessary because we had bulked up standard FORTRAN with lots of VAX extensions and our own enhancements.

Our management style was also fairly relaxed and democratic for those times. We held on to a scruffy start-up culture even as our staff grew past 300. But this grounding in openness harbored a tectonic fault: top managers were closer to their investors than their employees. A recent merger had lengthened the distance between investors and line staff even more. This distance caused chronic grumbling and unkind jokes among the lower echelons of the company. But for important engineering decisions, the managers and investors were always smart enough to listen to their preeminent technical staff.

In Edom Engineering's heyday, it seemed there was nothing our engineers couldn't do. When the thread paradigm established itself as an important element of programming, the compiler team added standard pthreads support to the C compiler in just a few months, and the graphics group was well on its way to making calls thread-safe in the gigantic Motif library (the leading graphics library on Unix at that time) when their project fell victim to the industry crunch that the company ran into during the late 1980s.

It is this economic crisis, and the self-destructive reaction taken by management, to which I now turn. Our industry suffered the kind of change that is grievously disruptive but by no means rare—the kind of paradigm shift that my readers will probably go through several times in their careers, no matter what field they work in—so this change deserves a few paragraphs to help you understand how limited the options left to us were.

Rewiring

Throughout the 1980s, requirements rose while competition intensified in our segment of the engineering field, which can broadly be called scientific data processing. As hardware got faster, generic workstations became better at meeting customer requirements without need for the clever tricks we used at Edom Engineering to achieve maximum performance. Meanwhile, the standard libraries and advanced features of Unix operating systems grew to the point where even our crack programming staff couldn't reproduce everything customers expected.

Our core scientific and engineering market was also shrinking because of an unrelated external factor: the U.S. military in the 1980s reduced the research funding upon which many of our customers depended.

It was in the late 1980s when Edom Engineering managers decided on a leap that they hoped would establish a new beachhead in advanced computing. Throughout its existence, we had been happy basing our systems on Motorola chips. But the new wave of Reduced Instruction Set Computing (RISC) processors promised much better performance. The sages among our hardware engineering staff checked out these processors and selected one that they said could deliver the performance we needed.

The impetus behind RISC processors was the increasingly multilayered decision-making required within conventional chips from Intel and Motorola, which computer scientists now categorized with the demeaning term *Complex Instruction Set Computing* (CISC). Conventional chips got that name because they contained large numbers of instructions, some narrowly tailored to particular software tasks. Different instructions sometimes require different numbers of cycles, forcing the chip's engineers on the hardware side, as well as compiler developers on the software side, to build in more complex scheduling. The weight of all these components led to a need for more wires connecting the processing unit to memory.

By the 1980s, computer scientists determined that increased overhead from these trends was eating up processor power, and concluded that they could create a competitive new generation of chips using a stripped-down set of very short, simple instructions that behaved in rigorously similar ways in a fixed number of cycles. Implementations from various companies hit the market in that decade. RISC became the major story in the trade press, and benchmarks bore out the inventors' predictions.

Thus began the Longjump project at Edom Engineering. It was fraught with uncertainty from the start. We were basing a system on a new product based on a new computing paradigm, and depending on a small firm with an unknown track record. At the same time as the hardware team wrapped the chip into an audacious new system trying to take advantage of every possible feature for speed, the software teams had to port our unique, finely tuned operating system, compiler, and libraries. Because RISC was so different an architecture from the Motorola chips we had always used, we had to base our compiler and a lot of our system utilities on those provided by the RISC vendor. The porting effort steered through uncharted waters.

An engineer I'll call George was appointed project leader for Longjump. George was a relatively young project leader, an earnest, restless fellow with an unusual personality for an engineer in those days. He bore a trim mustache, kept his shoulders slightly hunched as he sat in meetings, and looked about with tight lips that got tighter when he listened to news he didn't want to hear. He had a foot in marketing as well as engineering, and tended to wear suit jackets in an age when traditional computer nerd attire was even sloppier than it is today. He must have known that a more professional look would bolster his credibility when meeting with top management. And because this was his first attempt as project leader, he felt the need to convey credibility.

At the company meeting where Longjump was presented, George stood before the assembled management and staff to make a brief speech that included a seemingly formulaic phrase: "I'd like to thank the company's managers for entrusting me with the leadership of this project."

I don't think he anticipated how the rest of us would react to this gracious statement. We all knew Longjump was a hazardous undertaking, and this was no moment for even a hint of timidity. By thanking management for their trust, he planted in our minds the seed of doubt that he could live up to it.

But ultimately, if George played any counterproductive role, it was by showing too much deference to his managers as they directed the project into stagnant channels.

Coping

My philosophy, as stated at the beginning of this chapter, is both community-oriented and process-oriented. It's community-oriented because I believe every success and failure can be exploited to improve team building, and process-oriented because I believe every project decision should take into account the way it treats team members and resources.

In earlier, sunnier times, our technical writing group once held a meeting (similar to many such meetings held by Unix writers, I'm sure) about the reorganization of manpages, which are an ungainly collection of historical Unix documentation. After some 45 minutes where we dissected the competing issues and established some precepts, I said, "The decision we eventually come up with is less important than the fact of our holding this conversation."

Some of the group were shocked by that luxurious approach to how we spent our time, but I believe it appealed to the technical writing manager, Alan. He talked regularly about bringing one's full self into the workplace, including one's emotional reactions and personal values. He once asked his staff to read a recently published management book whose central claim was that companies needed to be based on a vision in order to enjoy long-term success, and that this vision must pivot on some valuable contribution to customers, workers, or the larger society.

Alan designated me the team leader for the Longjump documentation—my first stint as a team leader, like George. I decided it was my job to protect my team as much as possible. We had no room to negotiate our workflows or deliverables. But I would try to save us from wasteful bureaucracy. Furthermore, I pledged to share with all the writers any information that could identify upcoming crises before they hit.

It turned out I had something to offer on the latter point. As team leader for the documentation, I attended meetings throughout the software side of the project. I took meticulous notes and filtered them down to the items that I thought would have an impact on my fellow writers. I made sure all the writers on the train were offered a view as far ahead on the railroad tracks as any of us.

The aspect of team management that most engineers approach with a groan is regular meetings. At such meetings, typically, staff drone on about their accomplishments for the week and go back to their cubicles no more informed than before. For the Longjump writers, I announced that I would post an empty agenda each week and that we would hold a meeting next week only if someone added an item to the agenda.

This small innovation signaled my striving for both efficiency and democracy. Writers thanked me for eliminating pointless meetings. However, any writer had the power to call a meeting simply by posting an agenda item.

In practice, I was the only person to post agenda items. When we did have meetings, I reported news of specific interest to the group, and we were usually finished in 15 minutes. We didn't use any cool Scrum-like techniques, but we hit on our own formula for maximizing the value of our time together.

Coding

It's always useful to have a few tools to support changes in organizational behavior. As a modest example, I implemented my agenda-driven meeting schedule by posting a file in a shared directory. The likelihood of two people editing the file at the same time was negligible, but the concepts of operating systems and threads had been drilled into me and I therefore felt a heightened sensitivity toward race conditions. Consequently, I bundled access to the agenda in a simple script that used some basic command such as `chmod` to provide a simple locking mechanism using the filesystem.

A bigger tools challenge was posed by the manpages I mentioned earlier. All of our language tools were based on a new compiler suite that came from our vendor. We decided that editing our manpages to reflect the new system would take a prohibitive amount of effort, so the decree came down from somewhere that we should convert the vendor's manpages to fit our system.

The problem was that the vendor had given us pages only in output format, and to accommodate our customers' needs we required the pages in source format. The typical output we had looked like this:

```
O^HO^HOP^HP^HPT^HT^HTI^HI^HIO^HO^HON^HN^HNS^HS^HS
```

```
-^H-^H-o^Ho^Ho _^Hf_^Hi_^Hl_^He
Output binary image to _^Hf_^Hi_^Hl_^He.
```

That's a brief description of the classic -o compiler option. What appears as ^H here is actually a backspace character (ASCII value 8) that causes the terminal to superimpose the following character on the preceding one. Superimposing the same character three times, in the format shown, causes it to appear in bold on the terminal. Superimposing a character on an underscore produces underlining.

What we needed instead were the original `troff` macros used to generate manpages, in which the preceding sequence would look like this:

```
.SS Options
.TP
/fB-o/fP /fI-file/fP
Output binary image to /fI-file/fP.
```

How could a writer convert dozens of pages documenting hundreds of options from output to source format? Typically for the Longjump project, the human and organizational costs—the veritable absurdity of such a job—were ignored by management, and a junior writer, Kimberly, was tasked with doing the conversion by hand.

By the time news of this job reached me, Kimberly was beside herself. She was in her first year of the job, which was her crucial first year in the computer field, and was the type of new hire who was eager to demonstrate her industriousness and loyalty. She would go to any length to satisfy a request from management. But as we sat together scoping out the job, paging through screen after screen of garbage at her terminal, she cried out, "I don't see how I can ever finish this job. I don't even know where to start."

Why didn't the company go back to our vendor and insist they give us the manpages in source format? I don't know. Perhaps my manager and I just didn't have enough experience to argue forcefully enough for this action. Perhaps no one had noticed the problem before signing the contract, and there was no recourse now. Or perhaps the vendor sensed that Edom Engineering posed a competitive threat, and maliciously withheld the source files. In any case, we seemed stuck.

I decided to apply my modest programming skills to bring the project within a human being's purview. The hoary old troff format, particularly in output form, resisted mechanized processing. Even advanced AI techniques would probably not suffice to recognize all elements of a page, such as the section heading (.SS) and tagged item paragraph (.TP).

But I found a woman/machine collaboration that worked, and wrote some Emacs Lisp macros to automate as much activity as possible. Kimberly needed only to find a familiar element—such as a section heading or tagged item—position the Emacs cursor (point) over it, and press a single key to convert a paragraph to the right format. When I showed her the basic keystrokes, she nearly jumped out of her seat in excitement, and her relief was so great that she launched into the conversion of her first manpage with actual pleasure. Later she told me, "Those macros saved my life."

Capitulating

War correspondents in every conflict wire home stories of chauffeurs who try to avoid known roadblocks by taking detours through back country. Often the new route proves more deadly than the one they avoided. Such was the case with Longjump.

Speed on this project only caused time to accelerate, rather than to slow down as Einstein said it would. After only a month or two, our engineers realized that our new system components were not working together, and that software porting was going badly. We had no time to lose; we could hemorrhage at any roadblock. The investors insisted on meeting our schedule, so someone at the top laid down a radical shift of direction.

Instead of incorporating the RISC chip into a custom-designed and custom-built system, we would become a value-added retailer for another successful computer firm that was selling a computer based on that chip. Adopting their computer system would require only some scrambling around at the top of the device and software stack, rather than the intensive mixing and baking that the chefs of our engineering staff had originally planned.

Many of us felt our hearts sink upon hearing this strategy. Although it was certainly a blow to our pride to be using another vendor's product, we had substantive reasons for fearing the switch as well. Without our secret sauce, our craftsmanlike reengineering of the system from bottom to top, we would lose most of our performance advantages. We were, in effect, offering customers a generic computer system that happened to be backwardly compatible with our previous systems. Only the new RISC architecture would (hopefully) provide enough of a performance boost to make the move worthwhile.

Grumbling was evident throughout the halls in those days. Staff at lower levels sensed that George was not playing the role a project leader should play, which would entail explaining to management the full consequences of their choice.

A popular cubicle decoration at that period was a fanciful series of brief reports moving up the management chain from an individual contributor to a company CEO. The individual contributor labeled his project a stinking pile of manure. This crass assessment softened in each report as it rose through the management hierarchy. By the time the news reached the CEO, he was enthusiastically announcing the project's potential for growing sweet-smelling flowers.

I mentioned at the beginning of this article that to survive projects like Longjump, staff must constantly reconcile short-term tasks with their professional judgment. A couple of months into the project, the effort of such reconciliation became exhausting. Not every request could be solved by solutions such as the Emacs macros I gave Kimberly.

Engineers started prefacing or ending their task descriptions with comments like "Not that this will do any good" and "I don't see how this will work." But soon the comments stopped. Saying them to cubicle neighbors was redundant, because they all were in agreement already. But the comments were also seen as a waste of time, because top management was responding only to investor pressure.

Worst of all, none of the individual contributors could offer a better way to meet our goals and deadlines. But being engineers rather than investors, we felt we'd have more chance of success by lengthening the project schedule and creating a system that maintained our unique advantages than by hoodwinking our customers with a "me too" product whose resemblance to our earlier products was only skin-deep. The moment for such an argument had passed, however. No longer did the engineers' opinions carry weight in the company's major engineering decisions, as they had throughout its history.

The Break

Attending virtually all the meetings on the Longjump project, I was in a position to hear the full range of the engineers' lamentations. After many weeks of sitting at vinyl-laminated tables in the blank-walled boxes of conference rooms, I felt overwhelmed by the burden of what I was taking in.

One day I broke it all to Alan. I expected a conventional "Buck up and carry on" speech, with a sprinkle of praise and commiseration from him, but Alan's response astonished me entirely.

"I think," he told me in his deliberate speaking style, into which he seemed to place each word with special consideration, "you should write up exactly what you told me and send it as an email to the entire company."

What a bizarre idea! Admittedly, in Edom Engineering's loose corporate culture, staff always felt comfortable using the companywide alias, which would instantly reach everybody from the manufacturing team to the CEO. The alias was used not only for official business, but to announce parties, reschedule soccer games, and exchange jokes. There was nothing sacred about the companywide alias.

But one could ask whether I had anything to say that deserved taking up people's time. Everything I told Alan had circulated freely in the halls. As I have already indicated, engineers stopped talking about these issues because they had held the conversation many times and felt it was over and done with.

Yet the thought of writing up my thoughts thrilled me. Every individual contributor felt the same away about Longjump, but each one felt it in isolation. They could not share feelings in any encounter group or therapy session (despite the provision of a corporate psychologist who did nothing). Living what we felt to be a lie, day by day, we had lost the tiny hold on sanity that our earlier grasp of the truth had left to us and were plummeting down a dark hole lined with impossible demands.

So it lifted my spirits to hope that all our frustrations and fears could be uttered once more. I think Alan could tell I was the one to put them into words. Not only was I a writer; my team leader responsibilities placed me at a little-noticed but crucial fulcrum in the exchange of information about the project.

I remember him expounding on his idea with his legs crossed casually and a straight-backed posture. He urged me not to pull my punches. "You laid out the problems that the teams faced very clearly when explaining them to me, and I encourage you strongly to be just as candid, just as direct, and just as uncompromising when you write it up for the company."

The course seemed dangerous, but by this time, any fear had been beaten out of me. Little thought of career repercussions entered my mind. I knew I had been appointed team leader because my work was respected, and in the middle of the crunch on this project, management couldn't afford to lose me or discipline me in any way. It was for Alan's safety more than my own that I asked him, "What will you say if top management complains?"

"Don't worry, I'll back you up completely, and I can't see any way management could take negative action." Delivered in the same modulated tone, Alan's words gave me complete confidence.

If I preserved the email I sent that afternoon, it must be on some format that few computer systems can read today, so I'm sorry to say I can't quote it directly. It was only a few paragraphs long. I wrote of a consensus among Longjump team members that the project had taken a wrong turn. I summarized the tasks remaining to be done over the next few weeks and the hurdles that various teams faced with performance issues, lack of knowledge about the platform, and incompatibilities. I then turned to the effect of our observations on team morale, ending with our love for our work, our customers, and our company, all of which we thought would be jeopardized by forcing us to stick to the current plan and schedule.

I don't believe much work got done in the facility the rest of the day. Printouts of my email went up on cubicle walls. People congratulated me in the hall with comments such as, "I showed this to my wife, and she asked how long it took before the person who wrote it got fired." Emails shot back from a sister facility in another state, where I was not well known, as people asked who this courageous and perspicacious writer was.

In fact, I don't feel this is at all a story about courage or perspicacity. I was not courageous because I had no expectation of harm. I was not unusually perspicacious because I merely reported what I heard from everyone, and I presented my observations from that standpoint.

What I do feel proud of—and thank Alan for pushing me to do—is to have given my colleagues a voice. In doing this I broke through each individual's feeling of isolated panic, and fought the virulent sense of helplessness pervading the company. In giving them a voice, I allowed them to survive.

Anticipating 21st-Century Management

It was only while writing up my recollections as a chapter for *Beautiful Teams* that I reckoned there was something deeper and more significant about my email blast than merely letting off steam. I think Alan and I were exploring a new management style and the role of a new communications technology. The significance wouldn't emerge for 20 years, until management consultants dubbed it a new trend in corporate behavior.

I pointed out at the beginning of this chapter that Edom Engineering management maintained a respect for engineers and a tolerance for their opinionated way of expressing themselves, a legacy of the company's start-up days. Something on Longjump caused this to break down—probably the reluctance of the CEO to argue with investors and for George to argue with the CEO, along with the new lines of command brought in by our merger. The engineers at the grass roots were not prepared to organize themselves to preserve their decision-making power in the face of this breakdown in corporate culture. But another force, technological in nature, stepped in to offer an alternative power arrangement.

We were living in a period before mass online participation, when the World Wide Web ran on only a few dozen sites. Yet already, online communities had experimented with a grassroots political activity that dispensed with traditional leaders and party centers. Although Howard Rheingold's influential book *The Virtual Community: Homesteading on the Electronic Frontier* (Addison-Wesley) was not published until 1993,[*] and John Perry Barlow didn't release his Declaration of the Independence of Cyberspace (now seen as something of a period piece) until 1996, knowledge of Rheingold's WELL was widespread among Internet users at the time I worked on Longjump, and I was already building a different way for people to work together with far-flung colleagues through email forums run by Computer Professionals for Social Responsibility.

I am convinced that Alan's challenge to send out my views through email was a response to the power he saw dormant in digital communications. Alan does not remember this time in his career well enough to say whether he was consciously working through its potential as I babbled away about deadlines and bug reports in his office, but the effect of our conspiracy was to let loose into the environment an unscheduled experiment in grassroots

---

[*] Alan was later to publish a critique of this book, but that doesn't detract from my observation that he was making use of online communication and noticing much of its potential.

participation. My immediate enthusiasm showed that I, too, prepped by my political work online, was equipped to create the experimental organism we unleashed.

The results of the experiment validated the premise. Digital networks are powerful enablers for democratic action, at least among groups of people that already have ties. In such a degenerate corporate environment, so constrained financially, we couldn't expect miraculous results. The observed effects on employee morale were the best outcome we could hope for. But one could easily see how the same use of technology could actually support constructive project management in a healthier company, if deployed at any earlier stage and supported by enlightened management and social norms.

The vision that Alan and I presented that day—unconsciously in my case, but perhaps consciously in his—now fills the pages of management texts. It has become, in the wake of the *Cluetrain Manifesto* (by Christopher Locke, Rick Levine, et al.; Basic Books), Eric Von Hippel's *The Sources of Innovation* (Oxford University Press), and other books expounding on the value of openness, a hallmark of enlightened management. Few companies have moved yet to tap so radically the potential of employees (or customers and other stakeholders) organized in these ways into articulate policymakers for the organization. But many companies are talking the talk, and eventually that behavior will be accepted as normal.

Final Notes

Edom Engineering staff weren't the types to wait around and let algae gather on the pond. On the day of my email, they read and responded to it, but then plunged back into the depths of their work.

No manager called on me to justify or explain my email—they probably knew very well what was going on, whether or not George had been forthright with them—but the direction of the Longjump project did not change, either. Ultimately, with the new business model based on reselling a competitor's system, we met our stated goals and finished the project on time with a formal success status. The product fizzled in the marketplace.

As a matter of fact, RISC chips in general never lived up to the hype. Conventional chip makers found ways to improve speed despite the supposedly crippling complexity of their designs, using such strategies as prefetching instructions, predictive scheduling, and multi-cores. Some of these strategies, such as breaking large instructions into smaller parts with a consistent structure, they borrowed from RISC design.

The conventional manufacturers kept costs low through economies of scale, and invested the profits they garnered through market dominance in high-priced, state-of-the-art facilities that could produce chips even more cheaply. RISC manufacturers never caught up. So, although RISC companies remain in the field, RISC as a new computer market turned out to be a miscalculation by a large group of computer industry pundits and investors. Edom Engineering's last, great hope turned out to be just a footnote in that story.

I was never fired. I stayed at the company a few more months, until the remaining project of interest that I was documenting—the thread-safe Motif library—got canceled.

At that point, I went to my manager's manager, who headed a large engineering team and had an excellent rapport with me. I said to him, "My major project just got canceled, and I don't have enough work—what would you like me to do?"

This, of course, was a code phrase for: *I don't see any future for myself in this company, and I need your reassurance to stay.*

My manager's manager smiled in his perennially congenial way and answered, "Don't worry about it. Take some time to do some studying."

I took that as a code phrase for: *I have nothing to offer you. Go ahead and look for a new job.*

My departure was part of a general exodus during the company's subsequent and vertiginous decline. Since then, I have barely followed the sequence of acquisitions by other lackluster companies in the field. I feel now that it would have been better for everyone— the employees, the investors, and the customers—if the exodus had occurred before the Longjump project; it did no one a favor to push for the preservation of a dying business model.

But because we all chose (out of our affection for the products on which we had worked so hard during the years) to participate in this last gasp of a company we had built, we could at least benefit from the models we developed for behaving under extreme business conditions. I can't claim that my email blast was the proper way to channel the anger and fear that I was absorbing from those around me, but I aver that it was a psychological survival tactic that helped many of my colleagues. More interestingly, it was a somewhat distorted precursor of open communications on modern digital networks that underlie the more bottom-up, contributor-driven, democratic corporation being promoted by business experts today.

PART FIVE

Music

We started this book by interviewing Tim O'Reilly because we felt that he covered a wide range of top-ics that we'd delve into later on. One of the things that Tim did was draw a parallel between teams of developers and how groups of musicians work together. That piqued our interest, and we wanted to dig a little deeper.

Tim: I have to say that my greatest weakness as a team leader, to be quite honest, has always been that I've always taken what's available and tried to make something of it, rather than an engineering approach—we need one of these, and one of these, and one of these—and building something out of nothing.

Jenny: That's actually my question. As you were talking, one of the things you said really resonated with me. The traditional way to handle deciding what you're going to build is getting everybody to agree on that up front. It sounds like you're more interested in the discovery process, allowing people to come to whatever truth comes from the experience. How do you reconcile that?

Tim: Well, yes and no. It's a good question. It's so paradoxical, because it sounds like when you say whatever truth comes from the experience—that sounds very California and New Age. When I say, "uncover the statue in the stone," it's really there. There's not more than one. Well, maybe there's a couple, but it's not like any old thing works. It's not like you can just go with the flow and do what you feel. There's an aesthetic vision that drives the process.

Jenny: So, the leader has to carry that vision?

Tim: Yes, absolutely. You have to know what you're going for. And what you're doing is going back to the idea of humming a tune and getting other people to follow it. Well, there is an idea there of harmony. There is an idea there because there is a tune, and somebody can be off-key. It's not like everyone can go hum their own tune. This is the tune. Find it, converge. And that's the skill in bringing a creative team together.

Going back to the analogy of humming the tune, and having people learn to play it on their own instruments: if people are accomplished musicians, they can do that. Then they can actually start to elaborate on the tune, they can build on what you've done. But it starts what in open source what Eric Raymond calls a "plausible promise." There is an aes-thetic vision there where people say, "Yeah, I get it, I want to be part of that." Then they can express their own creativity. And if you've done it right, you haven't overspecified, you haven't told people what to do or how to do it. You've just given them a vision of where you're going, and they find their own way there.

Andrew: OK, I've got a question. There are definitely some really skilled, really amazing band leaders. Like, say, Count Basie, who's famous for not using as much sheet music and charts, and really having musicians who work exactly like that. But I'm sure history is littered with the names of bands we don't know with people who tried to work like that and weren't able to. And that's one thing that we've seen a lot in software projects specifically. You'll have really talented people, and a leader who's really smart and talented, yet the team has a lot of trouble getting software out the door.

Tim: And a lot of what I've done in my career has been to tell stories that help people to organize their own activity. So, I'm a very non-directive leader or manager. In fact, I often joke that I'm kind of like the title character in the '50s musical *The Music Man*. You know the story, the guy was a con man who sold instruments, and said that he'd teach the kids to play music. But of course, he didn't know anything about music. He said he had this new system called the "Think System," where he'd hum the tune and the kids would figure out how to play it on their own instruments. And of course, it works out in the story; the kids do kind of figure it out, and it works out just in time to save him because he's fallen in love with the town librarian.

Andrew: Could you run a real band like that?

Tim: Well, you could, of course, if you had very skilled players. In fact, that's what jazz is all about.

Andrew: I guess you're right—that's pretty much how Count Basie ran his band.

Tim: A jazz band is the Think System applied. Somebody puts out an idea, and someone else picks up on it. I still remember, actually, when Jeff Bezos and I talked to various congressional people about the patent system. One of the congressmen, well known; we were trying to make the analogy of how invention works, and that it's a little bit like jazz. And he totally got it, because he was a big jazz fan. "Oh my God! What if all of those jazz riffs were patented, and you couldn't take them and run with them?"

So, I think in a lot of ways that gets to the heart of something. If you have good enough people who are motivated and excited and skilled, you can in fact hum a tune and have them pick up and improvise on it. And that's what I've done through a whole lot of my career. That's not to say there isn't a lot of hands-on. But even that is in the form of storytelling. The team of editor and writer, for example, introducing a book: the way that I would often do it is that I would rewrite something and show them, and then they'd say, "Oh yeah, I get that now." As an editor, that's also how I'd work with assistant editors— I'd kind of demonstrate stuff, and they'd demonstrate back what they took away from me. And then, when I said, "Yeah, you've got it," I'd have less and less to do.

I know I've said two very contradictory things here, because I said, "finding the statue that's in the stone," but I also said, "articulating a vision that other people can believe in." One of those things sounds like there is the ideal form sitting there in the form, where there's only one. In the other, you can make anything out of anything. And the truth is somewhere in between. What it feels like from the inside, when you get it right, is like doing harmony in music. There are a lot of different harmonies possible, but you do have to converge on something.

So in some sense, I think that analogy is probably a pretty good one. There are some underlying things that make a situation work, that make it come together. That's something else that's a big part of my thinking—Alfred Korzybski, with general semantics: "The map is not the territory." The map matches the territory. And when you create an aesthetic vision that somehow matches a territory, that somehow makes the thing more what it is, then you get people to follow you. And when you seed that moment, when you're able to articulate a vision, you get people to sign up for it. And together you build something that is true, and feels true.

As we were editing our interview with Tim, we felt that this one section really stood on its own, because it said something to us. We felt that it made a poignant statement about how teams can revolve around a single visionary leader, and that one leader can bring everyone together under an overarching vision. But he said something else that struck us: in a way, he erased the line between a vision for a project and an artistic vision.

We felt that these ideas needed more exploration. So, we sought out an expert in how musicians work together, and we were thrilled that Tony Visconti could take the time to talk to us. Both of us have been fans of a lot of his work over the years, even when we didn't necessarily know that he was behind the music. Tony has spent his entire career figuring out how to get groups—teams, if you will—of musicians to work together.

We weren't sure exactly how this would turn out. But what really took us by surprise is just how much of what Tony said echoed many of the things that our other contributors said throughout the book. While you're reading this interview, keep your eyes open for them: see if you can spot ideas, sentiments, and opinions that reflect other things you've read over the past few hundred pages.

CHAPTER THIRTY-ONE

Producing Music

an Interview with Tony Visconti

If you don't know Tony Visconti's name already, just go to his website (*http://www. tonyvisconti.com*) and click on the Discography link. If you've been alive in the past four decades, you almost certainly own at least a few albums that he's produced (including some of our own favorites). He's worked with some of the greatest stars—and biggest egos—in the music business, and he's created lasting albums that were both artistic and commercial successes. We wanted to know how he did it…and to our amazement, he sat down with Andrew and told us! And it turns out that what he has to say is surprisingly relevant to the way we build software.

Andrew: Thanks so much for taking the time to do this. Since you're a producer, I want to start out by talking about just what it is that you do. Because I think a lot of people don't really have any idea what a producer does. There's an old Rocky and Bullwinkle episode where Boris Badenov hires Bullwinkle as a movie producer. Bullwinkle asks Boris what a producer produces, and Boris says, "Money." I've definitely noticed that people who have job titles like "producer," "art director," "editor," and "project manager" seem to have a lot in common. So, how would you describe what you do?

Tony: Well, those job definitions are very vague at best, because what someone brings to a job needs to be defined. My style of production is different from, say, a Hugh Padgham style of production, or even George Martin's style of production. A producer of a record is more like—well, one of the jobs is money manager. We don't raise the money, but in the old days, producers used to raise the money. Nowadays, the record company is the actual producer of an album or a project.

They'll say, "We have so much money and we'd like you to make us this kind of an album." So, they define the nature of the job in the first place. I, as the producer of the record, manage the entire production of the record from the moment it's handed over to me to the moment it's delivered. The responsibility is mine.

Andrew: That sounds a lot like what a project manager does. Or what a team leader does, in a lot of ways—but when a lead developer is doing that, he's basically wearing a project manager hat.

Tony: Yes, I guess that's a project manager—it's probably the similar thing in your world.

Andrew: And what you said about vague job definitions definitely makes sense in this case. Ask any programmer on a team, "What does a project manager do?" If they can come up with an answer at all, what you said is pretty close to what they would say. And I suspect that if you ask a musician in a band working on an album, they would have a lot of trouble saying exactly what it is a producer does, too, except that he sometimes tells you what to do and disagrees with you a lot.

What do you think qualifies someone to be a good producer, or an effective project manager?

Tony: I believe that if someone is going to be a project manager, they should have very intimate knowledge of all the jobs that they are going to manage. All the different stages, all the levels of work that needs to be done, like differentiate between the creative team and the logistical team. I mean, there are members in the team who are responsible for creativity, and members who are responsible for logistics, how to proceed, that things have to be done in an orderly way. So, a producer should know how to do these things.

I think a producer—or a project manager—should come up from the ranks, and should have had practical day-to-day work on all the jobs they are about to manage. Otherwise, they really won't understand the situation, and they'll be at the mercy of a person who's trying to get away with murder, someone who's trying to shirk their responsibilities. I've done every single job in the music business. I've been signed as a recording artist.

I've played bass. I've played guitar. I've played piano. And at one point I learned how to become an engineer. I learned how to orchestrate and write for orchestras—actually write real music on real paper and have musicians play off the paper.

Nowadays, I don't actually do all of those jobs at the level I used to do, because they were solitary jobs. I would be a bass player in one situation or I'd be an orchestrator in another. I can manage a team full of people in a recording situation because I know exactly what it takes to do those jobs.

Andrew: But you wouldn't necessarily be the best person for any of those jobs, better than a better musician or a better orchestrator or a better engineer than the people you're working with. You don't need to be the best, just have a good working knowledge of each job.

Tony: As years go on, I find that I don't want to do those jobs because it's just too much to do all those things at the same time. But when you have a lower budget, people will have to double up on jobs. For instance, if the budget is so small that I can afford only one assistant and we have to record a band, then I will take on a couple of jobs involved there. I'll be managing myself, in a way. But ideally, you want to have a team of experts. I know I'm a good bass player, but I want someone who's actually a great bass player.

I know what I can expect of a person on my team because of my experience. I know what's possible, and often my requests verge on the impossible. I can get performances out of musicians only because I know, I just know what can be done. I don't necessarily have to be better than them, but I think I'm qualified to direct them and to coach them because I've done that job.

Andrew: So, it's almost like a respect thing. Someone's really only going to take your direction or take your advice if they respect your ability, at least respect that you know enough to give them that kind of direction.

Tony: Yes. It's akin to martial arts. You won't respect somebody who's been doing martial arts for six months to teach you. Even as a novice, you can see that their body is uncoordinated and they can't really do what they're talking about. But when you study with a great martial arts teacher who's practiced for 35 years, then there's respect; you will do anything that person says. And if that guy's really experienced in everything he talks about, you have to respect that person. And he will respect you, because you come to him to learn or to achieve something.

So, that's the way I see it. I don't know if it sounds arrogant, but this happened to me quite early on because I studied music at a very early age. I would say I was qualified to be a record producer by the time I was 25 years old. The thing I did not have was people skills. For me, that came out of the school of hard knocks. Learning how to speak to people is actually a very important lesson to learn. How to actually communicate to people without anger, without sounding dishonest, disingenuous.

Andrew: What happens if you don't communicate well with people, with respect or honesty? What if you're transparent or disingenuous? What goes wrong on your team, with your project?

Tony: Well, if you don't correct problems directly and efficiently, then you'll lose their interest. They'll lose respect for you, and they'll lose interest in what you say. They'll think you don't know what you're talking about. That's the worst thing in the world to happen to a producer or project manager—where you're perceived as some kind of a dork who hasn't a clue. You don't ever want that to happen. You've lost the team once that happens.

And I'll tell you, if you do happen to put your foot in your mouth, a way to regain the respect of the team is to simply say, "I've made a mistake, could we start again on this? I've given it a lot of thought and I made a judgment error." That's how you gain the respect of a team again after you've lost it: you have to admit that you've made a mistake. Your honesty and courage to admit mistakes will maintain your team's respect. If you try to cover up your ignorance, or if you try to look cool all the time, you just get deeper and deeper into phoniness and your team will drift away from you.

Andrew: I definitely see really similar things on programming teams. It's not enough for a team leader to be respectable. You have to have—I don't want to call humility, but at least a willingness to see that somebody else is right.

Tony: Yes.

Andrew: And I know a lot of programmers have trouble with that. I'm assuming that a lot of rock stars do, too.

Tony: There're always going to be differences of opinion, but the hierarchy is always the same. The person who is managing the project is in charge. That always has to be clear and understood. But that does not give you a license to be a tyrant. One of the most positive goals of a good project manager is to bring out the best in the people in the project, not to stifle them, not to hold them back, not to squeeze them between two walls. It's very dangerous to do things like that. What you want to do is to create heroes on your team, to make people on your team—well, all of them if possible—make them shine, to really make your team look like the A team.

And you're not going to get that if you don't listen to them. In order for them to be members of the A team, you have to let their opinions be heard; you have to, you must. This also means that you have to be a flexible thinker and able to modify the goal of the project. If some maverick kind of idea comes up that can be incorporated—some stroke of genius comes from a team member—you have to be open to that. Even if it seems like a ridiculous idea at first, don't make snap decisions. Don't say, "Oh no, this isn't in the plan, it's not going to work." Take time to consider all ideas.

If a maverick idea turns out to be a bad idea, don't humiliate the proposer. You have to get across to your team that an idea is only an idea and they arise spontaneously. You don't want to make it personal when you're rejecting someone's idea. You can sincerely say it was a good idea, but not really germane to this project. There are ways of communicating, where you bring out the best in someone and you don't stifle them when you really feel that they're going down the wrong path.

Andrew: What happens if you feel the whole project is going in the wrong direction? You know you need to get it on the right track, but you just have a feeling that a lot of people on the team are going to be hard to convince. Even if they'll be happy with the final product after you change direction, the idea of making the change just isn't going to sit well with them. How do you handle it if there's just something that they don't want to do, some change that you know is going to meet with resistance? You have to be the bearer of bad news. How do you handle a situation like that?

Tony: Well, the nature of my business is it's very visceral. Music is an emotional product. People laugh and cry and make babies and dance to music. Music serves a lot of purposes in life, and it's very, very emotional. And I think everyone has a common feeling when they're making music. You kind of feel it in your gut that things are going well. I mean, it's very, very clear after a playback, when somebody's played really well—they come in and usually you see smiling faces. If you don't see smiling faces, and you yourself are not smiling, then something is going wrong. That's all I think a project manager has to say: "We're doing it wrong. We have to go back to the drawing board."

Don't moan about lost time, because the important thing is that the team has derailed and has to get back on the right track. I feel that way; I mean, I've stayed up all night recording a track, a vocal, or something. We'd come back the next day and we think it should be good because we stayed up all night. But you have to tell the truth—is it really good? I find in moments like these there is a common experience in the team. These harsh moments are easier to take after the team has had a good night's sleep.

It's simple: it's either good or it's bad, and somebody has to say that. I'm a firm believer in honesty when that happens. When that takes place, then I think people do fall into line.

Andrew: Have you ever been in a situation where you feel the team has that unity, but the final product just isn't any good? Everybody is happy with how it came out. But somebody's paying for this—a record company—and when you bring it to them you proudly play the album for whoever it is you're dealing with there, you can see on their faces that this is exactly what they were not looking for, and clearly they don't think they can sell this.

Tony: Yes.

Andrew: How do you handle a situation like that? Say they tell you you're going to have to take this back to the drawing board, and you've got another couple of months and enough budget to do it right. But you know that the team is just not going to want to hear that. Nobody wants to be told to go back to the drawing board after they think they just nailed it. So, does that happen? How do you deal with it?

Tony: It often happens if you've waited too long to present it to the person who commissioned this work. If you leave that right to the end, then you are going to risk that. Your employer doesn't want to know how late you stayed up. They don't want to know about your little internal squabbles. That's nothing. If your results are not what they expected, they'll say to you, "Is this what you brought me after all this time? Is this what we paid for?" Now, this is a very tough situation. In some way, you have to convince your employer that the results are "just different," and you have to tell your team that some modifications are necessary.

I have turned in some albums that were all but rejected and reluctantly released to the public. Sometimes, you're just ahead of your time. An artist person I produced was about three years ahead of his time when he was younger. He wasn't in sync with what the labels or the public wanted. You might hand in what you consider to be your greatest work ever, but by the time it's released it is met with blank stares. The trouble was my artist wasn't like anyone else. He was too iconoclastic, not trendy at first.

I've learned two ways to avoid that great misunderstanding at the end happening. Halfway or maybe three-quarters of the way through the project, I bring what I have to the record company and ask them, "What do you think? Are we going in the right direction?" Some artists are loathe to do that, but it's really important before you go too far. You have to get it out of your head that the people paying for the whole shebang are the enemy.

Psychologically, it's going to go a long way, because if the people who commissioned it feel included at an early stage, they will be more receptive at the end if they feel involved in the middle stages. I didn't like to do that in the old days. I liked to wait until the finished product, because I was quite young and arrogant. But really, you need feedback, and that feedback goes both ways—because what you're telling the client is, "I respect your opinion, and I'd like you to tell me what you think of the project so far." So, that's one way I avoid having that ego clash at the end.

Andrew: I like that idea a lot. The idea of an iterative process where you do part of the work, until you have something that sounds sort of like a finished partial product. Once you've gotten to a milestone—something finished enough that you can bring it to the client—you say, "This is what we've got so far. Here, are we going in the right direction? We're at a point where we can change direction if we need to." Then they can get their fingerprints on it, feel some sense of ownership of the final product. If you do that several times, iterate through the project that way, you'll zero in on something that everybody can agree on.

Tony: I wonder if your programmers have a similar attitude to some rock stars I've worked with, who feel that the record companies are corrupt and stupid and they wouldn't know what a hit record sounds like if it ran them down. But the record producer (or project manager) has to be the person who floats between those two worlds. The record company, they're all about the bottom line, the cash, whereas the programmers or the artists are all about culture and innovation and art and creativity. The project manager has to be the filter between the two worlds, because if the programmers communicated directly with the record company, they'd be thrown off the balcony. They'd be fired for insolence.

And if the record company were allowed to talk to the artists (the programmers), then the artists would throw them off the balcony. You have to understand the way both people's minds work. It's definitely a left-side/right-side brain situation, and that's where a project manager could really shine with their people skills. As I've said, you have to have technical skills. You have to understand the programmer's problems. But on the other hand, you have to understand the company's bottom-line problems, and what they want to sell to the public. So, there you go.

The second thing I do is I always budget in more than I need. It's a little trick of mine. And I book in maybe three extra weeks that I probably won't need, and then what I end up doing is I deliver the project under budget and early.

Because I really know deep down inside how long it's going to take—and I've only learnt this from experience, of course. This way, if you need those three extra weeks, it's available, and it kind of makes everyone breathe a little easier. If you budget just how long it's going to take and you have no contingency, then there's no Plan B. You're setting yourself up to fail. If you come to that crunch, where the client does not like your product and there's no budget left, you have failed, and everyone's going to look bad.

Andrew: So, what happens when your team members just don't get along? What happens when you've got conflicts? One person wants to do it one way, another person wants to do it another way. You've got irreconcilable differences, and the clock is ticking and the budget is burning.

Tony: Well, if they don't get along, that's something that should have been observed in the first place. I pick my team members very carefully. I have a lot of people in my phone book that I use. I know certain drummers will not get along with certain singers, I just know that. For instance, for this new project I'm working on, this drummer was recommended, but he was kind of, well, I won't say any names, but he was kind of a beer-drinking, happy-go-lucky guy who's always telling fart jokes. He plays great drums, and all that. But the singer was the complete opposite—a very sensitive person, a person who doesn't like gross people. It would have been insane to put those two people on the same job. And this drama would be taking the wind out of this performer's sails all the time. So even though I like this guy's drumming, he was the wrong drummer for this artist. The sessions would have collapsed into a kind of men's club, and the artist I'm working with is a very sensitive female.

I try to pick the team members for personality. Personalities are very, very important. So, the personalities have to be right, and of course, the style has to be right—not that everyone has to be in the same style, but the styles have to be complementary. It could be a yin-yang thing. Maybe that's the right thing to do. Maybe that's the wrong thing to do, putting such extreme types, personality types, and creativity types together.

But that has to be worked out, and that's your responsibility as a project manager. Learn as much as possible about these potential team members. Meet them. Have lunch with them. Have dinner with them. Go out with them. Learn about these people. You're going to be very, very intimate with them once the project starts, and you don't want any surprises. If someone potentially has a temper that's going to flare up, if I know that beforehand, then I will expect it to happen. But if that suddenly rears its head unexpectedly in the middle of a project, if suddenly I'm stuck with a diva, then it's a little too late in the game. It's a very awkward situation.

Do I have to fire this person? Do I have to sit and give him or her a lecture? But I should have known in the first place that this was going to happen. You have to try to build your team based on whether these people will be harmonious. Once it's gone wrong, I think you have the ultimate weapon: to fire a team member. And that's not a bad thing. That could be a very good thing, because if you get rid of the troublemaker, it'll strengthen the team. They'll know that you have the courage to do such a thing, and they probably didn't like the person anyway. And the next person who comes in is a Johnny-come-lately to the team, so he or she will be more obedient, do his or her best to fit in.

So, it's hard when you have different personalities, but if you're ready for the worst you can manage it better, a lot better.

Andrew: Firing people—that's not a topic a lot of people like to talk about.

Tony: You know, firing people is inevitable. You have to consider that can happen.

Andrew: I had a boss once who told me that the only way to get a team's respect is to make it clear that you're the boss. In his mind, I think that meant asserting his authority, and yelling at people until they did what he wanted.

Tony: You can't yell at people. If you yell at people, they don't hear the words, they hear the anger. You have to control your anger, and it's really not easy to do. You could be angry when you tell the truth, but you can't afford to show it. And you have to learn how to take a breath, go out of the room, come back in when you've calmed down a bit, and then tell the truth. You can't scream at people—it does not work. It just brings up memories of their parents or their teachers or bullies. You can't come off as that.

Andrew: But you do sometimes have a genuine difference of opinion, and a decision does have to get made. How do you handle that? What if you know things have to go one way, and you know that there's somebody you have to work with who just wants to see things go another way? What do you do if you know that it will just not work out if we keep going in that direction, but the people you're working with are just having a lot of trouble even seeing that?

Tony: That's delicate, because in my case, sometimes I have to back off every now and then, to realize that the artist's name is going to be bigger than mine in the credits. My team always contains a "star." Sometimes I have to change; I must admit if an idea comes that's not what I had in mind, I have to completely examine it and say, "This might not be a bad idea. I could be wrong."

So, I always keep that option open, but if I'm dead certain that this is going down the wrong way, I will have to remind everyone because every project begins with defining the goals. You have such meetings at the beginning of the project. And it should be down on paper, and charts, schedules, should be made up. We need to do this by that date, and to have a person go off the charts at some late stage in the project is really in breach of the contract which makes a team cohesive. I'm talking about the social contract of getting the job done. And if you had these things written down, you have to remind people that they've gone off the page.

That's very, very important, and that usually reels people back in, even the "star." But I do my best to see the difference between a frivolous idea and a brilliant idea. And of course, Andrew, if the idea is so amazing, you have to say, "I wish this idea came up at the beginning. We should spend some time on this." But you can't entertain frivolous ideas. It's really out of the question. You have to be very firm.

I'm a chart person. I have charts on the walls. In my studio right now, I have every song that we're recording up on a chart. I have horizontal columns for the songs, and vertical columns for what needs to be done to the songs. And every time an activity is done, it gets a mark—I put a random colored sticky star over the activity, which inadvertently turns into a grading system because the artist wants the gold stars. It gets kind of playful, too, because I encourage the use of the chart as an ideas section; anyone can jot down an idea. It makes everyone feel creative, involved, but mainly accountable, as it is always visible.

Everyone can see at any time at what stage we're at in the project, not just me. I think it's everyone's business to know how they fit into the whole. And my charts have been great for that. The other chart is a custom-made calendar from day one to the last day of the project, and it is numbered backwards, so the last day is one and the next-to-the-last day is two, so everyone can actually visually see what day we're in. "Oh, we have 45 days left. We have 42 days left. We have three days left." This is the bare visible truth about the deadline.

Now, I do this because I'm in a physical room, and I have these on the wall. But you could have an updated, interactive chart on your computer desktop that's emailed amongst your team every day, something that they open up several times during the day. We refer to our progress chart on the average of once an hour. If they're building a video game—"Oh, so Jimmy added the feet to that character, and Sue added a musical theme. OK, now I know what I have to do"—I really believe that a "public" progress chart holds everyone accountable.

Andrew: Is this something that you put up on the wall as a one-way communication to the team, or does everyone get involved in planning? Is it you talking to the team, or is it everyone talking to each other?

Tony: The progress chart starts out with all the ideas from the planning meetings. It is not a blank page. Everyone is involved with creating it. But as time goes by, I encourage everyone on the team to add new ideas that modify the original concept for the better.

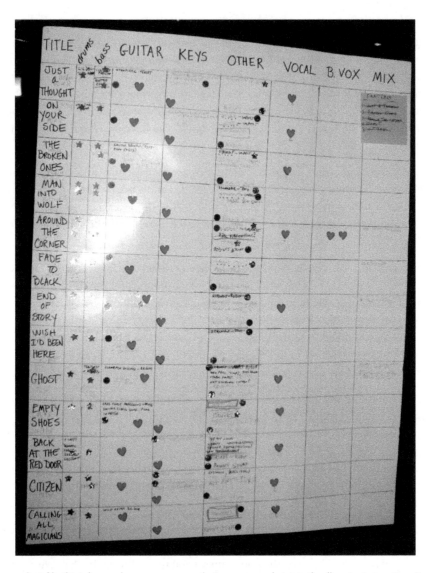

Tony uses charts like this to keep make sure everyone on the team can see what stage the album is at, at any time. How is this similar to Mike Cohn's task boards? How is it different?

Andrew: A lot of people would probably be surprised to hear that rock and roll album, this music, is made with charts and schedules and goals, writing down goals and building schedules. I think people would almost be relieved to find out that they're not the only ones who deal with those things, and that using a tool like that you can actually produce great art—and that it sometimes helps the creative process, rather than hurting it.

Tony: Well, anything that involves huge sums of money requires organization, and that includes rock and roll. There was a period when there was carte blanche, when Led Zeppelin's manager had an actual sculpture made out of cocaine in the form of a swan (and added to the recording budget). But those indulgences went a long way towards ruining the music business. Now the budgets have to be very streamlined and approved in the music business, because we're competing with video games and all kinds of other media. Pop music isn't raking in the kind of huge profits we saw two decades ago. Kids have more distractions now. Recordings have to be produced efficiently these days, especially rock and roll, I'm afraid.

But it's good. If people ask me, "We have enough money to put you in the studio with a group for seven days, what can you give us?" I'll tell them honestly, "I can produce four songs to a high level of quality." "Oh, but we want an album!" I can negotiate for more time, but if they insist on an album of, say, 12 songs, then I'll tell them that in that time we can record two songs to a high standard but the rest will be a jam, no sophistication. The premier album of the artist Jewel [*Pieces of You*] was just such a thing. They blew their small budget on the hit single, "Who Will Save Your Soul," and the rest of the album was taken mainly from her live performance in a club. You can't take a project on without being truthful about what restraints the budget will have on it. If you run out of money halfway through, there will be a drama and you will get a bad reputation.

Andrew: So, how did you learn this stuff? Clearly you've worked out a lot of systems, and know this isn't the sort of thing you can learn without making some mistakes. This is definitely the sort of thing where you have to have learned this from experience. I'm pretty sure that there aren't any books that teach you this stuff.

Tony: Well, I think it's pretty typical of people in their 20s to always want to come off as a cool person and as a nice guy, and that blocked me from taking complete charge. Eventually I saw that I wasted a lot of time and I allowed bad records to be made, because I was afraid to tell the truth.

Because eventually I grew tired of being, I guess *cowardly* is the word I want, and not having the courage to just call it as I see it. Once I did, though, I opened up the floodgates. I mean, I couldn't control it after that. I then had to learn diplomacy.

Andrew: But the charts—you basically came up with those yourself?

Tony: I innovated this chart in the '80s. I see a lot of other people using it now, the "public" chart. The people on my team were relying on my private notes for what was coming next and some were making private notes of their own. I thought, why don't we just put all the plans and ideas up on the wall for all to see? It worked great the very first time I did this. Now, when I work with the same artists again, they expect to see the chart!

I'm a bit fanatical about charts. I've got the backwards calendar that I already told you about. And there's one I have when I do a thing called "making a composite of a vocal." Say a singer sings a song seven times; I have a horizontal and vertical coordinate chart relating to virtually every word that the person sings, so I can cross-reference from, say, between eight vocals. After I pick the best-sung lines, words, even syllables, I am able to construct the "perfect" vocal. Anyone who wants to participate in the vocal comp can have the same chart and we compare our choices. I started doing the "comp chart" in the early '70s, but now loads of artists and producers use variations of this chart.

I find that these are interactive things that really bring the team together. They get really, really keen if they feel included in decisions. Still, I have veto power because I am ultimately responsible for bringing the project home. The charts I use are amazing team tools.

Andrew: That sounds really effective. It sounds like you've figured out a way to bring visibility into the project, and get your whole team involved; and it sounds like you need to do it in a way that balances out everyone's ego. Actually, it occurs to me that you need to deal with a lot of the same personality issues that you'll see on a programming team. When you're working with programmers, especially superstar programmers, sometimes the best people on your team are also some of the most socially awkward people on your team. They're not going to respect you unless you make it clear that you deserve their respect. Does that sound like some sort of situation you've had to deal with?

Tony: The human mind works in strange ways, and highly creative people generally have bad social skills because a lot of the brain is involved in being highly creative. They don't observe the effect that their impetuous outbursts have on other people, how they are alienating themselves from the rest. They don't see that. It is a social problem, but it's not very different from a young child who is very, very selfish. I'm not trying to make fun of creative people, but often, emotionally they haven't progressed much further than that in their social skills.

Often it becomes all about them, and like a lot of young kids, they need reassurance that you love them. That's really what this is about. It's a cry asking, "Do you love me?" That's what they want to hear you say. Now, of course, we're all adults, so you can't go around saying all the time, "I love you, Jim." You have to show it in other ways; you should make your appreciation quite overt. It might mean addressing Jim first in a meeting. You might have a group of them in the room; you say, "Let's discuss the next stage. I'd like to know how you all feel about it—Jim?" Jim might not have anything to say in that moment, but he'll notice he was the first to be consulted.

I probably sound arrogant, but as a father, I've learned to deal with children and divas. Every band I've worked with have sober, mature-thinking members and one or two diva-like personalities. There is a pecking order; it naturally forms as it does in all forms of social interaction. In a successful team we've all learned that we wouldn't be a team without our "star." Fortunately, a real smart "star" knows that they'd find it very hard to succeed, or even survive, without a great team.

I am a well-known record producer, but I can't afford the luxury of being a "star" myself. I have to be the soberest member of the team and lead my group of mavericks on into glorious victory.

Andrew: You know, I recognize some of that in myself. Early on in my career, when I was the top programmer on a small team, I acted like a prima donna. It was all about me. And I wonder if I would have gotten along better with the people around me if I'd said to myself, "You know what? I am a little bit overdemanding. I get impatient with people and I'm demanding, but I produce and they put up with me because I produce." What advice could you give people who are like that early-career version of me, advice that might make dealing with others a little easier?

Tony: I think they have to learn about the impact it has on the rest of the team, by being petulant and selfish. Even the most understanding people on the team will take only so much childish behavior.

And the programmer must realize that he might be a great programmer, but in a world of billions of people, there are other great programmers who will gladly fill his vacant seat after the mutiny. In this big resourceful world of talent, any team member could be replaced. Everyone has the responsibility to learn how to get along with each other, even the "stars."

You're in competition with other A teams; there's always competition. You cannot afford to have internal squabbling. You cannot have infighting to the point where one individual is destroying the morale and the productivity of the team. Someone who's got a better attitude will replace you. Everyone's replaceable.

Andrew: Before we finish this off, do you have any advice for somebody who is a good musician, or somebody who's a good programmer, or somebody who's good at whatever job they do? Someone who sees the next step in their career is going towards what you do, going towards leading a team or managing a team or making sure work gets done well? What advice would you give them?

Tony: Well, nowadays there are so many distractions, and it's really, really hard to concentrate given what we are exposed to. My motto for musicians who make music on the computer, for instance, is that computer skills aren't really that difficult to attain—compared to real musical skills. A smart 8-year-old can work Garage Band; it's no big deal dragging a loop into a space and another loop into another space and all that. My motto is "Put down the mouse and pick up a guitar." We're in danger of losing the ability to concentrate on mastering something. Nowadays the temptation is so great to just get lost in skateboarding, video games, drinking—a lot of people start drinking too heavily, too early now. But the greatest musicians that have ever lived have spent a long time learning, practicing, and perfecting what they did.

And I think that even though you reached a certain level—like there's a lot of young musicians who can play 12 chords and they think, well, that's all I need. My advice is that the more you know and the more you study, you'll have a better chance at succeeding in life. That's it. So devote your downtime, devote it to learning more stuff. I'm still learning new stuff to make better productions.

Contributors

 Scott W. Ambler is the practice leader agile development with IBM Software Group, and he works with IBM customers around the world to improve their software processes. He is the founder of the Agile Modeling (AM), Agile Data (AD), Agile Unified Process (AUP), and Enterprise Unified Process (EUP) methodologies. Scott is the (co-)author of 19 books, including *Refactoring Databases* (Addison-Wesley Professional), *Agile Modeling* (Wiley), *Agile Database Techniques* (Wiley), *The Object Primer*, Third Edition (Cambridge University Press), and *The Enterprise Unified Process* (Prentice Hall). Scott is a senior contributing editor with *Information Week*. His personal home page is *http://www.ibm.com/software/rational/leadership/leaders/#scott* and his Agile at Scale blog is *www.ibm.com/developerworks/blogs/page/ambler*.

 Scott Berkun is the best selling author of O'Reilly's *Making Things Happen* (formerly titled *The Art of Project Management*) and *The Myths of Innovation*. He worked as a manager at Microsoft from 1994 to 2003; during this time, he also worked on the first five versions of Internet Explorer. Since 2003 he has been on his own as independent writer and public speaker. His work has appeared in the *New York Times*, the *Washington Post*, *Wired* magazine, and on National Public Radio. He taught a course in creative thinking at the University of Washington, teaches seminars on innovation to the Fortune 500, and is currently a regular contributor to Harvard Business Digital. He has appeared frequently as a management and creative thinking expert on MSNBC and CNBC, and runs a popular blog, with videos, podcasts, and essays, at *www.scottberkun.com/blog*.

Barry Boehm is the TRW professor of software engineering in the computer science department at USC, as well as the director of USC's Center for Systems and Software Engineering.

Dr. Barry Boehm served within the U.S. Department of Defense (DoD) from 1989 to 1992 as director of the DARPA Information Science and Technology Office and as director of the DDR&E Software and Computer Technology Office. He worked at TRW from 1973 to 1989, culminating as chief scientist of the Defense Systems Group, and at the Rand Corporation from 1959 to 1973, culminating as head of the Information Sciences Department. He entered the software field at General Dynamics in 1955.

His current research interests involve recasting systems and software engineering into a value-based framework, including processes, methods, tools, and an underlying theory and process for value-based systems and software definition; architecting; development; validation; and evolution. His contributions to the field include the Constructive Cost Model (COCOMO) family of systems and software engineering estimation models, the Spiral Model and Incremental Commitment Model of the systems and software engineering process, and the Theory W (win-win) approach to systems and software management and requirements determination. He has received the ACM Distinguished Research Award in Software Engineering and the IEEE Harlan Mills Award, and an honorary Sc.D. in computer science from the University of Massachusetts. He is a Fellow of the primary professional societies in computing (ACM), aerospace (AIAA), electronics (IEEE), and systems engineering (INCOSE), and a member of the U.S. National Academy of Engineering.

Grady Booch is recognized internationally for his innovative work in software architecture, software engineering, and collaborative development environments. He has devoted his life's work to improving the art and science of software development. Grady served as chief scientist of Rational Software Corporation since its founding in 1981 and through its acquisition by IBM in 2003. He now is part of the IBM Thomas J. Watson Research Center, where he serves as chief scientist for software engineering, and where he continues his work on the *Handbook of Software Architecture* and also leads several projects in software engineering that are beyond the constraints of immediate product horizons.

Grady continues to engage with customers working on real problems, and is working to build deep relationships with academia and other research organizations around the world. Grady is one of the original authors of the Unified Modeling Language (UML) and was also one of the original developers of several of Rational's products. Grady has served as architect and architectural mentor for numerous complex software-intensive systems around the world in just about every domain imaginable. He also is the author of six best-selling books, including *The Unified Modeling Language User Guide* and the seminal *Object-Oriented Analysis and Design with Applications* (both from Addison-Wesley), and writes a regular column on architecture for IEEE Software. Grady lives in Thorne Bridge, Colorado, and Maui. His interests include reading, traveling, singing, playing the Celtic harp, Bikram yoga, and kayaking. At random times, the laws of physics do not apply to him. He is not dead yet.

Mike Cohn is the founder of Mountain Goat Software, a process and project management consultancy and training firm. He is the author of *Agile Estimating and Planning* (Prentice Hall), *User Stories Applied: For Agile Software Development* (Addison-Wesley Professional), and *Succeeding with Agile* (Addison-Wesley). With more than 20 years of experience, Mike has previously been a technology executive in companies of various sizes, from start-up to Fortune 40. A frequent magazine contributor and conference speaker, Mike is a founding member of the Scrum Alliance and the Agile Alliance. He can be reached at *mike@mountaingoatsoftware.com*.

Michael Collins is the chief scientist for RedJack, LLC, a network security consulting firm in the Maryland area. In this role, he develops traffic monitoring systems and analytical techniques for very large networks. Prior to working for RedJack, Dr. Collins worked for the CERT/Network Situational Awareness team at Carnegie Mellon University, where he developed tools and technologies for the DoD CENTAUR and DHS EINSTEIN projects. Dr. Collins has a Ph.D. in electrical and computer engineering from Carnegie Mellon University; he regularly publishes and lectures on network security and situational awareness.

Mark Denovich is currently living and working in Europe as a senior business consultant in the Auto ID industry, focusing on voice recognition technology. He is involved in developer training, product development, and R&D. Mark began developing software as a way of financing a physics degree at Carnegie Mellon University. Sound advice from his advisor—"uh, I don't think you are cut out for academia"—and an inability to grow a respectable beard led to dropping physics and pursing software development as a career. In those classes, he learned that software development was part art, part science. In the real world, he learned it was actually a business. His dream is to one day live on his own Walden Pond with a high-speed Internet connection, of course.

Bill DiPierre started writing software in high school more than 25 years ago. Along the way, he has held just about every job that exists within the software development life cycle. Bill lives in Philadelphia with two dogs, both of whom support his career, but encourage him to remember that there's more to life than being good at your job.

Cory Doctorow (*http://craphound.com*) is a science fiction novelist, blogger, and technology activist. He is the coeditor of the popular weblog Boing Boing (*http://boingboing.net*), and a contributor to *Wired*, *Popular Science*, *Make*, the *New York Times*, and many other newspapers, magazines, and websites. He was formerly director of European affairs for the Electronic Frontier Foundation (*http://www.eff.org*), a non-profit civil liberties group that defends freedom in technology law, policy, standards, and treaties. In 2007, he served as the Fulbright Chair at the Annenberg Center for Public Diplomacy at the University of Southern California.

Cory has won the Locus and Sunburst awards for his writing, and has been nominated for the Hugo, Nebula, and British Science Fiction awards. He cofounded the open source peer-to-peer software company OpenCola, and presently serves on the boards and advisory boards of the Participatory Culture Foundation, the MetaBrainz Foundation, Technorati, Inc., Stikkit, the Organization for Transformative Works, Areae, the Annenberg Center for the Study of Online Communities, and Onion Networks, Inc. In 2007, *Entertainment Weekly* called him "The William Gibson of his generation." He was also named one of *Forbes Magazine*'s 2007 Web Celebrities, and one of the World Economic Forum's Young Global Leaders for 2007. He is presently working on narrative documentary films with Kirby Dick (*This Film Is Not Yet Rated*) and Philippe Parreno (*Zidane*), and on a new young adult novel, *For the Win* (about union organizing in video games).

On February 3, 2008, he became a father. His little girl is named Poesy Emmeline Fibonacci Nautilus Taylor Doctorow, and is a marvel that puts all the works of technology and artifice to shame.

Patricia Ensworth is president of Harborlight Management Services, a consultancy specializing in risk management, global logistics, and multicultural teamwork for software engineering. She is the author of *The Accidental Project Manager: Surviving the Transition from Techie to Manager* (John Wiley & Sons) as well as essays in publications ranging from *CIO* to *Salon* to *Natural History*. After receiving a master's degree in cultural anthropology from Columbia University, she began working at Merrill Lynch as a software tester. Her subsequent career has included roles as a quality assurance manager, program manager, vendor relationship manager, trainer, and consultant. She has held management positions at Merrill Lynch, Moody's Corporation, and UBS Investment Bank; her consulting clients have included Citigroup, the American Management Association, Memorial Sloan-Kettering Cancer Center, and the U.S. Navy. She has earned PMP, CSQE, and ISTQB certifications. When not interacting with a device containing a keyboard and a screen, she can often be found sailing in New York Harbor.

Trevor Field is a British businessman with extensive experience in the outdoor advertising industry. He has also worked in the printing and publishing industries in South Africa and in the U.K.

In 1990, Trevor began developing the PlayPump system (*http://www.roundabout.co.za*), an innovative water system that doubles as a water pump and merry-go-round for children. Over the next four years, he designed and built the first two PlayPumps that were installed in Masinga, a rural area of KwaZulu-Natal, a province of South Africa. In 1995, he decided to focus full time on the Roundabout PlayPump system. He joined forces with Paul Ristic in 1996, and in 1997, Roundabout Outdoor was founded. Roundabout Outdoor went on to win the inaugural World Bank Development Marketplace competition in 2000 for the PlayPump. The system has since achieved worldwide successes in other competitions, and has attracted donor funding (via the NGO, PlayPumps International) from all quarters; one of the most significant to date was the $16.4 million donation announced by First Lady Laura Bush at the Clinton Economic Forum in New York in September 2006. Trevor is currently working to expand the PlayPump model into the rest of Africa and the world. Thus far, more than 1,000 PlayPumps have been installed in South Africa, Mozambique, Swaziland, Lesotho, and Zambia, with systems in other countries including Tanzania, Kenya, Uganda, and Ethiopia in development.

Karl Fogel is launchpad ombudsman at Canonical Ltd., an author on open source topics, a long-time open source developer, and a copyright reform activist. After working on CVS and writing *Open Source Development With CVS* (Coriolis; *cvsbook.com*), he went to CollabNet, Inc. as a founding developer in the Subversion project. Based on his experiences there, he wrote *Producing Open Source Software: How to Run a Successful Free Software Project* (O'Reilly; *producingoss.com*). After a brief stint as an open source specialist at Google, he left to found the non-profit QuestionCopyright.org, where he continues to be active since joining Canonical in 2008. He writes and speaks regularly on copyright reform and on the application of open source principles to areas outside software.

Peter Glück is a senior software engineer at NASA's Jet Propulsion Laboratory in Pasadena, California. Peter led the overall software development on the Phoenix Mars Lander project and has been involved with many successful NASA interplanetary missions over the past 20 years. Peter has also contracted with numerous software and technology companies on software development and implementation projects since 2002. He has received group and individual achievement awards from several aerospace organizations such as NASA, AIAA, and JPL, and he is a frequent public speaker and published author on software-related topics. Peter has a B.S. in Mathematics from CSU Northridge and an M.S. in Aerospace Engineering from USC.

James W. Grenning is the founder of Renaissance Software Consulting, where he trains, coaches, and consults worldwide. With more than 30 years of software development experience, both technical and managerial, James brings a wealth of knowledge, skill, and creativity to software development teams and their management. James's mission is to bring improved technical and management practices to development teams. As his professional roots are in embedded software, he is leading the way to introduce agile development practices to that challenging world. He is currently writing a book on applying test-driven development to embedded software. James was one of the original Extreme Programming coaches and trainers, always working with the best. He invented Planning Poker, an agile estimating technique used around the world. He also participated in the creation of the *Manifesto for Agile Software Development* (*http://agilemanifesto.org*).

Mark Healey is creative director at Media Molecule. He joined the games industry in 1988, and has established himself as one of the industry's most multitalented game developers. His main area of specialization is art, but during his career Mark has coded, designed, and contributed to game audio tracks. Mark joined Bullfrog Productions in 1994, and worked on some of its biggest hits, including *Theme Park*, *Magic Carpet*, and *Dungeonkeeper*. In 1997, he left Bullfrog to join Lionhead Studios, where he worked on *Black & White* and *Fable*. His small contribution to the cult Internet title *Live for Speed* gave Mark a taste for development on a smaller scale. In 2002, he began work on his own game, *Rag Doll Kung Fu*, working on the game's graphics, code, design, and music with help from some friends. *Rag Doll Kung Fu*'s blend of playability and off-the-wall humor proved to be a winning formula, and the game was nominated for the Develop Awards Best New PC IP and Innovation categories. The development and subsequent success of *Rag Doll King Fu* showed Mark that he worked best in a small, intense, but fun environment. Inspired by this, he formed a new development studio, Media Molecule, with the friends who had helped him make *Rag Doll Kung Fu* such a success: Alex Evans, David Smith, and Kareem Ettouney, joined by Chris Lee. The studio's first game, *LittleBigPlanet*, was launched in November 2008.

Auke Jilderda is a sales engineer and technical account manager at CollabNet. Auke began his career at Philips Research studying open source software engineering in an attempt to understand why some projects are spectacular successes while many others fail to gain momentum. Having identified the key aspects that make an open source project successful, he moved on to Philips Medical Systems to deploy these key aspects, as the "inner source" approach, at a major product family program to improve the company's ability to collaborate across organizational boundaries and locations. In addition, he worked on evolving the division's software strategy, exploring if, why, when, and where open source solutions can be used to implement commodity parts of a product as viable alternatives to developing them yourself or buying them from a specialized third party.

Four years ago, Auke joined CollabNet's European field team, and today handles a combination of sales engineering, technical account management of strategic accounts, and consulting on collaborative software engineering.

Andy Lester is a software developer and author. For more than 20 years, he has worked on and managed teams large and small, from tiny offices to worldwide collaboration. Andy blogs about issues facing the technology worker in The Working Geek (*http://theworkinggeek.com*). His experiences hiring developers led him to write *Land the Tech Job You Love* (Pragmatic Bookshelf).

Alex Martelli is a member of the Python Software Foundation and works in Mountain View, California, for Google, most often as über tech lead, but currently as senior staff engineer. Alex wrote *Python in a Nutshell* (O'Reilly), and many other books, articles, essays, keynotes, and other conference talks, on Python, numerical computing, and technical management of software development. Alex has an M.S. (Laurea) degree in electrical engineering from Bologna University; before Google, he worked for Texas Instruments, IBM Research, think3, and as a freelance consultant. He has also taught courses on programming, development methods, object-oriented design, and numerical computing, at Ferrara University and many other venues.

Steve McConnell is CEO and chief software engineer at Construx Software, where he writes books and articles, consults, teaches classes, and oversees Construx's software development practices. Steve is the author of *Software Estimation: Demystifying the Black Art*, *Code Complete*, *Rapid Development*, *Software Project Survival Guide* (all from Microsoft Press), and *Professional Software Development* (Addison-Wesley Professional). His first two books won *Software Development* magazine's Jolt Excellence award for best programming books of their years.

Steve has worked in the desktop software industry since 1984 and has expertise in project estimation, software construction practices, agile and rapid development methodologies, and outsource software management. In 1998, readers of Software Development magazine named Steve one of the three most influential people in the software industry along with Bill Gates and Linus Torvalds. Steve was editor-in-chief of *IEEE Software* magazine from 1998–2002.

Steve is on the panel of experts that advises the Software Engineering Body of Knowledge (SWEBOK) project and was chair of the IEEE Computer Society's Professional Practices Committee. Steve earned a bachelor's degree from Whitman College and a master's degree in software engineering from Seattle University.

Andy Oram, an editor at O'Reilly Media, has also been writing articles on technology and its social implications since the mid-1990s (*http://www.praxagora.com/andyo/professional/article.html*). He spent 10 years in the computer industry as a technical writer before trying the publishing field to achieve the same goals of enabling programmers and computer users to reach their goals effectively.

At O'Reilly, Andy specialized for many years in the open source area, having edited the first books put out by an American publisher on Linux and such ground-breaking works as *Peer-to-Peer*, *Mastering Regular Expressions*, *Intellectual Property and Open Source*, and *Beautiful Code*. He is also interested in providing better education for online communities, an issue he has researched at *http://www.praxagora.com/community_documentation/*. He is also a longtime member of Computer Professionals for Social Responsibility.

Tim O'Reilly is the founder and CEO of O'Reilly Media, thought by many to be the best computer book publisher in the world. The company also publishes online through the O'Reilly Network and hosts conferences on technology topics. Tim is an activist for open source, open standards, and sensible intellectual property laws.

Since 1978, Tim has led the company's pursuit of its core goal: to be a catalyst for technology change by capturing and transmitting the knowledge of "alpha geeks" and other innovators. His active engagement with technology communities drives both the company's product development and its marketing. Tim has built a culture where advocacy, meme-making, and evangelism are key tenets of the business philosophy.

Tim has served on the board of trustees for both the Internet Society and the Electronic Frontier Foundation, two organizations devoted to making sure the Internet fulfills its promise. He was on the board of Macromedia until its merger with Adobe. He is currently on the board of CollabNet.

Tim graduated cum laude from Harvard College in 1975 with a B.A. in classics. An archive of Tim's online articles, talks, and interviews can be found at Tim's archive page (*http://tim. oreilly.com*).

Dr. Maria H. Penedo is a Distinguished Technical Fellow and a senior staff/scientist at Northrop Grumman (NG) Corporation. At NG, she has been a leader in the design, insertion, and use of software engineering and information technology into programs, proposals, and the IT organization, especially in the areas of process-based environments, architecture, integration, collaboration, agent, and Web 2.0 technologies. She has applied her enthusiasm and passion for new technology and trends in the research and project worlds. Her work in the area of distributed collaboration was recognized with a 1998 NG Chairman's Award for Innovation; other honors include multiple Internal Research and Development Honor Roll awards, Woman Technologist of the Year, and a mentorship award.

She has been recognized as a leader in the international software engineering research community, and is an active participant of the leading professional societies in her field. She has published and lectured internationally and served on the program committees of major national and international conferences. She was an editor of IEEE's *Transactions on Software Engineering* and Wiley's *Software Process: Improvement and Practice Journal*, and a Distinguished Visitor of the IEEE Computer Society. She has a B.S. in mathematics and an M.S. in computer science from Brazil, and a Ph.D. in computer science from UCLA.

Dr. Karl Rehmer spent several years teaching mathematics and computer science after earning a Ph.D. in mathematics. Leaving the academic world to get a job at a location where his wife could work on her Ph.D. in computer science, he joined Honeywell Air Transport Systems in Phoenix, Arizona, in 1988. While working there, he was a member of the HADS team that developed the software tools used to develop avionics software for the Boeing 777 aircraft. Following that, Dr. Rehmer joined the Honeywell Research Center, where he developed the scheduler for the Deos real-time embedded operating system that has been used for many avionics applications. In 1996, he joined DDC-I, a vendor of software tools for the safety-critical market. He has been the chief architect of the DDC-I Mixed Language Debugger project. Additionally, he has worked on a number of subcontracts for DDC-I customers. He currently is adding support for additional languages and target operating systems to the DDC-I Mixed Language Debugger.

Eric Renkey is a software developer who currently manages a small development team at an integrated energy company. He learned to program many years ago on his family's Atari 800 and has worked as an IT professional since 1995. He is a pleasure to work with, as he'll be happy to tell you. Eric received a B.A. in psychology from The Pennsylvania State University.

Ned Robinson graduated from Hunter College's honors program (NYC) with a B.A. in English literature. As the computer revolution erupted in the 1980s, Ned decided to alter his career goals and taught himself how to program. At first, he programmed in Lotus 123 and dBase 3, but quickly progressed to C and C++. Ned worked for a variety of Wall Street banks until the early 1990s. He then became a lead developer and product manager for Sheridan Software, a Microsoft ISV that specialized in value-added VBX and ActiveX solutions.

As a classically trained pianist, Ned was always interested in merging his technical abilities and his love of music. In 1995, he founded RePlay Technologies, a software company dedicated to the practicing musician. RePlay Technologies ran for five years before Ned sold it and returned to work in the financial district. It was at a small financial services software company that he met Andrew Stellman and, like Andrew, became an advocate for software process. Since he is a developer at heart, he sees process engineering as a way to give back to the development community, as good software process allows developers to really shine and exercise their incredible resourcefulness in bringing business requirements to life.

Johanna Rothman helps leaders solve problems and seize opportunities. She consults, speaks, and writes on managing high-technology product development. She enables managers, teams, and organizations to become more effective by applying her pragmatic approaches to the issues of project management, risk management, and people management.

Johanna publishes "The Pragmatic Manager," a monthly email newsletter and podcast, and writes two blogs: Managing Product Development and Hiring Technical People. She is the author of several books, including *Manage Your Project Portfolio: Increase Your Capacity and Finish Projects* (Pragmatic Bookshelf), 2008 Jolt Productivity Award-winning *Manage It! Your Guide to Modern, Pragmatic Project Management* (Pragmatic Bookshelf), *Behind Closed Doors: Secrets of Great Management* (with Esther Derby; Pragmatic Bookshelf), *Hiring the Best*

Knowledge Workers, Techies & Nerds: The Secrets and Science of Hiring Technical People (Dorset House), and *Corrective Action for the Software Industry* (with Denise Robitaille; Paton Press).

Neil G. Siegel is vice president and chief engineer at Northrop Grumman's Information Systems sector. He has been responsible for many successful fielded military and intelligence systems, including the Army's Blue-Force Tracking system and the Hunter unmanned aerial vehicle. Programs for which he was responsible have won numerous awards, including the Crosstalk Award in 2001 for one of the five best software projects across the entire U.S. government, and the 2003 Monticello Award (given in recognition of an information system that has a direct, meaningful impact on human lives). His inventions have led to billions of dollars worth of new business for the company, and more than a dozen patents. Among many other honors, he was elected to the U.S. National Academy of Engineering in 2005.

Tom Tarka worked at MP3.com for just over two years, and the experience—the people, the place, the work—left an indelible mark on the person he became. Upon his departure, he picked up his travels where he had left off and spent the better part of a year roaming the United States in a 1971 VW Camper, eventually landing back on the East Coast.

After a brief stint as a mechanic, someone took a chance on Tom and his dusty chemical engineering degree and gave him a job in a field that had intrigued him since childhood: energy. He now works for the U.S. Department of Energy on next-generation power systems and global climate change and is a licensed professional engineer.

Tom resides in Pittsburgh, where he owns a home and a small collection of VW buses.

Tony Visconti's career as a record producer spans four decades. He is the producer of 12 David Bowie albums, 10 T. Rex albums, and many, many more by British recording artists. In the past two years, Tony has worked with Morrissey, Razorlight, Alejandro Escovedo, Anti-Flag, and Fall Out Boy. He has written his autobiography for Harper Collins, titled *Bowie, Bolan and the Brooklyn Boy*.

Karl Wiegers is principal consultant with Process Impact, a software process consulting and education company in Portland, Oregon, where he specializes in requirements engineering, process improvement, and project management. Karl is the author of the books *Software Requirements* (Microsoft Press), *More About Software Requirements* (Microsoft Press), *Peer Reviews in Software* (Addison-Wesley), *Practical Project Initiation* (Microsoft Press), and *Creating a Software Engineering Culture* (Dorset House), as well as numerous articles on many aspects of software, chemistry, and military history. Karl has a Ph.D. in organic chemistry, which he regards as the perfect background for a career in software development. You can reach him at *http://www.processimpact.com*.

INDEX

COLOPHON

The cover image is from *http://www.photos.com*. The cover fonts are Akzidenz Grotesk and Orator. Nisha Sondhe was the photographer for the Parts pages. Erik R. Ogan was the photographer for Tom Tarka's Contributor photo. The text font is Adobe's Meridien; the heading font is ITC Bailey.

Get even more for your money.

Join the O'Reilly Community, and register the O'Reilly books you own. It's free, and you'll get:

- $4.99 ebook upgrade offer
- 40% upgrade offer on O'Reilly print books
- Membership discounts on books and events
- Free lifetime updates to ebooks and videos
- Multiple ebook formats, DRM FREE
- Participation in the O'Reilly community
- Newsletters
- Account management
- 100% Satisfaction Guarantee

Signing up is easy:

1. **Go to: oreilly.com/go/register**
2. **Create an O'Reilly login.**
3. **Provide your address.**
4. **Register your books.**

Note: English-language books only

To order books online:
oreilly.com/store

For questions about products or an order:
orders@oreilly.com

To sign up to get topic-specific email announcements and/or news about upcoming books, conferences, special offers, and new technologies:
elists@oreilly.com

For technical questions about book content:
booktech@oreilly.com

To submit new book proposals to our editors:
proposals@oreilly.com

O'Reilly books are available in multiple DRM-free ebook formats. For more information:
oreilly.com/ebooks

Spreading the knowledge of innovators   oreilly.com

Have it your way.

O'Reilly eBooks

- Lifetime access to the book when you buy through oreilly.com
- Provided in up to four DRM-free file formats, for use on the devices of your choice: PDF, .epub, Kindle-compatible .mobi, and Android .apk
- Fully searchable, with copy-and-paste and print functionality
- Alerts when files are updated with corrections and additions

oreilly.com/ebooks/

Safari Books Online

- Access the contents and quickly search over 7000 books on technology, business, and certification guides
- Learn from expert video tutorials, and explore thousands of hours of video on technology and design topics
- Download whole books or chapters in PDF format, at no extra cost, to print or read on the go
- Get early access to books as they're being written
- Interact directly with authors of upcoming books
- Save up to 35% on O'Reilly print books

See the complete Safari Library at safari.oreilly.com

O'REILLY®